The Garden of Eating

The Garden of Eating

A Produce-Dominated Diet & Cookbook

Rachel Albert-Matesz & Don Matesz

Planetary Press, Phoenix, AZ

For information about permission for excerpts or bulk orders write to
Planetary Press, PO Box 97040, Phoenix, AZ 85060-7040.
Call (602) 840-4556, or email: PlanetaryPress@earthlink.net

ISBN: 0-9641267-1-0
Library of Congress Catalog Number: 2003096604

Albert-Matesz, Rachel, 1965-
    The garden of eating : a produce-dominated diet &
cookbook / Rachel Albert-Matesz & Don Matesz. -- 1st ed.
    p. cm.
    Includes bibliographical references and index.
    LCCN 2003096604
    ISBN 0-9641267-1-0

    1. Nutrition. 2. Cookery (Natural foods)
I. Matesz, Don, 1961- II. Title.

RA784.A375 2004   613.2
                         QBI03-200939

Editor: Marilyn Weishaar, Aberdeen, SD, The Weis Revise, weisrevise@nvc.net or www.theweisrevise.com
Cover, interior design, and layout: Brenda Weishaar, Aberdeen, SD, dakkid@nvc.net. Interior images from clipart.com, all rights reserved
Food styling for cover photo: Harriet Granthen, Curt Granthen Photography, Phoenix, AZ, granthenstudios@mindspring.com
Cover photos: Curt Granthen, Curt Granthen Photography, Phoenix, AZ, granthenstudios@mindspring.com
Indexing: Nan Badgett, Word·a·bil·i·ty, Tucson, AZ, nbadgett@earthlink.net

CONTENTS

Part III: APPENDIX

Acknowledgements

For more than 12 years, our friends, Rachel's cooking students, and coaching clients near and far have devoured our meals and recipes, adopted many of our methods, provided feedback, requests, great questions, and encouragement for this project.

For those who inquired about the possibility of moving in with us for a month or two to see how we shop, cook, and eat so well every day—without spending all day in the kitchen—you motivated Rachel to distill our practices into prose. We hope this book shows you the way!

Second helpings go to those special friends who provided ongoing encouragement during our book's long gestation and labor: Mary Swirsky, Marilyn Glidewell, Heather and Terry Crimson, Judy Genova, Katie Coyle-Todd, Megan Stamos, Mary Goodell, Dave Lerner, L.Ac.; Anastasia Rudinger, Annette Foster, Melissa Wokna, and others too numerous to mention who pleaded with us to find more time to finish so they could have complete books.

For unconditional love, emotional support, and unqualified belief in our vision: Patricia Poggi and Peter Langsam.

Many thanks for those who helped relieve the aches and pains caused by endless hours pecking away at the computer and pouring over text: Sarah Hoppe, Marsha Tilley, L.M.T; Mark Dumas, D.C.; Jason Wokna, Yunxia Li, L.Ac.; Quati Makeeta, D.C.; and Mary Hogue, L.M.T., and future L.Ac.;

For completing her labor, birthing her book first, and demonstrating "there is light at the end of the table," we applaud Rachel's friend, colleague, and fellow food coach, Judy Stone, M.S.W., C.N., author of *Take Two Apples and Call Me in the Morning.*

For sharing recipes: Stacie Tolen for Ben's Tomatillo Chili, Bruce Sherrod for his marvelous Moroccan Barbecue Spice Mix, Moroccan Spiced Salmon, and Moroccan Barbecue Sauce (which we modified), and Nancy Matesz for Mashed Sweet Potatoes with Lime.

For keying in our enormous database: Chris Corey and Cheryl Catlin.

The following farmers shared extraordinarily delicious naturally raised meat and locally grown produce and wild ocean fish for our recipe testing and development, cooking classes, and daily dining in Ohio: Chuck Wooten of Portage Acres Piedmontese, Jack Knorek of Oak Moon Farms, Jeff McKahon of Toledo's Rohr Fish & Seafood, Bev Garno of Garno Farms Poultry, Bilau Farms, Zemnecki Farm and the rest of the folks at The Erie Street Market in Toledo, and Claudia's Natural Foods Market.

From our new home in Phoenix, Arizona, we thank those who provided wild ocean fish harvested in a manner that ensures the future of the species, 100 percent grass-fed beef, and local, organic produce: Raymond Wiley of Alaska Flyin Fish Company, Kenny Aschbacker of American Surf N' Turf, Will Holder of Ervin's Beef, Young's Farm Poultry, Jana Anderson of Pinnacle Farms, One Windmill Farm, Blue Sky Farms, McClendon's Select Citrus growers and honey harvesters, and others who serve the farmers' market crowd in the greater Phoenix-Scottsdale area.

Our thanks also go to another ecologically responsible harvester, Larch Hansen of Maine Seaweed for harvesting American sea vegetables.

We thank the folks at Thai Kitchen for awesome coconut milk, Jay Robb Enterprises, and other companies large and small listed in the Appendix.

Huge hugs, endless Arizona dates, and extra jars of citrus honey go to our patient and dedicated editor Marilyn Weishaar for wise and thorough revising, commitment to excellence, and friendship, and to our diligent designer Brenda Weishaar, for creativity, care, and attention to detail with the book's cover and interior design.

We applaud our food stylist Harriet Granthen and cover photographer Curt Granthen for capturing our ideas and helping us create the most delicious cover shot we could imagine. We enjoyed sharing the process and eating the set with both of them.

For generously sharing knowledge, we thank Dr. Loren Cordain, Ph.D.; Melissa Darby, M.A., and the folks at The Price-Pottenger Nutrition Foundation.

To our indexer Nan Badgett, the caboose may be last to arrive, but it's often one of the most crucial ingredients in the success of a book. Thanks!

Last but not least, we thank everyone who provided financial support by pre-ordering and prepaying for books months before it went to press.

Foreword

We offer this book for educational purposes only. It is not meant to be used as a guide for diagnosis or treatment of any disease. If you have a medical condition, seek the advice of a health-care professional. Before making any changes in your diet or exercise program, you may wish to consult your physician.

Our purpose is to guide you toward greater health through optimal nutrition. *The Garden of Eating* is more than a diet book and more than a cookbook. It's a comprehensive guide to natural eating. It's principles are not new. They are derived from the ancient, time-tested food ways of pre-agricultural people free of modern degenerative diseases. This plan is vegetable-rich but not vegetarian.

We're going to show you the way to *The Garden of Eating*. You might not want to go all the way. That's up to you—but the farther you go, the more natural your diet will be, and the more benefits you will experience.

What's in this for you?

1. **Reduced digestive discomforts:** By eliminating (or, at least, reducing) consumption of foods incompatible with the human digestive system and metabolism, many people will gain relief from acid stomach, heartburn, constipation, diarrhea, or other gut reactions.

2. **Fat loss and long-term weight control:** Many who adopt this plan in full will lose fat without going hungry. High fiber, phytonutrient, protein, vitamin, mineral, and essential fatty acid levels satisfy the body's nutritional requirements and help to regulate appetite. Meanwhile the predominance of low calorie density food, inclusion of satisfying protein and fat, and control of appetite-stimulating concentrated carbohydrates makes it difficult to overconsume calories. This is the most important key to long-term weight control.

3. **Muscle and bone mass increase:** Many people who adopt this plan along with sensible exercise will notice a small increase in muscle and/or bone mass. Increased consumption of highly alkaline fruits and vegetables reduces systemic acidity and stops the corrosion of muscle and bone tissue. Increased muscle mass increases your metabolic rate so you burn more calories and fat.

4. **Enhanced resistance to infectious and degenerative diseases:** Many who adopt this plan will notice a reduction in frequency and severity of colds and flu. Elimination of commonly allergenic foods and general improvement in nutrition often reduces allergy symptoms. Degenerative diseases plaguing modern man are very rare among primitive groups that eat according to the principles given in *The Garden of Eating*. This plan can reduce your risk as well. Although your results may vary, some people have experienced remission or reversal of degenerative or immune system diseases following primitive diets similar to what we outline. You have nothing to lose on our approach because it is one of the most nutritious ways you can eat.

5. **Superior reproduction and child development:** This plan provides maximum nutritional support for healthy sperm, egg, and fetal development, necessary for preventing birth defects. Primitive groups from which we have drawn the dietary principles of *The Garden of Eating* have the lowest rates of birth defects. Coupled with natural breast-feeding for more than 12 months, and applied to children's nutrition, our plan will support excellent child development. Children raised on breast milk for 3 years and later a primitive diet can have superior physiques, facial, cranial, and brain development, and straight teeth highly resistant to decay, as shown by Dr. Weston Price, DDS, in his work *Nutrition and Physical Degeneration*. These children incur minimal risk of childhood infections as well as degenerative diseases.

1 Finding The Garden of Eating

chapter

I
n ancient times, people lived simply. They hunted, fished, and were with nature all day. When the weather cooled, they became active to fend off the cold. When the weather heated up in summer, they retreated to cool places. Internally, their emotions were calm and peaceful, and they were without excessive desires. Externally, they did not have the stress of today. They lived without greed and desire, close to nature. They maintained jing shen nei suo, or inner peace and concentration of mind and spirit. This prevented pathogens from invading. Therefore they did not need herbs to treat their internal state, nor did they need acupuncture to treat the exterior. When they did contract disease they simply guided properly the emotions and spirit and redirected the energy flow, using the method of zhu yuo to heal the condition.

The Yellow Emperor's Classic of Medicine

Chapter Overview
The life of so-called primitive people was free of many modern day maladies. This chapter will take a closer look at some of the studies that reveal how the primitive diets, especially those of hunter-gatherers, promoted remarkable health.

Not long ago, many groups of so-called primitive people were immune to the diseases and disabilities common in modern civilization. Whole tribes had no obesity, diabetes, heart disease, cancer, or neurological degenerative diseases. They never needed glasses, dentists, or orthodontists. Their children almost never had birth defects. They were lean and fit throughout life.

It may sound like a fantasy, but it's a fact.

In the early 20th century, the high number of Americans suffering from tooth decay, crooked and crowded teeth, and deformities of the palate and face disturbed an American dentist, Dr. Weston Price. He noticed that many people with dental and facial deformities also suffered from other medical conditions, reduced or retarded intelligence, or moral delinquency. Concerned with the prevalence and severity of dental, general, and social disease in America, he resolved to find the causes.

Unable to find any Americans unaffected by dental disease, Dr. Price studied native groups that were reported to be free of dental decay. He and his wife visited Swiss in isolated mountain villages, Gaelics in the Outer Hebrides, Eskimos, Indians of North and South America, Melanesians and Polynesians, many African tribes, Australian Aborigines, and New Zealand Maori. Dr. Price took thousands of photographs of people eating primitive diets, and of people of the same genetic stock who had switched to modern diets. He also recorded what they ate and analyzed many of their foods. In 1936, Dr. Price published his findings in a landmark book, *Nutrition and Physical Degeneration* (republished by Keats in 1999).

Price examined many mouths looking for dental disorders and spoke with physicians knowledgeable about the natives' general health. He found numerous people isolated from modern influences that had handsome faces, straight, decay-free teeth, and robust physiques. They also had a high resistance to both infections and degenerative disease, and fine moral characters.

He found that hunter-fisher-gatherers had the lowest rates of dental decay. Some of these tribes had no tooth decay, and none had a rate greater than 1 percent. Herding tribes living largely on milk and meat from pastured animals along with fruits and vegetables had rates similar to hunter-fisher-gatherers. Rates were higher among people involved in primitive grain farming, especially in places in Africa where animal foods were scarce and the diet was composed primarily of cereals, beans, sweet potatoes, and bananas. However, these were still low compared to modernized peoples of the same races, who had epidemic rates of dental disease.

The vast differences are remarkable:

- In tribes living entirely or largely by fishing, hunting, and gathering wild game, vegetables, fruits, and nuts, less than one-half percent of teeth were attacked by decay. That means 1 tooth in 200, or about 1 person in 60, had tooth decay.
- Gaelics eating oats with fish had a dental decay rate 120 times that of the Maori fisher-hunter-gatherers who ate no grains. Modernized people had rates up to 58 times higher than the primitive Gaelics.
- The Loetschental Valley Swiss living on milk products, whole rye bread, vegetables, and fruits had a rate 460 times that of the Maori. Modernized people had rates 15 times that of the isolated Swiss.
- The dental decay rate of the largely vegetarian Kikuyu was

Smile
Out of all the groups American Dentist Dr. Weston Price studied, hunter-gatherers had the lowest rates of dental decay, all coming in under 1 percent. Even the highest rates of tooth decay in primitive groups were dwarfed by the rates of modernized people.

550 times that of the Maori, but even the Kikuyu had teeth immensely better than modernized people, who have decay rates up to 13 times higher than the Kikuyu. (See Table 1.1)

Table 1.1

Percent of Teeth Attacked by Decay in Different Peoples Studied by Dr. Weston Price, DDS.

	Primitive	Modernized
Fisher/hunter/gatherers		
Amazon Jungle Indians	0.00	40.0
Australian Aborigines	0.00	70.9
New Zealand Maori	0.01	55.3
Eskimos	0.09	13.0
Malays*	0.09	20.6
Northern Indians	0.16	21.5
Polynesians*	0.38	21.9
Melanesians*	0.38	29.0
Herdsmen		
Masai	0.4	n.a.
Neurs	0.5	n.a.
Grain farmers		
Gaelics (seafood, oats, produce)	1.20	30.0
Swiss (milk products, rye, produce)	4.6	29.8
Kikuyu (chiefly vegetarians)	5.5	n.a.

*Although these groups cultivated some fruits and vegetables, their main livelihood was fishing-hunting.

Table adapted from Crawford M, Marsh D, *Nutrition and Evolution* (New Canaan, CT, Keats Pub. Inc., 1995), p. 209, and Price W, *Nutrition and Physical Degeneration* (New Canaan, CT, Keats Publishing, 1998).

You can see why none of the primitive tribes had dentists. Dr. Price's many photographs illustrate why they also had no need for orthodontists. As long as they remained on their primitive cuisine, their children had broad palates and perfectly aligned teeth. Dr. Price found that only the children of largely vegetarian grain farmers or modernized people regularly suffered from crowded or crooked teeth.

What a contrast to modern civilization! Ninety-five percent of modern civilized people have at least 1 decayed or filled tooth, and a large proportion has crooked, crowded teeth. Many also have incomplete or unbalanced development of facial, jaw, or skull bones—causing overbites, under bites, sunken cheekbones, and pinched nostrils.

Dr. Price showed deficient nutrition, *not* genetics, is the cause of these disorders. Hunter-gatherers were immune to these disorders so long as they ate their nutrient-dense native diets, but wherever they switched to paltry modern processed foods, their pure-blood children developed all the dental and facial disorders common in civilization.

Hunter-gatherers and herdsmen also had powerful vision and hearing, regardless of age. At a distance of half a mile, many could see more things than white people could see. Even more remarkable, some Maori were capable of seeing the moons of Jupiter without the aid of telescopes. Dr. Price searched for signs of cancer, heart disease, diabetes, and arthritis among the primitives, and found none wherever people remained on primitive diets.

He cataloged and analyzed foods eaten by people immune to modern diseases. He discovered that, compared to modern diets, native diets typically contained at least 50 percent more protein, 2 to 5 times more essential fatty acids, minerals, and water-soluble vitamins, and 10 times the fat-soluble vitamins A and D. A generous intake of animal foods such as insects, organ meats, finfish and shellfish, or meat, eggs, or milk from wild or pasture-grazing animals played an important role in this superior nutrition.

Although he searched for 20 years, Dr. Price found no traditional cultures existing on purely vegetarian diets. He wrote:

> "As yet I have not found a single group of primitive racial stock which was building and maintaining excellent bodies by living entirely on plant foods. I have found in many parts of the world most devout representatives of modern ethical systems advocating the restriction of foods to the vegetable products. In every instance where the groups involved had been long under this teaching, I found evidence of degeneration in the form of dental caries, and in the new generation in the form of abnormal dental arches to an extent very much higher than in the primitive groups who were not under this influence."[1]

Dr. Price was particularly impressed by the superior health of coastal people eating liberally of sea foods. The tribes he visited especially prized fatty seacoast animal products, such as fish eggs, fat baby mutton birds, various marine birds, marine bird eggs, large coconut crabs, and dugong (also known as sea cow). They also ate liberally of other types of shellfish and finfish, and sea vegetables. Inland tribes regularly traded with coast-dwellers to obtain sea foods. One of the Melanesian guides that Dr. Price worked with said those living inland knew they had to have sea foods at least once every three months. In Peru, too, Dr. Price found highland tribes were aware of a need for sea foods and traded with coastal people to obtain fish eggs and kelp.

Isolated hunter-gatherers with broad handsome faces and strong physiques were also remarkably free of emotional, mental, social, and moral disorders. Their honesty, unselfishness, and self-control were exemplary. In many tribes, one could leave a dwelling or possessions unattended and unlocked for days or months and know that no primitive person would touch them. None of the truly primitive groups needed prisons.

One thing important to note: Although all the healthy groups that Dr. Price studied had superb nutrition, none had a superabundance

Beyond Physical
Isolated hunter-gatherers have also been found to be free of many of the emotional, social, mental, and moral disorders that plague modern society.

of food. All were limited to local foods, which naturally ebbed and flowed depending on season and weather events. If they wanted something to eat, they had to go out and hunt for or gather it, or be involved daily in herding or farming. Generally they ate no more than necessary. Sometimes food was restricted by natural cycles. Overall, their caloric intakes were in equilibrium with their activity levels.

Scientists Agree: Dr. Weston Price Was Right

Although we have been led to believe that without modern medicine, primitives had no hope for good health, anthropologists have confirmed Dr. Price's findings: Hunter-gatherers simply did not have the degenerative diseases prevalent in affluent Westernized nations.

Civilized people suffer vision problems even at early ages; hunter-gatherers do not. A 2002 study led by Dr. Loren Cordain, Ph.D., a professor of Health Promotion at Colorado State University, links the early onset of myopia in modern nations with high intakes of refined carbohydrate.[2] Omega-3 essential fatty acids, vitamin A, and various carotenes are all critical to optimal development and function of the eyes, but modern diets are sorely lacking in these nutrients that are abundant in hunter-gatherer diets.

How about skin? Have you been told that diet has little effect on skin health, particularly acne? Acne is almost universal among modern populations. A 2002 study of two non-grain-eating primitive groups, the South Pacific Kitavans and the South American Ache hunter-gatherers, found them completely free of acne in all age groups.[3] Acne has been called "skin diabetes" because studies indicate people with acne have elevated glucose levels in the skin. One study found that a high-protein, moderate-carbohydrate diet (35 percent of calories as carbohydrate) similar to a hunter-gatherer diet reduced levels of the most potent form of testosterone (DHT) that is thought to promote acne.[4]

Since many primitive groups ate relatively liberal amounts of meat and fat, many assume they were prone to cardiovascular diseases. However, much research has shown that contemporary hunter-gatherers have enjoyed immunity to high blood pressure, non-obstructive coronary atherosclerosis, coronary heart disease, cerebrovascular disease, peripheral vascular disease, and varicose veins.[5, 6]

How about digestive disorders? Civilized people suffer from cholesterol gallstones, constipation, diverticular disease, appendicitis, and hemorrhoids, but despite careful searches such things have never been found among hunter-gatherers.[5]

Metabolic disorders such as obesity, insulin resistance, diabetes mellitus (Type II), and gout were also unknown among hunter-gatherers. Contemporary hunter-gatherers have also been found to be completely free of diseases of the immune system, including rheumatoid arthritis, multiple sclerosis, various other autoimmune diseases, and cancers of colon, lung, breast, and prostate.[5, 6, 7]

More Than a Pretty Smile
Studies show that contemporary hunter-gatherer groups do not suffer from many modern-day ills including—but not limited to—acne, vision problems, high blood pressure, heart disease, and digestive disorders.

How do we know their high immunity is not due to genetics? Dr. Price and other scientists observed that whenever and wherever these groups have abandoned their primitive diets for modern Western foods, they have developed the full range of modern diseases. When they have returned to their native nutrition plans, the diseases abate.

Famine or Feast?

You may be thinking, "That's all well and good, but Stone Age hunter-gatherers always lived on the edge of hunger, their lives were 'nasty, brutish, and short,' and besides, they were savage and dim-witted. Who wants to live like that?" Although these prejudices are common, they evaporate upon close examination.

When asked why they did not adopt agriculture, an !Kung Bushman replied "Why should we, when there are so many mongongo nuts in the world?"[8] The !Kung inhabit the Kalahari Desert yet have little difficulty finding food. We just don't know where to look.

The !Kung average 2000 calories per day, plenty for their needs—though admittedly, not enough to make them fat. Before farmers took over the most fertile areas of earth, hunter-gatherers had the run of the place. Nineteenth century American pioneers heading west recounted huge bison herds. Accounts from early American settlers tell of flocks of game birds literally darkening the sky. There was no shortage of food. All a man had to do was go for it.

Besides, agriculture certainly hasn't eliminated hunger. Substantial evidence indicates famine is created, not solved, by agriculture aimed at continuously increasing food supplies.[9] After 10,000 years of farming, culminating in our high-tech agriculture, in 2003 more than 3 billion people—one-half of the world population--suffered from malnutrition.[9] It is estimated that fewer than 10 million people roamed the Earth 10,000 years ago. Think about it: The number of malnourished people in 2003 was about 300 times the estimated world population when farming first started!

Although it is likely true that all pre-industrial people—hunter-gatherers and farmers alike—experienced occasional food supply reductions due to seasonal or local climate variations, for hunter-gatherers the shortages usually inflicted no serious damage; they kept them slim and healthy throughout life. These days in the Land of Plenty, people deliberately diet or starve themselves attempting to achieve the same effect. Which approach makes more sense?

Anthropologist Mark N. Cohen, Ph.D., notes the majority of archaeological studies have shown that diseases of nutritional deficiency were less common among hunter-gatherers than among their farming neighbors or descendants.[10] Extreme shortages were more rare for hunter-gatherers than for farmers. Although hunter-gatherers did not store food, this was not because they lacked foresight; they relied on Mother Nature to do the storing and always knew where to look.

Farmers vs. Gatherers
Many times farmers must rely on crops, often hybrids not native to the area and there-fore are susceptible to climactic changes, such as drought, freezing or flooding. Meanwhile, hunter-gatherers rely on hundreds of wild plants that are adapted to the climate variations common to their areas.

In recent times, when climatic changes have produced crop failures and starvation for farmers, neighboring hunter-gatherers have often remained relatively unscathed. Why? Hunter-gatherers use hundreds of different wild plants that are adapted to climate variations common in their habitat, according to Dr. S. Boyd Eaton, M.D., and Dr. Melvin Konner, M.D., Ph.D., in *The Paleolithic Prescription*. They further explain: Farmers rely on only a few crops, often hybrids imported from distant regions that are not adapted to local climate variations. Conditions such as cold, drought, or flooding can decimate a farmer's delicate crops and animals while having little effect on hardy wild plants and animals. For example, one year when extreme drought killed crops and cattle belonging to Bantu-speaking farmers in Botswana, they were able to survive only by adopting the hunting and gathering techniques of their neighbors, the !Kung San.[11]

Aboriginal Affluence

In *Stone Age Economics*, anthropologist Marshal Sahlins, Ph.D., of the University of Michigan (Ann Arbor) dubbed hunting and gathering "the original affluent society" achieved by orienting work to meeting genuine needs and stopping when enough was enough.

Anthropologists who have lived with hunter-gatherers in the most challenging environments—deserts, Arctic tundra—report that they often meet all their needs working an average of 20 to 30 hours a week. Hunter-gatherers spent a lot more time sleeping, talking, visiting relatives, and dancing than do modern people because they were not paying for cars, VCRs, and other techno-toys.

Hunting for Longevity

It's a myth that all hunter-gatherers died by the age of 30. Unless killed by infection or injury, hunter-gatherers lived as long as modern people—but in much better shape.

Scientific studies have found that rate of aging and maximum life span can be best estimated by use of a figure called Mortality Rate Doubling Time (MRDT), the time it takes for the mortality rate, i.e. the probability of death, to double. The MRDT of modern man is 8, so if someone is 40 today, at 48 he is twice as likely to die, at 56 he is 4 times more likely to die, and at 64 he is 8 times as likely to die. Steven Austad, Ph.D., from the University of Idaho (Moscow) is a leading expert on aging, and has determined that the MRDT of prehistoric people was about the same as ours.[13] They could live as long as we do, but their lifestyle may have involved more fatal infections or accidents related to hunting.

Nutrition and Physical Degeneration includes photos of elder hunter-gatherers from around the globe. American Indians had special respect for elders and grandparents.

In fact, about 20 percent of contemporary hunter-gatherers reached age 60 or beyond, but unlike many civilized elders, they

Original Affluent Society
Hunter-gatherers only worked to meet needs and stopped when they had enough. They generally worked 20-30 hours a week and had plenty of time for sleeping, talking, dancing, and visiting relatives.

were slim and in excellent health, without need of eyeglasses, hearing aids, or other supports for degenerating faculties, and virtually free of degenerative diseases as long as they adhered to their native diets.

The Modern Longevity Myth

Age Myth
Contrary to popular belief, hunter-gatherers, unless killed by infection or injury, lived as long an people in a modernized society. What's more, many elders in ancient civilizations maintained a high level of activity during life's later years.

The prevalent opinion that we live longer than our ancient ancestors misses the mark. Today the people with the longest life span are those living in Okinawa where the average life expectancy is 81.2 years—86 for women, 75 for men. In modern America, the average is 80.45 years.

In *Natural Eating,* Geoff Bond notes ancient people had a similar life expectancy. About 3000 years ago, the author of the Bible's Psalm 90 wrote that the expected life span was between 70 and 80 years. Around the same time in Greece, the poet Homer composed the *Iliad,* in which he tells us Odysseus' wife Penelope remained faithful though he was absent 20 years, during which time she had offers of marriage from many men, some the same age as her son Telemachus. Bond says, "In other words, in ancient Greece 3000 years ago, a 40-plus woman was such a marriageable attraction that she was pursued by men half her age."[14] More than 2300 years ago in Greece, the philosopher Aristotle recommended men not marry until reaching 35—as Bond says, "hardly the strategy of people expecting a short life or decrepit old age."

Ancient people not only lived long, they were active late in life. The great Chinese philosopher Kung Chiu, commonly known as Confucius, died at 73 in 479 B.C. Kung Chiu wrote his famed *Spring and Autumn* annals in the last years of his life. Siddhartha Gautama, now known as the Buddha, lived 80 years from 560 to 480 B.C. Gautama traveled from village to village by foot, teaching the Eightfold Path of enlightenment until his last day. In 399 B.C. the great Greek philosopher Socrates was put to death at 70 by the Athenian government for supposedly having "led the youth astray" through his relentless public questioning of received views. Plato was 41 when he set up his first school of philosophy in 386 B.C.; he taught and wrote until he died in 347 B.C. at 80.

Bond adds: "Look again at some of Alexander the Great's generals. Antigonus Monophthalmos was a battling veteran who, encouraging his troops from his war-horse, finally succumbed to a hail of javelins at the Battle of Ipsus. He was 81 years old. His opponent, Lysimichos was later killed at the Battle of Coropedium at the age of 70. His ally Selfcos Nicator survived all battles only to be assassinated at the age of 78."[14]

How many modern 70-year-old men would be capable of riding a horse into battle carrying the heavy ancient armaments? These old men had the virility of youth. We live no longer but lack their vigor in our old age!

We have generated the false impression we have longer lives than our forebears by misunderstanding our own average life-span calculations. For example, it is often claimed that the average life span for white Americans increased more than 25 years (for men from 48 to 74; for women from 51 to 80) between 1900 and 2000. The 1900 figures paint an inaccurate picture because they are averages that include all deaths from infancy to old age.

To illustrate, if 50 percent of people die in infancy, and 50 percent live to 80 years, the average life span will be only 40. But when only those who lived past childhood are taken into account, people in 1900 had the same life expectancy as we do today; many lived to 70 and older. By improving sanitation and bringing down the infant mortality, we have created the illusion that adults are living longer. Once out of childhood, our potential life span has not really changed in at least 3000 years.

Women's and Children's Health

The hunter-gatherer diet and lifestyle had special benefits for women, providing adequate iron from meat, lacking in many farm-based diets (see Chapter 2). In many tribes women contributed a large part of the food eaten—various plant and small animal products—and thus enjoyed status and respect.

Thanks to low body fat and consequently lower estrogen levels, hunter-gatherer women did not start menstruating until at least 16 years old.

Low body fat also resulted in early menopause, as early as 40. In contrast, farmer women typically have more body fat and elevated estrogen levels, causing more menstruation, beginning as early as 10 years of age and ending as late as 50 years of age—a reproductive life time up to 16 years longer than a hunter-gatherer. Consequently, farmer women suffer more blood loss and more iron deficiency than hunter-gatherer women.

Hunter-gatherer women typically nursed each child very intensively for 1 to 2 years, and continued nursing each child for 3 to 4 years total. Human milk is the only food designed by Nature specifically for infants and proven through eons to support complete development. On-demand intensive nursing as performed by hunter-gatherer women is a very effective contraceptive and also is extremely important to a child's physical and social development.

Designer Food
Human breast milk is the only food designed by Nature specifically to enhance infant development.

In *The Continuum Concept*, Jean Liedloff explained that in all pre-industrial cultures people understood that babies are helpless and require almost continuous contact with a caregiver, usually mother, during the first 2 or more years of life, to achieve optimal physical, mental, and emotional development. While living with South American Yequana Indians, Liedloff discovered that their babies raised in this manner did not manifest the behavioral and socialization problems, such as the "terrible twos" common in modern nations.

Later, Liedloff visited Bali and found that Balinese parents raised their babies in the same basic fashion as the Yequana, with the same result: healthy, happy children and a society without any generation gaps. Among both the Yequana and the Balinese, Liedloff found that in healthy families every baby was:

- free to breast-feed around the clock as needed in response to his own body's signals;
- carried in arms or otherwise in contact with someone, usually mother, and allowed to observe (or nurse, or sleep) while the person carrying him went about normal adult business—until he began creeping, then crawling on his own impulse, usually at 6 to 8 months;
- allowed to sleep in the parents' bed, until he left of his own volition (often about 2 years);
- given necessary attention immediately in response to his signals (squirming, crying, etc.), without judgment, displeasure, invalidation of his needs, undue concern, or making him a frequent or constant center of attention;
- expected by elders to be naturally amiable and helpful and to have strong self-preservation instincts; and,
- always accepted and appreciated.[15]

Liedloff explains how failure to follow this natural pattern of child care can produce people who have unmet developmental needs, poor self-understanding, anger at elders and the world, a sense of impotence, and difficulty forming healthy relationships.[16] Modern American child-rearing practices are so distant from what Nature demands it is little surprise American children are suffering en masse from behavioral disorders, depression, and suicide.

In the absence of intensive nursing and contraception, farmer women are pregnant more often and can have more children than hunter-gatherer women—sometimes several per birth (due to over nutrition) and more than a dozen per lifetime.[12] This puts a strain on women's iron stores and often results in deficiencies or depletions. It also has strained Mother Earth with overpopulation.

Returning to the Past
While it's true we no longer live in the Stone Age, we still live better on a hunter-gatherer diet than anything modern society has produced.

Not by Food Alone

In *A Cry Unheard: New Insights into the Medical Consequences of Loneliness* (Bancroft Press, 2000), Dr. James J. Lynch, Ph.D., presents compelling evidence that families or communities united by affection and altruism have the best health. He shows that lonely people have the highest rates of heart disease, cancer, and numerous other physical, emotional, and social maladies.

The lonely are legion in modern nations. Our competitive consumer culture creates conflict between the sexes, generations, classes, races, nations, and man and nature that destroys families and communities. In his book *The Gospel of the Red Man*, Ernest Thompson Seton noted, "The culture of the Red Man is fundamentally spiritual; his measure of success is, 'How much service have I rendered to my people?'"

This was the norm for tribal life. It fostered congenial kinship and culture that contributed greatly to hunter-gatherer health.

So What? We're Not Stone Agers!

It is commonly believed that during the past 10,000 years we have evolved to adapt to the agricultural diet and are genetically different from hunter-gatherers. One fashionable diet book claims the four blood types are products of human nutritional variations developed after the agricultural revolution.

However, several factors have conspired to inhibit genetic adaptation to farmed foods, including:

♦ cross-cultural marriages,
♦ our expanding population,
♦ increasing interregional travel,
♦ food-processing techniques designed to adapt foods to us,
♦ and the fact that diseases caused by eating farmed or industrial foods rarely kill people before they have had opportunity to have children.

The four blood types are found in all racial groups, including those only recently involved in agriculture, such as American Indians, disproving the hypothesis that some of the four ABO blood types are adapted specifically to farmed foods.[17]

Experts in human genetics and biology assert that we differ very little from Stone Age people. If farming and civilization have altered human biology, then people from recent hunter-gatherer groups––such as the Eskimos, Cherokees, Kalahari San, and Australian Aborigines—should be genetically and anatomically different from people whose ancestors have been farming for millennia, such as Near Easterners, Chinese, and New Guineans. However, we are aware of no evidence of any nutritionally important genetic, anatomical, or physiological difference between these groups.

In their must-read, ground-breaking book *Nutrition and Evolution,* leading biochemists Michael Crawford and David Marsh say: "Biologically, man is still a wild animal and there is no reason to suppose that his biology is adapted to anything other than wild foods. There simply has not been time for any selective evolution to have changed mankind as mankind has changed its pattern of eating."[18]

In short, despite our civilized sophistication and regardless of race, we still are designed for a primitive hunter-gatherer diet.

The bottom line?

Our departure from primitive nutrition is largely responsible for the emergence of many diseases of modern civilization—including many not commonly thought to be diet-related. To reclaim our health, we need to return to *The Garden of Eating.*

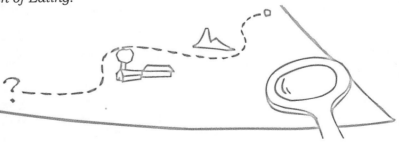

2 Native Nutrition

Thanks to Dr. Weston Price (Chapter 1) and the many other scientists who have studied hundreds of hunting and gathering, herding, and primitive farming communities during the past 150 years or so, we have a good understanding of native diets associated with extraordinary health.

Archaeology and history clearly indicate people have always eaten both animal and plant food. Diets of all primitive groups studied in contemporary times have included animal and vegetable foods. Dr. Price and other experts have reported that in many communities, animal foods were considered the most important and sacred.

Briefly, here are some of the remarkably successful diets studied by Dr. Price[1]:

Hunter/Fisher/Gatherers

1. Amazon Jungle Indians ate freshwater fish, birds, and land animals, yucca tuber, and fruits including bananas. All edible parts of animals were consumed, including organ meats and fats.

2. Australian Aborigines lived on dugong (a sea mammal), sea turtles, enormous shellfish, finfish, wallaby, kangaroo, small animals, rodents, some insects, birds, eggs, sea and land vegetables, and wild fruits and nuts. Again all edible parts of animals were consumed, including organ meats and fats.

Chapter Overview
Many native diets are associated with good health. Chapter 2 provides a closer examination of the food and food groups that were at the heart of the these diets.

3. Maori of New Zealand ate dugong, fat mutton birds, many other land and sea birds, shell and finfish, and fat sea turtles, along with wild roots, green vegetables, and fruits.

4. Eskimos ate mostly red meat and organs from whale and seal, along with liberal amounts of blubber and seal oil. They also ate some caribou, fish (fresh, dried, and frozen), and fish eggs. Some berries and plants were eaten fresh in summer and dried or stored in fat for winter.

5. South Pacific natives ate dugong, shell and finfish, sea turtles, wild pigs, coconut, starchy taro tuber, sea and land vegetables, and tropical fruits.

6. Indians in northern Canada lived almost exclusively on wild game meat and fat, mainly moose and caribou for 9 months of the year. They emphasized organ meats and bone marrow and fed much of the lean muscle meat to their dogs. During the summer they ate wild plants and in winter bark and buds from trees.

Herdsmen
1. The Masai, Neurs, and Somali tribesmen lived primarily on blood, milk, and meat from strictly pasture-fed cattle, goats, or camels, supplemented with local vegetables and fruits.

Grain Farmers
1. Gaelics in the Outer Hebrides ate liberally of sea foods, including fish heads and livers, some oats, and fresh greens in summer. Vegetables were grown and stored for winter.

2. Swiss in the Loetschental Valley ate large amounts of cultured dairy products from pasture-fed animals, especially cheese, whole rye bread, meat about once weekly, and a variety of vegetables, some fresh in summer and others stored for winter.

3. African Kikuyu lived primarily on sweet potatoes, corn, beans, bananas, millet, and Kafir corn (a type of millet). Animal foods including some pasture-fed goat milk and meat. Insects were a small part of the diet.

Generally, the tribes with the lowest rates of dental decay (see Table 1.1, Page 3) ate a variety of wild sea foods or game meats, vegetables, and fruits.

How Much Meat Did They Eat?
In 2000, a team of experts on hunter-gatherer nutrition, led by

> **What's a Dugong?**
>
> Dugongs, also known as sea cows, were a favorite food of several South Sea tribes studied by Dr. Price. They weigh between 500 and 1800 pounds and inhabit shallow tropical waters. Although numbers have been greatly reduced by human hunting, herds of several hundred dugong still exist. Dugong meat is likened to tender veal, and its hide makes a good grade of leather. An average adult dugong provides 24 to 56 liters (6 to 15 gallons) of oil. They are hunted with harpoons and gill nets.[2]

Colorado State University Professor Loren Cordain, Ph.D., published an analysis of 229 contemporary hunter-gatherer diets. It found "whenever and wherever ecologically possible, hunter-gatherers consumed high amounts (45 to 65 percent of energy) of animal food," including fish and sea foods, which ranged from 6 to 55 percent of their diets.[3]

A potential problem with this estimate is it is based on recorded habits of recent hunter-gatherers after contact and conflict with farmers. Most groups included in the database lived on marginal lands not wanted by farmers and civilization. Most had little or no access to sea foods or fertile soils producing edible fruits and vegetables and were forced to rely largely on hunting land animals. Consequently, they may not illustrate optimum diets.

Dr. Price was particularly impressed with the physical and mental development and high immunity to degenerative diseases among coast-dwelling people who ate liberal amounts of seafood, the best source of iodide. He found natives all around the world were aware they needed foods from the sea to maintain health. When Dr. Price asked highland Peruvians why they went to great lengths to obtain fish eggs and kelp from coastal people, they told him it was necessary to maintain female fertility and prevent the "big neck" disease—i.e. goiter—often developed by white people.[4]

Seafood is also the best source of omega-3 essential fatty acids. Iodide and omega-3s are required for full development of the brain and nervous system. Deficiency of these nutrients in pregnancy and childhood impairs brain and intelligence development. Severe iodide deficiency causes irreversible mental and physical retardation called cretinism. Hence the wisdom in the adage that seafood is brain food.

When the first Europeans arrived in Australia, the Aborigines dwelt on the seacoast, feasting on fish, sea turtles, and dugongs, as well as kangaroos, wallabies, lizards, and other land animals. The English moved in, drove the natives from their preferred sites along the coasts and rivers, and pushed them inland where pickings were slim and nutritionally different.[5]

Dr. Price recounted how, when the French landed in New Caledonia, Melanesia, they forced the natives who lived on the coast to move inland. The French established a colony and sugar plantation on the coast. One night in 1917 a band of the angry displaced Melanesians swept down on the French colony and massacred almost the entire white population. Dr. Price explained, "Their contact with the required foods from the sea had been cut off. They believed they required seafood to maintain life and physical efficiency."[6] Price found the natives who had been forced inland had a "marked increase in the incidence of dental caries" compared to those still living on the coast.

This story may shed light on early American history. When Europeans first landed in the Americas, Indians were dwelling along

Brainfood
Many primitive groups lived near coastal areas and ate abundant amounts of seafood, the best source of iodide and omega-3 essential fatty acids. Iodide and omega-3s have been linked to healthy development of the brain and nervous system.

the Eastern Seaboard. Though the Europeans probably would not have survived long without the Indians' help (among other things, they taught the Europeans how to use fish remains to fertilize gardens), the whites did not respect the natives' need to hunt and gather along the coast. The Indians responded with depredations similar to what the Melanesians inflicted on the French in New Caledonia.

The natives were forced inland because Europeans also preferred rich coastal habitats. Evidence indicates that the oldest human settlements were along coasts or estuaries, and most of the great cities of the world were and are close to the sea, rivers or lakes.[7] To this day, waterfront property commands the highest price. People are drawn to the coast for recreation and sustenance.

Reams of research done in the late 20th century suggest people who regularly eat fish have a lower incidence of the cardiovascular and nervous system problems than people who do not. This is important to keep in mind because the sea animal fat eaten liberally by many of the groups studied by Dr. Price can be quite different from grassland animal fat eaten by tribes such as Plains Indian hunters.

Wild Meat and Fat
When considering only the trimmed muscle, wild game meat is much leaner than many modern mass-market meats (Table 2.1). In general, wild game muscle has about 50 percent fewer calories, and less total fat and saturated fat than modern grain-fed meat.

Table 2.1:

Protein and Fat in Wild Game and Modern Feedlot Meats (3.5 ounce portion)		
Meats	**Grams of Protein**	**Grams of Fat**
Wild game		
Goat	20.6	3.8
Wild boar	16.8	8.3
Rabbit	21.0	5.0
Deer	21.0	4.0
Bison	25.0	3.8
Whale	20.6	7.5
Modern feedlot meats		
Prime lamb loin	14.7	32.0
Ham	15.2	29.1
Regular hamburger	17.9	21.2
Choice sirloin steak	16.9	26.7
Pork loin	16.4	28.0

Sources: Eaton SB, Konner M, Shostak M, *The Paleolithic Prescription* (New York, Harper & Row, 1988), p. 108; U.S. Department of Agriculture; American Meat Institute; National Livestock & Meat Board: Pennington JAT, *Food Values of Portions Commonly Used* (New York, Harper & Row, 1989).

Hunter-gatherers ate only lean meat, and very little saturated animal fat. Right?

Not quite.

Although the muscle meat of wild game is very lean, the animals can have substantial stores of subcutaneous, back, visceral, or kidney fat. The most obvious examples are the sea mammals already discussed, which have enormous amounts of blubber and oil. Among land animals, camel and bison have prominent humps on the back—those are special fat storage depots.

In "The Preference for Animal Protein and Fat: A Cross-Cultural Survey," nutritional anthropologist H. Leon Abrams points out that anthropologists and other qualified witnesses have reported hunter-gatherers universally prized animal fat.[8]

The human liver has a limited ability to metabolize protein and detoxify the amino acid and ammonia by-products. A diet too high in lean meat would cause what early American explorers called rabbit starvation, now known as protein poisoning, resulting first in nausea, then diarrhea, and finally death. To prevent this, lean meats must be eaten with fats or carbohydrate. Since wild fruits and vegetables were only modest sources of carbohydrate, Cordain's team calculated that hunter-gatherers had to hunt larger game that was at least 10 percent fat, such as whales, dugong, manatee, seals, rhinos, mammoth, horses, aurochs, bison, camels, elephants, and the like, to obtain enough fat to prevent protein poisoning.[3]

Was that fat less saturated than modern animal fats? That depends on where they were living. Sea mammal blubber is partially saturated, but it has a higher proportion of unsaturated oils than land animal fat, so hunters of sea mammals may have eaten relatively fewer saturated fats. By the way, the idea that Eskimos subsist mainly on fatty fish is wrong. Seals, whales, and caribou—all red meat—are the main staples of the traditional Eskimo diet.

All land mammals—caribou, bison, rhinos, deer, aurochs (ancestors of cattle), elephants, etc.—favored by hunter-gatherers store a highly saturated fat. An analysis performed by Cordain and colleagues found that the storage fat of North American deer, elk, and antelope is 60 to 65 percent saturated.[9] In comparison, modern beef fat is only about 45 percent saturated.

How much fat could inland people get from hunting large grazing animals? Even if a 1500-pound bison had only 3 percent of its body weight as stored fat (a very lean animal), the yield would be 45 pounds of highly saturated fat, providing 157,500 calories. By inciting the animals to stampede off a cliff or into a trap, the American Plains tribes typically killed from a few dozen to 200 bison at a time—yielding from 1600 to 9000 pounds of depot fat. They would eat some of the meat fresh, but most was dried. Bones were always cracked then boiled to extract the marrow fat, which supplies both monounsaturates (just like olive oil) and saturates.

Not by Lean Meat Alone To avoid protein poisoning, a healthy diet must include carbohydrates and fats that lean meat cannot provide. Fruits and vegetables provided a modest source of carbs, but hunter-gatherers also hunted larger game, with at least 10 percent fat in order to meet nutritional needs.

The dried meat was ground to a powder and mixed with berries and an equal weight of saturated fat to make pemmican, a cake that is solid at ambient temperatures. It's impossible to make pemmican without highly saturated fat. Plains tribes made and stored enough pemmican for their own needs *and* had a surplus that was a favored trade item. During the historic fur trade, *tons* of pemmican were traded by Plains tribes.

Stone age people hunted large game on all continents, making saturated animal fats part of human diets for more than 30,000 generations. But the amount varied from season to season; wild animals typically carry more fat in the fall and much less in the spring. Hunters preferred to capture fatter animals, but since they didn't control breeding and feeding, they didn't always get lots of fat (or food).[8] In addition, they didn't eat all the fat, because they used some for other purposes, such as tanning leather and making candles, soap, and salves.

Cordain's team estimated that most recent hunter-gatherers with high immunity to heart disease and other modern degenerative diseases typically had diets providing about 38 to 49 percent of calories as fat, mostly from animals.[3]

Is this a high-fat diet? Though people who should know better often state that any diet providing more than 30 percent of calories as fat is a high-fat diet, they are mistaken. Here's why.

In a diet providing 3000 calories, 30 percent from fat, the fat provides 900 calories and the absolute amount of fat is 100 grams. In a diet providing 2000 calories, 45 percent from fat, fat provides 900 calories and the absolute amount of fat again is 100 grams. Although the proportions of fat differ, the 45 percent fat, 2000-calorie diet has no more fat than the 30 percent fat, 3000-calorie diet.

Not many foraging tribes had surplus calories because few wild foods are energy-dense. Most groups had to eat animal fat to maintain adequate calorie intakes. Although their diets may have had a higher proportion of fat they didn't necessarily eat more fat grams than a present-day person who consumes more total calories.

Omega-6 v. Omega-3

Omega-6 and omega-3 are essential polyunsaturated fatty acids. Essential indicates that neither can be produced in the body—they must be consumed through diet.

Omega-6s, found in many vegetable oils as well as grain-fed animals, are far more commonplace in modern diets than are omega-3s. Although essential, omega-6s have been linked to the promotion of degenerative diseases when consumed in excess.

Omega-3s are more difficult to find, but are more beneficial to one's health. They can be found in wild marine animal fat, and oils such as flax and canola.

Big Fat Differences

One of the most important differences between wild marine animal fats, wild grassland animal fats, and modern mass-market animal fats is the ratio of omega-6 to omega-3 fatty acids.

Wild marine animal fats typically have at least 7 times more omega-3s than omega-6s. In wild or strictly grass-fed land animal fats, the ratio is typically reversed—2 to 3 times as much omega-6 as omega-3—but some can have about equal parts omega-6 and omega-3. And, because feeding grain to animals dramatically raises the amount of omega-6s and reduces the omega-3s deposited in their tissues, typical conventional meats and fats have between 4 and 20 times as much omega-6 as omega-3.[9, 10]

This ratio is very important. Diets too high in omega-6s and too low in omega-3s appear to promote degenerative diseases (discussed in Chapter 5). Wild marine animals provide an important counterbalance to the high omega-6 levels in modern animal fats that may account for the beneficial effects of eating fish.

A Fat Similarity

Wild game storage fat and butter have surprisingly similar compositions. When Cordain and colleagues analyzed wild game storage fat, they found a profile of 60 to 65 percent saturated, 25 to 30 percent monounsaturated, and less than 5 percent polyunsaturated, with an average of 2.5 times more omega-6 than omega-3.[9] Butter has a parallel profile of 63 percent saturated, 29 percent monounsaturated, and 3 percent polyunsaturated, but only 1.5 times more omega-6 than omega-3.[11]

Butter may be better. It has a more desirable omega-6 to omega-3 ratio, and more short-chain, low-molecular weight saturated fats than storage fat, which makes butter soft at room temperature and easier to digest and metabolize to energy. As we'll discuss in Chapter 5, butter is among the good fats with an undeserved bad reputation—in moderation it doesn't cause heart disease. It's a tasty substitute for blubber, bone marrow, or storage fat.

Did They Cook It?

Cooking is practiced by every known culture. Cooking meat has enormous advantages: It destroys parasites and makes proteins more digestible. Many cuts of meat contain so much fibrous connective tissue that they are inedible unless thoroughly cooked or ground finely by machines. This is especially true of organ meats and meat from older male game animals. (Testosterone makes meat fibers tougher.)

Although most recent hunter-gatherers (including Eskimos) ate most of their meat cooked—typically roasted over fire or baked in pits—many tribes ate some cuts raw.[12] It is unclear whether this has any nutritional basis, but the long tradition of eating some raw meat is preserved in some civilized cuisines. Some famous raw foods include Middle Eastern Kibbeh, French Steak Tartare, Italian Carpaccio, Korean Raw Beef, Spanish Ceviche, Hawaiian Lomi Lomi, Japanese Sushi and Sashimi (the last four all being raw fish).

Vegetables and Fruits

Wherever possible, healthy contemporary hunter-gatherers have eaten a very wide variety of produce, including leafy vegetables, stems, shoots,

Can't Believe it's Butter
Butter gets a bad rap among fats. It has a similar, and possibly more favorable, omega-6 to omega-3 ratio than wild game storage fat. When included in moderation it is not a contributing factor to heart disease.

roots, tubers, corms, bulbs, barks, mushrooms, fruits, and berries.[13] Modern plant foods in these categories include:
* Leaves: kale, collards, mustard greens, lettuce, and spinach
* Stems: leeks, celery
* Shoots: asparagus
* Roots: carrots, turnips, parsnips, rutabaga, and radishes
* Tubers: sunchokes and sweet potatoes
* Bulbs: onions and garlic
* Mushrooms: button, cremini, and shiitake
* Fruits: winter squash, tomatoes, melons, bananas, apples, peaches, plums, nectarines, cherries, pears, pineapple, oranges, and others
* Berries: blueberries, strawberries, raspberries, and others

Many native tribes used more than 100 species of plant foods on a regular basis. The !Kung in Africa ate some 30 species of berries and fruits, and an assortment of melons, leafy greens, and edible gums.[14] Australian Aborigines used 28 species of fruits, 9 species for stems, buds, or shoots, and 7 for roots or tubers.[15] American Prairie Indian women gathered and cultivated prolific camas bulbs, prairie turnips, and various berries (often added to pemmican). Anthropologist Melissa Darby, M.A., of Lower Columbia Research and Archaeology (Oregon) says that a woman gathering carbohydrate-rich camas could net 5,279 calories per hour. Eskimos eagerly sought what little plant food they could find in their environment, including sea vegetables, the partially digested plants found in caribou intestines, and wild berries available in the short arctic summer.[1]

Although hunter-gatherers used many types of plant foods, they preferred those richest in carbohydrate or fat, such as fruits, tubers, roots, bulbs, and nuts. Cordain's team estimated that fruits and underground storage structures made up about 65 percent of plant foods in hunter-gatherer diets, fruits being 41 percent and tubers, roots, and bulbs 24 percent.[16]

In 1996, Darby demonstrated that hunter-gatherers in the Northern Hemisphere had access to *Sagittaria latifolia*, a prolific wetlands plant that produces a tuber very similar to the white potato, which the Chinook Indians called *wapatos*. This plant grows in Europe as well as North America. It is easy to harvest and abundant from late fall through spring when other high-carbohydrate plant foods may be scarce. Darby has harvested approximately 5,418 calories per hour gathering wapatos from a knee-deep pond. The tubers do not need grinding or mashing to be palatable, and can be cooked fresh, stored fresh in a cool place, or dried. They are thoroughly cooked in a bed of hot ashes in 10 minutes, and do not need stones for long oven cooking. Pollen data indicates the wapato was prolific in the last Ice Age through North America, the North American Great Basin, Siberia, and Northern Europe.[17]

All known hunter-gatherer tribes have eaten many vegetables

and fruits cooked. Many raw vegetables and some raw fruits contain coarse nutrient-binding fibers or starches that are resistant to our digestive processes. Cooking breaks down fibers and starches, releasing nutrients from binders; cooked vegetables or fruits are generally more nutritious than raw.

Nuts and Seeds

Many hunter-gatherer tribes collected fat-rich seeds and nuts. In some instances these formed a major part of the diet. For example, the mongongo nut supplied most of the fat and up to 50 percent of the calories in the primitive !Kung diet. Some Polynesian groups used substantial amounts of coconut meat, milk, and oil. Australian Aborigines used 15 different species of nuts or seeds, including several varieties of walnuts, almonds, chestnuts (a starchy, low-fat nut), and the candlenut, which is so oily it can be set aflame and used as a light.

Many raw wild nuts and seeds are bitter and contain toxins or anti-nutrients, so they're inedible without extensive processing. Although nutmeats are calorie-rich, some wild varieties—for example, hickory nuts—have thick shells and only small amounts of nutmeat, often providing less energy than was spent in gathering and processing.

Prior to the industrial revolution, people didn't have the technology for efficiently extracting oils from nuts, seeds, or other plant foods. Consequently, prior to about 1900, only animal fats and oils were available or plentiful in many regions.[8, 18] Thanks to selective breeding, we now enjoy many varieties of nutritious, delicious, meaty, easily-shelled nuts. Most still contain some anti-nutrients that must be eliminated by soaking, sprouting, or toasting.

The Plant Food Paradox

How much plant food did hunter-gatherers eat? Cordain's team estimated they typically obtained 22 to 40 percent, or a mean of 31 percent, of their calories from carbohydrate. From these numbers you might think that fruits and vegetables were rarely consumed and formed the smallest portion of hunter-gatherer diets. In actuality, these figures indicate plant foods were likely the largest portion of those diets. How can that be? Vegetables and fruits have a very low caloric density compared to meat and fat. If fruits and vegetables are the only sources of carbohydrate in a diet, it's impossible to get 22 to 40 percent of calories from carbohydrate unless the plant foods are the largest portion of the diet by weight (or volume). This fact is best illustrated by an example. Consider the meal in Table 2.2 on the next page.

Consider this meal's caloric proportions: 61 percent of calories from meat (sirloin) and fat (we used olive oil, although hunter-gatherers probably would have used animal fat), and only 22 percent from carbohydrate. From this perspective, it looks like a meat-and-fat dominated diet.

Table 2.2

Plant-Animal Ratio of a Meal By Weight & Calories				
Item	**Weight**	**%Total Wt**	**Calories**	**%Total Cal**
5 ounces (raw) lean sirloin	140 g	25	176	35
Spinach salad:				
2 cups raw spinach	110 g	20	32	6
1/2 medium tomato	63 g	11	12	2
1/4 yellow bell pepper	34 g	6	12	2
1/4 cup scallions	24 g	4	0	0
1 tablespoon olive oil	14 g	3	126	25
1 tablespoon lemon juice	—	—	—	—
Fruit salad:				
3/4 cup cantaloupe	133 g	24	58	12
1/3 cup grapes	30 g	5	23	5
1/4 ounce macadamia nuts	7 g	1	56	11
Total meal	**555 g**	**100**	**499**	**100**

*Percentage totals are not exactly 100 due to rounding.
Macronutrient analysis: Protein: 39 g/31 percent; Fat: 27 g/49 percent; Carbohydrate: 28 g/22 percent.

However, when we consider this meal's proportions by weight, we find it is 72 percent vegetables and fruits and only 28 percent meat and fat. Apparently, to get to a level of 22 percent carbohydrate using only fruits and vegetables, a hunter-gatherer had to eat more than twice as much plant food as meat and fat.

Cordain's team estimated that a typical temperate or tropical hunter-gatherer diet would provide 20 to 31 percent of calories as protein, 38 to 49 percent as fat, and 22 to 40 percent as carbohydrate. This menu falls right in that range, but is on the high end for protein and lower than the mean for carbohydrate (31 percent).

Let's look at another example (Table 2.3), this time including a root vegetable. How about some grilled lamb loin, roasted carrots,

Table 2.3

Plant-Animal Ratio of a Meal by Weight & Calories				
Item	**Weight**	**%Total Wt**	**Calories**	**%Total Cal**
4 ounces lamb loin	102 g	17	186	31
3/4 cup carrots, roasted in 1 teaspoon olive oil	130 g	22	109	18
1 cup cooked kale greens	130 g	22	40	7
1 tablespoon butter on vegetables	14 g	2	108	18
1 cup blueberries	200 g	34	129	21
1 tablespoon coconut flakes	11 g	2	32	5
Total meal*	**587 g**	**100**	**604**	**100**

*Percentage totals are not exactly 100 due to rounding.
Macronutrient analysis: Protein: 35 g/23 percent; Fat: 28 g/42 percent; Carbohydrate: 54 g/36 percent.

kale dressed with butter, and blueberries with coconut flakes for dessert?

This meal is 23 percent protein, 36 percent carbohydrate, and 42 percent fat—right in the middle of the hunter-gatherer ranges estimated by Cordain's team. Again we find the plant food paradox: Meat and fat (lamb loin, olive oil, and butter) provide 56 percent of the calories, but plant foods provide 79 percent of the meal by weight. Another surprise: Without any dairy product other than butter, it provides 184 milligrams of calcium from lamb, carrots, kale, blueberries, and butter.

More Evidence Fruits & Vegetables Dominated Hunter-Gatherer Diets

More evidence that hunter-gatherers ate lots of fruits and vegetables comes from a research team led by Dr. Anthony Sebastian, M.D., at the Department of Medicine and General Clinical Research Center, University of California, San Francisco. In 2002 these scientists analyzed 159 possible hunter-gatherer diets with various proportions of meat, fat, vegetables, fruits, and nuts. They found 87 percent of these diets—including those in which meat and fat provided 50 to 60 percent of energy—had a net alkaline residue attributed to high intakes of fruits and vegetables.[19] The team's findings indicate that most hunter-gatherer diets were more than 65 percent produced by weight.

Here's why: All meats are acid forming, and all fruits and vegetables alkaline forming (see Acid-Base Confusion side bar). On a per-weight basis, the acid delivery of meat greatly exceeds the counterbalancing alkaline delivery of fruits or vegetables. On average, metabolism of a 3.5 ounce (100 gram) portion of fresh meat or fish produces an acid load of +8.9 milliequivalents (mEq), but an equal portion of fresh or dried fruit produces an alkaline residue of only -5.2 mEq, and an equal portion of fresh vegetables delivers an alkaline load of only -3.2 mEq. Fats are neutral.[20] This is a bit technical. Table 2.4 (next page) may be the best way to illustrate the point.

Diet 3 on the next page is 65 percent fruits and vegetables by weight but it yields a very slight net acid residue.

Sebastian's team calculated that a hunter-gatherer diet in which meat and fat provided 55 to 60 percent of calories produced an alkaline residue of -9 to -23 milliequivalents per day. Our calculations indicate that a diet must be at least 70 percent fruits and vegetables by weight to obtain that level of alkaline residue.

So, if you ask, "Were most hunter-gatherer diets meat-dominated or plant-dominated?"

Paradoxically, the correct answer appears to be "Both!"

Acid-Base Confusion

Many people incorrectly believe that tart fruits and tomatoes increase the acidity of urine. Although these foods contain weak organic acids, such as citric and malic acids, they are in the form of potassium salts. Your body metabolizes these compounds to alkaline potassium bicarbonate, which neutralizes (reduces) metabolic acids.

Animal products, cereals, legumes, and nuts all contain sulfur-rich amino acids (scarce in fruits). When these are metabolized for energy, strong sulfuric acid is released. Salt supplies chloride, which increases body and urine acidity.

Hence, meats, fish, eggs, grains, legumes, nuts, dairy, and salt are acid-forming; vegetables and fruits, including tomatoes and tart fruits, are base-forming. Fats are neutral. We need both acid and alkaline foods, but because the blood must be kept slightly alkaline and the kidneys have a limited ability to excrete acids, the balance is best tipped slightly in favor of alkaline foods.

Table 2.4

Acid-Base Balance of Diets with Different Plant-Animal Ratios by Weight

Positive (+) values indicate net acid residue,
negative (-) values indicate net base residue, in milliequivalents (mEq).

Diet 1: 25 percent meat, 75 percent produce

Amount of food	x	Ave. acid load/100 g	=	Total (mEq)
400 g meat	x	+8.9	=	+35.6
600 g vegetables	x	−3.2	=	−19.2
600 g fruit	x	−5.2	=	−31.2

Net load = +35.6 − 19.2 − 31.2 = −14.8 alkaline

Diet 2: 30 percent meat, 70 percent produce

Amount of food	x	Ave. acid load/100 g	=	Total (mEq)
480 g meat	x	+8.9	=	+42.7
560 g vegetables	x	−3.2	=	−17.9
560 g fruit	x	−5.2	=	−29.1

Net load = +42.7 − 17.9 − 29.1 = −4.3 alkaline

Diet 3: 35 percent meat, 65 percent produce

Amount of food	x	Ave. acid load/100 g	=	Total (mEq)
560 g meat	x	+8.9	=	+49.8
520 g vegetables	x	−3.2	=	−16.6
520 g fruits	x	−5.2	=	−27.0

Net load = +49.8 − 16.6 − 27.0 = +6.2 acid

Diet 4: 50 percent meat, 50 percent produce

Amount of food	x	Ave. acid load/100 g	=	Total (mEq)
800 g meat	x	+8.9	=	+71.2
400 g vegetables	x	−3.2	=	−12.8
400 g fruits	x	−5.2	=	−20.8

Net load = +71.2 - 12.8 - 20.8 = +37.6 acid

Your Needs May Vary

Please note these menus are presented only to illustrate the plant food paradox inherent in the description of hunter-gatherer diets given by Cordain's team. People can vary widely in their nutrient needs and tolerances. Only you can tell how much protein, fat, and carbohydrate you need or tolerate. We've found we feel better usually eating somewhat less fat and more carbohydrate (fruits and vegetables), than in these illustrations. You'll later find that reflected in our menu suggestions

Probably most of their calories came from animal foods, but by weight the bulk of their food was vegetables and fruits.

But Aren't We Different?

At this point, you might be wondering if hunter-gatherers are somehow different from modern people. Since we're not chasing down dinner or going gathering, do we still need to eat meat? Now that we're sedentary, aren't we better off eating grains and legumes to meet our protein needs?

First, studies of hunter-gatherers have shown that they didn't work as many hours as primitive farmers. In fact, they spent a lot more time sleeping, resting, and socializing, than most people today. On average they spent 20 to 30 hours per week working to meet their needs for food, clothing, and shelter.

Second, think about this: A lion doesn't become a vegetarian just because it is confined in a cage at the zoo. A zoo lion has the same digestive system and basic nutritional needs of a wild lion. The same is true of humans. Even if you're a desk jockey, your body would prefer a hunter-gatherer diet.

Let's take a look.

chapter 3 Friendly Foods

Through some 50,000 generations spanning 1.5 million years, during which our ancestors lived by hunting and gathering, the human body adapted to the diet provided by that lifestyle. We still have hunter-gatherer guts, for which the friendliest foods are meats, fats, fruits, and vegetables.

The Great Ape Myth

Have you heard that we should eat a vegetarian diet because we are closely related to the chimpanzees or gorillas? The argument sounds logical to people who have been led to believe that we are descendants of some ancient ape, but is refuted by anatomical evidence.

In Figure 3.1 on the next page you can see a very marked difference in body shape between man and apes. For our purpose the most important thing to notice is the belly size and shape. All apes have large bellies compared to those of man. Those bellies house the digestive apparatus required to process a diet composed of bulky, low-calorie, raw plant foods.

The differences between human and ape gut design are quantified in Table 3.1. The great apes have 4 times more gut space devoted to the large intestine than humans. Further, the apes have significant cecums—large fermentation sacs attached to the colon—but people don't.

Why the difference? Animals designed to live exclusively or almost exclusively on plant foods—such as most apes, cattle, horses,

> **Chapter Overview**
> Even though we live in a modern society, our health is still geared toward the hunter-gatherer diet. Chapter 3 will explore the food groups that hunter-gatherers relied on for healthy living.

and sheep—have guts capable of digesting and extracting nutrition from cellulose, the fiber that makes up the majority of plant matter. They feature enlarged or multi-chambered stomachs, or voluminous colons and cecums, vats heavily colonized by symbiotic, fiber-fermenting bacteria and protozoa. Herbivores can't survive without this equipment.

Figure 3.1

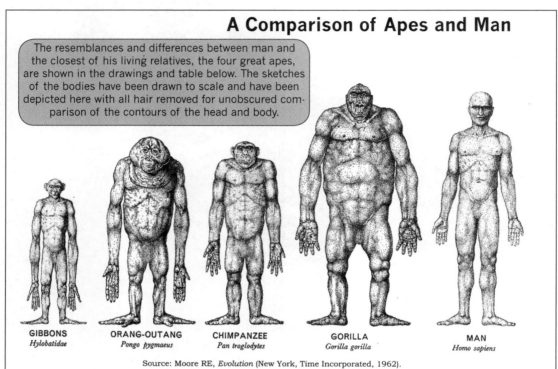

A Comparison of Apes and Man

The resemblances and differences between man and the closest of his living relatives, the four great apes, are shown in the drawings and table below. The sketches of the bodies have been drawn to scale and have been depicted here with all hair removed for unobscured comparison of the contours of the head and body.

| GIBBONS | ORANG-OUTANG | CHIMPANZEE | GORILLA | MAN |
| Hylobatidae | Pongo pygmaeus | Pan troglodytes | Gorilla gorilla | Homo sapiens |

Source: Moore RE, *Evolution* (New York, Time Incorporated, 1962).

Table 3.1

Relative Gut Volume Comparison of Chimp, Gorilla & Man

Percentage of Total Volume

Species	Stomach	Small Intestine	Cecum	Colon
Chimpanzee	20	23	5	52
Gorilla	25	14	7	53
Man	17	67	n.a.	17

Source: Milton K, "Primate Diets and Gut Morphology," in *Food and Evolution*, ed. by Marvin Harris and Eric Ross (Temple University Press, 1987), p. 99.

The human gut has no special fermentation vats, and is designed to limit microbial colonization. In good health the stomach produces enough strong acid (pH 1.5 to 3.5) to kill ingested microbes and initiate meat digestion. Any microbes that survive this acid bath are attacked in the small intestine by enzymes and the immune system. Remarkably, some bacteria survive to colonize the large intestine. However, if the microbial colony in your intestines gets very large, you'll suffer painful bloating from microbe-produced gases inflating your normally compact gut. Unlike herbivores, we can digest food without these gut flora. We have no cellulose-digesting enzymes, so we have a limited ability to extract nutrients from raw plants.

Another main difference is gall bladder development. Because their foods—leaves, fruits, roots—are very low in fat, vegetarian animals have little or no gall bladder. In contrast, we have a very well-developed gall bladder designed to help us digest fats, which are more abundant in meats than plant foods.

Contrary to popular belief, neither chimpanzees nor gorillas are strict vegetarians. Chimps eat insects, grubs, eggs, and occasionally actively prey upon Colobus monkeys, wild pigs, and small antelope. Gorillas in the wild consume many protozoa (micro-animals) that take up residence in the ape's stomach and not only help it digest plants but also provide its animal protein. However, in captivity gorillas do not maintain the intake of protozoa and must be fed meat or milk to maintain health.[1] Captive apes fail to thrive or successfully reproduce unless given meat or other animal products.

Why Meat?

Meat is our best source of iron and zinc. Unlike apes, we lack enzymes for releasing iron from plant foods, and absorb iron from meat at least 3 times more efficiently than from vegetables. When meat is scarce in the diet, inadequate iron intake is very common and can be devastating to both physical and mental development and function.[2, 3, 4]

Women and children, especially, need some meat. Women lose more blood in menstruation and childbirth than females of any other species—about 20 gallons of blood, an enormous amount of iron, over a lifetime. On average even women in wealthy industrialized nations have red blood cell counts 15 percent lower than men's—low enough to cause mental and physical problems. Children also have high iron needs because they are building blood and tissues from scratch.

In regions where meat is scarce, zinc nutrition is seriously compromised with particularly devastating effects on young boys and men. Zinc is essential for normal brain development and function, immune function, digestion, and sexual maturation. In Middle Eastern countries where very little meat has been available, young boys have suffered severe growth retardation and dwarfism from zinc deficiency. In some cases boys who are 17 years old have the physical stature of 7-year-olds and genital development like that of 6-year-olds.[5]

Vitamin B12 is critical for nervous system function, however, no plant foods provide vitamin B12 in the form needed by humans. Although some authorities claim that spirulina, sea vegetables, and fermented plant products (e.g. miso, tamari, and tempeh) provide B12, research has shown that the B12 in these is an analog molecule that does not satisfy human requirements. A recent study showed that long-term Seventh-day Adventist vegetarians suffer from dietary deficiency of B12.[6] Meat also provides several other B complex

Building Blocks
Meat provides the best source of zinc and iron. Zinc helps create a healthy immune system as well as being essential for normal brain development and function. Iron carries oxygen in the blood to all cells and helps prevent muscle fatigue. It's also crucial in the building of blood and tissue in children.

vitamins, including vitamins B3 and B6, which are limited in plant foods.

The beta-carotene in vegetables is not equivalent to vitamin A, which is found only in animal fats. In 2000 and 2002, two small studies checked the ability of 11 healthy women and 11 healthy men to convert beta-carotene to vitamin A.[7, 8]. Of the 11 in each group, 5 (45 percent) were unable to convert beta-carotene to vitamin A. Another study found no increase in blood vitamin A levels among people supplementing their diets with beta-carotene for 4 consecutive years.[9] Without animal foods probably 45 percent of people will develop vitamin A deficiency that weakens teeth, bones, eyesight, skin, and immunity over time.

It can be difficult to meet the body's protein needs eating only plant food. You would have to eat roughly 10 (8-ounce) potatoes totaling 4.4 pounds to obtain the average daily requirement of 50 grams of protein. That's why many vegetarians use eggs or dairy products.

Plants are inadequate sources of several important essential amino acids, in particular tryptophan (the raw material for serotonin, the deficiency of which is thought to cause depression), methionine, and threonine. A 2000 study found low methionine levels in typical vegans and vegetarians.[10]

Finally, research suggests people may need some animal fats to obtain adequate amounts of certain essential fatty acids not found in plants—particularly one called docosahexaenoic acid (DHA), an omega-3 fatty acid that is an essential component of brain and nervous tissue. This will be discussed in some detail in Chapter 5.

Does Meat-Eating Cause Bone Loss?
Some vegetarians claim that animal protein causes bone loss, and that a vegetarian diet protects against osteoporosis. They point out that Eskimos eating their traditional 90 percent meat diet have been found to have the world's highest rate of osteoporosis.[11]

However, Eskimos are not a fair example. First, their diet almost completely lacks plant foods, which supply materials necessary for bone health. Second, since the Arctic is frigid, lacks sunshine for more than 6 months of the year, and has only weak sun exposure even in summer, the people probably don't get enough sun exposure to generate the amounts of vitamin D necessary for bone maintenance (see Chapter 5). When scientists have studied people in temperate climates eating high-protein diets, they've found no ill effects on bone density. In fact, high-protein mixed diets appear to promote better bone density than vegetarian diets.

In 1999, scientists from Utah State University, Logan, and the University of Iowa College of Medicine, Iowa City, published a study of protein intake and hip fracture using data from the Iowa Women's Health Study. In this study of nearly 32,050 women aged 55 to 69, women who suffered hip fractures ate an average of 74 grams of protein per day, 51 grams from animal products. Those eating less than 49 grams of animal protein per day had five times the hip breaks of those eating more than 70 grams daily. Those without fractured hips ate an average of 82 grams of protein per day, including 60 grams from animal sources. In this study calcium intake had no relation to hip fracture risk. The scientists also noted that the women with hip fractures had lower intakes of animal fat and higher intakes of carbohydrate than the others.[12]

In 2003, researchers from the USDA's Grand Forks (N.D.) Human Nutrition Research Center and University of North Dakota Physics Department, Grand Forks, published results of an experiment designed to test the hypothesis that eating a meat-rich diet increases urinary calcium losses. Fifteen post-menopausal women were first put on a low-meat diet (12 percent of calories as protein) for 12 weeks, then on a high-meat diet (20 percent of calories as protein) for 12 weeks. The diets did not affect urinary calcium loss or indicators of bone metabolism. The team concluded: "Calcium retention is not reduced when subjects consume a high-protein diet from common dietary sources such as meat."[13]

The same year, researchers from the School of Allied Health at the University of Connecticut, Johns Hopkins Bloomberg School of Public Health, and Yale University School of Internal Medicine published results of experiments dealing with urinary calcium losses. The studies indicated that increased losses might be associated with high-protein intake only because it significantly improves calcium absorption. This team found that within 4 days of starting a low-protein diet, healthy adults developed high parathyroid hormone levels that were linked to a reduction in calcium absorption and persisted for 2 weeks. High parathyroid levels stimulate breakdown of bone to release calcium. The researchers noted that recent epidemiological studies "demonstrate reduced bone density and increased rates of bone loss in individuals habitually consuming low-protein diets."[14]

Studies also contradict the claim that vegetarians or people with a low meat intake have lower rates of osteoporosis. A 1997 study of Taiwanese Buddhist vegetarians found they have a 2.5-fold higher risk of osteoporosis of the lumbar spine, and 4-fold higher risk of osteoporosis of the femoral neck.[15] In 2002, researchers from Institute of Metabolism and Endocrinology, The Second Xiang-Ya Hospital, Central South University, Changsha, Hunan, People's Republic of China, reported on the rate of osteoporosis in Chinese women, who typically eat much less meat than Western women.[16] They found osteoporosis in at least one site in approximately 24 percent of those 50 to 59 years of age, 56 percent of those 60 to 69, 72 percent of those 70 to 79, and 83 percent of those older than 80. Lack of calcium is not the problem; the calcium intake of Chinese women is similar to that of Western women.[17]

Ironically, these findings indicate people following the grain-dominated diets recommended by vegetarian authorities are likely to suffer extreme bone loss. Since grains and legumes are poor sources of calcium and contain anti-nutrients that disrupt vitamin D metabolism, causing poor utilization of dietary calcium, cereal-dominated diets can cause tooth and bone diseases.[18] For more on the importance of vitamin D see Chapter 5.

Why We Need Fruits and Vegetables

With all the recent rage about low-carbohydrate diets, some people may wonder, do we really need to eat all those vegetables and fruits?

Yes. As omnivores we require certain nutrients that are not available in adequate quantities from meat, including carbohydrates, vitamin C, calcium, magnesium, potassium and other minerals, carotenes, other antioxidants, and fiber.

Since we have well-developed sensors for the sweet flavor, which is most strongly represented by carbohydrate, there is little doubt that we are designed to seek the natural sources, which are fruits and vegetables. We require about 50 to 100 grams of carbohydrate daily to prevent ketosis, and about 150 grams total to provide all the glucose required for brain and nervous system function.

Protein isn't a good substitute for carbohydrate. Although the liver can convert protein to glucose if necessary, this conversion, known as *gluconeogenesis,* is inefficient, resulting in loss of 30 to 40 percent of the calories originally present in the protein. Overuse of this process is hazardous because it produces large amounts of sulfuric acid and ammonia waste, which must be detoxified by the liver and excreted by the kidneys.

Fat also fails as a carbohydrate replacement. Most tissues are unable to completely metabolize fats without glucose. Glucose metabolism supplies a compound called pyruvate that cells need for completely converting fat to energy. The unused part goes to the liver to be converted to ketones.

If forced by starvation or a low-carbohydrate diet, most tissues can use ketones for energy, but the brain can derive no more than 75 percent of its energy from ketones (the rest must come from glucose). Since the primary purpose of ketosis is to ration your own fat to survive starvation, in ketosis your body acts *as if* it was starving.

Consequently, in healthy people and non-insulin dependent diabetics, ketosis suppresses thyroid hormone levels and metabolic rate, and stimulates the release of insulin, which slows the release of fat from fat cells, reduces conversion of fat to ketones, and pushes ketones into the urine.[19] In other words, ketosis reduces the rate at which your body burns fat.

Eskimos have demonstrated that the human body is not designed to follow a long-term very low-carbohydrate diet. Despite many generations of living on a 90 percent meat and fat diet, Eskimos have not completely adapted to it, and suffer ill effects. Several investigators have reported that primitive Eskimos suffered from liver enlargement related to their diet. The liver is responsible for

Produce Power
Our bodies also need a variety of nutrients that meat does not provide in adequate amounts. This is where fruits and vegetables enter the equation as they offer nutrients such as vitamin C, potassium, antioxidants and fiber.

metabolism of by-products of fat and protein metabolism. When Eskimos traded in some fat and protein for carbohydrate, their livers reduced to normal size.[20]

Dietary carbohydrate is required for delivery of tryptophan to the brain and production of serotonin. Inadequate intake and storage of carbohydrate (as glycogen in the liver) can depress serotonin levels. This can cause depression, anxiety, irritability, impatience, impulsivity, abusive behavior, poor attention span, confusion, hyper-reactivity, tendency to anger, insomnia, and increased appetite, especially cravings for sweets—Nature's demand for brain-fueling carbohydrate.[21]

Unlike many other species, we are unable to make our own vitamin C so require a dietary source. Although some primitive people living in northern regions obtained enough vitamin C to prevent scurvy by eating rare or raw meat, especially adrenal gland, much more C can be gotten from fruits and vegetables. In fact, some wild fruits and vegetables have extraordinary amounts. Although raw or rare meat certainly can meet minimum vitamin C needs, only fruits and vegetables can provide the probably optimum intake of 500 mg daily.

Fruits and vegetables provide an enormous number of antioxidant compounds. There are thousands of bioflavonoids, 600 carotenoids, 5000 phenol compounds, and 7000 terpenes (which appear to strongly inhibit cancer cells or cause them to revert to normal). Although meats and fats from strictly grass-fed animals contain many fat-soluble antioxidants—e.g lutein, a carotene, is richly supplied by egg yolks from grass-fed chickens—the most direct sources are fruits and vegetables.

Can Fruits and Vegetables Make You Fat?

Fruits top the list of plant foods eaten by hunter-gatherers (41 percent of their total intake), followed by underground storage

Table 3.2

Glycemic Indices and Loads (glycemic index x carbohydrate content in 10 g portion) of refined foods and selected fruits and vegetables (glucose as reference standard =100)					
Industrial refined foods	**Glycemic index**	**Glycemic load**	**Fruits & Vegetables**	**Glycemic index**	**Glycemic load**
Rice Krispies	88	77.3	Parsnips	97	19.5
Cornflakes	84	72.7	Baked potato	85	18.4
Shredded Wheat cereal	69	57.0	Sweet potato	54	13.1
Bagel	72	38.4	Banana	53	12.1
White bread	70	34.7	Carrots	71	7.2
			Beets, boiled	64	6.3

Source: Foster-Powell K & Brand Miller J, "International tables of glycemic index," *Am J Clin Nutr* (1995):62:871S-893S. Adapted from Cordain L, Eades MR, Eades MD, "Hyperinsulinemic diseases of civilization: more than just Syndrome X," *Comparative Biochemistry and Physiology*, Part A, 136 (2003): 95-112, p.97.

structures such as tubers, roots, and bulbs (24 percent). Some foods from these groups, such as bananas, winter squash (a fruit), beets, carrots, parsnips, and sweet potatoes have been attacked by some nutritionists who say these foods should be avoided because they score high on the glycemic index. Supposedly these foods will promote elevated insulin levels and consequently make people fat.

This is a mistake. To promote elevated insulin and fat formation, a food must have a high glycemic *load*, which is calculated by multiplying its glycemic index score by the amount of carbohydrate in a 10-gram portion. Although some fruits, roots, and tubers score relatively high on the glycemic index, all have relatively low glycemic loads compared to modern refined foods (see Table 3.2 on previous page).

Although parsnips and white potatoes both score high on the glycemic index, they deliver a glycemic load about half that of a bagel or slice of white bread, and about one-fourth that of a bowl of Rice Krispies or Cornflakes. Carrots and beets deliver glycemic loads one-tenth of those of processed cereals. It's clear that processed grain

Table 3.3

Calorie Concentration (calories per gram)

Vegetable Foods

Vegetable oil	9.0	Sweet potatoes	1.0
Nuts (average)	5.8	Yams	0.9
Salad dressing	5.5	Banana	0.9
Sugar	4.0	Corn	0.8
Honey	3.0	White potatoes	0.6
Raisins	2.9	Apples	0.6
Dried apricots	2.7	Apricots	0.5
Dried apples	2.7	Orange	0.5
Whole wheat bread	2.4	Kale	0.5
Avocados	1.7	Onions or carrots	0.4
Brown rice	1.2	Pumpkin	0.3
Spaghetti	1.1	Asparagus	0.3
White rice	1.1	Spinach or lettuce	0.2

Animal Foods

Lard	9.0	Skinless chicken thigh	2.0
Butter	7.2	Skinless turkey thigh	1.9
Bacon	6.0	Skinless chicken breast	1.6
Conventional T-bone steak	4.7	Skinless turkey breast	1.6
Salami	4.5	Eggs	1.6
Cheddar cheese	4.0	Fresh tuna	1.3
Hamburger	2.9	Venison	1.3
Turkey w/ skin	2.6	Reindeer	1.3

Adapted from: McDougall J, *The McDougall Plan* (New Win, Clinton NJ, 1983), p. 24.

foods are the likely culprits for blood sugar disorders and obesity, not fruits, roots, and tubers.

People rarely eat roots or tubers alone as is done in tests to determine the glycemic index. When carbohydrate-rich foods are eaten in a meal with protein- or fat-rich foods, the glycemic response is reduced. The glycemic index of any food in a meal may be less important than the impact of the entire meal.

It would be a major challenge to overeat vegetables and fruits. The average woman who needs at least 1500 calories per day would likely find it very difficult to eat 15 large potatoes or bananas. In general, vegetables and fruits fill you up long before you can eat enough to fill you out. Based on caloric density, an overuse of fat-rich food is far more likely to cause gain of body fat, since fats are up to 45 times more calorie dense than vegetables and fruits (see Table 3.3 on previous page).

We have seen a number of people attempt very low-carbohydrate diets in hopes of losing body fat, only to fail. In several instances, they gained body weight. We think there are at least 3 reasons this happens. First, without adequate carbohydrate, the body is starved of a vital nutrient and responds by reducing metabolism and retaining fat. Second, when over-restricting carbohydrate, people tend to crave sweets, and often attempt to satisfy those cravings with very high-fat, high-calorie foods. Third, without adequate vegetables and fruits, the body becomes slightly acidic, impairing enzyme activity and fat metabolism.

Maintaining Acid-Base Balance

In Chapter 2 we showed that you have to eat more than twice as much fruits and vegetables as meat to avoid a net acid overload to your system.

Why does this matter?

Normal metabolism produces acids, including sulfuric acid, a by-product of protein breakdown. Too much acid accumulation will irritate, inflame, and erode tissues and impair the function of energy-generating and life-sustaining systems. To neutralize and excrete these acids, the body needs a reserve of alkaline elements or compounds.

Fruits and vegetables provide potassium citrate and malate that the body metabolizes to potassium bicarbonate, which effectively neutralizes acidic by-products of metabolism. If this bicarbonate is not available, calcium may be drawn from the bones to neutralize acids before excretion.

Dr. David A. Bushinsky, M.D., is a professor of medicine and of pharmacology and physiology at the University of Rochester (New York) School of Medicine and Dentistry. Dr. Anthony Sebastian, M.D., is a professor in the Department of Medicine and General Clinical Research Center, University of California, San Francisco. Dr. Bushinsky and a team of scientists led by Dr. Sebastian have found that a slight systemic acidosis corrodes bones and muscles, reduces rejuvenating growth hormone production, and accelerates aging.[22-24] Other studies show that people who eat the most fruits and vegetables have the lowest rates of osteoporosis.[25, 26]

Eskimos confirm these findings. Although they are physically stronger than most college athletes and ingest at least 2000 milligrams of calcium daily from fish bones, they have the world's highest rate of osteoporosis. Without eating alkaline fruits and vegetables, even that high calcium intake is insufficient to neutralize the acid produced by their high protein intake. This may be why they suffer bone calcium loss.[11]

According to renowned anthropologist Vilhjalmur Stefansson, who lived with Eskimos for several years, they have an average lifespan at least 10 years shorter than Americans. Stefansson specifically noted that Eskimo women "usually seem as old at 60 as our women do at 80."[27]

More Perks of a Produce-Dominated Diet

Although many official diet guidelines recommend whole grains be the foundation of healthy eating, a produce-dominated diet is superior. Here's why:

1. Produce provides more nutrients.

Although fruits, vegetables, and whole grains all provide essential carbohydrate, as shown in Table 3.4, calorie for calorie, vegetables and fruits generally are far more nutritious.

Table 3.4

Nutrients in 50-Calorie Portions of Carbohydrates									
Food	Pro. (g)	Fib. (g)	Provit. A (RE)	B2 (mg)	Fol. (ug)	Vit. C (mg)	Potass. (mg)	Iron (mg)	Calc. (mg)
Brown rice	1.0	0.7	0	.01	2	0	20	0.19	4
Whole wheat	2.0	2.0	0	.02	6	0	60	0.58	6
White potato	1.0	1.0	0	.02	5	6	205	0.62	5
Winter squash	1.0	1.0	435	.03	35	12	536	0.40	17
Sweet potato	0.9	1.3	1069	.03	11	12	180	0.22	14
Broccoli	5.0	5.0	250	.20	90	134	526	1.51	83
Carrots	2.0	4.0	1546	.06	16	10	387	0.54	30
Collards	5.0	6.0	812	.16	102	35	241	1.52	286
Kale	2.0	5.0	1145	.12	21	64	340	1.40	160
Blueberries	0.6	1.8	9	.04	6	12	81	0.16	6
Cherries	1.0	1.0	14	.04	3	5	152	0.26	10
Strawberries	1	4	4	.1	.09	84	250	0.57	21

Source: Whitney and Rolfes, *Understanding Nutrition* (West Publishing , 1993), Appendix H.

2. Vegetables and fruits contain more and friendlier fiber than grains.

Table 3.4 shows that many fruits and vegetables provide more fiber per serving than whole grains (let alone refined grains). Fiber found in vegetables and fruits is friendlier to our guts. Why?

Vegetables and fruits come from dicotyledonous plants, or dicots, whereas grains and legumes are from monocotyledonous plants, or monocots. The fiber in dicots is primarily the non-woody, soluble type, unlike the woody, primarily insoluble fiber found in most grains with the exception of oats, barley, and rye.

Whereas we can't digest the woody fibers predominant in grains and legumes, we can to some extent degrade the non-woody fibers predominant in vegetables and fruits. Soluble fibers slow down intestinal transit, enabling the body to extract more nutrients from foods. Insoluble fibers accelerate food movement, reducing assimilation. Soluble fruit and vegetable fibers have the most health benefits. For example they lower blood lipids whereas the woody, insoluble fibers from grains do not.

Whole grain fiber also contains phytate, a compound that interferes with absorption of essential minerals such as iron, calcium, and zinc (more on this in Chapter 4). Fruits and vegetables don't have this undesirable effect.

3. Vegetables and fruits provide more potent cancer protection.

When 150 scientists reviewed 4500 research studies of the influence of dietary variables on 18 different cancers, vegetables were found to provide a convincing protective effect for 5 cancers, a probable preventive effect for 4 others, and a possible preventive effect for another 7. For fruits the analysis revealed 4 convincing, probable, and possible preventive relationships. For cereal grains there were no convincing or probable preventive relationships, and only 1 possible preventive effect (that for cancer of the esophagus).[28]

To prevent cancer, the World Cancer Research Fund and American Institute for Cancer Research recommend 400 grams (nearly 1 pound) of fruits and vegetables daily, providing at least 10 percent of daily calories.[29] If you follow our plan you will consume more than 1200 grams of fruits and vegetables daily, providing more than 30 percent of your daily energy intake, and gain a substantial cancer-preventive effect.

4. Vegetables and fruits are alkaline-forming.

Although all plant foods provide essential carbohydrate,

vegetables and fruits are rich in alkaline substances, whereas almost all grains and legumes are acid-forming. An alkaline produce-dominated diet may facilitate fat loss and stave off aging; an acidic grain-based diet may have the opposite effect.

Potato Problems

Clearly, the most common criticisms leveled at fruits and vegetables, even tubers like white and sweet potatoes, lack substance. However, America's favorite vegetable, the white potato, has a problem you should know about.

The white potato contains a dangerous glycoalkaloid called solanine. At sublethal doses solanine causes nausea, vomiting, diarrhea, and abdominal pain; at higher doses it causes low blood pressure, fever, rapid weak pulse, hallucinations, delirium, coma, and even death. The solanine content of potatoes is elevated by exposure to light and sprouting. Potato sprouts and potatoes with green skin have the highest levels of solanine. Never eat potatoes with green skins or sprouts and always store them in a dark place. People have been severely poisoned by white potatoes that have turned green.

On the plus side, potatoes are rich in potassium, alkaline, and easy to prepare. Dr. Price found potatoes were a staple food for Highland Peruvians who had a high immunity to degenerative diseases. They ate them along with meat, organs, and fat from llama, alpaca, vicuna, and guinea pigs. Although aware of the potato's problems, we eat them when we can find them free of sprouts or green skins. Only you can decide if they work for you.

Table 3.5

Profiling Potatoes

Food	Calories	Carb (g)	Fiber (g)	Carotenes	Potassium (mg)
Banana (114 g)	104	27	2	9	451
Russet potato, baked (101 g)	110	25	2	0	422
Sweet potato, baked (114 g)	117	28	3	2486	396
Raisins (100 g)	300	79	4	.7	750

Source: Whitney and Rolfes, *Understanding Nutrition* (West Publishing, 1993), Appendix H

Sweet Potatoes

Sweet potatoes are not related to white potatoes. They contain a class of toxins called cyanogenic glycosides that are also present in stone fruits. At levels very much higher than found in fresh sweet potatoes or stone fruits, these glycosides can cause gastrointestinal inflammation. However, so far we've been unable to find any evidence of people being poisoned by eating sweet potatoes. Nor have we seen any link between sweet potatoes and any degenerative disease.

Sweet potatoes are alkaline and much more nutritious than white potatoes. They played an important role in several successful primitive and modern diets. Several of the very healthy African tribes studied by Dr. Price regularly ate sweet potatoes. The primitive Kitavan people eat a diet of sweet potatoes, fish, and coconuts, and they remain thin and immune to the diseases of civilization throughout life.[30] In Chinese medicine the sweet potato is considered a longevity food.[31] Until recently the sweet potato was the main food for the healthy longevous Okinawans.[32]

Cooked without added fat, these foods are not fattening; they are too bulky and filling. Each 4-ounce banana, white potato, or sweet potato has only 100 to 120 calories. However, when deep-fried, they become calorie bombs: 1 ounce of deep-fried sweet potato chips has 20 to 50 percent more calories than a 4-ounce fresh baked sweet potato. You can eat a fist-sized fresh sweet potato with a couple teaspoons of butter and take in fewer calories than in 28 potato chips.

chapter 4 Problems with Farmed Foods

About 10,000 years ago, some people began raising cereal grains. Since then, cereals have become mankind's main foods. Numerous other items unknown to hunter-gatherers—dairy products, sugar, salt, and alcohol—have entered human diets. Although people have been eating some farmed foods for about 333 generations, this has not had any noticeable impact on the structure of our digestive system or our nutritional needs. Our bodies have not adapted to many farmed foods.

Grappling with Grains and Beans

Most of us have been raised on slogans suggesting cereals are "the staff of life." Grains are the base of many modern diet guidelines put out by government and medical organizations. It's difficult for many of us to imagine anything could be wrong with them.

However, when scientists looked at the effects of a transition from hunting-gathering to agriculture on 18 different cultures spread across the globe and separated in time, they found differently. In general, grain farmers were less healthy; they had more nutritional stress, higher incidence of infections, more dental decay, weaker bones, more infant mortality, and a shorter life expectancy than their hunter-gatherer forebears.[1]

How can that be?

A little botany will help. Cereals, legumes, and many seeds (such as flax) are classified as monocotyledonous plants, or monocots.

Chapter Overview
Although we've been eating farmed foods for hundreds of genera-tions, our bodies have yet to adapt. Chapter 4 will examine why these farmed foods are not the best options to maintain a healthy lifestyle.

Monocots are composed largely of lignified cellulose, an insoluble fiber commonly known as bran. Lignified cellulose is almost completely resistant to the mechanical and chemical action of the human gastrointestinal tract. Consequently, raw grains or legumes will pass through the entire digestive tract unchanged.

To ensure the continuation of the species, plants equip their seeds with enzyme inhibitors and other toxins designed to prevent the seeds from being digested by animals. Raw cereals and legumes contain amylase and protease inhibitors that block our starch and protein digestive enzymes.[2] A meal of raw cereal or legume flour will cause serious digestive distress. (Please don't try it!) These enzyme blockers are not entirely destroyed by normal cooking. They can be reduced by soaking 24 hours or removed by sprouting, but today these are uncommon methods because people want fast food.

Whole grains and beans contain other antinutrients not removed by cooking, including phytates, lectins, and alkyl resorcinols. Phytates block mineral absorption, and lectins and alkyl resorcinols can damage the intestines and pancreas, trigger auto-immune responses, and attack and damage red blood cells.[2]

Raw grains and beans are unfit for human consumption. Our guts have never really had to adapt to them because for 10,000 years we have been devising and testing methods to *adapt them to us*, i.e. processing techniques. Let's look at lectins, which are carbohydrate-binding proteins found in high concentrations in grains and beans.

The *British Medical Journal* reports that some legume lectins are immediately toxic: "In 1988 a hospital launched a 'healthy-eating day' in its staff canteen at lunchtime. One dish contained red kidney beans; 31 portions were served. At 3 p.m. one of the customers, a surgical registrar, vomited in theatre [surgery room]. During the next four hours 10 more customers suffered profuse vomiting, some with diarrhea. All had recovered by next day. No pathogens were isolated from the food, but the beans contained an abnormally high concentration of the lectin phytohaemagglutinin."[3]

Some lectins are absorbed into the blood, deposited in internal organs, and have chronic toxic or inflammatory effects. One wheat lectin causes kidney disease. Other lectins are linked to autoimmune diseases of thyroid, pancreas (insulin-dependent diabetes), stomach ulcers, rheumatoid arthritis, and common respiratory viral infections. Diets high in lectins have been found to cause loss of the healthy mucous coating of the small intestine along with overgrowth of abnormal bacteria and protozoa.[3]

Cooked grains and beans—especially beans—also contain high levels of indigestible carbohydrates that promote bacterial fermentation in the intestines causing uncomfortable gas and bloating (recall chili's revenge). Although experts often blame meat and fat for soaring sales of over-the-counter indigestion remedies, Christian Allan, Ph.D., and Dr. Wolfgang Lutz, M.D., see it differently. They point out that USDA surveys suggest the average American

Blame Game
While meats and fats get most of the blame for indigestion, it's more likely that beans and grain products are the culprits.

consumes only about 30 grams of beef, 82 grams of total fat, and 12 grams of saturated fat daily, compared to approximately 300 grams of grain products. That's 10 times more grain than beef or saturated fat, and 3 times more grain than total fat.[4]

Many Seventh-day Adventists (SDAs) follow low-fat, high-cereal, vegetarian diets. If meat and fat were the main causes of indigestion, SDAs should be free of it. However, William Jarvis, Ph.D., a professor at Loma Linda Seventh-day Adventist University in California, says digestive distress is "legendary" among modern vegetarian Seventh-day Adventists.[5]

During the 12 years we spent experimenting with grain- and bean-based vegetarian diets, we had the same gut reaction. None of the popular methods that are supposed to de-gas beans worked for us.

Among the grains, wheat and related grains (spelt, kamut, rye, barley, oats, and triticale) are perhaps the most hazardous. They contain gluten, a protein that causes celiac sprue and has been linked to at least 20 auto-immune diseases: Alopecia areata, arthritis, atresia, autoimmune thyroid disease, biliary sclerosis, cirrhosis, Crohn's disease, diabetes mellitus, fibromyalgia, hypoparathyroidism, idiopathic thrombocytopenic purpura, microscopic colitis, multiple sclerosis, nephropathy, optic neuritis, oral cankers, sarcoidosis, systemic lupus erythematosus, trigeminal neuritis, and vasculitis. Gluten has also been linked to various cancers (esophageal, mouth, pharynx, breast, small intestinal lymphoma), osteoporosis, schizophrenia, infertility, recurrent miscarriage, amenorrhea, and low birth weight.[6]

Although whole grains and legumes contain B-complex vitamins, they also contain substances that block absorption of those nutrients. For instance, up to two-thirds of the vitamin B6 in grains is unavailable because it is bound by pyridoxine glucosides impervious to human digestion.[7] Similarly, proteins, iron, and zinc in cereals are in forms difficult to assimilate.

What to Do About Whole Grains?

We highly recommend that you try going grain-free for several weeks or months to find out how you feel and perform without grains. You may be amazed at the benefits. However, we realize few will say sayonara to cereals permanently. If you continue eating cereals, or have them occasionally, we recommend you eat only properly processed whole-grain products. Proper processing involves two main steps.

First, to eliminate phytates and other antinutrients, grains or legumes must be soaked at least 24 hours, or fermented. Second, the product must be thoroughly cooked, preferably with low, moist heat to further reduce the starches to more digestible forms. Generally, this means cooking a minimum of 30 minutes, even if using a partially processed grain such as rolled oats.

Wheat Woes
Wheat and other related grains contain a protein called gluten, which has been linked to at least 20 auto-immune diseases.

For preparing dry whole grains (such as brown rice, millet, or oats), see Appendix H. If making whole grain bread, your best choice is to use sprouted grain flour, long fermentation (preferably sourdough), then baking or preferably Chinese-style steaming. See Appendix G.

Even if you make whole-grain products using the best methods, monitor your response to these foods. You may be surprised to find that even small servings of properly processed whole-grain products can cause digestive problems.

Beyond the Milky Way

Milk mongers chant the mantra "milk does every body good," and suggest it is essential for building bones and preventing osteoporosis. However, neither Stone Age nor contemporary hunter-gatherers used milk, and today about 75 percent of the world's population lives without it. What's up?

As mammals, we are designed to take raw mother's milk when we are infants. Infants produce *renin*, a curdling agent necessary for digestion of milk protein, and *lactase*, an enzyme for digesting *lactose* (milk sugar). By the time most people reach 4 years old, production of lactase and renin production stops. Human milk, unlike the milk of any other animal, is specially designed to nourish human infants.

Cows' milk is designed to help a baby cow double its birth weight of 100 pounds in about 47 days. At 2 years, a calf can weigh more than 400 pounds but have a brain weighing less than 1 pound. A child the same age weighs only 30 pounds but has a brain weighing more than 2 pounds. Cows' milk is designed to build big bodies, not big brains; human milk is for big brains, not big bodies.

Dairy-linked disorders most commonly appear in the digestive, respiratory, circulatory, nervous, and immune systems. Pasteurized cows' milk has been linked to Sudden Infant Death Syndrome, intestinal bleeding, infant anemia, allergies, asthma, heart disease, several cancers (breast, ovarian, prostate), Type I diabetes, criminal behavior, multiple sclerosis, rheumatoid arthritis, schizophrenia, and osteoporosis.[8-16]

Brain chemistry and nutrition researcher Dr. Michael Crawford, Ph.D., notes these problems are surprising only "if you don't know that human milk is designed for the growth of the brain and vascular system whereas cows' milk is for muscles and skeletal growth."[17]

Lacking lactase, most adults get gas, bloating, diarrhea, or constipation after drinking pasteurized milk. Aged cheese adds insult by delivering enormous amounts of salt, calories, and saturated fat in a small package. Aged cheeses are the most acid-forming items in modern diets. Since each ounce of cheese—a tiny 1-inch cube—contains 100 calories and 8 grams of fat, it is very easy to overeat.

Primitive Milk

Some primitive herdsmen living largely on raw, whole, and often

Milk – Brains vs. Brawn
Just as human milk is only intended to nourish human infants, cows' milk is intended only to nourish baby cows. Human milk aids brain and vascular growth, while cows' milk is designed for muscle and skeletal growth.

cultured milk products were free of some of the disorders commonly associated with dairy products. In Africa Dr. Price found that the Masai and Samburu cattle herdsmen and Somalian camel herdsmen had excellent physical and mental health comparable to hunter-gatherers. They ate enormous amounts of butterfat with no ill effects. For example, the Masai consumed more than 300 grams of butterfat daily, and the Samburu topped 400 grams daily from whole milk. These tribesmen had very low cholesterol levels (about 150 milligrams per deciliter) and virtually no heart disease. Autopsies have proven they do not develop the atherosclerosis so common in modern people who eat less animal and more vegetable fats (as well as much more carbohydrate).[18, 19]

Dr. Price also found good physical and mental health among the Swiss in Loetschental Valley. They lived largely on milk products, including aged cheese, with whole rye sourdough bread and vegetables. A research team found these primitive Swiss had a diet high in calories, saturated fat, and cholesterol, but their blood cholesterol levels were low and they had little cardiovascular disease.[18]

In the 1960s it was found that the Udaipur people in northern India ate a diet rich in milk products and butter, with a high intake of saturated butterfat. The Madras people in the south ate little fat and mostly unsaturated vegetable oil—only 2 percent of their calories came from saturated fats. Surprising to those who think fat and butter are bad, the intake of fat was up to 19 times higher among the Udaipur people, but the people in Madras had the higher coronary heart disease (CHD) rate—in fact, CHD was up to 15 times more common in Madras.[19, 20]

Milk is rich in animal protein and relatively low in carbohydrate compared to grains. It may be that primitive herdsmen had good health similar to hunter-gatherers because their diets were similar—high in protein and natural fats, and lower in carbohydrate.

But modern milk has similar proportions of protein, fat, and carbohydrate. Why then is modern milk linked to so many diseases apparently absent in these primitive dairying cultures?

In primitive cultures, all children were intensively breast-fed for 1 to 3 years. An infant's digestive tract is very sensitive and more permeable than an adult's. Its greater permeability allows the infant to absorb important immune system proteins found in mother's milk. Human mother's milk contains growth factors required for proper development and maturation of the digestive tract. Nature intends that infants be fed only human milk until the digestive tract is mature enough to tolerate non-human proteins.

Human milk protein is about 70 percent alpha-lactalbumin, and only 30 percent human casein. Cows' milk protein is 70 percent bovine casein, and 30 percent beta-lactalbumin. If an infant is given proteins other than those in human milk before about 8 months of age, he will absorb some of those non-human proteins. When those proteins enter the infant's gut and blood, his immune system attacks the foreigners. The infant immediately suffers terrible indigestion (colic), skin disorders, and breathing problems.

Meanwhile, the immune system creates antibodies designed to recognize and attack the offending proteins. The problem is the amino acid sequences in the casein protein of cow's milk are very similar to many of the natural, essential proteins in the human body. The immune system is thus stimulated to attack the body tissues that resemble cow's milk casein.

The insulin-producing beta cells of the pancreas and the joints contain proteins similar to cows' milk protein. Some people suffering from juvenile-onset diabetes and rheumatoid arthritis have elevated levels of antibodies to cows' casein. In such cases, the person's immune system may have attacked and destroyed parts of the pancreas or joint tissues that are similar to cows' milk protein. This may help to explain many of the other problems associated with dairy products.

Modern milk production is a world apart from traditional herding. You might have an image of contented cows grazing freely on a family farm, but in fact most modern dairy cows "stand around on concrete pads in corporate-owned confinement dairies where they are implanted with synthetic hormones, dosed with antibiotics, and fed an artificial grain diet."[21] Hormones are used to force the cows to produce abnormal amounts of milk. In the 1940s, a cow was considered productive if it gave 4500 pounds of milk per lactation; today's force-fed, drugged cows produce a prodigious 17,000 pounds each, 20 times more than is needed to feed a calf. When a cow is forced to produce this volume the milk is inevitably less nutritious.

The milk used by all healthy primitive groups came from animals raised entirely on pasture and hay, with no grain or hormones. Such milk is much healthier than mass-market milk, which is sorely deficient in several good fats. Milk from exclusively grass-fed cows has 3 times more omega-3 fats beneficial for the vascular and nervous systems, and 5 times more conjugated linoleic acid, a fat that may help humans burn body fat, build muscle, and prevent cancer. There's more. Milk from completely grass-fed cows is also much higher in vitamin A, carotenes, vitamin E, and other antioxidants—all because grass provides nutrients not found in grains.[21]

Modern milk processing has side-effects. Pasteurization involves heating milk to only 145° F (62° C) for 30 minutes or 161° F (72° C) for 15 seconds. This fails to destroy all microbes and only partially denatures the milk's protein. When this altered protein contacts stomach acid, it forms a gluey mass that is very difficult to digest.

Boiling completely sterilizes milk while reducing its protein to very easily digested peptides and amino acids, but it must be done in small batches (1 gallon or less) and quickly cooled. This isn't practical for industrial milk processing so it should be left to the consumer, who has the right to have milk raw or cooked at his own discretion.

Milking it Too Much
Modern production methods force cows to produce abnormally high volumes of milk. The volume alone is bound to make this milk less nutritions than that of a grass-fed cow. Furthermore, milk from a grass fed-cow provides a higher level of nutrients than what is found in cows living on a grain-fed diet and hormones.

Boiled milk may be as beneficial as raw without the risk of bacterial infection. According to Dr. Rudolph Ballentine, M.D., a specialist in Ayurvedic medicine and author of *Diet & Nutrition: A Holistic Approach* (Himalayan International Institute, 1978), in India where people have used milk for thousands of years, it is always boiled first, in spite of the fact that cows are cared for personally. Dr. Ballentine also says that although the famous Swiss Bircher-Benner Clinic stresses a largely raw-foods diet, it nevertheless serves patients boiled milk products.

Homogenization reduces the size of milk's fat globules, rendering them easier to absorb, and facilitates absorption of an enzyme, xanthine oxidase, suspected to damage arteries. Removing fat from milk (fractionation) also removes its fat-soluble vitamins and factors required for assimilation of its minerals.[22]

Pasteurization laws also damage family farms. Large confinement dairies raising hundreds of hormone-enhanced cows on cheap feeds can produce enormous amounts of pasteurized, homogenized, devitalized milk, flooding the market and driving the price down. Small family farms raising a few dozen contented cows on their favorite food—grass—can't compete even though they produce superior milk, largely because pasteurization laws prohibit them from selling raw milk directly to the public. The pasteurization laws force farmers to sell their milk at wholesale prices to the milk-processing middlemen.

White Flood

Pasteurization laws help large dairies flood the market with less nutritious and lower-priced milk. This effectively washes out many family farmers' efforts to raise small herds of grass-fed dairy cows and still offer competitive prices.

California and Georgia allow the retail sale of certified raw whole milk. Certified raw milk is verified to have bacterial counts lower than what are allowed in pasteurized milk. Twenty-six other states allow farmers to sell raw milk directly to the consumer. Twenty-two states have banned the retail sale of raw milk for human consumption, on grounds that raw milk carries more disease than pasteurized. However, in *The Milk Book*, Dr. William Campbell Douglass, M.D., cites the public record showing that pasteurized milk is no safer than raw milk from clean dairies. Milk from strictly pasture-fed animals rarely contains pathogens unless contaminated by human hands. Corporate confinement dairies and milk processors seeking to monopolize the interstate milk market benefit from the sham safety issue and the pasteurization laws that make it difficult for small family dairy farms to survive.

There are creative ways to leap this legal barrier. In Arkansaw, Wisconsin, the Brunner family raises grass-fed dairy cows. They have formed Midvalleyvu Farms, Inc., which legally sells equity shares in its milk producer license to the public; this allows all share owners to purchase exceptional quality raw grass-fed cows' milk products from the corporation.

Keep in mind that the care and feeding of the livestock is the most important consideration. Pasteurized milk from a family farm raising strictly grass-fed animals is by far nutritionally superior to raw milk from confined, primarily grain-fed animals. You can boil and ferment pasteurized milk to eliminate bacteria and render its protein more digestible. Beware, "organic" milk may be drawn from cows that have eaten more grain than grass.

Also remember that most people have at least some difficulty digesting unmodified milk. This is especially true of people not breast-fed for at least 12 months or given unmodified cows' milk as infants. In cultures where milk is used as a primary food, it is almost invariably prepared by fermentation to make products such as yogurt, kefir, and koumiss. The fermentation process predigests milk proteins and sugars, so they are less likely to cause discomfort or disease.

Many people have difficulty digesting even the best quality raw fermented milk products from grass-fed cows. Many others have no digestive problems from consuming milk, but may still experience sinus congestion, skin rashes, allergies, asthma, arthritis, or other immune system disorders associated with milk products.

If you want to use milk products, look for a pasture-based dairy farmer near you, and if you can, get raw milk. Bear in mind also that goats' milk is easier to digest than cows' milk. To find a real milk producer near you, check the Real Milk Web site, www.realmilk.com. When you get good raw milk, boil it, cool it quickly, and then convert it to yogurt, kefir, or similar fermented products.

But don't fret if you can't get raw milk from grass-fed animals, or simply can't tolerate any non-human milk product. People don't need non-human milk to be healthy. You can get everything you need from other foods that don't present the risks associated with dairy products.

Greenery Boost
A common misconception is that without milk, people cannot get enough calcium, however dark leafy greens of the cabbage family supply plenty.

The Milk Myth

Think you need milk to prevent osteoporosis? Surprise! The Harvard School of Public Health Nurse's Health Study found that osteoporosis was at least as common among women who drank milk daily as among those who drank milk less than once a week.[23] In 2003, Harvard scientists again reported that a study of 72,337 postmenopausal women found neither pasteurized milk nor high calcium intakes protected against hip fracture (but vitamin D did have a protective effect).[24]

In 2000, scientists from the Department of Nutrition Sciences, University of Alabama at Birmingham reviewed 57 studies of the effects of dairy foods on bone health. Fifty-three percent showed no significant effect, 42 percent were favorable, and 5 percent unfavorable. Only 21 of those studies had strong evidence, and of those, 57 percent showed no significant effect, 29 percent were favorable, and 14 percent unfavorable. Since most of the studies focused on white women, there was practically no evidence modern milk would benefit men or ethnic minorities.[25]

What to Do Without Milk?

Can people get enough calcium without milk? Of course. Hunter-gatherers did it for more than a million years. How? By eating dark green leafy vegetables and transforming bones into broth.

In *The Garden of Eating* plan, dark green leafy cabbage-family vegetables (such as kale, collards, turnip greens, mustard greens, and broccoli) and Bone-Building Broth supply abundant calcium. A 1-cup serving of dark greens can supply at least as much calcium as a half-cup of milk, and is at least as well absorbed as calcium from milk.[26] To supplement vegetable sources of calcium, all traditional dairy-free cuisines include calcium-rich bone broths. One cup of properly made bone broth can contain as much or more calcium than a cup of milk and is delicious when used to prepare vegetable and meat dishes and salad dressings. Try dark greens cooked in Bone-Building Broth, for a delicious, high-calcium dish.

Our plan easily provides 600 to 800 milligrams of calcium from vegetables and fruits alone without counting contributions of bone broth. Although the National Academy of Sciences Nutrition Board recommends an average daily intake of 1000 milligrams of calcium per day for adults, this panel of experts also states that worldwide studies have not found high calcium intakes associated with protection against osteoporosis.[27]

Your acid-base balance is likely more important than calcium intake for bone health. Eskimos have demonstrated you can develop osteoporosis even if you eat 2000 milligrams of calcium daily if your diet is highly acidic because of lack of fruits and vegetables. You can build and maintain excellent bones eating less than 1000 milligrams of calcium daily if your diet is alkaline by virtue of being very rich in fruits or vegetables.

Moreover, no matter how much calcium you ingest, you won't absorb much unless you're getting adequate vitamin D, the most important nutrient for calcium absorption. Contrary to common belief, neither brief facial sun exposures of 15 minutes a day nor the RDA of 400 units of D is effective in maintaining adequate vitamin D levels (see Chapter 5).

Bones are like muscles: If you don't use them, you'll lose them even if you have the best possible bone nutrition. Bones become stronger when they are gradually subjected to progressively heavier loads through weight-bearing exercise. Walking is not adequate, first because it doesn't involve any load other than your body, which you carry around every day, and second because it does little for the bones (or muscles) above your hips.

Unless you are extremely frail, you probably won't build bones

Calcium Schmalcium
Even though the recommended amount of daily calcium is 1000 mg, worldwide studies have not found that high calcium intakes offer protection against osteoporosis. Your acid-base balance is likely more important. You can build and maintain excellent bones by eating less than 1000 mg of calcium a day on an alkaline diet rich in fruits and vegetables.

with 5-pound dumbbells either. You need a resistance that is greater than what you normally encounter, and a 5-pound dumbbell weighs less than a gallon of water. In pre-industrial cultures, men and women regularly engaged in hard work lifting and carrying substantial loads of food, stones, wood, water, or other objects that taxed their abilities.

You can satisfy your body's need for hard work with a strength training program. Few exercise instructors know how to design and implement safe and effective resistance exercise programs. We recommend instructors certified by the International Association of Resistance Trainers (www.exercisecertification.com), the Super Slow Exercise Guild (www.superslow.com), or the National Strength Professionals Association (www.nspainc.com).

Wayne Wescott, Ph.D., has written several good books—widely available in public libraries—on the principles of safe, effective training for general fitness: *Building Strength and Stamina*, *Strength Training Past 50*, and *Strength Training for Seniors*. Another very good resource found in many public libraries is *A Practical Approach to Strength Training* by Matt Bryzicki. You can also get good information, based on the American College of Sports Medicine guidelines, on the Web site www.ExRx.net.

The bottom line? Bone loss is probably caused by chronic systemic acidity, inadequate dietary animal protein, lack of sunshine/vitamin D, or lack of weight-bearing exercise, not by milk or calcium deficiency.

Sugar Blues

Prior to the industrial revolution, people regularly obtained sugar in the natural whole food forms of vegetables and fruits, and infrequently had small amounts of raw honey. They didn't have the abundant sources of isolated sugar available today.

Isolated sugar (sucrose, fructose, honey, corn, barley malt, or rice syrup, maple syrup, or any other) provides practically no vitamins or minerals. Careful studies have shown that when lab animals are fed sugar-rich foods or especially fluids (think soda), they develop voracious appetites and become extremely obese.[28]

The typical modern American consumes about 5.5 ounces of refined sugar daily, amounting to 595 unnecessary, easily consumed, appetite-stimulating calories, enough to produce more than 1 pound of fat gain per week. It shouldn't be a surprise that more than 50 percent of Americans are overweight.

Heavy refined sugar consumption also has been linked to dental decay, heart disease, Type II diabetes, lung and stomach cancers, several female cancers, digestive disorders, premenstrual disorder, osteoporosis, hyperactivity, and immune suppression.[29-40]

Unlike low-carbohydrate plans, our recipes, menus, and meal-planning tips will help satisfy your sweet tooth while avoiding the dangers of refined sugar and potentially dangerous synthetic sugar

Sugar Surplus
Isolated sugar sources provide few if any vitamins or minerals, and further stimulate the appetite. The average American diet includes 5.5 ounces of refined sugar daily—enough to produce more than 1 pound of fat gain per week.

substitutes. In *The Garden of Eating* you can eat your fill of sweet fruits and vegetables. We also show you how to use stevia, dried fruits, honey, and agave nectar (cactus syrup) sparingly to season vegetables, meats, and desserts.

Beware: If you use agave nectar or honey in place of refined sugar and attempt to reconstruct your favorite cookies or pastries using natural ingredients, you'll still get the sugar blues. Although agave nectar and honey are better than white sugar in some respects they still are essentially types of refined carbohydrate.

Salt Shake-up

If you have a salt tooth, you're not alone. But did you know that mineral salt is not an essential nutrient? It's an additive, preservative, and flavoring, originally added to food to prevent spoilage by killing microbes. There are some good reasons you might want to shake your salt habit.

Historically, only farmers, not hunter-gatherers, ate salt as a matter of course. Some experts believe early farmers used salt to satisfy a need created by the lack of meat. It has been most heavily used throughout history for preservation of meats, such as ham, bacon, sausage, and fish. It is by no means an adequate nutritional substitute for lean meat.

Modern civilized people are the only animals that add salt to food daily. Even after the advent of agriculture, before A.D. 1000 few farming people ate salt regularly or liberally, because it was too scarce and expensive. For thousands of years Eskimos, Yanomamo of Brazil, and many other native tribes have traditionally lived *sans* salt without any deficiencies.

Except in cases of extreme fluid loss from diarrhea or sweating, dietary mineral salt is unnecessary because all sodium requirements are easily met or exceeded through food.[41] Human milk has 4 times more potassium than sodium yet provides plenty of sodium for an infant. Fresh meat, eggs, fish, and milk have about 4 times more potassium than sodium, generally 50 to 100 milligrams of sodium per 4 ounce serving; one egg has about 60 milligrams. Nuts and some vegetables and fruits also provide some sodium but far less than animal products, from 0 to 50 milligrams per serving.

The National Academy of Sciences says a healthy adult can maintain sodium balance "with an intake of little more than the minimal requirement of an infant," i.e. 300 to 500 milligrams daily.[42] An unsalted meat-rich diet can provide more than 1000 milligrams of sodium daily, twice the amount required to maintain sodium balance under normal circumstances. Chloride is never naturally lacking in the diet as it is adequately supplied by fresh, unsalted foods.

Contrary to common belief, rising blood pressure is not a natural consequence of aging. The International Salt Study, or INTERSALT, found a close dose-related correlation between salt intake (measured by 24-hour urinary sodium) and blood pressure. Only the tribes with

Put the Shaker Away
Until modern times salt was used mainly as a preservative. An unsalted meat-rich diet meets or exceeds the daily sodium requirement.

little or no added salt in the diet were immune to hypertension and coronary heart disease throughout life.[43]

Dr. Richard D. Moore, M.D., Ph.D., is a former professor of biophysics at the State University of New York at Plattsburgh and visiting professor at the University of Vermont's medical school who has been active in biomedical research for more than 30 years. In *The Salt Solution*, Dr. Moore explains how a high-sodium, low-potassium diet interferes with the sodium/potassium pumps of all the body's cells. According to Dr. Moore, a high-sodium, low-potassium diet promotes a wide range of problems, including atherosclerosis, hypertension, stroke, asthma, osteoporosis, cataracts, migraines, erectile dysfunction, migraines, senile dementia, kidney stones, ulcers, insulin resistance and Type II diabetes (NIDDM), stomach cancer, and possibly other cancers.[43]

Only 40 percent of mineral salt is sodium, 60 percent is chloride, or chlorine ion. The chloride may be responsible for much of the harm attributed to salt. A team of researchers led by Dr. Anthony Sebastian, M.D., Professor in the Department of Medicine, University of California, San Francisco, has shown that salt's chloride increases the irritating, corrosive acid load of a diet.[44]

It's no secret that salt stimulates the appetite. Restaurants, bars, fast-food eateries, and processed-food companies liberally add salt to excite your palate, pique your interest in processed foods, and motivate you to eat more than you need. Conversely, reducing your salt use can help normalize your appetite, making it easier to tell when you are truly hungry and when you've had enough of any particular food. Ousting the excess water held in your body's over-salted tissues can often amount to significant weight loss.

As with any other substance, the dose makes the poison. Provided your diet is produce-dominated, you may be able use small amounts of unrefined sea salt without ill effects. Dr. Moore recommends a potassium-to-sodium ratio of at least 4:1—similar to human milk, and common in hunter-gatherer diets—and advises an upper limit of 2000 milligrams of sodium daily. Fresh natural foods contain at least 3 and up to 150 times more potassium than sodium. However, since unsalted animal foods provide significant sodium, if you eat much meat, eggs, or milk, you have to use mineral salt very sparingly to achieve an optimum potassium-to-sodium ratio.

The Garden of Eating plan satisfies Dr. Moore's guidelines, typically supplying no more than 1200 milligrams of sodium and at least 6000 milligrams of potassium daily. We sparingly use a truly unrefined sun-dried sea salt, such as Celtic sea salt, primarily where it is necessary for its preservative properties, for example in salad dressings and sauces we want to last for 1 to 2 weeks in the refrigerator, or when making beef jerky. Should you wish to leave the salt out of these recipes, you will need to use homemade salad dressings within a week and refrigerate or freeze dried meats unless you use them within a month.

In a Pinch
If salt is needed, we recommend using an unrefined sun-dried sea salt.

Our recipes will show you how to make delicious foods with minimal or no added salt, using herbs and spices rich in nutrients that help prevent degenerative diseases. You may initially miss the high-salt taste, but if you persist, within a short time your taste buds will adjust.

Foolish Ferments?

For more than a million years, our hunter-gatherer ancestors lived without alcoholic beverages. Although people have been led to believe that "moderate" alcohol consumption helps to prevent cardiovascular disease, a 1998 review found that the evidence for a cardio-protective effect for alcohol is weak.[45] Even if we grant alcohol the benefit of doubt, the cardiovascular advantage is minor and only associated with very small doses, 10 to 20 grams of alcohol—3 to 4 ounces of wine daily. Larger amounts are linked to more damage than benefit.[46] There is strong evidence that even moderate alcohol consumption is harmful in one way or another.

Alcohol promotes obesity because it almost completely stops the body from using fat for fuel. It also poisons and destroys liver and brain cells. Those who cite the French as support for drinking alcohol to prevent cardiovascular disease almost always appear unaware of the fact that their death rate from liver cirrhosis increased by 163 percent overall (208 percent for French men and 186 percent for French women) between 1925 and 1982.[47]

It is well-known that for many people even small amounts of alcohol can cause intoxication, impair judgment, and facilitate other self-destructive behaviors. Also, scientists have found that women who regularly drink alcohol are more likely to have more severe premenstrual discomfort than teetotalers.[40]

The benefits of red wine are likely not from its alcohol but from other components, such as antioxidant flavonoids, which are also found in grape juice.[48] In 2001, scientists at the Department of Chemistry, University of Scranton (Pennsylvania) found that the beneficial effects of red wine are due entirely to its content of polyphenols. At the same polyphenol dose, grape juice was more effective than red wine or dealcoholized red wine in inhibiting atherosclerosis and improving lipids and antioxidant parameters.[49] In the same year another team from the Departments of Pharmacology and Medicine, Georgetown University Medical Center, Washington, D.C., found that grape juice flavonoids inhibit blood clotting and enhance release of nitric oxide, which increases blood vessel diameter.[50] The beneficial polyphenols and flavonoids are present in red grape juice, fresh grapes, raisins, and many other berries.

Although we do not recommend drinking alcohol, you will find some recipes in which we use wine for flavoring. In these recipes, the alcohol is eliminated in the cooking process. If you prefer, you

It's in the Grapes
The benefits of red wine most likely stem not from the alcohol content, but from components such as antioxidant flavonoids and polyphenols, both of which are also found in grape juice, fresh grapes, and raisins.

may replace red wine with apple cider or red grape juice, and white wine with white grape juice, or replace either type of wine with good homemade poultry stock or broth.

Fake Foods

Modern diets include a bewildering variety of artificial foods. We have synthetic sweeteners, protein isolates, fake fats, mock meats, and isolated vitamins and minerals, which are often combined with refined carbohydrates to form "food" bars and shakes. Also popular are fluorescent colors, not-quite juices, highly processed pastries, chips, and puffed snacks. A hunter-gatherer wouldn't even recognize these things as food. Your great-great-grandmother would probably be amazed people accept them as edible.

These are unnecessary and impediments to good nutrition. If you pay close attention, you'll find they all have a distinct processed-food flavor and unpleasant aftertaste. They're the most important things to let go to experience *The Garden of Eating.*

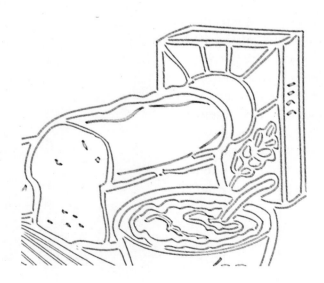

chapter 5   A Short Fat Primer

There is no nutrition topic more clouded by misunderstanding and prejudice than fat. Thanks to a relentless campaign of incomplete information, most Americans believe that saturated fats and cholesterol are akin to poisons, and unsaturated vegetable oils and artificial fats made from them (margarine, shortening) are practically panaceas.

However, saturated fat is natural to the human body, and people have eaten saturated animal fats for many centuries. Animal fats have been highly valued in all traditional cultures.[1] Since hunter-gatherers and herdsmen who got most of their calories from partially saturated animal fats were immune to all the degenerative diseases blamed on those nutrients, modern conceptions are clearly amiss.

We are going to do our best to dispel big fat myths and replace them with some real fat facts.

Saturated Facts

As animals, we produce saturated animal fats. On a fat-free diet, or whenever the body synthesizes fats from excess carbohydrate or protein, it produces saturated and monounsaturated, but not polyunsaturated, fatty acids. According to Dr. Germain J. Brisson, Ph.D., former professor of nutrition at Laval University (Quebec, Canada) and author of *Lipids in Human Nutrition*, when we eat large amounts of polyunsaturated fatty acids, enzymatic processes in the intestines will, as much as possible, convert them into saturated fatty

Chapter Overview
Contrary to messages in today's society, saturated fats are needed by humans. Furthermore, unsaturated fats are not as beneficial as touted. Chapter 5 will examine and dispel some big fat myths, and shine the light on some real fat facts.

acids before absorption.[2] The body makes saturated fats because they are essential to health. They are used to make cell walls resistant to penetration by parasites, viruses, and bacteria. The fat pads that protect bony surfaces (palms, soles, sitting bones) and fat deposits that cushion the internal organs are made up largely of saturated fat.

Saturated fats are also very important in the nervous system and brain. The gray matter of the nervous system is made up largely of sphingomyelin, a compound that incorporates 1 fatty acid, most commonly saturated stearic acid or palmitic acid (the same as in palm oil).[3,4] The white matter of the brain is composed largely of phospholipids incorporating palmitic or stearic acids.[5] All told, about a third of the brain's fat is saturated.

How does human body fat stack up against common dietary animal and vegetable fats? Look at Table 5.1

Table 5.1

Average Fatty Acid Profiles of Some Common Fats and Oils		
Saturated Fats(%)	**Monounsaturated Fats(%)**	**Polyunsaturated Fats(%)**
Animal		
Human 42.9	46.9	10.2
Beef Tallow 47.8	49.6	2.6
Butter 62.6	28.6	3.4
Lard 40.0	50.0	10.0
Chicken fat 29.6	44.5	21.0
Vegetable		
Corn 8.0	24.2	58.8
Flax 9.6	17.0	68.8
Olive 14.3	77.1	9.3
Palm 49.3	36.8	9.6
Sesame 14.0	39.7	41.2

Sources: Human fat: Bettelheim FA, Brown WH, March J, *Introduction to General, Organic, & Biochemistry*, sixth edition (Brooks/Cole, 2001), p. 474. All others: Enig M, *Know Your Fats* (Silver Spring, MD, Bethesda Press, 2000), Appendix C.

Surprise! Forty-three percent of the fat produced and stored by our bodies is saturated! Beef tallow, butter, lard, and human fat are all quite similar. Lard is most like human fat. Palm oil also is very similar to human fat, but most vegetable oils are a world apart. Fats much like our own are loudly denounced; fats most unlike our own are most loudly praised. What's up?

In Nature, tissues of temperate or northern plants, fish, and other cold-blooded animals typically produce highly unsaturated fats, whereas warm-blooded animals (including people) and tropical plants (palm, coconut) typically produce more saturated fats. Why?

Chemist Karel Sporek explained that this distribution is due not to nutritional properties but to the melting points of the fats.[6] Creatures inhabiting cold climates or having low body temperatures (northern plants, reptiles, ocean fish) are endowed with more unsaturated fats (oils) because they are sufficiently fluid at low temperatures. Saturated fats are too stiff at those temperatures. If an Alaskan salmon contained much saturated fat, it would freeze solid in the cold Pacific waters; saturated fats would be immovable in a flax plant on the Canadian plains.

In contrast, at tropical temperatures—including human core body temperature (98.6° F, 37° C)—unsaturated fats alone are too fluid or jiggly for making fat pads, storage depots, or strong cell membranes. Unsaturated fats are prone to produce dangerous, carcinogenic peroxides in warm oxygen-rich environments—such as our innards—so Nature combines them with saturated fats which act as antioxidants and protect the essential unsaturates.

For those readers who are more technically inclined, consider this. Some experts claim that saturates with different carbon chain lengths have different health effects. They say myristic acid (14 carbons) and palmitic acid (16 carbons) are the major factors raising total and LDL cholesterol and risk of cardiovascular disease, but stearic acid (18 carbons) is supposed to have little or no harmful effect.

Putting aside the fact that the body can convert the myristic or palmitic acids into stearic acid—or vice versa—consider Table 5.2 showing the average percentage of these fatty acids in human fat, tallow, and lard.

Table 5.2

Average Percentage of Major Saturated Fatty Acids in Common Animal Fats			
Fat	**Myristic**	**Palmitic**	**Stearic**
Beef tallow	6.3	27.4	14.1
Human fat	2.7	24.0	8.4
Lard	1.3	28.3	11.9

Source: Bettelheim FA, Brown WH, March J, *Introduction to General, Organic, & Biochemistry,* sixth edition (Brooks/Cole, 2001), p. 474.

Beef tallow has more "bad" myristic and palmitic acids than human fat, but also more neutral or "good" stearic acid. Lard actually has less "bad" myristic acid than human fat, as well as more "good" stearic. But the differences are so small it is unlikely our body fat has properties significantly different from tallow or lard.

Here's why we bring this up: Although this seems forgotten by critics of saturated fats, animals store fat mainly as a reservoir of energy for use between meals or when food is scarce. Between meals and whenever food intake is restricted, even if you fast, your body will essentially run on lard—your lard—that is about 43 percent saturated fats. The heart, liver, and resting muscles together consume most of the energy used by the body. These tissues prefer fat for fuel.[7] There is no way to keep your blood vessels clear of saturated fatty acids.

Since not only humans but all mammals store saturated fats for famine survival, and the heart prefers fats for fuel, it is extremely unlikely that saturated fats are intrinsically toxic and cause cardiovascular disease.

In the 1990s, experts stopped heavily promoting polyunsaturated oils and switched to promoting monounsaturates such as oleic acid. Human tissues can convert saturated palmitic and stearic acids into monounsaturated oleic acid—just like in olive oil.[8] Hence, 95 percent of tallow and 90 percent of lard is either monounsaturated or readily convertible to monounsaturated. Olive oil is only 77 percent monounsaturated.

If you're confused, you're not alone. The experts themselves are confused. While hypnotically fixed on the real and imagined effects of degrees of saturation, they apparently have forgotten many basic fat chemistry facts.

Dr. Michael I. Gurr, Ph.D., is a professor of biochemistry at the school of Biological and Molecular Sciences at Oxford Brookes University, UK, and former editor-in-chief of *Nutrition Research Reviews*. Gurr says that the idea that saturated fats promote cardiovascular diseases is not supported by the preponderance of research on the topic.[9] Brisson shares this view.[10]

Since 1990, Dr. Uffe Ravsnkov, M.D., Ph.D., has published more than 30 critical articles and letters addressing the alleged link between saturated fats and cholesterol and cardiovascular disease in peer-reviewed Scandinavian and international medical journals. In *The Cholesterol Myths*, Dr. Ravsnkov shows that despite millions of dollars spent on research, scientists have repeatedly failed to produce good evidence that diets rich in saturated fats or cholesterol promote heart disease or cancer.[11]

History fails to support the idea that saturated fats are responsible for soaring rates of cardiovascular disease in western nations. In 1909, cardiovascular disease was rare in America, but by 2000 it affected 60 million people and was the leading cause of death. Table 5.3 shows that while total daily per capita fat consumption increased by about 33 percent between 1909 and 1999, saturated fat consumption remained nearly constant. A marked (67 percent) rise in

Big Saturated Fat Lie
Saturated fats make up 43% of the body's storage fat. What's more, the heart prefers saturated fat for fuel. Scientists have repeatedly failed to produce solid evidence that diets rich in saturated fats promote cardiovascular disease or cancer. While saturated fats may not be as bad as perceived, this doesn't mean you can eat an unlimited amount of saturated fat without ill effect.

Table 5.3

Changes in U.S. Dietary Fats during the Twentieth Century (grams/capita/day)			
Year	Total Fat	Saturated Fat	Unsaturated Fat
1909-19	120	50	60
1990-99	159	51	100

Adapted from Cordain L, Eades MR, Eades MD, "Hyperinsulinemic diseases of civilization: more than just Syndrome X," *Comparative Biochemistry and Physiology*, Part A, 136 (2003): 95-112, p. 100.

intake of unsaturated fats (from vegetable oils) accounted for almost all (97 percent) of the increased dietary fat during this time.

Be aware, we're not endorsing supermarket (feedlot) animal fats, or suggesting you can eat unlimited saturated fats without undesirable consequences. Feedlot animal fats are too rich in omega-6 fatty acids, too low in omega-3 fatty acids, and lack important fat-companion antioxidant nutrients. All fats supply 9 calories per gram, and are readily converted to body fat if consumed in excess of your energy needs—even if you are on a low-carbohydrate diet.

We recommend only grass-fed animal fats, which are nutritionally far superior to feedlot animal fats. Remember that although some native people got a higher proportion of their calories from fat, their caloric intake was limited because they did not control livestock feeding and breeding. We recommend eating natural fats in balance with your energy needs.

Essential Fat Facts

The body does not make polyunsaturated fatty acids. Two kinds are essential for health, the omega-3s (n-3 or w-3) and the omega-6s (n-6 or w-6). These must be obtained from foods.

The omega-3 family includes alpha-linolenic acid, eicosapentaenoic acid (EPA), and docosahexaenoic acid (DHA). Alpha-linolenic acid is available from both vegetable and animal sources. Some blue-green algae and sea plankton contain traces of DHA, but only animal fats—especially sea animal fats—contain enough EPA or DHA to be significant sources for humans.

The omega-6 family includes linoleic acid, available from both vegetable and animal sources, and arachidonic acid (AA), found only in animal sources. None of these can be synthesized in laboratories, and because they are very sensitive to heat and light, improper processing of foods (i.e. over-exposure to heat and light) destroys them.

Alpha-linolenic acid and linoleic acid are considered the parent fatty acids of their respective families because they have the shortest chains (18 carbons), which can be elongated to form the longer family members, essential for numerous body functions and structures.

DHA is particularly important in the nervous tissue, brain, and eyes of higher mammals. Herbivorous animals can convert alpha-linolenic acid first to EPA (20 carbons) and then to DHA (22 carbons), and linoleic acid to AA (20 carbons). Carnivorous animals have more sophisticated nervous systems than herbivores and consequently have a higher DHA requirement. Yet according to biochemist Dr. Michael Crawford, Ph.D., a leading expert on essential fatty acids, meat-eating animals are less efficient at converting alpha-linolenic acid into EPA and especially DHA. Although cats have a high need for DHA, they are completely incapable of producing it from alpha-linolenic acid.[12]

We have the most sophisticated central nervous system of all

Importance of O-3s
Omega-3s are polyunsaturated fatty acids that are vital for cardiovascular health as well as the health of the nervous system, brain, and eyes in higher mammals.

animals. Do we produce enough EPA and DHA to meet our needs? According to Dr. Eleanor N. Whitney, Ph.D., R.D., and Sharon R. Rolfes, M.S., R.D., authors of the textbook *Understanding Nutrition*, although we can make the conversion, the process is so inefficient, "the most effective way to sustain body stores of arachidonic acid, EPA, and DHA is to obtain them directly from foods."[13] DHA is the most difficult to produce, yet the most important for health of the brain and nervous system.

In 1999, scientists from the Departments of Food Science and Medical Laboratory Science, RMIT University, Melbourne, reported that vegetarians produce little DHA even if fed diets rich in vegetable source omega-3 alpha-linolenic acid.[14] Studies performed in the 1990s supported this finding and reported that the milk of vegetarian women contains only one-third the DHA of omnivores.[15] This is a concern because DHA is necessary for growth and development of the brain and eyes.

The omega-3s are also very important for cardiovascular health. In 1996, Italian scientists compared free-living vegetarians and fish-eaters in Tanzania and found that the vegetarians had lower blood levels of omega-3s, higher blood pressure, and blood profiles suggesting increased risk of cardiovascular diseases.[16] Animal fats rich in omega-3s may be essential for prevention of heart disease.

Unfriendly Fats

For years doctors and dietitians have been blaming animal fats for heart disease and cancer, and recommending people eat vegetable oils instead. However, history and research suggest vegetable oils are more likely the culprits.

For more than 2 million years before the industrial revolution, these oils were very rare and fake fats made from those oils, such as margarine and shortening, were unknown. Each tablespoon of vegetable oil provides about 15 grams of fat and 130 to 150 calories—3 times as much fat and twice the calories of an egg!

As shown in Table 5.4, in America during the past 100 years animal fat intake has remained virtually constant, while consumption of processed unsaturated vegetable oil products has increased four-fold, parallel with rates of major degenerative diseases—obesity, heart disease, cancer, and diabetes.[17]

Table 5.4

Changes in U.S. Dietary Fats 1909-1988 (grams/capita/day)		
Year	Animal fat	Vegetable fats/oils
1909-13	100	20
1957-59	100	40
1988	90	80

Source: Enig M, *Know Your Fats* (Bethesda Press, 2000), p. 94.

Polyunsaturated oils are highly susceptible to rancidity from exposure to heat, light, and oxygen. They must be extracted without being heated, then refrigerated in dark bottles to prevent formation of highly toxic, sticky lipid peroxides, which are a lot like plastic.[18] This is why boiled linseed (flaxseed) oil is still used as a varnish. After the boiled oil is applied to wood it reacts with oxygen in the air to produce a thin plastic-like coat.

In the industrial processes used to extract vegetable oils for sale in supermarkets, oils are exposed to enough heat, light, and oxygen to produce peroxides. These give the oils a bad taste and smell so they are bleached and deodorized before being put on the market or used to make synthetic fats (margarine and shortening).

Even if the oils were to survive industrial processing undamaged, they are typically packaged in clear bottles and stored in brightly lit groceries at room temperature. They are more or less rancid by the time someone takes them home. Then people at home usually store them at room temperature, and often use them for cooking. If you want to see oil turn to plastic, brush a baking pan with safflower oil, then bake it at 350° F—you'll have trouble getting the glue off the pan with any solvent.

Even if you get cold-pressed oils packaged in dark bottles and keep them refrigerated, as soon as you eat them conditions are correct for converting them to the pesky peroxides. Remember, your innards are always hot (98.6° F), and loaded with oxygen. What happens when peroxides get loose in your blood? Damage to arterial tissue and plaque.

That's right—unsaturated oils are a large part of the plaque that blocks coronary arteries. Lipid expert Dr. Mary Enig, Ph.D., president of the Maryland Nutritionists Association says: "The major fatty acids in the cholesterol esters in the atheroma blockages are unsaturated (74 percent of total fatty acids). Proportionally, there are, by far, many more polyunsaturates (41 percent) than saturates (26 percent) in these lesions."[19]

Since polyunsaturates are so unstable and easily damaged by oxygen, they increase the body's need for antioxidants, especially vitamin E. Whole foods rich in fat typically are also rich in vitamin E. But when oils are industrially refined, virtually all the natural vitamin E that was in the source is destroyed. Synthetic vitamin E is about half as effective as natural E and lacks the full E complex of multiple tocopherols and tocotrienols. Consequently, unless people who eat a lot of vegetable oils also take a full-spectrum natural vitamin E supplement, they may suffer from vitamin E deficiency.

The brain may incorporate more polyunsaturated fats when they are a significant portion of the diet.[20] If so, the brain may become more vulnerable to dangerous peroxidation reactions. The brain has low levels of vitamin E required to prevent these reactions. One study reports chickens fed polyunsaturated oil developed brain damage very quickly.[21]

Unsaturated Unsafe
Contrary to popular belief, unsaturated oils are the largest part of the fats in the plaque that blocks coronary arteries.

When food fabricators hydrogenate those oils to produce synthetic fats marketed as shortening and margarine, they produce *trans* fats unknown to Nature. Brisson states that when *trans* fats are taken up into heart muscle cells, the rate of energy production drops dramatically—by about 200 percent. When under stress, the heart's need for energy rises rapidly; if *trans* fats are the major part of its fuel supply, it may not be able to generate adequate energy.[22]

The National Academy of Sciences Institute of Medicine states that *trans* fats increase the risk for cardiovascular disease and there is *no safe level* of these fake fats in the diet.[23] *Trans* fats have also been linked to infertility, depressed sperm counts and testosterone levels, abnormal sperm formation, lactation insufficiency, low birth weight, and reduced visual acuity in developing infants. They also impair the enzyme system that detoxifies carcinogens and drugs.[24]

Omega-6 Overload

We only need a few grams of omega-6 fat daily; we can get more than enough from animal fats, nuts, and seeds. But these days people are eating about 80 grams of vegetable oils daily (Table 5.3). These oils supply lots of omega-6s and little or no omega-3s. Modern animal fats also provide up to 20 times more omega-6s than omega-3s. Consequently, the typical American consumes about 20 times as much omega-6s as omega-3s. Based on analysis of primitive diets such as those studied by Dr. Price, experts have estimated the optimal ratio is no more than 4:1.

Dr. Artemis Simopoulos, M.D., is the editor-in-chief of *World Review of Nutrition and Dietetics* and president of The Center for Genetics, Nutrition, and Health in Washington, D.C. She was chairwoman of the Nutrition Coordinating Committee of the National Institutes of Health for nine consecutive years. In a review of essential fatty acid research appearing in the *American Journal of Clinical Nutrition*, Dr. Simopoulos says critical body functions such as heart rhythms, blood clotting, blood vessel tone, and inflammation, are upset by diets that have more than 4 times as much omega-6s as omega-3s.[25]

Medical detectives have found that excess omega-6s increase blood clotting, cell proliferation, vasoconstriction, vasospasm, inflammation, and cardiac arrhythmia.[25, 26] Omega-6 overload suppresses immune functions and promotes atherosclerosis, cancer (including skin cancer), inflammatory diseases, insulin resistance, and some neurological disorders. [27, 28, 29, 30, 31] The bottom line: Omega-6-rich refined oils, man-made vegetable fats, and feedlot animal fats are dangerous. Your body will thank you for dumping them out.

More Omega-3s Please!

Many leading scientists believe that most modern people need to redress longstanding omega-3 fatty acid deficiency. It has been estimated that only 40 percent of Americans get enough omega-3s, and the MRFIT study found 20 percent of subjects had none detectable in their tissues.[32]

An optimum intake of omega-3s reduces inflammation, blood clotting, blood fats, and cell proliferation, dilates blood vessels, and corrects heart rhythms. Dr. Simopoulos says omega-3s have been shown effective in preventing and treating coronary heart disease, cancer, hypertension, Type II diabetes, renal disease, rheumatoid arthritis, ulcerative colitis, Crohn's disease, and chronic obstructive pulmonary disease.[33]

Correcting the Imbalance
The fats of wild marine animals are highest in omega-3s and lowest in omega-6s. One teaspoon of cod liver oil is thought to help prevent cardio-vascular disease.

According to Dr. Simopoulos and other experts, research suggests omega-3 DHA is essential for normal brain development and function and may be required to prevent and reverse attention deficit disorder, violent aggressive personality disorders, schizophrenia, and some forms of depression.[25, 33, 34] A 2001 study suggests omega-3s may also be essential for normal bone metabolism to prevent osteoporosis.[35]

Although flax oil is rich in omega-3s, it is also high in omega-6s most people don't need. You have to take at least 7 grams of the alpha-linolenic acid in flax to get 1 gram of EPA. Fats from wild marine animals—fatty ocean fish, seal, whale, etc.—are very low in omega-6s and high in omega-3s, including preformed EPA and DHA in beneficial amounts. They are best for correcting the imbalance created by modern diets.

We suggest eating fatty wild ocean fish regularly, and taking 1 teaspoon of Carlson brand cod liver oil, or 2 capsules of Carlson brand fish oils each day. This will provide the intake of EPA and DHA (650 milligrams per day) thought to help prevent cardiovascular disease and promote optimal health. Carlson's lemon-flavored cod liver oil tastes so good many people like it right from the spoon. We enjoy it drizzled over vegetables at the table.

Dangerous A and D?

Can't you get toxic amounts of vitamins A and D from cod liver oil? There is no way 1 teaspoon per day will produce any vitamin toxicity, because it contains only one-quarter the recommended daily intake of vitamin A and just 100 percent of the daily D requirement of 400 International Units (IU).

Some experts now believe the vast majority of people in modern nations need much more dietary vitamin D, which is the most important factor in your ability to absorb calcium. It also is necessary for activating thyroid hormone, for cholesterol metabolism, and optimum immune function. Laboratory research has shown it also inhibits cancer development.[36]

Pre-industrial people spent many hours outdoors hunting, gathering, herding animals, or farming, often in little clothing. Many modern people do not spend enough time in intense sunlight to get adequate vitamin D. Production of vitamin D requires exposure to UV-B light. At or above the latitude of Boston between November and

February the sunlight is too weak to stimulate significant vitamin D synthesis. Before 10 a.m. and after 2 p.m. the angle of the sun's rays greatly reduces UV-B exposure. Clothes, clouds, smoke, smog, and sunscreens with sun protection factors (SPF) of 8 or above block UV rays. To get the same amount of vitamin D that fair-skinned people produce in 30 minutes, dark-skinned people must be exposed for 3 hours.

Due to concerns about skin cancer, many people are avoiding sun exposure or using sunscreens, especially during the 10 a.m. to 2 p.m. window when vitamin D production is most efficient. Nonmelanoma skin cancer is the most common cancer in the United States. Although it is typically associated with sunlight exposure, both epidemiological and experimental studies have shown that omega-6 fatty acids promote and omega-3s prevent nonmelanoma tumor development.

In 2001, scientists at the University of Minnesota Hormel Institute in Austin published a study in the Proceedings of the National Academy of Sciences showing how the omega-6 fat arachidonic acid promotes while the omega-3s EPA and especially DHA inhibit nonmelanoma skin cancer cell development. The authors concluded "the dietary ratio of omega-6 to omega-3 fatty acids may be a significant factor in mediating tumor development."[31] This research partly explains why skin cancer is more common in 2003 than in 1903, although people in 2003 spend less time in the sun.

The skin also collects fat-soluble antioxidants (vitamin E, carotenes, etc.) which protect against burning and cancer, but many modern people have low skin levels of these nutrients because they don't eat many vegetables, nuts, or fruits. We've found we are very resistant to sunburn and attribute this to our high intake of vegetables, nuts, and fruits.

In 2000, a team of researchers from Saint Joseph University, Beirut, found vitamin D deficiency in 73 percent of people 30 to 50 years of age in sunny Lebanon; 31 percent had severe deficiency.[37] In this study, urban dwelling, low dietary vitamin D, and veil wearing (among Muslim women) were linked to vitamin D deficiency—showing that even people in sunny countries can develop vitamin D deficiency due to diet and lifestyle. Studies of urbanites in San Diego, California, found they spend very little of their time in full sunlight.[38]

The National Institutes of Health says: "Homebound individuals, people living in northern latitudes such as in New England and Alaska, women who cover their body for religious reasons, and individuals working in occupations that prevent exposure to sunlight are at risk of a vitamin D deficiency."[39] This means many homemakers, factory workers, and desk jockeys are at risk.

A full-body sunlight exposure barely sufficient to trigger tanning—for a fair-skinned individual as little as 15 minutes—is equivalent to consuming as much as 10,000 IU of vitamin D.[38] According to Dr. Reinhold Vieth, Ph.D., in the tropics where humans originally emerged, people who spend most of their days outdoors (farmers,

Skin Cancer and Omegas

Studies show omega-6s seem to promote the development of non melanoma tumors, while omega-3s help to inhibit them. This might explain why skin cancer is more common in 2003 than in 1903. Even though today we generally spend less time in the sun, we ingest far greater amounts of omega-6s than needed.

lifeguards, and others) produce about 4000 IU of vitamin D daily (tanning reduces vitamin D production) and have circulating vitamin D levels at least twice the typical modern urbanite.[40]

Vieth has accumulated substantial evidence indicating all people require that much vitamin D to maintain health. He says: "The potential benefits of greater vitamin D nutrition include a reduction in the occurrence of breast, prostate, and bowel cancers and the autoimmune conditions of multiple sclerosis and insulin-dependent diabetes."[41]

In 1998, physicians from Massachusetts General Hospital, Harvard Medical School, University of Western Australia (Perth), and Sir Gairdner Hospital (Perth) reported finding low blood levels of vitamin D in about 40 percent of people who were taking multi-vitamins containing 200 to 400 IU of D.[42] In an editorial in the same issue of *The New England Journal of Medicine*, Dr. Robert Utiger, M.D. wrote: "On the basis of what we know about vitamin D, sick adults, older adults, and perhaps all adults probably need 800 to 1000 IU daily, substantially more than the newly established levels of adequate intake. A widespread increase in vitamin D intake is likely to have a greater effect on osteoporosis and fractures than many other interventions."[43]

The Food and Nutrition Board of the Institute of Medicine says the tolerable upper intake level for dietary vitamin D is 1000 IU for infants up to 12 months of age and 2000 IU for children, adults, pregnant, and lactating women.[39] A number of studies have shown that vitamin D toxicity does not occur below doses of about 40,000 IU daily.[38]

Hence, unless you regularly spend more than 30 minutes in midday sun nearly naked without sunscreen, it is unlikely you would overdose taking 1 teaspoon of cod liver oil daily as your only dietary source of vitamin D. If you do spend a lot of time in the sun or still don't feel safe with cod liver oil, Carlson also makes pure liquid fish oil that contains no vitamin A or D, or you can take Carlson fish oil capsules. If you don't choose some dietary source of vitamin D, make sure you get your daily dose of sunshine. Remember you only need small amounts of omega-3s, maximally about 2 to 3 grams daily. Be aware that too much may be as harmful as omega-6s. High doses of fish (or flax) oils can suppress the immune system.[44]

Grass-fed Animal Fats

Unlike white, bland feedlot animal fats, fats from grass-fed animals are very similar to those in wild game.[45] Grass-fed animal fats—including butter—are yellow and richly flavored because they are loaded with beneficial carotenes, vitamin A, and vitamin E. Grass-fed animal fat contains 4 times more antioxidant vitamin E than feedlot fat. Grass-fed animal fat typically has 2 to 6 times more beneficial omega-3s than factory farmed fats. Eggs from pastured birds can have up to 20 times more omega-3s than factory-farmed eggs.[46]

Grass-fed vs. Feedlot
Grass-fed animal fats have 4 times as much Vitamin E as feedlot animal fats, as well as 2 to 6 times as much omega-3s.

Grass-fed animal fats contain 3 to 5 times as much conjugated linoleic acid (CLA) as conventional animal fats.[46] Preliminary research suggests this CLA blocks cancer growth. Animals fed a diet containing only 0.1 percent of calories as CLA had a significant reduction in tumor growth, and at 1.5 percent of calories tumor size was reduced by as much as 60 percent.[47] A 1996 study including more than 4500 Finnish women found those eating the most CLA had a 60 percent lower risk of breast cancer.[48] A case-control study of 360 women in France found those with the highest levels of CLA in breast tissue had a 74 percent lower risk of breast cancer.[49] And, when Irish researchers treated human breast cancer cells in a test tube with 20 parts per million CLA from the milk of grass-fed cows, by the eighth day of treatment, 93 percent of the cells were dead.[50]

Based on animal studies, people have to eat about 3 grams of CLA daily to reap cancer-preventing benefits. Grass-fed animal fats are the most efficient way. People eating feedlot animal fats consume an estimated maximum of 1 gram of CLA daily. To get 3 grams of CLA daily from conventional animal fats you'd have to eat much more fat and calories than you need.

Benefits of Butter

If you can find it near you, go out of your way and spend a little more for butter from strictly grass-fed animals. Even if it's not from grass-fed animals, butter is similar to wild game fat (see Chapter 2) and has other health benefits. It is rich in low-molecular weight fatty acids that are more easily digested and burned for energy than the high molecular weight fatty acids that make up most other fats and oils.

Butter has short-chain saturated fats that inhibit growth of pathogenic fungi, and medium-chain fatty acids that weaken harmful viruses and microbes. While it is a dairy product, it does not contain lactose or enough milk protein to be a problem for most people. If you can't find butter from grass-fed animals, butter from animals raised by organic standards is better than from any other land animal fat in the supermarkets.

Friendly Plant Fats

Although most vegetable oils are just too rich in omega-6 fatty acids to be fit for human consumption, some are acceptable. We recommend all kinds of true nuts, and olive, flax, sesame, coconut, and palm oils.

Five studies done between 1996 and 2001 found that consumption of nuts 5 or more times per week reduces risk of cardiovascular disease.[51-55] Although peanuts were included in these studies, they actually are not a nut, but a legume. Although we occasionally use peanuts, we prefer to use tree nuts, such as almonds, pecans, walnuts, pine nuts, macadamias, and Brazil nuts.

Olive oil is rich in monounsaturated oleic acid and low in omega-6s, and fairly well-known as a healthful oil. So long as it

Friendly Veggie Oils
Many vegetable oils are too rich in omega-6s fatty acids; however there is a group of friendly plant fats suitable for human consumption. These oils include true nut oils, olive, and coconut.

is extracted without solvents, it is rich in antioxidants, including vitamin E, carotenoids, and phenolic compounds, so it stores well and resists rancidity. Because its smoke point (where peroxides are produced) is just 280° F, it should be used raw or in low- to medium-temperature cooking, preferably not exceeding 212° F. In sautéing, you can keep the temperature from exceeding that level by adding the vegetables and stock early.

Cold-pressed flax seed oil (edible linseed oil) is the richest vegetable source of omega-3 alpha-linolenic acid. It must be used raw because heating it produces the dangerous peroxides. Sesame has a high proportion of oleic acid, but it is too rich in omega-6 linoleic acid for regular use. We only use it when making something raw that requires milder oil than extra-virgin olive, and then we combine it with some flax oil to provide counterbalancing omega-3s.

Because they are largely composed of saturated fatty acids, palm and coconut oils have been denounced like animal fats.

Palm oil has been used as food for centuries in Africa and Asia. Because it is about 50 percent saturated, it is more resistant to heat damage than other vegetable oils, making it good cooking oil.

Enig notes that coconut oil is unique in several ways.[56] First, 65 percent of coconut fat is short- and medium-chain saturated fats (caprylic, capric, and lauric acids), which are easily assimilated, rapidly converted to energy in the liver, and can increase metabolic rate. Second, 40 percent of coconut fat is lauric acid, a fat with antimicrobial, antifungal, and antiviral actions that naturally occurs in human mothers' milk and is included in infant formulas. Finally, coconut fat has fewer calories per unit weight than saturated fats predominant in conventional animal fats.

Fears that coconut oil causes cardiovascular disease are mistaken. Studies of primitive Polynesian peoples have absolved coconut oil as a cause of heart disease. For instance, the Tokelauans obtain about 57 percent of their daily calories from fat derived primarily from coconut. Coconut saturated fats provide about 50 percent of their total calories (130 grams of saturated fat daily), and they consume only 6 grams of unsaturated fat daily. These and other coconut-consumers in Polynesia are practically immune to heart disease.[56, 57, 58]

Heart disease is rampant among Americans and in baffling defiance of common sense conventional nutritionists have blamed coconut oils, which are a tiny portion of the typical American diet. According to Enig, the coconut scare was created by the makers of the artificial competitors, margarine and shortening, which do raise heart disease risk.[56]

Fat Moderation

Since our goal is to return to *The Garden of Eating*, remember that although pre-industrial people relished animal fats, their supplies weren't as fat as ours. Keep in mind:

* Although they ate wild animal fats, most of the muscle meat was very lean. They did not have fatty muscle meat *and* extra storage fat.

* Most hunter-gatherers had no significant amounts of vegetable fats/oils in their diets. Some ate ribs, but they didn't eat them along with vegetables soaked in olive oil as a side dish. In the South Pacific, where coconut was heavily used, omega-3 rich sea foods were the main animal protein.

* Primitive people didn't control animal breeding and feeding, they let Nature take its course. So they sometimes had lean and sometimes had fat. All in all, they generally had caloric intakes in balance with their activity levels. Like the modern French, their diets had a moderate proportion of fat and moderate calorie counts.

* Today we have animals with fatty muscle meat *and* a lot of storage or skin fat, *and* we have vegetable oils, all at once. Many modern people have the opportunity to create meals that have far more fat and calories than would have been possible for a hunter-gatherer most of the time.

To balance caloric requirements and meet our nutritional needs while still pleasing our palates, we have to exercise some self-discipline. We'll give you some practical guidelines starting with Chapter 7.

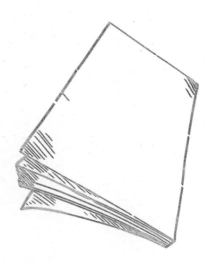

6 Organic Matters

All foods eaten by hunter-gatherers are more or less wild, grown with little or no human interference, and no synthetic fertilizers or pesticides. Before 1945, fields were fertilized with ground minerals and composted plant and animal wastes. Plants were protected from pests by good nutrition from rich soil, diversified planting with companion crops, small animals left to roam the fields (e.g. chickens are excellent slug control), and their natural pesticides to which humans have adapted through eons of experience.

Almost all meat, poultry, eggs, or fish consumed by humans came from wild game or 100 percent pasture-fed animals. Most people grew some or all of their own food. What they didn't grow, they bought from neighbors. Most produce was eaten at the peak of freshness, straight from the garden in season.

These days things are done a lot differently, and consequently, foods in many markets just aren't what they used to be. If you want the best from *The Garden of Eating*, we recommend eating locally grown and organic foods, especially grass-fed animal products, as much as possible.

Down on the Pharm

Unlike old-time diversified farms, many modern farms operate much like factories. Produce is raised in an artificial mono-crop style, on nutritionally incomplete synthetic fertilizers and doused with synthetic pesticides. This has resulted in less nutritious, more risky

Chapter Overview
Chapter 6 will look at the benefits and advantages of eating locally grown and organic foods, especially grass-fed animal products.

foods, massive erosion of topsoil, a waste of valuable manure, and chemical poisoning of our drinking water.

Chemical fertilizers typically supply nitrogen, phosphorus, potassium, and in some instances calcium—only 3 minerals out of the 14 essential to human health. Each generation of crops removes some of all the soil minerals, but conventional farmers generally add back only 3 or 4 of them. As the soil becomes progressively depleted, each generation of conventionally grown produce is weaker and less nutritious.

Many artificial pesticides are compounds of chlorine or bromine, highly toxic minerals that are not part of natural pesticides produced by plants. Our bodies are not capable of detoxifying these compounds. Most attack the nervous, endocrine, reproductive, or immune system.

Even conservative scientific organizations have recognized these present a serious problem. According to Jeremy Rifkin, president of the Foundation on Economic Trends, "In 1987, the National Academy of Sciences issued a warning that 90 percent of all fungicides, 60 percent of all herbicides, and 30 percent of all insecticides may cause cancer."[1]

In 1999, *Consumer Reports* found dangerous levels of these toxins on some U.S. fruits and vegetables.[2] The study found that even a single serving of some produce can contain toxic synthetic pesticide or herbicide residues at levels unsafe for children. Some of these permeate the produce and can't be removed by washing.

Some foods analyzed carried residues 125 times what is deemed safe for young children. The most-contaminated items were fresh peaches, apples, grapes, green beans, pears, spinach, and winter squash. Spinach had up to 14 different pesticide residues.

Bugs rapidly become resistant to chemical pesticides. Between 1950 and 1986, annual pesticide use increased from 200,000 pounds to more than 6.4 billion pounds. However, crop losses remained steady at about one-third of total production, because pests became immune to the chemicals. At least 305 species of insects, mites, and ticks now have strains resistant to one or more pesticides.[3]

Organic Answer

The Consumers Union scientists found that commercially grown organic food is largely free of the toxins tainting conventional produce. In 2001, Japanese scientists reported that organically grown Chinese cabbage, carrots, Welsh onions, spinach, and other pesticide-free produce were superior to conventionally grown produce at suppressing activity of mutagenic chemicals.[4]

Is organic produce more nutritious? That depends on when and where you get it. If you purchase out-of-season organic produce at a conventional or natural foods supermarket, chances are it will have little chemical contamination, but it may not be more nutritious than conventional produce.

Factory Farming
Many modern farms operate more like factories, mass producing one crop, usually with the help of synthetic fertilizers and pesticides. All of this contributes to a decrease in the food's nutritional value.

In 1998, organic farming proponent Virginia Worthington compiled the results of 30 different studies comparing 300 store-bought vegetables.[5] She found certified organic crops had a higher nutrient content 40 percent of the time and conventionally grown produce was more nutritious 15 percent of the time. Forty-five percent of the time store-bought organic produce was no more nutritious than conventional supermarket fare.

As detailed by organic farmer Henry Brockman in his booklet *Organic Matters*, there are several reasons you can't rely on supermarkets to supply you with super-nutritious organic produce.[6] First, farms raising mass-market organic produce may use high-nitrogen fertilizers to accelerate crop growth, which means fruits and vegetables reach marketable size without having had time to absorb minerals or synthesize nutrients to maximum possible levels.

Second, mass-market organic farms may use the same crop varieties as conventional farms. Most of those varieties are hybrids selected for productivity, external appearance, and durability in transcontinental transportation, not taste or nutritional value. At peak of ripeness, one peach variety may have 20 times the carotene of another; one kind of carrot may produce as much as 10 times the carotene as another. But mass-market producers usually don't select the most nutritious cultivars—unless they also happen to be the most durable for shipping.

Third, most mass-market organic produce is picked before it is ripe and reaches maximum nutritional value and then shipped 1500 miles before it is purchased for consumption. During that trek it loses more nutritional value. Produce can lose 50 percent of its carotene (pro-vitamin A) and 60 percent of its vitamin C within 3 days of being harvested. A week after harvest, these nutrients can be completely lost. Rarely is mass-market organic produce in consumers' mouths within a day of harvest when nutritional value is greatest (assuming the produce was allowed to ripen fully).

Grow Your Own or Buy Local

If you want maximum nutritional value from your produce, you need to grow it yourself or buy it at your local farmers' market. Whether organically grown or not, we have found that fresh, locally grown fruits and vegetables are nearly always more colorful and flavorful than their supermarket counterparts.

Locally and organically grown produce is the best choice. Since this is not always available or affordable, we often choose locally grown produce from small farmers. Local producers typically use smaller amounts of hazardous chemicals than large mono-crop farms that produce fruits and vegetables only for transcontinental shipment and supermarket sales.

Not All Organic Better
Depending on the procedures used to grow organic foods, the produce may not be any more nutritious than that of conventional farms. Your best option is to buy from a local farmer, a farmers' market, or grow your own produce. It is almost always more flavorful and colorful.

Locally grown, non-organic produce often has more color and flavor, and contains more vitamins and phytonutrients than organic produce shipped 1500 miles or more and allowed to waste away in trucks, warehouses, and supermarkets for 1 or 2 weeks before it reaches your grocery cart or mouth.

Presently organic produce is more expensive than conventional, but as demand and supply grow, prices will fall. In the meantime, you can cut your costs on organic produce by subscribing to a Community Supported Agriculture project (CSA), frequenting your local farmers' market, or joining or forming a co-op food-buying club. Information on buying clubs can be found in Chapter 10 and Appendix E.

Can Organic Feed the World?

Organic farming can feed the world if the food is produced on diversified farms, then consumed locally. For 40 centuries, the enormous population of China was supported by organic agriculture. Chinese farmers kept their soils highly productive for so many centuries by keeping Nature's nutrient cycle intact.

Human wastes contain many nutrients taken from the soil. In Nature, our wastes—urine, manure—simply go back to the Earth as part of the nutrient cycle. Our modern waste-disposal and agricultural systems ignore this natural process. Consequently the soil is progressively depleted.

Chinese farmers have long used human manure on their fields. Although uncomposted human manure is unsafe fertilizer, composting expert J.C. Jenkins says proper thermophilic composting generates enough heat to kill all infectious bacteria and parasites, rendering human manure completely safe for use in farming.[7]

Food Supply and Population

We don't have to keep increasing food production. Future generations will be better off if, over time, we gradually reduce it. Why? Biology has discovered that, for any species, every increase in food supply promotes population growth. Conversely, reductions in food supply result in decline of populations.

Vegetarians assert we should stop eating meat to increase the supply of food for humans. In the mid-1990s, U.S. livestock consumed 130 tons of grain annually, enough to feed about 400 million people. Food supply experts Dr. Russell Hopfenberg, Ph.D., of Duke University (Durham, North Carolina), and Dr. David Pimentel, Ph.D., of Cornell University (Ithaca, New York) explain why the vegetarian idea is misguided: "Certainly there would be even more human food available if dependence on livestock was decreased. However, because human population is a function of food availability, the resulting increase in available human food would induce a commensurate rise in population. This population increase would ultimately exacerbate the starvation and malnutrition predicament."[8]

If we stabilize our food production, the population can stabilize without any increase in starvation. Studies of monkeys show that when food supply is kept relatively constant, starvation does not occur.[8] Daniel Quinn, author of *Beyond Civilization*, explains why: If the food supply is held constant at an adequate level, even if the population increases at a rate of 1 to 2 percent per year, the reduction in caloric intake for each individual is so small it is practically unnoticeable for up to 9 years.[8, 9]

In fact, even if the food supply *drops* at a rate similar to the rate of population growth, impact on individual caloric intake is minor for up to 5 years. Suppose 1000 people have a food supply of 3000 calories per person per day (a total of 3 million calories). If the group increases annually by 1.4 percent (our current rate) and the food supply decreases by 1.5 percent, in the second year there are 1014 people—the added 14 all being infants who require only about 600 calories daily—and a total food supply of 2.955 million calories per day, or 2914 calories per person. In the third year, there are 1028 people, 14 of them infants and 14 only 1-year-olds; and each person will have 2831 calories available. If this continues for 2 more years, in the fourth year, there are 1042 people and 2751 calories for each, and in the fifth, 1057 people each supplied with 2671 calories; a reduction of only 329 calories, or 11 percent, from the first year.

Regardless of nutritional quality of foods eaten, such gradual caloric reduction can reduce body fat levels, fertility, and reproductive activity. Leaner people generally have fewer children.[10] Birth rate and population can gradually decline in equilibrium with decreasing food supply, without any increase in malnutrition. If we wisely focus on reducing production and consumption of unnecessary and empty calories—such as white sugar—people could be leaner and healthier.

The alternative is to continue vainly increasing food production, focusing on caloric quantity instead of quality (nutrient density). That will generate an even larger population with a higher proportion malnourished and malformed—many of whom will die of diseases resulting from poverty and pollution. Already an unprecedented 3 billion people are malnourished. Infections and pollution, side effects of overpopulation, cause 75 percent of deaths each year.[8]

There's a saying, "Insanity is doing the same thing over and over and expecting different results." During the past 10,000 years, we have repeatedly increased food production. Always the result has been more people, poverty, malnutrition, pollution, infectious disease, and deaths from the last 3 factors. We are bound by Nature's laws. It is time to try something else.

Nature's Meat vs. Feedlot Meat
According to Nature's plan, livestock is designed to roam freely outdoors and eat fresh grass or other wild pasture foods. However, on modern factory farms animals are confined and fed an unnatural diet of dry cereals (e.g. corn and soy) laced with salt, meat scraps,

synthetic hormones, antibiotics, and garbage. No, that wasn't a mistake—several independent investigations have found so-called farmers feeding cement, cardboard, newspaper, spoiled dumpster food, and other trash to their animals.[11] Livestock are also regularly sprayed with pesticides that are retained in the animals' fat. The result is obese, ill animals from which we get nutrient-depleted, steroid-laden, over-marbled meats that present a high risk of salmonella, E. coli, or mad cow infection.

Feedlot animals are typically butchered in assembly-line style slaughterhouses by unskilled laborers who endure dangerous working conditions for minimum wages. After being trucked hundreds or thousands of miles, the animals may arrive at these facilities covered in manure. The production line moves so quickly that workers can't maintain clean techniques. Intestinal contents from any contaminated animals on the kill line can taint processing equipment and spread salmonella or E. coli throughout the plant. Ground meat (the usual source of E. coli outbreaks) from dozens or hundreds of animals is co-mingled; bacteria from one contaminated animal can infect the whole batch.

Feedlot meat is used to make processed products such as bacon, sausages, and various lunch meats. These are loaded with various highly suspect salts (sodium chloride, nitrates, nitrites, etc.) and other fillers, preservatives, and additives.

Do you have a choice? Yes. You can get meat directly from farmers raising animals on pasture, the way Nature intended.

Grass-fed is Best

In her excellent book *Why Grassfed is Best*, Jo Robinson presents many good reasons to go an extra mile and spend an extra dollar to buy pasture-fed animal products directly from your local farmer. Here are the main benefits for you and Mother Earth, too, taken from her book and Web site (www.eatwild.com), the USDA, and other sources:

1. Improved nutrition

Grass-fed livestock is better nourished than grain-fed. Fresh pasture foods are much more nutrient dense than grains. Moreover, livestock has better digestion and assimilation when raised on pasture foods for which their guts are designed. The result is more nutritious meat and eggs.

Robinson has compiled many studies showing that meat, eggs, or milk from wild or strictly grass-fed animals have many nutritional advantages over feedlot products. Refer to previous chapters—especially Chapter 5—for details.

2. Avoid food poisoning

Grain feeding alters farm animals' intestinal flora and pH, promoting pathogenic strains of acid-resistant E. coli and Salmonella. Strictly pasture-fed animals are much less likely to harbor legions of these malicious microbes that can survive our first line of defense, stomach acid. Mad cow disease is not found in cattle fed entirely on pasture and hay.

Small farmers selling grass-fed animal products have their animals carefully butchered by local USDA-inspected processing houses where sanitation violations are rare compared to mass-market facilities. These skilled butchers process one animal at a time and sterilize their equipment between animals.

3. Ecology

Some authors claim that raising livestock is a misuse of land, causes global warming, ground water loss and pollution, loss of species diversity, and depletion of fossil fuels. They say it is more ecological for humans to eat a grain-based, largely or totally vegetarian diet.

Surprise! Grass feeding animals can be more ecological than row cropping grains and beans for several reasons.

Only about one-third of the Earth's land mass can be used for food production. Of that, only about one-third (about one-ninth of the total land mass) is suitable for growing crops. Suburban sprawl and erosion from row cropping will continue to take away cropland. The remaining two-thirds of usable land supports only growth of plants that are not edible for humans, but are edible for ruminant animals, i.e. bison, cattle, deer, elk, zebras, elands, sheep, goats, and the like.[12]

Grazing ruminants release methane, a greenhouse gas, but their pastures are 50 percent more effective than cultivated fields at removing carbon-rich greenhouse gases from the atmosphere. The USDA Conservation Reserve Program (CRP) found that when cultivated soils are returned to pasture, they gain an average of one-half ton of carbon per acre per year for the first 5 years after restoration. Returning cropland to grassland helps combat global warming.

Most cultivated plants have sparse root structures and are planted relatively far apart; non-cultivated plants (weeds) naturally fill the gap but farmers fight back with herbicides. Wind and rainfall can't be stopped and carry exposed soil and chemicals off the farm and into our waterways.

Native grassland plant species do not require chemical input. They have dense root structures that prevent weed growth and erosion, enable the soil to retain water, refill subterranean aquifers, and protect surface waterways. Compared to cultivated lands, properly managed pastures make almost no contribution to soil erosion, ground water loss, or water pollution.

Properly managed grazing also results in natural distribution and incorporation of animal urine and feces into the soil. Factory farms and feedlots produce high

Return to Grassland
Two-thirds of the Earth's land mass that is suitable for food production is better suited to the growth of plants edible for ruminant animals (bison, cattle, sheep, etc.) than as cropland. Cropland converted to grassland can fight global warming and reduce soil erosion and water pollution.

concentrations of wastes that often end up in waterways. Fortunately, wastes from these operations can be successfully incorporated into pasture lands, helping reduce water pollution.

Do grazing cattle damage range lands? Only if improperly managed. Grazing animals are a natural, essential part of healthy grassland ecology. If they are managed in a way that mimics natural patterns of native animals (deer, elk, bison, etc.), grazing cattle can improve rangelands. Well-managed grazing increases the number and vigor of native perennial grasses, reduces weed species, improves vegetative cover of stream banks, hastens manure decomposition, and extends the pasture's growing season.

According to the USDA's Agricultural Research Service, ungrazed pasturelands are degraded through loss of native plant species diversity, increased weed growth, and reduced carbon storage. Pasture plants, ruminant animals, and predators are interdependent by Nature's design.

4. Energy efficiency

Raising animals entirely on pasture is probably the most energy efficient of all food production methods. In raising row crops, farmers commonly invest 5 to 10 calories of fossil fuel (for large machinery used for tilling, planting, and harvesting) for each calorie of food or fiber harvested. Pasture-based animal husbandry is 10 to 20 times more energy efficient, producing 2 calories of energy profit (food, fertilizer, and fiber) for every calorie of fossil fuel invested.

Why? Diverse grassland complete with ruminant animals is an ecosystem evolved by Nature. It requires practically no human effort to maintain. Vast single-crop farms are artificial and can be maintained against Nature's design for diversity only by investing enormous amounts of human labor and energy.

Grains and legumes all require extensive, energy-intensive processing (such as grinding) or cooking. This is true even of so-called quick-cooking rice and cereals, which are "quick" because they are processed and precooked by the food industry. The food-processing industry is the fourth largest U.S. industrial energy user—after metals, chemicals, and oil. Farming uses less than one-fifth of the energy consumed by our food system. The other 80 percent is spent in processing, packaging, distributing, and preparing food.[13]

Meat, eggs, and milk are all edible with little or no processing or cooking. When you buy fresh or frozen raw animal products directly from the farmer, total energy spent in getting it to your plate is a tiny fraction of what's spent in the industrial food loop.

Natural Energy
Raising animals on pastureland is one of the most energy efficient methods of food production. Because pastureland is natural, it can be maintained with little human effort. In contrast, enormous energy inputs are required to grow mass amounts of a single crop.

5. Supports Local Family Farms

Perhaps most important, when you purchase pasture-based animal products you will be supporting local family farmers who take care of their animals and their environment. Large corporations have converted farms into mass-production animal factories that supply food to supermarkets. These corporations are running family farms out of business by focusing on producing large quantities of low-quality food, regardless of the damage inflicted on rural economies and families.

For example, a 1992 University of Missouri (Columbia) study found that when a corporation invests $5 million to build a large confinement hog operation, 40 to 45 low-paying jobs are created. An analysis by the Land Stewardship Project (White Bear Lake, Minnesota) found that this kind of operation will put 126 independent, small-scale hog farmers out of business—a net loss of at least 80 livelihoods. Corporate hog factories usually rely on distant suppliers, putting more local people out of business.[14]

By dumping enormous quantities of cheap products on the market, agricultural corporations can drive prices down to a level where family farmers are unable to make a profit. Once they control the market, they are able to set prices to levels for maximum profits. Some care little about worker or food safety. Some intend to shove genetically engineered foods down your throat.

How about a featherless chicken? We're not kidding. In corporate chicken factories 10,000 birds are packed into close quarters. As you can imagine, they generate a lot of heat, and if fans or air conditioners fail, the chickens will die within a few hours. To reduce the losses, scientists have developed a featherless hybrid bird that can stand more heat. You can see a picture of this new bald breed at www.eatwild.com (search for "Meet Tomorrow's Chicken"). Before you know it, they'll hatch boneless chickens.

The list of scientifically documented health, economic, and environmental benefits of pasture-based animal husbandry and grass-fed animal products is so large we can't present it all here. Visit Robinson's site, www.eatwild.com, for up-to-date information.

If you want to support sustainable, local agriculture based on healthy family farms, purchase more locally produced, pasture-based animal products (as well as fruits and vegetables). Grass-farming supports small, local farmers (and the businesses in their communities), relationships

Want to Learn More? Read Orville Schell's *Modern Meat: Antibiotics, Hormones, and the Pharmaceutical Farm* (New York: Random House, 1984), and *Fast Food Nation* by Eric Schlosser (Boston: Houghton Mifflin, 2001). Check out the magazine *Acres USA* (www.acresusa.com). Log onto www.organicconsumers.org and sign up for the *Biodemocracy Newsletter*. Another good source is www.foodandwater.org.

between growers and consumers, and the health of people and our precious planet.

Organic vs. Grass-fed

Organic animal products are not necessarily the same as grass-fed. By law the organic label can be used only on meats, eggs, and milk from animals raised on feed grown without synthetic fertilizers or pesticides, without hormones or antibiotics. Usually organic livestock is grain-fed.

Although many grass-fed animal products qualify for the organic label, some do not. The farmer might use pasture fertilizers, medications to treat parasites, or some non-organic hay for winter feed, or he might have been unable to find a certified organic butcher. Yet his "non-organic" grass-fed animal products will be far superior to certified organic animal products.

To be certain you are getting grass-fed meat, buy meat directly from the farmer. Ask the producer how much grain his animals eat. You're looking for an answer like "none" or "only in a pinch, when we run out of pasture and hay."

If you can't find grass-fed products from a farmer near you, organic products are your next best choice. At least you'll avoid drug and pesticide residues found in conventional feedlot products.

If you are unable to purchase grass-fed or organic meat, natural meats from animals raised on vegetarian diets without synthetic hormones or antibiotics are better-than-average alternatives. Still it is to your advantage to purchase your meats directly from a local farmer rather than a supermarket.

Because of growing consumer demand, some better quality grain-fed meats such as beefalo (a cross of beef and buffalo), grain-fed buffalo, Coleman Natural Beef, Piedmontese beef, Laura's Lean Beef, and ostrich are now available in modern supermarkets. Many of these are as low in total fat as wild game meats.

Remember, although lean, these new supermarket meats are all grain-fed and may have undesirably high levels of omega-6s and low levels of omega-3s, as well as other nutrients, both in the muscle and in the trim fat. White fat means the animal was grain-fed. Yellow fat is high in carotenes and a sign the animal was grass-fed.

For millennia our ancestors ate only wild game or pasture-fed animal products. That is the kind of meat we are designed to eat. The closer you get to this, the better your health will be. To get the best, we strongly recommend you connect with a producer of strictly grass-fed meat.

Grass-fed vs. Organic
Not all grass-fed animal products qualify as organic. Usually organic livestock is grain fed. Even so, "non-organic" grass-fed animals will be superior to certified organic products.

7Return to The Garden of Eating
General Principles

In a nutshell, here are our recommendations for a diet similar to that of native people known to be practically immune to degenerative diseases:

1. Make fresh locally grown vegetables and fruits 65 to 75 percent of the weight and volume of your meals/diet.
2. Make clean, lean grass-fed animal products 20 to 35 percent of the weight and volume of your meals/diet.
3. Use friendly fats in moderation, according to individual needs.
4. Minimize use of salt and use only unrefined, sun-dried gray sea salt.
5. Eliminate refined grain products, conventional dairy products, mass-market meats, refined sugars, unfriendly vegetable oils, alcohol, and all synthetic foods.

Properly prepared whole grains and dairy products from grass-fed animals are optional as discussed in Chapter 4.

Since many people have no idea how to translate the recommended ratios of fruits, vegetables, and animal products into menus and grocery lists, we've come up with the following practical principles:

1. **Estimate your daily meat requirement.**
   If you use the American measurement system:
   a.) Minimum: Take your body weight in pounds (minus desired fat loss) and divide by 10.

Chapter Overview:
Chapter 7 offers practical principles and guidelines that will lead you along the path of *The Garden of Eating*. Also included are sample meals that illustrate the quantity of food needed.

b.) Maximum: Take your body weight in pounds (minus desired fat loss) and divide by 8.

That will give you an estimated range for your daily meat requirements in ounces.

EXAMPLE:

120-pound woman (or 150-pound woman who needs to lose 30 pounds)
   a.) 120/10 = about 12 ounces of meat minimum
   b.) 120/8 = about 15 ounces of meat maximum

These are round numbers just to get you started. You might need to fine-tune them for yourself.

If you use the metric system:

Multiply your weight in kilograms by 2.2, which gives you your weight in pounds, then after you get the range of meat intake in ounces, multiply by 28 to convert the range to grams.

These numbers tell you how much to eat daily and how much to have on hand for a week or more.

EXAMPLE:

55-kilogram woman
   a.) Weight in pounds = 55 x 2.2 = 121 (round down to 120)
   b.) Range:
      i.) 12 ounces x 28 g/ounce = 336 grams
      ii.) 15 ounces x 28 g/ounce = 420 grams

So, a 120-pound (55 kg) woman should plan to eat about 12 to 15 ounces (330 to 420 grams) of meat, poultry, fish, or eggs daily. Spread over 3 main meals, she'll eat about 3 to 5 ounces (about 100 to 140 grams) 3 times a day. Her week's supply would be about 7 pounds (3.2 kg) of meat, poultry, fish, or eggs (not counting the weight of bones and skin, which would increase the amount you need to buy).

2. Estimate your daily fruit and vegetable requirements:
   a.) Minimum: Take your body weight in pounds (minus desired fat loss) and divide by 4.
   b.) Maximum: Take your body weight in pounds (minus desired fat loss) and divide by 3.

That will give you an estimated range for your daily fruit and vegetable requirements in ounces.

EXAMPLE:

120-pound (55-kg) person, or 150-pounder who needs to lose 30 pounds
   a.) Minimum: 120/4 = 30 ounces (840 grams or 1.9 pounds)
   b.) Maximum: 120/3 = 40 ounces (1120 grams or 2.5 pounds)

Again, these are estimates using round numbers and you'll have to fine-tune them for yourself. They are a relatively good approximation of our own practice, and you have to be near these figures to have a produce-dominated diet producing a net alkaline balance, as we discussed in Chapter 3. Here's why:

If our 120-pound woman eats 12 to 15 ounces of meat (almost 1 pound) and 30 to 40 ounces of produce (1.9 to 2.5 pounds) daily, her diet's minimum plant-animal ratios will range as follows:

15 ounces meat, 30 ounces produce = 33 percent meat, 67 percent fruits/vegetables = slightly acid

12 ounces meat, 30 ounces produce = 28 percent meat, 72 percent fruits/vegetables = net alkaline

Although to many people 30 ounces of fruits and vegetables may appear a prodigious, perhaps impossible amount to eat, in fact it is not. The perception is due mainly to lack of knowledge about the average weights of common foods. Few people know that a large apple can weigh 8 ounces (half a pound).

> **Buy More**
> You'll actually need to buy more than 14 to 18 pounds of produce to account for inedible portions of the plants you normally discard: rinds, skin, seeds, woody stems, etc.

Food Portions that Weigh 8 Ounces (one-half pound):

1 large apple, banana, or pear
1 medium to large sweet potato
1 medium-size baked potato
1 1/3 cups cubed cantaloupe
1 1/2 cups blueberries
1 1/2 cups steamed asparagus or broccoli
1 1/2 cups sautéed kale or collards with onions
1 cup cooked apple compote
1 large salad

We have experimented with various proportions of high- and low-carbohydrate plant foods and found we—like hunter-gatherers—prefer about half our produce allotment as roots, bulbs, tubers, or fruits (winter squashes are fruits), and the other half as non-starchy vegetables.

Our 120-pound person will be eating 10 to 13 ounces of fruits or vegetables at each of 3 main meals, and may have some at snacks as well. Each time she eats, she'll have 5 to 7 ounces of roots, bulbs, tubers, or fruit, and 5 to 7 ounces of non-starchy vegetables. For a week, she'll need 210 to 280 ounces, or 13 to 18 pounds (6 to 8 kg) of fresh fruits or vegetables, excluding inedible trim.

3. Estimate your daily friendly fat requirements

Here generalizations are a bit more difficult. Everyone has a different fat requirement and tolerance. What's too much? You will have to experiment to find out how much you need to feel well. Based on our experience, we suggest the following rough guidelines for adding fat to your main foods:

a.) Minimum: Multiply body weight in pounds (minus desired fat loss) times .35.

b.) Maximum: Multiply body weight in pounds (minus desired fat loss) times .70.

EXAMPLE:

120 pound person
a.) Minimum added fat = 120 x .35 = 40 grams
b.) Maximum added fat = 120 x .70 = 84 grams

These give you an estimated range of daily requirements for added fat in grams.

In this system, any fat beyond what naturally occurs in lean trimmed meat, skinless poultry, fish, and eggs is added fat. Thus, any trimmable meat fat or skin is added fat. Butter, avocado, olives, nuts, nut butters, tahini, coconut, coconut milk, and olive, coconut, fish, flax, and sesame oils also count as added fat for these estimations.

Most hunter-gatherers only ate animal fats most of the time. They didn't eat meals including both naturally occurring meat fat *and* vegetable oil salad dressing. To replicate hunter-gatherer diets, if we eat vegetable oils we have to swap them for animal fats teaspoon for teaspoon.

Again, these are estimates only. You may find you need more or (rarely) less than these amounts.

A teaspoon of any pure fat measures about 5 grams, so our example person needs at least 8 teaspoons of added fat per day. She can plan to have 2 to 3 teaspoons of added fat at each of 3 main meals. But she may find she needs more than this, especially if she is very active. Or, like us, she may eat 4 times a day and have some fat—perhaps in the form of nuts or nut butter—as a snack.

You'll know you are eating too little fat if you can't go more than a couple of hours without getting hungry or feeling your energy peter out. You should eat enough fat to make food enjoyable and enable you to function at a high level for at least 3 hours after eating.

Your taste can help you discover your fat limit. Adding fat to your food will increase your enjoyment to a point, beyond which there will be no increase in enjoyment.

You may be eating too much fat if you feel sluggish after meals (but that also could be from too much carbohydrate). Over a period of time, too much fat can put stress on your liver and gallbladder and make you feel stressed, irritable, or "bilious" as was said in times past. For others, excess dietary fat triggers acne outbreaks.

Only you know your requirement, which may actually

Fat Exchanges Providing 5 Grams of Fat

1 teaspoon oil, clarified butter, or ghee

1 1/3 teaspoons butter

1/2 tablespoon nut butter or tahini

1 tablespoon nuts or seeds

6 almonds

2 tablespoons full-fat coconut milk

2 heaping tablespoons dried, flaked coconut

3 tablespoons mashed avocado

1/5 to 1/6 of a large avocado

1/3 cup lite coconut milk

1/2 ounce macadamia nuts

change from meal to meal and day to day. If you've been eating a low-fat diet before adopting our plan, you may have to limit your fat intake in the early stages because your body is not used to it. Over time eating by our guidelines you may find your tolerance and need for fat increases.

Putting it together

1. Trimmed meat, poultry, fish, or eggs: 4 to 5 ounces (about the size of the palm of your hand)
2. Roots, tubers, bulbs, or fruits: 5 to 6 ounces
3. Green leaves and other fibrous vegetables: 5 to 6 ounces
4. Friendly fat: 2 to 3 teaspoons, or more as needed.

For example:

1. 1 (4-ounce) piece of grass-fed T-bone steak
2. About 1 cup roasted mix of carrots, onions, and potatoes
3. About 1 cup sautéed kale with onions and shiitake mushrooms
4. 1 to 2 teaspoons of friendly fat used to cook root vegetables
5. About 1 teaspoon of friendly fat or oil used to sauté greens
6. About 1 handful of grapes for desert

This is not an insurmountable pile of food. Refer back to Chapter 2 to see similar menus along with nutritional and plant-animal ratio analyses. Remember: Each person has to adjust the ratios and amounts to meet his or her own needs.

Using the above formula, you can generate a start-up grocery list for your first foray into *The Garden of Eating*.

Calculate weekly meat, fruit, and vegetable needs of each person in your family, add them together, and take the list with you to the market.

For example, a family of 4 with a 120-pound mother, 160-pound father, 80-pound son, and 100-pound teenage daughter would need at least 25 pounds of meat, poultry, and fish, 66 pounds of fruits and vegetables, and 4 pounds of friendly fats for a week's supply.

Bear in mind you'll need to buy more vegetables and fruits to account for the trim you toss or compost.

You will also have to buy slightly more meat, poultry, or fish because there will be some shrinkage in cooking; if bones or skin are present you can't count these as edible portions. For example, on a 4-pound bone-in chicken, half the weight will be skin and bones. The same ratio applies for heavy-boned roasts.

> **How to Eyeball a Produce-Dominated Meal**
>
> You're about to eat and faced with an empty dinner plate. What do you do?
>
> 1. Choose a protein portion about the size of the palm of your hand. That should fill 1/4 to 1/3 of your plate.
>
> 2. Fill the remaining 2/3 to 3/4 of your plate with fresh vegetables (don't forget the leafy greens), fruits, or a combination of the two. If you include a high-density carbohydrate (e.g., potato, sweet potato, sweet corn, banana, or whole grain) choose a portion about the size of your protein portion, then fill the remainder of your plate with fibrous, non-starchy vegetables (e.g., cooked or raw leafy green or mixed vegetables).
>
> 3. Add a small amount of nuts, seeds, avocado, olive or coconut oil, butter, or salad dressing, or use a modest amount of acceptable fat or oil to cook or marinate 1 or 2 dishes. If you leave the skin on the chicken or eat a rich cut of meat, count that as added fat.

Maintaining a Strong Appetite and Good Digestion

Many people, particularly women, underestimate how much food they need to eat, then end up bingeing to fill in what they're missing. Some people feel guilty and chastise themselves for eating a large meal, even if they are consuming the same or fewer calories than before.

We urge you to cultivate a good appetite. Satisfying it with nourishing food is what Nature intended. You don't want to suppress your appetite, even if your intention is to lose weight (body fat). You still need to consume generous amounts of wholesome foods. You'll just need to be more sparing in the use of added fats and foods with a very high calorie density, such as nuts, nut butters, oils, fatty meats, juices, and dried fruits.

To cultivate a good appetite and maintain a healthy metabolism, you have to avoid overeating, excessive raw, cold, or frozen foods, and late-night eating. Here are some guidelines and explanations:

* Eat only enough food at any meal to feel 80 percent full, not more and usually not less. Leaving that 20 percent empty allows the digestive system to work at peak efficiency. The exact amount you need to reach the feeling of being 80 percent full will vary with your needs, which are generated by your level and type of activity. Only you can sense exactly how much you need. No expert or supposedly scientific formula can predict your changing needs.

* If you have a hard time pushing yourself away from the table, or have a history of compulsive snacking, overeating, or bingeing, one of the best things you can do for yourself is to eat 3 nourishing, sit-down meals a day at regular intervals. This will help to regulate your appetite, blood sugar, and energy level, making your hunger more manageable and predictable. That in turn helps you avoid extreme dips in energy that might otherwise trigger overindulgence, especially in the evening.

* Eat most foods cooked and warm. Proper cooking kills parasites, neutralizes toxins, makes food more digestible, and increases nutrient delivery. Warm food transfers energy to the body and improves the function of digestive enzymes. Most people can tolerate some raw fruits and salad vegetables, but the amount varies from person to person. Excessive intake of raw foods can cause gas, bloating, frequent loose stools, and nutritional deficiencies from impaired digestion and assimilation.

* Minimize use of frozen or very cold foods, e.g. ice cream, iced drinks, foods straight from the refrigerator. Foods below body temperature are harder to digest because they cause withdrawal of blood from the digestive system and inhibit enzymes, which require warm temperatures for activity.

Cold and frozen foods suck heat and energy out of the body—particularly the digestive organs—and promote phlegm formation and unhealthy blood coagulation in the abdomen.

Warming Up
Cooked and warmed foods are easier to digest than raw foods.

The occasional frozen treat in warm weather usually has no serious consequences. However, according to traditional Chinese medicine, frequent ingestion of cold foods, especially in cold weather, injures the digestive organs, depresses metabolism, aggravates arthritis, and promotes menstrual disorders, obesity, and formation of abdominal tumors and cysts.

* Generally avoid eating after 7 p.m. The digestive system is at its lowest energy level from then until morning. Even if you follow all of the other rules, eating late will usually cause indigestion, compromise the digestive organs, and according to traditional Chinese medicine, promote phlegm-related disorders, including tumors, cysts, obesity, atherosclerosis, and other circulatory diseases.

Cold Facts
Minimizing intake of cold and frozen foods will contribute to healthier metabolism and better digestion.

Sample Meals

To help you gauge a reasonable amount of food for 2 adults whose activity level is light and who spend most of their time sitting at a desk or standing, we've included 2 sample days of meals taken from our actual experience, representative of our typical pattern.

Typically, we both walk for 30 to 60 minutes 5 or more times a week, do yoga or stretching 4 to 6 times a week, and Don lifts weights for about 30 minutes, twice a week. We occasionally swim, dance, or take a hike.

Note that the Daily Values (DVs) are set by the FDA for purposes of labeling processed foods and some are not representative of nutritional requirements. The FDA has set the DV for carbohydrate at 60 percent of calories, based on the assumption that high-carbohydrate, low-fat, low-protein diets are healthier.

The absolute requirement for dietary carbohydrate is a matter of debate but probably falls in the range of 50 to 150 grams daily. The DV for sodium merely represents a customary sodium intake for Americans eating highly refined, processed, and heavily salted foods. Individual sodium requirements vary based on water losses through sweating or diarrhea, but in most cases do not exceed 500 milligrams daily.

In the following calculations, calcium intakes include only the calcium present in the foods listed. Several recipes used in these menus incorporate our Bone-Building Broth for which we do not have a nutritional analysis. Actual calcium intakes were higher by an undetermined amount.

Nutrition analyses performed using Cybernetic Dietician® nutrition software program for Macintosh available from www.satoripublishing.com/CyberDiet.

~Sample Meals next 4 pages~

Sample Day 1:
Food Analysis for Rachel Matesz

Height: 65 inches (5'5")
Age: 38
Weight: 118
Activity level: light

	Actual intake	Daily value
Calories	1830 kcal	1844 kcal
Protein	133 g (28 percent)	50 g
Carbohydrate	174 g (38 percent)	274 g
Fat	72 g (35 percent)	61 g
Cholesterol	565 mg	277 mg
Fiber	35 g	23 g
Calcium	658 mg	738 mg
Sodium	1174 mg	2190 mg

* **Note:** Foods prepared without salt.
Eggs and dried, powdered egg whites are
naturally rich in sodium.

Breakfast 7 a.m.
2 large eggs, fried (100 g) in 1/2 teaspoon coconut oil (2.5 g)
2 ounces Roasted Smoky Turkey Breast (56 g)
1 1/2 cups steamed broccoli (117 g) plus 1 teaspoon lemon-flavored cod liver oil (5 g)
1 1/2 cups cantaloupe cubes (266 g)

Lunch 11 a.m.
4 1/2 ounces Orange Roughy baked with basil, garlic and pepper (128 g)
   in 1/2 teaspoon olive oil (2.5 g)
1 lemon wedge (7 g)
Large salad:
   2 cups spring greens
   1/4 cup minced celery (112 g)
   1/3 cup toasted, crumbled dulse leaf (7 g)
   1/2 cup Roasted Onion (50 g), includes 1 teaspoon olive oil (5 g)
   1/2 cup Roasted Carrots (56 g), includes 1/2 teaspoon olive oil (2.5 g)
1/2 cup Apple & Apricot Compote (115 g) plus 2 teaspoons macadamia nut butter (10 g)

Snack 3 p.m.
Blueberry-Peach Smoothie:
   1/4 cup coconut milk (56 g)
   1 teaspoon flax oil (5 g)
   1 ounce vanilla egg white protein (28 g)*
   1 cup sliced frozen peaches (170 g)
   3/4 cup frozen blueberries (140 g)
   2 thin slices fresh gingerroot
   Dash stevia plus 1/4 cup water

Dinner 6:30 p.m.
3 1/2 ounces Roasted Smoky Turkey Breast (84 g)
1 heaping cup Sautéed Kale with Onions (168 g), includes 1 teaspoon coconut oil (5 g)
4-ounce baked sweet potato (114 g) + 1 teaspoon flax oil or butter (5 g)

Weight of 1 day's food = 1833 grams (4.09 pounds)

Animal protein	466 grams	25 percent by weight
Vegetables	624 grams	34 percent by weight
Fruits	644 grams	35 percent by weight
Nuts, seeds, oils	99 grams	5 percent by weight

Sample Day 2:
Food Analysis for Rachel Matesz

Height: 65 inches (5'5")
Age: 38
Weight: 118
Activity level: light

* **Note:** First sodium intake figure represents foods prepared with no added salt. If sea salt is used in Better Barbecue Sauce and Mustard-Tahini Dressing, the second figure will be accurate.

	Actual intake	Daily value
Calories	1797 kcal	1844 kcal
Protein	115 g (28 percent)	50 g
Carbohydrate	182 g (38 percent)	274 g
Fat	67 g (35 percent)	61 g
Cholesterol	259 mg	277 mg
Fiber	42 g	23 g
Calcium	554 mg	738 mg
Sodium	603 mg (or 821 mg)	2190 mg

Breakfast 7 a.m.
4-ounce 96 percent lean hamburger, pan seared (112 g)
1/4 cup Better Barbecue Sauce (56 g)
1 1/4 cups sautéed Better Brussels Sprouts (168 g), includes 1 teaspoon coconut oil (5 g)
2 small peaches (224 g)

Lunch 11 a.m.
4 ounces roasted chicken thigh meat with sage, thyme, and pepper (112g)
Large salad (220 g):
    2 cups shredded romaine
    1 grated carrot
    1/4 cup minced parsley
    1/4 cup sliced red radish
    1/3 cup minced celery
    1/3 cup toasted dulse leaf, crumbled (7 g)
    1/4 cup Mustard-Tahini Dressing (17 g tahini)
1 medium apple (138 g)

Snack 3:30 p.m.
2 small bananas (1 1/4 cups sliced) (202 g)
1/4 cup Fluffy Almond Butter: 2 tablespoons almond butter (32 g) + water and vanilla

Dinner 7 p.m.
5 ounces (raw weight) salmon, baked with tarragon and lemon pepper (140 g)
3/4 cup Marinated Beet Root Salad (117 g) plus 1 tablespoon Toasted Walnuts (7 g)
1 1/2 cups steamed asparagus with bell pepper (236 g) plus 1 teaspoon lemon-flavored cod liver oil (5 g)

Total weight of day's food = 1791 grams (4 pounds)

Animal protein	364 grams	21 percent by weight
Vegetables	772 grams	43 percent by weight
Fruits	564 grams	31 percent by weight
Nuts, seeds, oils	59 grams	3 percent by weight

Note: Numbers add up to slightly less than 100 percent because of rounding.

Sample Day 1:
Food Analysis for Don Matesz

Height: 69 inches (5'9")
Age: 42
Weight: 158
Activity level: light

	Actual intake	Daily value
Calories	2580 kcal	2668 kcal
Protein	177 g (29 percent)	66 g
Carbohydrate	248 g (36 percent)	401 g
Fat	99 g (36 percent)	89 g
Cholesterol	635 mg	400 mg
Fiber	50 g	33 g
Calcium	892 mg	1067 mg
Sodium	1143 mg	3168 mg

* Note: Foods prepared without salt. Eggs and dried, powdered egg whites are naturally rich in sodium.

Breakfast 7 a.m.
2 large eggs (100 g) fried in 1/2 teaspoon coconut oil (2.5 g)
4 ounces Roasted Smoky Turkey Breast (112 g)
1 1/2 cups steamed broccoli (117 g) plus 1 teaspoon lemon-flavored cod liver oil (5 g)
1 1/2 cups cantaloupe cubes (265 g)
5 small dried Black Mission figs (40 g) + 2 tablespoons toasted pecans (14 grams)

Lunch 11 a.m.
6 ounces Orange Roughy, baked with basil, garlic, and pepper (170 g) in 1 teaspoon
    olive oil (5 g)
1 lemon wedge (7 g) plus 1/3 cup toasted dulse leaf, crumbled (7 g)
Large salad:
    2 cups baby spring greens
    1/4 cup minced celery (112 g)
    1/2 cup Roasted Onions (55 g), includes 1 teaspoon olive oil (5 g)
    1 cup Roasted Carrots (117 g), includes 1 teaspoon olive oil (5 g)
1 cup Apple & Apricot Compote (230 g) + 2 teaspoons macadamia nut butter (10 g)

Snack 3 p.m.
Cherry Smoothie:
    1/4 cup coconut milk (56 g)
    1 tablespoon almond butter (16 g)
    1 ounce vanilla egg white protein (42 g)*
    1 cup pitted, frozen sweet cherries (150 g)
    2 thin slices fresh gingerroot
    1/4 cup water

Dinner 6:30 p.m.
5 ounces Roasted Smoky Turkey Breast (140 g)
1 packed cup Sautéed Kale with Onions (168 g) in 1 teaspoon coconut oil (5 grams)
4-ounce baked sweet potato (114 g) plus 2 teaspoon coconut oil or butter (10 grams)

Total weight of day's food = 2417 grams (5.4 pounds)

Animal protein	620 grams	29 percent by weight
Vegetables	672 grams	32 percent by weight
Fruits	685 grams	32 percent by weight
Nuts, seeds, oils	134 grams	6 percent by weight

Notes: Weight of protein adjusted upward. One ounce of dried, powered egg white is equivalent to 3.5 ounces of fresh meat. Totals are slightly less than 100 percent because of rounding.

Sample Day 2:
Food Analysis for Don Matesz

Height: 69 inches (5'9")
Age: 42
Weight: 158
Activity level: light

* **Note:** First sodium figure represents foods prepared with no added salt. If sea salt is used in Better Barbecue Sauce and Mustard-Tahini Dressing, the second figure will be accurate.

	Actual intake	Daily value
Calories	2661 kcal	2668 kcal
Protein	183 g (28 percent)	66 g
Carbohydrate	241 g (36 percent)	401 g
Fat	107 g (36 percent)	89 g
Cholesterol	373 mg	400 mg
Fiber	50 g	33 g
Calcium	645 mg	1067 mg
Sodium	871 (or 1088 mg*)	3168 mg

Breakfast 7 a.m.

6-ounce 96 percent lean hamburger, broiled (168 g)
1/4 cup Better Barbecue Sauce (56 g)
1 1/3 cups Better Brussels Sprouts (168 g), includes 1 teaspoon coconut oil (5 g)
2 large peaches (336 g) plus 2 tablespoons toasted almonds (18 g)

Lunch 11 a.m.

6 ounces roasted chicken thigh meat with sage, thyme, and pepper (168 g)
Large salad:
    1 1/2 cups shredded romaine
    1/2 grated carrot
    1/4 cup minced parsley
    1/4 cup sliced red radish
    1/3 cup minced celery (192 g)
    1/3 cup dulse leaf, toasted (7 g)
    1/4 cup Mustard-Tahini Dressing (17 g tahini)
1 large apple (212 g)
4 whole dried apricots (24 grams)
2 tablespoons toasted pecans (14 g)

Snack 3:30 p.m.

2 medium bananas (272 g)
Vanilla Protein-Nut Spread:
    2 tablespoons almond butter (32 g)
    1 ounce vanilla egg white protein (28 g)
    1/4 cup water plus 1/2 teaspoon vanilla extract

Dinner 7 p.m.

7 ounces (raw weight) salmon, roasted with tarragon and lemon pepper (196 g)
1 cup Marinated Beet Root Salad (176 g) plus 1 teaspoon coconut or olive oil (5 g)
1 1/2 cups steamed asparagus with red bell pepper (234 g) plus 1 teaspoon
    lemon-flavored cod liver oil (5 g)

Total weight of day's food = 2417 grams (5.4 pounds)		
Animal protein	644 grams	27 percent by weight
Vegetables	833 grams	34 percent by weight
Fruits	844 grams	35 percent by weight
Nuts, seeds, oils	96 grams	4 percent by weight

Making the Change

When you change your diet, you will re-educate your taste buds and your body will have to make some changes to adapt to new foods and proportions of nutrients. You won't necessarily be wild about the change at first. It can take from several days to several weeks to readjust. Many people who try a cold turkey approach experience more or less strong cravings for grains, sugar, dairy products, or other non-primitive, processed foods.

Most people who start *The Garden of Eating* plan will experience tangible benefits—especially in digestion and mental performance—from day one.

Cold Turkey or Transition?

Minor changes in diet usually produce only minor improvements in health, which may not provide sufficient motivation to keep you moving forward. More sweeping changes in diet will usually lead to more noticeable and dramatic improvements in health, which will provide more motivation to keep you going.

Does this mean you will never eat any of the foods you are accustomed to consuming? Probably not. On some occasions you may have limited food options or may want to eat some of the less-wholesome foods you used to eat. That's reality.

For some, just the idea of being unable to eat spaghetti, macaroni and cheese, pizza, potato chips, baguettes, brownies, bonbons, ice cream, or whatever, creates a feeling of restriction and a desire to break free (binge). To minimize these feelings, we suggest incorporating 1 or more Free Meals—opportunities to eat some of the things you have been avoiding in your new eating plan—into your food plan.

The Free Meal

Here is how it works. You strictly follow a super-nutritious natural foods plan all week. If you eat 3 meals a day, that would mean 19 or 20 produce-dominated natural food meals per week, then give yourself permission to enjoy 1 or 2 Free Meals on the weekend, or whatever days you clearly designate. (Keep track. You don't want every day to become a Free Day and lose all the benefits of eating wholesome foods.)

By planning for 1 or 2 Free Meals each week you'll keep your deviations within reason. The goal is not to pig out and stuff yourself to the point of discomfort. We recommend choosing reasonable portions of one or more of the foods you feel you've been missing.

If you consume these foods with awareness—eating slowly, sitting down, chewing well, and being conscious of the entire eating experience (wise to do at all meals)—you may be surprised to find you don't need as much as you thought you'd need to feel satisfied.

Your Free Meal might consist of sushi with white rice and soy dipping sauce, or a bagel with lox and cream cheese, a dill pickle and cookie, an enchilada, or a spaghetti dinner. It could be a few buckwheat pancakes with butter and real maple syrup, blueberry muffins with yogurt, or a large bowl of real buttered popcorn (not the hydrogenated, artificially flavored stuff!). Or, something as modest as 1 or 2 slices of buttered whole-grain toast with your morning eggs and a couple of strips of bacon. The choices will be yours. If you know you'll be visiting friends or attending a dinner party, office function, or wedding reception, make this your chosen time to indulge in a Free Meal—in moderation!

Over time, the thrill of a weekly Free Meal may wear off. You might even forget to take one, or find the foods you want for a treat are not much different from those you're eating on a daily basis. You will notice that we include recipes for special treats we enjoy making for ourselves or sharing with friends—Frozen Banana Delight with Cocoa, Chocolate-Protein Pudding, Chocolate Protein-Nut Spread, Chocolate-Avocado Mousse, Dark Chocolate-Dipped Dates, and Dairy-Free Cocoa-Coconut Pots de Creme, among others. You may eventually prefer these lower-impact treats to the conventional types.

You may experience such an improvement in energy, vitality, digestion, and elimination that major deviations in diet result in strong bodily sensations you never noticed before. After eating too extremely or excessively, you may notice congestion, constipation, irritability, lethargy, depression, foggy thinking, or other unpleasant consequences. If so, your body is talking to you and you have the wisdom to understand the message. From here you can make the choices that best support your overall health.

What to Expect

How you initially respond to this change depends somewhat on what you have been doing up to this point. Although your results may vary, here's what our experience suggests you can expect upon changing from various other diets to *The Garden of Eating*:

If you were following a typical American diet expect to:
* Enjoy a wider variety of foods and flavors after you shake the desire to have everything taste like salt.
* Purchase much larger amounts of fresh vegetables, fruits, lean meats, nuts, herbs, and spices.
* Eat a larger amount of food because the food is more bulky and less calorie dense.
* Spend more time preparing food but less time in the doctor's office.
* Have larger and more frequent bowel movements.
* Make more trips to the toilet if you are not currently drinking at least 8 (8-ounce) glasses of pure water a day.
* See a loss of body fat.
* Have more energy, mental clarity, better sleep, and a general sense of well-being.

* See a reduction in mucous production, congestion, colds, flu, and allergies.
* Have a temporary increase in intestinal gas from the increased fiber. As your intestinal flora changes, this will dissipate—usually within a month. Remember, vegetables and fruits require more thorough chewing than refined white and processed foods.
* Have gentler periods within 3 to 4 months if you have suffered from PMS.
* Experience relief from heart-burn, hemorrhoids, bloating, and other minor digestive disorders.
* Have fewer joint and muscle aches and pains because of the increased alkalinity of this way of eating.
* Miss and crave salt, coffee, sugary, and fried foods until your mind and body adjust to this way of eating. These cravings are not indicative of any nutritional need.

If you were following a low-carb or ketogenic diet expect to:
* Experience the same kinds of things described above.
* Experience an immediate and slight weight gain because your body will be replenishing depleted glycogen stores, which include water. Over the long term you will lose more body fat as lower caloric intake and increased alkalinity allow your body to release fat and water.
* Feel more full during or after meals.
* See an increase in lean body mass (muscle).
* Feel more relaxed and calm.

If you were following a vegan, vegetarian, or macrobiotic diet expect to:
* Experience many of the same things described above.
* Experience a rise in body temperature, if you suffered from chronic coldness.
* Catch fewer colds, flu, and infections.
* See a reduction in other symptoms of deficiency such as anemia, chronic fatigue, sweets' cravings, short-term memory loss, and loss of libido.

chapter 8 Organizing Your Kitchen

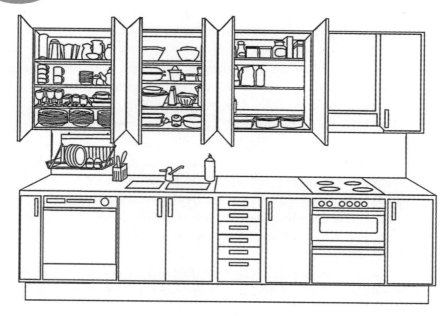

How are you going to fit all of those vegetables, fruits, and meats into your refrigerator and freezer? Where will you keep all of the herbs, spices, and seasonings you'll be using once you start making more food from scratch?

One of the first things I do with my clients is help them organize their refrigerator, freezer, and cupboards. It's easier and more enjoyable to work in a well-organized kitchen where you can find what you need when you need it.

Think of your shelves as storefront space. How are shelves organized in a grocery store? Which items are grouped together and why? Copy that. You'll be amazed at how much more you can pack into the same space by shuffling things around. Restocking before you run out of essentials will be much easier if everything is in its place.

Chapter Overview
To make time in the kitchen easier and more enjoyable, a well-organized area is key. The steps in this chapter offer ideas and tips that will provide an inviting place to make healthy meals.

Step 1: Revamp Refrigerator

Take everything out. Wipe the inside with a biodegradable all-purpose cleaner. Stash the most perishable items in an ice chest and defrost the freezer. Once it's clean, you'll feel better about restocking and have more empty space for new foods.

Sort through the bottles and packages in your fridge. You may be tying up valuable refrigerator space with items that don't need refrigeration and neglecting to refrigerate highly perishable goods. See "Foods That Need Refrigeration, Foods That Don't," Page 99.

Ideally, you'll throw out items containing multiple sugars, hydrogenated and partially hydrogenated oils, margarine, shortening, artificial flavorings and colorings, MSG, and chemical ingredients. Save the jars. Soak them to remove old labels, then use them to store foods in and out of the refrigerator.

If you have a cupboard, freezer, or fridge full of grain and cereal products, you have several options. You can give away foods you don't want to eat or be tempted by or stash them away somewhere and ration their use until they're gone. You can make the transition to your new diet by reducing your grain consumption to once a day, then once every other day, then once or twice a week, eventually eliminating them altogether when you're ready for that step. Or you may choose to consume high-quality whole grains once every day.

Line up jars of nuts, seeds, nut butters (which require refrigeration to prevent spoilage, once they've been opened), salad dressings, marinades, sauces, freshly squeezed lemon or lime juice, and minced parsley. For easy access, store foods for packing lunches, single-serving portions of snacks, and leftovers near the top or front of the fridge.

If you designate shelves or portions of shelves for specific items, it will be easier to find and use foods before they spoil. We have a protein shelf where we keep at least two kinds of meat—thawing, thawed, freshly purchased or cooked, and ready to eat. We place meat packages in deep-dish pie plates, loaf pans, or lightweight baking pans to keep the fridge clean and prevent stray juices from contaminating other foods. If you have a special meat compartment, use it. Every day or two, I transfer 1 or 2 packages of frozen meat from the freezer to the refrigerator to allow ample time for defrosting (usually 1 to 3 days, depending upon size and thickness).

Keeping cooked meats near the front encourages us to consume them promptly. Sometimes, I store 1 or 2 portions of cooked meat in containers to make it easier to pack lunches or reheat meal-size amounts in the toaster oven or over a steamer rack. We stack egg cartons on the meat shelf.

Note: Eggs keep better in the carton than in the door where they can lose moisture or absorb odors from other foods.

Since our diet consists of mostly vegetables and fruits, we reserve most refrigerator space for fresh produce. I keep a filled salad spinner on the top shelf. (Slip a clean kitchen towel or placemat under the spinner to absorb moisture if it has a flow-through design that lets water out.) I stash jars of washed and chopped salad vegetables near the spinner or in the side door, ready to toss into salads, a steamer basket, wok, skillet, or roasting pan.

We stuff several cotton/canvas shopping bags filled with kale, collards, broccoli, Brussels sprouts, romaine lettuce, or spinach (without plastic bags) on the bottom shelf of the fridge. Vegetables keep better in breathable bags; they don't trap moisture or invite

Reduce & Reuse
Feed your trash can: The first step in making the transition to your new eating plan is to throw away or give away unhealthy foods (refined foods, grains, etc.) or at least reduce daily consumption. But don't toss glass jars—soak them to remove old labels and then reuse to store foods.

mold. I fill the crisper bin with root vegetables, citrus fruits, celery, zucchini, and anything else that fits. I line bins with cotton or linen towels or placemats (for ease of cleanup) and wash mats every few weeks.

We store foods in stainless steel and Pyrex pint, quart, or larger bowls covered with heat-proof saucers, dinner plates, or fitted lids. Or, we use round and square heat-proof Pyrex containers with snap-tight lids. Leftovers can go directly from the refrigerator to the toaster oven or top of a steamer basket, then to the table without dirtying more dishes or using plastic wrap, which can leach toxic chemicals into food. Since the tops of the containers are firm, we stack them to fit more food in the fridge. This handy system saves time and resources.

We refrigerate fruits but keep some at room temperature because there's rarely enough room in the refrigerator. Hanging wire baskets and pottery bowls are great for storing oranges, grapefruits, apples, peaches, pears, nectarines, bananas, mangoes, and tomatoes. As fruits ripen, we eat or transfer them to a crisper bin as it empties.

Step 2: Face Freezer

After defrosting and cleaning the inside of the freezer and turning it on again, you can restock by grouping similar items together—all frozen fish, fowl, and meat together (cooked in one section, raw in another), frozen fruits in one place, frozen vegetables in another. I store extra nuts, homemade jerky, and dried fruit in the freezer to retard spoilage. Organizer shelves from a kitchen shop, department store, or mail-order catalog can help you pack more into the freezer.

A side-by-side refrigerator-freezer provides more side door and shelf space than an upright model. Make do with what you have for now. Later, you may want or need to invest in a larger secondhand refrigerator-freezer and chest freezer. The additional storage will allow you to keep more fresh produce on hand, buy grass-fed meats in quantity, stock up on sale items, freeze extra fruit during the summer and fall, or buy frozen produce in bulk to reduce food costs and shopping frequency.

Check newspapers and auction listings for restaurant, moving, and estate sales, and let your friends know what you're looking for. I've received great appliances free or for a small fee from friends of friends or relatives.

If you buy a chest freezer, get one with a warning light so you'll know if it's on the blink. A back-up generator is ideal (but not essential) for possible power outages. You don't want to lose half a side of grass-fed beef, 10 pounds of salmon, 6 chickens, 10 pounds of frozen blueberries, and all that hard-earned money if your power goes out for any length of time.

Step 3: Unclutter Cupboards

Empty, clean, and restock your cupboards in an orderly fashion.

Cold Storage Search
You might find you need additional freezer space in order to keep more fresh produce on hand. Watch newspaper ads and auction listings for restaurant, moving, and estate sales.

Empty items sold in plastic bags—apple fiber, carob powder, unsweetened cocoa, powdered egg whites, dried fruits and nuts—into wide-mouth pint and quart jars. Add labels or wide masking tape and use bold permanent markers to indicate what's in each jar (some things are obvious; others may not be to you or family members) and the date you purchased it so that older foods are used first.

Group unopened jars of nut butter together. Store tomato paste near tomato sauce. I put coconut milk near the dried fruits, gelatin, flavoring extracts, and other items frequently used for smoothies, Frosty Fruit Whips, blender puddings, and Protein Popsicles (See Index for recipes). If you use whole grains, store them in glass jars at room temperature. Refrigerate or freeze flour. Make it as convenient as possible to find and eat healthy foods. Keeping an ample supply of non-perishables will mean fewer trips to the store and more options for meals and snacks. A pantry or broom closet can provide extra space.

Store items you use most on shelves at eye level, close to your work area. Why trek across the kitchen unnecessarily? Use high shelves to stash items you'd rather not be tempted to eat. If you have a large family or small children, you might want to label shelves so everyone will know where to put things.

Step 4: Make More Space

Having difficulty finding room for everything? Think about what you can get rid of. If you haven't discussed this with your nearest and dearest, set questionable items aside for now. If your significant other isn't ready to give up his/her grains or junk foods, designate a special cupboard for those foods.

Look for things tying up valuable counter, cupboard, or drawer space, particularly knickknacks. Ask yourself, "Does this need to be in the kitchen?" (My clients have had combs, lost keys, dead pens, toys, and a laundry list of oddities vying for valuable kitchen-front space.) If the item doesn't have to be in the kitchen, move it. If you're lucky—like most of my clients—uncluttering will free up 2 or 3 drawers. Use organizer shelves to stack more plates, bowls, mugs, cups, pots, and pans in your cupboards. You may still need to open up a few shelves in the laundry room, a cubbyhole in the hallway, the stairwell, wherever you can. Turn a coat closet into a pantry for additional storage. Be creative.

Move it Out
Some clients have reclaimed two to three kitchen drawers by removing a variety of items that do not belong in the kitchen.

Step 5: Clear Counters

If you remove everything that's not essential for food preparation from the counter, you'll have more work space. If your kitchen is uncomfortably small, you might save up for a kitchen remodel, trade in your microwave oven for a smaller convection toaster oven, or invest in a solid wood utility cart with a butcher block top. My movable cart measures 32-inches wide, 22-inches deep, and 32-inches high. It has a drawer, two sturdy slatted shelves for pots and pans or bowls of onions, sweet potatoes, winter squash and fresh fruit, and serves as an extra chopping station.

Don and I like to keep frequently used items on the counter near the stove and cutting board, things such as balsamic vinegar, apple cider vinegar, extra-virgin olive oil, coconut oil, tamari soy sauce, a bowl of fresh garlic and ginger root. Two large crocks filled with the utensils we use the most: wooden spoons, metal and rubber spatulas, ladles, tongs, salad spoons, whisks, tea strainers, skimmers, and the like also sit on the counter. We keep a Vita-Mix on the counter, where it performs almost daily duty.

I keep 2 sets of sturdy measuring spoons hanging from hooks near the crocks and stove. Why two? A couple of reasons: To avoid having to wash and dry spoons in between measuring wet and dry ingredients, and so Don and I can both work in the kitchen at the same time. A flame deflector hangs nearby to slip between the gas flame and pot when I need to simmer something thick (like a stew with little liquid) on low heat. I hang 2 heavy-duty oven mitts and a few cloth trivets near the stove and keep a couple of wire mesh strainers on the wall.

We've kept a large 18x12x1-inch wood cutting board on the counter for more than 12 years. No sense putting it away when it gets used every day. We use a separate cutting board with a built-in drip tray for meats.

A food scale—invaluable for weighing vegetables, fruits, and meats for recipes where the weight before chopping is important—sits on another counter. I stack Pyrex bowls in one place, small skillets and saucepans in another. Store your pots and pans in an easily accessible place. Pull-out drawers are perfect if you have them or can build them in. To save space, install a rack under one of the kitchen cabinets to hold lids for pots and pans. You'll be amazed at how much you can store in a relatively small kitchen if you are systematic and organized.

Step 6: Containers & Storage

Allocate ample space for containers. We reserve an entire cupboard for food-storage containers: pint and quart Mason jars, nut butter, mustard, and spice jars; heat-proof Pyrex and Corningware custard cups and dishes with fitted lids. We use these containers in the refrigerator, freezer, and pantry. Most of them are clear so we can find what we need at a glance. They're also non-toxic and unlike soft plastic, they won't leach harmful phthalates (cancer-causing chemicals) into food.

We keep and reuse thick 16-ounce and 24-ounce high density polyethylene (HDPE) containers, saved from Omega Nutrition Coconut Butter (now called coconut oil). These heavy containers won't pass chemicals into food or absorb odors. We use round containers for single-serving portions of Smoothie Bases, Better Balanced

Space Solutions
Be creative with the space available. Install a rack under a kitchen cabinet for pot and pan lids. Use crocks to hold kitchen utensils and hooks to hang oven mitts, measuring spoons, trivets, or anything you need to have within reach every day.

Smoothies, Frosty Fruit Whips, and Blender Puddings (see Index for recipes), as well as frozen bananas, and other snacks.

Step 7: Clean out Utensil Drawer

Unclutter the kitchen drawers while you're at it. Keep small, frequently used tools (that aren't sharp) in one drawer. Store large utensils in ceramic crocks by the stove. Hang large or odd shaped items on the wall for easy access.

We reserve an entire drawer for jar lids, another for rubber bands (tucked into a zip-closing bag), twist ties (for closing cellulose bags and half-used packages of frozen fruit), cellulose (plant-based) food bags, and Ziploc bags, which we use sparingly and reuse. Aluminum foil, unbleached parchment paper, and cloth napkins go in another drawer.

Step 8: Keep Things in Their Place

You don't want your efforts to be in vain. So, after you organize the kitchen and stock up on healthy foods, call everyone in your household into the kitchen and explain what you've done and why. Teach them the system. Adopt the following rule: If you use the last bit of something or find a jar almost empty, add the item to the shopping list posted on the refrigerator.

You may have to remind everyone (gently) to put things in their new places until they get the hang of it. The goal is to find foods and tools you need quickly and easily. By taking time to create and implement a system, you will make your kitchen time less stressful and more enjoyable. As things get out of place, you can go back and regroup.

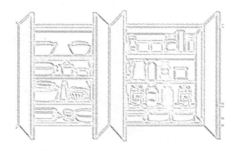

Foods That Need Refrigeration, Foods That Don't

To avoid premature spoilage of highly perishable foods and avoid using refrigerator space unnecessarily, you need to know which foods do and do not require refrigeration

Foods Requiring Refrigeration

* vegetable oils (such as flax oil and any others except olive and coconut)
* nuts, seeds, and trail mix (refrigerate or freeze)
* nut and seed butters (Refrigerate after opening or if acquired from bulk bins.)
* fresh cracked, shredded, or flaked coconut (refrigerate or freeze)
* cod liver oil and fish oil capsules (refrigerate or freeze)
* butter and clarified butter (Refrigerate or freeze; small amounts may be kept at room temperature.)
* cooked grains, sprouted grains, all flour, and all breads
* sliced, blended, or cooked fruit and vegetables
* peeled, sliced, or mashed avocados
* ripe fruits that are starting to soften
* lemon juice, lime juice, unpasteurized fruit juices, and opened juice bottles
* open cans of tomatoes and coconut milk
* berries, grapes, and cherry tomatoes
* dried fruits (only during hot or humid weather or if you have a lot of bugs)
* green onions, scallions, and fresh spring onions
* fresh herbs: basil, oregano, thyme, and chives
* zucchini, cucumbers, bell peppers, other salad veggies, and roots
* leafy greens: kale, collards, mustard greens, spinach, and lettuce
* garlic (peeled, sliced, minced, or pressed only)
* eggs, fish, poultry, meat, and dishes containing them
* frozen fish, fowl, or meat you want to thaw
* sauces, salad dressings, marinades, fruit and vegetable purées, and opened jars of mustard
* smoothies, blender puddings, fruit and vegetable juices

Note: *To retard spoilage flax oil is best stored in the freezer where it will remain liquid and pourable because it contains super-unsaturated fatty acids.*

Foods Not Needing Refrigeration

* olive oil, coconut butter, and coconut oil
* unopened jars of nut and seed butter
* ghee (stable for 6 to 12 months at room temperature)
* fresh ginger root, garlic, and shallots
* crisp apples (unless you have space in the fridge)
* whole, firm, unripe avocados, melons, pineapples, bananas, mangoes, stone fruits, and hard pears
* oranges and grapefruits (Refrigerate if space permits or they start to soften.)
* dried fruits (Refrigerate in hot and humid weather or if you have a bug problem.)
* fresh tomatoes (Refrigerate cherry tomatoes and very ripe tomatoes.)
* unopened cans of fish, tomatoes, coconut milk, hot sauce, and bottled mustard
* onions with dry skins
* whole, uncut winter squash and spaghetti squash, sweet potatoes, yams, and potatoes
* dried chives, parsley, freeze-dried onions, bell pepper flakes, and dried mushrooms
* uncooked fresh chestnuts in the shell and dried (steam-peeled) chestnuts
* dried herbs, spices, and herbal teas
* carob and unsweetened cocoa powder
* coconut, if fresh, whole, and in the shell (Refrigerate after opening.)
* apple fiber and dried shan yao
* stevia extract powder and liquid
* kiwi concentrate (trutina dulcem)
* honey, maple syrup, and agavé nectar
* flavoring extracts, liquid smoke seasoning
* vinegars
* sea vegetables and sea weeds (dried and uncooked)
* unflavored gelatin powder
* uncooked whole grains (e.g., millet, quinoa, amaranth, whole brown rice, spelt or wheat berries)

Note: *In hot or humid weather, or if you have a problem with bugs in your area, store dried fruits and whole grains in the refrigerator or freezer.*

chapter 9 Tools of the Trade

The right equipment makes a world of difference. In some cases it can be the difference between the success and failure of a recipe. A variety of tools will allow you to maximize your time in the kitchen by giving you more options for cooking multiple dishes to meet multiple needs. Friends, cooking students, and acquaintances always ask me what brands and tools I recommend.

What follows is our list of essentials. Don't think you have to invest in everything right now. Start with what you have and add to your collection as the need arises and your budget permits. We didn't acquire all of our tools overnight.

For some products, I have listed specific sources for unusual or hard-to-find tools, Don's and my favorite brands, and great buys. If I haven't indicated a brand or store, check kitchen shops or the retail stores in your area and on-line sources. Contact information for stores/brands/catalogs/ is listed at the end of this chapter.

It also pays to search thrift stores, discount merchandise outlets, garage and estate sales to find great tools (often seldom or never used) for a fraction of the suggested retail cost. You might even stumble across some fabulous freebies from friends and family members.

MISCELLANEOUS TOOLS

Some tools seem so obviously essential, yet you would be amazed at how many people I meet who do not own sharp knives, cutting boards, pots with lids, steamer baskets, or basic measuring devices.

Chapter Overview
The kitchen tools you use can be the difference in creating a good recipe and a great recipe. This chapter outlines essential equipment that you should have or should add to your supplies as money permits.

~101~

Stainless steel and wood tools are preferable to plastic; they're more durable, safe for hot and cold items, and eliminate exposure to harmful plastic chemicals.

Best knives: 7" Hollow Henkel Ground Santoku Knife (combination light cleaver and all-purpose chef knife) made by Messermeister and sold through Kitchen Classics, $68 to $90; Wusthof Santoku and Henkel Santoku, $84.95 to $100 from Williams Sonoma and Sur La Table.

NHS Professional Knife, $52.95; Japanese Caddie Knife, $18 to $22; or Mac Superior Knife, $46.95; from Natural Lifestyle Supplies Mail Order Market, Gold Mine Natural Foods, and Diamond Organics.

Great sharpeners: Chantry Knife Sharpener, $42, from Kitchen Classics; Global Ceramic Sharpener, $29.95, and Multi-Edge Diamond Hone Sharpener, $39.95, from Sur La Table; Chef's Choice Manual Knife Sharpener, $30, from Williams Sonoma and Sur La Table; Ceramic Knife Sharpener, $19.99, from Chefs Catalog.

Great guards: 4" sheath, $1.57; 8" sheath, $2.50; or The Knife Safe by Lamson Sharp (comes in many sizes), from Broadway Pan Handler, Kitchen Classics, and kitchen shops everywhere. Prices vary with size.

Great cleavers: 8" Chinese Kitchen Knife by Joyce Chen, $29.95; 8" Chinese Chef's Knife by Dexter/Russel, $36.95; or Henckels 3-Riveted Pro S Cleaver, $49.95, all from Cooking.com; Messermeister meat cleaver $130 from Kitchen Classics.

Great paring knives: Mac paring knife, 4" blade, $11.95, from Natural Lifestyle Supplies Mail Order Market, others available from Williams-Sonoma, Sur La Table, and Kitchen Classics.

Super shears: Henckels 8" Kitchen Shears, $24.95; Henckels Twin Kitchen Shears with Carbon Steel Blades, $39.95; or Diamond Cut Multi-Purpose Kitchen Shears that double as a nut cracker and bottle opener and come with a lifetime warranty, $5.95, Cooking.com or Aircore Inc.; Come-Apart Shears, $19.99, Chefs Catalog.

Japanese Vegetable Knife: You'll never really enjoy chopping or cooking until you have good knives. Quality cutlery allows you to cut food faster, more easily, efficiently, attractively, and safely. You don't have to spend a fortune or buy an entire set. One good Japanese-style vegetable knife will do almost everything. We have used them to cut fruits, nuts, meats, and awkward items, like hard winter squashes, for more than 18 years. They're durable, lightweight, and easy to wield.

Look for tempered stainless chrome-moly or high-carbon surgical stainless steel with a 6 1/4- to 7-inch long blade and 10- to 12-inch overall length. Buy a knife with a wood handle and full-tang construction. The latter will keep the knife from coming apart.

Care: Do not put knives with wood handles in the dishwasher, or drop sharp knives into a sink or pan of dishwasher. Wipe a sharp knife with a sponge, rinse, dry with a towel, and return to the cutting board or designated knife drawer.

You're more likely to cut yourself with a dull knife. Sharpen once a week with a rod, stone, machine, or other appropriate device. Some meat shops and kitchen shops will sharpen your knives free or for a small fee.

Knife sharpeners: Most people have difficulty using sharpening rods and standard steels without dulling or damaging their knives. Sharpening with a machine is an easier option. Non-electric machines are inexpensive and easy to operate. You run your knife between 2 tension-mounted sharpening steels that simultaneously hone both sides of the blade at the correct angle.

Knife Guards (sheaths): Plastic guards protect your fingers and knife blades and are better than a knife block that takes up too much space.

Meat cleaver: Use it to cut through bone and cartilage when you chop a whole chicken into fryer parts. Look for a sturdy and wide blade riveted into a wooden handle. Wash by hand and towel dry.

Paring knife: Get 1 or 2 sturdy small knives preferably with full-tang construction. Check with shops and brands listed under best knives.

Kitchen shears: Open packages without dulling good knives. Cut dried fruits and fresh herbs. Slice raw or cooked poultry and meat without dirtying a cutting board. Get heavy gauge carbon steel—suitable for right- and left-handed use—with thick handles and that come apart for easy cleaning and sanitation.

Cutting board: Get one large, thick, sturdy wood cutting board—preferably 12x18x1-inch—to leave on the counter for daily chopping of vegetables, fruits, and nuts. Get a second wood board with a drip tray for meat, poultry, and fish. Wood boards are more attractive and durable and they won't dull your knives as quickly as plastic boards.

But aren't plastic boards more sanitary? Although they have been touted as being more sanitary, plastic cutting boards trap bacteria, according to a study conducted by microbiologists at the University of Wisconsin's Food Research Institute (Madison). "Tests proved that wood cutting boards are actually so inhospitable to contaminants like poultry and meat juices that bacteria disappeared from wood surfaces within minutes. On the other hand, bacteria from the plastic boards multiplied at room temperature." (Source: *The Food Lovers Tiptionary: An A to Z Culinary Guide with more than 4,500 Food and Drink Tips, Secrets, Shortcuts, and Other Things Cookbooks Never Tell You* by Sharon Tyler Herbst, Hearst Books 1994)

Better boards: 16"x12"x1" board, $18, from Crate & Barrel;11"x16"x¾" hardwood board, $14.95 and 13"x19"x¾" inch hardwood board, $19.95, from Natural Lifestyle Supplies; 18" square x 2¾" deep heavy-duty board with neoprene-padded feet to prevent slipping, $99.99 from Chefs Catalog. More options available at Cooking.com and kitchen shops everywhere.

Ceramic crocks: Keep frequently used tools in ceramic crocks on your counter, one near the stove and the other near your workspace for convenience. Lehman's Hardware & Appliances and kitchen shops everywhere.

Mixing and serving spoons: Buy assorted sizes and shapes of wood and metal spoons for mixing, mashing, and serving. Include large and small ladles for soup, stew, sauces, and dressings, salad spoons or tongs, and slotted spoons.

Wire whisk: Look for a small- and a medium-size stiff general-purpose whisk, and a flat whisk for deglazing pans and making cooked sauces. A French or balloon whisk is optional for vinaigrettes.

Spatulas: Get a sturdy metal spatula (pancake turner) for turning burgers, steaks, or chops, serving eggs, etc. Include 1 slotted stainless steel turner. Mini spatulas of the same design are optional. Get at least 2 heat-proof rubber spatulas, one narrow, one wide, for scraping food from saucepans, bowls, jars, blender, or food processor, and a mini spatula to reach into small jars.

Vegetable scrub brush: A small, round, natural bristle brush for cleaning vegetables will cost you a few dollars at most from Natural Lifestyle Supplies or GoldMine Natural Foods.

Vegetable peeler: A new U-shaped peeler with a thick handle for speed and ease of use is great for cucumbers, apples, turnips, rutabaga, beets, nubby looking carrots, etc.

Apple corer: Quickly core apples for Total Juice, baked or dried

Cutting Board Care
Do not soak wood boards or put them in the dishwasher. Clean with a sponge or dishcloth and citrus-based dish soap or all-purpose cleaner and water, then wipe with a towel. Regularly saturate the board with olive, coconut, or block oil. Allow oil to soak in overnight to moisten wood and prevent warping and cracking.

apples, compotes, and fruit leather. Look for a thick ergonomic handle.

Pastry brush: A good-quality pastry brush is handy for greasing baking and roasting pans, and brushing fish, fowl, or roasts with oil. Wash in warm soapy water or the dishwasher (if dishwasher safe) after contact with food, particularly meat, fish, or fowl.

Bulb baster: Baste turkey breasts or whole chickens with pan juices using a hard-plastic baster with rubber bulb.

Funnel: A narrow funnel will help you pour dried herbs and spices into bottles, and soups, stocks, and sauces into jars without making a mess. I prefer stainless steel.

Citrus reamer: Save 20 seconds every time you juice with a wooden reamer. Halve citrus fruit, pick out seeds, and use this tool to quickly squeeze the juice into a bowl. You can also use a hand-held citrus press that comes in different sizes for lemons, limes, and oranges. Sold in kitchen shops everywhere.

Grater: Get a large sturdy box grater for shredding carrots, beets, apples, and zucchini. A microplane grater is a must for finely grating gingerroot and citrus zest.

Garlic press: You can live without one, but if you get one, be sure it has a thick handle to reduce wrist strain.

Trivets: Have half a dozen heavy-duty trivets to keep hot pots and pans from burning counters, table tops, and tablecloths. They can be wood, thick cork, ceramic, tile, or quilted cloth.

Skimmer: A shallow 8-inch wide open-weave basket with a long handle is essential for making parboiled vegetable salads and whole boiled greens.

Metal strainers with handle: Use a large strainer to rinse and drain produce, strain stock or broth, and whole grains, if you use them. Use a small strainer for herb teas or Chicory & Dandelion Root "Coffee". Available from Lehman's Hardware & Appliances or other kitchen shops.

Flame tamer: Also called a heat-deflector, this thick metal plate has tiny holes covering the surface and a sturdy wooden handle. Slip it between a simmering pot and burner on "low" to evenly spread the heat/flame. It reduces heat and prevents burning. This is particularly handy if you have a gas range and/or boil rice, oatmeal, or other grains.

Terrific flame tamer: $2.99, GoldMine Natural Foods; $3.99, Natural Lifestyle Supplies Mail Order Market, Kitchen Classics, Sur La Table, and other kitchen shops.

Superb separator: 2-cup size, $16.95, and 4-cup size, $18.95 from Cooking.com.

Fat separator: Invaluable for removing fat from meat pan juices without having to chill the liquid overnight. Save and use the cooking juices to moisten greens (sautéed kale, collards, or Brussels sprouts), for reheating leftover chicken, turkey or making a sauce or gravy. Most separator cups are plastic (which I despise), but glass and dishwasher-safe products are available.

Colander with legs: Stainless steel lasts longer than plastic, won't absorb odors, or leach chemicals into your food. Use a colander to wash and drain vegetables, fruits, boiled beets, and parboiled vegetables, and to strain stock and bone broth.

Heavy-Duty Oven Mitts: For serious protection against heat, steam, and splatters don't mess with cheap cotton or polyester mitts. Get heavily insulated flame-proof mitts for barbecuing and grilling and moving hot pans into and out of the oven. Mitts rated to 450° F work well even when wet. Keep 2 on hooks near the stove.

Dishtowels: Have at least 7 sturdy, unbleached cotton dish towels. Change them daily.

Cotton placemats: Besides using these at the table, I place 1 under a flow-through salad spinner in the fridge and use several to line the crisper bins to absorb excess moisture and simplify cleaning bins.

Unbleached parchment paper: This works well for lining baking trays for fish, burgers, macaroons, Silver Dollar Sweet Potatoes, and squash halves in order to reduce cleanup and avoid oiling pans. Avoid carcinogenic dioxin bleaches by choosing unbleached parchment sold in kitchen shops and natural foods markets. If you make muffins (best with sprouted whole grain flour), look for unbleached muffin liners. The muffins won't stick like they do with bleached and colored papers, and you'll avoid toxic dyes and bleaches.

Unbleached paper towels: Use cloth napkins, rags, and dish towels as much as possible to reduce paper waste. When you must use paper towel to blot fish or poultry dry before seasoning, use unbleached paper products sold in most grocery and natural foods stores.

Burn cream: Every kitchen needs an exceptional ointment for contact and steam burns—not just a soothing cream, but something that can prevent painful blistering, peeling, and scarring.

Perfect protection: Tucker Invincible Retail Oven Mitt, $12.95 and $15.95, each from Chefsresource; 12-inch Kool-Tek Oven Mitts, $12.95 each, 15-inch Pyro Guard Oven Mitt, $21.95 each, Cooking.com.

Perfect parchment: Order from The Well Tempered Kitchen Store, Island Market Foods, Dorothy McNett's Place, or Kitchen Classics. Average price for 71 square feet, $4 to $5.95.

Best burn cream ever: Ching Wan Hung (Chinese Burn Cream). Nearly a decade ago, I accidentally wrapped my entire right hand around the piping-hot handle of a cast iron skillet that had just come out of a 350° F oven. I promptly dropped the pan, began shaking and sweating, and realized I'd received what would have been a third-degree burn. With repeated application of this ancient herbal product, I was able to relax my arm within 4 hours and the pain abated within 8 hours. The next day I was able to hold a chef knife, chop, and teach a cooking class. There was no blistering or scarring. The same product also works for sunburns. Available from Chinese herb shops, such as East Earth Trade Winds, and The Herb Stop.

MEASURING DEVICES

Instant-read thermometer: This is an absolute must for bread making and testing to tell if a roast is done. Do not leave this thermometer in a roast in the oven; it will break. Insert to test meat, remove if/when you return meat to the oven, and wash well between insertions.

Oven thermometer: Another must is a thermometer that stays in the oven at all times. Test your oven for accuracy. Older ovens may be off by 50 or more degrees, which can ruin a dish. Place thermometer in oven set to 350°F. Check the reading after 30, 45, and 60 minutes. If your oven is hotter or cooler than the temperature you set, you'll know how much to adjust it up or down for baking and roasting. You'll also know when your oven is fully preheated.

Refrigerator thermometer: It pays to keep an eye on the temperature in the refrigerator. A refrigerator thermometer will tell you when your fridge is on the fritz, so you can call a repairman and quickly fetch a cooler and ice. If your refrigerator is not cold enough (between 35° and 40°F), foods will spoil prematurely and you may risk food poisoning.

Measuring spoons: Buy sturdy, heavy-gauge stainless steel measuring spoons that go from 1/8 teaspoon up to 1 tablespoon. I suggest getting 2 sets—at least 1 narrow enough to reach into spice jars—so you can measure wet and dry ingredients without having to stop, wash, and dry in between ingredients, or have 2 cooks working in the kitchen at the same time. Hang spoons on hooks near blender, stove, and cutting board.

Measuring cups: Get a sturdy heavy-gauge stainless steel set of measuring cups that includes 1/4, 1/3, 1/2, and 1 cup measures, and Pyrex 2- and 4-cup sizes, which are also handy for mixing and pouring. Store them in an easily accessible place.

Metal measuring cups are generally for dry ingredients; glass versions are for wet. Metal and glass are more accurate than plastic. They're non-toxic, better for your health and the environment.

Super scales: Salter Chrome Elite Digital Scale, $49.95, Chefsresource.

Budget options: Soehnle 11-pound Culina or 4-pound Culina Scale, $19.99, Amazon.com; Salter Housewares Electronic Scale, $59.95, Sur La Table; Salter Digital Scale, $69.95, Williams-Sonoma. Also check Kitchen Classics or your local kitchen shop.

Kitchen scale: Many recipes require precision and call for vegetables, fruits, or meats in pounds. Look for a scale that weighs from 1 ounce to 11 pounds. I keep mine on the counter at all times. Digital scales are generally more accurate than spring-loaded scales, particularly for lightweight foods.

Fish pliers: Removing pin bones from fish fillets may seem like a daunting task. Red snapper and salmon are often the worst offenders. The solution? Invest in a new pair of needle nose pliers reserved for food and the kitchen. Better yet, pick up a pair of fish pliers from your favorite kitchen shop. Prices start as low as $8.

Note: If possible remove bones before marinating or cooking. Run your fingers back and forth across the flesh to feel for bones. Remove them just like you would remove a splinter using a tweezers.

ASSORTED GADGETS

Timer: Get 2 to keep track of cooking times. Store on the counter and discipline yourself to use them.

Steamer basket/inserts: A stainless steel accordion-style open-weave basket with overlapping petals will expand to fill a pot and collapse for storage. It will turn any covered pot or saucepan into a steamer. Look for 1-inch legs and a central handle that unscrews, so you can place large, flat foods or a heat-proof bowl or dish in the basket to warm leftovers or cook. Double steamers provide twice the capacity in the same pot. You can also use a pot with 1 or 2 steamer/pasta inserts.

Stacking bamboo or metal steamer baskets: Look for a set of 2 stacking trays that measure at least 10 inches from inside edge to inside edge so you can rest a 9-inch dinner plate on each tray if/when you cook things that might stick or soil the trays. Rest the steamers inside the rim of a wok or over a pot with the same diameter as the trays, then fill pot with 2 or 3 inches of water.

Asian markets frequently sell stainless steel sets that include the pot that sits on the stove. You can use these trays to steam vegetables, reheat leftover poultry, meat, roots, tubers, or grain in heat-proof bowls, or revive dry bread, muffins, and other baked goods wrapped in a cotton or linen napkin. Some also sell a bamboo set.

If you make your own bread and use the recipe for Steamed Buns (See Appendix), you'll need and want at least one 12-inch set of stacking bamboo steamer trays with a lid (2 sets for a double batch).

Oil mister: This isn't essential, but it's handy to add oil judiciously to salads, shish kabobs, fish, chicken breast, sautés, skillets, and baking pans. Fill sprayer with heart-healthy olive oil and avoid commercial chemical-laden vegetable oil sprays. You'll use less oil and avoid unhealthy aerosols.

Salad spinner: Still blotting lettuce dry with paper towels? Save time and paper, and wash salad greens and dry in seconds. By spinning off all moisture from lettuce, spinach, parsley leaves, and other leafy veggies, you'll enjoy crisper greens, extend shelf life, prevent lettuce rust, and help dressing adhere to salad. Separate and rinse a bunch of lettuce, pull cord or turn top, spin dry, then store greens in spinner in fridge for days. A spinner with a flow-through design dries greens more quickly and thoroughly than a unit with a closed top and bottom.

Splatter screen: If you cook lean meat, you won't need this. If you sometimes sear lamb or higher-fat ground beef, this will keep fat from splattering all over the range.

Suribachi: An oversized ceramic Japanese grinding bowl is invaluable for pulverizing toasted nuts, making Gomashio (sesame salt), mashing sweet potatoes or winter squash, emulsifying nut butters, making tahini dressings, Protein-Nut Spread, and nut

Super steamer inserts: RVSP brand 9" collapsible vegetable steamer, $5.95, 11" folding steamer, $8; Norpro 8" Double Steamer Insert, $13.95, from Cooking.com or most kitchen shops.

Super sources for bamboo steamers: 12" steamer set $22.95 from Kitchen Classics, $18.95 from Qi Journal.

Economical mister: Brushed aluminum, $9.99, stainless steel, $14.99, Misto, or Chefsresource.

First-choice spinners: Emsa Salad Shower Plus with flow-through design, $19.95, and Zyliss Stainless Steel Salad Spinner, $34.99, from tabletools.com; Fresh-Spin Automatic Salad Spinner, $29.95, Williams-Sonoma.

Second choice: Swiss made Zyliss (plastic) Salad spinner, Oxo Good Grips Pump Action Salad Spinner (one-handed operation), or Emsa Salad Washer and Berry Drainer, $24.95, Cooking.com. Also sold in kitchen shops everywhere.

Super screens: Heavy-duty stainless steel Splatter Guard with Feet by Cuispro, 11 ½", $15.95, and 13", $18.95, Cooking.com. Also sold in kitchen shops everywhere.

Super suribachis: 7" suribachi with wooden pestle, $9.99, and 9½" suribachi, $19.95, GoldMine Natural Foods or Natural Lifestyle Supplies Mail Order Market.

butter-based sauces. Suribachis smaller than 7 inches in diameter are impractical.

Food dehydrator: This is your best ally for making homemade beef or turkey jerky, dried fruit and vegetable chips, fruit leather, and dried produce from your garden or farmers' market. An adjustable thermostat is a must! Buy extra add-on trays and fruit roll trays as needed.

Jerky Press/Jerky Gun: A jerky press or gun is a must if you plan to make ground beef or turkey jerky. It comes with several attachments that allow you to press uniformly shaped pieces that will dry evenly. You can make thin round tubes or long flat strips that are easy to eat and store. Manufacturers that sell food dehydrators usually sell these inexpensive, time-saving tools. Available from Nesco/American Harvest.

Japanese salad press: We use this handy invention when we make coleslaw. Mix shredded vegetables with sea salt, pack into bucket and lock down lid. Leave for 3 to 8 hours or up to 3 days. The combination of salt and pressure causes the vegetables to soften and release water. The press also works for making sauerkraut, Kim-Chee, and pickles.

Popsicle molds: Great for making healthier frozen treats for family members (fun but not essential). These are hard to find.

> **Dandy dehydrator:** Nesco Ameri c Harvest, $79.95. If your budget permits, an Excalibur dehydrator is highly rated, Excalibur Products, A Division of KBI.
> **Best salad press:** 2½-quart hard plastic press, $22.95 from GoldMine Natural Foods; 2-quart press $33.95, 3-quart press $39.95, Natural Lifestyle Supplies Mail Order Market.
>
> **Best popsicle pick:** Frozen Pop Mold, $19.99, Chefs Catalog.

BOWLS and ASSORTED STORAGE CONTAINERS

We have more than 15 metal and glass bowls plus a dozen heat-proof containers with lids. We use them daily for mixing, serving, and marinating and storing leftovers in the refrigerator. Top with plastic or rubber lids or heat-proof saucers or dinner plates to eliminate the need for plastic wrap, which contains toxic compounds that can leach into foods. After removing plastic or rubber lids, you can transfer bowls from the refrigerator to the toaster oven or a steamer rack for warming, and then to the table, reducing the number of dishes dirtied (and use of a microwave oven). Corningware Pop-Ins and Classics are heat-proof, freezer-proof, and stack well.

Wide-mouth jars: Invest in at least 2 dozen pint and 1 or 2 dozen quart Mason jars for storing chopped, raw, or parboiled vegetables, salad dressings, marinades, sauces, raw or roasted nuts, dried fruits, compotes, iced herbal tea, broth, stock, and assorted leftovers.

Benefits:

(1) Wide-mouth glass jars are inert, non-toxic, and won't give off chemical fumes or hold residual flavors or odors from previously stored foods.

(2) They're easy to line up in the side door and shelves of the fridge and cupboards.

(3) Contents are easily and quickly identified.

(4) Vibrant colored vegetables, fruits, and nuts will invite you to eat more wholesome foods.

(5) They're inexpensive.

Also save nut butter and mustard jars, and bottles from condiments you no longer use.

Spice jars: Buy 2 or 3 dozen dark amber jars with labels for the tops and sides. Dark glass protects herbs and spices from light, which causes oxidation, loss of flavor and fragrance. We use at least 2 dozen herbs and spices on a weekly basis for flavor, added vitamins, minerals, antioxidants, and numerous health benefits. If you cannot find dark jars, use clear jars but store them in a cupboard or pull-out drawer to protect them from sunlight.

Heat-proof and freezer-proof custard cups and storage containers: Get at least a dozen assorted clear heat-proof bowls and 8-, 12-, 16-, and 32-ounce freezer and heat-proof Pyrex or Corningware bowls for storing, serving, reheating, and/or freezing single, double, or larger portions of leftovers. Heat-proof square and oblong Pyrex baking pans with snap-on lids are handy for marinating, baking, and storing meats without plastic or foil and for roasting then refrigerating vegetables, or baking and storing apples or sweet potatoes in the same container.

Mixing and storage bowls: Invest in inexpensive and durable stainless steel nesting bowls and Pyrex mixing bowls. Glass and Pyrex are important for storing foods that contain acidic ingredients, i.e., tomato sauce, marinades, anything with vinegar, lemon, lime, orange juice, or wine. Bowls may be used for mixing, marinating, storing, and serving cooked fryer parts, roasts, root vegetables, stews, compotes, and salads, or stashing chopped vegetables in the fridge.

Get at least 1 (preferably more) 8-, 12-, 16-, 24-, and 32-ounce bowl. Snap-on lids for smaller bowls are ideal. Bowls without lids may be topped with saucers or dinner plates and stacked in the fridge.

Invest in 6-, 8-, and 12-quart stainless steel bowls for washing leafy greens, and making large tossed salads, parboiled greens, and parboiled salads. If you make bread, you'll need them for mixing and kneading.

Thermos bottles: Get a 16-ounce stainless steel thermos for each household member for transporting hot soup, stew, as chilled smoothies, and Frosty Fruit Whips (see Index for recipes). Smaller insulated pint-size food containers will hold other food items; get them if you'll use them.

You can also pack smoothies, blender puddings, or other snacks in thick black HDPE plastic containers, which are more stable than

---

Savvy spice jars: Order 4-ounce amber spice jars with caps and labels from a wholesale co-op buying club or retail mail order outlet; 12 for $17.60, Frontier Co-Op.

Versatile containers: L'Ovenware, Corningware Classics and Pop-Ins with rubber lids, which are removed before transferring container to oven, and heat-proof square, round, and oblong baking pans with snap-on lids.

Top thermos: Nissan Stainless Steel 9.5 ounce Wide-Mouth Snack Jar, $22.95, 16.9 ounce Travel Mug Food Jar, $26.95, GoldMine Natural Foods and Natural Lifestyle Supplies Mail Order Market.

Fab food tins: 5½"x8" Bento, $39.95, from Natural Lifestyle Supplies Mail Order Market and Asian markets.

soft plastic. Stash them in an insulated lunch tote with reusable ice packs.

Stainless steel lunch boxes: Stainless steel "Bento" (Oriental) lunch boxes are wonderful for packing meals for work or school. Look for oblong tins with individual clamp-on lids or a set of 2 or 3 stacking stainless steel containers with a metal handle that locks them together for traveling. Food sits directly in these tins, which are also handy for storing and heating leftovers. Pack foods that need to be warmed in one container and foods to serve cold in another. Stash them in an insulated lunch tote with utensils, a cloth napkin, and a dry ice pack. Use cellulose (plant-based) bags with twist ties to replace plastic bags.

Cellophane bags: 100 percent plant-based biodegradable, non-toxic bags that seal shut with twist ties, $8.95 and $9.95 (small and large), from Natural Lifestyle Supplies Mail Order Market.

Canvas and cotton tote and produce bags: Invest in a dozen small and large cotton, linen, or canvas shopping bags. They're stronger than plastic or paper and will last for years. Keep some on a hook or doorknob in the kitchen, by the front door, and in the car. Stuff fresh produce and other items from the farmers' market into these bags.

> **Cool cloth bags:** Canvas grocery bags, $8 each or 3 for $21, cotton produce bags 3 (12x12) and 2 (8x8) bags, $18, Tomorrows World; canvas tote bags $8 each or 6 for $46, Giam/Harmony Inc. Many environmental groups will give you a sturdy tote bag for a $15 donation.

Filled with fresh, perishable produce—kale, collards, mustard greens, broccoli, lettuce, cucumbers—the bags can go directly into the refrigerator. Produce will keep longer and stay fresher in breathable bags than in plastic. Bags filled with less perishable items—onions, sweet potatoes, or apples—may be set on the floor, hung on hooks, or emptied into wire baskets or ceramic, pottery or glass bowls. Don't worry about getting the bags dirty with sandy vegetables, beets, or purple cabbage; they're machine washable and will last for years.

ESSENTIAL POTS and PANS

Sauce pots and pans: Look for heavy-gauge stainless steel; the thicker the better to reduce burning and facilitate cleanup. Insulated handles and an extended warranty are ideal. My essentials include a 1-cup and a 2-cup saucepan, two 1 1/2-quart, one 2 1/2-quart, and one 3-quart saucepan for steaming, simmering, boiling, stewing, and parboiling.

Other essentials include an 8-quart and a 12-quart stockpot for making stock and Bone-Building Broth, and a 3 1/2- to 4-quart enamel-lined cast iron or stainless steel Dutch oven for sautéing large batches of sturdy greens, making stews, roasts, casseroles, and compotes.

Skillets: Heavy-duty stainless steel pans are a must. They should include one or two 8-inch skillets, one 10-inch sauté pan, and at least one 12- to 13-inch sauté pan. You'll need 1 tight fitting lid for each pan. Skillets with all-metal handles and lids are ideal for transferring a pan to the oven.

Baking pans: A large collection of baking pans will allow you to bake or roast several dishes simultaneously. I use them to toast nuts, roast vegetables, and store freshly purchased meat or packages of meat transferred from the freezer to the fridge. I usually keep at least 2 pans on the meat shelf of the refrigerator to prevent cross contamination and keep the refrigerator clean.

My essentials include one 8x12-inch glass, ceramic, or stainless steel baking pan, two 13x19x2-inch stainless steel roasting pans, two 8- or 9-inch square or round stainless steel baking pans, and two 10-inch deep-dish glass pie plates.

Roasting pan with lid: You'll need at least 1 roasting pan with a lid to roast 1 or 2 chickens or turkey breasts, a whole turkey, or a beef, pork, or bison roast. A roasting rack keeps rich roasts above the pan juices.

OPTIONAL EXTRA PANS

Loaf pans: If you regularly make meatloaf, get a 9x5-inch stainless steel or Pyrex loaf pan. This is also handy for defrosting and safely storing packages of fish or meat in the fridge. A glass lid is optional but desirable for baking vegetables or storing meatloaf.

Cast iron skillets: Cast iron skillets are invaluable for sautéing, stir-frying, roasting, or broiling, as well as toasting seeds on top of the range. See next page for instructions on how to care for cast iron skillets.

Waterless cookware: These pans need less oil for cooking. They retain flavors, vitamins, minerals, and moisture, while reducing shrinkage. Heat-channel design bonds aluminum alloy between two or more layers of stainless steel for efficient, even, rapid heat distribution without burning. This eliminates the need for high temperatures, saves energy, and cuts cooking time and cleanup. They can be used in the oven or on the range top to bake meatloaf, roasts, potatoes, sweet potatoes, chicken, etc. Non-breakable, stay cool handles reduce the risk of injury.

Egg poacher: Poaching is one of the best ways to cook eggs and this handy tool helps turn out perfectly shaped, gently cooked eggs with minimal cleanup. You can use a conventional saucepan, but a tough film will

---

The best saucepans, skillets, and stockpots: Heavy-duty stainless steel pots, pans, and skillets with tight-fitting lids and sturdy, stay-cool handles are important for even heat distribution, reduced sticking, ease of cleanup, safety, and durability. Some of my favorite brands include Cuisinart, All-Clad, Multi-Clad, and Neova. All but the Neova are sold in kitchen shops and Chefs Catalog.

Super stainless steel baking pans: For hard-to-find pans without non-stick coatings, contact Natural Lifestyle Supplies Mail Order Market. 8" square cake pan, $7.95; 9" round cake pan, $7.95; 12"x14" cookie sheet, $9.95; 8¾"x4½" loaf pan, $9.95; 13"x9"x2" baking pan, $19.95; 15½" x10½"x1" jelly roll pan, $19.95. Check local kitchen shop or the cookware department of chain stores.

Best cast ironware: 3-piece skillet set, $27.95; 5-quart Dutch Oven, $28.95; 9" round skillet, $9.95; 10½" square and round skillet, Lodge Manufacturing or Lehman's Hardware & Appliances, Kitchen Classics, Williams-Sonoma, and Sur La Table.

Cookware for life: VITA-MIX Neova Cookware sets start at $279 and come with a lifetime guarantee. Free ground shipping worth $25 when you use this code to order: #ITRMA01.
  Second choice: Williams-Sonoma Waterless Cookware with lifetime warranty.

Good egg poacher: Norpro 10-inch Stainless Steel Egg Poacher, $34.95, from Cooking.com; 10-inch Korona Stainless Steel 5-Egg Poacher, $34.95, Amazon.com.

Seasoning a new cast iron skillet:

1) Warm the cookware then peel off label.

2) Wash with
brush; rinse, and dry thoroughly.

3) Coat cookware with a thin layer of coconut or olive oil.

4) Warm pan, then spread the oil over the entire surface, including all corners, with a clean cloth or unbleached paper towel.

5) Place pan in oven and heat to 300 to 350°F for 30 to 60 minutes. Remove from oven while warm; pour off excess oil. Wipe pan with a cloth or paper towel, and store.

Note on enamel-lined cast iron skillets: There is no need to season these pans such as the ones made by Le Creuset. Wash and clean them with non-abrasive sponges and dish soap and air dry or dry with a towel. Do not heat them when they are empty.

Cleaning cast iron: Do not put cast iron skillets in the dishwasher. Do not soak unless absolutely necessary to remove crusty baked on food. Wash with a sponge and running water. Towel drying is sufficient only for enamel-lined cast iron. Dry a wet cast iron skillet over medium heat on the stove top. After drying, lightly oil.

Using cast iron cookware: Use moderate rather than high heat. Use little or no water when cooking in a newly seasoned cast iron skillet and avoid cooking acidic ingredients, such as tomatoes, or vinegar, unless combined with a larger volume of non-acidic foods. Uncover hot foods after removing them from the stove, otherwise the steam may remove the protective layer you created when you seasoned the pan. Over time, a cast iron skillet will turn black. This indicates the pores are sealed. If rust builds up, the pan was improperly seasoned or it was used to cook acidic foods.

Treating a rusty cast iron skillet: Scrub off as much of the rust as possible with a wire-bristle brush and rinse well. Repeat steps 1 to 5 for seasoning a new cast iron skillet.

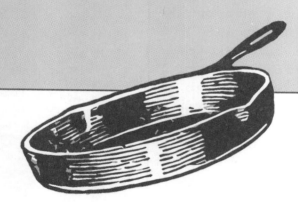

build up on the bottom of the pan. You can buy an egg-poaching insert to use with one of your own skillets or a complete set that includes a skillet with its own insert. We prefer egg poachers without non-stick coatings. Poachers that cook 4 to 6 eggs are $35 to $40 new; inserts cost less but are more difficult to find.

APPLIANCES

These tools can help you prepare foods more quickly, make them more attractive, or last longer.

Range/stove: If you have the option, buy or convert to a gas stove and range top to reduce your exposure to electromagnetic radiation and make your food taste better. Gas provides better and faster temperature control so you're less apt to burn food. Burners are ready to use instantly and you always have visible feedback. Chefs prefer gas ranges for a good reason.

Convection toaster oven: It takes less time to preheat a convection toaster oven than a conventional full-size oven. The convection oven surrounds food with an evenly heated airflow, saves energy, retains more of the natural flavors than a microwave, and alleviates the risk of radiation leaks. Convection mode cooks and reheats up to 30 percent faster than a regular oven or toaster oven. Roast or bake a cut-up fryer, half a dozen chicken breast halves or 4 to 6 sweet potatoes while you eat breakfast, shower, and dress. Broil 4 fish steaks or turkey burgers while you toss a salad, or roast a 3 1/2-pound turkey breast or 3-pound beef roast without firing up a full-size oven.

Blender: Buy one with a glass container and ice-crushing mode. Container should be wider at the top than bottom to effectively purée frozen or dried fruits. You'll probably use it daily (unless you have a Vita-Mix) for smoothies, Frosty Fruit Whips, blender puddings, salad dressings, marinades, grinding nuts, and blending soups. Beware, cheap blenders burn out quickly with vigorous use.

Home drinking water filtration device: Tap water contamination is a major problem in America. The Environmental Working Group and other health-related organizations recommend the use of a home drinking water filter.

Best system: For more than 15 years we have used the Multi-Pure Home Drinking Water System to filter the water we use for both drinking and cooking. This solid carbon block system is NSF and UL certified to remove one of the widest ranges of contaminants. Multi-Pure's 880 model is the only solid carbon block system that is NSF certified to reduce arsenic.

Multi-Pure point-of-use systems range in price from $199.95 to

---

Super stoves: Lehman's Hardware & Appliances and kitchen stores.

Convection toaster ovens: Cuisinart Convection Toaster Oven/Broiler, $179.99; Black and Decker Dining-In Convection Toaster Oven & Broiler $149.95, Cooking.com; DeLonghi Airstream Convection Toaster Oven that doubles as food dehydrator, $159.95, Gourmet Kitchen Store, and all major cooking shops.

Best blenders: Waring Professional Bar Blender, $99.95 to $139.95, Cooking.com, Kitchen Classics, Williams-Sonoma, and Sur La Table. Also check discount merchandise outlets. If finances permit, upgrade to a Vita-Mix.

$575.95. Multi-Pure also makes a combination reverse osmosis and solid carbon block system for water supplies that require multiple treatment technologies; it sells for $699.95.

For comprehensive information about water filtration technologies, how to choose the best system for your needs, and how to order a Multi-Pure, e-mail us at PlanetaryPress@earthlink.net or write to us in care of Planetary Press, P.O. Box 97040, Phoenix, AZ 85060-7040.

Vita-Mix: Unlike other juicers, this high-speed, multi-purpose machine makes low-glycemic Total Juices, which leave in fiber, vitamins, and minerals that extraction juicers remove. It also replaces a blender, food processor, ice crusher, grain grinder, and several other appliances. After burning out 3 blenders in 9 years, we finally got a Vita-Mix. It's easier to clean than a blender, juicer, or food processor, and the blades never need sharpening.

Coffee-spice mill: Use this to grind whole spice seeds for the freshest flavor and best fragrance. If your family members use one for coffee, buy a second grinder dedicated to spices.

Note: To clean the inside of container between spices, add 1/4 cup of baking soda, cover, and grind, then empty.

Mandoline/kitchen slicer: Quickly cut vegetables into julienne for steaming or stir-frying, or make fancy waffle shapes for dipping, or thin rounds for salads or dehydrating. The easy-to-operate machine requires no electricity, and takes up less space than a food processor. Look for one with an easy-to-assemble upright stand that holds attachments, has a safety lock and safety vegetable holder to protect your fingers while you slice.

Chest freezer: You're going to be eating a lot of fish, fowl, and meat. If you're buying grass-fed beef, pastured poultry, stocking up on in-store specials, or going through a lot of frozen fruit, you'll want to buy in bulk. If you hunt, fish, or have joined a co-op buying club, an extra freezer is essential. Look for a second-hand unit to save money.

Slow cooker: Cook a chicken, fryer parts, a turkey breast, roast, or stew while you work, work out, or shop. Bake stuffed apples while you clean house or run errands. Mull cider for a crowd. Save time and energy. Slow cookers come in a variety of sizes and shapes. A 3 1/2- or 5-quart model will be most versatile. Removable stoneware inserts are easier to clean than one-piece models. Glass lids are preferable to plastic because glass won't absorb odors or release toxic chemicals.

One-and-only source: Vita-Mix. Mod $369 (reconditioned) to $449 (new). For FREE ground shipping worth $25, mention Rachel's code when you order: I TR MA

Spice Mill: $19.99, Cooking.com, Krups USA, and kitchen shops everywhere.

Savvy slicers: Boerner Original V-Slicer, $40, Minuteman Trading LLC.; Kyocera Ceramic Kitchen Slicer, $25, and De Buyer Stainless Steel Mandoline, $169, Williams-Sonoma; Benriner Vegetable Slicer, $24.95, GoldMine Natural Foods.

Super durable slow cookers: Rival Crock-Pot Slow Cooker.

Source List for Tools of the Trade

Aircore Inc., Dijon Enterprises, PO BOX 306, Dickson, TN 37056, (888) 957-8573, www.aircore-cookware.com

Amazon.com, www.amazon.com

Broadway Pan Handler, 477 Broome Street, New York, NY 10013, (866) 266-59273 or (212) 966-3434, www.broadwaypanhandler.com

Chefs Catalog, PO Box 620048, Dallas, TX 75262, (800) 338-3232, www.chefscatalog.com

Chefsresource, 22732-B Granite Way, Laguna Hills, CA 92653, (866) 765-CHEF or (800) 765-2433, www.chefsresource.com

Cooking.com, 2850 Ocean Park Boulevard, Suite 310, Santa Monica, CA 90405, (800) 663-8810, www.cooking.com

Crate & Barrel Catalog, 1250 Techny Road, Northbrook, IL 60062,
store locator: (800) 996-9960; order line: (800) 323-5461, www.crateandbarrel.com

Diamond Organics: The Organic Food Catalog, P.O. Box 2159, Freedom, CA 95019, (888) 674-2642 or (888) 674-2642, www.diamondorganics.com

Dorothy McNett's Place, 800 San Benito Street, Hollister, CA 95023, (831) 637-6444, www.happycooker.com

East Earth Trade Winds, PO Box 49315, Redding, CA 96049-3151 and 1714 Churn Creek Road, Redding, CA 96002, (800) 258-6878, email: eetw@snowcrest.net

Excalibur Products, A Division of KBI, 6083 Power Inn Road, Sacramento, CA 95824, (800) 875-4254 or (916) 381-4254, Fax: (916) 381-4256, www.excaliburdehydrator.com

Frontier Co-Op, 3021 78th Street, PO Box 299, Norway, IA 52318, (800) 669-3275, www.frontiercoop.com

Giam/Harmony Inc., 360 Interlocken Boulevard, Suite 300, Broomfield, CO 80021, (800) 869-3446, www.giam.com

Gold Mine Natural Foods, 7805 Arjon's Drive, San Diego, CA 92126, (800) 475-FOOD (3663), www.goldminenaturalfood.com

Gourmet Kitchen Store, PO Box 414, Kresgevilla, PA 18333, (888) 304-2922, www.gourmetkitchenstore.com

Herb Stop, 4769 20th Street, Phoenix, AZ 85016, (602) 468-1187, www.herbstop.com

Island Market Foods, PO Box 307, 9740 S.W. Bank Road, Vashon Island, WA 98070, (206) 463-2446 www.islandmarketfoods.com

Kitchen Classics, 4041 E. Thomas Road, Phoenix, AZ 85018, (602) 954-8141, www.kitchenclassics.com

Krups USA, PO Box 3900, Peoria, IL 61614, www.krupsusa.com

Source List for Tools of the Trade

LamsonSharp, 45 Conway Street, Shelburne Falls, MA 01370, (800) 872-6564, www.lamsonsharp.com

Lehman's Hardware & Appliances, One Lehman Circle, PO Box 41, Kidron, OH 44636. (330) 857-5757, www.lehmans.com

Lodge Manufacturing, PO Box 380, South Pittsburgh, TN 37380, (423) 837-7181 or www.lodgemfg.com

Minuteman Trading LLC, PO Box 328, Boyce, VA 22620, (540) 837-2451, email: minutemn@vissuallink.com

Misto, 8 Trobridge Drive, Bethel, CT 06801, (888) 645-7772, www.misto.com

Multi-Pure Corporation, Las Vegas Technology Center, PO Box 34630, Las Vegas, NV 89133, (800) 622-9206. For product information contact Don and Rachel Matesz, Independent Distributors c/o Planetary Press, P.O. Box 97040, Phoenix, AZ 85060-7040, email: PlanetaryPress@earthlink.net, or call (602) 840-4556.

Natural Lifestyle Supplies Mail Order Market, (800) 752-2775, www.natural-lifestyle.com

Nesco American Harvest, (800) 288-4545, 1700 Monroe Street, Two Rivers, WI 54241, www.nesco.com

Qi Journal, 26151 Carancho Road, Temecula, CA 92590, (800) 787-2600 or order on line at http://qi-journal.com

Rival Crock-Pot Slow Cooker, 32 B. Spur Drive, El Paso, TX 79906, (800) 557-4825, www.crock-pot.com

Sur La Table, 1938 Occidental Avenue South, Seattle, WA 98134, (800) 243-0852, www.surlatable.com

Tabletools.com, 223 South Beverly Drive, Beverly Hills, CA 90212, (888) 211-6603, www.tabletools.com

Tomorrows World, 9659 First View Street, Norfolk, VA 23503, (800) 229-7571, www.tomorrowsworld.com

VITA-MIX, 8615 Usher Rd., Cleveland, OH 44138-2103, (800) VITA-MIX or (800) 848-2649, www.vitamix.com

The Well Tempered Kitchen Store, 122 Atlantic Hwy, Waldoboro, ME 04572, (207) 563-5762 or (207) 563-6242, www.welltemperedkitchen.com

Williams-Sonoma, 3250 VanNess Avenue, San Francisco, CA 94109, (800) 541-2233, www.williamssonoma.com

chapter 10 Stocking the Produce-Dominated Pantry

Step 1: Reduce Temptation

If everyone in your house decides to adopt a produce-dominated whole-foods diet, you could donate unopened packages, cans, and bottles of highly refined, processed, and artificial foods to a food bank. Or you could store them, along with partially used packages, in a box, cupboard, or freezer, for a once- or twice-a-week Free Meal.

As you remove unwholesome foods from your kitchen and diet, you will free up money, and your appetite, for more nourishing foods. If your family members want to keep eating unwholesome ingredients, stash any offending (or tempting) items in out-of-the-way places: designated cabinets, or certain sections of the refrigerator or freezer.

Step 2: Customize Your Lists

The following lists are neither exhaustive nor are they required for every kitchen. Your lists will vary with tastes, preferences, ages, and activity levels of family members, number of people for whom you cook, the season, where you live, and your budget. Some of the foods listed may be unfamiliar. Keep an open mind and mouth. Commit to trying at least 1 new fruit and vegetable and a new herb and spice each week and your repertoire of familiar foods will mushroom!

Keep a grocery list on the refrigerator and jot down what you need as your supply dwindles. Copy the lists you'll find in the food sections later in this chapter and fill in the blanks. You'll save time, energy and money, and minimize the number of trips to the store if you

Chapter Overview
Now that you have some insight into the basis of the nutrition plan, it's time to look at the variety of foods included in the produce-dominated diet. Also included are sample shopping lists.

~117~

replenish before the cupboards, freezer, or refrigerator are bare.

Once you've organized your kitchen (Chapter 8) taking inventory will be a quick, almost effortless task.

Step 3: Overcome Your Fear of Buying

You'll want to buy the basics—fresh vegetables, fruits, and lean meats—in generous amounts. If you don't, you'll find it almost impossible to prep and cook with several meals in mind, deprive yourself of delicious and ready-to-eat leftovers, and need to shop almost daily. To eat well consistently, you need to have an abundance of wholesome food on hand.

On average, most adults, regardless of diet, eat 3 to 4 pounds of food each day. On a produce-dominated diet this usually amounts to 3/4 to 1 pound of animal products (i.e., eggs, fish, fowl, or meat) and 2 to 4 pounds of fresh produce (vegetables and fruit) per person, per day. Two people can easily consume 12 pounds of animal products and 40 to 50 pounds of fresh produce per week. We do!

Although eating this much may initially sound daunting, it is not difficult to achieve. If you eat 2 vegetables, or 1 serving of vegetables and 1 fruit at each meal, you can easily consume 1 pound of fresh produce at every meal. Do this at breakfast, lunch, and dinner and you will consume 3 pounds of produce per day. For a more detailed breakdown of how much food you and your family members might eat in a day or week, see Chapter 7, Page 79.

Don't be afraid to buy half a side of beef or 8 or more frozen chickens at a time. In most states and regions, pasture-fed animals are raised and butchered seasonally. In some parts of the country it's impossible to raise animals solely on pasture through the winter. If you live in one of these areas and want pasture-fed meat, you'll have to stock up, unless you find a farmer who feeds cattle only hay through the winter. Chapter 7 will help you see just how much of these foods you're going to be using every week. Since you're going to be eating meat at every meal it makes sense to ensure you have a steady and ample supply of the highest quality meat on hand.

Step 4: Be Open to Change

Some people say they don't like the taste of some of the foods we recommend—certain vegetables, fruits, or other things they are unaccustomed to eating. This can change. Your tastes aren't engraved in stone. They are conditioned habits that can be changed with persistence.

Although your mind may prefer processed foods, your body certainly does not! Your body prefers foods with real flavors that come with a high nutrient density. The effects of advertising and familial habits have put your mind out of harmony with your body. Your mind must be trained to accept natural foods. If you practice eating wholesome unrefined foods, you will grow to like them so much that you may rarely, if ever, want anything else.

Buy Ample Amounts
Buying fresh vegetables, fruits, and lean meats in ample quantities will save time and help in maintaining a consistent, healthy eating pattern.

Unfamiliar foods are like strangers. You don't know them and may be suspicious of them, unless you are an extremely adventurous eater. When you try a new food (or present one to your husband or children), try at least 3 mouthfuls (and encourage them to do the same). Do this at least 3 days in a row and make sure to try at least 3 different recipes using that particular food. If that seems too difficult, then every time you try a new food, eat at least 3 mouthfuls; try the food at least 3 days in a row, then try the food again in at least 2 more recipes, eaten at least 3 times.

Yes, we just repeated ourselves! The only way to change your habits is through repetition. If you want better health, you have to make choices that meet your body's nutritional needs. Some things will be unfamiliar at first, but your body will eventually thank you for changing.

Step 5: Go Gathering
Although many of the ingredients we use can be purchased in supermarkets, you will find fresher produce, and a wider variety of it, at your local farmers' markets, natural food stores, and co-ops that support local farmers.

Many of the dry goods are difficult (if not impossible) to find in supermarkets but readily available in natural foods stores, health food co-operatives, or catalogs for co-op buying clubs. If you have trouble locating any of the specialty items we recommend, refer to source section in the Appendix.

If you go to a supermarket, shop the periphery and select freezer sections, where you'll find the most nourishing foods. Sometimes you'll find a natural foods section. Some supermarkets even sell hormone- and antibiotic-free meat, poultry, free-range eggs, organic produce, and fish frozen at sea.

Wherever you shop, read labels. Even natural foods stores stock a lot of "health-food junk-food" products. Potato chips are potato chips, wherever they're sold. Corn chips, crackers, pretzels, breaded and fried entrées, white pasta, macaroni and cheese, instant pilafs, soda, cupcakes, and breakfast bars are not the building blocks of health, regardless of what their advertisers want you to believe. Look for products with the simplest and fewest ingredients, as close to the way God and Mother Nature made them as possible.

Money-Saving Moves
1. **Start a garden:** Don't limit yourself to a summer garden. Hearty plants, such as kale and collard greens, can be picked until the ground freezes in cold climates. These same plants may be picked in the winter, spring, and fall in hot, arid states like Arizona and the surrounding area.

    Carrots, beets, onions, winter squashes, turnips, and apples, may be harvested over the summer and late in the fall, then stored for months. Those who live where

Power of Threes
Some foods will be strange at first. Take a chance—try at least 3 mouthfuls of a new food, for 3 days, and in 3 different recipes. The repetition will give you a chance to adjust to the foods and will lead to improved nutrition.

the growing season is short can enjoy fresh produce all year by constructing a greenhouse if space and finances permit. Consult *Mother Earth News* or your local library for information on building greenhouses.

If you don't have yard space, start with a collection of windowsill or porch-side pots you can bring inside when the weather turns cold. In some cities you can rent a garden plot. Or, if your neighbor has a garden, you might offer to help with upkeep in exchange for a portion of the harvest.

2. **Take up foraging:** Consult a knowledgeable friend, expert, the Internet, or library or books before you pick; some plants are poisonous! Ask around to find food foraging classes in your area. Avoid picking foods if you don't know what they are or if you find them growing near highways or busy roads where they might accumulate high levels of lead and other contaminants from auto exhaust.

3. **Volunteer for yard duty**: Many people with fruit and nut trees eat only a fraction of the fare their trees bear. Many of these people will gladly allow you pick to your heart's content if you offer to remove windfall fruits and yard debris. You can freeze or dry fruit you can't eat within a week. Enjoy it all year round or give it as gifts for the holidays.

4. **Frequent local farmers' markets:** Locally grown, vine-ripened, just-picked produce from a farmer will be fresher, more flavorful, and often more economical than imported vegetables and gas-ripened fruits from the supermarket. Local produce is also better for Mama Earth. It requires little or no fuel for transport and no processing. It supports local farmers who would otherwise be put out of business by huge agribusinesses that don't care about you, our soil, or our future.

Since some farmers sell local and imported produce, you will need to familiarize yourself with what grows in your area and/or ask a lot of questions: "Where were these peaches grown?" "Did you grow this broccoli?" "Do you use herbicides and pesticides?" Look for a farmer who advertises "chemical-free, unsprayed" or "organically grown" produce. If you can't find one, there are still plenty of good reasons to buy local non-organic produce.

5. **Look for locally grown (pasture-raised) meat and eggs:** Pasture-raised poultry, grass-fed meat, and free-range eggs almost always cost less when you buy them from the farmer and eliminate the middleman. This supports local farmers, who are the stewards of the earth and keys to our future. It

Support Local Farms
When purchasing locally grown foods, you'll often find the produce will be fresher and more flavorful than that in the supermarket. Plus, purchasing locally grown foods will support your community.

also reduces the unnecessary shipping of foods from afar.

We buy most of our meat, poultry, and eggs directly from farmers, and supplement with hormone and antibiotic-free, grain-fed meat and eggs from a natural foods market when necessary. If possible, we get any grain-fed meat or eggs we buy from a local farmer. (See Appendix D for a national directory of farmers who produce 100 percent grass-fed meats).

6. **Join a co-op buying club**: You can create or join with a group of people who order from a wholesale natural foods warehouse at prices 20 to 40 percent below retail. Members stock up on frequently used items—such as frozen and dried fruits and vegetables, juices, herb teas, nuts and nut butter, olive oil, organic vinegars, coconut milk, free-range poultry and meat, non-irradiated organic herbs and spices, biodegradable cleaning products, natural toiletry items, etc.

You can purchase items in ones, twos, threes, or by the pound or case for your household or to split among several families. Once a month you place an order and once a month you pick it up at the home of one of your buying club buddies. Members divvy up duties—collecting orders, breaking down boxes, dividing up contents, adjusting invoices—for a total investment of 1 to 3 hours per month, at most.

Our Appendix includes a nationwide list of co-op buying clubs. Call to see which ones deliver to your city and state. Ask for an information packet, including names and telephone numbers for established groups in your area. You may be able to join a group without having to start your own.

For Related Information, See these Web Pages:

Find farms, farmers' markets, and CSA (Community Supported Agriculture) projects in your area
www.foodroutes.com
www.csacenter.org
www.nal.usda.gov/afsic
www.localharvest.org

10 REASONS TO BUY LOCAL FOOD
http://www.asapconnections.org/local.htm

FARMERS' MARKETS BY STATE
http://www.ams.usda.gov/farmersmarkets/map.htm

INDUSTRIAL AGRICULTURE: FEATURES AND POLICY
http://www.ucsusa.org/food/?ind.ag.html

THE FARMER AS STEWARD
http://www.familyfarmer.org/conference/campany.html

Eggs
☐Chicken eggs
☐Dried powdered egg whites
☐Duck eggs
☐Vanilla or chocolate egg white protein

Eggs

Selection criteria

1. *Best choice*: 100 percent pasture fed or barnyard chicken/duck eggs
2. *Second*: omega-3, DHA rich eggs
3. *Third*: organic or naturally raised hormone and antibiotic-free eggs
4. *Fourth*: dried, powdered egg whites

What to avoid

1. conventional mass-market (factory-farmed) eggs
2. irradiated eggs
3. dried or liquid egg products containing vegetable oils, hydrogenated fats, artificial flavorings and colorings, added salt, preservatives, sugar, fructose, artificial sweeteners, or soy protein.

Note: Dried, powdered egg whites do not contain oxidized cholesterol because the yolks have been removed. They are an acceptable compromise, provided they are free of artificial ingredients.

Best sources for whole eggs: Look for a local farmers' market or someone who raises livestock on pasture. For a list of suppliers of pasture-raised animals in your area, consult the book, *Why Grassfed is Best* and www.eatwild.com.

Best sources for dried, powdered egg whites and egg white protein: natural foods store

Second: co-op buying club, or supermarket with health food section

What to look for

* *Fresh eggs*—Yolks should be firm, golden orange, well-rounded, with a rich flavor. Once you become accustomed to eating such eggs, you won't want anything less.

* *Dried, powdered egg whites*—Look for dried, powdered egg whites with no additives.

* *Egg white protein*—Buy a product that is plain or flavored with pure vanilla extract and/or unsweetened cocoa, with or without stevia (for sweetness). Bromelain and papain (fruit-based digestive enzymes) and chromomium picolinate (a mineral lacking in most modern diets due to soil depletion) are acceptable ingredients.

Product should not contain artificial flavorings, colorings, or artificial sweeteners. Refer to Sources in Appendix D for acceptable brands.

Amount to buy

We buy chicken and duck eggs 2 dozen at a time for 2 people, and 2-pound tubs of dried, powdered egg whites and egg white protein.

Storage tips

Refrigerate whole eggs in cartons and use within 4 weeks. Store dried, powdered egg whites and egg white protein at room temperature

Are those eggs too old to eat?

Not sure? Put the eggs in a bowl of cold water. If they sink and stay on their sides at the bottom of the bowl, they're fresh. Aging eggs will start to turn upright. If they're old, they'll float and should be tossed or composted.

Fish and Seafood
   Selection Criteria
     1. *Best choice*: wild caught fish, sold fresh or frozen at sea
     2. *Second:* canned fish, in water, olive or fish oil, preferably with little or no salt
   What to avoid
     1. processed fish (e.g. surimi, cured, salted, sugared, and breaded products)
     2. fish canned with cottonseed, soy or vegetable oils, broth, MSG, and hydrolyzed soy or vegetable protein
     3. farmed fish (or at least limit the amount)
     4. lake fish (particularly from sources known to be contaminated)
     5. irradiated fish
     6. cooked shrimp, prawns, or lobster treated with preservatives

Best source: If possible buy directly from the person who caught the fish. Some small-scale fisherman harvest fish from pristine waters of Alaska, freeze it, and sell it at farmers' markets.

Second: Find a specialty seafood market or natural foods store with a fish counter. Develop a relationship with a knowledgeable merchant who can tell you the fish's origin, freshness, whether previously frozen, and how long it will keep. He should be willing and able to order wild ocean fish and introduce you to new varieties.

Third: Look in the supermarket freezer section for frozen fish, and in natural foods markets for canned fish free of MSG, preservatives, and additives.

   What to look for

* *Fresh fish*—Flesh should be firm and moist, with no traces of drying or browning around edges; steaks should adhere to the bone. Flesh should spring back to its original position when dented with a fingertip. Packages should be tightly wrapped with no pools of liquid. Check sell-by dates. Fish should have no offensive odor. Inland fish (lake perch, walleye, pickerel, bass) should smell mildly of cucumber.

FYI: We recommend avoiding lake fish because it typically contains higher levels of contaminants than deep ocean fish. Ocean fish may have a slight briny smell. Avoid fish with a strong ammonia-like smell (a sign of spoilage) with the exception of shark, skate, and ocean perch, which have a slight ammonia-like fragrance even when fresh.

Fish & Seafood

☐ Arctic Char

☐ Canned, no-salt tuna in water

☐ Canned, whole sardines, preferably unsalted

☐ Cod

☐ Deep Sea Dory

☐ Escolar (oil fish)

☐ Flounder

☐ Grouper

☐ Haddock

☐ Halibut

☐ Mackerel

☐ Ocean Perch

☐ Orange Roughy

☐ Pollock

☐ Prawns

☐ Red Snapper

☐ Salmon

☐ Scampi

☐ Scrod (baby cod)

☐ Sea Bass

☐ Shrimp

☐ Sole

☐ Tuna

Concerned about mercury levels in seafood?

Many health experts believe benefits of s
drawbacks. However, some varieties are more likely to be
contaminated than others. The following list includes the
mercury levels, listed in parts per million (ppm). The FDA
recommends young children and women of childbearing age
avoid tilefish, swordfish, shark, and king mackerel, which contain
the highest levels mercury.

* tilefish	1.45 ppm
* swordfish	1.00 ppm
* shark	0.96 ppm
* king mackerel	0.73 ppm
* grouper (mycteroperca)	0.43 ppm
* tuna (fresh or frozen)	0.32 ppm
* northern lobster	0.31 ppm
* grouper (epinephelus)	0.27 ppm
* halibut	0.23 ppm
* sablefish	0.22 ppm
* pollock	0.20 ppm
* dungeness crab	0.18 ppm
* tuna (canned)	0.17 ppm
* blue crab	0.17 ppm

Source: U.S. Food and Drug Administration.

Note: Although canned tuna comes from smaller fish
than fresh tuna steaks, it can still be a significant source
of mercury. Many health experts recommend that tuna
consumption be limited to once a week for children and no
more than 8 ounces of fresh or canned tuna per week for
adults. If you regularly consume tuna or other fish containing
mercury, consuming sea vegetables (also known as seaweeds)
at least 3 times a week can help chelate mercury and other
heavy metals. For more on the benefits of sea vegetables, see
Page 395.

Fish Farming Follies

Farmed fish are raised in net cages—floating feedlots that foster diseases and parasites and smother marine life with sewage and antibiotic residues. Farmed fish, such as salmon, are fed artificial colorings to disguise their gruesome gray flesh. Lastly, farmed fish are less nutritious than their wild cousins.

To learn more about the hazards of fish farming visit: www.farmedanddangerous.org

* *Frozen fish*—Fish should be solidly frozen in an intact package or encased in ice with no yellowing or freezer burn (ice crystals or water stains). Fish frozen at sea is often fresher than what is sold "fresh" at supermarket seafood counters.

* *Canned fish*—Look for unsalted fish packed in water, olive oil, or sild (fish oil). Avoid products canned in broth, which can contain MSG even if it's not listed on the label, and those that contain hydrolyzed vegetable protein, preservatives, additives, and vegetable oils.

Note: Sardines are a source of beneficial omega 3 fatty acids. Whole sardines with the bones are an exceptional non-dairy source of calcium and vitamin D, as well as other nutrients.

Amount to buy

Buy fresh fish for immediate use and extra packages for the freezer. Keep a couple of varieties on hand in large quantities so you can transfer packages from the freezer to the fridge every few days. Allow 12 to 24 hours to defrost enough fish for 2 meals.

Note: To economize, we sometimes buy odd shaped pieces (scraps, bellies cubes, or trim) of fish in an Asian or seafood market for a fraction of what you'd pay for steaks or fillets. They are moist, tender, delicious, and nutritious. They cook quickly and usually come skinned and without bones.

Storage tips

Cook fresh fish within 2 days. Consume cooked fish within 2 days. Use uncooked frozen fish within 1 year if tightly packaged, 3 months if not tightly wrapped.

Red Meats
Selection Criteria

1. *Best choice*: wild game or 100 percent pasture-fed lean meats, locally grown if possible
2. *Second*: "organic," "naturally raised" hormone and antibiotic free, locally grown if possible

What to avoid

1. processed meats (e.g. bacon, sausage, hot dogs, "lunch meat," salted, cured, or breaded meat, meat containing

MSG, hydrogenated oils, propyl gallate, artificial colorings, etc.)

2. fatty and conventional mass-market meat
3. irradiated meat

Best source: If possible, buy 100 percent pasture-raised meat directly from small dedicated farmers from your state or region. Due to seasonal availability, you will have to buy it frozen and in large quantities, stocking up for several months or more at a time. Some farmers who raise grass-fed beef will sell smaller amounts and let you choose the cuts you want (steaks, stew meat, and/or ground beef for example).

For a state-by-state listing of supplies near you, check *Why Grassfed is Best!* (Vashon Island Press) or visit www.eatwild.com.

Second: While not ideal, the next best thing to grass-fed is "organic" or "naturally raised" meat. It is available at farmers' markets, natural foods store, co-op buying clubs, specialty foods stores, or supermarkets under specialty labels, such as Laura's Lean Beef, Coleman Natural Meats, Organic Valley Farms, or Piedmontese beef. Another option is Bison (Buffalo).

What to look for

* *Fresh meat*—Meat should be moist, even color, free of browning or drying around edges, with no pools of liquid. The flesh should spring back when dented with a fingertip.

* *Frozen meat*—This should be tightly sealed, solidly frozen, free of water spots and discoloration.

Don't shy away from frozen meat; it is often the only way to buy quality local or naturally raised meat. Small farmers have to preserve their meat or much of it will spoil before it is sold. The only reliable alternative to freezing is drying, which is ecological but doesn't preserve the fresh qualities or texture of meat.

* *Beef and bison*—Meat should be bright red, verging on purple.

Note: Pasture-raised meat, like wild game, has a stronger flavor than grain-fed meat and the visible fat may be slightly yellow. These are signs of a higher essential fatty acid, vitamin, mineral, and antioxidant content. Although it may initially taste gamey or strange, with regular use it will begin to taste normal and grain-fed meat will eventually taste strange, even flat.

Lean, wild or pasture-raised meat will be tender if properly handled after slaughter and properly cooked. Since it cooks 30 percent faster than fatty meat, be careful not to overcook.

Note: Even if a producer says his meat is pasture raised, ask questions to make sure you are getting genuine grass-fed beef. "Are the animals 100 percent pasture raised?" "Do they receive any grain? If so, how much?" "Are the animals given any growth hormones or antibiotics?"

Amount to buy

Stock the freezer with enough meat so you can transfer packages to baking pans or bowls in the refrigerator every few days or weekly.

Red Meats

❑ Beef or bison, ground or preformed patties (80 to 96 percent lean)

❑ Beef or bison roast (boneless or bone in)

❑ Beef or bison stew meat

❑ Beef or bison steaks (boneless or bone in)

❑ Beef bones (for soup, stock, or broth)

❑ Lamb chops, steaks, or riblets

❑ Lamb, ground (extra lean)

❑ Lamb, roast leg of, (boneless or bone in)

❑ Lamb bones (for soup, stock, or broth)

❑ Pork, ground (93 to 96 percent lean)

❑ Pork loin or sirloin chops or steaks (preferably boneless)

❑ Pork roast, loin or tenderloin (boneless or bone in

We regularly buy a quarter or half side of grass-fed beef at a time and ask for all the bones for making stock and broth.

Storage tips

Cook fresh or thawed meat within 4 days, and consume within 3 more days. Pasture-raised meats and wild game will keep longer in the refrigerator than grain-fed meat without discoloration or spoilage. Tightly wrapped raw meat may be frozen for a year or more. Use cooked, frozen meat within 3 months.

Poultry
Selection Criteria

1. *Best choice*: wild fowl or 100 percent pasture-fed (or pastured) poultry, locally grown if possible
2. *Second*: "organic," "naturally raised," or "free-range" hormone- and antibiotic-free poultry, locally grown if possible

What to avoid

1. processed meats (e.g. bacon, sausage, hot dogs, lunch meat; anything salted, cured, breaded, or containing MSG, vegetable oils, hydrogenated oils, propyl gallate, phosphoric acid, nitrates, nitrites, sugar, artificial colorings, etc.)
2. fatty poultry (e.g., poultry ground with skin)
3. conventional mass-market poultry
4. anything labeled "self-basting"
5. irradiated poultry

Best source: Whenever possible, purchase 100 percent pasture-raised poultry directly from small farmers from your state or region. Due to seasonal availability, you may have to buy it frozen and in larger quantities, stocking up for several months or more at a time. For a state-by-state listing of suppliers, see *Why Grassfed is Best!* or visit Robinson's Web site www.eatwild.com.

Second: "organic," "naturally raised," or "free-range," hormone- and antibiotic-free fowl from a farmers' market, specialty food store, gourmet food store, or co-op buying club

Third: supermarkets, under special labels, such as Rocky the Range, or hormone and antibiotic-free Amish poultry

What to look for

* *Fresh poultry*—Product should be moist, even in color, free of browning or drying around edges, with no pools of liquid. Flesh should spring back when dented with a fingertip.

* *Frozen poultry*—This should be tightly sealed, solidly frozen, free of water spots and discoloration. Don't shy away from frozen poultry; it is often the only way to buy quality local or naturally raised poultry. Small farmers have to preserve their poultry or much of it will spoil before it is sold. The only reliable alternative to freezing is drying, which is ecological but doesn't preserve the fresh qualities or texture of meat.

Poultry

❑ Chicken, fryers or roasters, whole or cut up parts

❑ Chicken, split breasts, boneless breast halves or fillets

❑ Chicken thighs and/or drumsticks (boneless or bone in)

❑ Ground chicken or turkey, lean (skinless light or dark meat

❑ Chicken/turkey bones (for soup, stock, or broth)

❑ Ground chicken or turkey burgers (preformed; dark meat, light meat, or combination)

❑ Turkey breasts (boneless or bone in)

❑ Turkeys, whole, halved or quartered

Note: Pasture-raised poultry will have firmer flesh, stronger, thicker bones, and a more pronounced poultry flavor than confined, grain-fattened fowl. Robinson reports, "In a blind taste test of ordinary and free-range Thanksgiving turkeys, *New York Times* food editors chose a free-range bird as their number one choice. The meat was flavorful and juicy, and had a tender but meaty texture. Owners of fine restaurants concur."

Professional chefs at upscale restaurants prefer pasture-fed poultry because of its superior flavor. After eating it, you will be surprised at how flat and flavorless supermarket and other mass-market chickens and turkeys taste.

Amount to buy
Keep your freezer amply stocked so you can transfer packages to the fridge every few days.

Storage tips
Cook fresh or thawed poultry within 3 days and eat within 3 days or freeze leftovers. Use frozen, cooked meat within 3 months. Raw poultry may be frozen for 1 year, or longer, if tightly wrapped.

Fresh Vegetables

Selection Criteria
1. *Best choice*: local organic or biodynamically grown
2. *Second*: locally grown, non-organic
3. *Third*: imported organic
4. *Fourth*: imported conventional

What to avoid
1. canned vegetables (with the exception of unsalted tomato paste)
2. vegetables treated with salt, sulfites, MSG, petroleum-based wax or other preservatives
3. irradiated and genetically modified vegetables
4. wilted, dried out, soggy, or aged looking vegetables

What to look for
Fresh vegetables should look fresh, vibrant, and crisp. If the organic produce you find in local markets looks wilted and lifeless, select fresher looking non-organic alternatives.

Best source: directly from farmers or local farmers' market

Second: natural foods market or co-op buying club

Third: supermarket

Amount to buy
Keep a generous variety and quantity on hand for use at every meal. Most leafy greens shrink to one-fourth their original volume when cooked. Vary selections within each week, month, season, and year.

If your local farmers' market is only open once a week, buy as much as will fit in your refrigerator. After 4 or 5 days it will still be fresher and more flavorful than imported produce that traveled 2,000 or more miles.

Bulb Vegetables

☐Elephant garlic

☐Garlic

☐Leeks

☐Pearl onions

☐Scallions (green onions)

☐Shallots

☐Spanish onions: red, white, yellow

☐Sweet onions: Walla Walla or Vidalia

Bulb Vegetables
What to look for

* *Onions*—These should have hard, firm, dry skins, small necks and papery outer scales free of soft and moldy spots.

* *Young, fresh (uncured) onions*—Look for moist skins and necks.

* *Scallions*—Seek out firm bunches; outer leaves should be free of soggy, wet, or moldy spots.

* *Leeks*—Look for firm and crisp shoots with medium-size necks and 3 inches or more of white shoots extending from base.

* *Shallots*—Seek out firm, plump cloves, neither shrunken nor shriveled.

* *Garlic*—Go for compact heads with plump, firm cloves well covered in a crisp, paper casing, free of soft or moldy spots.

Amount to buy

We buy onions (with dry skins) by the dozen or in 5- to 10-pound bags for daily use. We buy leeks 2 or 3 at a time, shallots by the handful, and garlic several heads at a time.

Storage tips

Onions with dry skins, garlic, and shallots—Store at room temperature in bowls or baskets.

Leeks, young and spring onions and scallions—Refrigerate in cloth bags or directly in the crisper bin of the refrigerator. Refrigerate sliced onions and use within 5 days. Consume cooked bulb vegetables within 4 days.

Leafy Green & Flowering Vegetables

☐Arugula/rocket

☐Baby greens

☐Baby spinach

☐Bib lettuce

☐Bok choy

☐Boston lettuce

☐Broccoli

☐Broccoflower

☐Brussels sprouts

☐Buttercrunch lettuce

~Continued next page~

Leafy Green and Flowering Vegetables
What to look for

* *Lettuce and salad mixes and spinach*—Look for crisp, vibrant, fresh looking leaves free of yellowed, dried out, mushy, soggy, wilted, or moldy spots.

Note: Thoroughly wash and dry even prewashed lettuces, spinach, and other salad greens.

* *Broccoli*—Buds should be dark green or purplish in compact clusters with green leaves intact. Stems should not be too thick or tough. Smaller stalks and buds are best. Yellowed heads are past their prime and will taste bitter.

* *Cauliflower*—Heads should be solid with white to creamy-white clusters. Leaves should look fresh if attached. Avoid heads with significant amounts of black or brown spots.

* *Brussels sprouts*—Sprouts should have tight, firm, bright green leaves, free of wormholes and blemishes. Avoid sprouts with yellowed, wilted, or brown around the edges.

* *Kale and collard greens*—These should be deep, dark green, crisp, fresh looking and free of soggy, yellowed, or decayed spots. If the leaves have yellowed, they are not worth buying, even if the label says "organic."

* *Mustard and turnip greens*—Leaves will naturally be less green than kale or collards, but should still be fresh, crisp, free of soggy, wilted, or brown spots or large yellow patches.

Amount to buy

We buy 3 or 4 bunches of broccoli at a time. Kale, collards, and/ or mustard or turnip greens are purchased 2 or 5 pounds at a time (usually 3 to 10 bunches). Depending on size, we buy 2 or 3 heads of lettuce at a time. We buy spring salad mix by the quarter or half pound, and other assorted greens as needed.

Storage tips

Arrange vegetables loosely in crisper bin of refrigerator or store in cloth bags on the bottom shelf of the fridge.

Store heads of lettuce in cloth bags.

Store baby, spring, and mesclun greens in open plastic bags; if rinsed and drained, store in salad spinner in fridge.

Store chopped vegetables in pint or quart jars or other sealed containers.

Use greens before they wilt, within 4 to 5 days of purchase. Greens purchased directly from a farmer can last up to 1 week. Greens purchased from a store rarely keep as long, unless you get them the day they arrive in the store. Fresh locally grown greens will stay fresh longer than imported greens. Use cooked greens within 3 days or freeze.

~Leafy Green & Flowering Vegetables, cont.~

❑ Cabbage sprouts

❑ Cauliflower

❑ Chinese cabbage

❑ Choy sum

❑ Collard greens

❑ Endive

❑ Escarole

❑ Kale

❑ Mesclun mix

❑ Mustard greens

❑ Oak leaf lettuce

❑ Radicchio

❑ Red or green cabbage

❑ Red and green leaf lettuce

❑ Romaine/cos lettuce

❑ Savoy cabbage

❑ Spinach (flat or curly)

❑ Spring/field greens

❑ Tot soy

❑ Turnip greens

Shoots

What to look for

* *Asparagus*—Spears should be firm and well rounded with compact tips. Avoid flat limp stalks and soggy tips.

* *Celery*—Stalks should be crisp and thick, tightly nestled with green leaves, which are useful for flavoring salads, soups, stews, and egg dishes.

* *Fennel*—Stalks should be firm with bright green foliage with little or no yellowing, free of brown, black or decayed fronds. Smaller specimens are usually sweeter and less woody than larger heads.

Amount to buy

Buy as needed. For the best flavor, buy locally grown asparagus and fennel in season.

Storage tips

Store in cloth bags on bottom shelf of refrigerator or loosely in crisper bin lined with a cotton towel or placemat. Eat cooked shoot vegetables within 2 days.

Shoots

❑ Asparagus

❑ Celery

❑ Fennel

Fruit Vegetables

- ❑Avocados: Haas, Fuerte, Bacon, Gwen, Zutano, or Pinkerton

- ❑Bell peppers: red, yellow, orange, red

- ❑Cherry tomatoes: red, gold, orange

- ❑Fresh chili peppers

- ❑Tomatoes: red or low-acid gold or orange

- ❑Tomatillos

Miscellaneous

- ❑Cucumbers: regular, English, or "burpless"

- ❑Green beans and yellow wax beans

- ❑Pickling cucumbers (such as Kirby)

- ❑Pea pods and sugar snap peas

Summer squash

- ❑Crookneck squash (summer squash)

- ❑Patty pan squash (summer squash)

- ❑Spaghetti squash (a gourd)

- ❑Zucchini (summer squash)

Hard winter squash

- ❑Buttercup squash (winter squash)

- ❑Butternut squash (winter squash)

- ❑Delicata squash (winter squash)

- ❑Honey delight (winter squash)

- ❑Kabocha pumpkin or Hokaido pumpkin (winter squash)

- ❑Sweet dumpling (winter squash)

Fruit Vegetables

What to look for

Tomatoes—Fruits should be firm, brightly and evenly colored, and relatively heavy for their size, plump and free of blemishes. Heavier tomatoes have more "meaty" solids and less liquid. Vine-ripened tomatoes will have a fresh tomato fragrance.

Avoid: Out of season tomatoes. Substitute unsalted sun-dried or canned organic tomatoes.

* *Avocados*—Skins should be green to greenish-black in color. The skin of Haas avocados will turn from green to black when ripe. Some varieties, such as fuerte, bacon, gwen, zutano, or pinkerton, remain green. For immediate use these fruits should yield to gentle pressure; for use in 3 to 5 days, buy firm avocados free of cracks. Look for medium to large avocados for a high flesh to pit ratio.

Note: To test an avocado, pierce the stem end with a toothpick. If it inserts easily, the fruit is ripe. To speed ripening, place unripe avocados in a bowl with ripe fruits, or place avocados and a ripe apple or banana in a paper bag with holes punched in it and folded shut.

* *Cucumbers*—Look for unwaxed vegetables with trim, even shape, good green color, and firm texture; small whitish lumps on surface are fine. Buy the smallest ones you can find. (English or burpless cucumbers are always long.) Pickling cucumbers aren't just for pickling; they are perfect for salads, don't require peeling (provided they've not been waxed), and don't need to be seeded to be digestible.

* *Summer squash*—Choose specimens with good color, heavy for their size. The rind should be soft enough to puncture with a fingernail, but never soggy.

* *Pumpkins and winter squashes*—Look for squash that's heavy for its size. Butternut should be uniformly peachy. Kabocha, buttercup, Hokaido, honey delight, and sweet mama squash should be deep, dark green. Markings on delicata and sweet dumplings should be bright orange, which is a sign of sweetness.

Most squashes—except butternut—have splotches on the skin where fruit sat on ground; rich orange spots indicate ripe flesh. Syrupy spots on the stem end are also a good indication of sweetness.

Amount to buy

Buy what you will use within the week. We buy bell peppers 2 to 4 at a time, tomatoes 2 or more pints or pounds at a time, depending on what we're making and the season. Avocados and other fruit-vegetables are purchased 2 or more at a time or as needed.

Buy cucumbers, pods, zucchini, and summer squash in amounts you're likely to use within a week or so. Spaghetti squash and hard winter squash keep longer. We buy them several at a time (more in the winter) since they will keep for several months, if properly stored.

Storage tips

Peppers, eggplants, and tomatillo—Store in crisper bins or on refrigerator shelves in paper or cloth bags. Store sliced peppers in a sealed jar and use within 4 days.

Tomatoes—Store at room temperature in bowls or wire baskets. When ripe, use promptly. Refrigerate sliced raw tomatoes and use within 48 hours, or cook, freeze, or dehydrate.

Avocados—Store at room temperature if hard or unripe; keep away from direct heat. If ripe, but not mushy, whole avocados may be refrigerated for up to 5 days. Once sliced, consume within 2 days or mash with lemon or lime juice and freeze.

Miscellaneous vine vegetables and summer squash—Refrigerate in closed paper bags, cloth bags, or in crisper bins of your refrigerator. Line bins with cotton placemats to absorb moisture.

Spaghetti squash and hard winter squash—Store at room temperature on a table, in wire baskets, or on wooden racks that allow air circulation, or in a cold attic, an old-fashioned cold box, or enclosed porch. Colder temperatures are better; the heat of the kitchen can cause premature spoilage. Leave plenty of space or crumbled newspaper between squash to prevent collection of moisture and mold.

Refrigerate hard squash after cutting. Use cooked vine vegetables within 3 days or freeze.

Root Vegetables

What to look for

* *Carrots*—They should be firm and smooth, with deep orange color, fairly regular in shape. If greens are attached, remove them immediately so they don't steal nutrients and flavor from the roots.

* *Beets*—Young, slender, firm, and smooth beets are best. Avoid soft and flabby roots and those with traces of mold because they are past their prime.

* *White radishes*—Daikon should be firm and fresh; if they bend easily, they're old. Look for roots no wider than a cucumber, thinner if possible; fatter daikon are frequently woody and tough.

* *Jicama*—These roots should have fairly unblemished skin free of greenish or blackish moldy or moist spots.

* *Celeriac*—These will appear earthy, dirty, irregularly shaped, even hairy on the outside; this is normal. Scrub well and peel just before use.

* *Burdock root*—These roots resemble kindling. The sticks should be firm, the diameter of a large marking pen, with a brown, dusty exterior. If pieces are soft and easily bent, they are past their prime and not worth buying.

Root Vegetables
❑ Beets
❑ Burdock root
❑ Carrots
❑ Celeriac, celery root
❑ Daikon radish
❑ Icicle radish
❑ Jicama
❑ Parsnips
❑ Red radishes
❑ Rutabaga
❑ Turnips

* *Others*—All other roots should be firm, free of soft spots, fairly unblemished, and unwaxed; the smaller the better. Enormous turnips, rutabaga, and parsnips are usually mealy, dry, and bitter.

Amount to buy

We buy 2 to 4 pounds of carrots every week or two; beets 1 to 3 pounds at a time; 1 or 2 bunches of small radishes or 2 or 3 daikon radishes at a time; others as needed.

Storage tips

Store roots in cloth bags on the bottom shelf or directly in refrigerator crisper bin. Do not store carrots or beets near apples; they emit ethylene gas, which can give the carrots a bitter taste. Most roots will keep for several weeks if purchased when fresh, firm, and free of soft spots.

Tubers

What to look for

* *Sweet potatoes and yams*—The exterior should be firm, smooth, fairly unblemished, with bright skin, an even color and texture and free of black, moldy, or soft spots and sprouts. Small to medium and narrow tubers are sweeter and more flavorful than wide, fat, jumbo sweet potatoes. Color may range from tan to brown to copper or magenta, depending upon the variety.

* *Jerusalem artichokes (sunchokes)*—Find pieces that are firm, free of soft, dark brown, wet, or black spots. Size and shape may vary from small, potato-like tubers to knobby ginger root-like pieces.

* *Potatoes*—Select firm, smooth, unblemished tubers with an even color and texture, free of green spots and sprouts. The latter can be poisonous.

Amount to buy

We buy sweet potatoes, and what most people call yams, by the half dozen or dozen and sunchokes 1/2 to 1 pound at a time.

Storage tips

Sunchokes—Store in the refrigerator crisper bin.

Sweet potatoes and garnet and jewel yams—Keep at room temperature in a basket, bowl, on a rack with some room for air to circulate. If stored in a bowl or basket, check often to avoid spoilage.

Note: If stored in quantity, separate each sweet potato with crumpled newspaper to keep moisture from collecting on the skin, which can invite mold. Do not refrigerate uncooked sweet potatoes or yams.

Potatoes—Potatoes are not in the same family as sweet potatoes and should *not* be stored at room temperature or exposed to light.

Store potatoes in paper bags or gunny sacks, in a cool, dark place, such as a cold porch or cold attic (in the winter), a cold box (a cupboard vented to the outdoors and found in some old homes), or

Tubers

- ❏ Beauregard sweet potatoes
- ❏ Japanese sweet potatoes
- ❏ Jersey sweets (white sweet potatoes)
- ❏ Jerusalem artichokes (sunchokes)
- ❏ Potatoes: cara, wilja, atriona, record, desiree, new, ratte, russet, Idaho, yellow Finn, Yukon gold, butterball, fingerling, or other
- ❏ Red garnet or jewel "yams" (actually sweet potatoes)

a closet or pantry. Check them frequently and discard if the tubers sprout or the skin begins to green.

Note: Use cooked tubers within 3 to 4 days or freeze.

Dried Vegetables

What to look for

Seek out non-irradiated dried vegetables free of additives, preservatives, salt, vegetable oils, sugars, dyes, and sulfites. Sun-dried tomatoes should be dry or packed in extra-virgin olive oil without salt or other preservatives.

Best sources: natural foods store, co-ops, mail order, or Internet. Favorite brands: Frontier Herbs and The Spice Hunter. Refer to Appendix D for dried powdered yam/sweet potato sources.

Amount to buy

For economy and convenience, we buy dried onions in 1-pound bags, sweet potato powder or flour by the pound, and enough dried vegetables flakes and bits to fill 4-ounce spice jars or pint jars. Buy sweet potato/yam flour by the pound if you have a use for it.

Storage tips

Dried vegetables will keep for a couple of years stored in sealed glass jars at room temperature.

Note: Label may say "freeze-dried."

Dried Vegetables
- ❑ Dried bell pepper bits
- ❑ Dried carrot bits
- ❑ Dried celery bits
- ❑ Dried chives
- ❑ Dried onion flakes
- ❑ Dried parsley flakes
- ❑ Sun-dried tomato halves
- ❑ Yam/sweet potato powder/flour or Yammit put out by Jay Robb Enterprises

Mushrooms

What to look for

Caps should be closed around the stems or just slightly open to reveal even textured gills free of soft, soggy, brown, or black spots.

Amount to buy

Purchase as needed. If you use mushrooms infrequently, buy dried varieties.

Note: Farmers' markets featuring local produce usually provide the freshest and least expensive shiitake mushrooms.

Storage tips

Fresh mushroom—Store in paper bags in the refrigerator; use within 6 days. If you store them in plastic bags, open or poke holes in the bags to allow air to circulate.

Dried mushrooms—Store in jars at room temperature; they will keep for years.

Mushrooms
- ❑ Button or cremini
- ❑ Oyster, porcini, enoki
- ❑ Shiitake

Sea Vegetables

☐ Alaria or wakame

☐ Ao-nori flakes

☐ Dulse flakes or granules

☐ Dulse, whole leaf

☐ Dulse, whole leaf, applewood smoked

☐ Kelp (kombu)

☐ Kelp, nori, or dulse granules with spices

☐ Ocean ribbons

☐ Sea palm

☐ Sushi nori (sheets)

☐ Wild nori (laver)

Sea Vegetables

Selection Criteria

1. *Best choice*: dried sea vegetables from your region or continent
2. *Second:* imported (dried) sea vegetables

What to avoid

1. products containing added salt, soy sauce, MSG, dyes, sugar, or preservatives

Best source: small sea vegetable harvesters (see Sources in Appendix D)

Second: natural foods store, co-op, or co-op buying club

Third: Asian market (ideal for sushi nori sheets, sold in economical 50 sheet packs)

What to look for

You want dried sea vegetables with nothing added. Avoid those that contain artificial flavorings, colorings, sugar, or salt. Asian markets sell pure product as well as products with additives, so read labels carefully.

To learn about the benefits of sea vegetables, refer to the Index. You may also want to do an Internet search for books and Web sites.

Amount to buy

Start with small packages if you're unfamiliar with sea vegetables.

Kelp and kombu are great for soups, stews, stock, and broth. Dulse and green nori flakes, and herb-and spice-seasoned seaflakes are perfect for sprinkling over food at the table. Sea palm, ocean ribbons, and dulse leaf are great for sautés and cooked vegetable salads. Eventually you may want to buy your favorites by the pound or in assorted 4-pound family packs.

We buy 50-sheet packs of sushi nori for about $8 in Asian grocery stores (a real bargain). You can cut them into hearts, moons, stars, or edible decorations for the dinner table or individual plates. Snip them into bits, like confetti, with kitchen shears, then sprinkle over salads, cooked greens, eggs, or fish, at the table. Use the sheets as a sort of tortilla wrap for salad, cooked vegetables, fish, and poultry. Sushi nori is delicious and practically calorie-free. Figure 1/2 to 1 sheet per person for a meal.

Keep sea flakes and herbed granules, toasted dulse, laver, wild nori, and sushi nori sheets on the table to replace the salt shaker.

Storage tips

Store dry sea vegetables indefinitely in their original packages or in wide-mouth jars at room temperature.

Refrigerate sea vegetables after soaking or cooking in water, broth, or stock. Toasted sea vegetables need no refrigeration and will not spoil.

Canned Vegetables

Selection Criteria

1. *Best choice*: organic, no-salt tomato products
2. *Second:* non-organic, no-salt tomato products

What to avoid

1. products containing added salt, soy sauce, MSG, sugar, oils, or preservatives
2. irradiated tomato products

Best sources: natural foods store, co-op, buying club, or health food section of supermarket.

What to look for

Choose products containing only ripe tomatoes and perhaps garlic, onion, and herbs.

Amount to buy

Buy tomato paste 4 to 6 cans at a time for Better Barbecue Sauce and quick pan sauces when fresh locally grown tomatoes are unavailable.

Note: Canning destroys a significant amount of vitamins, fiber, and flavor and usually adds salt. Avoid canning vegetables and fruits, other than tomatoes. Freezing and drying are more ecological options that also preserve more nutrients.

Storage tips

Store in a cool, dry place. Refrigerate in glass jars after opening.

Canned Vegetables

❑ Canned crushed or diced tomatoes

❑ Canned whole tomatoes

❑ Tomato paste

❑ Tomato or spaghetti sauce

Frozen Vegetables

Selection Criteria

1. *Best choice*: organic
2. *Second:* non-organic

What to avoid

1. products containing added salt, soy sauce, MSG, sugar, oils, dyes, or dairy products
2. irradiated frozen vegetables

Best sources: natural foods store, co-op, buying club, or supermarket

What to look for

Select loose packed bags rather than frozen blocks that take longer to thaw and cook.

Amount to buy

When traveling by car, frozen vegetables—carrots, onions, broccoli, peppers, and cauliflower—may be thawed in a cooler and served without cooking (they come blanched or parboiled). You can toss them with salad dressing for a convenient vegetable dish to go with beef jerky, hard-boiled eggs, canned fish, previously cooked chicken, etc. How much you need will depend on your use, family size, and the number of freezers you own.

Frozen vegetables are not essential. We prefer fresh vegetables, however, frozen spinach, Brussels sprouts, broccoli, bell peppers,

Frozen Vegetables

❑ Bell pepper strips

❑ Broccoli

❑ Broccoli, carrot, water chestnut blend

❑ Broccoli, cauliflower blend

❑ Brussels sprouts

❑ Cauliflower

❑ Kale, collards, or mustard greens

❑ Oriental/stir fry blend or Italian Mix

❑ Spinach, cut leaf, in bags

❑ Winter squash

Fresh Fruits

- ❑Apples
- ❑Apricots
- ❑Bananas
- ❑Blackberries
- ❑Blueberries
- ❑Boysenberries
- ❑Cantaloupe
- ❑Canary melon
- ❑Cherries
- ❑Cranberries
- ❑Crenshaw melon
- ❑Dates (fresh)
- ❑Fresh figs
- ❑Grapes
- ❑Grapefruit
- ❑Honeydew melon
- ❑Kiwi fruit
- ❑Lemons
- ❑Limes
- ❑Lingonberries
- ❑Mangoes
- ❑Marionberries
- ❑Mulberries
- ❑Nectarines
- ❑Papayas
- ❑Peaches
- ❑Pears
- ❑Pineapple
- ❑Plums
- ❑Raspberries
- ❑Strawberries
- ❑Tangerines/Tangelos
- ❑Watermelon

and winter squash can be handy during winter or spring in a northern climate, or when you're pressed for time and can't get to the market or store.

If you have a garden, consider chopping, parboiling and freezing broccoli, cauliflower, spinach, collards, mustard greens, and kale during the fall, for use during the winter. I sometimes sauté kale, collards, or Brussels sprouts in quantity, then freeze in pint containers to thaw and serve (they don't need to be warmed, unless they are semi-frozen or the weather is cold) when I'm especially busy. They are delicious served cold like a salad.

Storage tips

Store in original packages (or freezer-proof containers) in the freezer. Use within 4 to 6 months.

Fresh Fruits
Selection Criteria
1. *Best choice*: organic or wild, vine-ripened locally grown
2. *Second*: locally grown, non-organic
3. *Third*: organic, imported

What to avoid
1. canned fruits and fruits treated with sulfites (sulfur dioxide), sugar, or dyes
2. irradiated fruits
3. waxed fruits

Best sources: farmers' market, natural foods store, or co-op
Second best: local produce outlet or supermarket

What to look for

* *Apples*—These should be firm, crisp, and free of soft spots, blemishes, and wrinkles. Bright color indicates maturity. Farmers' markets sell numerous varieties not sold in supermarkets. Color depends upon the particular variety. Small- to medium-size apples will generally have more flavor than large, overgrown fruits.

* *Bananas*—Be sure to buy bananas free of bruises with the skin intact at both ends. Green color indicates they were not gassed to accelerate ripening. They will ripen further at home. Avoid storing bananas in the refrigerator or freezing in skins if you don't want the skin to turn brown.

* *Grapes*—Look for plump, compact clusters, firmly attached to stems. They will not ripen further.

* *Kiwi*—When ripe these will yield gently to pressure.

* *Mangoes and papayas*—Skins should be smooth and orange to yellow or red, depending upon the variety. The more green or yellow, the less ripe they are. They are ready to eat when they yield to gentle pressure and smell fruity. If you buy them hard, allow them to ripen at room temperature.

* *Melons*—These may be ripe or unripe at the time of purchase. They will ripen further at room temperature. When they are ready to eat they will have a pleasant aroma and yield to pressure at the blossom end. Try heirloom varieties, if possible.

* *Cantaloupe*—Skins should be thick with firm netting that stands out like relief work.

* *Honeydew*—Skin should be soft and velvety smooth.

* *Watermelon*—Skin should be smooth with a slight dullness. When thumped with your finger, mature melon will have a muffled "ping". An immature watermelon produces a higher pitched sound.

* *Nectarines, peaches, and apricots*—Pick brightly colored fruits with slight softening along seam. They should be fairly firm or just starting to soften. Colors vary. Farmers' markets sell varieties not found in supermarkets.

* *Pears*—Pick fruits that are firm, but not rock hard. They will ripen further at home. Different varieties will have different colored skin, ranging from yellow to green to red. Asian pear apples will be very crisp, even when ripe.

* *Pineapple*—The skin may be gold, yellow, orange, or reddish brown, depending on the variety. You can buy them ripe or unripe. They will mature more at home. They are ready to eat when they emit a fruity fragrance, have a slight separation of the eyes and leaves, and the spikes pull out easily. Avoid brownish pineapple, which is too ripe and actually rotten. Check the bottom of a pineapple for mold.

* *Plums*—Look for stone fruits that are fragrant with slightly glowing skins that yield to gentle pressure. Color varies with the variety. Farmers' markets sell numerous varieties that may be yellow, blue, red, purple, even black.

* *Lemons, limes, oranges, and tangerines*—These should be firm, unblemished, free of soft spots. If they are soft, they should not be mushy. Ripe citrus fruits will smell fragrant and fruity. Avoid citrus fruits (other than limes) that have greenish markings, a sign of under-ripeness.

Amount to buy

We usually keep at least 3 varieties—and sometimes more—of fresh fruit on hand. Vary selections with the season, your appetite, and what you can find.

We buy oranges, bananas, and many other fruits by the half dozen or more. Depending on the season, source, and price, we buy berries one or more pints at a time. When we can get them directly from a grower, we buy stone fruits several pounds at a time. Melons, except for watermelon, are bought in duplicate. Depending on the season and source, we buy 3 to 6 pounds of apples at a time for eating and by the peck or bushel in the fall for dehydrating.

If you live in fruit-growing country, explore the many varieties of fruit that are available locally at farmers' markets or U-pick farms. Watch for the changing seasons.

Storage tips

Grapes, cherries, and berries—Sort through and discard decayed, moldy, or severely damaged pieces. Do not wash cherries or berries until ready to eat; excess moisture hastens decay and causes cracks in the skins. Refrigerate immediately after sorting. Store rinsed, drained fruits in glass bowls in the refrigerator.

Melons, pineapple, and other fruits—If unripe, store in bowls or hanging baskets at room temperature. Once ripe and sliced, refrigerate in glass jars and use within 3 days or freeze.

Apples, oranges, lemons, limes, and grapefruit—Store at room temperature or in refrigerate crisper bins, or bowls, space permitting. In late autumn and winter, extra apples may be stored in a cold attic or on a cold porch, where they might keep for a few months.

If you have too many lemons or limes, squeeze the juice into a large measuring container, pour into ice cube trays, freeze, then transfer to sealable freezer containers. They'll be ready when you want them for salad dressings, sauces, marinades, salsa, guacamole, or lemonade. (Standard ice cube trays produce cubes containing 1 1/2 to 2 tablespoons of liquid.)

Peel, slice, dice, or cube a ripe melon, mango, or pineapple. Refrigerate each in a covered bowl or wide-mouth pint or quart jars and eat within 3 days or freeze on cookie sheets, then transfer to freezer containers. They are great for smoothies, Frosty Fruit Whips, Vita Mix Total Juices, or to purée in a food processor for a split-second sorbet on a steamy day. Almost any ripe fruit may be sliced, pitted, and frozen. (See Index for recipes.)

Dried Fruits

☐ Apricots (we prefer Turkish), pitted

☐ Cherries (fruit sweetened)

☐ Cranberries (fruit sweetened)

☐ Currants

☐ Dates, pitted

☐ Date-Coconut Rolls

☐ Figs (we prefer black mission)

☐ Nectarines

☐ Peaches

☐ Pears

☐ Pineapple rings

☐ Prunes, pitted (aka dried plums)

☐ Raisins

Dried Fruits
Selection Criteria

1. *Best choice*: sulfite-free, unsweetened, biodynamically grown or organic
2. *Second*: sulfite-free, unsweetened, non-organic

What to avoid

1. products with added sugar, dextrose, sucrose, fructose, oil, sulfur dioxide (sulfites), and dyes
2. irradiated fruits

Best sources: Natural foods store, co-op, buying club. Read labels carefully. Buy dried fruit with nothing added (other than fruit juice for tart fruits, like cranberries). Natural food stores sell Date-Coconut Rolls (see Sources in Appendix D)

Second: Health food or produce section of supermarket

Amount to buy

We buy dried fruits by the pound or half-pound and keep at least 4 varieties on hand for cooking, snacks, and desserts. Date-Coconut Rolls are soft, pulverized, pitted dates rolled in sulfite-free unsweetened coconut. There are many delicious varieties of raisins, dried apricots, figs, dates, and other fruits.

Storage tips

Store dried fruits at room temperature in sealed, wide-mouth pint or quart jars. Dried fruit will keep almost indefinitely. In hot and/or humid weather, store in the refrigerator (space permitting) or freezer. (That's where I keep extra fruits I've dried.)

Frozen Fruits

Selection Criteria

1. *Best choice*: organic, unsweetened
2. *Second*: non-organic, unsweetened

What to avoid

1. products with added chemical preservatives, sugar, or salt
2. irradiated fruits

Best sources: natural foods store, co-op, buying club, or frozen food section of supermarket

What to look for

Select frozen fruit with nothing added, except possibly citric or malic acid to prevent discoloration.

Amount to buy

Buy your favorites in duplicate, triplicate, or in 2- to 5-pound bags from a supermarket, natural foods market, or co-op buying club. Keep at least 3 varieties on hand.

Rinse and drain fresh blueberries to freeze. Chop other seasonal fruits into bite-size pieces when bargains abound and freeze for future smoothies, Frosty Fruit Whips, or to thaw and serve with Vanilla-Protein Coconut Cream or a dusting of shredded, unsweetened coconut. (See Index for recipes.)

Note: Raspberries and blackberries generally have too many seeds for smoothies.

Storage tips

Freeze in original packaging. Seal opened bags with twist-ties. Use frozen fruit within 6 to 8 months. Fruit may be thawed or used frozen for smoothies.

Use only frozen (not thawed) fruit for Frosty Fruit Whips. To defrost fruit for a side dish, empty a frozen package into a glass jar or bowl with a cover (to save the juices) and refrigerate all day or overnight, then use within 24 hours.

Juices

Selection Criteria

1. *Best choice*: organic, unsweetened
2. *Second*: non-organic, unsweetened

What to avoid

1. products with added preservatives, sugar, or salt
2. irradiated fruits

Best sources: natural foods store, co-op, or buying club

Second: supermarket

Note: For fresh pressed cider, check your local farmers' market.

Frozen Fruits
- ❑ Blackberries
- ❑ Blueberries
- ❑ Mango chunks
- ❑ Melon, cherry, grape
- ❑ Melon balls
- ❑ Mixed berries
- ❑ Peaches, sliced
- ❑ Pineapple chunks
- ❑ Pitted sweet cherries
- ❑ Raspberries
- ❑ Strawberry, mango, pineapple
- ❑ Strawberries

Juices
- ❑ Apple cider or apple juice or concentrate
- ❑ Cherry juice or concentrate
- ❑ Orange juice or concentrate
- ❑ Pineapple juice or concentrate
- ❑ Red grape juice or concentrate
- ❑ Tomato juice (unsalted or low-sodium)

What to look for

Choose 100 percent real fruit juice or fruit juice concentrate and fresh or frozen carrot juice.

Amount to buy

Keep several bottles in the pantry and a couple of containers of concentrate in the freezer for poaching fish or fowl, sweetening chutney, barbecue sauce, salad dressings, or replacing wine, sugar, and syrups in cooking.

Note: Pure fruit juice makes an acceptable alternative to cocktails, wine, and soda. As a beverage, juice is best limited because of its high sugar and low fiber content.

Fruit juice may be diluted 50:50 with herbal tea for an occasional beverage.

Storage tips

Refrigerate bottles of juice after opening. Refrigerate unpasteurized juices immediately; when they turn hard (alcoholic) you can use them to replace wine in cooking.

Nuts & Seeds

❑ Almonds

❑ Cashews

❑ Chestnuts, cooked, peeled, frozen

❑ Chestnuts, dried, steam peeled

❑ Chestnuts, in shell

❑ Coconut milk (canned)

❑ Coconut, shredded

❑ Coconut whole, in the shell

❑ Macadamia nuts

❑ Pecans

❑ Pinon nuts (pine nuts)

❑ Pumpkin seeds (green, hulled variety)

❑ Sesame seeds (whole, with hull intact)

❑ Sunflower seeds

❑ Walnuts

Nuts and Seeds

Selection Criteria

1. *Best choice*: organic raw nuts and seeds in the shell
2. *Second*: non-organic raw nuts and seeds in the shell
3. *Third*: organic, raw, shelled, and refrigerated whole nuts, seeds, and nut halves
4. *Fourth*: non-organic shelled and refrigerated whole nuts, seeds, and nut halves
5. *Fifth*: shelled, raw, whole nuts, seeds, and nut halves sold at room temperature

What to avoid

1. roasted, salted or sweetened nuts, seeds, or coconut
2. nuts, seeds, and coconut containing sulfur dioxide (sulfites), dyes, maltodextrin and other starches, MSG, and preservatives
3. crushed or slivered nuts or nut pieces (usually rancid)
4. irradiated nuts and seeds

Note: If you enjoy roasted nuts, lightly dry toast them without oil or salt. (See Index for recipe.)

Best sources: natural foods store, co-op, buying club, or farmers' market

Second: supermarket

Look for plain coconut milk on the ethnic aisle of supermarkets or natural foods stores.

For locally grown nuts and seeds and fresh chestnuts in the shell, check your local farmers' market.

Look for steam-peeled, dried chestnuts in Asian and Italian markets. Gourmet and Asian markets usually sell peeled, frozen chesnuts.

What to look for

* *Shelled nuts*—Color and texture should be even and uniform. If mottled with oily or dry spots, they are probably rancid. Ideally, they'll be sold refrigerated to retard spoilage.

* *Shredded coconut*—The label should say "sulfite-free, unsweetened coconut," and nothing else. Large flaked pieces are great for trail mix; smaller flakes are best for garnishing fruit salads or making macaroons. You can turn large flakes into small flakes in a blender or food processor.

* *Canned coconut milk*—This product should contain only coconut and water with the possible addition of guar gum, a natural vegetable-based thickener.

* *Dried, peeled chestnuts*—These should have an even color and texture and be free of wormholes and black spots.

* *Frozen, peeled chestnuts*—These should be free of additives and sugar.

Amount to buy

We regularly keep 3 varieties of nuts on hand to garnish cooked vegetables, fruits, salads, and to make nut butter, smoothies, sauces, spreads, salad dressings, and desserts. Buy 1- to 5-pound bags, depending upon how often you use them and your family and freezer size. We buy fresh chestnuts 2 pounds at a time in the fall and winter, dried or frozen chestnuts one or more pound at a time, and canned coconut milk several cans at a time or by the case to economize.

Storage tips

* *Nuts, seeds, and flaked coconut*—Store in refrigerator or freezer, preferably in glass jars. Use within 12 months if refrigerated; 3 years if frozen. Nuts in the shell will last longer.

* *Chestnuts*—Store fresh chestnuts in the shell in the coolest part of house (the refrigerator, attic, or cold porch) for 2 to 4 weeks or freeze for up to 4 months. (See Index for preparation tips.) Keep dried, peeled chestnuts in sealed jars at room temperature for several months, or in the freezer for up to several years. Refrigerate cooked chestnuts and use within 1 week. Keep frozen chestnuts in the freezer until ready to use.

* *Canned coconut milk*—Store unopened cans at room temperature. Do not be alarmed if the milk is very thick or has separated in the can. If it doesn't easily emulsify with a fork or whisk, purée the entire contents of the can in a blender until smooth. Either way, refrigerate opened coconut milk in a sealed glass jar and use within 5 days or freeze in ice cube trays for longer storage. You can drop frozen coconut milk cubes into a soup pot, add to a blender with fruit for a smoothie, or defrost in a jar.

* *Whole coconuts*—Store fresh coconuts at room temperature if the brown shell is intact. Keep young, fresh coconuts without a hard

shell (exterior will be white) in the refrigerator and use promptly. The latter should be free of green, brown or black spots.

Nut & Seed Butters

☐Almond butter, roasted

☐Cashew butter, roasted

☐Hazelnut, pecan or pistachio butter, roasted

☐Macadamia nut butter, roasted

☐Peanut butter, roasted (organic)

☐Sesame tahini, roasted

Nut and Seed Butters

Selection Criteria

1. *Best choice*: organic, roasted, unsalted, unsweetened
2. *Second*: non-organic, roasted, unsalted, unsweetened

What to avoid

1. products containing vegetable oils, hydrogenated oils, salt, sugar, or honey
2. products containing soybeans, soy protein, or emulsifiers

Best sources: natural food store, co-op, or co-op buying club

Second: natural foods market, natural foods section of supermarket, or mail order

What to look for

Nut butter and tahini should contain dry roasted nuts or seeds, nothing more! We prefer the flavor of roasted nut butters over raw.

When purchasing peanut butter, it's worth paying more for organic because conventional peanuts are usually grown in rotation with cotton, one of the most heavily sprayed crops containing high levels of pesticides and herbicides.

Amount to buy

Buy your favorites in duplicate or triplicate (unless you plan to make your own). We usually keep almond butter and sesame tahini on hand, and sometimes cashew or macadamia nut butter. We use peanut butter less often.

Storage tips

Immediately refrigerate if sold in plastic tubs in the refrigerator section of natural foods stores. Refrigerate bottled nut butters and tahini after opening.

Note: Oil separation is natural. After opening a new jar of nut butter, immediately transfer contents to a food processor or bowl; process until smooth, return to the original jar, and refrigerate. The mixture will be easy to spread and will never separate again. Use opened jars within 6 months.

Fats and Oils

Selection Criteria

1. *Best choice*: organic extra-virgin oils packed in dark bottles
2. *Second*: unsalted, real creamery butter, clarified butter, or ghee, preferably organic
3. *Third*: unrefined or virgin-pressed palm oil

What to avoid

1. refined, bleached, and deodorized coconut and vegetable oils

2. oils sold in clear bottles (They're almost always rancid.)
3. margarine, shortening, and all hydrogenated and partially hydrogenated fats and oils, and butter substitutes made from vegetable oils other than olive and flax
4. vegetable oils: soy, safflower, sunflower, peanut, canola, cottonseed, generic "vegetable oils, "salad oil," Wesson, Mazola, Crisco, and other refined oils

Best sources: natural food store, health food co-op, co-op buying club, or gourmet market

Second best: extra-virgin olive oil and butter from a supermarket, ethnic market, mail order, or by Internet

Third: coconut oil from an ethnic market

What to look for

Virgin-pressed oils sold in dark bottles will have a darker, more vibrant green or gold color and a more pronounced fragrance and flavor than refined supermarket oils and health food store oils sold in clear bottles. They will also be more nutritious.

* *Fish oil*—Seek out Carlson's Lemon-Flavored Fish Oil (very palatable) or pharmaceutical-grade (molecularly distilled) fish oil. Either may be used at the table, spooned over individual servings of salad or steamed broccoli, or combined with olive oil in any vinaigrette recipe. Do not heat or cook with fish oil.

* *Flax oil*—Buy unrefined, virgin-pressed flax oil sold in dark bottles. The best tasting brands we've found are Barleen's (lignan-free version), Flora, and Omega Nutrition. Good fresh flax oil is neither harsh nor bitter tasting.

Don't try to eat flax oil off the spoon to get your essential fatty acids. Instead, use it to replace a portion of olive oil in salad dressings and mayonnaise, to replace all or a portion of coconut milk or nut butter in smoothies, smoothie bases, blender puddings, or to replace butter as a topping for sweet potatoes in meals or snacks.

Flax oil should never be used for cooking or baking. Polyunsaturated oils break down when heated, creating carcinogenic lipid peroxides and varnish-like coatings on baking pans.

* *Sesame oil*—The label should say "untoasted" and "unrefined" or "virgin-pressed," and the bottle should be dark brown or green to screen out light, which causes oxidation and spoilage. Eden Foods and Flora make the best sesame oil we've found.

* *Coconut oil*—Seek out unrefined, virgin-pressed coconut oil in a dark bottle or heavy duty plastic container. Use this to replace vegetable oils, margarine, shortening, and/or butter in cooking, baking, or at the table. (Refer to the Index and Appendix for sources and to learn more about the benefits of coconut oil.) Great brands: Garden of Life, Omega Nutrition, and Coconut Oil Supreme.

* *Butter*—Buy unsalted butter with nothing added. Try regular or cultured. Grass-fed is best.

* *Clarified butter or ghee*—Look for plain unflavored products. Ghee may be flavored with garlic or herbs for use at the table.

Fats & Oils

❑ Clarified butter and/ or ghee

❑ Extra-virgin olive oil

❑ Flax oil, virgin-pressed

❑ Molecularly distilled fish oil or lemon flavored cod liver oil

❑ Real creamery butter, unsalted

❑ Unrefined or virgin-pressed coconut oil

❑ Unrefined, extra-virgin or virgin-pressed sesame oil

❑ Vitamin E oil, 1-ounce bottle

* *Palm oil*—The label should say unrefined or virgin-pressed.

What to avoid

refined oils, even if the label says organic

Amount to buy

We buy 32-ounce bottles of olive and flax oils, 24- to 32-ounce tubs of coconut oil, 12-ounce bottles of lemon-flavored cod liver, and butter by the pound. Occasionally we use virgin-pressed sesame oil for salad dressings or mayonnaise where olive oil would be too strong.

Note: To prevent premature spoilage of oils, buy a small bottle of vitamin E oil, and add a few drops to any newly opened bottle and to all homemade salad dressings.

Storage tips

Coconut and olive oil—These may be stored at room temperature in dark bottles. Coconut oil will be thick below 74° F and liquid above 74°F. It is stable enough to withstand repeated thickening and melting at room temperature and has a shelf life of 3 years.

Fish oil—Refrigerate after purchasing.

Flax oil—Store in the freezer. Because it is super-unsaturated, flax oil will remain liquid and pourable in the freezer to prolong shelf life. The refrigerator is acceptable, but not as good.

Butter—Refrigerate or freeze what you won't use within a month. A single or partial stick may be kept at room temperature, loosely covered, in a glass container or crock away from direct sunlight or hot appliances. Ghee will keep at room temperature for 6 to 12 months. Clarified butter should be refrigerated.

Adding Spice to Your Life

Herbs and Spices for Better Nutrition

Most herbs and spices stimulate digestion and improve the flow of digestive juices, which make us feel better. They contain numerous nutrients including vitamins, calcium, minerals, enzymes, antioxidants, and phytonutrients that enhance health in ways too numerous to mention here. Added to our basic foods, these simple seasonings increase our enjoyment of eating.

Although herbs and spices aren't calorically dense, since they help us digest and get more nutrition and pleasure out of calorically dense foods, they are worth foraging to find.

Enhancing What is Natural

The art of whole foods cooking involves bringing out the natural flavors in foods with the least amount of interference.

That's where herbs and spices come in. It is only when used improperly or to excess that they mask or distort foods' natural flavors or cause irritation. Herbs and spices are natural flavors, yet many modern cooks lack an understanding of their importance or know how to use them.

Herbs & Spices

- ❏ Allspice
- ❏ Anaheim or ancho peppersl
- ❏ Anise seed
- ❏ Apple pie spice
- ❏ Basil leaf
- ❏ Bay leaf
- ❏ Cajun spice blend (unsalted)
- ❏ Cardamom pods
- ❏ Cardamom seeds (removed from pod)
- ❏ Cayenne, ground (great for cuts)
- ❏ Cayenne peppers
- ❏ Celery seed
- ❏ Chili powder, salt-free
- ❏ Chipotlé, ground
- ❏ Chives, freeze dried
- ❏ Cinnamon, ground
- ❏ Cinnamon, twigs
- ❏ Cloves whole or ground
- ❏ Cream of tartar (for macaroons and meringues)
- ❏ Cumin, ground
- ❏ Cumin seed, whole
- ❏ Curry powder
- ❏ Dill blend
- ❏ Dill weed

~Continued next page~

Our recipes will show you how to use herbs and spices. To learn more about the therapeutic properties of your favorite herbs and spices, consult the library, on-line information sources, books, and the magazines *Herbs for Health*, and *The Herb Companion*. Space does not permit us to go into detail about the many herbs and spices we regularly use.

Tempt Your Taste Buds

Herbs and spices help to enhance the enjoyment of a produce- and protein-rich diet. The tricks are to use a light hand, to measure, use time-tested herb and spice combinations, and follow recipes until you memorize your favorites and know the character of a wide array of herbs and spices.

As you get the hang of using a wider variety of herbs, spices, and other natural seasonings, you will know which seasonings go well together, what dishes each seasoning works in, what to add, when to add it, and how much to use for the desired effect. With repetition, using herbs and spices will become a habit.

Defining Herbs and Spices

Spice applies to dried roots, barks, pods, seeds, and berries, while herb refers to leaves, flowers, shoots, and stems. Black pepper, red pepper, chili powder, cardamom, cinnamon, ginger, fennel, cumin, mustard, and nutmeg are spices. Bay leaf, basil, oregano, thyme, dill, parsley, sage, rosemary, tarragon, chives, and marjoram are herbs.

Herbs are generally more volatile than spices and more easily injured by overcooking or too high heat. Fresh (as opposed to dried) herbs are the most volatile and should generally be added during the last few minutes of cooking. Spices are sturdier; they can take (and give) more heat. Whole spices, such as cinnamon sticks, bay leaves, vanilla beans, whole cloves, and peppercorns, often require longer cooking to release their flavors and should be removed before serving.

Herbs and Spices
Selection Criteria
1. *Best choice*: non-irradiated, preferably organic herbs and spices
2. *Second*: non-irradiated, commercially grown herbs and spices

What to avoid
1. products containing salt, MSG, sugar, corn syrup, FD & C dyes, artificial flavorings and colorings
2. products with hydrogenated or partially hydrogenated oils, chemical names and numbers
3. irradiated herbs and spices

Best sources: natural food store, co-op, buying club, ethnic market, or mail order

~Herbs/spices cont.~

❏ Dry mustard powder

❏ Fennel seed, whole

❏ Garam masala (a blend)

❏ Garlic, fresh

❏ Garlic, granules—or powder

❏ Ginger, ground, powder

❏ Gingerroot, fresh

❏ Herbs de Provençe (a blend)

❏ Lemon pepper (a blend)

❏ Marjoram leaf (optional)

❏ Mustard seeds, yellow

❏ Nutmeg, ground

❏ Orange peel, dried

❏ Oregano leaf

❏ Paprika, ground

❏ Peppercorns, white, black, red, green, or mixed (whole for pepper mill, stock, or broth)

❏ Pepper, black, ground

❏ Pure almond extract

❏ Pure maple extract

❏ Pure vanilla extract

❏ Rosehips, cut/ deseeded or rosehip powder

❏ Rosemary

❏ Sage, rubbed

❏ Sumac, ground

❏ Tarragon

❏ Thyme leaf

❏ Turmeric, ground

Second: health food section of supermarket, specialty kitchen shop or ethnic market

What to look for

Stores with a rapid turnover of product will have the freshest herbs and spices. You can buy flavoring extracts in alcohol or vegetable glycerine. Extracts bottled in glycerine add additional sweetness to your recipes without sugar and are preferable for recipes where the extract will not be cooked. Alcohol-based extracts can add an unpleasant taste to smoothies and other uncooked dishes or beverages. The glycerine is derived from coconut or other fruits.

Best brands: Frontier Herbs, Spicery Shoppe, The Spice Hunter

Second: *Salt-free* herbs, spices, and blends from Penzeys Spices or The Spice House. (Refer to Sources in Appendix D.)

Amount to buy

We have 50 herb and spice jars in our collection—some in both whole and powdered form—and use at least half of them regularly. We mainly use dried herbs and spices. In some recipes, spices are lightly dry roasted to produce a more intense flavor, ground to a powder in a spice-dedicated coffee grinder, then added to a recipe; in others we cook whole spices—such as bay leaf or peppercorns—then removed them before serving.

Ground spices are convenient; however, cumin, mustard, fennel, cardamom, and anise seeds, cloves, star anise, black pepper, and herbs such as dried rosemary and sage taste better if you grind them fresh and use them within 3 months.

To economize, buy herbs and spices from the bulk section of a natural foods store or co-op. You needn't buy a lot. You can purchase as little as a tablespoon or an ounce, or as much as a cup. This allows you to experiment with new seasonings without committing to an entire bottle. Once you know what you like, you can purchase amounts to fill your spice jars (usually 1/2 cupful per jar).

About fresh herbs

Some cooks prefer fresh herbs, however they are more perishable and must be used, or dried, soon after picking or purchase. If you rely only on fresh herbs, you won't enjoy as wide a variety, unless you have a large year-round garden.

Note: You can replace 1 teaspoon of dried herbs with 1 tablespoon of fresh herbs, and vice-versa.

Storage tips

Store dried herbs and spices in sealed, dark bottles that exclude light, in a cool, dry place. If you have only clear bottles, store in a cupboard to prevent discoloration and loss of flavor.

* Dried herbs and spices—Store in airtight jars at room temperature. Natural food co-ops and companies, such as Frontier Herbs, sell dark spice bottles with labels by the dozen. Do not store directly on or near a stove, dishwasher,

refrigerator, microwave oven, heater vents, or shelves receiving bright sunlight.

 * *Fresh gingerroot and garlic*—Keep fresh garlic and gingerroot at room temperature in bowls, ceramic crocks, or hanging wire baskets. Do not refrigerate.

Note: Bottled ginger and ginger juice must be refrigerated after opening.

 * *Fresh herbs*—R

clean moist cloth napkin.

Sweeteners
Selection Criteria
 1. *Best choice*: Stevia extract powder* or liquid or kiwi concentrate (trutina dulcem)
 2. *Second*: dates, date sugar, raisins, and pure fruit juice
 3. *Third*: honey, agavé nectar (cactus honey)*, date syrup, and fruit juice concentrate
 4. *Fourth*: maple syrup or maple granules

What to avoid
 1. brown and white sugar (sucrose), fructose powder, corn syrup, high fructose corn syrup
 2. dried cane juice (Sucanat), Rapidura, cane syrup
 3. artificial sweeteners: Equal, Aspartame, saccharin, malitol, Splenda (chlorinated sugar), sucralose, etc.

 *   ***Note:*** Refer to Index for information on stevia and agavé nectar.

Best sources: natural foods store, co-op, buying club, farmers' market, mail order, or kitchen shop

Second: health food section of supermarket (honey is sold everywhere)

Amount to buy
Our kitchen is always stocked with stevia extract powder and liquid, dried dates and/or Date-Coconut Rolls, date sugar, and raw honey or agavé nectar. Occasionally we buy kiwi concentrate, maple syrup, or maple granules.

About concentrated sweeteners
Dried or dried and powdered fruits, dried fruit purées, and mashed bananas are preferable to sugar, corn syrup, and other caloric sweeteners because they are unrefined and contain more vitamins, minerals, fiber, and antioxidants.

Date sugar and date syrup are easily made from dried, pitted dates and contain potassium and other minerals found in whole fruits. Honey is rich in antioxidants and enzymes that are absent from refined sugar. Nevertheless, concentrated sweeteners are calorie dense and easily over-used, so it's best to use them sparingly and infrequently, not as daily staples or in large amounts. When we use

---

Sweeteners

❏ Agavé nectar (cactus honey), light or dark

❏ Stevia extract powder

❏ Dates (dried whole, pitted, or date-coconut rolls)

❏ Date sugar (dried, powdered dates)

❏ Honey, preferably raw and unfiltered

❏ Maple syrup or maple granules

❏ Stevia extract liquid or stevia glycerite

❏ Trutina, kiwi concentrate (TriMedica, Slim Sweet, KiSweet)

concentrated sweeteners, we usually pair them with stevia extract powder or liquid, so we don't need as much.

Storage tips

Store all sweeteners at room temperature in jars or the original canisters. They will keep almost indefinitely.

Herbal Teas

Note: What follows are some of our favorites. Your selections may vary.

❑ Black currant tea

❑ Black seed tea with rooibos or peppermint

❑ Ethiopian tea

❑ Ginger tea bags

❑ Green tea (caffeine-free)

❑ Lemon zinger tea

❑ Maté/Yerba Maté tea

❑ Peppermint tea

❑ Raspberry or blackberry zinger tea

❑ Red zinger tea

❑ Roasted chicory root (granules, pieces, or tea bags)

❑ Roasted dandelion root (granules, pieces, or tea bags)

❑ Rooibos tea (African Red Bush tea)

❑ Rosehip tea

❑ Spearmint tea

Herbal Teas

Selection Criteria

1. *Best choice*: organic herbal teas
2. *Second*: non-organic, unsweetened, preservative-free herbal teas

What to avoid

1. teas containing sugars, artificial sweeteners, artificial flavorings and colorings
2. irradiated tea
3. products containing caffeine*

> *** Note:** Black tea and green tea both contain caffeine, but less than coffee, and may be a suitable substitute during your transition away from coffee. (See Index for more on coffee and coffee alternatives.) Red bush tea and most other herbal teas are caffeine-free.

Best sources: natural foods store, co-op, buying club, mail order, kitchen shops, or health section of supermarket

Second: specialty tea house or tea shop

Amount to buy

We like keeping half a dozen varieties on hand. Experiment with single herb teas and blends. Try your favorites hot or cold. Herbal teas sweetened lightly with stevia present a healthful alternative to soda, wine, beer, and sugary fruit drinks. Some herbal brews can replace the look or taste of coffee without the caffeine.

What to look for

* *Roasted chicory and dandelion root*—This is sold dry, as small diced pieces you can simmer or brew like coffee, as loose coffee-like grinds, or in tea bags you can steep like tea.

* *Herbal teas*—Look for products with the simplest, fewest, and purest ingredients.

Storage tips

Store at room temperature in original container. Store bulk or loose tea in jars.

Miscellaneous Foods

Selection Criteria

1. *Best choice:* organically grown ingredients
2. *Second:* non-organic, unsweetened, preservative-free product

What to avoid

1. products with added sugar (including maltose and dextrose), sulfites, or aluminum
2. products with artificial flavorings and colorings, artificial sweeteners, propylene glycol, MSG, polysorbate, and chemical names and numbers
3. irradiated products
4. sweetened or flavored gelatin products

Best sources: natural foods stores, co-ops, buying clubs, mail order, Internet, health food sections of supermarkets, and specialty or gourmet shops

Second: some found in supermarkets

What to look for

* *Arrowroot*—White, flavorless, odorless starch that is used as a thickener. It's a more-nutritious, less-refined alternative to cornstarch.

Look for bottles or bulk in natural foods stores, herb shops, and supermarkets. If possible, buy it in bulk, rather than in small jars, to save money.

Note: You may replace arrowroot with kuzu starch (see Table of Equivalents and Substitutions, Appendix C), however, kuzu costs many times more per pound, so we don't use it.

* *Vinegar*—Seek out organic, sulfite-free brands, including unpasteurized raw apple cider vinegar, balsamic and red wine vinegars. Unsweetened brown rice vinegar may also be used.

* *Prepared mustard and hot sauce*—Look for low-salt natural brands free of preservatives and additives, artificial colorings, and sugars. Some of our favorites include Eden, Westbrae, Edward and Sons, and True Natural Taste Organic White Mustards.

Add mustard to salad dressings and sauces, smear over fish, fowl, or meat before baking, roasting, or grilling, over steaks, burgers, and meatballs at the table, or use as a fat-free spread for sprouted bread.

* *Chocolate, unsweetened bars*—These should contain only unsweetened chocolate.

* *Cocoa powdered*—Look for unsweetened, preferably organic cocoa powder.

* *Carob powder*—Buy raw or roasted carob powder free of added sugars.

* *Unflavored gelatin*—This is sold as flakes or powder (also known as beef gelatin). Natural foods stores and mail order outlets sell it in bulk. You may also use Knox unflavored gelatin in our recipes. Avoid sugared or flavored gelatin products.

Misc. Foods

- ❏ Apple cider vinegar, organic, unpasteurized
- ❏ Apple fiber powder (NOW FOODS brand)
- ❏ Arrowroot powder/ starch
- ❏ Balsamic vinegar, preferably organic
- ❏ Carob powder, raw or roasted
- ❏ Hot sauce, mild or hot (low sodium)
- ❏ Mustard, prepared (Dijon style, stoneground, yellow or white)
- ❏ Mustard (sun-dried tomato, jalapeno, smoked green chilies, or red chilies and garlic flavors)
- ❏ Natural Liquid Hickory Smoke Seasoning
- ❏ Organic or free-range chicken broth
- ❏ Red wine vinegar, preferably organic
- ❏ Shan yao (Radix Dioscorea)
- ❏ Unflavored gelatin (aka beef gelatin)
- ❏ Unrefined sea salt (Celtic, Fleur de Sel de Camargue or Lima brand)
- ❏ Unsweetened Baker's chocolate squares
- ❏ Unsweetened cocoa powder

Note: Agar agar, a vegetarian version of gelatin sold in natural foods stores, can be used as a substitute for unflavored gelatin, however you must use 2 or 3 times as much of it and simmer it longer than gelatin. Agar agar is far more costly at $120 a pound ($7.50 to $10 per ounce), so we don't use it.

* *Shan yao (Radix Dioscorea)*—Look for elliptical-shaped pieces of dried shan yao, a starchy white tuber sold in Asian markets, Chinese herb shops, and by mail. The dried pieces are easily powdered in a blender and make an excellent grain-free binder for meatballs, meatloaf, and fish cakes.

* *Chicken stock or broth*—Look for preservative-free "organic" or "free-range" chicken broth. Buy the lowest sodium brand you can find and avoid products that contain MSG, artificial flavorings, or hydrolyzed vegetable protein. Good brands include Shelton's, Trader Joes, and Imagine Foods.

* *Liquid hickory smoke seasoning*—Wright's brand is the purest one we have found. It contains the simplest and fewest ingredients and is free of artificial ingredients. Look for it in supermarkets on the condiment aisles near the barbecue sauces.

* *Sea salt*—Avoid refined salt, refined sea salt, and kosher salt, which are stripped of their natural minerals and usually contain dextrose, aluminum, anti-caking agents, and/or bleaches. Unrefined, slightly gray, truly sun-dried sea salt contains more than 83 trace minerals naturally found in seawater. You can use it to replace salt and refined sea salt in recipes. Although it contains slightly less sodium per teaspoon, there is no need to use more of it. Unrefined sea salt brings out a richer flavor in foods. It is best to use even this salt sparingly and in cooking or mixing in the kitchen rather than at the table.

Note: Coarse, sun-dried sea salt will dissolve into foods cooked in generous amounts of water (soup, stew, long sautés, etc.). For a finer texture, pour coarse moist, sun-dried sea salt into a pie plate and dry at room temperature or in an oven with the pilot on for 12 to 24 hours. Store in a salt grinder or grind in a mortar or suribachi and store in a sealed jar at room temperature.

Amount to buy

We buy most of the items on the list in 1/2- to 1-pound bags. We buy natural liquid hickory smoke seasoning and prepared mustards in duplicate so we never run out.

Storage tips

Store at room temperature. If purchased in plastic bags, transfer to glass jars. Refrigerate mustard and hot sauce after opening.

Grains and Grain Products (optional)
Selection Criteria

1. *Best Choice*: 100 percent *sprouted* whole-grain flour to make your own steamed bread (see Index and Appendix G for recipe)

2. *Second:* 100 percent sprouted, flourless, whole-grain loaf bread, tortillas, rolls, English muffins, and bagels, leavened with sourdough or yeast

3. *Third:* 100 percent whole-grain sourdough or desem-method bread, especially rye or barley, or organic whole corn tortillas made from whole corn with lime or whole corn masa (and nothing else, except possibly sea salt)

4. *Fourth:* wild rice, quinoa, amaranth, teff, kamut, spelt, and other ancient or heirloom grains, old-fashioned rolled or steel cut oats, whole oat groats, whole grain brown rice, or millet (rinsed, soaked, and thoroughly cooked, or sprouted, dried, ground and prepared with leavening)

What to avoid

1. refined, bleached, enriched, or deodorized flour, unbleached flour, cake flour, pastry flour, white or wheat flour, and products that contain them

2. instant or quick-cooking cereals (including instant oatmeal, cream of wheat, etc.), instant rice, cous cous, white rice, pasta, and macaroni

3. baked goods and flour products made with vegetable oil, shortening, margarine, hydrogenated or partially hydrogenated oils, added sugars, polysorbates, MSG, hydrolyzed vegetable protein, artificial colorings and flavorings, artificial additives, preservatives, and dough conditioners

4. cold cereals, granola, puffed, fluffed, and extruded grains, corn chips, fried taco shells, crackers, pretzels, deep-fried grain, cereal products, etc.

Best sources: natural food store, health food co-op, co-op buying club

Second: small local and natural foods bakeries or health food freezer section of supermarkets

What to look for

If you make your own bread, look for 100 percent sprouted whole-grain spelt, kamut, wheat, and rye flours. Or, sprout, dehydrate, and grind whole grains at home if you have the equipment and time. (Refer to Appendix D for mail order sources of 100 percent sprouted whole grain flour.)

Better store-bought breads are made from 100 percent sprouted whole grains, without flour; brands include Food for Life Ezekiel, Oasis, and Alvarado Street Bakery. These breads are less carbohydrate and calorie dense, more nutritious, more digestible, and less likely to promote health problems than conventional grain, cereal, bread, and flour products.

Sprouted, unleavened breads, such as Essene or Manna are undercooked and can be difficult to digest. They are heavy and extraordinarily calorie dense despite being made without flour, oil, or sugar. Because the grains are not completely ground and are very

Grains

❑ 100 percent sprouted, whole-grain flour (spelt, rye, barley, kamut, or wheat)

❑ 100 percent sprouted, flourless whole-grain loaf bread

❑ 100 percent sprouted, flourless whole-grain tortillas, rolls, or English muffins

❑ 100 percent whole corn tortillas made with lime

❑ Amaranth

❑ Brown rice (short, medium, or long grain)

❑ Chinese black rice or Thai black sweet rice

❑ Kamut berries (whole grain kamut)

❑ Millet (regular or glutinous)

❑ Red rice (whole grain)

❑ Rolled oats (old fashioned or thick)

❑ Rye berries (whole grain rye)

❑ Spelt berries (whole grain spelt)

❑ Teff

❑ Wheat berries (whole grain wheat)

❑ Whole oat groats

❑ Wild rice

❑ Quinoa

resistant to chewing, some individuals find that the grain sprouts leave the body looking much like they went in.

Amount to buy

Your use will dictate the amount you buy.

Storage tips

Whole grains or sprouted, dehydrated whole grains—Store in glass jars at room temperature for up to 3 years or refrigerate in humid weather or if you have a problem with bugs or moths in your home.

Flour and sprouted grain flour—Refrigerate or freeze and use within 7 to 12 months.

Cooked whole grains—Refrigerate and use within 4 days.

Bread and tortillas—Refrigerate or freeze. If refrigerated, use within 2 weeks. If frozen, use within 6 months.

Miscellaneous Non-Food Items

Best sources: natural foods store, co-op, buying club, mail order

Second: supermarket

Make your own produce, fish, and poultry wash

Add 16 drops of grapefruit seed extract to a 16-ounce spray bottle. Fill to the top with filtered water. Spray fresh produce, rub with your hands, and rinse thoroughly. (Do not rub berries!)

To wash lettuce, including prewashed greens, spray, rinse thoroughly, then spin dry.

You may spray the surface of raw fish or chicken, allow it to stand for 5 minutes, then rinse thoroughly to remove grapefruit seed extract and any surface bacteria prior to preparation.

Clean consciously

As you clean up your diet, you will also want to clean up your immediate environment, your home, and our ecosystem. If you eat good food, then gum up the works with toxic cleaning agents or lawn and garden chemicals, you will certainly limit your progress on the path to greater health.

Toxic chemicals can upset your biochemistry and hormones, causing sensitivity symptoms and more serious diseases. Sometimes a cure is achieved simply by removing the cause(s)—the toxic chemicals. Many people have observed improvement in or relief from respiratory and skin allergies, headaches, and fatigue, as well as an improvement in learning and behavior disorders in children as a direct result of removing toxic conventional chemical cleaning products from their homes.

Toxic lawn and garden care products and herbicide and pesticide sprays are an even greater danger to your health and the safety of our common wealth, the air and water. (Their fumes or residues pollute air and ground water.) Many are nervous system toxins, hormone disrupters, or carcinogens. Constant use of these chemicals has created "superbugs" and "superweeds" that are immune to their effects. There are safer, effective ways to groom your garden. Check

Misc. Non-Food

❑ Aluminum foil

❑ Baking soda to deodorize refrigerator

❑ Biodegradable, non-toxic scouring paste

❑ Biodegradable, non-toxic dish soap

❑ Citrus-based all-purpose cleaner

❑ Distilled vinegar for cleaning

❑ Grapefruit seed extract

❑ Plant-based cellulose food storage bags

❑ Unbleached paper muffin liners

❑ Unbleached paper towels

❑ Unbleached parchment paper

out one of the many guides to organic gardening in your local library or bookstore.

Non-toxic, biodegradable dish, floor, counter, bathroom, all-purpose and laundry soaps, disinfectants, window cleaners, and fabric brighteners and softeners can be found in most natural foods stores, health food co-ops, and specialty mail-order catalogs. They will improve your indoor and outdoor air quality and our nation's water quality. We can't promise you'll see relief from any disorders, but you have nothing to lose by giving up the poisons.

Twelve Tips to Help You Pare Down Your Use of Plastic

Your consumption habits are more than personal. They affect the land, air, and water. Your purchases can increase your exposure to harmful chemicals that poison our air and water, harm wildlife, increase consumption of non-renewable resources, and produce excessive amounts of non-recyclable solid waste. During the last 50 years, use of plastics has increased exponentially.

Soft plastics and plastic wrap exposes us to Diethylhexyladepate (DEHA), a known carcinogen that is meddlesome at room temperature and more hazardous when heated.

Neither Don nor I have purchased plastic wrap (Cling wrap, Saran Wrap, etc.) in more than 15 years. We rarely use plastic food storage containers, never heat foods in plastic, use very few plastic bags, and reuse whatever bags we bring home. Here are some of our suggestions.

Whenever and wherever possible...

1. Buy foods that don't come in packages.

2. Buy in bulk, using paper bags or containers from home.

3. Reuse plastic shopping bags to line garbage pails.

4. Recycle plastic tubs and heavy-duty containers.

5. Store non-perishable foods at room temperature in jars.

6. Refrigerate chopped or cooked foods in jars, or glass, Corningware, Pyrex or stainless steel bowls. Cover the bowls with fitted lids, dinner plates, or saucers.

7. Pack lunches and snacks in wide-mouth, stainless steel thermos bottles, stainless steel bowls, or food tins with fitted lids, reusable plant-based cellulose bags, and waxed paper liners from boxed herbal teas.

8. Use Pyrex and Corningware freezer bowls, pint-size canning jars, or thick (HDPE) plastic containers to freeze foods.

9. Store meat and poultry bones for making Bone-Building Broth and stock in empty bags saved from frozen fruits and vegetables. Close with twist ties. Use and reuse zip-locking bags or plant-based cellulose bags.

10. Invest in a dozen cotton/canvas tote bags to bring home dry goods and fresh produce, and to store some of your vegetables in the refrigerator.

11. Set up recycle bins in your kitchen or garage for whatever your city refuse department or drop-off sites will accept.

12. Compost all non-meat food waste rather than dump it out in plastic bags that will wind up in the landfill. Set up a compost bin in your backyard to recycle the waste. Build the bin yourself or buy an enclose composting barrel with a hand crank to turn the waste food into fertilizer more quickly.

Twelve Ways to Reduce Your Dependence on Disposables

The average person throws out his/her weight in packaging every month. Do you? Paper, Styrofoam and plastic plates, bowls, cups, and utensils can be almost eliminated. The following suggestions can help you reduce, reuse, recycle—and add less to the collective trash heap.

1. Replace disposable plates, cups, and bowls with glass, pottery, wood, and stainless steel products.

2. Replace disposable utensils with stainless steel and wood.

3. For potlucks, picnics, and meals away from home, pack your own dishes, utensils, and cloth napkins.

4. When hosting events, use your own cups, plates, bowls, and cloth napkins; borrow some from a friend; or invite guests to bring them from home.

5. If you must buy disposable cups or plates, purchase paper rather than Styrofoam.

6. Use paper towels sparingly, infrequently, and only where necessary. For example, use them to blot fish, poultry, or meat dry before seasoning and cooking. In most cases, you can replace paper products with cloth napkins, dish towels, and rags. Use the good parts of a soiled tablecloth to make napkins.

7. Buy only unbleached and dioxin-free paper towels.

8. Minimize your use of aluminum foil, which in not recyclable.

9. Reheat leftovers in heat-proof bowls or containers.

10. Give up soda and other beverages sold in plastic bottles. Drink water filtered at home, herbal teas, and pure fruit juices. Use thermos bottles or heavy duty PC (polycarbonate) plastic bottles.

11. Limit use of foods sold in cans.

12. Use jars from mustard, nut butter, tahini, salad dressing, etc., to store nuts, seeds, sauces, soups, stews, salad dressings, and leftover meat juices.

If you follow these tips you will be amazed at how little trash you generate each week and how much longer a roll of aluminum foil or unbleached paper towels last.

11 Meal Planning Makeover

Planning meals isn't only a matter of what you eat, but also when you eat it.

Like the sun and the moon, every human body has regular cycles—a predictable sequence of chemical and physiological changes that alter and regulate organ functions, metabolism, moods, and the production and secretion of hormones. For example, melatonin, a pineal gland hormone, is secreted only after dark. It facilitates deep, restful sleep, is rejuvenating, and may counter cancer. Drinking alcohol or caffeinated beverages during the day or staying up with the lights on much past 10 p.m., inhibits production and secretion of melatonin, resulting in difficulty sleeping and possibly increasing your risk of developing cancer.

Traditional Chinese Medicine (TCM) has a deep understanding of these cycles and provides a sensible map of our biorhythms. Each day has cycles similar to the seasons. Hours between midnight and 6 a.m. correspond to spring, a time of rising and rebirth. Hours between 6 a.m. and noon are like summer, a time of growth, development, and activity. Hours between noon and 6 p.m. correlate to autumn, a time of harvest, and 6 p.m. to midnight parallels winter, a time of storage, restoration, recuperation, and hibernation.

After a long night of fasting, the powers of digestion, assimilation, and metabolism are rested, primed, and powerful. Your body is ready for action. Chinese scientists discovered that the digestive system is most energized between 7 and 9 a.m.—making that the ideal time for

Chapter Overview
Meal planning involves what you eat and when. Chapter 11 will explain the benefits of setting up a regular schedule and how to create meals that mix different flavors and textures.

breakfast because food eaten during this time is well digested and transformed into energy, not stored as fat.

Our metabolic powers gain strength throughout the morning and peak around noon, like the rising sun. The best time for lunch is between 11 a.m. and 1 p.m. Traditional cultures, like the French and Chinese, enjoy a large, leisurely lunch followed by a nap. That doesn't mesh with most modern American routines, which allow only a brief, light lunch. Americans' lunch schedules are synchronized with what's best for industry and commerce, not what is good for human health.

After noon, our digestive and metabolic powers gradually decline like the waning sun. About 7 p.m., body functions shift from energy expenditure to energy conservation, recuperation, and restoration. Because the digestive system is less energetic, food eaten after 7 p.m. is more difficult to digest. Undigested food feeds fermentation, growth of pathogenic bacteria, and parasites. It causes shallow, restless sleep, morning sluggishness, lack of morning appetite, and a gain of phlegm and fat.

Benefits of Breakfast

This isn't just ancient folklore. Numerous studies have confirmed the importance of a nourishing breakfast, linking it to lower cholesterol and body fat levels, increased attention span, better blood sugar control, and longevity.

Why are obesity rates and heart disease rates so much lower in France than in America? The French eat more real (and less processed) food. They typically eat sitting down, linger over meals, chew well, and have their largest meal at lunch. By 2 p.m., they have consumed nearly 60 percent of their total daily calories. Americans generally take in only 38 percent of their calories by 2 p.m., snack after lunch, eat their largest meal at dinner, and often nosh until bedtime.

Controlled scientific studies confirm that fat loss is easier to achieve when food intake is spread across 3 or more small meals a day. For example, when the fat-burning ability of women in their 60s was compared with that of women in their 20s, the groups were almost equal in their ability to burn fat when meals were between 250 and 500 calories each. When the groups ate 1000-calorie meals, the rate of fat burning declined significantly in the older women. [*Am J Clin Nutr* 1997; 66(4): 860-6].

People who eat a good breakfast and lunch are less likely to overeat or binge later in the day. If you skip meals or eat skimpy portions, you are likely to swing to the other extreme because your body perceives a state of starvation.

When food is scarce (whether from famine, very low-calorie dieting, or habitual meal skipping) our bodies increase the secretion of leptin, a fat-storage hormone. When we eat again, our bodies store up more calories than before in preparation for the next famine. This

Don't Skip Meals
Habitually skipping a meal causes the body to perceive a state of famine. In response, the body produces leptin, a fat-storage hormone. When you eat again, the body will store more calories in preparation for the next meal that is skipped.

is why many people find they stop losing weight after the first few weeks or months on very low-calorie diets, then gain back all they lost and more, even if they aren't eating more than before they started dieting.

When you provide your body with the nourishment it needs at regular intervals, it is assured there is no famine and it's safe to lose fat, so your metabolism is reset to a healthy level.

Daily Rhythm

Some people initially resist regular meals, saying "eating by the clock is unnatural." Nothing could be farther from the truth. All of nature runs in regular cycles. If you dine at regular times and eat about the same amount from day to day, you may be surprised to find you feel hungry at regular intervals. This makes it easier to plan what and when to cook and schedule exercise sessions and other activities. You'll have a better idea of your own energy cycles and when you need to stop and refuel. It's like putting gas in your car before it sputters to a stop with an empty tank.

If you have low blood sugar (hypoglycemia) or high blood sugar (diabetes), you know what it feels like to be running on empty and avoid getting to that point. People who frequently skip meals or under-eat are often driven to eat excessively when hunger strikes and they're faced with food. To break this pattern, it's helpful to plan and consume smaller, more frequent meals.

Why are smaller, more frequent meals desirable? The human stomach is small—unlike that of the pure carnivore—and requires frequent feeding. Large, infrequent meals can easily overload your system, impairing digestion, assimilation, and metabolism of nutrients.

We recommend 3 meals a day plus an intentional snack if you need it. Unlike constant noshing and unconscious eating on the run, intentional snacks are planned, eaten with awareness, and comprised of nutritious foods. When you're well nourished, you'll also find it easier to resist unwholesome foods.

A rhythmic schedule of meals and activity is virtually effortless once you have a system. A momentum will develop that carries you along. If you've never been regular in what, when, how much, or how often you eat, you will be amazed at the favorable effect a schedule can have on your energy, mental focus, moods, appetite control, and athletic performance.

Food Combining: How Important Is It?

Most food-combining plans should be called food-separating plans because their main rules are about avoiding certain combinations, such as fruits and anything else, or starches with meats. In actuality, the human digestive system is able to release enzymes for processing all food types at the same time.

Moreover, eating fruit with meat, for example, is beneficial

> **Regular Rhythm**
> Eating 3 small meals plus a designated snack at regular intervals will make it easier to plan what and when to cook.

because the organic acids in fruit facilitate the absorption of iron in meat. Eating meat with starches improves the absorption of iron in the plant foods.

Many people achieve a more stable energy level and regularity of hunger pattern by combining protein-, carbohydrate-, and fat-containing foods at the same meal than by separating fruits and starches from protein foods.

Researchers have observed that people frequently over-eat fat when fed meals with little or no carbohydrates (probably because the brain prefers running on glucose, supplied by carbohydrates). Conversely, people easily over-consume carbohydrates when meals are completely or virtually devoid of fat or protein. Using some fat or oil in meals stimulates release of cholecystokinin (CCK), a hormone thought to be partially responsible for feelings of satisfaction. (That's why fat-free meals may leave you feeling paradoxically full and unsatisfied.)

Meals containing a mix of carbohydrate, protein, and fat are best for stabilizing blood sugar levels. Here's why: Carbohydrate is digested quite quickly, and provides fuel immediately after the meal. As the supply of carbohydrate drops off, protein becomes available. When that drops off, fat provides the long-term energy. Having a modest but significant amount of protein and some fat at each meal retards the return of hunger.

What's a Meal?

Webster's dictionary defines a meal as "the food served and eaten in one sitting." Used since the 13th century, the term was originally an extension of the Old English idea of a "fixed time for eating," such as breakfast, lunchtime, and dinnertime.

Okay, now you're wondering what we eat for those meals.

What's *in* a Meal?

Although some modern meals are haphazardly planned, if at all, and appear to be made up of almost anything, or of a single food—such as cereal, toast, bagels, or muffins—there are some who plan meals by somewhat standard principles. What chef, mom, or home cook is not familiar with the model of basing meals (at least dinner) around a meat, a starch, and a vegetable? Our modular method of meal planning is actually quite similar and common worldwide.

General Meal Outline
1. **protein:** meat, poultry, fish, or eggs
2. **starchy or dense carbohydrate:** vegetable, root, fruit (or combination)
3. **fibrous carbohydrate:** green leafy and/or mixed non-starchy vegetables
4. **fat:** nuts, seeds, olives, avocados, butter, coconut, coconut milk, or coconut, olive or flax oil

---

Mix it Up
Many meal plans urge that you avoid certain food combinations. However, a mix of carbs, protein, and fat in each meal complement each other and have been shown to effectively stabilize energy and blood sugar levels.

Modular Meal Planning

With the exception of main-course salads, we rarely make one-dish meals. Most of the dishes we make fall into 1 of 3 modules or categories: protein (meat foods), carbohydrate (vegetables and fruits), or fat (animal or vegetable). We usually prepare foods as separate components because it allows us to mix and match the same dishes at different meals. One dish, such as sautéed collard greens, might be served twice the same day or even 2 days in a row, but with different accompaniments. Likewise, roasted chicken might be served 2 or 3 days in a row but with different greens and a different dense vegetable or fruit each time.

By mixing and matching food modules, you can use the same components to build different meals by changing the assembly, the colors, shapes, and forms. You coordinate protein-rich foods with cooked or raw dark leafy greens and bright orange, yellow, and red vegetables and fruits in simple or complex ways. You can dress it up with various combinations of herbs, spices, vinegars, salad dressings, sauces, salsas, chutneys, nuts, seeds, nut butters, flavored mustards, or edible garnishes.

If you get in the habit of keeping a generous supply of raw materials and cooked foods on hand, you don't necessarily have to know exactly what you're going to combine and serve at every meal.

Think of the formats as outlines. How you flesh them out is up to you, what's in season and on hand, the occasion, and your time constraints.

Switch it Up
When planning meals, prepare foods as separate dishes—this will let you create many combinations of the modules for different meals.

Putting It All Together

The basic meal formats that follow will help you map out breakfast, lunch, dinner, and snacks. They may be used to guide your selections at home, when you're packing lunches, or eating out in a restaurant or deli, at a potluck, picnic, or buffet. Recipes for specific dishes are in later chapters. See Index for page numbers.

Our typical breakfast consists of eggs, some kind of meat, or a combination of the two, with cooked leafy greens, fruit and 1 or 2 condiments.

Sample Breakfast Formats

Protein + Greens + Fruit + Condiments
1) Salmon & Egg Scramble, steamed asparagus, and sliced pineapple with shredded, unsweetened coconut
2) Turkey burgers with Cajun Ketchup, leftover Better Brussels Sprouts, and sliced peaches and blueberries with chopped, toasted pecans
3) 3-egg omelet with herbs, leftover Sautéed Kale with Onions & Mushrooms, and sliced melon with grapes

Protein + Greens + Starchy Vegetable + Fruit + Condiments
1) Scrambled eggs, leftover Herb-Roasted Potatoes, Sautéed

Collards with Sun-Dried Tomatoes, and Fruit Salad with shredded coconut

2) Leftover Seared Pork Chops, leftover Steamed Broccoli & Cauliflower with Herbed Mayonnaise, leftover Steamed Corn on the Cob, and fresh plums

3) Soft-Boiled Eggs, leftover steak, Sautéed Kale with Sunchokes, and fresh cherries and peaches

Protein + Fruit + Fat

If you're pressed for time, not yet used to eating breakfast, or resistant to the idea of eggs or meat with vegetables every morning, try one of the following:

1) Better Balanced Smoothie
2) fruit salad, bowl of berries, or winter squash with Vanilla Protein-Coconut Cream
3) 1 ounce of homemade beef or turkey jerky with a peach and a plum
4) Protein-Nut Spread with sliced apples

Our table condiments usually consist of homemade barbecue sauce, lemon or lime wedges, fruit chutney, salsa, sliced avocado, guacamole, homemade mayonnaise, salad dressing, prepared mustard, hot sauce, fresh herb garnish, toasted sea vegetables or sea vegetable flakes, lemon pepper, a sprinkle of toasted nuts or coconut, diluted nut butter, oil or butter used in cooking or at the table, or a garnish of edible flowers, minced scallions, chives, or parsley.

Initially, you might miss toast with jam, pancakes with syrup, granola, cold cereal, or doughnuts. The idea of eating meat and vegetables—particularly leafy greens—for breakfast may sound strange. Yet, they are common breakfast foods in many cultures.

Dark leafy greens are rich in vitamins and minerals found in primitive diets but sorely lacking in most modern diets. They add a refreshing taste, texture, and color to meals and provide a nourishing compliment to eggs and meats. Within a few weeks, you may be surprised to find you enjoy and even want vegetables at breakfast.

Few people snack on cooked leafy greens. Getting a serving in at breakfast will ensure that you meet your daily greens' quota.

Making Room for Breakfast

If you are not accustomed to eating breakfast, try skipping dinner 5 nights in a row. Or you might eat a light but nourishing snack, such as a large apple or banana with a tablespoon of nut butter, one-quarter to one-half cantaloupe or honeydew melon, 2 cups of fruit salad with 2 tablespoons of nuts, or a protein-rich fruit smoothie, no later than 7 p.m. Then fast until breakfast. This will stimulate your

---

Breakfast Bites
Toss out the pancake mix, cereals, and toast and munch on some dark leafy greens with your eggs and meat. It might seem unusual at first, but within a few weeks, you might find you like vegetables at breakfast.

metabolism, your immune function, and your appetite for breakfast.

Habitually reducing the size of your evening meal can give you *more* social time, not less. Couples and families can profit from making breakfast the family gathering time since many intramural and social events occur at night, putting a crunch on family time at supper.

If you frequently work in the evening like we do, consider eating an early breakfast and lunch, a light afternoon supper, and a fruit-based snack at your previous dinner hour. We typically eat 4 times a day: 3 meals and 1 planned snack.

Whenever possible, we prefer to have dinner between 3 and 4 p.m., and a nourishing evening snack at least 3 hours before bedtime when most people are sitting down to a big meal. Fruit smoothies are often the ideal solution if your evening activities don't allow you to sit down with a spoon, fork, or food that requires much chewing, but you know you need to eat. If you work a late shift or take classes in the evening, eating 1 or 2 pieces of fresh fruit, perhaps with some homemade jerky, or drinking a smoothie, is preferable to having a meal at 8 or 9 p.m.

After 7 p.m.

On days we can't eat supper in the afternoon, we usually have a light snack around 3, then dinner by 6:30 or 7 p.m. at the latest. Eating a full meal later leads to sluggish digestion and restless sleep.

Lunches and Dinners

Lunch is easy to assemble if you've washed, sliced, and cooked plenty of food ahead. If you pack lunch, invest in a couple of containers with tight-fitting lids, an insulated lunch tote, refreezable ice packs, and a wide-mouth thermos for each family member.

Most of the foods we eat taste great at room temperature or warm. If you have a toaster oven at the office, you can pack a portion of your lunch—usually the protein or protein and root, tuber, squash, or tomato sauce portion—in a heat-proof Corningware or metal container with a fitted lid. (Asian stainless steel food tins are ideal.) If the lid isn't heat-proof, replace it with foil before slipping the container into the oven at 200 to 225° F for 20 to 30 minutes, or at 300° F for 10 to 15 minutes. Avoid or minimize reheating cooked greens; overcooking leads to loss of flavor, nutrients, and color. Parboiled vegetables, tossed salads, and cooked fruits are delicious served at room temperature.

You can use the same meal formats for lunch and dinner, filling in with different foods.

Lunch & Dinner Formats

Any of the following meals may be packed into containers for lunch, or served at home.

No Eating Zone
When possible, do not eat after 7 p.m. as it leads to sluggish digestion and restless sleep. If you must eat later, do not eat a full meal. Try 1 or 2 pieces or fruit, a smoothie, or homemade jerky.

Protein + Greens + Fruit, Roots or Vine Vegetable + Condiments

1) Roasted Smoky Turkey Breast with Better Barbecue Sauce, Sautéed Collards, Stewed Pears with Anise and toasted pecans for garnish
2) Poached Chicken Breast Halves, Sautéed Kale with Onions & Mushrooms, Creamy Carrot Soup with Ginger
3) Baked Chicken with Lime, Simmered Carrots with Sunchokes, Coleslaw with Mustard-Tahini Dressing on a bed of romaine
4) Seared Pork Chops with Nutty Spring Green & Orange Salad with Sweet Citrus Vinaigrette

Protein + Greens + Tuber + Condiments

1) Baked or grilled salmon, Baked Sweet Potato with butter, flax oil, or coconut oil, Spinach Salad with Tahini Dressing
2) Baked Chicken, Basic Baked Sweet Potato with butter, and Mesclun Green Salad with Very Easy Vinaigrette
3) Beef, Carrot & Sunchoke Stew, Sautéed Collards with Leeks, Baked Apple with Date-Nut Filling
4) Steak, Sun-Dried Tomato, Potato & Green Salad with Onions & Avocado

Variety in a Meal

We incorporate different foods, colors, flavors, textures, and preparation techniques into a meal. This makes meals more inviting, enjoyable, and it provides a broader range of nutrients.

Balancing by Color

There are 3 primary color groups: red-orange-yellow, blue-green, and white-black. Advertisers and fast food restaurants use the colors of fresh produce—particularly red, orange, and yellow—to entice you to eat their processed products. You can use color psychology to stimulate your desire for more nutritious foods, while artfully painting your plate for optimal nutrition.

How inviting would a monochromatic meal of white meat fish, cauliflower, potatoes, cashews, and onions be? Salmon with beets, red peppers, and strawberries? Not very.

Foods with different colors concentrate different nutrients. Vegetables and fruits are great sources of potassium, magnesium, vitamin C, other vitamins and minerals, and countless carotenoids. Dark leafy greens usually concentrate the most calcium, magnesium, phosphorus, and folic acid. Bright orange, yellow, red, blue, and purple vegetables generally pack more beta-carotene, lutein, zeazanthin, and other health protective phyto nutrients.

Food Painting
Use the psychology of color to stimulate your desire for nutritious foods. Red-orange-yellow, blue-green, and white-black make up the 3 primary color groups.

Not used to thinking and cooking in color? Here's a start. The red-orange-yellow spectrum represents energy, warmth, life. It is found primarily in energy-dense foods such as fruits, dense roots, and sweet-starchy vegetables. Examples include red meats or fish, egg yolks, carrots, beets, sweet potatoes, mangoes, peaches, apricots, plums, watermelon, cantaloupe, chestnuts, red grapes, and cherries.

The blue-green colors are cool, soothing, and represent plant life. Green foods include romaine, green leaf lettuces, cabbage, arugula, kale, collards, mustard greens, parsley, cilantro, spinach, broccoli, Brussels sprouts, zucchini, asparagus, avocados, green apples and pears, and honeydew melons. Some "greens" like kale may actually be blue-green. Dark blue foods include blueberries and blackberries.

White is bright; black is dark. So, bright colors are whitish and dark colors are blackish. Bright red is white-red, dark red is black-red. Generally, blacker, darker foods are richer and more nutrient dense than whiter-brighter foods. Lettuce, cauliflower, and cucumber are far less nutritious than kale, collard greens, broccoli, and blueberries. White potatoes are anemic compared to sweet potatoes, but more nutritious than white rice.

What do we eat that's black? Sea vegetables, such as kelp or kombu, nori, sea palm, or alaria, black radishes, figs, raisins, and dates. What do we eat that's white? Onions, daikon radishes, cauliflower, turnips, cashews, macadamia nuts, pine nuts, and coconut.

The Five Flavors

Five basic flavors have been identified: sweet, sour, bitter, salty, and pungent or spicy. Chinese medicine teaches that an excess of one flavor, such as sweet or salty, can create imbalances in our diets and bodies. Employing all 5 flavors can increase enjoyment of meals and ensure nutritional adequacy. Most modern people need to cultivate a taste for bitter foods.

Sweet: A natural sweet taste can be found in brightly colored vegetables, particularly roots, squashes, tubers, and round vegetables, such as onions, particularly cooked onions, and nuts and fruits. If you are attentive, you may even recognize the sweetness in meats. If you satisfy your taste for sweets with these foods, you will take in more nutrients and be less likely to overdose and create nutritional imbalances than if you relied mainly on honey, maple syrup, molasses, corn syrup, high fructose corn sweetener, sugar, and other concentrated and caloric sweeteners.

Sweet herbs, such as stevia extract and licorice root, may provide a sweet taste with virtually no digestible calories or carbohydrates. They make a great substitute for concentrated sugars and are needed in only minuscule amounts.

Sour: Try lemon, lime, or orange juice, organic, raw apple cider vinegar, red wine vinegar, and balsamic vinegar, or herbs and spices, such as rosehips, ground sumac, lemon pepper, dill, tarragon,

Fab Five Flavors
There are 5 basic flavors: sweet, sour, bitter, salty, and pungent/spicy. Incorporating mixtures of these flavors will increase meal enjoyment and improve nutrition.

and turmeric. Or try mildly sour vegetables, such as bell peppers, tomatoes, sorrel, rutabaga, butternut squash, and fruits such as ginger gold and granny smith apples, berries, or dried figs and apricots.

Bitter: This is the most neglected flavor. Most modern people shy away from bitter, unless they've developed a penchant for coffee or chocolate, sweetened with sugar! More nourishing foods with a slight bitter flavor include brassica family vegetables—kale, collards, mustard and turnip greens, Brussels sprouts, broccoli, cabbage, cauliflower—and salad greens, such as arugula, endive, escarole, radicchio, watercress, and nettles. Other examples include burdock, celeriac (celery root), celery, sesame tahini, lightly toasted nuts, roasted chicory and dandelion root drinks ("coffees"), turmeric, cumin, oregano, mustard, red and black pepper, cinnamon, nutmeg, and cloves.

Salty: Sea vegetables, eggs (especially the whites), meats, bone broths and stocks, celery, parsley, leafy greens, and herbs and spices, such as ground sumac berries, fennel, cumin, mustard, and cardamom seeds, can lend a salty taste.

We urge you to minimize use of mineral salt. We use it mainly as a preservative in some salad dressings, condiments such as barbecue sauce, and occasionally in beef jerky and some meat and vegetable dishes. Even here, salt may be omitted but you will just have to consume the dressing or jerky sooner. We do not use salt at the table, in all of our foods, or on a daily basis.

Mineral salt is nutritionally unnecessary and potentially harmful, particularly in the amounts used by most modern people. (See Chapter 4.) Your body's sodium and electrolyte needs can be met through land and sea vegetables, fruits, eggs, and meats.

Mineral salt is not the only or best way to satisfy the natural desire for the salty flavor. Many foods rich in essential minerals other than sodium also have a salty flavor. For example, the Moroccan Spice Mix (Page 399), in the condiment chapter, provides 600 milligrams of calcium in a recipe that serves 6 or 8 people.

Sea vegetables are also very good sources of minerals. In fact, they pack far more minerals relative to sodium than mineral salt. Dulse is just one of many sea vegetables that can satisfy your desire for a salty taste in cooking or at the table. If a salty taste is what you're after, reach for mineral-rich whole foods.

Some authors claim unrefined, sun-dried sea salt, such as Celtic sea salt, is mineral-rich. In truth, although unrefined salt does contain a greater variety of minerals than refined salts, which are typically more than 99 percent sodium chloride, unrefined salts are still 86 percent sodium chloride by weight. It is unwise to rely on unrefined sea salt as a source of your daily mineral requirements—the amount of minerals (other than sodium chloride) contained in a teaspoon, quarter teaspoon, pinch, or reasonable serving is insignificant. It would not meet the daily requirement for any nutrient.

However, if you use salt, we recommend Celtic sea salt or some other unrefined sea salt, because it is sun-dried, free of anti-caking agents, bleaches, aluminum compounds, and sugar, and tastes remarkably different—better and less biting.

Once you minimize mineral salt, you will be amazed at the naturally salty and sweet flavors you notice in foods. Eventually you may find salted—or at least highly salted—foods unpleasant, even inedible. At the very least, you'll want increasingly less salt.

Pungent and spicy: These flavors come mainly from leafy vegetables, such as turnip, mustard, chicory and dandelion greens, arugula (rocket), cabbage, red and white radishes, turnips, ginger, horseradish, onions, scallions, garlic, chives, and other herbs and spices.

A single flavor predominates in some foods. Several flavors vie for your attention in others. A food with more than one flavor will usually have a primary and secondary flavor. Tomatoes, granny smith apples, and currants taste sweet and sour. Onions and radishes are pungent when raw, but more sweet when cooked. Many leafy green vegetables taste pungent and bitter when raw but mild when cooked. If you pay attention you will find meats are sweet and salty at the same time. Some spices are both bitter and pungent. Sugar kelp, a sea vegetable, tastes salty first, sweet second.

Incorporating the 5 flavors into meals is not difficult. Simply include 1 or more dark leafy green vegetables, 1 or more bright orange, yellow or red vegetables or fruits, and an animal protein at each meal and season with 1 or more herbs or spices.

Textures

If all of your meals were puréed, you'd probably feel more like an infant than a well-nourished adult. This is not to say that puréed foods are only for babies; they most certainly are not! Who doesn't enjoy a velvety smooth pudding, custard, or mousse, a soft frozen dessert, or creamy fruit smoothie? Children and adults usually enjoy a variety of textures; however, young children with their immature digestive systems need more mashed and puréed foods than adults.

Foods with contrasting textures pair well. Crisp, tender, steamed vegetables complement a creamy carrot soup or a chunky stew. Mashed sweet potatoes make a good match for a solid, dense dish of roasted turkey and crunchy coleslaw. Crunchy nuts make a great garnish for stewed or poached fruit. A creamy salad dressing or spoonful of guacamole will enhance a crisp leafy green salad.

For crunchy textures, try grated, sliced, or diced raw vegetables, such as carrots, daikon (an Asian white radish), red radishes, celery, jicama, sunchokes, or bell peppers, leaf lettuce, minced scallions or raw onion rings, or parboiled or stir-fried vegetables. Sprinkle seeds or chopped nuts over fruit or salad. Scatter toasted and crumbled sea vegetables over cooked greens or tossed salad, or nibble on raw fruits or dried apple chips.

Opposites Attract
Contrasting textures add interest to meals. Serve something crunchy with something soft; serve something smooth with something chunky.

For a soft, smooth, and creamy texture, try soft-boiled or poached eggs, lightly cooked fish, beef or poultry liver, ground beef, well-cooked winter squash, baked or mashed sweet potatoes or carrots, puréed chestnuts, coconut milk, guacamole or avocado sour cream. Incorporate some sesame tahini or nut butter into a sauce, dip, dressing, vegetable soup, or pudding. Make a fruit smoothie, applesauce, or Frosty Fruit Whip. Or, frost a date-coconut roll with macadamia nut butter for dessert.

Try sliced raw vegetables, cooked poultry, meat, or hard-boiled eggs, baked, roasted, or sliced raw root vegetables, a casserole, meatloaf, beef jerky, roasted, baked, or stewed beef, lamb, or chicken kidneys or hearts, or a jelled pudding if you want a firmer texture.

For a chewy texture, serve cooked poultry, red meat, organ meats (such as kidneys), firm-fleshed fish steaks, or beef jerky. Also try dried figs, apricots, dates, papaya or sweet potato slices, or prunes, fruit leather, sun-dried tomatoes, or other fibrous foods.

Use several textures when you plan a meal. Imagine the foods on the table, your plate, and in your mouth. With practice and attention, you will consistently create interesting and varied meals that you and your guests will enjoy.

What about Dessert?

We haven't said much about dessert. Although we do include them in our diet, for the most part we satisfy our sweet tooth with fresh raw, cooked, or dried fruits, or sweet vegetables (cooked onions, winter squashes, carrots, and sweet potatoes) incorporated into meals and intentional snacks. Beyond that, we enjoy naturally sweetened puddings, macaroons, and other treats with some of our meals or as snacks. We actually get tired of and lose interest in sweets given the amount of sweet vegetables and fruits we regularly eat.

Many people find their cravings for cookies, cakes, pies, pastries, candies, ice cream, and extreme sweets diminish when they:

* increase their consumption of protein and fresh produce (fruits & vegetables),
* eliminate refined, processed, and highly sugared and salted foods, and
* eat 3 nourishing meals at regular intervals throughout the day.

11 Common Causes of Sweets Cravings

Cravings for sugary and starchy foods are common. Ever wonder how to get a handle on them?

1. **Irregular or missed meals.** Skipping meals can contribute to poor food choices and a reliance on sugar for quick energy. The solution: Eat 3 nourishing meals a day.
2. **Lack of sufficient carbohydrates.** Very low-carbohydrate diets often create cravings for sweets (fuel for your hungry brain). One solution is to incorporate a wider variety of fresh vegetables and fruits into your meals and snacks.

Dessert Deserted?
There are some desserts included in the meal plan, but for the most part your sweet tooth can be satisfied with sweet vegetables and fruits that are part of the meals and snacks.

3. **Lack of sufficient protein.** Combining a complete protein with 3 or 4 times as much fresh produce at meals can curb the cravings for sweets by creating more stable energy and blood sugar levels.

4. **Excessive use of salt.** Salt can over-stimulate your appetite. Reducing your use of salt and salted foods can help regulate your appetite.

5. **Eating refined carbohydrate.** Replace refined carbs with unrefined whole foods and you can expect more even energy levels, better moods, and a healthier appetite.

6. **Habitual use of sugar**. The more sugar you eat, the more you want. Cravings are like stray cats. Feed them and they keep coming back. If you stop feeding them, eventually your stray desires will disappear!

7. **Chronic under-eating.** Under-eating frequently leads to over-eating or out-of-control eating of high-starch and sugary-rich foods. Eating at regular intervals throughout the day can help avert low-energy emergencies that may be at the root of your cravings.

8. **Mineral and trace mineral deficiencies.** There is no single magic bullet mineral or vitamin pill. If you're deficient in one nutrient, you'll be deficient in others. Whole foods are your best offense and defense. Nevertheless, a good multi-vitamin with calcium and magnesium may provide additional support for those in transition to a produce-dominated diet. We recommend the Shaklee Vita-Lea because of its excellent quality and design.

9. **Emotional problems.** No amount of dessert will satisfy your emotional needs or take away your troubles. If you find that you medicate yourself with food when you're not hungry—to stuff fear, anger, loneliness, boredom, or stress—we urge you to explore non-food ways to release pent up energy, nurture yourself, and create balance and peace in your life.

10. **Physical depletion.** Adrenal exhaustion can contribute to cravings for stimulants, such as salt, sugar, alcohol, coffee, or drugs. You may benefit from more sleep, gentle exercise, meditation, relaxation tapes, massage, psychotherapy, acupuncture, and herbs.

11. **Lack of purpose and definite goals.** What do you want in your life? Are your daily food choices supporting your vision for the present and the future? "Every bite you take is a choice you make about how well you care for yourself," says Judy Stone, M.S.W., C.N., author of *Take Two Apples and Call Me in the Morning!*

Stop Feeding Strays
It's better to ignore cravings for unwhole-some foods, than to give in to them. Continue feeding them and they just keep coming back. If you resist, eventually those urges will vanish.

Assembling snacks

Snacks don't have to be as structured as meals. You can vary the format and the foods. The important thing is to make your snacks nourishing and intentional, to avoid aimless and constant noshing that can spoil your appetite for meals or lead you to over-consume calories from high-density foods, like nuts, which pack 400 calories per one-half cup. (That's a single handful!)

You can prepare your snacks in advance, pack them for work, school, a park, playground, bus, train, or airplane. A wide-mouth thermos bottle will be helpful for some items.

Snack Formats
Carbohydrate (fruit)
1) 2 chunks of fresh watermelon
2) 1 or 2 cups of grapes, berries, or a banana
3) 2 peaches, plums, apricots, or nectarines
4) An 8- to 16-ounce Vita-Mix Total Juice

Carbohydrate (fruit or veggies) + Fat (nuts or nut butter)
1) 1 to 2 cups fresh or frozen sliced banana and 2 to 4 tablespoons Fluffy Nut Butter
2) 1 Baked Apple with Date-Nut Filling
3) 3/4 cup Apple Compote and 2 to 4 tablespoons Fluffy Almond Butter
4) 1/2 cup of guacamole with carrot, celery, and jicama sticks

Protein (jerky, eggs, or meat) + Carbohydrate (fruit or vegetables)
1) 1/2 to 1 ounce homemade beef jerky and 1 apple or carrot
2) 1 or 2 hard-boiled eggs and fresh fruit or sliced vegetable sticks
3) 4 to 6 meatballs rolled in lettuce leaves and served with veggie sticks and a dip

Protein (egg white protein or meat) + Carbohydrate (fruit) + Fat
1) 12- to 16-ounce Better Balanced Smoothie
2) 1 medium to large apple or banana plus 1/4 cup Protein-Nut Spread
3) 1 ounce homemade jerky with 1 1/2 cups grapes or 1 large fruit
4) 1/2 to 1 ounce chopped turkey jerky mixed with 1/4 cup toasted nuts, and 1/4 cup dried fruit

THE GARDEN OF EATING PLAN

By weight, about 65 to 75 percent of a produce-dominated meal or snack is produce, about 5 percent will be nuts, seeds, oils, or sweeteners, and about 25 to 35 percent will be clean, lean animal products.

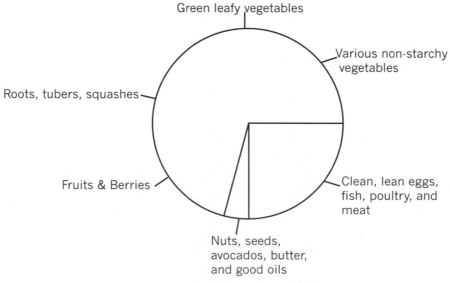

Green leafy vegetables

Various non-starchy vegetables

Roots, tubers, squashes

Clean, lean eggs, fish, poultry, and meat

Fruits & Berries

Nuts, seeds, avocados, butter, and good oils

Agave and honey (too small to depict)

By calories, about 60 to 70 percent will be protein and fat (mostly from animal products and nuts), and about 30 to 40 percent will be carbohydrates (from vegetables and fruits).

You won't eat all types of produce at every meal or snack. Refer to our meal planning guidelines, Basic Meal Formats in this chapter, and sample weeks of menus in Chapter 13 for specific details.

chapter 12 Meal Preparation in a Nutshell

Most of us get up early, stay up later, work odd hours and spend less time around the home fires than we'd like. We do most of our hunting and gathering in supermarkets, natural foods stores, farmers' markets, by mail, or the Internet.

Fast-paced modern lifestyles can make the prospect of getting nourishing and delicious meals on the table, 3 times a day, 7 days a week, seem like an ominous endeavor. Who, in America, grows up learning how to purchase fresh ingredients and prepare wholesome produce-dominated meals? Who has time to acquire these skills later in life? Who knows where to start?

What you need is a time-tested system and practical guiding principles. You need flexible, family-friendly, user-friendly recipes that taste as good leftover as fresh and just as good hot, as warm, cold, or room temperature. You need dishes and meals you can prepare in whole or in part in advance.

You don't have to reinvent anything. The system we are about to share with you is something we've honed during more than 12 years together in the kitchen. It allows us to dine on delicious, extraordinarily nutritious produce-dominated meals 3 times a day, and enjoy wholesome snacks 7 days a week without spending all day in the kitchen or using a microwave oven.

Where do you start?

The Pemmican Principle.

Pemmican is the paleolithic equivalent of a protein bar. American

> Chapter Overview:
> Chapter 12 shows you the principles and systems to follow so you will have healthy food ready to eat or prepare at anytime.

Indians made this portable, high-energy meal replacement bar from dried, pulverized buffalo meat mixed with tallow, rendered fat from around the kidneys of a buffalo, and dried berries. (Before you say, "yuck!" a lot of people, kids included, take to this stuff from the very first bite. Others develop a taste for it the more they eat it.) Many American Indians relied heavily on pemmican when they were busy or traveling.

Do you think they made pemmican fresh every day? No way. They cut meat from multiple freshly butchered buffaloes into thin strips and dried it, then rendered all the fat; they wasted nothing. During the height of berry season, they picked as much fruit as they could and dried berries that they didn't eat on the spot. To make pemmican, they pulverized the meat (a lot of meat), mixed it with enough warm tallow to hold the meat together, then tossed in some dried berries, and maybe some herbs they'd collected and dried in the sun.

The idea isn't for you to hunt down a buffalo or buy and dry

Beyond the Microwave Oven

Neither of us has owned or used a microwave oven in more than 18 years—with good reason.

Since natural immunity is the cornerstone of life and health, and microwave ovens appear to undermine health, why take the risk?

1.) Microwaving destroys non-nutritive but beneficial substances in foods, leaving them devitalized. One study reported in the *Lancet* (Dec. 9, 1989) showed that microwave-heated milk develops D-amino and cis-amino acids, known to have neuro- and hepato- (liver) toxic effects. Another study, reported in the *Journal of American Dietetic Association* (May 1989), concluded that microwaving human milk destroys vital immunoglobin A, a protein essential for building immunity and required for physical development. Warming breast milk on top of a stove did not produce these ill effects.

2.) Microwaved foods usually taste bland, have unpleasant textures, and lack flavor and fragrance. Warm a dinner roll in a microwave oven. If not devoured in minutes, it turns into a petrified rock. Wrap the same bread in a cotton or linen napkin and heat it over steam for 2 or 3 minutes and it becomes moist, tastes freshly baked (even it was dry before), and won't become unpalatable or inedible, even if it sits out for hours.

Most other foods lose flavor and fragrance cooked by microwave. In tests, blindfolded participants almost universally preferred the flavors and aromas of foods cooked by conventional methods. Ask any professional chef what s/he uses, or peek into his or her kitchen. It's a gas stove not a microwave or even an electric stove.

"Conventional cooking gives flavor to food through a series of chemical reactions between the sugar molecules and the amino acids [present in the foods]." ("Microwaving Means Micro Flavors," *Natural Health*, Sept./Oct. 1992). One of these reactions, the Maillard effect, creates compounds that account for browning and flavor development, particularly rich, meaty, nutty, buttery, and caramel-like flavors missing from microwaved foods.

To bypass last-minute emergency defrosting or split-second warming, we transfer frozen meats to the refrigerator 24 to 48 hours before we plan to cook them.

We often cook or reheat foods in the convection oven and always make enough for 2 or 3 days or meals. A convection toaster oven heats up faster and cooks 25 to 30 percent faster than a conventional oven. We reheat other foods in minutes in heat-proof bowls or containers on metal or bamboo steamer trays, in a double boiler, or in a saucepan with a minimum of water, stock, or broth. When pressed for time (or in hot weather), we eat many of our leftovers—meats and vegetables—at room temperature.

a whole carcass, and make several months worth of beef jerky or pemmican tomorrow. In fact, you don't have to make pemmican at all to benefit from the wisdom employed by early Americans.

The point is that the American Indians prepared food in batches for multiple meals and days. Sometimes they dried enough meat and berries to last for months. When they had the time, energy, and resources they made the most of what was on hand and prepared foods ahead for the times when it wouldn't be convenient to scavenge, hunt, pick, gather, or cook.

They also utilized the idea of component cooking. They prepared foods that could be mixed and matched to make different meals and snacks. Dried meat could be eaten as jerky, made into pemmican, or added to a stew. Rendered fat could be used to make pemmican, in cooking, or to tan hides, make soap, candles, and other necessities. Dried berries, which keep exceedingly well, could be eaten out of hand, alone or mixed with nuts, added to pemmican, or to stew. These individual foods could be dried or otherwise prepped in advance and assembled later.

Cooking every meal from scratch, sun up to sun down is impractical. And why cook for a single meal when you can make enough for 2 or 3 meals at a time? What's the biggest stumbling block that stops you from eating healthy meals after you've resolved to change your way? Not having healthy food on hand when hunger strikes.

The obvious solution: Shop, chop, prep, and cook more food in advance of meals, before you're hungry, and before you're ready to reach for whatever processed, packaged, and preserved food is within easy reach, even if it's not part of your new resolution.

The rest of this chapter is dedicated to showing you what you need to know and do to make sure you always have healthy food on hand, ready to eat or heat, or to expertly assemble for meals and snacks.

Handling Hunger
Having plenty of healthy, delicious & wholesome foods prepared in advance will help you knock out hunger.

Use Procedure-Oriented Cookery

Our style of cooking relies on basic cooking techniques that when followed precisely produce predictably good (even great) results. Our emphasis on basic procedures, techniques, proportions, and variations provides greater variety in the kitchen and at the table.

You don't need as many recipes when you can get 3, 4, 5, or 10 options from a single master recipe. This style of cooking almost guarantees you will have a more varied and interesting diet.

Develop a Recipe Repertoire

I've heard it said that most cooks have a repertoire of 10 basic dishes they use repeatedly. But why stop there when you could have a repertoire of 5, 6, or 7 dishes from each food group? Expand your repertoire each week and you'll eventually master 40 or more recipes!

I always encourage my students to take 2, 3, or 4 recipes they like and make them every week for a month, changing one ingredient each time: an herb or spice, the type of vegetable, fruit, meat, fish, or poultry. Try a different kind of apple or dried fruit in a compote, use a new variety of leafy greens when you sauté, a new spice blend with baked or poached chicken parts. Replace ground beef with ground turkey or bison when you make burgers, meatloaf, meatballs, or chili. Substitute Arctic char or escolar for salmon in a fish recipe. Add a different fresh or dried fruit or vegetable to a green salad. Try a variation on one of our many salad dressing recipes. Buy a new variety of potatoes or sweet potatoes. Add cocoa instead of vanilla to a fruit smoothie or Protein-Nut Spread (See Index for recipe).

Stress-free Subs
Consistently measure and pay attention to the ingredients in each recipe. Soon you'll have enough knowledge and confidence to know what seasonings work with what foods.

If you measure consistently, every time, every day, and pay attention to the elements in each recipe, you will develop the confidence to make the substitutions we suggest without stress. Experimenting within the structure we've provided will enable you to turn out great food without having to taste and taste as you work. You will start to learn what seasonings go well together and with what foods. You'll become familiar with recipes you repeat. You'll know the basic steps and ingredients and eventually know your favorites by heart.

If you keep at it, you will be able to pull 2 or 3 meals together simultaneously and pick up speed. If you don't know a recipe, you'll glance at the page to remind yourself of the ingredients, proportions, or steps. Eventually, you'll be a walking recipe Rolodex. You will know how much of each food to buy, thaw, and prepare for the number of people you regularly serve each week. You'll have a system that takes the guesswork out of shopping and cooking meals with leftovers to spare and little or no food waste.

Utilize Component-Style Cooking
    (1) protein (eggs, fish, poultry or meat)
    (2) starchy or dense vegetables (tubers, roots, or winter squash)
    (3) fruits
    (4) leafy green and fibrous vegetables (tossed salads, cooked leafy greens, or mixed vegetables)
    (5) fats (nuts, seeds, oil, butter, avocado, and coconut)
    (6) free foods (mustard, lemon pepper, balsamic vinegar, sea vegetables, edible flowers, and other garnishes—parsley, scallions, chives, cilantro, etc.)
    (7) condiments (free foods or caloric foods from other categories, such as vegetables, fruits, or fats—e.g., chutney, barbecue sauce, salsa, tahini dressing, mayonnaise, relish, or vinaigrette)

Simple dishes are more versatile and more easily transformed into new eating experiences. Whereas casseroles and one-pot meals can become tiresome, modular meal planning provides almost endless variety. Component cooking and modular meal planning make it easy and fun to mix and match leftovers with fresh foods, meal to meal and day to day. Condiments become your accessories, unifying contrasting foods, colors, flavors, and textures, so you never run out of options and leftovers don't have to mean reruns.

Cook Once Eat Thrice

The final element that will allow you to enjoy super-nutritious and extraordinarily delicious food every meal, every day, is to make every dish with 3 or 4 meals in mind. These intentional leftovers are the key components you will mix and match at multiple meals over the course of 2 or 3 days, or over an entire week or 2 in the case of salad dressing, barbecue sauce, ketchup, toasted nuts or seeds, and some sea vegetable dishes.

To make sure you eat your greens at least twice a day and have vegetables ready to eat tomorrow, you'll want to get in the habit of making extra portions each day. The same goes for meats. In a fast-food world, planned leftovers are the greatest guarantee that you'll have the nourishment you need for the next day's breakfast, lunch, or dinner.

Plan for Leftovers, but Don't Go Overboard

Intentional leftovers are always a plus. We don't mind some repetition. After all, we love the food. Sometimes we eat the same foods or meals 2 or 3 days in a row with only slight variation. (Who doesn't?) We're also adept at color coordinating, accessorizing, and transforming leftovers into new meals, so we don't have to repeat the same meals, even if we eat some of the same foods 2 or 3 days in a row. For example, we might turn yesterday's cooked winter squash into a delightful soup, stew or pudding pie, or turn a roast into stew or topping for a main-course salad. But don't take batch cooking to the extreme; this can lead to significant nutrient losses, food spoilage, and waste. While the same soup or stew might be agreeable 3 days in a row, by day 4 you're likely to be tired of it and find it lacking flavor.

Although some foods freeze well—barbecue sauce, cooked chicken, turkey, chili, stew, beef brisket in barbecue sauce, homemade ketchup, fruit chutney, mashed sweet potatoes seasoned with lime juice, sautéed kale, collards, Brussels sprouts, and parboiled vegetables—most foods do not. With little or no salt or concentrated sweeteners, a low fat content, no cheese, heavy sauces, or preservatives, most vegetable, fish, and meat dishes fail the taste test after cooking, freezing, and rewarming.

Prepare foods in manageable batches that can and will be consumed within 2 or 3 days, give or take extra portions for the freezer. That way you can enjoy convenience without sacrificing good nutrition. You'll minimize food waste and enjoy more flavorful food if you make it a priority to use freshly prepared foods promptly. Explore creative ways to use leftovers, rotating fresh foods and leftovers into your daily meals, such as incorporating small bits of leftover fish or meat into breakfast with eggs, omelets, scrambles, small batches of

Reheating Cooked Greens
When defrosted completely in the fridge or an ice chest, leftover cooked greens taste best if they are not reheated. If you want them warm, heat them while they are still frozen to avoid overcooking.

soup, or a salad. Don't extend your leftovers too far; aim to use them up promptly.

Note: Our Lean & Creamy Salad Dressings (see Index for recipes), unlike most dressings, freeze well.

Sensible Shelf Life for Prepared Foods Stored in the Fridge

* Cooked fish	2 to 3 days
* Cooked poultry and red meat	3 to 4 days
* Hard-boiled eggs	1 week, if shelled
	2 weeks, stored in the shell
* Cooked leafy green and fibrous veggies	2 to 3 days
* Cooked roots, tubers, and squashes	3 to 4 days
* Roasted vegetables	3 to 4 days
* Homemade soup, stew, or chili	3 to 4 days
* Chopped raw vegetables (stored in jars without water)	4 to 6 days
* Cooked fruit	4 to 5 days
* Sliced melon or pineapple	3 days (longer if frozen)
* Homemade salad dressings, barbecue sauce, and chutney	1 to 2 weeks (longer frozen)
* Homemade mayonnaise	7 to 10 days
* Opened can of coconut milk	4 to 6 days (longer if frozen)

Cooking in Blocks

The best way to get a running start for the week is to set aside a 4-hour block of time on Saturday or Sunday. You're not going to make a week's worth of food in an afternoon. The food wouldn't be fresh, flavorful, or nutritious if you did that. What you are going to do is turn your refrigerator into a healthy salad bar and deli and set yourself up for the first half to three-quarters of the week. The exceptions are salad dressings, marinades, toasted nuts, salsa, chutney, ketchup and barbecue sauces, which can be made to last for a week or 2 at a time. If you get a head start, it won't take as much effort to keep the food flowing throughout the week.

If you can't spend that much time all at once, set up a couple of 2-hour blocks of time to wash, chop, and cook foods and dishes with 2, 3, or 4 meals or days in mind. You might cook 2 chicken or turkey breasts at once, bake 6 or 8 sweet potatoes, and fix 2 batches of sautéed greens, then freeze half of the food in meal-size portions so you have fresh food for a few days and frozen food for future meals. Alternatively, you might prepare 2 protein dishes, 2 dense vegetables, 2 greens dishes (1 cooked, 1 not), and 2 condiments one day, mix and match the components at different meals over the course of 3 days, then repeat.

Do a Little Each Day

Even with a big block of cooking behind you, you'll still need to do some prep every day or two. The good news is that fill-in dishes—tossed salads, parboiled vegetables, baked sweet potatoes, roasted vegetables, steamed or sautéed greens, fried, scrambled, or soft-boiled eggs, simmered salmon, and seared burgers—require minimal hands-on prep. The exact amount of time will depend on your family size, their appetites, the complexity of dishes you select, and your skill and efficiency in the kitchen. If you organize your kitchen, stock up, and practice, you can learn to turn out twice as much food in the time it now takes you to make a single meal.

Cold Potato or Hot Turkey?

Many of the foods we eat taste great warm, chilled, or close to room temp—as is, or transformed into something new. Some foods—like cooked leafy greens—look and taste more appealing if you don't reheat them. Others—like sweet potatoes and root vegetables—may be warmed or served close to room temperature as a side dish, or scattered over a green salad.

Last night's beef roast, steak, or chicken breast can be turned into a main course, served over salad greens with assorted raw, roasted, or parboiled vegetables.

Poached salmon is pricey in restaurants. Leftover baked salmon is priceless (and delicious unheated) and pairs well with almost any kind of cooked leafy green vegetable or salad, and a starchy or dense vegetable or fruit. You can turn any kind of fish or fowl into a chicken or tuna-type salad and serve on a bed of baby greens, or sprouted whole-grain bread.

Toss yesterday's steamed asparagus, or cauliflower with pea pods with a light vinaigrette or pesto. Chop and toss last night's baked potatoes or steamed green beans with minced celery, onions, and herbed mayonnaise or creamy tahini dressing for a delicious (fibrous or starchy) side salad. Dip cold parboiled broccoli and cauliflower in tahini dressing or guacamole for a snack or appetizer. Your options are multiplied if you shop, chop, prep, and cook ahead.

With minimal effort, leftover winter squash can become a quick breakfast paired with Protein-Coconut Cream, or a Tomato, Squash & Ginger Bisque, or a stew with leftover roast turkey or lamb, Bone Building Broth, Roasted Onions, and herbs, or a Squash Pudding Pie (see Index for recipes) for dessert.

You probably already eat (or once ate) a lot of foods lukewarm or straight from the fridge: hard-boiled eggs, tuna, chicken, potato, or pasta salads, sandwiches, yogurt, Thanksgiving leftovers, chicken legs, cold cuts, buffet and deli fare.

Cold or room-temperature meals are convenient and easy to assemble, especially on hot days. Banish the belief that you have to serve a hot dinner, particularly if your family members dine at different times. When you reframe it, a room-temperature dinner becomes a picnic, potluck, salad bar extravaganza, or beautiful buffet, indoors or out.

Not Always Hot
Room-temperature or cold meals are easy to assemble and great on hot days. If you just can't get past thinking that a meal should be hot, think of it as a picnic, salad bar, or buffet.

Seven Steps for Making More Food More Efficiently

1. **Create a mental map**

   Aim to prepare as much food as you comfortably can whenever you enter the kitchen. Rehearse mentally. Visualize what you need to do, then run through a step-by-step plan of action before you start. Make a list of what you're going to do and in what order. As you become more efficient and pick up speed, you can free flow and work from a bare outline.

2. **Do things in order**

   Start with dishes that require longer cooking, need time to cool, or will be served chilled. When cooking for multiple meals, start baking, roasting, or simmering foods before washing and chopping produce, or assembling salads, dressings, and sauces. Start water or a pot of beets boiling or squash steaming before chopping vegetables for a salad or sauté. Prepare dishes with shorter cooking times—and those that don't reheat well, like fish—close to serving time, unless you plan to serve them chilled.

3. **Multi-task**

   Start a batch of Bone Building Broth (Page 278 or Page 306) or stock in the morning or before bed. It can simmer all day or overnight. Put a pan of sweet potatoes or a beef roast in the oven or toaster oven, slip 2 pans of seasoned chicken parts into a full-size oven, or assemble a turkey breast in the slow cooker before you sit down to breakfast or lunch. Set timers and make notes so you know when each dish will be done.

4. **Strike while the oven (or grill) is hot**

   Grill 2 meats at the same time, or one after the other. Serve one hot for lunch and the other cold for dinner. Always cook enough for 2 or 3 meals, and then set extra portions aside for the next 2 days. Broil steak for 2 meals, reduce the temperature, then roast 2 pans of vegetables and some chicken and sweet potatoes that you can mix and match over the course of several days. You'll save energy and enjoy having a refrigerator full of healthy food.

5. **Reduce, reuse, recycle**

   Wash at least some of the dishes by hand so you can use the same cups, spoons, pots, and bowls for multiple tasks. If you're planning to make both Vanilla- and Chocolate-Protein Nut Spread (see Index for recipes), make the vanilla version, then the chocolate, to avoid having to wash the bowls and utensils in between. If you use the blender to make 2 batches of salad dressing in a row, start with the mildest one so you'll

Double Time
Prepare several dishes at once to get the most out of prep time.

only need to give the container a light rinse in between. **Note:** A thorough soap and hot water wash is a must for anything that comes in contact with raw or cooked eggs (say in mayonnaise), fish, poultry, or meat.

6. **Clean as you go**

   Cooking won't seem so overwhelming if you clean your knife, wipe off the cutting board, and clean the counters as you go. Keep a wet dishcloth by the board, so you can wipe the knife and board in between chopping tasks, and then toss it in the wash when you're done. Wash dishes, empty the dish drainer, put things away, or sweep the floor when you have a moment. It won't feel like so much work and you will be able to think more clearly and move more effortlessly in an uncluttered kitchen.

7. **Crock around the clock**

   You don't have to stand over a pot to cook. Most of our recipes require very little stirring. Even so, when you're pressed for time or it's hot indoors or out, there's nothing like a slow cooker. You can use it to simmer a beef and vegetable stew, slow cook chili, roast a whole chicken or a turkey breast, or bake stuffed apples. You can run errands, clean house, start laundry, write letters, or take a walk while your lunch, dinner, or dessert cooks. You can leave bone broth to cook while you're away all day or while you sleep at night.

   The flavors produced by a slow cooker aren't as intense as those you'd get from cooking in the oven or on top of the range, particularly a gas range or stove, but the convenience makes it worth the trade off at times.

Ten Tips to Turn Your Refrigerator into a Healthy Salad Bar & Deli

1. **Shop ahead**

   To eat produce-dominated whole foods meals 3 times a day, you need to buy foods, particularly vegetables and fruits, in enormous amounts. A well-stocked kitchen is your best defense against junk food and low-quality meals. Don't wait until you run out to restock. See Chapter 7 for tips to help you guesstimate how much vegetables, fruits, and meat you will need to buy per week. After several weeks or months, you'll become adept at figuring out how much your family members can consume in a week or month.

Fast Food
Shopping and chopping in advance cuts down on prep before mealtime.

2. **Chop ahead**

   Wash, dry, and chop an assortment of vegetables whenever you have 10, 15, or 30 minutes to spare. For example, cube and thinly slice enough onions to fill 2 pint or quart jars, ready for sautéing, stir-frying, or roasting. Chop 2 bunches of broccoli and 1 small head of cauliflower into bite-size pieces for parboiling, steaming, or stir-frying. Peel, seed, and thinly slice 1 large or several small cucumbers for salads. Seed and slice enough tomatoes for 2 days of salads or enough bell peppers for steaming, stir-frying, or parboiling over the course of 4 days. Mince extra parsley, scallions, chives, or arugula to use for garnishes throughout the week.

I typically cook greens in the morning. When time permits, I wash, destem and chop the greens (1 1/2 to 2 pounds of kale, collards, or Brussels sprouts) and a medium-size onion the night before so assembly will go more quickly in the morning. Even if you plan to cook the greens in the evening, chopping ahead makes sense and reduces the time it takes to get dinner on the table when everyone's hungry.

If time permits, I'll wash, trim, and slice 2 pounds of carrots or onions, readying them for roasting first thing in the morning or later in the day. You don't need to chop every vegetable in the house, just prep enough for 3 to 5 days, then repeat.

Note: Although most vegetables may be chopped several days ahead, lettuce and celery should be chopped to serve for only 1 or 2 days; after that they usually rust.

3. Quit canning...but use jars

Canning leads to significant nutrient losses and calls for excessive amounts of salt. Tomatoes are the only vegetables we buy and eat from a can. Everything else is best dried, frozen, or eaten fresh.

Don't toss those jars; they're perfect for storing chopped raw vegetables, parboiled vegetables, salad dressings, sauces and marinades, nuts, seeds, shredded coconut, homemade jerky, melon or pineapple cubes, cooked fruit compote, bone broth, stock, and leftover meat cooking juices in the fridge, and for shelving dried herbs, spices, fruits, vegetables, and assorted baking supplies in the cupboard.

What's so great about glass jars?

They:

(1) are non-toxic and won't off gas chemicals or leach carcinogenic phthalates (plasticizers) and xenoestrogens into your food;

(2) won't retain residual flavors or odors from previously stored foods;

(3) are easy to line up in the refrigerator and on pantry shelves;

(4) allow you to see what you have and find what you want fast;

(5) are great attention grabbers, inviting you to eat more colorful foods, particularly produce you've prepped ahead;

(6) are inexpensive and durable; and

(7) represent an ecological alternative to plastic wrap and plastic storage containers.

4. Choose containers consciously

Store leftovers in heat-proof Pyrex or stainless steel bowls covered with snap-on lids or heat-proof dinner plates or saucers which stack well. The same containers can often be used to store food (in the fridge or freezer), to reheat (in the oven, toaster oven, or on a rack over steam), and to serve. Don't use a large container when a smaller one will do. Transfer contents to smaller jars or bowls as they empty to free up more space, so you can pack more food into your refrigerator and shop less often.

Before warming, remove lids that are not heat-proof, replacing them with heat-proof saucers or aluminum foil if a cover is needed. Heat foods uncovered if the cooking time is brief, you're using dry heat (an oven), or you're warming food over steam and want to add moisture to it, e.g., leftover cooked rice that's dry. Cover the container if you're heating for more than 10 minutes, or using moist heat (steam) and you don't want the food (say a soup or stew) to absorb excess moisture. To reheat frozen food, use a cover to keep it from drying out since it will take longer to heat than defrosted or refrigerated food.

5. Label, label, label

Attach small squares of paper with rubber bands or use wide masking tape and indelible markers to note the contents. Date perishable items, then make it a priority to consume them in a timely fashion.

6. Spin-off

Make salads a permanent fixture in your daily diet. Rinse salad greens in a bowl, transfer to a salad spinner, spin dry, then store them in the spinner on the top shelf of the fridge. If your spinner has a flow through design (holes on the top and bottom), slip a cotton placemat or cloth dish towel under the container to absorb excess moisture.

For a split-second salad, slice or tear lettuce leaves, enough for a meal or 2 (no need to chop small leaves). Top or toss with colorful raw, roasted, grilled, parboiled, or steamed vegetables, and garnish or dress. For single-dish dining, top or toss with sliced, diced, or flaked fish, poultry, or meat.

Can You Freeze Foods in Glass Jars?

You can freeze foods in glass canning jars as long as you leave an inch of space for expansion. We usually freeze extra barbecue sauce, ketchup, chutney, applesauce, jerky, or our Lean & Creamy Salad Dressings in 16-ounce canning jars, rather than plastic containers. **Caution:** If you freeze foods in jars, store them in the side door or back of the fridge in such a way that they won't tumble out and break when you open the door or fish around for things.

7. **Plump-up the protein shelf**

   Every day or two, transfer 1 or 2 packages of frozen fish, poultry, or meat from the freezer (or grocery bags) to baking pans, loaf pans, or pie plates on a designated meat shelf with 2 or 3 meals in mind. After you cook meat, transfer another package to the refrigerator to allow ample time for thawing.

8. **Double up**

   Hard boil eggs by the dozen or half-dozen. Serve the fresh or leftover meats as hot or cold side dishes, or slice and serve them over individual salads for one-dish dining. Add leftover salmon to scrambled eggs with herbs, or a tuna-like salad. Add Sunday's turkey to Monday's salad and Tuesday's omelet. Create an impromptu stew with leftover lamb, roasted vegetables, and broth. Add yesterday's steak to a stir-fried vegetable medley or slather it in barbecue sauce for a delicious side dish.

9. **Veg ahead**

   Serve leftover sautéed or steamed greens at room temperature. Serve roasted onions, carrots, or mushrooms hot one day, and cold over salad greens the next. Turn Sunday's baked winter squash into Monday's Creamy Squash Soup with ginger or curry, and garnish with fresh chives or parsley you've minced ahead. Transform baked sweet potatoes into Mashed Sweet Potatoes with Lime (see Index for recipes). Turn leftover baked or simmered potatoes into potato salad or a main-course green salad with last night's meat.

10. **Dress ahead**

    Make 2 or 3 salad dressings at a time, then pour them into wide-mouth pint jars or bottles saved from commercial dressings, and add your own label. If you have at least 2 salad dressings and a variety of vegetables on hand, you probably won't mind having salads twice on some days.

    Use these delicious drizzles and sauces to top tossed green salads, parboiled vegetables, steamed vegetables, or as a mayonnaise replacement for chicken, turkey, egg, or potato salad.

    Make a double batch of barbecue sauce or ketchup to top burgers, steaks, chops, roasts, meatballs, or chicken for 2 weeks running or freeze a jar for the future. Line up all the condiment jars in the refrigerator for a salad bar effect and let the fun begin.

Tantalizing Toppers
Have an ample supply of dressings and sauces on hand to turn ordinary salads into scrumptious, healthy meals.

Nine Cool Tips for Cooking in Hot Weather

Don't stop cooking when it's hot. You still need nutritious foods and you can't live by salads alone. If you eat out, someone else will have to cook, so you won't save energy (or money). Instead of dining out every day and night, try these tips:

1. **Do it ahead:** Do all or most of your cooking early in the day. You won't have to turn on the oven during the hottest part of the day and you'll have healthy, convenient food to spare and to share.

2. **Turn the parcel into parts:** Cut a whole chicken into fryer parts so it cooks more quickly.

   Cut a turkey breast into cubes perfect for stir-frying, sautéing, or making shish kabobs. Do the same for a pork roast, or cut it into thin slices to sauté, sear, or grill. Transform chuck roast into chuck steaks, then marinate for the grill.

3. **Convection is the cure:** A large convection-type toaster oven increases your options, heats up in minutes and cooks foods 30 percent faster than a conventional oven. It also generates less heat, so it won't overheat your kitchen in hot weather.

   We use our convection toaster oven all year round, and especially in hot weather, to bake or roast sweet potatoes, onions, carrots, chicken or turkey breasts, cut-up fryer parts, fish fillets and steaks, small beef roasts, steaks, and chops. I also use it to toast sea vegetables and nuts. On a hot day, I might cook 2 or 3 dishes sequentially. Or I might bake or roast one thing each day, several days in a row, so I have an overlap of fresh and leftover foods each day.

4. **Make more stovetop and grill-top meat dishes:** You'll find plenty of these in the Index:
   Quick Smoky Simmered Salmon with Chipotlé (Page 234)
   Macadamia-Orange Roughy in Orange & White Wine Reduction Sauce (Page 248)
   Sautéed Fish Fillets (Page 249)
   Herbed Meat Balls (Page 288)
   Tuscan Chicken Casserole (Page 274)
   Poached Chicken Parts in White Wine with Herbs (Page 264)
   Quick Smoky Turkey (Page 261)
   Honey-Mustard Chicken with Ginger (Page 272)
   Sautéed Chicken Breast Fillets (Page 273)
   Herbed Burgers (Page 290)
   Stir-Fried Beef with Broccoli & Mushrooms (Page 286)
   Stir-Fried Veggies with Last Night's Meat (Page 287)
   Pan Grilled Chicken Breasts with Mango-Ginger Chutney (Page 270)

5. **Grill it:** Grill more meats, plain or seasoned—indoors in a grill pan or electric grill, or outdoors—and remember to make

Cut-ups
Divide a whole bird or roast into smaller pieces for quicker cooking.

everything with 2 or 3 meals in mind. Hot or cold, grilled fish, fowl, and meat are delicious, nutritious, and convenient.

6. **Parboil:** When the temperature climbs prepare more parboiled and fewer roasted and baked vegetables. Parboiled veggies taste great cold or close to room temperature—dressed or undressed—as side dishes, added to green salads, or as dippers in place of chips.

7. **Chill out:** If you don't want piping hot meals, make chilled, raw vegetable soups, such as Gazpacho, or serve cooked soups, such as Creamy Carrot Soup (Page 370), close to room temperature. Enjoy more homemade buffet, salad, and picnic-style meals. Serve cooked dishes close to room temperature. (We do this a lot). Serve cold baked potatoes, sliced and fanned over a salad or as a side, drizzled with a flavorful mayonnaise or tahini dressing. Enjoy more fruit salads, raw vegetable salads, parboiled vegetable medleys, and main dish salads that include a mix of meat and raw or raw and cooked vegetables.

8. **Steam it:** Not just for vegetables, steaming works for cooking fish in a heat-proof dish, in a parchment and foil wrap, or directly on a metal steamer tray. It also works for some puddings placed in heat-proof custard cups covered with foil. Countless other foods may be steamed. If you make bread, make Steamed Buns, which are cooked on top of the range in a fraction of the time required for baked dinner rolls or loaf breads.

9. **Center more meals on salad:** Light lettuce salads will feel more substantial when you add roasted, grilled, steamed, or parboiled vegetables fresh or leftover fish, poultry, or meat, and a friendly fat source: avocados, toasted nuts, seeds, olive or flax oil, diluted nut butter, or homemade pesto or pistou. Fresh or dried fruits are at home in many green salads. Refer to Chapter 19 for great ideas.

chapter 13
Sample Month of Menus with Prep Lists

Preparing produce-dominated meals takes practice. The more you do it, the easier it gets. To help you apply the principles outlined in the last 2 chapters, we offer 4 sample weeks of menus and prep lists representing a composite of many weeks from our actual experience.

The following menus are based on recipes in this book and designed to serve 2 people. When making shopping lists, jot down the ingredients and amounts for each recipe you plan to make for the week. If you're cooking for 4 people, you may wish to double the recipes. If you have a well-stocked kitchen, you won't have to buy all the ingredients in every recipe because there will be some overlap of ingredients from week to week.

To order ready-made shopping lists for the sample month of menus, send your request with $5 plus $1.50 shipping (please convert foreign funds to United States' currency) to Rachel Albert-Matesz, c/o Planetary Press, PO Box 97040, Phoenix, AZ 85060-7040.

Although it would seem wise to offer a sample week of menus for each season, it's not as easy as you'd think. We were amazed at the difference in local, seasonal produce when we moved from the Midwest to the Southwest. What grows in Ohio and Michigan in the fall, spring, and summer varies widely from what you'll find in farmers' markets and gardens in Arizona and Southern California. We've aimed for a more general set of menus you can modify for the season and your region.

Chapter Overview:
It will take practice to create meals that are produced-dominated. This chapter provides sample menus and prep lists to help you apply the principles of *The Garden of Eating*.

You will notice some of the same vegetables repeated in many of our menus. We prepare many of the same foods and dishes throughout the year, such as sautéed or boiled kale or collard greens and carrots. These vegetables are hearty enough to be grown and harvested in the late fall and winter, even after a frost (and as far north as Scotland), protected from snow and frigid temperatures with cold frames. The hardy greens are also strong enough to survive summer heat when lettuce sometimes burns out.

While not as sturdy as kale, collards, or Brussels sprouts, we were able to get fresh, locally grown broccoli, cauliflower, spinach, and bok choy as late as November and December in Ohio. Carrots grow year-round in Arizona, but not in the Midwest, unless you have a greenhouse or cold frames, but they're worth eating year-round. If the demand for these and other vegetables was greater, more farmers might make them year-round crops in areas with suitable climates. Given the nutritional value of these foods, we buy them from other regions when we can't get them locally.

Most of our recipes are amenable to year-round use with slight adjustments in ingredients or cooking method. For example, we substitute soaked sun-dried tomatoes for fresh in salads, stews, and stove-top casseroles. Instead of using a full-size oven in hot weather, we use a slow cooker for baking a chicken or turkey breast, or a toaster oven for baking sweet potatoes or chicken fryer parts.

If you have a garden, access to a farmers' market, or belong to a Community Supported Agriculture (CSA) project that delivers fresh, locally grown produce to your door each week, replace imported produce with locally grown fruits and vegetables whenever possible. Make additional substitutions for any food sensitivities or aversions of your family members. If it's simply a matter of not liking something, bear in mind that food preferences can change with the right recipes, repeated exposure, and the desire to broaden your diet and acquire a taste for more nutritious food.

If you're cooking for one, you'll probably want to freeze extra portions of poultry or meat, share the experience by setting up a food exchange with a friend, or cut all of the recipes in half. If your leftovers don't follow the outline exactly, make appropriate adjustments and substitutions. You can freeze extra poultry, beef, sautéed greens, soups, stews, and some sauces, although there will be a slight loss of flavor.

If you buy too much fruit—melons, berries, grapes, bananas, stone fruits—or it starts to ripen and soften faster than you can consume it, slice and freeze the surplus on baking sheets. Transfer it to freezer containers, label, date, and freeze for future Frosty Fruit Whips, Better Balanced Smoothies, and Vita-Mix Total Juices (see Index for recipes).

For the best results, follow each week of menus 3 times (You don't have to do it 3 weeks in a row, although you might want to). Each time, change 1 or more ingredients in a menu using the variations at

Year–Round Recipes
With slight adjustments in ingredients and/or cooking methods, most recipes are suitable for year-round use.

Mark Your Place:
To make it easy to shop and prepare the sample month of menus, mark the recipes for each week with a different colored page flag (available in office supply stores). For example, you might use red flags for week 1, blue for week 2, yellow for week 3, and green flags for the recipes for week 4.

17 Simple Tips to Help Vary Your Menus:

1. Burgers: Use ground turkey, then buffalo, then beef. Try different herbs and spices.

2. Roast turkey breast: Make Roasted Smoky Turkey Breast, then Herbed-Orange-Roasted Turkey Breast, then Slow-Cooked Apple & Mustard-Glazed Turkey Breast (see Index for recipes).

3. Baked chicken parts: Use breast halves once, then thighs, then a cut-up fryer once. Or, use breasts or mixed parts all 3 times, with different seasonings.

4. Beef and vegetable stew: Vary the vegetables, meats, or seasonings.

5. Pork chops: Season a different way each time, three weeks in a row.

6. Replace steak with a roast. Buy ground buffalo to replace ground beef for burgers, meatballs, or meatloaf. Grill, then broil, then pan sear your steaks or burgers.

7. Enjoy the same fish prepared with different techniques or seasonings. Or, use the same recipe with 3 different kinds of fish (e.g., salmon, then Arctic char, then sea bass).

8. Sauté kale with different seasonings, or take a kale recipe and try it with collards, then with mustard or turnip greens; compare the results.

9. Repeat the Basic Green Salad (or one of the other salads) using different kinds and combinations of salad greens, different colorful mix-ins, or different dressings.

10. Make Vinaigrette or Lemonette with 3 different herb or spice combinations. Do the same with Tahini Dips & Dressings and Homemade Mayonnaise (see Index for recipes).

11. Prepare the basic Apple Compote with a different kind of apple, a different dried fruit, or a different spice each time.

12. If you don't like pork, substitute lamb or chicken breast. If you don't like lamb, substitute beef. If you don't like one kind of fish, try another. If you have one in the house but not the other, feel free to substitute.

13. Try fruits and nuts you've never eaten—various apples, pears, plums, peaches, berries, cherries, and melons from your local farmers' market or natural foods store. Try different types of dates and dried figs. (You will be amazed at how many varieties exist.)

14. Try a new variety of sweet potatoes each week (red garnets, jewels, Japanese and white sweet potatoes taste remarkably different). Try new types of winter squash.

15. Replace chicken eggs with duck eggs. Try goose eggs if you get the chance.

16. Roast carrots with ginger, then garam masala, followed by mustard seeds. Try carrots in combination with onions, parsnips, or turnips.

17. If a menu says baked squash and baked salmon, in hot weather, substitute simmered squash and simmered salmon. Similarly, replace a beef roast or leg of lamb with broiled, grilled or roasted steak or chops.

the end of each recipe, or the tips listed on the previous page. This will help you master new techniques, learn some of the recipes by rote, add to your recipe repertoire, pick up speed, and enjoy a more varied diet.

Practice

Eventually, you will be able to plan meals in your head. You won't have to create a week's worth of menus in advance unless you want to. You will automatically take inventory every evening and mix and match dishes for the next day to use up what you have on hand. Down the road you may prefer to make a "coming attractions" list for the next week. Until then, try the suggestions that follow.

After following the sample menus for several weeks or months, post a Meal Planning Worksheet on the refrigerator. This is nothing more than an 8 1/2 x 11-inch sheet of paper with Breakfast, Lunch, Dinner written across the short side and days of the week across the long side. When filled in, this sheet will help you decide what to defrost, wash, chop, and cook ahead.

Create a rough plan for the week or sketch out a few days at a time, whatever works for you. Fill out the sheet in pencil so you can switch things around. Each morning or evening take inventory of what's leftover for the next day, and what you must make to fill in—a mental dress rehearsal. I do this automatically every day!

Be specific. Fish, chicken, turkey, bison, or pork? Burgers, meatloaf, steak, or roast? Chicken thighs, breasts, or mixed parts? Kale, collards, Brussels sprouts, or broccoli? Note the particular recipe you plan to use, until you've memorized your favorites. As you become more skilled, you may prefer generalities that allow more flexibility: green salad, sautéed greens, or parboiled salad; baked (or poached) chicken parts with herbs, beef roast, or meatballs; mayonnaise or tahini dressing. You can decide on the seasonings at the last minute. If you have broccoli from the previous day, work it into a meal, even if your worksheet says sautéed greens or salad. If you run out of broccoli, but have cauliflower and asparagus, steam or parboil them.

Don't let cooked food sit around so long that it loses flavor, fragrance, or spoils. Repetition is only a problem if you're eating a severely limited and nutrient-deficient diet, which this is not! If you eat sautéed kale (or salad) 6 days in a week, or many weeks in a row, you won't suffer, provided you prepare a fresh batch every 2 or 3 days and vary

---

Tips for Busy Times

* In anticipation of a particularly busy week, bake or roast extra chicken or turkey breast and freeze in portions, each to serve 2 meals.

* Make and freeze extra beef stew, chili, sautéed kale or collards, Mashed Sweet Potato with Lime, Smoothie Bases, or our Better Barbecue Sauce (see Index for recipes).

* Make multiple batches of beef or turkey jerky, fruit leather, or toasted nuts.

* Stock up on and substitute frozen spinach, Brussels sprouts, broccoli, or mixed vegetables for cooked greens (they're not bad with salad dressing).

* Place frozen, unsweetened mango, pineapple, or peach slices in a jar and defrost overnight in the refrigerator to use in place of fresh fruit or fruit salad.

* Buy preformed beef, bison, and turkey patties, skinless boneless chicken breasts and thighs, and prewashed (ready to cook) kale, collards, trimmed spinach, mustard or turnip greens.

* Ask a friend or family member to help you in the kitchen.

The more of these steps you take, the better.

the seasonings or side dishes. It's no different than people who eat cold cereal, sandwiches, or bread day in, day out. Hunter-gatherers often ate the same food for prolonged periods in various seasons and regions.

If you don't want the exact same meals 2 days in a row, mix and match the leftover meat, vegetable, and fruit dishes, the way you do with garments in your closet. Coordinate the colors and dishes in new and different ways. Accessorize with different salad dressings, sauces, fruits, nuts, herbs, relishes, flavored mustards, etc.

How Much Food Can You Make in 90 minutes?

If your kitchen is well stocked and organized, you have a good sharp vegetable knife (or chef's knife), and you work methodically, you can turn out an amazing amount of food in 1 1/2 hours of hands-on time—enough for 6 or more meals. Here's an example of what I did late one afternoon in under 90 minutes; it might take you longer, but with practice, you'll pick up speed.

* chopped 2 pounds of carrots; started Roasted Carrots (6 to 8 servings)
* peeled and chopped 2 pounds of potatoes; started Herb-Roasted Potatoes (6 to 8 servings)
* chopped 2 pounds of onions; assembled Balsamic Roasted Onions (6 to 8 servings)
* blended a double batch of Sesame, Garlic & Chive Dressing (16 servings)
* chopped 1 onion and 2 pounds of collards; set aside to cook the next day (6 servings)
* assembled a Basic Green Salad (4 to 6 servings)
* cooked bison burgers on top of the range (4 to 6 servings)
* Seasoned Smoky Roasted Turkey Breast and started it when the carrots, onions, and potatoes came out of the oven (12 servings)
* baked 6 small to medium sweet potatoes with turkey (6 servings)

Prepared according to our recipes, we enjoyed burgers with green salad, roasted vegetables, and tahini dressing for dinner, with fresh fruit for dessert. We had enough to repeat the meal the next day, with leftover roasted veggies for a third day and dressing for 2 weeks. While we ate dinner, the turkey and sweet potatoes baked and we had enough of that meal for 3 meals, and turkey for the freezer.

I cooked the greens and onions the next morning for breakfast and had enough to serve with dinner and a meal the day after.

WEEK 1 MENUS – FALL/WINTER

	Breakfast	Lunch	Snack (optional)	Dinner
S u n d a y	Smoky Omelet with Chipotlé (Page 224) Sautéed Collards with Onions, Mushrooms & Sage (Page 316) Sliced oranges and grapefruit **or** sliced mango dusted with shredded unsweetened coconut	Stewed Chicken with Carrots, Parsnips & Ginger (Page 275) Leftover Sautéed Collards with Onions, Mushrooms & Sage Rosehip-Apple Compote (Page 430) garnished with toasted almonds (Page 406)		Roast Leg of Lamb (Page 305) **or** Broiled **or** Grilled Lamb Chops (Page 303) Basic Baked Squash Halves (Page 380) **or** Simmered Squash with Pie Spice (Page 379) Coleslaw (Page 362) with Sesame, Garlic & Chive Dressing (Page 411) Roasted Dandelion & Chicory Root "Coffee" (Page 495)
M o n d a y	Fried or Poached Eggs (Page 219 or 217) with leftover lamb Leftover Sautéed Collards with Onions, Mushrooms & Sage Beet-Apple Blend (Page 506) or sliced fresh fruit	Leftover Lamb Leftover Baked Squash **or** Simmered Squash Leftover Coleslaw with Sesame, Garlic & Chive Dressing	Speedy Smoothie (Page 475)	Leftover Stewed Chicken with Carrots, Parsnips & Ginger Steamed Broccoli & Cauliflower with lemon-flavored cod liver oil Leftover Rosehip-Apple Compote garnished with toasted almonds
T u e s d a y	Poached or Fried Eggs (Page 217 or 219) with leftover lamb Better Brussels Sprouts with Sunchokes & Sage (Page 324) Sliced oranges and grapefruit **or** sliced mango dusted with shredded unsweetened coconut	Leftover Stewed Chicken with Carrots, Parsnips & Ginger Leftover Better Brussels Sprouts with Sunchokes & Sage Leftover Rosehip-Apple Compote garnished with toasted almonds	Speedy Smoothie (Page 475)	Baked Salmon with Sumac (Page 235) Leftover Coleslaw with Sesame, Garlic & Chive Dressing Leftover Baked or Simmered Winter Squash with Pie Spice and butter, or coconut or flax oil
W e d n e s d a y	Paprika Scrambled Eggs (Page 224) Leftover Better Brussels Sprouts with Sunchokes & Sage Beet-Apple Blend (Page 506) or sliced apples Dried Figs with Anise Seeds & Nuts, optional (Page 454)	Leftover Baked Salmon with Sumac Leftover Coleslaw with Sesame, Garlic & Chive Dressing Herb-Roasted Potatoes (Page 390), cooked Tuesday evening	Speedy Smoothie (Page 475)	Seared Pork Chops with Cranberry, Onion & Chipotlé Sauce (Page 284) Steamed Broccoli with Yellow Bell Pepper (Page 326) and lemon-flavored cod liver oil Baked Spiced Sweet Potato Halves (Page 385)

WEEK 1 MENUS – FALL/WINTER CONT.

	Breakfast	Lunch	Snack (optional)	Dinner
Thursday	Poached Eggs or Soft-Boiled Eggs (Page 217 or 218) with leftover pork Leftover Steamed Broccoli with Yellow Bell Pepper (Page 326) and lemon-flavored cod liver oil Carrot-Orange Blend (Page 508) or sliced oranges	Basic Green Salad made with sliced red radishes, scallions, and parsley, topped with leftover Herb-Roasted Potatoes, leftover Baked Salmon, and Sesame, Garlic & Chive Dressing	Speedy Smoothie (Page 475)	Leftover Pork Chops with Cranberry, Onion & Chipotlé Sauce Sautéed Kale with Onions & Mustard, topped with lemon-flavored cod liver oil Leftover Baked Spiced Sweet Potato Halves
Friday	Pork & Egg Scramble (Page 228) Leftover Sautéed Kale with Onions & Mustard topped with lemon-flavored cod liver oil Sliced fresh fruit or Apple-Orange Blend (Page 506)	Leftover Green Salad topped with leftover Herb-Roasted Potatoes, thawed ready-to-eat shrimp or canned tuna, topped with leftover Sesame, Garlic & Chive Dressing Fresh pear	Banana with almond or cashew butter	Tuscan Chicken Casserole (Page 274) Leftover Sautéed Kale with Onions & Mustard and lemon-flavored cod liver oil Simmered Carrots with Sunchokes (Page 371)
Saturday	Scrambled Eggs with Herbs (Page 224) and any leftover shrimp Steamed Cauliflower, Red Cabbage & Celery (Page 326) topped with lemon-flavored cod liver oil Fruit Salad (Page 435) dusted with unsweetened, shredded coconut	Leftover Tuscan Chicken Casserole (Page 274) Leftover Steamed Cauliflower, Red Cabbage & Celery with Very Easy Vinaigrette (Page 422) Leftover Simmered Carrots with Sunchokes		Caveman Chili (Page 300) served over Baked Spaghetti Squash (Page 377) Mustard-Glazed Broccoli (Page 329) Chocolate-Avocado Mousse (Page 432)

~Prep Lists and Information start on next page~

PREP FOR WEEK 1

Recipes for Sunday Morning Prep Session

> Smoky Omelet with Chipotlé (Page 224)
>
> Sautéed Collards with Mushrooms, Onions & Sage (Page 316)
>
> Toasted almonds (Page 406)
>
> Roast Leg of Lamb (Page 305) or Broiled or Roasted Lamb Chops (Page 303)
>
> Baked Squash Halves (Page 380) or Simmered Squash (Page 379)
>
> Stewed Chicken with Carrots, Parsnips & Ginger (Page 275)
>
> Sesame, Garlic & Chive Dressing, double batch (Page 411)
>
> Coleslaw (Page 362)
>
> Extra onions, scallions, and parsley and vegetables for Monday
>
> Vegetables for Better Brussels Sprouts (Page 324)
>
> Rosehip-Apple Compote (Page 430)
>
> Roasted Dandelion & Chicory Root "Coffee" (Page 495)
>
> Smoothie Bases for the week (Page 467 and 468) for snacks
>
> Bone-Building Broth (Page 278 or 306), if desired

Sunday Morning (3 to 4 hours):

1. Wash and chop onions, mushrooms, and collards; prepare as for Sautéed Collards recipe. Meanwhile, slice fruit for breakfast. Cook eggs.

2. Toast nuts in oven (325° F). Season enough lamb for 3 to 4 meals.

3. When nuts are done, raise heat and start roasting lamb (if you're cooking chops, wait to cook lamb until dinner). Assemble and bake enough squash for 3 meals. Set timers.

4. Assemble and start enough Stewed Chicken with Carrots, Parsnips & Ginger for 3 meals.

5. If you have enough bones in the freezer, start a batch of Bone-Building Broth on top of the stove or in a slow cooker; let it cook all day or night.

6. Make a double batch of Sesame, Garlic & Chive Dressing for the week or 2 different flavored dressings.

7. Prepare enough coleslaw for 4 or 5 days.

8. Thinly slice 1 or 2 quart jars full of onions for sautés. Wash, trim, and chop 2 pounds of Brussels sprouts for Better Brussels Sprouts you'll cook Tuesday morning. Wash, spin dry, and mince a jar of scallions and parsley for garnishes.

9. Check squash, Stewed Chicken with Carrots, Parsnips & Ginger, and lamb.

10. Prepare enough Apple Compote for 3 days.

11. To have fruit smoothies for snacks all week for 2 people, make 1 batch of Don's and Rachel's Smoothie Bases (for 2 people). Refrigerate or freeze individual portions.

12. Serve chicken stew, some of the leftover collards from breakfast, and Apple Compote for lunch, and refrigerate everything extra.

Sunday Evening (30 minutes):

1. If you haven't already cooked lamb, broil or grill enough chops for supper and 2 more meals.

2. Warm enough leftover squash for dinner. Dress coleslaw for dinner and 3 more meals.

3. Make enough Roasted Chicory & Dandelion Root "Coffee" for 2 or 3 days

4. Pack lunches for the next day.

Monday Morning (15 to 20 minutes):

1. If you want a smoothie for a snack later, blend a premeasured portion of Smoothie Base with 1 cup fresh or frozen fruit. Pour into a wide-mouth thermos and chill. Repeat for each person

2. Remove leftover cooked collards from the fridge and slice fruit or make a Vita-Mix Total Juice.

3. Slice leftover lamb (heat briefly, if desired).

4. Cook eggs for breakfast.

Monday Evening (15 to 20 minutes):

1. Heat leftover chicken stew and Apple Compote for dinner.

2. Wash, chop, and steam broccoli and cauliflower. Lightly dress with cod liver oil at the table.

3. Pack salad and compote portion of lunches for Tuesday. (Heat stew the next morning).

Tuesday Morning (30 to 45 minutes):

1. If you want a smoothie for a snack later, blend a premeasured portion of Smoothie Base with 1 cup fresh or frozen fruit. Pour into a wide-mouth thermos and chill. Repeat for each person

2. Sauté and simmer Better Brussels Sprouts, using vegetables you chopped on Sunday.

3. If you don't have a toaster oven at work, boil water to fill thermos bottle(s); seal and let stand. Meanwhile, heat stew for lunches. When stew is hot, empty thermos bottle(s); fill with stew, and seal.

4. Slice fruit for breakfast. Cook eggs.

Tuesday Evening (30 minutes):

1. Remove leftover coleslaw and winter squash from refrigerator and preheat oven.

2. Wash, peel, dice, season, and roast potatoes for Wednesday through Friday

3. Wash 6 sweet potatoes (for 3 days), poke with fork holes, and bake in a dry pan.

4. Season enough salmon for 3 meals. Bake in hot oven.

5. After dinner, pack lunches for Wednesday.

Wednesday Morning (30 minutes):

1. For optional smoothie snack, blend a premeasured portion of Smoothie Base with 1 cup fresh or frozen fruit, pour into a wide-mouth thermos, and chill. Repeat for each person

2. Gently warm leftover Brussels Sprouts for breakfast. Prepare a Vita-Mix Total Juice or slice apples or other fruit.

3. Prepare eggs. Serve figs, toasted almonds, and anise seeds, if desired.

Wednesday Evening (30 to 40 minutes):

1. Preheat oven. Sear pork chops, and transfer to oven along with enough leftover sweet potatoes for dinner.

2. Prep ingredients for Cranberry, Onion & Chipotlé Sauce; prepare when chops are done.

3. Wash and chop broccoli and yellow peppers; steam close to serving time.

4. Wash and spin dry salad greens and slice red radishes for salads. Pack lunches for Thursday.

Thursday Morning (20 minutes):

1. If you want a smoothie for a snack later, blend a premeasured portion of Smoothie Base with 1 cup fresh or frozen fruit, pour into a wide-mouth thermos and chill. Repeat for each person.

2. Take out leftover broccoli and bell peppers.

3. Prepare a Vita-Mix Total Juice or wash and slice fresh fruit. Cook eggs.

Thursday Evening (30 minutes):

1. Prepare enough Sautéed Kale with Onions & Mustard for 3 meals.

2. Gently warm leftover sweet potatoes and pork chops with sauce.

3. Defrost frozen shrimp (for Friday lunch), if desired. Pack lunches

Friday Morning (15 to 20 minutes)

1. Take out leftover cooked kale.

2. Slice fresh fruit or make a Vita-Mix Total Juice. Cook eggs.

3 Pack fruit and nut butter for snacks if desired.

Friday Evening (30 minutes):

1. Take out leftover cooked kale. Prepare enough Simmered Carrots with Sunchokes for 3 meals.

2. Prepare Tuscan Chicken Casserole.

Saturday Morning (15 to 20 minutes):

1. Prepare a fruit salad or make a Vita-Mix drink with whatever fruits are at hand.

2. Chop and steam cauliflower, red cabbage, and celery for breakfast and lunch.

3. Cook eggs and take out any leftover shrimp.

Saturday Lunch (15 minutes):

1. Warm leftover Carrots with Sunchokes and Tuscan Chicken Casserole.

2. Prepare Very Easy Vinaigrette to toss with leftover steamed vegetables.

Saturday Evening (1 to 1 1/4 hours):

1. Prepare Chocolate-Avocado Mouse. Chill.

2. Follow recipe for Caveman Chili. While it cooks, bake spaghetti squash.

3. Chop broccoli and measure out seasonings. Set aside.

4. Just before serving, prepare Chicory & Dandelion Root "Coffee."

5. Halve squash, scoop out and discard seeds, rake the flesh onto plates, and prepare broccoli.

WEEK 2 MENUS – FALL/WINTER

	Breakfast	Lunch	Snack (optional)	Dinner
S u n d a y	Spinach & Egg Pie Italiano (Page 232) Fruit Salad (Page 435) garnished with shredded, unsweetened coconut	Roasted Chicken with Thyme (Page 262) Mesclun Greens with Herb-Roasted Mushrooms & Onions (Page 349) and Lean & Creamy French Dressing (Page 419) Baked Apples with Date-Nut Filling (Page 428)		Beef, Carrot & Sunchoke Stew (Page 296) Steamed Broccoli and Cauliflower with butter, lemon-flavored cod liver oil (Page 326), or Macadamia-Dill Dressing (Page 413) Roasted Dandelion & Chicory Root "Coffee" (Page 495)
M o n d a y	Leftover Spinach & Egg Pie Italiano Leftover Fruit Salad garnished with shredded, unsweetened coconut	Leftover Mesclun Greens with Herb-Roasted Mushrooms & Onions, Lean & Creamy French Dressing Leftover, Roasted Chicken with Thyme	Fresh pear with or without Ground Beef Jerky (Page 486)	Leftover Beef, Carrot & Sunchoke Stew with parsley garnish Steamed Broccoli with Cauliflower and butter, lemon-flavored cod liver oil, or Macadamia-Dill Dressing Leftover Baked Apples with Date-Nut Filling
T u e s d a y	Poached or Fried Eggs (Page 217 or 219) with leftover Roasted Chicken with Thyme Better Brussels Sprouts (Page 323) Beet-Apple Blend or sliced oranges and apples	Leftover Mesclun Greens with Herb-Roasted Mushrooms & Onions and Lean & Creamy French Dressing Leftover Roasted Chicken with Thyme	Fresh pear with or without leftover Ground Beef Jerky	Leftover Beef, Carrot & Sunchoke Stew with parsley garnish Leftover Better Brussels Sprouts Leftover Baked Apples with Date-Nut Filling
W e d n e s d a y	Chicken & Egg Scramble (Page 228) Leftover Better Brussels Sprouts Beet-Apple Blend or sliced apples Dried Figs with Anise Seeds & Nuts, optional (Page 454)	Basic Green Salad with cucumber, celery, red radish, scallions, and grated carrot (Page 344) topped with sliced, leftover Roasted Chicken and leftover Lean & Creamy French Dressing	Pear, or pear with Ground Beef Jerky	Moroccan-Spiced Salmon (Page 237) with Moroccan Barbecue Sauce (Page 400) Oil-Free Sautéed Chinese Greens (Page 321) Baked Squash Halves (Page 380) or Simmered Squash (Page 379) with pie spice and butter or coconut oil

Week 2 Menus – Fall/Winter – cont.

	Breakfast	Lunch	Snack (optional)	Dinner
Thursday	Protein-Coconut Cream (Page 470) over leftover Baked Squash Halves or Simmered Squash	Leftover Moroccan-Spiced Salmon flaked over Basic Green Salad with cucumber, celery, red radish, and scallions with leftover Lean & Creamy French Dressing or Macadamia-Dill Dressing Fresh apple or pear	Grapes with Ground Beef Jerky	Turkey Burgers (Page 277) with leftover Moroccan Barbecue Sauce Leftover Oil-Free Sautéed Chinese Greens with lemon-flavored cod liver oil Dried Figs with Anise Seeds & Nuts (Page 454) or fresh fruit
Friday	Leftover Baked Squash Halves with leftover Protein-Coconut Cream	Leftover Moroccan-Spiced Salmon served over Basic Green Salad with leftover Lean & Creamy French Dressing Leftover steamed carrot sticks	Apple or orange with or without Ground Beef Jerky (Page 486)	Leftover (or freshly cooked) Turkey Burgers with leftover Moroccan Barbecue Sauce Steamed Broccoli, Cauliflower & Red Onions with leftover Macadamia-Dill Dressing Apple-Apricot Compote (Page 429) garnished with toasted walnuts
Saturday	Better Balanced Smoothie (Page 471 to 474)	Leftover Chicken with Thyme or Herbs de Provençe (from freezer) Mesclun Greens topped with leftover Steamed Broccoli, Cauliflower, Celery & Red Onion and leftover Macadamia-Dill Dressing Leftover Apple-Apricot Compote garnished with toasted walnuts		Creamy Carrot Soup with Ginger (Page 370) Roasted Red Snapper with Rosemary, Garlic, Lemon & Pepper (Page 243) Sautéed Collards with Onions, Cumin & Pepper (Page 314) Roasted Chicory & Dandelion Root "Coffee" (Page 495) Dark Chocolate-Dipped Dates, optional (Page 453)

~Prep Lists and Information start on next page~

PREP FOR WEEK 2

Recipes for Sunday Morning Prep Session

Spinach & Egg Pie (Page 232)

Fruit Salad (Page 435)

Roasted Balsamic Onions (Page 373)

Herb-Roasted Mushrooms (Page 375)

Beef, Carrot & Sunchoke Stew (Page 296)

Roasted Chicken with Thyme (Page 262)

Baked Apples with Date-Nut Filling (Page 428)

Lean & Creamy French Dressing, double batch (Page 419)

Macadamia-Dill Dressing, double batch (Page 413)

Moroccan Spice Mix (Page 399)

Toasted walnuts (Page 406)

Toasted Dulse (Page 397)

Salad bar setup for week (chopping assorted vegetables below)

Steamed Broccoli with Cauliflower (Page 326)

Bone-Building Broth, optional (Page 278 or 306)

Sunday Morning Prep (3 to 4 hours):

1. Preheat oven. Assemble and bake Spinach & Egg Pie.

2. Prep onions and mushrooms for 3 meals to roast after pie is done.

3. Make fruit salad for breakfast and Monday morning.

4. When pie is done, raise oven temperature to 400° F. Transfer onions and mushrooms to oven; set a timer.

5. After 20 minutes, stir onions and mushrooms. Assemble and roast 1 large or 2 smaller chickens. If roasting 2 chickens, use different seasonings on each one. (Freeze half or more of the meat).

6. Assemble Baked Stuffed Apples. Remove onions and mushrooms from oven; lower heat to 350° F; bake apples and chicken. Set timers!

7. Wash and chop vegetables for Beef, Carrot & Sunchoke Stew. Brown meat. Start stew on the stove or in a slow cooker for Sunday dinner, and Monday, and Tuesday.

8. Make a single or double batch of Lean & Creamy French Dressing and a double batch of Macadamia-Dill Dressing. (They keep for 2 weeks in the fridge.)

9. Toast spices for Moroccan Spice Mix to season salmon and make barbecue sauce midweek.

10. Check chicken. Prep vegetables for salads and sautés for several days. Wash, spin dry, and finely chop 2 bunches of scallions and 1 bunch of parsley. Wash and spin dry 1/4 to 1/2 pound of Mesclun or Baby Greens. Mince 2 cups of celery. Stuff into wide-mouth pint and quart jars. Seed and chop 2 cups of tomatoes for the salad for lunch.

11. Chop 2 bunches of broccoli and half a head of cauliflower. (You'll steam some for dinner and more on Monday night.) Thinly slice 1 quart of red onions for later in the week. Wash, trim, and chop 2 pounds of Brussels sprouts and 1 large onion to cook Tuesday morning.

12. When chicken is done, dry toast enough walnuts for 2 to 3 weeks. Lower heat to 200° F and toast a pan of dulse leaf. Stay close; these foods burn easily. Refrigerate cooled nuts in jars. Store cooled dulse in a jar on the dining table.

13. Assemble salad to serve with chicken for lunch. Debone chicken, and refrigerate leftovers.

14. If you have enough bones on hand, start a batch of Bone-Building Broth (Page 278 or 306) and let it cook all afternoon and evening, or overnight, on top of the range or in a slow cooker.

Sunday Evening (20 to 30 minutes):

1. Warm stew for supper and Baked Apples for dessert.

2. Steam broccoli and cauliflower for dinner.

3. Pack lunches for Monday.

4. If you want beef (or turkey) jerky for snacks during the week, prepare Ground Beef or Turkey Jerky and start it drying before dinner. (It will take all night to dry).

Monday Morning (15 minutes):

1. Take out leftover Spinach & Egg Pie, and leftover fruit salad.

2. Pack snacks, if desired.

Monday Evening (15 to 30 minutes):

1. Heat leftover stew for dinner. Gently warm enough Baked Apples for dessert and take out leftover broccoli, cauliflower, and dressing for dinner.

2. Pack lunches for Tuesday. If you have fruit salad that's too ripe, freeze for future smoothies.

Tuesday Morning (45 minutes):

1. Prepare Better Brussels Sprouts using vegetables you chopped on Sunday.

2. Prepare a Vita-Mix Total Juice. If you don't have a Vita-Mix, wash and slice fresh fruit.

Tuesday Evening (30 minutes):

1. Take out leftover Brussels Sprouts from breakfast; heat gently if desired. Warm leftover stew and Baked Apples for supper.

2. After dinner, chop extra salad vegetables (cucumbers, radishes, scallions, celery), wash and spin dry lettuce for 2 more days, as needed.

3. Pack lunches for Wednesday and snacks, if desired.

Wednesday Morning (15 to 30 minutes):

1. Gently warm leftover Brussels Sprouts for breakfast.

2. Make a Vita-Mix Total Juice or slice apples or other fruit.

3. Prepare Chicken & Egg Scramble.

4. If you're still hungry, take out dried figs, toasted walnuts, and anise seeds.

Wednesday Evening (1 to 1 1/4 hours):

1. Wash, halve, season, and bake Squash Halves for supper and 2 more meals.

2. Assemble Moroccan Barbecue Sauce. Prepare Moroccan-Spiced Salmon.

3. Prepare Oil-Free Sautéed Chinese Greens for dinner and 1 or 2 other meals.

4. Make Protein-Coconut Cream for Thursday's and Friday's breakfasts.

5. Transfer cooked, frozen chicken (made Sunday) to refrigerator for Thursday, Friday, and Saturday.

Thursday Morning (1/4 hour):

1. Pack lunches. Warm leftover squash if desired; top with Protein-Coconut Cream.

Thursday Evening (15 to 20 minutes):

1. Take out leftover Oil-Free Sautéed Chinese Greens. Cook enough preformed turkey burgers (sear in skillet) for dinner and Friday night.

2. Take out dried figs, toasted walnuts, and ground anise seeds or fresh fruit for dessert.

3. Pack lunches and a snack if desired.

Friday Morning (15 minutes):

1. Take out leftover winter squash; serve at room temperature or heat briefly. Top with leftover Protein-Coconut Cream.

Friday Evening (30 minutes)

1. Prepare Apple Compote. Chop nuts for garnish.

2. Gently warm leftover burgers (cook more if needed) and heat barbecue sauce.

3. Chop and steam enough broccoli, cauliflower, and red onion for dinner and 1 more meal.

Saturday Morning (15 minutes):

1. Make Better Balanced Smoothie(s) or use up assorted leftovers.

Saturday Lunch (15 minutes):

1. Assemble main-course salad from salad greens, leftover steamed vegetables, leftover chicken, and Macadamia-Dill Dressing or Lean & Creamy French Dressing.

2. Serve leftover Apple Compote for dessert.

Saturday Evening (1 to 1 1/4 hours)

1. Prepare Creamy Carrot Soup. While it cooks, chop enough onions, collards, and garlic for 3 meals and set aside.

2. If desired, prepare Dark Chocolate-Dipped Dates and cool in freezer.

3. Preheat oven to 400° F. Season fish and roast in oven.

4. Start greens cooking. Start Roasted Chicory & Dandelion Root "Coffee."

WEEK 3 MENUS – SPRING/SUMMER/EARLY FALL

	Breakfast	Lunch	Snack (optional)	Dinner
Sunday	Your Basic Omelet (Page 223) Sautéed Kale with Onions & Garlic (Page 314) Honeydew Melon	Quick Smoky Simmered Salmon with Chipotlé (Page 234) Leftover Sautéed Kale with Onions & Garlic Marinated Beet Root Salad (Page 366) with Fluffy Tahini (Page 409)		Creamy Carrot Soup with Cumin & Dill (Page 370) Poached Chicken Breasts in White Wine with Herbs (Page 264) Basic Green Salad (Page 344) with Lean & Creamy Mustard Dressing (Page 417) Date-Coconut Roll stuffed with toasted almonds, optional (Page 451)
Monday	Garlic & Pepper Scrambled Eggs (Page 224) Leftover Sautéed Kale with Onions & Garlic Sliced honeydew melon with red grapes	Leftover Basic Green Salad with leftover Marinated Beet Root Salad and Fluffy Tahini Leftover Poached Chicken Parts in White Wine with Herbs	Speedy Smoothie (Page 475)	Leftover Creamy Carrot Soup with Cumin & Dill Leftover Quick Smoky Simmered Salmon with Chipotlé Sautéed Collards with Mushrooms & Ginger (Page 316) Date-Coconut Roll stuffed with toasted almonds, optional
Tuesday	Smoky Salmon & Egg Scramble (Page 228) Leftover Sautéed Collards with Mushrooms & Ginger Sliced cantaloupe Dried Fig Halves with Anise Seeds & Nuts, optional (Page 451)	Leftover Creamy Carrot Soup with Coconut, Cumin & Dill Leftover Sautéed Collards with Mushrooms & Ginger Leftover Poached Chicken Breasts in White Wine with Herbs Red grapes	Speedy Smoothie (Page 475)	Broiled Steak with Pepper (Page 291) Salad greens topped with leftover Marinated Beet Root Salad with Fluffy Tahini
Wednesday	Soft-Boiled Eggs (Page 218) with leftover chicken Leftover Sautéed Collards with Mushrooms & Ginger Leftover sliced cantaloupe Date-Coconut Roll stuffed with toasted almonds, optional	Steak, Sun-Dried Tomato & Green Salad from leftovers with Lean & Creamy Mustard Dressing Fresh peach, optional	Speedy Smoothie (Page 475)	Baked Deep Sea Dory with Herbs (Page 242) Parboiled Vegetable Medley (Page 332) with Very Easy Vinaigrette (Page 422) Leftover Marinated Beet Root Salad with Fluffy Tahini

Week 3 Menus – Spring/Summer/Early Fall cont.

	Breakfast	Lunch	Snack (optional)	Dinner
T h u r s d a y	Tarragon & Chive Scrambled Eggs (Page 225) with leftover fish or steak Leftover Parboiled Vegetable Medley with Very Easy Vinaigrette Carrot-Peach Blend (Page 507) or fresh peaches dusted with unsweetened coconut	Steak, Sun-Dried Tomato & Green Salad from leftovers, with Lean & Creamy Mustard Dressing	Speedy Smoothie (Page 475)	Leftover Baked Deep Sea Dory with Herbs Leftover Parboiled Vegetable Medley with Very Easy Vinaigrette Baked Spiced Sweet Potato Halves (Page 385)
F r i d a y	Smoky Scrambled Eggs with Chipotlé (Page 224) and leftover fish Simmered Broccoli with Herbs (Page 328) with butter or lemon-flavored cod liver oil Berries topped with shredded unsweetened coconut (honey optional)	Chicken, Sweet Potato & Green Salad with Lean & Creamy Mustard Dressing, from leftovers	Speedy Smoothie (Page 475)	Broiled Lamb Chops or Steaks (Page 303) Leftover Simmered Broccoli with Herbs, tossed with any leftover salad dressing Steamed Corn on the Cob (Page 391), butter, optional
S a t u r d a y	Don's Faux Frittata (Page 230) or leftover Lamb Chops Steamed Spinach with sliced scallions, topped with butter or lemon-flavored cod liver oil Fruit Salad made from leftover fruit, garnished with shredded, unsweetened coconut	Chicken, Sweet Potato & Green Salad from leftovers with Lean & Creamy Mustard Dressing	Frosty Fruit Whip (Page 476 or 477)	Smoky Turkey (or Beef) Burgers (Page 277) Whole Boiled Greens with Cauliflower (Page 311) and Spicy Peanut Sauce (Page 416) Steamed Corn on the Cob (fresh or leftover), butter, optional Chilled Cherry Gel (Page 438) garnished with chopped toasted almonds

~Prep Lists and Information start on next page~

PREP FOR WEEK 3

Recipes for Sunday Morning Prep Session

> Your Basic Omelet (Page 223)
> Sautéed Kale with Onions & Garlic (Page 314)
> Marinated Beet Root Salad (Page 366)
> Toasted almonds (Page 406)
> Creamy Carrot Soup with Cumin & Dill (Page 370)
> Salad bar setup for the week (chopping assorted vegetables, below)
> Fluffy Tahini, double recipe (Page 409)
> Lean & Creamy Mustard Dressing, single or double recipe (Page 417)
> Smoky Simmered Salmon with Chipotlé (Page 234)
> Poached Chicken Breasts in White Wine with Herbs (Page 264)
> Don's Smoothie Base, optional (Page 467)
> Rachel's Smoothie Base, optional (Page 468)

Sunday Morning Prep (3 1/2 to 4 hours):

1. Before breakfast, wash and put beets on to boil for Beet Root Salad.

2. Prepare Sautéed Kale with Onions & Garlic. While they cook, slice melon for breakfast and make omelets.

3. When beets are tender, remove from heat and let cool. Slice onions for beet salad (parboil if you don't like them raw). Make the vinaigrette; toss with onions. Rinse and drain beets, trim, peel, slice, and toss with onions. Marinate at room temperature or in the refrigerator for at least 3 hours.

4. Dry toast almonds to last 2 weeks or longer. While you wait, prepare Creamy Carrot Soup. Remove almonds from oven or toaster oven. Let cool, then refrigerate in a jar.

5. Make a double batch of Fluffy Tahini and a single or double batch of Lean & Creamy Mustard Dressing. Chill.

6. Wash and chop an assortment of vegetables for several days' salads. Halve and thinly slice 1 pint of red radishes. Mince 4 celery stalks with their tops. Peel, seed, and slice 1 large or 3 small cucumbers. Spin dry, trim, and mince 1 bunch of parsley and 2 bunches of scallions. Wash and spin dry 1 head of romaine and/or 1/4 to 1/2 pound spring greens. If tomatoes are in season, wash, quarter, seed, and slice 2 or 3 tomatoes. Store everything but lettuce in wide-mouth jars. Store lettuce in a salad spinner or wrapped in a cotton towel in the fridge.

7. Halve and thinly slice 1 large onion. Trim and chop 1 pint of mushrooms. Destem and chop 2 pounds of collard greens to sauté Monday evening.

8. Purée Creamy Carrot Soup; adjust seasonings and refrigerate for later.

9. To make quick smoothies for snacks for 2 people during the week, make 1 batch of Don's and Rachel's Smoothie Bases. Refrigerate or freeze in individual portions.

10. Thirty minutes before lunch, assemble and cook Poached Chicken Breasts and Quick Smoky Simmered Salmon. Take out half the Sautéed Kale with Onions & Garlic from breakfast, Beet Salad, and Fluffy Tahini. Serve with Salmon. Refrigerate all leftovers.

Sunday Evening (30 minutes):

1. Take out leftover Poached Chicken for supper (gently warm meal-size portions, if desired.

2. Gently heat enough Creamy Carrot Soup for 1 meal.

3. Assemble a green salad using vegetables you washed and prepped earlier and take out Lean & Creamy Mustard Dressing.

4. For dessert, stuff a tablespoon of toasted almonds into a Date-Coconut Roll for each person. Serve with tea.

5. Pack lunches for Monday. (Pack Fluffy Tahini in separate containers).

Monday Morning (15 to 30 minutes):

1. If you want a smoothie for a snack later, blend a premeasured portion of Smoothie Base with 1 cup fresh or frozen fruit, pour into a wide-mouth thermos, and chill. Repeat for each person.

2. Take out leftover Sautéed Kale with Onions & Garlic. Wash and slice fruit. Scramble eggs for breakfast.

Monday Evening (30 minutes):

1. Prepare Sautéed Collards with Mushrooms & Ginger using greens chopped on Sunday.

2. Take out enough Smoky Simmered Salmon for dinner, heat briefly or serve chilled.

3. Warm leftover Creamy Carrot Soup.

4. Pack chicken and greens for tomorrow's lunches. Heat soup in the morning.

Tuesday Morning (30 minutes or less):

1. If you want a smoothie for a snack later, blend a premeasured portion of Smoothie Base with 1 cup fresh or frozen fruit, pour into a wide-mouth thermos, and chill. Repeat for each person

2. Boil water. Fill a thermos for each person with hot water and seal. Warm soup for lunches. When it's hot, empty each thermos, fill with soup and seal.

3. Take out leftover Sautéed Collards for breakfast and slice fruit.

4. Scramble eggs with leftover salmon and seasonings.

Tuesday Evening (30 minutes):

1. Take out enough steak for dinner and 2 more meals and preheat broiler. Take out prewashed greens, layer on plates, and top with minced parsley and leftover Beet Salad with Fluffy Tahini.

2. While steak broils, pack lunches for Wednesday. Store dressing in separate containers.

Wednesday Morning (15 to 30 minutes):

1. If you want a smoothie for a snack later, blend a premeasured portion of Smoothie Base with 1 cup fresh or frozen fruit, pour into a wide-mouth thermos, and chill. Repeat for each person

2. Take out leftover Sautéed Collards and melon. Slice leftover chicken. Cook eggs for breakfast. If you're still hungry, have a Date-Coconut Roll stuffed with toasted almonds.

Wednesday Evening (1 hour):

1. Chop vegetables for parboiled salad for dinner and 3 more meals. Put a pot of water on to boil.

2. Make a batch of Very Easy Vinaigrette. Parboil each kind of vegetable separately but in the same water, as instructed. Plunge each in ice water, and drain well.

3. Take out leftover Beet Salad and Fluffy Tahini. Bake fish for dinner.

4. Toss parboiled vegetables with vinaigrette to coat.

5. Serve meal when fish is ready. Refrigerate leftovers after dinner.

Thursday Morning (15 to 30 minutes):

1. If you want a smoothie for a snack later, blend a premeasured portion of Smoothie Base with 1 cup fresh or frozen fruit, pour into a wide-mouth thermos, and chill. Repeat for each person

2. Take out leftover parboiled salad. Make a Carrot-Peach Blend in your Vita-Mix or rinse, slice, and serve fresh peaches. Cook eggs for breakfast.

3. Using leftovers, pack main course salads for lunch, if you haven't already done it.

Thursday Evening (30 to 45 minutes):

1. Wash, halve, season, and bake enough Sweet Potato Halves for 3 meals.

2. Season and bake enough chicken breast halves for 3 meals.

3. Take out Parboiled Salad with Vinaigrette and leftover fish. (Heat fish briefly, if at all.)

4. Pack lunches.

Friday Morning (15 to 30 minutes):

1. If you want a smoothie for a snack later, blend a premeasured portion of Smoothie Base with 1 cup fresh or frozen fruit, pour into a wide-mouth thermos, and chill. Repeat for each person.

2. Wash and drain fruit; wash, chop, and simmer broccoli, then cook eggs for breakfast.

Friday Evening (15 minutes):

1. Season and broil or grill lamb chops for 2 meals.

2. Take out leftover broccoli and toss with any dressing you have on hand.

3. Steam corn on the cob for dinner and for the next day if you like.

Saturday Morning (30 minutes):

1. Wash and trim spinach; set aside. Prepare Don's Faux Frittata or warm leftover lamb.

2. While frittata cooks, steam spinach and make enough fruit salad for 2 meals.

3. Assemble chicken, sweet potato, and green salads for lunch. Chill.

Saturday Evening (1 to 1 1/2 hours):

1. At least 4 hours before dinner, prepare Cherry Gel and Spicy Peanut Sauce and chill.

2. At least 1 hour before serving, prepare Whole Boiled Greens with Cauliflower.

3. Season and shape burgers. Close to serving time, cook burgers and steam fresh sweet corn, or gently rewarm leftover corn in a pot with 1/4-inch of water.

Week 4 Menus – Spring/Summer/Fall

	Breakfast	Lunch	Snack (optional)	Dinner
Sunday	Garlic & Chive Scrambled Eggs (Page 224) with leftover meat or fish Sautéed Kale with Onions & Sage (Page 314) Carrot-Peach Blend (Page 507) or fresh peaches	Baked Sea Bass with Mustard & Herbs (Page 240) Leftover Sautéed Kale with Onions & Sage Basic Baked Sweet Potatoes (Page 386)	Apple or grapes	Roasted Smoky Turkey Breast (Page 258) with Better Barbecue Sauce (Page 401) Roasted Onion, Sweet Pepper & Spring Green Salad (Page 353) with Lean & Creamy Italian Dressing (Page 419) Stewed Pears with Anise (Page 431) garnished with toasted pecans (Page 406)
Monday	Leftover Roasted Smoky Turkey Breast with Better Barbecue Sauce Leftover Sautéed Kale with Onions & Sage Carrot-Peach Blend or fresh peaches and plums	Leftover Roasted Onion, Sweet Pepper & Spring Green Salad with leftover Roasted Smoky Turkey Breast and Mustard-Tahini Dressing (Page 411) Leftover Stewed Pears with Anise garnished with toasted pecans	Protein-Nut Spread (Page 464) with sliced apple	Leftover Baked Sea Bass with Mustard & Herbs Basic Green Salad (Page 344) with Lean & Creamy Italian Dressing Mashed Sweet Potatoes with Lime (Page 387) made from leftover Baked Sweet Potatoes
Tuesday	Leftover Roasted Smoky Turkey Breast with leftover Better Barbecue Sauce Southern-Style Greens (Page 320) Fresh nectarines or plums	Leftover Basic Green Salad with leftover Roasted Smoky Turkey Breast and Mustard-Tahini Dressing Leftover Mashed Sweet Potatoes with Lime	Leftover Protein-Nut Spread with fresh banana	Basic Beef Roast (Page 294) Leftover Southern-Style Greens Roasted Carrots with Ginger (Page 369) Leftover Stewed Pears with Anise garnished with toasted pecans
Wednesday	Poached Eggs or Soft-Boiled Eggs (Page 217 or 218) Leftover Beef Roast and Better Barbecue Sauce, optional Leftover Southern Style Greens Fresh nectarine Dried Fig Halves with Anise Seeds & Toasted Nuts (Page 406), optional	Basic Green Salad with leftover Roasted Carrots, (sliced) Beef Roast, and Lean & Creamy Italian Dressing Fresh plums, optional	Protein-Nut Spread with sliced apple	Tomato, Squash & Ginger Bisque (Page 381) garnished with scallions Broiled White Meat Fish Fillets with Garlic & Pepper (Page 247) and butter or olive oil Parboiled Broccoli, Cauliflower and Red Radishes (Page 330) with leftover Mustard-Tahini Dressing

WEEK 4 MENUS – SPRING/SUMMER/FALL CONT.

	Breakfast	Lunch	Snack (optional)	Dinner
Thursday	Basic Omelet (Page 223) with leftover Better Barbecue Sauce Steamed Spinach with Red Onions (Page 337) with lemon cod liver oil and pepper Sliced Pineapple with Strawberries and flaked, unsweetened coconut	Leftover Basic Green Salad topped with leftover sliced Beef Roast, Roasted Carrots, Lean & Creamy Italian Dressing Fresh Apple or grapes, optional	Fresh Peach or peach with leftover Protein-Nut Spread	Leftover Tomato, Squash & Ginger Bisque garnished with parsley Leftover Broiled White Meat Fish Fillets Leftover Parboiled Vegetable Medley with leftover Mustard-Tahini Dressing
Friday	Soft-Boiled Eggs or Poached Eggs with leftover fish or beef Leftover (or fresh) Steamed Spinach with lemon-flavored cod liver oil and pepper Beet-Apple Blend (Page 506) or apple and orange slices	Leftover Tomato, Squash & Ginger Bisque garnished with parsley Basic Green Salad with canned tuna or thawed shrimp, avocado, and leftover Mustard-Tahini Dressing Fresh apple, optional	Better Balanced Blueberry Smoothie (Page 474)	Grilled or Broiled Pork Chops or Chicken Breasts with Mango-Ginger Chutney (Page 404) Leftover Parboiled Vegetable Medley with Tahini Dressing or Sautéed Cabbage with Curry (Page 338)
Saturday	Vanilla Omelet with leftover Mango-Ginger Chutney (Page 223) Leftover (or freshly cooked) Sautéed Cabbage with Curry	Leftover Pork Chops or Chicken Breasts sliced and served over Mesclun Green & Pear Salad (Page 348) with leftover Lean & Creamy Italian Dressing		Baked Chicken Thighs with Cumin & Lime (Page 265) Slow Simmered Carrots with Sunchokes (Page 371) Leftover Sautéed Cabbage with Curry or Steamed Broccoli Dark Chocolate-Dipped Dates (Page 453) or My Favorite Macaroons (Page 447)

~Prep Lists and Information start on next page~

PREP FOR WEEK 4:

Recipes for Sunday Morning Session

Sautéed Kale with Onions & Sage (Page 314)

Carrot-Peach Blend (Page 507)

Garlic & Chive Scrambled Eggs (Page 224)

Toasted pecans (Page 406)

Baked Sweet Potatoes (red garnet or jewel "yams" Page 386)

Roasted Onions (Page 373)

Roasted Bell Peppers (Page 376)

Roasted Smoky Turkey Breast (Page 258)

Better Barbecue Sauce, double recipe (Page 401)

Mustard-Tahini Dressing, single or double recipe (Page 411)

Lean & Creamy Italian Dressing, single or double recipe (Page 419)

Salad bar setup for the week (chop assorted vegetables)

Toasted Dulse, optional (Page 397)

Chocolate or Vanilla Protein-Nut Spread, optional (Page 464)

Baked Sea Bass with Mustard & Herbs (Page 240)

Stewed Pears with Anise (Page 431)

Sunday Morning (4 hours):

1. Wash, chop and sauté onion, kale, and sage. While they cook, prepare Carrot-Peach Blend in a Vita-Mix or wash and slice fresh fruit. Cook eggs for breakfast.

2. Dry toast enough pecans for 2 or more weeks in a 325 or 350° F oven. Watch closely.

3. Rinse 6 sweet potatoes for Sunday, Monday, and Tuesday; poke with holes, if desired.

4. Cool nuts on the counter; raise oven temperature to 400° F, and bake sweet potatoes.

5. Chop onions and prep bell peppers according to recipes; roast in oven with sweet potatoes.

6. Season turkey breast; roast in oven with vegetables or in a slow cooker, for dinner, a few more days, and the freezer.

7. Make a double batch of Better Barbecue Sauce (you can freeze half), a single or double batch of Lean & Creamy Italian Dressing, and a single or double batch of Mustard-Tahini Dressings. (These dressings will last for 2 weeks in the fridge.)

8. Wash, spin dry, and mince 2 bunches of scallions and 1 bunch of parsley for salads and garnishes. Peel, halve, seed, and thinly slice 4 pickling cucumbers or 1 large cucumber. Thinly slice 1 large, white radish for salads. Refrigerate in jars.

9. Check peppers and stir onions. Remove when done. Follow instructions to cover and cool, then peel and slice peppers. Refrigerate when cool.

10. Halve and thinly slice 2 quart jars full of onions. Wash, destem, and thinly slice 2 pounds of collard greens to cook Tuesday morning. Store in covered containers in the refrigerator.

11. Rinse salad greens and spin dry. Check turkey breast and sweet potatoes.

12. If desired, prepare a Chocolate or Vanilla Protein-Nut Spread for snacks during the week.

13. Season and bake sea bass for lunch with leftovers for the next day. Meanwhile, assemble and cook pears, for Sunday dinner's dessert and 2 more days.

14. Check turkey breast; when done, allow to cool. Cook down pan juices. Slice and refrigerate cooled turkey breast.

15. For lunch, take out cooked greens from breakfast. Reheat sweet potatoes and serve with fish.

Sunday Evening (15 to 30 minutes):

1. Assemble roasted vegetable and green salad for supper; take out dressing and cooked pears.

2. Reheat enough Smoky Turkey and barbecue sauce for dinner.

3. Pack lunches for Monday.

Monday Morning (15 to 30 minutes):

1. Take out leftover cooked kale. Warm leftover turkey breast and barbecue sauce, if desired.

2. Prepare a Carrot-Peach drink in a Vita-Mix or wash and slice fresh fruit for breakfast.

3. Pack lunches. If desired, include Protein-Nut Spread and an apple for a snack.

Monday Evening (30 minutes):

1. Prepare Mashed Sweet Potatoes with Lime. (Make 1/2 to 2/3 of the recipe using leftover Baked Sweet Potatoes).

2. Briefly heat leftover Baked Sea Bass, if desired. Assemble a green salad using greens you washed on Sunday and assorted sliced and/or grated raw vegetables; serve with Tahini Dressing.

3. Pack lunches for Tuesday.

Tuesday Morning (30 minutes or less):

1. Prepare enough Southern-Style Greens for breakfast and 2 more meals using onions and collards you chopped on Sunday.

2. Reheat enough leftover turkey and barbecue sauce for breakfast. Rinse fruit for breakfast.

3. Pack a snack for later, if desired

Tuesday Evening (30 to 45 minutes):

1. Start Basic Beef Roast. Cut 2 pounds of carrots into sticks and roast both for dinner, Wednesday, and Thursday.

2. Pack lunches for the next day. Prepare snacks, if desired.

3. Stir carrots, take out leftover sautéed greens from breakfast, Pears with Anise from Sunday, and nuts for a garnish.

Wednesday Morning (15 to 20 minutes):

1. Take out leftover Southern-Style Greens for breakfast.

2. If desired, reheat a portion of beef roast and barbecue sauce. Wash fruit and cook eggs.

Wednesday Evening (30 to 45 minutes):

1. Follow recipe for Tomato, Squash & Ginger Bisque using frozen squash.

2. Season fish and preheat broiler or toaster oven.

3. Chop and cook enough broccoli, cauliflower, and red radishes for a Parboiled Vegetable Medley for 3 meals. (See recipe for cutting and cooking instructions.)

4. Broil fish and take out leftover Tahini Dressing. Purée soup and serve.

5. Pack lunches for Thursday.

Thursday Morning (15 minutes):

1. Take out leftover barbecue sauce. Wash and slice fruit; refrigerate extra pineapple in a jar.

2. Wash, trim, chop, and steam asparagus. Make omelets for breakfast. Serve with leftover turkey breast, if desired.

3. Pack a snack for later if desired.

Thursday Evening (15 minutes):

1. Take out leftover parboiled vegetables, Tahini Dressing, and fish.

2. Gently warm soup and serve.

3. Pack lunches for Friday.

Friday Morning (20 to 30 minutes):

1. Take out leftover spinach and leftover beef or fish. Follow recipe for Beet-Apple Blend if you have a Vita-Mix. If not, wash and slice fresh fruit.

2. Cook eggs.

3. If you want a smoothie for a snack later, prepare it now, and chill in a thermos.

Friday Evening (30 minutes):

1. Assemble Mango Chutney.

2. Chop cabbage and onions; set aside.

3. Season and broil or grill enough pork chops or chicken breasts for 2 to 3 meals.

4. If you have enough leftover parboiled salad and Tahini Dressing for dinner, refrigerate and cook cabbage in the morning, otherwise, cook cabbage for dinner.

Saturday Morning (15 minutes):

1. Take out leftover Mango Chutney; heat briefly, if desired. Take out leftover Sautéed Cabbage with Curry. If you didn't cook cabbage last night, cook it now.

2. Prepare the Vanilla Omelet and serve with Mango-Ginger Chutney and cabbage.

Saturday Lunch (15 minutes):

1. Slice leftover pork chops or chicken breasts.

2. Assemble Mesclun Green & Pear Salad; top with chicken and Lean & Creamy Italian Dressing.

Saturday Evening (1 hour):

1. Three to 8 hours before dinner, prepare Dark Chocolate-Dipped Dates or My Favorite Macaroons.

2. Season chicken and marinate in the fridge.

3. One hour before dinner, start chicken, sunchokes, and carrots.

4. Take out leftover Sautéed Cabbage with Curry. (If you don't have enough for supper, chop and steam or simmer broccoli with cauliflower or spinach.) Make enough of everything for Sunday or Sunday and Monday.

14 The Incredible Egg

Best Bites

Factory-Farmed Eggs

Most commercial eggs come not from farms, but from factories: light-, temperature-, and humidity-controlled windowless warehouses. Tens of thousands of chickens may reside in a single building. They are packed and stacked so tightly in small wire cages they cannot flap their wings. Their diet of corn and soy is dispensed through automatically controlled grain troughs, and laced with hormones, antibiotics, pesticides, and herbicides. The drugs stimulate rapid growth and stem the tide of disease caused by overcrowding and undernutrition.

The birds never see sunlight or set foot on soil. Beneath artificial light, often kept on for more than 17 hours a day, laying hens are stimulated to lay more eggs than Mother Nature intended. Because their natural sleep cycle is destroyed, the natural seasonal fluctuations in egg laying are prevented and they literally wear out. Hens raised on factory farms have a life span one-sixth that of birds raised under more natural conditions. They also produce less-nutritious, less-flavorful eggs.

Eggs from factory-farmed birds contain detectable levels of antibiotics, and antibiotic-resistant bacteria, including staphylococcus anureus, Enterococcus faecalis, E. coli, and Citrobacter freuendii, according to a 1997 report published in a medical journal (*Comp Immunol Microbiol Infect Dis* 20 (1): 35-40).

Irrational Irradiation

In July 2000, the USDA approved irradiation of eggs. To kill bacteria and increase shelf life, irradiation exposes food to a radiation dose equivalent to that of up to one billion chest X-rays. At the time, there was sufficient evidence to prove that irradiation destroys 80 percent of the vitamin A in eggs. Irradiated eggs are more difficult to cook with and contain elevated levels of free radicals, unstable molecules that weaken cell membranes, accelerate aging, and promote cancer and diabetes.

Current laws do not require irradiated foods or products that contain multiple food ingredients to be labeled. If you buy anonymous mass-market eggs, you increase the risk of buying and consuming nutrient-deficient and potentially damaging food.

That Golden Yolk

Many important nutrients are concentrated in egg yolks. All the vitamin A and D, 84 percent of the vitamin B12, 87 percent of the pantothenic acid, 81 percent of the folic acid, 92 percent of the calcium, 45 percent of the protein, and 23 percent of the potassium in an egg are concentrated in the yolk! All the vitamin E and omega-3 essential fatty acids in pasture-raised or wild bird eggs are in the yolk.

Egg yolks also provide choline, lecithin, and other phospholipids. These are vital to cell membranes throughout your body. They are especially important in nerve cells. Phospholipids emulsify other fats, keeping them suspended in blood and body fluids, allowing fat-soluble substances—such as vitamins and hormones—to pass easily into and out of cells.

The functioning of all your cells and the integrity of your cell membranes can only be maintained if you eat foods rich in natural phospholipids. There is evidence that age-related cognitive decline, so common in people today, is the result of a lack of phospholipids, due to an insufficient intake of nourishing animal-source foods, such as egg yolks. Don't toss out those golden yolks.

Perfectly Poached Eggs

Prep: 3 minutes ~ **Cooking:** 3 to 5 minutes ~ **Yield:** 2 servings

Ingredients & Directions

Extra-virgin olive oil **or** unrefined coconut oil if using egg poaching cups

Filtered water

1 tablespoon lemon juice **or** 1/2 tablespoon raw apple cider vinegar

4 to 6 medium to large free-range chicken eggs **or** duck eggs

Lemon pepper, ground black pepper, or paprika

1 handful toasted, crumbled dulse **or** wild nori sea vegetable (Page 397) **or** 1 to 2 tablespoons dulse or nori flakes, optional

Minced scallions, chives, arugula flowers, other edible flowers, lemon pepper, or hot sauce

1. Fill a skillet with water to a depth of 1 to 2 inches. Add vinegar or lemon juice. Bring almost to boil over medium-high heat. Crack eggs into 2 small bowls or custard cups.

2. One by one, slide eggs into simmering water. Cover skillet or begin spooning hot water over eggs and cook over medium or medium-low heat for 3 to 5 minutes, until whites are set and centers are still soft but covered with a thin film.

3. Transfer eggs to plates, garnish as desired, and serve.

Nutrition

2 medium chicken eggs:

128 calories
12 g protein
2 g carbohydrate
8 g fat
44 mg calcium
110 mg sodium

2 large chicken eggs:

146 calories
12 g protein
2 g carbohydrate
10 g fat
50 mg calcium
126 mg sodium

Poaching requires no added fat, unless you're using an egg poacher, in which case, you need to lightly oil the cups. Poached eggs often stick to the skillet, so if you make them often, it's worth investing in a skillet with a stainless steel egg-poaching insert sold in kitchen shops everywhere. Poached eggs are delicious spooned on steamed asparagus or broccoli, or sautéed leafy greens.

Soft-Boiled Eggs

Prep: 3 minutes ~ **Cooking:** under 10 minutes ~ **Yield:** 2 servings
---

Ingredients & Directions

Filtered water to cover eggs

4 medium to large free-range chicken eggs **or** duck eggs

Cold water and 4 to 6 ice cubes

Ground black pepper, lemon pepper **or** hot sauce, optional

Toasted Dulse, crumbled (Page 397), **or** Dulse, Dried Onion & Sea Cress Flakes, (Page 398), **or** dulse flakes, optional

1. Place eggs in a 1-quart saucepan. Add water to cover by 1 inch. Cover pot and bring to a rolling boil over high heat.

2. Reduce heat to medium-low (number 4 on an electric range numbered 1 to 8) and start timing: 3 1/2 minutes for small to medium eggs, 4 minutes for large eggs, 4 1/2 to 5 minutes for extra large or jumbo eggs. Add 30 seconds for eggs taken straight from the refrigerator.

3. Drain eggs and cover with cold (preferably filtered) water and ice cubes. After ice melts, drain again, and transfer to serving plates.

4. Tap outside of each egg in a circle and cut in half with a butter knife. Scoop eggs from shells and serve immediately, sprinkle with pepper, hot sauce and/or dulse or wild nori if desired.

5. If you've prepared enough for 2 days, refrigerate extra eggs in their shells and use within 24 to 48 hours.

Variations

* Use a 1 1/2-quart saucepan and 6 eggs. Omit extra meat from the meal.

* **Medium-Boiled Eggs:** For slightly firmer eggs, increase cooking time to 5 to 6 minutes, plunge in cold water, drain, crack, and peel as for hard-boiled eggs.

* For a double batch, use a larger saucepan. Keep eggs in a single layer.

Nutrition

2 medium chicken eggs:

128 calories
12 g protein
2 g carbohydrate
8 g fat
44 mg calcium
110 mg sodium

2 large chicken eggs:

146 calories
12 g protein
2 g carbohydrate
10 g fat
50 mg calcium
126 mg sodium

Soft-boiled eggs are more moist than hard-boiled eggs; their protein is more assimilable. But—you have to eat them immediately because they don't keep for more than a day or so. Sometimes we cook enough for 2 days in a row, but no longer. We spoon the eggs over steamed broccoli, asparagus, or sautéed leafy greens, and serve with fresh fruit or potatoes.

Fried Eggs

Prep: 5 minutes ~ **Cooking:** 4 to 8 minutes ~ **Yield:** 2 servings

Ingredients & Directions

1 teaspoon extra-virgin olive oil, unrefined coconut oil, ghee **or** clarified butter

4 to 6 medium to large free-range chicken eggs **or** duck eggs, rinsed

Ground chipotlé (smoked dried jalapeno pepper), black pepper **or** lemon pepper, optional

1 tablespoon boiling water, optional

1 to 2 tablespoons minced scallions, chives, parsley, or arugula flowers, for garnish

1. Crack eggs into a small bowl. Heat oil in a 9-inch skillet over medium heat until hot but not smoking. Tilt pan to spread oil. Slip eggs into skillet; sprinkle with pepper, if desired.

2. Cook uncovered until whites lose their translucence, about 1 or 2 minutes. Reduce heat to low and cook for 2 to 4 minutes more, until the whites are firm and yolks almost set. *For firmer whites,* cover skillet immediately.

3. Transfer eggs to serving plates, garnish, and serve.

Nutrition

2 medium chicken eggs:

146 calories
12 g protein
2 g carbohydrate
10 g fat
44 mg calcium
110 mg sodium

We fry our eggs in a fraction of the fat found in most recipes. We serve the eggs over steamed broccoli or asparagus (great for dipping into the yolks) or with sautéed kale, collards, or Brussels sprouts. For more protein, we add a side of homemade beef jerky or leftover chicken, turkey, roast beef, or salmon instead of bacon or sausage and round out the meal with fresh or dried fruit.

Hard-Boiled Eggs

Prep: 5 minutes ~ **Cooking:** 1 minute (plus 25 minutes to rest) ~ **Yield:** 6 servings

Ingredients & Directions

Filtered water

6 medium to large free-range chicken eggs **or** duck eggs, rinsed

4 to 6 ice cubes

Ground black pepper, lemon pepper **or** hot sauce, optional

Toasted Dulse, crumbled (Page 397) **or** dulse flakes, optional

1. Arrange eggs in a 2-quart saucepan. Cover with 1 to 1 1/2 inches of cold water. Cover pot and bring to a rolling boil over medium heat. Cook 30 to 60 seconds. *(That's right, SECONDS!)* Remove from heat, and allow eggs to rest in covered pot for 15 minutes.

2. Drain, and cover eggs with ice water for 10 minutes; then drain and refrigerate them in the shell. Or, tap lightly and peel, or roll eggs between your palms to free shells and skin.

3. Refrigerate peeled eggs in tightly covered container. A wide-mouth Mason jar or Pyrex container works well. Use peeled eggs within 1 week, unpeeled eggs within 10 days.

Nutrition

2 medium chicken eggs:

128 calories
12 g protein
2 g carbohydrate
8 g fat
44 mg calcium
110 mg sodium

2 large chicken eggs:

146 calories
12 g protein
2 g carbohydrate
10 g fat
50 mg calcium
126 mg sodium

Most people boil eggs far too long resulting in dry, greenish-tinged, difficult-to-digest yolks. This recipe is easy, only the instructions are long. You'll learn it by rote after a few tries.

Consider cooking 6 or even 12 eggs at a time, ready for breakfasts on the go, quick snacks, or to garnish salads for lunch.

Angeled Eggs

Prep: 30 minutes ~ **Cooking:** under 10 minutes ~ **Yield:** 6 servings

Ingredients & Directions

6 large Hard-boiled Eggs (Page 220)

1 3/4 teaspoons Dijon **or** stoneground mustard

1/4 teaspoon ground turmeric

1/4 teaspoon ground black pepper **or** ground chipotlé (smoked dried jalapeno)

1 tablespoon minced scallions, chives, parsley, tarragon **or** chervil **or** 1 teaspoon dried, crumbled herbs

1/2 cup Toasted Dulse (Page 397) **or** 2 tablespoons dulse flakes

1/4 cup minced sweet white onion **or** 2 teaspoons minced shallots, optional

2 teaspoons lemon juice **or** organic apple cider vinegar, optional

1/4 cup plus 2 tablespoons Mustard-Tahini Dressing (Page 411)

Paprika to dust egg halves

Nutrition

2 egg halves:
103 calories
7 g protein
4 g carbohydrate
7 g fat
34 mg calcium
111 mg sodium

Angled....deviled? *Deviled* sounds so much less inviting and puts the eggs in such an unfavorable light. There's nothing evil about these eggs since we're using free-range or pasture-raised eggs and homemade tahini dressing in place of commercial mayonnaise.

Dulse, a crinkly, purple sea vegetable, isn't essential, but it adds a slightly smoky and salty taste along with healthful minerals and potassium.

1. Peel eggs and slice in half lengthwise. Add yolks to a medium bowl with remaining ingredients except paprika. Mix and mash with a fork or potato masher to create a coarse cream.

2. Portion and spoon heaping teaspoon-size balls of yolk mixture into the egg white halves; evenly divide any remaining mixture. Dust with paprika.

3. Cover and refrigerate. Use within 3 days.

Variations

* For wet mustard substitute 1/2 teaspoon dry mustard. For a spicy kick, double the pepper.

* Replace Tahini Dressing with Homemade Mayonnaise (regular, herb, garlic, or horseradish flavor, Page 424). Fat content will be slightly higher. If you buy mayonnaise, choose a natural foods brand made without hydrogenated or partially hydrogenated oils; an omega-3 rich brand is ideal.

* **Egg Salad (serves 2):** Mash whites with yolks and seasonings. Serve on individual beds of raw salad greens with colorful raw or parboiled vegetables. Add a side of baked potatoes or assorted veggie sticks (cucumber, Jicama, carrot, and celery). For rollups, wrap tablespoon-sized portions of egg salad in large lettuce leaves and secure with toothpicks.

Note: Turmeric is an antioxidant; oregano, rosemary, and cumin possess similar properties, so you can substitute different herbs and spices.

Seafood & Egg Salad

Prep: 15 minutes ~ **Cooking:** 0 ~ **Yield:** 2 servings

Ingredients & Directions

2 hard-boiled, free-range chicken eggs **or** duck eggs (Page 220), made ahead and peeled

6 to 8 ounces leftover cooked white meat fish, flaked with a fork:
> deep sea dory, blue hake, cod, pollock, sole, orange roughy, or tuna

1/4 teaspoon dry mustard **and/or** ground turmeric

1/4 teaspoon ground chipotlé, black pepper, **or** lemon pepper

1 tablespoon minced **or** 1 teaspoon dried parsley, chives, tarragon, basil, **or** 2 celery ribs, minced finely

1/2 cup Toasted Dulse, crumbled (Page 397) **or** 2 tablespoons dulse flakes, or to taste

1/4 cup yellow, red, or sweet white onions, minced, optional

1/2 cup Sesame, Garlic & Chive Dressing (Page 411) **or** Sesame-Pesto Dressing (Page 414)

Ground paprika **or** ground sumac

Nutrition	**1 serving:**
	271 calories
	30 g protein
	11 g carbohydrate
	18 g fat
	1 g fiber
	78 mg calcium
	231 mg sodium

1. Mash eggs in a shallow 1-quart bowl. Add cooked fish or drained tuna and remaining ingredients except paprika or sumac. Stir well, cover, and refrigerate until serving time.

2. Serve mixture in mounds (I use an ice cream scoop) on 2 large beds of salad greens with other colorful vegetables. Dust lightly with paprika or ground sumac before serving.

3. Refrigerate leftovers and use within 2 days.

Variations

* Use 4 eggs. Reduce fish to 4 to 6 ounces if desired.

* Replace Tahini Dressing with 3 to 4 tablespoons Homemade Mayonnaise (master recipe or horseradish, garlic, or herb flavor, Page 424).

* **Tuna & Egg Salad:** Replace fresh fish with canned, water-packed, no-salt tuna.

* **Seafood & Egg Salad Wraps:** Cover 2 large lettuce leaves with 1 rounded tablespoon of seafood and egg salad. Wrap to make a package and pin with toothpicks. Repeat with remaining salad. Serve with fresh fruit.

Here's a great way to stretch whole eggs and use up leftover fish. I've served this for lunch, and even breakfast, on a bed of salad greens with sliced, minced, or grated raw vegetables and a side of fruit. If you've hard boiled eggs in advance—an easy and wise thing to do—and washed and chopped vegetables ahead, you can assemble this in a hurry.

Note: If you use canned tuna, be aware that a 6-ounce can contains only 4 to 5 ounces of fish.

Your Basic Omelet

Prep: 5 minutes ~ **Cooking:** 10 minutes or less ~ **Yield:** 2 servings

Ingredients & Directions

6 large free-range chicken eggs **or** 4 large duck eggs

1/4 to 1/3 teaspoon ground black pepper, lemon pepper, **or** chipotlé

1 tablespoon minced fresh parsley, chives, **or** scallions

2 to 3 teaspoons extra-virgin olive oil, unrefined coconut oil, ghee **or** clarified butter

1 cup roasted onions, peppers, mushrooms, or other vegetables (see Index for recipes) for optional filling

Toasted Dulse **or** Toasted Wild Nori (Page 397), crumbled, optional

Nutrition

1 serving (without filling):
262 calories
18 g protein
3 g carbohydrate
20 g fat
78 mg calcium
190 mg sodium

1. Rinse eggs, crack, and add to a small bowl with pepper. Whisk until well blended.

2. Heat oil over medium-high heat in a heavy-bottom 12- or 13-inch stainless steel or cast iron skillet. Tilt pan to completely coat the bottom and sides. When hot, but not smoking, whisk eggs again, pour into pan, and cook undisturbed, for 30 seconds.

3. Use a fork or thin-bladed spatula to push edges of the egg mixture toward the center of the pan as they set; tilt pan so uncooked portion runs into empty spaces. Repeat. Remove from heat when eggs no longer run but are still moist and glossy, usually 2 to 3 minutes total.

4. *To fill, optional:* When the eggs are still wet, but not runny, sprinkle filling over half of the omelet. Using a spatula, carefully fold omelet in half to cover filling. For a firmer consistency, partially cover skillet and cook until the filling is warm and eggs are set, about 4 to 5 more minutes.

5. Divide the omelet in half and serve immediately; sprinkle with sea vegetable if desired.

Variations

* **Your Basic Omelet with Salmon:** When eggs have set up, add 1/2 to 3/4 cup flaked, cooked salmon and 1 thinly sliced scallion or 1 tablespoon of minced fresh chives.

* **Vanilla Omelet with Fruit Chutney:** Omit pepper, parsley, turmeric, chives, and scallions. Whisk 1 teaspoon pure vanilla extract in alcohol **or** 2 teaspoons nonalcoholic vanilla extract, 1/4 teaspoon stevia extract powder **or** 4 teaspoons honey **or** agavé nectar, and 1/2 teaspoon ground cinnamon **or** apple pie spice with eggs. For filling, replace roasted vegetables with 2/3 to 1 cup Mango-Ginger Chutney (Page 404), Apple Compote (Page 429), or Stewed Pears with Anise (Page 431).

If you have a large skillet, you can make 2 omelets at the same time.

We like to serve this with steamed or sautéed leafy greens, zucchini, or asparagus, and a side of fresh fruit or a Vita-Mix Total Juice. Better Barbecue Sauce makes a great topping for the omelet. If you prefer 2 egg omelets, use only 4 eggs in the following recipe and then add a side of leftover cooked meat to each plate. Potatoes also pair well with omelets and greens.

Garlic & Pepper Scrambled Eggs/Omelet

Prep: 4 minutes ~ **Cooking:** 4 minutes ~ **Yield:** 2 servings

Ingredients & Directions

4 medium to large free-range chicken eggs **or** duck eggs, rinsed

1/4 teaspoon ground turmeric

1/4 teaspoon garlic powder **or** minced garlic

1/4 teaspoon chipotlé **or** ground black pepper **or** lemon pepper

1 teaspoon extra-virgin olive oil, unrefined coconut oil, ghee **or** clarified butter

1. Crack eggs into a small bowl. Add turmeric, garlic, and pepper.

2. Heat oil in a 10-inch slope-sided skillet over medium-high flame until hot but not smoking. Tilt skillet to completely coat bottom and sides. Whisk eggs with a fork until well blended.

3. **For an omelet:** Pour egg mixture into skillet. Reduce heat to medium or medium-low. As eggs begin to set up (almost immediately), push cooked portion toward center with a metal spatula and tilt pan to allow uncooked portion run underneath. Repeat until eggs no longer run. Remove from heat when eggs are firm but still appear glossy and moist, about 3 to 4 minutes for a single batch. Gently lift and fold 1 side of the omelet over the other.

4. **For a scramble:** Add whisked eggs to hot skillet and reduce heat to medium-low. As eggs begin to set up, push the cooked portion aside with a wooden spoon or metal spatula and tilt pan to allow uncooked eggs run underneath. Break up curds as they form until eggs are cooked through but still glossy and moist, about 4 minutes for a single batch.

Remove from heat and transfer eggs to serving plates.

Variations

* For more protein, fat, and calories, use 6 eggs and increase oil by 1/2 teaspoon. It is not necessary to increase the amount of herbs or spices.

* **Smoky Scrambled Eggs/Omelet with Chipotlé:** Omit garlic; add 1/8 to 1/4 teaspoon ground chipotlé and 1/4 teaspoon Wright's Liquid Hickory Smoke Seasoning (the only brand we've found that's free of sugars, colorings, MSG, preservatives and additives).

* **Turmeric & Cumin Scrambled Eggs/Omelet:** Replace garlic with ground cumin; reduce pepper to 1/8 teaspoon.

* **Turmeric & Ginger Scrambled Eggs/Omelet:** Replace garlic with dried ginger **or** 1 teaspoon ginger juice; add a scant 1/8 teaspoon black pepper.

~Variations continued next page~

Nutrition

2 medium eggs:
140 calories
12 g protein
3 g carbohydrate
9 g fat
53 mg calcium
110 mg sodium

2 large eggs:
159 calories
12 g protein
3 g carbohydrate
10 g fat
59 mg calcium
126 mg sodium

This is Don's master recipe. He varies the seasonings every time or two. If you're cooking for more people, double or triple the recipe and use a 12-inch skillet. For more protein, we figure 3 eggs per person or add 2 or 3 ounces of leftover fish, skinless chicken, turkey breast, or lean meat to each plate.

To complete the meal, we add a generous serving of cooked leafy greens and a colorful fruit.

Note: The spice turmeric provides antioxidants and blocks the production of inflammatory prostaglandins (hormone-like substances) in the body. Many spices possess similar properties.

Variations

Garlic & Pepper Scrambled Eggs/Omelet ~ continued

* **Curried Scrambled Eggs/Omelet:** Omit turmeric and garlic from original recipe; reduce pepper to 1/8 teaspoon (use black pepper); add 1/3 teaspoon mild or spicy curry powder.

* **Pepper & Sage Scrambled Eggs/Omelet:** Replace garlic with dried, rubbed sage; reduce pepper to 1/8 teaspoon (use black, white, or red pepper).

* **Herbes de Provençe Scramble/Omelet:** Replace turmeric with 1/2 teaspoon dried, powdered Herbes de Provençe; add 1/8 teaspoon ground white or black pepper.

* **Tarragon & Chive Scrambled Eggs/Omelet:** Omit turmeric and garlic; add 1/2 teaspoon dried tarragon **or** 1/2 tablespoon minced fresh tarragon leaves, plus 1/2 teaspoon dried **or** 1/2 tablespoon minced fresh chives.

* **Garlic & Chive Scrambled Eggs/Omelet:** Omit turmeric; add 1 teaspoon dried **or** 1 tablespoon minced fresh chives. Use black or white (rather than red) pepper.

* **Italian Scrambled Eggs/Omelet:** Omit turmeric; add 1/4 teaspoon each of dried, crumbled basil, oregano, and thyme **or** 3/4 teaspoon each of fresh, minced herbs (stems removed). Prepare as above. If you have flavored olive oil leftover from a jar of sun-dried tomatoes, use this for cooking, or add 3 tablespoons minced sun-dried tomatoes to the scramble.

* **Paprika Scrambled Eggs/Omelet:** Omit turmeric and garlic; add 1/4 teaspoon ground paprika with 1/8 to 1/4 teaspoon ground black pepper. If desired, add 2 tablespoons minced onion and/or sweet red or green bell pepper or onions.

* **Tex-Mex Scrambled Eggs/Omelet:** Omit turmeric; add 1/4 teaspoon cumin, 1/4 teaspoon dried, crumbled oregano (or 3/4 teaspoon, minced fresh); replace black pepper with 1/4 teaspoon ground chipotlé. Prepare as above.

Using Dried, Powdered Egg Whites

Dried, powdered egg whites are a convenient source of protein. We use them when we are low on eggs, when we want a fat-free or fast protein source for smoothies or cooking, or we have a recipe that calls only for whites but we don't want to toss out any yolks. Use powdered whites anywhere you'd use fresh eggs: in scrambles, omelets, quiches, casseroles, blender puddings, smoothies, shakes, or baking, or as a binder for meatloaf or meatballs. For a savory protein-rich breakfast, stir 1/4 to 1/3 cup of dried, powdered egg whites into a bowl of oatmeal. Add a few tablespoons of crumbled, Toasted Dulse (Page 397), a teaspoon of minced scallions or chives, and 2 or 3 teaspoons of butter, coconut oil, or flax oil. Sprinkle with black pepper, stir, and serve with steamed or sautéed leafy greens.

Although package instructions say you can reconstitute and beat dried, powdered whites for desserts, we find that fresh whites produce the best results for delicate desserts such as macaroons, mousses, and meringues.

Free of fat and cholesterol, commercial dried, powdered egg whites are made by separating egg whites from yolks, freeze drying, and powdering. Commercial products are pasteurized (no longer raw) so you needn't worry about salmonella or cooking. Look for a brand that contains no added ingredients. My favorites are NOW Foods, JUST WHITES, Jay Robb, and Hickman's, sold in natural foods markets and the health food section of some supermarkets.

To reconstitute powdered whites, mix with water (or other liquid) and beat with a wire whisk, electric beaters, or in a blender until dissolved, and frothy. Cook or bake in your favorite recipe. Alternatively, add powdered whites to the dry ingredients in a recipe, then be sure to add water or fruit juice in the amounts specified to any other liquids called for in your recipe.

Because they are fat free and dehydrated, dried, powdered egg whites are stable at room temperature, where they may be kept for years without risk of spoilage.

Dried egg white equivalents

2 teaspoons powdered whites	= 3.2 g protein, 14 calories, 51 mg sodium	= 1 egg white
1 tablespoon powdered whites	= 6 g protein, 21 calories, 75 mg sodium	= 1 medium egg
4 teaspoons powdered whites	= 6.4 g protein, 28 calories, 102 mg sodium	= 1 egg or 2 whites

To replace whole eggs or fresh whites, follow the proportions below

Dried whites	plus water	to replace this amount of eggs
2 teaspoons	2 tablespoons	1 egg white
4 teaspoons	1/4 cup	2 whites or 1 whole egg
2 tablespoons	1/4 cup plus 2 tablespoons	3 whites
8 teaspoons	1/2 cup	4 whites or 2 whole eggs
1/4 cup	3/4 cup water	6 whites or 3 whole eggs
1/3 cup	1 cup water	8 whites or 4 whole eggs
1/2 cup	1 1/2 cups	12 whites or 6 whole eggs

Note: Use warm water or juice if whisking dried, powdered egg whites in a bowl. Use cold, cool, or warm liquid if mixing in a blender or food processor. The latter produces the best results.

Scrambled Eggs by the Sea

Prep: 15 minutes ~ **Cooking:** 4 minutes ~ **Yield:** 2 servings

Ingredients & Directions

4 to 6 medium to large free-range chicken eggs, rinsed

1/4 teaspoon ground turmeric

1/4 teaspoon ground chipotlé **or** black pepper

1/2 teaspoon dried, crumbled herbs or ground spices, optional:
> basil, oregano, cumin, sage, thyme, chives, Herbes de Provençe, **or** Italian blend

1/2 cup dulse **or** wild nori (laver) sea vegetable, raw, cut into bits with kitchen shears, sorted to remove any small shells or stones **or** toasted, coarsely crumbled sea vegetable

1/4 teaspoon Wright's Natural Liquid Hickory Smoke Seasoning, optional

1 to 1 1/2 teaspoons extra-virgin olive oil, unrefined coconut oil, ghee **or** clarified butter for oiling skillet

Nutrition	**1 serving (2 medium eggs):**
	157 calories
	14 g protein
	5 g carbohydrate
	9 g fat
	62 mg calcium
	171 mg sodium

1. Crack eggs into a bowl. Add remaining ingredients except for oil, ghee or butter. Whisk until frothy.

2. Heat oil in a 9- or 10-inch (preferably slope-sided) skillet over medium-high flame until hot but not smoking. Tilt skillet to coat bottom and sides of pan. Pan must be hot or eggs will stick.

3. Pour egg mixture into skillet. Reduce heat to medium or medium-low. As eggs begin to set up (almost immediately), push cooked portion aside with a metal spatula or large wooden spoon and tilt skillet to allow uncooked portion run underneath. Repeat until eggs are set. Cook until eggs are no longer runny but still glossy and moist, about 3 to 4 minutes for single batch, 5 minutes for double batch. Transfer to plates and serve.

Here's a delicious and easy way to incorporate sea vegetables into your diet. I love the caviar-like color, slightly salty taste, and knowing I'm getting extra trace minerals. Dulse, a crinkly purple colored sea vegetable, adds the most bacon-like taste but you can substitute wild nori, or a sheet of sushi nori, minced with kitchen shears. Kelp, kombu, alaria, wakame, sea palm, and ocean ribbons require precooking. If you have some on hand, give them a try here.

Double the recipe for 4 people and use a 12-inch skillet, or cook 2 separate batches.

Smoky Salmon & Egg Scramble

Prep: 10 minutes ~ **Cooking:** 4 to 6 minutes ~ **Yield:** 2 servings

Ingredients & Directions

3 medium to large free-range chicken eggs, rinsed

3/4 cup filtered water

1/4 cup dried, powdered egg whites

1/3 teaspoon ground chipotlé (smoked dried jalapeno pepper)

1/4 teaspoon ground turmeric

1/4 teaspoon dry mustard

1/2 cup dulse leaf **or** wild nori sea vegetable, cut into tiny pieces with kitchen shears and sorted to remove any small shells or stones, optional

1/4 teaspoon Wright's Liquid Hickory Smoke Seasoning, optional

5 ounces cooked wild salmon (from 6 ounces raw)

2 teaspoons extra-virgin olive oil, unrefined coconut oil, ghee **or** clarified butter

Edible flowers for garnish, optional

Nutrition

1 serving:
283 calories
34 g protein
2 g carbohydrate
16 g fat
50 mg calcium
273 mg sodium

1. Crack eggs into a blender. Add water, dried, powdered egg whites, spices, herbs, sea vegetable, and liquid smoke if desired. Blend until frothy, stopping to scrape sides with a spatula. Flake salmon and set aside.

2. Heat oil in a 9- or 10-inch skillet over medium-high flame until hot but not smoking. Tilt skillet to completely coat bottom and sides. Add egg mixture and sprinkle with flaked salmon and reduce heat to medium or medium-low. As eggs begin to set up, almost immediately, push cooked portion aside with a metal spatula and tilt pan to allow uncooked portion to run underneath. Repeat as eggs set up. Remove from heat when eggs are no longer running but still glossy and moist, about 4 minutes for single batch.

3. Transfer to serving plates and garnish if desired. Repeat process for second batch of eggs as desired.

Variations

* Omit water and dried, powdered egg whites and use 4 whole eggs.

* Add 1 tablespoon dried onion flakes and 1 tablespoon water.

* **Chicken & Egg Scramble:** Replace salmon with cooked, diced chicken breast.

* **Pork & Egg Scramble:** Replace salmon with cooked, minced lean pork loin, roast, or chops.

The dish is perfect for breakfast or lunch and provides a thrifty way to use up leftover bits of cooked salmon. If you don't have salmon on hand, substitute leftover cooked shrimp, Arctic char, chicken, turkey, or pork, and change the name of the recipe accordingly. I don't like to use canned or smoked salmon because it's so high in sodium; if you use it rinse well and reduce or omit salt from other dishes in the meal.

Scrambled Eggs with Tarragon & Tomatoes

Prep: 10 minutes ~ **Cooking:** 4 to 6 minutes ~ **Yield:** 2 to 3 servings

Ingredients & Directions

2 Roma tomatoes, halved, seeded, and chopped finely

6 medium to large free-range chicken eggs **or** duck eggs, rinsed

1 1/2 tablespoons minced fresh **or** 1 1/2 teaspoons dried, crumbled tarragon

1 teaspoon extra-virgin olive oil, unrefined coconut oil, ghee **or** clarified butter

Dash finely ground black or white pepper

1. Wash, halve, seed, and chop tomatoes and set aside.

2. Combine eggs and tarragon in a bowl. Whisk with a fork and set aside.

3. Heat oil in a 10- to 12-inch skillet over medium-high heat until hot but not smoking. Tilt skillet to completely coat bottom and sides. Add egg mixture. Reduce heat to medium or medium-low. As eggs begin to set up (almost immediately), sprinkle with tomatoes and begin pushing cooked portion aside with a metal spatula and tilting pan to allow uncooked portion to run underneath. Repeat as eggs start to set. Keep moving spatula. Remove from heat when eggs are no longer running but still glossy and moist, about 4 minutes for single batch.

4. Divide into 2 or 3 portions, transfer to serving plates, garnish with pepper, and serve.

Nutrition

1 serving (1/2 recipe):

243 calories
20 g protein
9 g carbohydrate
15 g fat
90 mg calcium
176 mg sodium

1 serving (1/3 recipe):

162 calories
13 g protein
6 g carbohydrate
10 g fat
60 mg calcium
117 mg sodium

Fresh tomatoes and tarragon add a tantalizing taste to everyday eggs.

Removing seeds from tomatoes—called seeding—makes a more attractive presentation. It only takes 2 minutes: slice the tomato in half across its middle. (Think of the tomato as the Earth and cut it in half across the equator.) With the end of a chopstick, scrape the seeds into a bowl, and discard. (I do this for salads to make serving and eating less messy.) Substitute basil or chives if you don't have fresh tarragon.

Variations

* **Scrambled Eggs with Chives and Tomatoes:** Replace tarragon with fresh or dried chives.

* **For a fluffier texture:** Blend eggs with tomatoes in a blender or food processor. Stir herbs in by hand and cook as above.

Don's Faux Frittata

Prep: 10 minutes ~ **Cooking:** 15 to 20 minutes ~ **Yield:** 4 servings

Ingredients & Directions

6 medium to large free-range chicken eggs **or** medium size duck eggs

3/4 cup filtered water

1/2 cup dried, powdered egg whites

4 small plum or Roma tomatoes, cored and halved (1 heaping cup)

2 tablespoons dried onion flakes **or** 1 small onion, finely minced

1/4 teaspoon ground turmeric

1/2 teaspoon ground chipotlé (smoked dried jalapeno pepper) **or** black pepper

1 teaspoon ground cumin, ground sumac **or** dry mustard

1/2 cup dulse leaf **or** laver (wild nori) sea vegetable, sorted to remove small shells or stones and cut into tiny pieces with shears, optional

2 to 3 teaspoons extra-virgin olive oil, unrefined coconut oil, ghee **or** clarified butter

1. Rinse eggs and crack into blender. Add remaining ingredients except oil. Cover and blend until smooth and frothy, stopping to scrape down sides with spatula.

2. Heat oil in heavy 12-inch skillet or chef pan over medium heat until hot but not smoking. Tilt skillet to coat evenly with oil. Pour egg mixture into skillet. Cover and reduce heat to medium (number 4 on an electric range). Cook undisturbed for 12 to 15 minutes, until slightly puffy and firm on top. Turn off heat.

3. Remove skillet from burner if you're using an electric range. Keep covered for 5 minutes, to allow steam to condense and lift stuck portions off bottom of skillet.

4. Cut into 8 wedges and serve. Cover and refrigerate leftovers and use within 2 days.

Variations

* Omit water and dried, powdered egg whites. Use 8 large eggs. (See box for nutrition information.)

Nutrition

1 serving (2 wedges):
215 calories
20 g protein
11 g carbohydrate
(2 g fiber)
10 g fat
64 mg calcium
261 mg sodium

Variation 1 serving (2 wedges):
213 calories
14 g protein
12 g carbohydrate
(2 g fiber)
13 g fat
76 mg calcium
140 mg sodium

This looks a lot like a frittata—the Italian version of an omelet, cooked in a heavy skillet until firm and fluffy, then cut into wedges—but contains a fraction of the fat. If you're cooking for 2 and prefer to make this fresh each day, prepare half a recipe in a 10-inch skillet and reduce the cooking time. I like to serve this with steamed asparagus or leftover sautéed kale, collards, or mustard greens, and fresh fruit or a Vita-Mix Total Juice.

Egg & Vegetable Pie Italiano

Prep: 15 minutes ~ **Cooking:** 25 to 30 minutes ~ **Yield:** 4 servings

Ingredients & Directions

Extra-virgin olive oil, unrefined coconut oil, ghee **or** clarified butter to grease baking pan

1 1/2 cups diced fresh tomatoes, **or** drained, canned diced no-salt-added tomatoes, divided

1 tablespoon dried parsley or chives **or** 1/4 cup washed, dried, minced fresh parsley leaves **or** chives

1/4 cup dulse flakes **or** 1/2 cup dulse leaf **or** laver (wild nori) sea vegetable, sorted to remove small shells or stones and cut into tiny pieces with shears, optional

6 medium to large free-range chicken eggs **or** duck eggs **or** 8 small eggs

1/2 cup dried, powdered egg whites

2 tablespoons dried onion flakes

2 garlic cloves, minced

1 teaspoon dried basil **or** 1 tablespoon fresh basil leaves, stems removed

1 teaspoon dried oregano **or** 1 tablespoon fresh oregano leaves, stems removed

1/2 teaspoon dried thyme **or** 1/2 tablespoon fresh thyme leaves, stems removed

1/4 teaspoon ground turmeric

1/2 teaspoon ground chipotlé (smoked dried jalapeno pepper) **or** black pepper

1/2 teaspoon Natural Liquid Hickory Smoke Seasoning, such as Wright's, optional

Nutrition

1 serving (2 slices):

211 calories
21 g protein
14 g carbohydrate
(2 g fiber)
8 g fat
3 g fiber
220 mg calcium
274 mg sodium

Variation 1 serving (2 wedges):

204 calories
14 g protein
14 g carbohydrate
(2 g fiber)
10 g fat
76 mg calcium
153 mg sodium

This dairy-free pie looks like a cross between a crustless quiche and pizza, but contains a fraction of the fat. Assemble and bake it first thing in the morning—before breakfast—or the night before. We figure 2 slices per person for a meal, served with sautéed leafy greens or steamed asparagus, and fresh fruit or a Vita-Mix Total Juice. For a richer taste, try the variation below.

1. Place rack in center of and preheat oven to 350° F. Oil a 10-inch deep-dish pie plate or 9x9x2-inch baking pan. Scatter half the tomato and parsley or chives over bottom of pie plate. Sprinkle with dulse if desired.

2. Combine reserved tomato and remaining ingredients in blender. Process until smooth and frothy, stopping to scrape sides with spatula. Do not overmix.

3. Pour egg mixture over vegetables in pie plate. Bake for 25 to 30 minutes, until puffy, firm in the center, and lightly golden on top. Cut into 8 slices and serve, or cool, cover, and refrigerate for later. If desired, top each serving with 1/4 of a sliced avocado. Use within 4 days.

Variations

* Omit chopped tomato and dried, powdered egg whites. Scatter 8 to 12 chopped sun-dried tomato halves over the pie plate and use a total of 8 large eggs. Cooking time will be slightly less. Check pie at 20 minutes. (See box for nutrition information.)

* Omit dried onions and scatter 1 to 2 cups of roasted vegetables (onions, mushrooms, carrots, or mixed vegetables) over pie plate with fresh or dried tomatoes.

Spinach & Egg Pie

Prep: 15 minutes ~ **Cooking:** 20 minutes ~ **Yield:** 4 servings

Ingredients & Directions

Extra-virgin olive oil, unrefined coconut oil, ghee **or** clarified butter to grease baking pan

8 large free-range chicken eggs **or** duck eggs

2 to 3 tablespoons freeze-dried onion flakes (We love onions.)

2 tablespoon dried parsley or chives **or** 1/2 cup washed, dried, minced fresh parsley leaves or chives

1 tablespoon dried Greek or Italian herb blend **or** Herbes de Provençe, crumbled

2 to 3 level tablespoons prepared mustard (Dijon, yellow, jalapeno, or red pepper)

1/2 teaspoon ground turmeric **and/or** cumin

1/2 teaspoon ground chipotlé (smoked dried jalapeno pepper) **or** black pepper

3 small garlic cloves, minced

12 sun-dried tomato halves, cut into bite-size pieces with kitchen shears (about 1/4 cup)

1 (16-ounce) bag frozen cut leaf spinach, thawed

1/2 cup dulse leaf, sorted to remove small shells and stones, and minced with shears, optional

Nutrition

1 serving
(2 slices without dulse):

200 calories
14 g protein
14 g carbohydrate
(2 g fiber)
10 g fat
88 mg calcium
234 mg sodium

Variation
1 serving (2 slices):

178 calories
21 g protein
11 g carbohydrate
(2 g fiber)
6 g fat
71 mg calcium
245 mg sodium

This dairy-free pie makes a fast breakfast entrée—if you make it the night before or first thing in the morning before you hop in the shower. All you need to complete the meal is fresh fruit or a Vita-Mix Total Juice. Figure 2 slices per adult or growing teen.

1. Preheat oven to 350° F. Liberally oil a 9x9x2-inch baking pan or 10-inch deep-dish pie plate.

2. In a mixing bowl or blender, combine eggs and next 7 ingredients (eggs through garlic) and whisk or blend until smooth. Pour into a medium-size mixing bowl. Add dried tomato pieces, spinach, and dulse if desired, then stir to evenly distribute. Pour into pie plate and smooth with a spatula.

3. Bake for 25 to 30 minutes until firm in center and top is golden. Cut into 8 slices and serve, or cover and refrigerate. Use within 4 days. Serve leftovers cold or heated briefly.

Variations

* Replace frozen spinach with frozen mustard or turnip greens, broccoli, or broccoli with cauliflower.

* Scatter 4 to 8 ounces of cooked salmon over pie before baking for more protein.

* Scatter 1/2 cup rinsed, drained and chopped, pitted black olives over pie before baking.

* For a higher protein, lower fat pie, use only 6 whole eggs, then add 3/4 cup filtered water **or** lite coconut milk, and 1/2 cup dried, powdered egg whites. Purée in blender with onion, herbs, and spices. Stir in tomatoes, spinach, and dulse, if desired. (See box for nutrition information.)

15 Fishing for Compliments

Bᴇꜱᴛ Bɪᴛᴇꜱ

Quick Smoky Simmered Salmon with Chipotlé

Prep: 10 minutes ~ **Cooking:** 7 to 12 minutes ~ **Yield:** 4 servings

Ingredients & Directions

4 center-cut salmon fillets **or** 4 steaks
(about 1 1/2 pounds)

1/2 cup filtered water, or enough to cover bottom of pan by 1/4 inch

1 bay leaf

1 teaspoon dry mustard

1/3 to 1/2 teaspoon ground chipotlé

1 1/2 teaspoons Wright's Natural Liquid Hickory Smoke Seasoning

1/2 teaspoon finely ground, unrefined sea salt
or 1 tablespoon tamari soy sauce, optional, but desirable

1. Rinse fish, pat dry, and set aside.

2. Stir water, bay leaf, mustard, chipotlé, and liquid smoke in a 12- or 13-inch skillet. Add optional sea salt or tamari if desired. Add 2 to 4 tablespoons additional water if using an electric range.

3. Arrange salmon pieces in skillet without overlapping. Cover and bring to a boil, reduce heat, and simmer fillets 7 to 9 minutes or steaks 8 to 12 minutes, or until a thin-bladed knife penetrates with little or no resistance and fish is nearly opaque throughout.

4. Transfer fish to plates. If excess liquid remains, simmer and reduce to about 1/4 cup and spoon over fish. Serve warm or cover and refrigerate for later. Use within 2 days.

Variations

* **Quick Smoky Simmered Char with Chipotlé:** Replace salmon with Arctic char.

* **Quick Smoky Simmered Sea Bass with Chipotlé:** Replace salmon with center-cut South American or Chilean sea bass fillets or steaks at least 3/4-inch thick.

* **Smoky Salmon with Barbecue Sauce:** After removing fish from pan, add 1 cup Better Barbecue Sauce (Page 401) to skillet. Simmer and stir to thicken and warm. Spoon over fish and serve.

Nutrition

1 serving:
220 calories
31 g protein
10 g fat
34 mg calcium
75 mg sodium

When I was growing up I never tired of smoked salmon. I still love the flavor—but not all the sodium nitrates, nitrites, or sugar, so I created this dish. Don and I enjoy it hot or as a cold side dish with cooked greens or a tossed salad, and sweet potatoes, squash, root vegetables, or fruit. Leftover salmon is also delicious with fried or poached eggs or in scrambled eggs or an omelet for breakfast.

FYI: Look in the condiment aisle of a supermarket for a brand of natural liquid hickory smoke seasoning, such as Wright's, that's free of MSG, polysorbates, additives, sugar, salt, dyes, and chemical names or numbers.

Note: Double the recipe for more people or meals, but do not double the water. Use only enough to barely cover the bottom of the skillet.

Baked Salmon with Sumac

Prep: 10 minutes ~ **Cooking:** 8 to 30 minutes ~ **Yield:** 4 servings
---

Ingredients & Directions

4 center-cut salmon fillets **or** steaks (about 1 1/2 pounds)

2 to 3 teaspoons extra-virgin olive oil

1 1/2 teaspoons ground sumac

1 teaspoon dried oregano **or** thyme, crumbled

1/3 teaspoon ground black pepper

Light sprinkle of finely ground, unrefined sea salt, optional (omit if sumac is salted)

1/2 cup Fluffy Tahini (Page 409) **or** Tahini Tartar sauce (Page 410), optional

Nutrition

1 serving:
220 calories
31 g protein
10 g fat
34 mg calcium
75 mg sodium

1. Preheat oven to 350° F for 1/2-inch thick fillets or 400° F for anything thicker.

2. Lightly oil a shallow baking pan or line with parchment. Rinse fish, pat dry, and place in pan. Brush or mist with oil. Sprinkle and rub seasonings in with the back of a spoon.

3. Bake 1/2-inch thick fillets 8 to 10 minutes, 1/2- to 1-inch thick fillets, 15 to 20 minutes, and 1 1/2- to 2-inch thick fillets about 30 minutes, or until firm to the touch, a thin-bladed knife penetrates easily, or flesh is nearly opaque throughout.

4. Top with tahini sauce at the table as desired.

5. Cover and refrigerate leftovers and use within 2 days.

Variations

* **Baked Sea Bass with Sumac:** Replace salmon with South American or Chilean sea bass steaks or fillets.

* **Baked Salmon with Basil & Garlic:** Replace sumac and oregano with dried, crumbled basil, **or** 2 1/2 tablespoons minced fresh basil. Add 2 cloves of garlic, finely minced or pressed.

Red sumac berries come from a bush that grows wild throughout the Mediterranean (not to be confused with poison sumac, which bears white berries). The crushed berries are dried and used in Italian, Arabic, Turkish, Syrian, and Lebanese cuisines as the major souring ingredient in place of lemon, vinegar, or tamarind.

Look for ground sumac in Middle Eastern grocery stores or on line. It's sold with salt and without. Ask before you buy. Also see Appendix D for mail order sources.

Arctic Char with Garlic & Ginger

Prep: 15 minutes ~ **Cooking:** 6 to 12 minutes ~ **Yield:** 4 to 6 servings

Ingredients & Directions

4 (6-ounce) Arctic char fillets **or** (6- to 8-ounce) steaks, 3/4- to 1 1/2-inches thick

1 tablespoon extra-virgin olive oil **or** unrefined coconut oil

2 medium garlic cloves, coarsely chopped

1 1/2 to 2 teaspoons peeled, finely minced fresh gingerroot **or** 1 tablespoon ginger juice

1/4 teaspoon ground black pepper **or** chipotlé (smoked dried jalapeno pepper powder)

Light sprinkle of finely ground, unrefined sea salt, optional

Squeeze of fresh lemon, optional

Juice of 1/2 lemon, optional

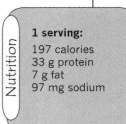

Nutrition

1 serving:
197 calories
33 g protein
7 g fat
97 mg sodium

1. Preheat oven to 350° F for 1/2-inch thick fillets or 400° F for anything thicker.

2. Lightly oil a shallow baking pan or line with parchment. Rinse fish, pat dry, place skin side down in prepared pan. Brush or mist fish with oil. Sprinkle with garlic, ginger, pepper, and optional sea salt. Rub seasonings in with back of a spoon. Mist or brush with oil again. Drizzle with lemon juice if desired.

3. Bake 1/2-inch thick fillets 8 to 10 minutes, 1/2- to 1-inch thick fillets 15 to 20 minutes, 1 1/2- to 2-inch thick fillets about 30 minutes, or until firm to the touch, a thin-bladed knife penetrates easily, or flesh is nearly opaque throughout.

4. Top with tahini sauce at table as desired.

5. Cover and refrigerate leftovers and use within 2 days.

Variations

* **Baked Grouper with Garlic & Ginger:** Replace char with grouper.

* **Baked Salmon with Garlic & Ginger:** Replace char with salmon.

* **Baked Arctic Char with Basil & Garlic:** Omit ginger and add 1 1/2 teaspoons dried, crumbled **or** 1 1/2 tablespoons chopped, fresh basil leaves without stems. Serve with lemon.

* **Baked Escolar with Ginger & Lime:** Replace Arctic char with escolar; omit the garlic; double the amount of ginger, and replace lemon juice with the zest and juice of 1/2 to 1 fresh lime.

* This same recipe also works with white meat fish at least 1/2-inch thick, such as mahi mahi, halibut, or cod.

Arctic char is an omega-3 rich relative of salmon that most people don't know about. If you get to know your local seafood merchant, you can have him order this and other wild fish for you to try. I suggest you keep extra packages in the freezer for regular use.

Wild fish is more nutritious because it has a more favorable fatty acid profile. It's more ecological and it tastes better than farmed fish.

Moroccan-Spiced Salmon

Prep: 15 minutes, plus time to make spice rub & sauce ~ **Cooking:** 10 minutes ~ **Yield:** 6 servings

Ingredients & Directions

6 (6-ounce) center-cut salmon fillets, each 1- to 1 1/2-inches thick (about 2 1/4 pounds)

1/2 teaspoon ground black pepper, or to taste

1/4 teaspoon finely ground, unrefined sea salt, optional

1 1/2 to 2 tablespoons unrefined coconut oil **or** ghee or clarified butter

1 recipe Moroccan Barbecue Spice Mix (Page 399)

1 recipe Moroccan Barbecue Sauce (Page 400), optional

Nutrition

1 serving:
280 calories
31 g protein
6 g carbohydrate
15 g fat
133 mg calcium
240 mg with salt

1. Preheat oven to 400° F. Rinse fish; pat dry with unbleached paper towel and place on platter.

2. Heat 1 tablespoon oil in each of two (10-inch) ovenproof cast iron or heavy-bottom stainless steel skillets (or 2 tablespoons oil in one 12- to 13-inch chef pan) over medium-high heat.

3. Meanwhile, season salmon with pepper and optional salt. Sprinkle fish with half the spice mix, turning to coat all sides. Add more as needed to thoroughly coat; press firmly to coat evenly.

4. When oil is hot, add 3 salmon fillets skin side up to each medium skillet or add all 6 pieces to 1 large skillet. Sauté for 2 minutes; turn skin side down. Brown second side for 1 to 2 minutes. Quickly transfer skillet to preheated oven and roast for 10 to 12 minutes, or until skin is crisp and fish is easily pierced with a thin-bladed knife. Remove skillet with thick oven mitts. (Don't touch those handles!)

5. Serve plain or with Moroccan Barbecue Sauce. Refrigerate leftovers and use within 2 days.

Variations

* **To reduce fat:** Use a baking sheet lined with parchment in place of skillets with oil. After liberally seasoning fillets with spices, lightly rub or brush pieces with 1 tablespoon olive **or** coconut oil, clarified butter, **or** ghee. Bake 10 to 20 minutes, or until fish tests done.

Chef Bruce Sherrod of Berkeley, California, shared his secrets for creating crispy spice-coated salmon steaks packed with flavor and calcium. You can prepare the spice rub and barbecue sauce a few days ahead or make extras for future use.

This fish is delicious with or without the sauce.

Round out the meal with a green salad or sautéed or steamed leafy greens, and roasted root vegetables or mushrooms, sweet potatoes, or a colorful beet, carrot, or squash soup. For company, consider a finale of My Favorite Macaroons, Stewed Pears with Anise & Apricots, or Apple-Prune Compote with Chinese 5-Spice.

Herbed Salmon Cakes with Citrus

Prep: 30 minutes ~ **Cooking:** 12 to 20 minutes ~ **Yield:** 12 servings

Ingredients & Directions

2-pounds wild salmon bellies, scraps **or** boneless skinless fillets

1/2 cup finely minced or grated red **or** white onion

1/2 cup minced fresh parsley leaves

1/2 cup celery ribs and top leaves, finely minced

1 medium carrot, grated (about 1/2 cup)

2 large eggs **or** 4 egg whites, whisked

1 cup raw dulse leaf, sorted to remove shells, and minced with kitchen shears

1/2 teaspoon dried, crumbled basil

1/2 teaspoon dried, powdered rosemary

1/2 teaspoon dried, crumbled thyme

1/2 teaspoon dried, crumbled oregano

1/2 teaspoon lemon pepper, or to taste

Grated zest from 1/2 medium orange (colored part only) **or** zest from 1 lemon **or** 2 teaspoons dried orange rind **or** citrus powder

2 tablespoons powdered shan yao (Radix Dioscorea) **or** arrowroot starch **or** powdered rolled oats

3 tablespoons filtered water **or** preservative-free chicken stock or broth

1 1/2 tablespoons extra-virgin olive oil, unrefined coconut oil, ghee, **or** clarified butter

Nutrition

1 serving:
120 calories
16 g protein
16 g carbohydrate
  (2 g fiber)
5 g fat
36 mg calcium
81 mg sodium

Ask the merchant at your local seafood shop to save salmon trimmings or bellies. They should be free...or inexpensive. I like to make a large batch of fish cakes and freeze some of the cooked patties. If you use fish that wasn't previously frozen, you can freeze uncooked patties. This recipe is easy to assemble, only the ingredient list is long. Try Cajun Ketchup or Better Barbecue Sauce, an herb infused Mayonnaise, or Tahini Tartar Sauce at the table (see Index for recipes).

1. Pulverized fish in food processor or mince with sharp knife.

2. Combine all ingredients except oil in large bowl. Blend with bare hands. Divide into 12 portions, form into balls, and press into 1-inch thick patties. Cover and refrigerate for several hours or overnight if time permits.

3. Preheat oven to 350° F. Line a 13x9x2-inch baking pan or cookie sheet with unbleached parchment or lightly oil 12 muffin tins. Arrange patties on prepared sheets or press into tins.

4. Bake until firm on top and around edges and opaque throughout, about 15 minutes.

5. Serve warm or cover and refrigerate. Use cooked patties within 3 days. Use raw patties within 2 days or separate with parchment or wax paper and freeze.

Note: Do **not** substitute salted and canned salmon; it's too high in sodium.

Variations

* Replace dulse with 1 teaspoon finely ground, unrefined sea salt **or** 1 tablespoon tamari.

Salmon Ceviche with Tomato, Onions & Avocado

Prep: 20 minutes ~ **Marinating:** 10 to 14 hours ~ **Yield:** 6 servings

Ingredients & Directions

Fish and citrus juice:

1 1/2 to 2 pounds wild salmon fillets (preferably sushi-grade), rinsed, cut into 1-inch cubes, and skinned

3/4 to 1 cup lemon or lime juice (from about 4 lemons or 5 to 6 limes)

Vegetables and seasonings:

3 large or 4 medium red or orange tomatoes, peeled, seeded, and diced (about 4 cups)

1 1/2 teaspoons dry mustard **or** 2 teaspoons paprika

1/4 cup minced fresh dill weed **or** 1 tablespoon dried dill weed

1/2 teaspoon ground chipotlé **or** black pepper

1/2 teaspoon finely ground, unrefined sea salt, additional 1/2 teaspoon if desired

Garnish:

2 medium-large avocados, halved, pitted, peeled and sliced

Nutrition

1 serving:
321 calories
24 g protein
17 g carbohydrate
(6 g fiber)
18 g fat
50 mg calcium
237 mg sodium

1. Place salmon in a glass pie plate or shallow bowl, and cover with lemon or lime juice and a plate or lid. Refrigerate for 6 to 12 hours, turning the fish twice with a non-metallic spoon to evenly marinate it in the juices. When ready, the fish will appear almost translucent, inside and out.

2. Drain fish in colander. Discard the juices. Combine vegetables and seasonings in a large glass bowl. Add salmon and toss to coat. Cover and refrigerate for 2 to 4 hours before serving.

3. Serve salmon over salad greens and garnish with sliced avocado. Cover and refrigerate leftovers in a glass bowl or jar and eat within 3 days.

Variations

* **Omit salt.** Add 1 cup of packed, raw dulse (a purple sea vegetable), sorted to remove shells and small stones and snipped finely with kitchen shears.

* Replace mustard, paprika, and dill with 1/3 cup minced fresh basil and 3 minced garlic cloves.

* Replace salmon with fresh tuna, bay scallops, orange roughy, true cod, **or** sea bass.

Raw fish marinated in an acidic solution to kill potential parasites and pathogens and predigest the fish is served in many cultures. If possible, buy sushi-grade fish from a seafood market or fisherman; it's flash frozen at 10° F to 20° F below zero and retains an excellent texture after thawing. For economy, I sometimes use filleted salmon bellies from an Asian market. This dish makes a delicious breakfast, lunch, or dinner served over salad greens or with cooked leafy greens and fresh fruit.

Note: Out of season, replace fresh tomatoes with 12 soaked, sliced sun-dried tomato halves.

Baked Sea Bass with Mustard & Herbs

Prep: 5 minutes ~ **Cooking:** 12 to 30 minutes ~ **Yield:** 4 to 6 servings

Ingredients & Directions

1 1/2 to 2 pounds Chilean sea bass fillets **or** steaks, cut into 4 to 6 portions

3 to 4 tablespoons minced fresh tarragon, basil leaves, or dill weed **or** 1 to 1 1/2 tablespoons dried, crumbled herbs

1/4 to 1/2 teaspoon coarsely ground black pepper **or** ground chipotlé

2 to 4 rounded tablespoons Dijon, creamy white **or** stoneground mustard

Olive oil, coconut oil, clarified butter or ghee for oiling skillet

Nutrition

1 serving:
320 calories
24 g protein
25 g fat
2 g carbohydrate
19 mg calcium
111 mg sodium

1. Preheat oven to 400° F. Lightly oil shallow baking pan or line with parchment.

2. Rinse fish, pat dry, and place in pan without overlapping pieces. Sprinkle with herbs and pepper. Generously coat top and sides of each portion with mustard.

3. Bake 3/4-inch thick pieces about 12 minutes. Allow 15 to 20 minutes for 1-inch thick pieces, and 30 minutes for 1 1/2-inch thick or larger pieces, or until firm to the touch, a thin-bladed knife penetrates with little or no resistance, and flesh is opaque throughout.

4. Serve warm. Cover and refrigerate leftovers. Use within 2 days.

This almost-effortless dish is delicious and impressive if you can find South American or Chilean sea bass, which has a rich, buttery flavor, and a generous dose of omega-3 essential fatty acids. These fish have jet black, scaly skin and pearly white flesh. Lean varieties are drier, usually sold without the skin, and more closely resemble mahi mahi or Swordfish steaks. They benefit from the addition of olive oil.

Note: If you can't find South American or Chilean sea bass, substitute wild salmon, Atlantic or Mediterranean butterfish, or escolar (oil fish). If using a low-fat variety of salmon, such as coho, or a low-fat variety of sea bass, add 1 tablespoon of olive oil to the mustard.

Baked Haddock with Balsamic Vinaigrette

Prep: 10 minutes ~ **Marinating:** 4 to 6 hours ~ **Cooking:** 3 to 30 minutes ~ **Yield:** 4 to 6 servings

Ingredients & Directions

1 1/2 pounds haddock fillets or other white meat fish

2 to 3 tablespoons extra-virgin olive oil

2 tablespoons balsamic vinegar

3 tablespoons minced fresh herbs **or** 1 tablespoon dried, crumbled herbs:
    oregano, basil, thyme, chervil, chives, or a
    combination of three of these

2 small or 1 large clove of garlic, finely minced or pressed

1/2 teaspoon coarsely ground black pepper **or** white pepper

1/4 teaspoon finely ground, unrefined sea salt, optional

Nutrition

1 serving:
217 calories
32 g protein
2 g carbohydrate
9 g fat
73 mg calcium
117 mg sodium

If you're cooking for fewer than 4 people, cook half the fish one night and the remainder the next, or cook it all at once and use the leftovers to make main-dish salads the second day or night. I serve this on a bed of steamed spinach, bok choy, or mixed vegetables or with a crisp green salad, and a colorful root, tuber, squash, or fruit dish.

1. Rinse fish, pat dry, and arrange skin-side down in 1 oblong or 2 (9- to 10-inch) non-metallic baking pans. Whisk remaining ingredients, pour over fish, and rub in with a spoon.

2. Cover each pan with a snap-on lid, plate, or foil. Refrigerate for 4 to 8 hours, turning once.

3. Remove pan(s) from the refrigerator 15 to 30 minutes before cooking. Preheat oven to 350° F for 1/4- to 1/2-inch thick fillets or 400° F for anything thicker.

4. Uncover and bake 1/4-inch thick fillets about 3 minutes, 1/2-inch thick fillets 8 minutes, fillets up to 1-inch thick 15 to 20 minutes, and 1 1/2- to 2-inch thick pieces 30 minutes. Thin fillets are done when outside appears opaque or thinnest part flakes easily with a fork. Thick pieces are done when firm to the touch, a knife penetrates easily, or flesh is nearly opaque throughout.

5. Serve fish warm with pan juices. If pan juices are excessive, simmer to reduce. Use fish within 2 days.

Variations

    *   Replace haddock with blue hake (ocean white fish), deep sea dory, cod, scrod, orange roughy, pompano, flounder, **or** ocean perch.

Baked Deep Sea Dory with Herbs

Prep: 10 minutes ~ **Cooking:** 4 to 20 minutes ~ **Yield:** 4 servings

Ingredients & Directions

1 1/2-pounds deep sea dory fillets or other white meat fish

1 to 1 1/2 tablespoons extra-virgin olive oil, melted unrefined coconut oil, **or** butter

3 tablespoons minced fresh herbs **or** 1 tablespoon, dried, crumbled herbs:
    parsley, chervil, chives, basil, dill, thyme, or fennel, used alone or in combination

1/2 teaspoon coarsely ground black pepper **or** 1 teaspoon lemon pepper

Light sprinkle of finely ground, unrefined sea salt, optional

1 lemon, quartered

1/2 cup Fluffy Tahini (Page 409) **or** Tahini Tartar sauce (Page 410), optional

Nutrition

1 serving:
155 calories
24 g protein
7 g fat
4 mg calcium
121 mg sodium

Look for deep sea dory, a mild-tasting, reasonably priced wild caught fish, in the freezer section of your local supermarket. Adjust cooking time to the thickness of the fillets.

If you don't have other things to bake at the same time, use a toaster oven. Reduce everything by 1/3 for a small toaster oven, thin fillets, or if you're using only 1 pound of fish.

1. Preheat oven to 350° F for 1/4- to 1/2-inch thick fillets or 400° F for anything thicker.

2. Lightly oil 1 large or 2 small shallow baking pans or line with parchment paper. Rinse fish, pat dry, and place in pans without overlapping pieces. Lightly brush or mist with oil or dot with butter. Sprinkle with herbs, pepper, and optional salt. Rub seasonings in with back of spoon.

3. Bake 1/4-inch fillets 3 to 4 minutes, 1/2-inch fillets 8 to 10 minutes, fillets up to 1-inch thick 15 to 20 minutes. Cook 1 1/2- to 2-inch thick pieces for 30 minutes. Thin fillets are done when outside appears opaque or thinnest part flakes easily with a fork. Cook thicker pieces until firm to the touch, a knife penetrates easily, or flesh is nearly opaque throughout.

4. Garnish with lemon wedges and Fluffy Tahini or Tahini Tartar Sauce as desired.

5. Cover and refrigerate leftovers and use within 2 days.

Variations

* Replace dory with orange roughy, true cod, black cod, ling cod, flounder, haddock, scrod (baby cod or other baby fish), salmon, Arctic char, escolar, halibut, or sea bass. Reduce or omit oil if using Chilean or South American sea bass **or** escolar, which are already rich.

Roasted Red Snapper with Rosemary, Garlic, Lemon & Pepper

Prep: 15 minutes ~ **Cooking:** 10 to 20 minutes ~ **Yield:** 4 to 6 servings

Ingredients & Directions

1 1/2 pounds red snapper, 1 large **or** 2 smaller fillets (3/4- to 1 1/2-inches thick)

1 tablespoon extra-virgin olive oil, unrefined coconut oil, ghee, **or** clarified butter

2 to 3 medium to large garlic cloves, coarsely minced (about 1 tablespoon)

1 1/2 tablespoons minced fresh rosemary leaves **or** 1 1/2 teaspoons dried, ground rosemary

1/2 cup crabmeat, optional

1/2 teaspoon ground white **or** black pepper

1/4 teaspoon finely ground, unrefined sea salt, optional

1/2 lemon, quartered

1/2 cup Fluffy Tahini (Page 409), Tahini Tartar Sauce (Page 410) **or** Homemade Mayonnaise (Page 424), optional

Nutrition

1 serving:
194 calories
34 g protein
2 g carbohydrate
9 g fat
59 mg calcium
108 mg sodium

A mild all-purpose fish with a moderate fat content, red snapper is firm enough to grill, and beautiful baked or broiled. Thaw frozen fish completely in the refrigerator before cooking.

For a gourmet touch, Chef Jeff McKahon stuffs the fillets with preservative-free real crabmeat.

I like to serve this with a crisp green salad or cooked leafy green or mixed vegetables, baked or roasted sweet potatoes, mushrooms, or a creamy carrot or squash soup, with or without raw or cooked fruit for dessert.

1. Preheat oven to 400° F. Lightly oil shallow baking pan or line with unbleached parchment. Rinse fish, pat dry, and place in pan. Lightly mist or rub with oil or spread with ghee or butter.

2. Make 2 long, 1/4-inch deep slits down center and sides of each fillet. Gently pull slits apart. Fill with garlic and optional crabmeat, and press to close. Sprinkle fish with rosemary, pepper, and optional sea salt. Rub in with spoon and drizzle with juice of 1/4 lemon.

3. Bake 1/2-inch thick fillets for about 6 minutes, fillets up to 1-inch thick 15 to 20 minutes, 1 1/2-inch thick or thicker fillets about 30 minutes. Thin fillets are done when outside appears opaque or thinnest part flakes easily with a fork. Thicker fillets are done when firm to the touch, a thin-bladed knife penetrates with little or no resistance, or flesh is nearly opaque.

4. Remove promptly. Serve with lemon or sauce. Refrigerate leftovers and use within 2 days.

Note: Don't chop the garlic too finely or it will burn as it cooks.

Variations

* **Roasted Red Snapper with Rosemary, Garlic, Lemon, Pepper & Crab Meat Filling:** In step 3, stuff approximately 1/2 cup of real crabmeat into incisions. Mist or brush fish lightly with oil before baking.

* **Roasted Red Snapper with Basil, Garlic, Lemon & Pepper:** Replace rosemary with fresh **or** dried basil leaves.

Baked Fish Fillets with Practically Paleo Pesto

Prep: 15 minutes ~ **Cooking:** 3 to 25 minutes ~ **Yield:** 4 to 6 servings

Ingredients & Directions

Extra-virgin olive oil, or unrefined coconut oil (to coat pans)

1 1/2-pounds white meat fish fillets (2 large or 4 to 6 smaller fillets), 1/2- to 1 1/2-inches thick:
  deep sea dory, orange roughy, cod, flounder, sea trout, grouper, scrod (baby fish), sole, pollock, red snapper, ocean perch, wild salmon, escolar, or Arctic char

1/4 teaspoon coarsely ground black pepper

1/4 to 1/3 cup Practically Paleo Pesto **or** Pistou (Page 415)

1. Preheat oven to 350° F for 1/2-thick fillets or 400° F if thicker. Lightly oil a shallow baking pan or line with unbleached parchment paper.

2. Rinse fish, pat dry, place in pan(s). Sprinkle with pepper. Spread at least half the Pesto or Pistou over fillets.

3. Bake 1/4-inch thick fillets 3 to 4 minutes, 1/2-inch thick fillets 8 to 10 minutes, fillets up to 1-inch thick 15 to 20 minutes, 1 1/2-inch thick or thicker pieces about 30 minutes. Thin fillets are done when outside appears opaque or thinnest part flakes apart when separated with a fork.

4. Spread additional Pesto, Pistou, or herb paste over 1-inch or thicker fillets after 10 minutes. Cook until firm to the touch, thin-bladed knife inserts easily, or flesh is opaque throughout.

5. Promptly remove fish from oven and serve. Refrigerate leftovers and use within 2 days.

Nutrition

1 serving (cod):
176 calories
30 g protein
6 g fat
32 mg calcium
207 mg sodium

1 serving (Arctic char):
184 calories
33 g protein
3 g fat
4 mg calcium
207 mg sodium

Since Don and I usually avoid cheese and like to keep our salt intake modest, when we're in the mood for it, I make dairy-free, low-salt pesto, or pistou (the French Provençal version without nuts). If you're out of basil, try the Quick Herb Paste inspired by *The Joy of Cooking.*

Variations

* **Baked Fish Fillets with Quick Herb Paste:** Substitute 1 to 2 tablespoons extra-virgin olive oil mixed with 2 tablespoons chopped fresh herbs (any combination of parsley, chervil, basil, chives, or thyme) and 1 or 2 finely minced cloves of garlic for pesto or pistou. Quarter 1 lemon for garnish.

Note: If strong fishy fragrances put you or your loved ones off, avoid using ocean perch or red snapper or turn your air purifier on high!

Sesame-Buttered Seafood

Prep: 20 minutes ~ **Cooking:** 10 to 25 minutes ~ **Yield:** 4 servings

Ingredients & Directions

Fish and garlic:

Extra-virgin olive oil, unrefined coconut oil, ghee **or** clarified butter to oil pan

4 cod or halibut steaks (about 1 1/2 pounds), 3/4 to 1 inch thick

2 medium-large garlic cloves, coarsely chopped (about 1 1/2 to 2 teaspoons)

Light sprinkle of finely ground, unrefined sea salt, optional

Tahini Sauce (2/3 cup):

1/4 cup roasted sesame tahini (not sesame butter), thoroughly mixed

2 to 3 tablespoons warm filtered water

1/4 to 1/2 teaspoon finely ground, unrefined sea salt

2 to 3 tablespoons lemon juice

1 teaspoon lemon pepper **or** 1/2 teaspoon ground black pepper

2 teaspoons mild Hungarian paprika

1 teaspoon dried **or** 1 tablespoon minced fresh dill weed, optional

1/4 cup finely minced fresh parsley leaves, scallions, or chives for garnish

4 tablespoons crumbled, Toasted Dulse (Page 397), optional

Finely grated zest (colored part only) of 1 lemon for garnish, optional

Nutrition

1 serving:
(cod):

250 calories
34 g protein
7 g carbohydrate
        (1 g fiber)
10 g fat
55 mg calcium
213 mg sodium

Sesame Tahini—a paste made from hulled, ground sesame seeds—adds a rich buttery flavor to lean white meat fish and low-fat varieties of salmon like coho. Bake fish in the oven or on the grill in aluminum foil packets lined with parchment paper.

1. Preheat oven to 350° F. Lightly oil a shallow baking pan or line with unbleached parchment for easy cleanup. Rinse fish, pat dry, place in baking pan. Sprinkle with garlic.

2. Mix tahini, warm water, and salt until smooth. Zest lemon; reserve zest for garnish. Stir in lemon juice, pepper, paprika, and dill. Divide evenly and spread over fish. Sprinkle with parsley, scallions, or chives.

3. Cover pan with a lid or foil. Bake 18 to 20 minutes, or until flesh flakes with a fork.

4. Garnish with dulse, scallions and/or lemon zest and serve. Refrigerate leftovers and use within 2 days.

Note: When you open a new jar of tahini, transfer the contents to a bowl or food processor, mix until smooth, return to the original jar, and refrigerate. It will never separate again.

Variations

* Substitute orange roughy, flounder, deep sea dory, sole, **or** wild salmon fillets or steaks. Check 1/2-inch thick fillets after 10 minutes.

Arctic Char in Parchment Packets

Prep: 15 minutes ~ **Cooking:** 10 to 15 minutes ~ **Yield:** 4 servings

Ingredients & Directions

4 (5- to 6-ounce) Arctic char fillets
(1 1/4 to 1 1/2 pounds), at least 2/3-inch thick

1/2 teaspoon coarsely ground black pepper **or** 1
teaspoon lemon pepper

3 tablespoons minced fresh herbs **or** 1 tablespoon,
dried, crumbled herbs:
   one or a combination of several:
      basil, oregano, chervil, chives, tarragon, or
      fennel fronds

1/4 to 1/2 teaspoon finely ground unrefined sea salt

4 to 6 teaspoons extra-virgin olive oil, **or** unrefined
coconut oil, butter, clarified butter **or** ghee

1 small or 1/2 large red onion, cut into 1/8- to 1/4-inch
thick rings

2 medium or 3 small tomatoes, cut into 1/2-inch thick
slices

1 lemon, quartered

Nutrition

1 serving:
189 calories
29 g protein
5 g carbohydrate
6 g fat
26 mg calcium
304 mg sodium

Arctic char (also known as blueback, trout, or Quebec red trout), looks, cooks, and tastes remarkably like lean varieties of salmon such as coho. This recipe accommodates a wide range of herbs, spices, vegetables, and varieties of fish.

To complete the meal, include a crisp green salad, a parboiled vegetable medley, or sautéed greens, and a colorful root, tuber, squash or fresh fruit.

1. Rub grates with paper towel moistened with oil and preheat grill.

2. Cut 4 pieces of aluminum foil and line with 4 sheets of unbleached parchment paper, each twice the size of a fish fillet. Put a portion of fish on each. Drizzle or rub with oil or spread with butter. Sprinkle with pepper, herbs, and sea salt. Top with onion and tomato slices.

3. Fold parchment-lined foil together over fish. Roll it down to within 1 inch of vegetables. Crimp and roll sides and pull sides up to form handles.

4. Cook packages on hot grill or in a shallow baking pan in preheated 350° F oven for 20 minutes. Check 1 envelope for doneness (flesh will flake with a fork). If not done, rewrap and cook for 5 more minutes.

5. Open packets at table. Garnish with lemon wedges and serve. Refrigerate leftovers and use within 2 days.

Variations

* **Pompano in Parchment:** Substitute pompano for char.

* **Salmon in Parchment:** Replace Arctic char with salmon. For contrast, use low-acid gold tomatoes, or replace tomatoes with fresh thinly sliced shiitake or cremini mushrooms. If using mushrooms, omit salt and mist vegetables with tamari soy sauce in a spray bottle.

* **Escolar in Parchment:** Replace char with escolar for a delicious buttery flavor and soft texture.

Broiled White Meat Fish Fillets with Garlic & Pepper

Prep: 15 minutes ~ **Cooking:** 6 to 12 minutes ~ **Yield:** 4 to 6 servings

Ingredients & Directions

Fish:

1 1/2 to 1 3/4 pounds wild caught fish fillets with or without skin, cut into 1 or more pieces:
> haddock, deep sea dory, orange roughy, scrod (baby fish), red snapper, flounder, sea trout, sole, ling cod, true cod, grouper, pollock, or other

1 to 1 1/2 tablespoons extra-virgin olive oil, unrefined coconut oil, ghee **or** clarified butter

1/4 teaspoon lemon pepper **or** coarsely ground black pepper

1 to 2 garlic cloves, chopped coarsely (not minced)

Light sprinkle finely ground unrefined sea salt, optional

2 teaspoons fresh lemon juice

1/4 cup minced fresh parsley leaves for garnish

2 to 4 tablespoons dulse **or** laver/wild nori flakes for garnish

1. Position broiler rack 3 to 4 inches from heat source. Preheat. Lightly oil shallow baking or broiling pan.

2. Rinse fish, pat dry, and place skin side down in pan. Brush or lightly mist fish with oil or butter. Sprinkle with pepper, garlic, and optional sea salt. Rub in with back of spoon.

3. Leave door of electric range ajar; close for gas range. Cook undisturbed for 4 minutes. Fillets 1/4- to 1/2-inch thick are done as soon as exterior turns opaque. Check 1-inch fillets after 6 minutes. Baste or mist thicker fillets with oil and cook 2 to 3 minutes more. Turn 1 1/2-inch thick fillets, mist with oil, and cook another 5 minutes, until a thin-bladed knife is easily inserted into thickest point and all, or nearly all, traces of translucence are gone.

4. Drizzle with lemon juice, garnish, and serve. Refrigerate leftovers and use within 2 days.

Variations

* **Broiled Oily or Dark Meat Fish Fillets**: If using salmon, char, escolar, or Chilean sea bass, reduce oil to 2 teaspoons and sprinkle fish with 2 teaspoons lemon juice before cooking.

* Replace garlic with a generous sprinkling (1 to 2 teaspoons) of dried, crumbled oregano or dried, powdered rosemary, **or** 1 tablespoon ginger juice.

Broiling is best reserved for steaks or fillets at least 1/2-inch thick, anything thinner should be baked or sautéed to avoid overcooking.

Nutrition

1 serving (haddock):
198 calories
32 g protein
1 g carbohydrate
7 g fat
60 mg calcium
117 mg sodium

Broiling rules:
1) Preheat broiler for at least 15 minutes for full-size oven or 5 minutes for a toaster oven.
2) Cook fillets 6 to 8 minutes per inch of thickness.
3) Stay close to supervise.
4) Remove fish promptly when done.

Note: Be sure to include some garlic, or ginger, oregano, or rosemary, to block the production of harmful HCAs (heterocylic amines, produced when meats are cooked at high temperatures).

Macadamia-Orange Roughy in Orange & White Wine Reduction Sauce

Prep: 15 minutes ~ **Cooking:** 7 to 10 minutes ~ **Yield:** 6 servings

Ingredients & Directions

2 pounds orange roughy fillets, about 1/2-inch thick (about 6 to 8 fillets)

1 cup orange juice (preferably freshly squeezed with pulp)

1 cup dry white wine (Chardonnay, Fume Blanc, Sauvignon Blanc, Pinot Grigio, or other white table wine)

2 bay leaves

1/2 teaspoon lemon pepper **or** ground white pepper

1/4 teaspoon unrefined, mineral-rich sea salt

1 1/2 teaspoons dried, ground rosemary or crumbled tarragon **or** 1 1/2 tablespoons minced fresh rosemary or tarragon

1 tablespoon arrowroot starch dissolved in 2 tablespoons cold water **or** cold orange juice

1/2 small orange, cut into thin slices for garnish

1/4 to 1/2 cup coarsely chopped, lightly toasted, unsalted macadamia nuts for garnish

Nutrition

1 serving:
253 calories
23 g protein
12 g carbohydrate
(2 g fiber)
8 g fat
72 mg calcium
207 mg sodium

My sister-in-law, Nancy, taught me this modified poaching technique. I added orange juice and herbs, and thickened the pan juices. Nancy and I like to serve this with Mashed Sweet Potatoes with Lime, and a large green salad with a creamy tahini dressing or vinaigrette. For dessert, try Dark Chocolate-Dipped Dates, Stewed Pears with Anise, or Rosehip-Apple Compote drizzled with macadamia nut butter (see Index for recipes).

1. Rinse fish, pat dry, and set aside. Combine juice, wine, bay leaves, pepper, salt, and herbs in a 12- to 13-inch skillet or 2 smaller pans. Cover and bring to low boil.

2. Lower fish into bubbling juice, reduce heat to medium-low, cover, and cook 4 minutes until tops of fillets begin to turn opaque. Turn fish with slotted spatula. Cook 3 to 4 minutes more, until almost translucent inside and easily pierced with a fork.

3. Transfer fish to platter. Simmer juices until reduced to about 1 cup. Add dissolved arrowroot, simmer, and stir until thick and clear; spoon over fish. Garnish with orange slices and nuts; serve.

4. Cover and refrigerate leftovers and use within 2 days.

Variations

* Add 1 tablespoon dijon or white mustard to pan sauce in step 3.

* Substitute fillets of cod, deep sea dory, Chilean sea bass, escolar, blue hake (ocean whitefish) or salmon. Turn 2/3- to 1-inch thick fillets or steaks after 5 minutes and cook a total of 10 to 14 minutes or until fish tests done. Be careful not to overcook.

* Replace rosemary and tarragon with 2 tablespoons of minced fresh fennel fronds.

* Omit macadamia nuts, then dot cooked fish with 2 tablespoons of real butter.

Sautéed Fish Fillets

Prep: 15 minutes ~ **Cooking:** 3 to 6 minutes ~ **Yield:** 4 servings

Ingredients & Directions

4 small fish fillets, 1/2- to 1 1/4-inch thick (about 1 1/2 pounds):
> orange roughy, cod, deep sea dory, pollock, flounder, sole, perch, or scrod

Finely ground, unrefined sea salt (about 1/4 teaspoon)

1/2 teaspoon ground black pepper **or** 1 teaspoon lemon pepper

1/3 cup arrowroot starch

2 to 3 tablespoons unrefined coconut oil, olive oil, clarified butter, ghee **or** combination of 2 of these

4 lemon wedges, optional

1/2 cup Better Barbecue Sauce or Cajun Ketchup (Page 401) or Tahini Tartar Sauce (Page 410), **or** Mango-Ginger Chutney (Page 404), optional

Nutrition	**1 serving (orange roughy without sauce):**
	231 calories
	26 g protein
	12 g carbohydrate
	9 g fat
	53 mg calcium
	247 mg sodium

1. Rinse fish, pat dry, and place on platter. Sprinkle both sides with salt and pepper. Add arrowroot to a clean, dry pie plate. Dredge fillets in flour one at a time to coat.

2. Heat oil in a heavy 10- to 13-inch skillet over medium heat. Two minutes before cooking fillets, increase heat to medium-high. Arrange fillets in skillet and cook until lightly golden and a crust forms, about 2 to 3 minutes. Turn with metal spatula and cook until a light crust forms on second side, 1 to 3 minutes depending on thickness.

3. Transfer fish to a clean plate. If cooking fish in a smaller skillet in half the oil, cook in 2 batches and set cooked portions in a 200° F oven while cooking remaining pieces. Add additional oil to skillet only as needed. Add remaining fish and repeat process.

4. Pass lemon wedges, barbecue sauce, tahini sauce, or chutney at the table. Refrigerate leftovers and use within 2 days.

You don't need wheat or corn flour to create crispy crusted fish filets. Arrowroot starch, ground from a traditional hunter-gatherer tuber, works well. Use it anywhere you'd normally use cornstarch; it's less allergenic and hasn't been tampered with by mad scientists doing experiments with Genetically Modified Organisms (GMOs).

You can use almost any lean, white meat fish, provided the pieces are at least 1/2- and no more than 1 1/4-inches thick. Allow about 4 minutes of cooking time for 1/2-inch thick fillets, 6 minutes for 1-inch thick fillets.

Fish cooks quickly, so be sure to have your side dishes—cooked leafy greens or tossed salad, and a root vegetable, tuber, or fruit—ready before you start the fish. This method was modified from a recipe in Pam Anderson's *How to Cook Without a Book*.

Steamed Fish Fillets & Steaks on a Bed of Herbs

Prep: 15 minutes ~ **Cooking:** 7 to 12 minutes ~ **Yield:** 4 servings

Ingredients & Directions

2 to 3 large bunches of herbs (2 or 3 cups full, enough to liberally cover each tray), thoroughly rinsed and patted dry with tough stems removed:
>   fresh basil, oregano, thyme, parsley, dill, fennel, mint, or tarragon leaves

4 (6-ounce) fillets **or** 4 (7- or 8-ounce) steaks:
>   salmon, Arctic char, swordfish, snapper, sea trout, sea bass, halibut, escolar, tuna, grouper, flounder, mackerel, or cod

1 teaspoon lemon pepper **or** 1/2 teaspoon ground black pepper

Finely ground sea salt, optional

Optional sauce (select 1):

1/2 cup Tahini Tartar Sauce (Page 410) **or** Sesame-Garlic Sauce (Page 409) for topping

1/4 to 1/2 cup Homemade Mayonnaise (Pages 424 to 425)

1/4 cup Dairy-Free Pesto **or** Pistou (Page 415)

Nutrition

1 serving (salmon without sauce):
220 calories
31 g protein
11 g fat
34 mg calcium
75 mg sodium

A quick and energy-efficient cooking method, steaming retains moisture and provides a wider margin for error than broiling or grilling. As this fish cooks, the fragrance of the herbs—not fish—will permeate your kitchen. Stacking bamboo or stainless steel trays will allow you to cook vegetables, along with the fish, using the same pot, burner, and steam. Otherwise, use a fish poacher or accordion-style vegetable steamer.

1. Rest a bamboo steamer tray inside a large wok or on rim of large saucepan the same diameter. Place a large metal vegetable steamer in a large pot, or place meat rack or fish poaching tray on top of 3 empty tuna cans (tops and bottoms removed) in a roasting pan or fish poacher set over 2 burners.

2. Generously line bamboo or metal steamer with herbs, covering every inch. For a roasting pan or fish poacher and thin or delicate fillets, rest herbs on individual "trays" made from sheets of aluminum foil lined with parchment, cut to size and folded up at edges for ease of removal.

3. Rinse fish, pat dry, season both sides with pepper, and salt if desired; arrange over herbs.

4. Add 1 to 2 inches of boiling water to bottom of wok or pot. Water should not touch bottom of tray. Do not stack more than 3 trays. Cover top tray (or pot) with a lid.

5. Turn heat to medium-high and cook fish over rapidly simmering water with steam rising. Cook approximately 10 minutes per inch of thickness or until fish tests done. If water starts to cook away before fish is done, add additional boiling water to bottom of pot. Check often.

6. Remove fish when slightly translucent in center, steaks are medium-rare at bone, or a thin-bladed knife inserts easily. Fish will continue cooking after removal from heat.

7. Discard spent foliage unless cooked to perfection. Serve fish with your choice of toppings.

8. Refrigerate leftovers and use within 2 days. Leftovers are best served unheated.

Note: Do **not** put fish directly on bamboo trays or they will forever remind you of fish!

Broiled Scampi with Herb Paste

Prep: 30 minutes ~ **Cooking:** 8 to 12 minutes ~ **Yield:** 4 to 6 servings

Ingredients & Directions

1 1/2-pounds scampi (8 to 10 jumbo green shrimp to the pound), preferably unsalted

1/4 cup Practically Paleo Pesto or Pistou (Page 415)

Extra-virgin olive oil, ghee, **or** clarified butter to lightly brush or mist shrimp

1. Rinse shrimp thoroughly to remove excess salt and pat dry. Preheat broiler. If oven has several settings, set to "high broil."

2. **To remove shells:** Grasp the wide end of 1 shrimp with thumb and forefinger of one hand and grasp tail with other hand. Bend shell to break it above last phalange. Peel off all but end of tail; repeat with remaining shrimp.

3. **To devein:** One at a time, lay shrimp on side on meat-designated cutting board. With paring knife, make a thin slit down each back. Remove vein with point of paring knife or by running each shrimp under cold water. Place cut side down on a plate.

4. **To butterfly:** Some shrimp come butterflied. If yours do not, make a thin slit down the inside curl of each shrimp to loosen attached membrane.

5. Arrange shrimp on broiler tray belly (curved side) up. Dab about 1/2 teaspoon pesto or pistou down each slit. Lightly mist or brush top and sides with olive oil.

6. Broil 8 to 12 minutes, until shrimp turns white and tails curl. Serve warm or chilled. Cover and refrigerate leftovers. Use within 2 days.

Nutrition

1 serving:
287 calories
27 g protein
20 g fat
61 mg calcium
214 mg sodium

Scampi is an Italian sautéed shrimp dish, but today the term often refers to jumbo green shrimp sold in the shell, 8 or 10 to the pound. I figure 3 to 5 scampi per person for an entree, 1 or 2 for an hors d'ouevre.

Variations

* **Quick Boiled Shrimp or Scampi (with no added fat):** Peel and devein shrimp, or buy deveined shrimp in the shell, then remove shells. Immerse shrimp in boiling water; cook 2 to 3 minutes until flesh turns pink and tails curl. Drain, and serve immediately, or plunge in cold water, then drain. Omit pesto and pistou.

    Serve over a green salad with one of our lean & creamy dressings (Pages 417 to 419) or a tahini dressing (Pages 411 to 415) with a cooked root vegetable, tuber, squash, or fruit. Or, serve with assorted parboiled vegetables and Spicy Peanut Sauce (Page 416) and Fruit Kabobs (Page 434) for dessert.

FYI: The vein of a shrimp is its intestinal tract. If it's clear, it's empty and you don't need to remove it. If it's dark, it can impart a bitter flavor; remove it, or buy deveined, raw scampi. Save shells for making Shrimp Shell Stock (Page 253).

Note: You can make the pesto or pistou several days ahead.

Strawberry, Shrimp & Pineapple Kabobs
with Poppy Seed-Orange Drizzle

Prep: 30 to 60 minutes ~ **Cooking:** 3 minutes ~ **Yield:** 4 servings as an entrée, 6 to 12 as a starter

Ingredients & Directions

Shrimp:

1 pound uncooked (preferably wild and unsalted) shelled jumbo shrimp) **or** 1 1/2 pounds deveined, raw shrimp with tails attached (24-26), lowest sodium variety you can find

Broth:

1 1/2 quarts filtered water

1 bay leaf

6 peppercorns

1 stalk celery, halved

1/4 teaspoon unrefined sea salt, optional

Fruit, skewers and dressing:

1 pound fresh strawberries (about 24), washed, drained, hulls removed

1/2 of a 3-pound pineapple, peeled, cored, and cut into 1-inch cubes (about 2 heaping cups)

12 (10- to 12-inch) bamboo or wood skewers

1 1/2 to 2 cups Poppy Seed Orange or Pineapple Drizzle (Page 420) without salt

Nutrition
1 kabob:
119 calories
8 g protein
11 g carbohydrate
5 g fat
47 mg calcium
54 sodium
1 serving (3 kabobs):
335 calories
24 g protein
34 g carbohydrate (3 g fiber)
14 g fat
141 mg calcium
162 mg sodium

1. **Shrimp:** Rinse well and drain. Remove tails and peels, if present.

2. **Broth (for uncooked shrimp only):** Boil broth ingredients over medium heat. Add shrimp; reduce heat, and simmer for 2 to 3 minutes until shrimp turn orange and tails curl. Rinse or plunge in cold water for 2 minutes. Drain, pat dry, and set aside.

3. **Assembly:** Thread 1 strawberry, 1 shrimp, and 1 pineapple cube, then repeat on each skewer. Rest kabobs in oblong glass or Pyrex pan. Add enough of the drizzle to liberally coat. Serve immediately, or cover and chill for 4 to 6 hours, before serving. Do not reheat.

4. Use leftovers within 24 hours.

Variations

* **To grill or broil:** Soak bamboo skewers in water for 30 minutes so they won't catch fire. Thread peeled, deveined, uncooked shrimp and fruit on skewers. Brush shrimp and fruit with butter, olive or coconut oil. Grill or broil, 2 to 4 minutes per side, until tails curl and skin turns pink. Avoid overcooking.

Jeff McKahon of Rohr Fish & Seafood in Toledo, Ohio, showed me how to make these dazzling dessert-like kabobs—a surprising starter followed by Herbed Salmon Cakes with Citrus (Page 238) and a green salad or cooked leafy greens—or a delicious entrée served on a bed of baby greens with sliced fresh water chestnuts and avocado, and Creamy Carrot Soup (Page 370). Prepare drizzle at least 6 hours ahead to give it time to thicken.

To save time, buy deveined raw shrimp in the shell (removal is easy) or ready-to-eat shrimp with only the tails attached (pinch and pull to remove shells). Shrimp shells can be frozen for making Shrimp Shell Stock (Page 253) for Savory Shrimp & Coconut Bisque (Page 254).

Shrimp Shell Stock

Prep: 10 minutes ~ **Yield:** 4 cups

Ingredients & Directions

4 cups uncooked shrimp shells, rinsed well and drained (from 2 pounds of shrimp)

4 1/2 cups filtered water

Optional additions:

1/2 cup dry white wine such as Chardonnay, Fume Blanc, Sauvignon Blanc or Pinot Grigio

1 medium carrot

1 celery stalk

1 small onion

5 peppercorns

1 bay leaf

1 clove garlic, crushed or chopped

Nutrition breakdown not available

1. For quick cooking, finely chop vegetables. If you have more time and want more flavor, cut vegetables into chunks or wedges and cook longer.

2. Combine everything—adding as many optional ingredients as you like—in a 2-quart saucepan. Bring almost to boil. Partially cover and reduce heat so mixture bubbles but doesn't boil hard. Simmer 20 minutes with finely chopped vegetables, 45 to 60 minutes for larger vegetables pieces and more flavor.

2. Strain mixture over a large bowl, pressing on vegetables to extract as much juice as possible. Pour into clean wide-mouth jars, adding additional water as needed to yield 4 cups stock. Allow to cool and refrigerate until ready to use.

3. Use within 3 days, bring it to a full boil it if it's still around on day 4, or freeze.

Variations

* **Basic Fish Stock:** Substitute 1 pound of fish scraps from your local fish merchant (heads, tails, or some combination). Add 2 to 3 sprigs of fresh thyme **or** 1/2 teaspoon dried thyme. For a stronger flavor, use twice as much water and wine; double vegetables, herbs, and spices, and simmer 45 to 60 minutes.

* Use Shrimp Shell stock to make Cajun Ketchup (Page 401).

I prefer to buy raw shrimp in the shell, so I can stash the shells in the freezer. When I have at least 3 cups, I make this delicious stock. It makes a fantastic flavoring for Don's Savory Shrimp & Coconut Bisque (Page 254) or any seafood soup or stew that calls for stock or broth.

Double the recipe if you like; it freezes well. If you have mushrooms or parsley to use up, add 1 to 3 handfuls for extra flavor.

Savory Shrimp & Coconut Bisque

Prep: 30 minutes ~ **Cooking:** 15 minutes ~ **Yield:** 6 to 8 servings

Ingredients & Directions

3/4 to 1 pound raw (preferably unsalted) small shrimp, peeled, deveined, and patted dry. (Save shells for making stock.) Cut large shrimp in half to make bite-size pieces.

1 tablespoon unrefined coconut oil, **or** clarified butter or ghee

1 teaspoon unrefined sea salt (less if using salted shrimp)

1 cup finely chopped onion

2 to 3 small garlic cloves, minced

1 cup thinly sliced button, cremini, **or** shiitake mushroom, caps and most of the stems

1 cup carrots, cut into 1/4-inch cubes

1 (14-ounce) can (1 3/4 cups) unsweetened premium or lite coconut milk, well blended

3 cups Shrimp Shell Stock (Page 253), poultry Bone-Building Broth (Page 278), **or** preservative-free chicken broth

1 tablespoon paprika

1 tablespoon lemon juice **or** brown rice vinegar **or** 1 1/2 teaspoons raw apple cider vinegar

1/4 to 1/2 teaspoon ground chipotlé **or** 1 teaspoon hot sauce

1/4 teaspoon ground black pepper **or** 1/2 teaspoon lemon pepper

3 tablespoons arrowroot starch (4 tablespoons if using lite coconut milk), dissolved in 1/4 cup filtered water, stock or broth

1/4 cup minced scallions, chives **or** parsley for garnish

Nutrition

1 serving (premium):
296 calories
13 g protein
20 g carbohydrate
(1 g fiber)
18 g fat
42 mg calcium
416 mg sodium

1 serving (lite):
206 calories
13 g protein
14 g carbohydrate
(3 g fiber)
11 g fat
31 mg calcium
398 mg sodium

Instead of cream, I use coconut milk, which is nondairy and contains less than half the fat and calories. This delightful recipe is easy to make, only the ingredient list is long. If you set all the ingredients in small bowls, assembly will be almost effortless. As a starter, this pairs well with muffin-sized salmon cakes, a crisp green salad or steamed asparagus, baby bok choy, or broccoli, with a fruit salad or Mashed Sweet Potatoes with Lime (see Index for recipes).

1. Chop vegetables and set aside in individual bowls.

2. Heat oil in a 2-quart saucepan over medium heat. Add onion, garlic, mushrooms, salt, and carrot, stirring for 1 minute after each addition. Cover, reduce heat, and simmer 10 minutes.

3. Shake unopened can of coconut milk. Rinse top and remove lid. If contents have separated, whisk or purée in blender or food processor until smooth.

4. Add coconut milk, stock or broth, paprika, lemon juice or vinegar, chipotlé and black pepper. Bring to boil, add shrimp and dissolved arrowroot. Reduce heat, simmer, and stir until thick and shrimp turns pink, 5 to 7 minutes. Remove from heat. Ladle into bowls, garnish, and serve.

Variations

* For a briny taste of the sea without stock or to omit salt: After adding carrots, add 1 cup of raw dulse leaf, sorted to remove small shells and stones, and minced with shears.

* For a thicker texture, reserve and purée 1 cup of coconut milk or stock with 1 to 1 1/2 cups leftover cooked cauliflower. Add with arrowroot, simmer and stir to thicken.

Tuna Waldorf Salad

Prep: 20 minutes ~ **Yield:** 4 servings

Ingredients & Directions

2 (6-ounce) cans no-salt, water-packed tuna, drained or 12 ounces cooked fresh tuna, flaked with a fork

1 1/2 large **or** 2 small tart or tart-sweet apples (about 12 ounces), washed, cored, peeled, and diced:
    pink lady, braeburn, salmon, jonagold, or gala

1/2 cup finely minced sweet white onion (vidalia, Maui or Walla Walla sweet)

1/4 cup unsalted lightly toasted walnuts **or** pecans (Page 406), halved

2 celery stalks **or** 1/2 cup fennel bulb, finely minced

1/4 cup raisins, optional

1 teaspoon dried **or** 1 tablespoon fresh, minced dill, optional

1/2 cup Mustard-Tahini Dressing (Page 411) **or** 1/3 cup Homemade Mayonnaise (Page 424) or to taste

8 to 10 cups of tossed salad greens, comprised of 2 or more lettuces:
    red leaf, green leaf, Boston, bib, buttercrunch or oak leaf lettuce paired, with endive, escarole, or radicchio if desired

Nutrition

1 serving (with tahini dressing & nuts):
294 calories
27 g protein
22 g carbohydrate
    (5 g fiber)
12 g fat
33 mg calcium
206 mg sodium

Variation 1 serving:
347 calories
28 g protein
23 g carbohydrate
    (6 g fiber)
16 g fat
41 mg calcium
206 mg sodium

More than 20 years ago, after my mother lunched on a similar salad sandwiched between 2 slices of toasted, sprouted grain bread at a café in Albuquerque, New Mexico, she came home and made her own rendition. I've enjoyed this with and without the bread (the same kind my mother bought—Food for Life Ezekiel bread, sold in natural foods stores and the health food freezer section of major supermarkets).

1. In a 1-quart mixing bowl, combine all ingredients, except salad greens and toss to coat. Add more tahini dressing, mayonnaise, or lemon juice as needed.

2. Evenly divide greens between 4 large plates (or bowls with snap-on lids for pack lunches). Top with one-quarter of the tuna and serve. Or, serve green salad on the side and spoon tuna on toasted 100 percent sprouted whole grain bread.

3. Cover and refrigerate leftovers and use within 24 hours.

Variations

* Replace apples with 2 cups of halved seedless red grapes and omit raisins.

* For a richer taste increase nuts to 1/2 cup. (See box for nutrition information.)

* **Chicken or Turkey Waldorf Salad:** Replace tuna with diced or shredded leftover roasted or grilled chicken or turkey breast; use toasted almonds, walnuts **or** pecans.

16 Birds of a Feather

Best Bites

Roasted Smoky Turkey Breast

Prep: 20 minutes ~ **Cooking:** 1 1/2 to 2 hours ~ **Yield:** 12 or more servings

Ingredients & Directions

4- to 4 1/2-pound bone-in or boneless turkey breast

1 cup apple cider **or** apple juice, divided, slightly more if needed

2 tablespoons extra-virgin olive oil

1 tablespoon dry mustard

1 teaspoon ground chipotlé (smoked dried jalapeno pepper)

1 tablespoon Wright's Natural Liquid Hickory Smoke Seasoning

1 to 2 tablespoons tamari soy sauce
or 1/2 to 1 teaspoon finely ground, unrefined sea salt

1 tablespoon arrowroot starch, optional

Nutrition

4 ounces without skin:

209 calories
35 g protein
3 g carbohydrate
6 g fat
25 mg calcium
147 mg sodium

This smoky-tasting turkey is low in sodium and free of nitrates and nitrites. It's delicious warm or at room temperature, plain or with Better Barbecue Sauce or Cajun Ketchup, or over individual green salads with raw or roasted vegetables and guacamole, a creamy Tahini Dressing, or Lean & Creamy Dressing, or with eggs, cooked greens, and fruit for breakfast. (See Index for recipes.)

1. Rinse breast, pat dry. Place in Dutch oven or roasting pan that closely matches size of breast. Place rack in middle of oven and preheat to 450° F.

2. Whisk 1/2 cup apple juice with oil, mustard, chipotlé, liquid smoke, and sea salt or tamari. Pour over breast. Add 1/2 cup reserved juice to pan. Cover pan with lid or foil that does not touch breast.

3. Bake for 15 minutes, then reduce heat to 350° F and roast 30 minutes longer. Uncover and begin basting with pan juices every 15 minutes, until instant-read thermometer inserted into center of breast registers 160° F and interior is white or pale pink. Do not let probe touch bone. If juices begin to cook away, add 1/4 to 1/2 cup juice to pan.

4. Transfer turkey to meat-designated cutting board to rest for 15 minutes. Heat pan juices in roasting pan or transfer to saucepan on range top over medium heat. Stir to loosen stuck bits and reduce to 3/4 cup. For a thicker sauce, dissolve arrowroot in 1/4 cup cool apple juice, add to pan juices, simmer, and stir to thicken.

5. Thinly slice meat, or cut into 1-inch thick slices then cube. Freeze bones for making broth or stock. Toss meat with juices, turn to coat, and serve warm or cover and chill. Refrigerate leftovers. Use within 3 days or freeze.

Variations

* **Roasted Smoky Turkey Legs:** Replace breast with turkey thighs or legs. Omit oil. Allow 45 to 60 minutes for thighs or drumsticks, slightly longer for legs.

* **Slow Cooker:** Place turkey breast in 3 1/2- to 5-quart slow cooker. Use only 1/2 cup apple juice. Cover and cook on LOW for 6 to 8 hours or until tender and meat tests done (allow 4 to 6 hours for turkey thighs). Simmer pan juices in saucepan to reduce to 3/4 cup. Thicken with arrowroot if desired, pour over sliced or cubed meat, and turn to coat.

Note: In hot weather, I bake this in a large toaster oven or slow cooker. If baking multiple dishes in a full-size oven at 400° F, cover breast for 1 hour, then uncover and begin basting with pan juices.

Herbed-Orange Roasted Turkey Breast

Prep: 20 minutes ~ **Cooking:** 1 1/4 to 1 3/4 hours ~ **Yield:** 12 servings

Ingredients & Directions

4- to 4 1/2-pound bone-in or boneless turkey breast, skin removed

2 tablespoons extra-virgin olive oil

2 tablespoons dried, ground rosemary, thyme, rubbed sage, **or** combination

1/2 teaspoon coarsely white pepper **or** 1 teaspoon lemon pepper

1/2 teaspoon finely ground, unrefined sea salt

1 1/4 cups orange juice, divided, or slightly more as needed

1 1/2 tablespoons arrowroot dissolved in 1/4 cup cold orange juice

1 orange, cut into thin slices for garnish

Nutrition

4 ounces skinless breast:
215 calories
35 g protein
5 g carbohydrate
6 g fat
33 mg calcium
152 mg sodium

For a memorable meal, serve this turkey with Silver Dollar Sweet Potatoes or Roasted Carrots & Potatoes, with a crisp green salad, or sautéed kale, collards, or Brussels sprouts.

1. Rinse breast, pat dry with unbleached paper towel. Place in Dutch oven or roasting pan that closely matches size of breast. Place rack in middle of oven and preheat to 450° F.

2. Mix oil, herbs, pepper, and salt. Lift skin and spread mixture over breast; re-cover breast with skin. Add 1 cup juice to roasting pan. Cover pan with a lid or foil that does not touch the meat.

3. Bake for 15 minutes, then reduce heat to 350° F and roast 30 minutes longer. Uncover and begin basting with pan juices every 15 minutes, until instant-read thermometer inserted into center of breast registers 160° F and interior is white or pale pink. Do not let probe touch bone. If juices begin to cook away, add an additional 1/4 to 1/2 cup juice to pan.

4. Heat juices in roasting pan or transfer to saucepan on range top over medium heat. Stir to loosen stuck bits and reduce to 3/4 cup. Add dissolved arrowroot. Simmer and stir until thick.

5. Thinly slice meat, or cut into 1-inch thick slices, and cube if desired. Garnish with orange slices and serve with sauce. Freeze bones for making broth or stock. Use meat within 3 days or freeze.

Variations

* **Slow Cooker:** Arrange breast in 3 1/2- to 5-quart slow cooker. Reduce juice to 3/4 cup. Cover and cook on LOW for 6 to 8 hours until done; continue with steps 4 and 5.

* For additional gravy, combine 3/4 cup orange juice, 1/2 cup chicken stock, broth, **or** white wine, 1 teaspoon dried, crumbled herbs (see list above), 1/4 teaspoon pepper, and 1/2 teaspoon sea salt **or** 1 tablespoon tamari soy sauce. Simmer to dissolve salt; add 1 1/4 tablespoons arrowroot dissolved in 2 tablespoons cold water or stock, simmer, and stir until thick and clear.

Note: In hot weather, I bake this in a large toaster oven or slow cooker. If baking multiple dishes in a full-size oven at 400° F, cover breast for 1 hour, then uncover and begin basting with pan juices.

Slow-Cooked Apple & Mustard-Glazed Turkey Breast

Prep: 20 minutes ~ **Cooking:** 5 to 6 hours ~ **Yield:** 12 servings

Ingredients & Directions

2 tablespoons extra-virgin olive oil

2 bay leaves

4- to 4 1/2-pound bone-in turkey breast, completely thawed

1/2 teaspoon ground black pepper **or** lemon pepper, or to taste

1/2 cup apple cider **or** apple juice

2 teaspoons dried ground rosemary

2 teaspoons dried crumbled oregano

1 to 2 garlic cloves, minced

1 tablespoon dry mustard **or** 2 tablespoons Dijon or creamy white mustard

2 teaspoons Wright's Natural Liquid Hickory Smoke Seasoning

1/2 teaspoon unrefined sea salt **or** 1 tablespoon tamari soy sauce, optional

1/2 tablespoon arrowroot starch dissolved in 3 tablespoons cold water **or** apple juice

Nutrition

4 ounces skinless breast:

209 calories
35 g protein
4 g carbohydrate
6 g fat
30 mg calcium
76 mg sodium

Turkey breast is one of the leanest choices on the block. It has a higher ratio of meat to bone than chicken and usually costs less. A 4-pound breast will usually yield 2 quarts of cooked meat (about 3 pounds), allowing ample leftovers for the week, the freezer, or both.

1. Lightly oil 3 1/2- to 6-quart slow cooker. Add bay leaves. Rinse turkey breast under cold water; pat dry with unbleached paper towel. Place, breast side down in slow cooker.

2. Combine and stir remaining ingredients except arrowroot and water or apple juice. Pour over breast. Cover and cook on LOW (200° F) for 5 to 6 hours or until instant-read thermometer inserted into thickest part of breast away from bone registers 160 to 170° F or pop-up thermometer comes up.

3. Remove turkey from cooker. Allow to cool for 15 minutes. Discard bay leaves; simmer pan juices in saucepan, uncovered, about 15 to 20 minutes. Add dissolved arrowroot and stir until thick and clear, about 4 minutes. Remove breast halves from bone one at a time and slice diagonally. **To cube:** Cut crosswise in to 1-inch thick slices; cut each in to strips and then cubes.

4. Freeze bones for making broth or stock. Pour sauce over breast meat and serve, or transfer meat to several containers and refrigerate or freeze for later.

5. Use refrigerated portions within 3 days and use frozen portions within 4 months.

Variations

*   Replace turkey breast with turkey thighs or drumsticks. Reduce cooking time as needed.

Quick Smoky Turkey

Prep: 5 minutes ~ **Cooking:** 6 minutes ~ **Yield:** 3 servings

Ingredients & Directions

1 1/2 cups (about 12 ounces) cooked, skinless turkey, shredded or diced

1/3 cup poultry Bone-Building Broth (Page 278) **or** preservative-free chicken broth

1/2 teaspoon Wright's Natural Liquid Hickory Smoke Seasoning

1/4 to 1/3 teaspoon ground chipotlé **or** black pepper

1/2 teaspoon dry mustard powder

1/2 cup Better Barbecue Sauce (Page 401), optional

Dulse flakes **or** toasted, crumbled dulse (Page 397), optional

1. Combine broth or stock, liquid smoke, chipotlé, or black pepper, and mustard in 10-inch skillet. Stir to dissolve; add turkey. Cover and bring to low boil over medium-high heat; reduce heat and simmer 5 to 6 minutes, until warm and juicy.

2. Remove lid and cook away excess. Pass Better Barbecue Sauce at the table or sprinkle with toasted and crumbled dulse, if desired.

3. Refrigerate leftovers and use within 2 days.

Variations

* **Quick Smoky Chicken:** Replace turkey with leftover poached or roasted chicken.

Nutrition

4 ounces skinless breast:

198 calories
35 g protein
6 g fat
23 mg calcium
75 mg sodium

4 ounces skinless dark meat:

217 calories
34 g protein
9 g fat
38 mg calcium
94 mg sodium

Don devised this recipe more than 6 years ago to enhance Thanksgiving leftovers. It's delicious with sautéed greens, steamed broccoli, parboiled vegetables, or a tossed salad. For a substantial side dish, I serve Basic Baked Sweet Potatoes, Silver Dollar Sweet Potatoes, Mashed Sweet Potato with Lime, Simmered Squash, or Soothing Ginger, Squash & Apple Soup. If you want dessert, consider Cranberry-Apple Compote, Rosehip-Apple Compote, or My Favorite Macaroons (see Index for recipes).

Note: Double recipe if you want leftovers for main dish salads, scrambles, omelets, or a bacon alternative for breakfast.

Roasted Chicken with Lemon & Thyme

Prep: 15 minutes ~ **Cooking:** 1 1/2 hours ~ **Yield:** 6 servings

Ingredients & Directions

3 1/2- to 4-pound roasting chicken, thawed completely, rinsed, and patted dry

1 lemon rinsed and patted dry

Zest of 1 lemon (colored part only)

3 tablespoons chopped fresh herbs **or** 1 heaping tablespoon dried, crumbled thyme

1 teaspoon ground black pepper **or** white pepper

2 garlic cloves, crushed

1 teaspoon finely ground unrefined sea salt, optional

Sauce:

1/4 cup balsamic vinegar, apple cider/juice, **or** dry white wine

1/4 cup unsalted, unsweetened, canned, crushed, or puréed tomatoes, optional

Nutrition

4 ounces skinless breast without sauce:

190 calories
35 g protein
3 g carbohydrate
4 g fat
30 mg calcium
88 mg sodium

4 ounces skinless dark meat without sauce:

299 calories
31 g protein
3 g carbohydrate
13 g fat
6 mg calcium
103 mg sodium

I usually cook 1 (5- to 7-pound) chicken or 2 (3- to 4-pound) birds so I have enough meat for several meals, including some for the freezer. I find chicken cooked at a 325° F more moist. At this temperature, allow about 30 minutes of cooking time per pound.

1. Preheat oven to 325° F. Remove and reserve giblets. Remove excess skin. Grate lemon zest over a small bowl. With a skewer or toothpick, prick holes all over lemon.

2. Combine lemon zest, herbs and pepper, adding sea salt if desired. Use mixture to season cavity and skin of chicken. Stuff lemon, crushed garlic, and giblets into body cavity. Using 2 toothpicks or trussing needles, pin neck skin over the back to close cavity. Tie legs together with cotton twine or dental floss.

3. Place chicken breast side down on rack in shallow roasting pan. Allow space between 2 birds cooked in the same pan. Roast uncovered about 1 1/2 hours for small chicken, longer for large bird. If desired, turn breast side up after 60 minutes. Use oven mitts and paper towel to protect from burns.

4. Test small chicken after 1 1/2 hours by inserting a metal stem thermometer or sharp knife at least 2 inches into breast or inner thigh. Do not let probe touch bone. Chicken is done when juices run clear when pierced deeply with knife, or thigh registers 170 to 175° F and breast is 160 to 165° F. If not done, remove thermometer and return roast to oven. Wash thermometer in hot soapy water after each use.

5. When done, remove toothpicks or skewers, and cut twine. Insert 2 wooden spoons into cavity; lift and tilt so juices run into pan. Discard lemon. Reserve giblets to serve. Tent chicken with foil and let rest for 10 to 15 minutes to allow juices to settle.

Note: One 6-pound chicken takes twice as long as 2 (3-pound) birds. If you're pressed for time, you can crank the heat up to 400 or 425° F for the first 20 minutes, then reduce it to 350° F and figure about 20 minutes per pound from there on out. Compare the results.

FYI: On a hot day, I might roast a small to medium chicken in a large convection toaster oven. When it's done, I bake a pan of whole sweet potatoes and we have lunch or dinner for a few days.

~ Directions continued next page ~

Directions

6. Skim fat from roasting juices or pour juices into gravy pitcher, skim off fat, and return to pan. Add 1/4 cup balsamic vinegar, juice, or wine to juices in pan. Simmer and stir over moderate heat, scraping browned bits from bottom of pan. Cook until reduced to about 3/4 cup.

7. Remove skin if desired. Carve meat on meat-designated board or platter with sides to catch drips. Pour juices from board or platter into sauce. Spoon sauce over sliced meat and serve. Freeze neck and bones for making stock or broth. Refrigerate leftovers and use within 3 days or freeze.

Variations

* Replace half of thyme with fresh or dried, rubbed sage or marjoram; combination of dried, rubbed sage, thyme and marjoram; or dried cumin, oregano, and thyme.

* **Roasted Chicken with Oregano or Basil:** Replace thyme with fresh or dried oregano or basil.

* **Roasted Chicken with Herbes de Provence:** Use lemon and replace thyme with 1 tablespoon dried, powdered, Herbes de Provence (blend of thyme, rosemary, winter savory, tarragon, and basil; lavender may be included).

* **Roasted Chicken with Moroccan Spice Mix:** Omit lemon. Replace herbs with 2 tablespoons Moroccan Spice Mix (Page 399), and season chicken with 1 teaspoon ground black pepper. For sauce, replace vinegar, cider, **or** wine with tomato purée, **or** combination of vinegar, cider, **or** wine with tomato purée.

* **Roasted Chicken with Orange & 5-Spice Blend:** Replace lemon and lemon zest with orange and orange zest; replace thyme, pepper, and garlic with 1 tablespoon Chinese 5-Spice Blend. If desired replace salt with 2 tablespoons tamari soy sauce. For sauce, use 1/2 cup orange or pineapple juice. For a sweeter taste, use orange or pineapple juice concentrate.

* **Roasted Chicken with Curry:** Omit lemon. Replace thyme, garlic, and pepper with 2 tablespoons curry powder. Stuff 1 cup fresh or frozen cubed pineapple or mango into cavity of chicken; discard fruit after cooking. For sauce, use apple, pineapple, or mango juice.

* **Slow Cooker:** Transfer seasoned chicken to 3 1/2- to 5-quart slow cooker. Cover and cook on LOW for 5 to 6 hours (longer for larger chicken), or until meat tests done. Transfer chicken to bowl with paper towels, oven mitts, and large utensils. Simmer juices in large saucepan over medium heat until reduced by at least one-half. Skim off fat with gravy pitcher or refrigerate in wide-mouth jars and skim off fat after it congeals; make gravy if desired.

* Use defatted chicken juices to replace stock or broth when sautéing kale, collards, **or** Brussels sprouts.

Roasted Chicken with Lemon & Thyme ~ continued

Poached Chicken Parts in White Wine with Herbs

Prep: 10 minutes ~ **Cooking:** 30 to 40 minutes ~ **Yield:** 6 to 8 servings

Ingredients & Directions

Pan Sauce:

1 to 1 1/2 cups dry white wine, such as Chardonnay, Fume Blanc, Sauvignon Blanc, or Pinot Grigio

1 bay leaf

1 tablespoon dried herbs or herb-spice blend, crumbled:
Italian blend, Herbes de Provençe, Fine Herbs,
or Quatre Epice

1/4 teaspoon ground chipotlé **or** black pepper
or 1/2 teaspoon lemon pepper

1 to 2 garlic cloves, quartered or coarsely chopped

1 tablespoon extra-virgin olive oil (if using only breast meat)

1/2 teaspoon finely ground, unrefined sea salt
or 1 tablespoon tamari soy sauce, optional

Chicken:

4 pounds bone-in, chicken breasts, thighs, or mixed parts, skin removed **or** 2 to 2 1/2 pounds boneless, skinless breast halves or thighs

This is an effortless way to cook chicken without turning on the oven. White wine moistens the meat and produces a delicious reduction sauce. I vary the herbs and spices every time or two.

Nutrition

4 ounces skinless breast meat:

222 calories
34 g protein
6 g fat
30 mg calcium
72 mg sodium

4 ounces skinless dark meat:

270 calories
31 g protein
13 g fat
29 mg calcium
101 mg sodium

1. Combine pan sauce ingredients in a 13-inch chef pan, 4-quart Dutch oven, or divide between two 10-inch skillets. Rinse chicken and pat dry. For best texture, pound boneless breast halves to 1/2-inch thick with a meat tenderizer. Add chicken to pan(s) with little or no overlapping.

2. Cover and bring to boil over medium-high heat. Reduce heat to medium-low and simmer until tender, 25 to 40 minutes, depending on size, turning pieces after 10 minutes. Cut into thickest part of thigh or breast. Chicken is done when meat is firm to the touch, juices run clear when pierced deeply near bone, and breasts are beige throughout.

3. Transfer chicken to a platter. Raise heat and simmer to reduce pan juices to 1/3 cup, 10 to 15 minutes, then spoon over meat, and serve. Or, refrigerate liquid and use to sauté greens. Freeze bones for broth or stock.

4. Use leftover meat within 3 days or freeze.

Variations

* **Poached Chicken Parts with Tarragon and Wine:** Replace herbs and pepper with 3 tablespoons minced fresh **or** 3 teaspoons dried tarragon, 1 teaspoon dry mustard, and 1/4 teaspoon ground white pepper.

* **Poached Chicken Parts in White Wine with Basil, Garlic & Sun-Dried Tomatoes:** Add 12 sliced sun-dried tomato halves and 6 whole cloves of garlic to saucepan. Replace herbs with 1 1/2 tablespoons dried basil, **or** add 1/4 cup chopped fresh basil during last 5 minutes of cooking.

* **For a delicious reduction sauce**, in step 3, after transferring chicken to a platter, thinly slice and add 1 medium onion and 4 shallots to pan juices; stir, simmer, and sauté over medium-high heat until tender and juices are absorbed, then spoon over chicken.

Note: For wine, substitute water, chicken broth, or white grape juice, if you prefer. If you double the recipe, do not double liquid—use only enough to cover bottom of pan by 1/4 inch. Use 2 skillets if necessary.

Baked Chicken Thighs with Cumin & Lime

Prep: 15 minutes ~ **Cooking:** 35 to 45 minutes ~ **Yield:** 6 servings

Ingredients & Directions

Chicken:

2 pounds boneless, skinless chicken thighs (about 12 thighs) **or** 4 pounds bone-in, thighs **or** hindquarters (about 6), with or without skin

Cumin-Lime Seasoning:

1 1/2 teaspoons ground cumin

1 1/2 teaspoons dried, crumbled oregano

1/2 to 1 tablespoon coarsely chopped garlic (about 3 large cloves)

1/3 to 1/2 cup lime juice (from about 3 medium limes)

1 tablespoon tamari soy sauce **or** 1/2 teaspoon finely ground, unrefined sea salt, optional

1/4 cup finely minced parsley **or** cilantro, optional

Nutrition

4 ounces skinless dark meat:

249 calories
31 g protein
2 g carbohydrate
13 g fat
28 mg calcium
101 mg sodium

1. Rinse chicken, pat dry with unbleached paper towel, and arrange in one 9x13-inch pan or two 10-inch Pyrex pie plates or non-metallic cake pans. Remove skin if desired.

2. Combine everything but parsley and cilantro in a small bowl. Stir and spoon over chicken. Let rest at room temperature for 30 minutes or in refrigerator for up to 12 hours.

3. Position rack in center of oven. Preheat to 375 to 400° F. Cover pan for skinless chicken. Bake 35 to 45 minutes, or until juices run clear when meat is pierced near the bone with a sharp knife. Dark meat will still be slightly pink inside and a thermometer will register 170° F.

4. Simmer juices in skillet to reduce to about 1/4 cup and spoon over chicken, or reserve for sautéing cabbage, kale, collards, or Brussels sprouts.

5. Garnish chicken with parsley or cilantro and serve or chill. Freeze bones for making broth or stock. Use chicken within 3 days or freeze.

This mouth-watering dish has pleased picky children...and finicky adults. Make a double batch if you're serving more than 3 people. Leftovers are perfect for pack lunches or quick meals at home, cold or warmed in a toaster oven. They also freeze well.

While the chicken cooks, I roast enough sweet potatoes, winter squash, onions, or assorted root vegetables for 2 or 3 days. I round out the meal with a parboiled salad, sautéed greens, or a tossed green salad.

Variations

* **Baked Chicken Breasts in Lime:** Replace thighs with 6 (5-ounce) breast halves or 6 (6-ounce) bone-in breast halves. If you remove the skin (you don't have to) add 1 1/2 tablespoons olive oil to seasoning mix. Marinate 4 to 6 hours, cover, and bake 30 to 35 minutes, or until beige throughout and juices run clear when pierced deeply. (Reduce cooking time for pounded breast filets.) Simmer to reduce juices, or save for cooking greens.

Baked Chicken Parts with Rosemary

Prep: 15 minutes ~ **Cooking:** 35 to 45 minutes ~ **Yield:** 6 to 8 servings

Ingredients & Directions

3 1/2- to 4 1/2-pound chicken, cut into fryer parts (weight includes bones):
    breast halves, thighs, drumsticks, or combination

1 1/2 tablespoons dried rosemary, ground to a powder

1/2 teaspoon ground lemon pepper **or** black pepper

1 to 2 garlic cloves, minced (about 1/2 to 1 teaspoons)

1/2 teaspoon finely ground, unrefined sea salt
or 1 tablespoon tamari soy sauce, optional

3 tablespoons balsamic vinegar, optional

1. Preheat oven to 375 to 400° F. Rinse chicken and pat dry. For best texture, use meat mallet and pound boneless breast halves to 1/2-inch thick. Arrange chicken in 9x13x2-inch pan or two 10-inch Pyrex pie plates.

2. If you plan to remove skin before serving, pull skin back to reveal meat, leaving it attached. Sprinkle meat with rosemary, pepper, and garlic, then sea salt or tamari if desired. Drizzle with vinegar if desired. Re-cover chicken with skin. If leaving skin on, rub seasonings over skin and drizzle with vinegar if desired.

3. Bake uncovered for 35 to 45 minutes or until firm to the touch and juices run clear when pierced deeply with a knife near bone. Breasts will be beige throughout; dark meat may contain traces of pink. Remove skin before serving if desired. (Allow less time for pounded chicken breasts.)

4. Defat juices if desired. Pour into saucepan, simmer to reduce to 1/4 cup, and spoon over chicken, or refrigerate juices for sautéing kale, collards, or Brussels sprouts.

5. Deposit bones in a bag in freezer for making broth or stock. Use chicken within 3 days or freeze. Use chicken juices within 5 days or freeze.

~ Variations on next page ~

Nutrition

4 ounces skinless breast meat:
179 calories
35 g protein
4 g fat
26 mg calcium
84 mg sodium

4 ounces skinless dark meat:
288 calories
31 g protein
13 g fat
2 mg calcium
99 mg sodium

I love the simplicity of this recipe. Sometimes I use a cut-up fryer, sometimes thighs, other times only breast halves. If I'm using a full-size oven rather than a toaster oven, I usually start 2 pans cooking first thing in the morning or before lunch—each with different seasonings— so we have convenience food for the next few days and the freezer.

Note: If the chicken comes with giblets, place in a small oiled baking dish, dust with herbs and spices; bake until juices run clear, about 20 minutes.

Variations

* If using boneless skinless parts, use only 2 pounds of meat and cook covered.

* **Baked Chicken Thighs with Rosemary:** Use 2 pounds of boneless skinless thighs **or** 4 pounds of bone-in thighs or hindquarters, with or without skin.

* **Baked Chicken Breast Halves with Rosemary:** Substitute 6 large skinless, boneless breast fillets with rib meat (2 to 2 1/2 pounds) **or** 6 bone-in halves (3 pounds). If you remove skin, place breast halves in large bowl, sprinkle with 1 1/2 to 2 tablespoons olive oil and seasonings, and toss to coat.

* **Baked Chicken Parts with Tarragon and Lime:** Prepare as for mixed fryer parts, thighs, or breast halves, but omit rosemary, lemon pepper, garlic, and vinegar. Substitute 1 1/2 to 2 tablespoons dried, crumbled tarragon, 1 teaspoon dry mustard, and 1/2 teaspoon ground black pepper. Drizzle chicken with juice of 1/2 lime.

* **Baked Chicken Parts with Herbs de Provence:** Replace rosemary with powdered Herbes de Provençe in original recipe or any of the variations. Prepare with or without garlic and pepper. Add balsamic vinegar if desired.

* **Baked Chicken Parts with Thyme:** Prepare as for mixed fryer parts, thighs, or breast halves, but replace rosemary with dried thyme. Omit vinegar. Add garlic and pepper, if desired.

* **Baked Chicken Parts with Paprika & Pepper:** Prepare as for mixed fryer parts, thighs, or breast halves. Substitute 1 heaping tablespoon (sweet or hot) Hungarian paprika mixed with 1 teaspoon dry mustard, and 1/4 teaspoon black pepper **or** 1/2 teaspoon lemon pepper for the rosemary, lemon pepper, garlic, and balsamic vinegar.

* **Baked Chicken Parts with Chili Powder:** Prepare as for mixed fryer parts, thighs, or breast halves, but omit rosemary, lemon pepper, garlic, and balsamic vinegar. Substitute 1 tablespoon salt-free chili powder (a blend, *not* straight chili pepper), 1 or 2 teaspoons minced garlic, and 1 teaspoon ground cumin. Add 1/4 teaspoon cayenne **or** ground chipotlé if you like it hot. Drizzle juice of 1 lime over chicken.

Moroccan-Spiced Chicken Thighs

Prep: 15 minutes ~ **Cooking:** 25 to 45 minutes ~ **Yield:** 6 to 8 servings

Ingredients & Directions

4 1/2 pounds bone-in chicken thighs **or** 2 1/2 pounds boneless, skinless thighs

1/2 teaspoon finely ground, unrefined sea salt

1/2 teaspoon ground black pepper

2/3 cup or slightly less Moroccan Barbecue Spice Mix (Page 399)

1 to 1 1/2 cups Moroccan Barbecue Sauce (Page 400), optional

1. Preheat oven to 400° F. Line one 9x13x2-inch pan or two 10-inch Pyrex pie plates or cake pans with parchment paper for easy cleanup. If using both light and dark meat, use 2 pans.

2. Remove skin. Rinse chicken, pat dry, and arrange on large platter. Sprinkle chicken with sea salt and pepper. Pour spice mix onto center of plate. One at a time, dredge chicken pieces in spice mix to coat thoroughly. Arrange on dry baking sheets.

3. Bake uncovered, 20 to 30 minutes for boneless pieces, 35 to 45 minutes for bone-in pieces, or until firm to the touch and juices run clear when pierced deeply with a knife near bone. Dark meat will still be slightly pink inside. Serve with or without Moroccan Barbecue Sauce.

4. Freeze bones for making broth or stock. Use chicken within 3 days or freeze.

Variations

* **Moroccan-Spiced Chicken Breasts:** Replace thighs with 2 to 2 1/2 pounds boneless, skinless breast halves. Place breast halves between 2 layers of parchment or wax paper and pound to 1/2-inch thick with meat mallet or heavy skillet. Repeat with remaining pieces. In medium bowl, toss chicken with 2 tablespoons olive oil. Dredge in spice mix to coat, and bake.

Nutrition

4 ounces skinless dark meat without sauce:

289 calories
30 g protein
6 g carbohydrate
16 g fat
114 mg calcium
264 mg sodium

**Variation
4 ounces skinless breast meat:**

246 calories
35 g protein
6 g carbohydrate
9 g fat
118 mg calcium
253 mg sodium

Toasted and ground coriander, fennel, cumin, cardamom seeds, and cloves create a delightfully crispy crust for chicken thighs without frying or sautéing.

To complete the meal, serve coleslaw, sautéed greens, or a steamed or parboiled vegetable medley with a creamy tahini dressing, and a potato, squash, sweet potato, or carrot side dish. Barbecue Sauce is optional.

FYI: You can make the spice mix several hours or days ahead, but the fresher it is the more fragrant and flavorful it will be. See Index for additional recipes using this spice mix.

Broiled or Grilled Chicken with Herbs

Prep: 15 minutes ~ **Cooking:** 18 to 25 minutes ~ **Yield:** 6 servings

Ingredients & Directions

Chicken:
3 to 4 pounds bone-in, skin-on chicken breast halves, thighs, or combination

Seasonings:
2 tablespoons lemon juice, orange juice, **or** balsamic vinegar

1 tablespoon dried rosemary, tarragon, Fine Herbs, Herbes de Provençe **or** Italian blend **or** 3 tablespoons minced fresh herbs (one or a combination of several)

1/3 teaspoon ground black pepper **or** 2/3 teaspoon lemon pepper blend

1 or 2 garlic cloves, minced, optional

1/2 teaspoon finely ground, unrefined sea salt **or** 1 tablespoon tamari soy sauce, optional

Extra-virgin olive oil to grease pan or grill grates

Nutrition

4 ounces skinless breast:

204 calories
36 g protein
6 g fat
31 mg calcium
78 mg sodium

4 ounces skinless dark meat:

240 calories
30 g protein
13 g fat
28 mg calcium
100 mg sodium

To keep herbs and spices from burning, slip them under the skin before broiling or grilling, then remove skin at the table if you wish. Chicken breast is so lean, you might want to eat the skin.

I recommend always cooking enough chicken for the next day's lunch or dinner. Leftovers are great served warm or close to room temperature in a pack lunch or for dinner with sautéed greens, a parboiled vegetable medley, or green salad, and a root vegetable, tuber, squash, or fruit.

1. Lightly grease broiler pan or grill grates. If using oven, move broiler rack 6 to 8 inches below heating element. Preheat oven on broil or fire up grill.

2. While grill or oven is heating, rinse chicken, pat dry, and place on platter. Loosen and slit skin around edges on 1 side of each piece of chicken using a sharp paring knife.

3. Mix liquid and seasonings to make a paste. Evenly distribute, slipping about 1 teaspoon or slightly more under the skin of each piece.

4. Place chicken skin side down. (If broiling, close oven door for gas range; leave door of electric stove ajar.) Broil or grill for 10 to 12 minutes on skin side. Turn pieces and cook 8 to 12 more minutes depending on size and thickness, until juices run clear when pierced deeply with a knife, meat is firm, breast meat is beige throughout, and dark meat is still slightly pink inside.

5. Remove skin leaving herbs on meat. Or leave skin on and prepare side dishes with less fat or oil. Freeze bones for making stock or broth. Use meat within 3 days or freeze.

Note: If desired, allow chicken to stand at room temperature for 30 to 60 minutes before cooking, or cover and refrigerate for several hours or overnight. Preheat oven when ready to cook.

Grilled or Broiled Chicken Breasts w/ Mango-Ginger Chutney

Prep: 30 minutes (includes chutney) ~ **Cooking:** 25 minutes ~ **Yield:** 6 servings
---

Ingredients & Directions

1 recipe Mango-Ginger Chutney (Page 404)

6 small to medium boneless, skinless chicken breast halves or cutlets (1 1/2 to 2 pounds)

Finely ground unrefined sea salt, optional

Finely ground black pepper, optional

Extra-virgin olive, coconut oil, clarified butter **or** ghee to brush chicken breasts

1. Assemble chutney (or prepare up to 24 hours ahead, and refrigerate until 30 minutes before serving). While chutney cooks or comes to room temperature, proceed with chicken.

2. Lightly grease broiler pan or grill grates. Position broiler or grill rack 2 to 4 inches from heat source. Preheat oven on broil or fire up grill or oil and preheat grill pan 4 minutes.

3. Meanwhile, remove tenderloin from each breast half and pound with a meat mallet or heavy skillet until even textured and flat. Slip each breast half between 2 sheets of parchment or wax paper and pound to 1/2-inch thick. Turn and pound reverse side until 1/3-inch thick.

4. Sprinkle and rub fillets with sea salt and pepper and brush or rub with oil. Grill or broil quickly, about 3 to 4 minutes per side, until firm, juices run clear when pierced with a fork, or beige throughout. Avoid overcooking.

5. Transfer chicken to plates, top with chutney, and serve.

Nutrition

3 1/2 ounces breast meat plus 1/3 cup sauce:

265 calories
32 g protein
23 g carbohydrate
(3 g fiber)
5 g fat
30 mg calcium
78 mg sodium

This recipe is incredibly easy. A crisp green salad or sautéed or stir-fried leafy greens complete the meal. Grilled or roasted onions, mushrooms, or carrots make great accompaniments. I make enough of everything for the next day's lunch or dinner and sometimes enough for the day after that.

Variations

* **Broiled (or Grilled) Pork Chops with Mango-Ginger Chutney:** Substitute 6 boneless pork loin chops (1- to 1 1/4-inches thick) for chicken. Grill 5 to 6 inches from heat source, 5 to 7 minutes per side, or until firm, juices run clear, and, interior is still slightly rosy when sliced. Or cook in grill pan on range top, about 5 minutes per side.

* **Grilled Salmon with Mango-Ginger Chutney:** Substitute salmon for chicken. Rub 1 1/2 to 2 pounds of salmon fillets with oil, sea salt, and pepper. Grill until salmon tests done, about 10 minutes per inch of thickness. Serve with chutney.

Note: If you want more chutney per person, divide sauce among 4 chicken cutlets and reserve extra cutlets for salads or the freezer.

Grilled or Broiled Chicken Breasts in Spicy Peanut Sauce

Prep: 30 minutes (includes peanut sauce) ~ **Cooking:** 10 minutes ~ **Yield:** 6 servings

---

Ingredients & Directions

1/2 recipe Spicy Peanut Sauce (Page 416) made with lime or orange juice, additional 3/4 cup as needed at the table

1 tablespoon Dijon, creamy white, or yellow mustard, optional

6 small to medium boneless, skinless chicken breast halves or cutlets (about 2 pounds)

Extra-virgin olive **or** coconut oil to grease grill grates or broiler pan

2 tablespoons water **or** orange juice as needed for sauce

Nutrition

3 1/2 ounces breast meat plus 2 tablespoons sauce:

244 calories
35 g protein
3 g carbohydrate
(1 g fiber)
10 g fat
26 mg calcium
221 mg sodium

Peanut Sauce keeps otherwise lean chicken breasts from drying out on the grill or under the broiler.

You can assemble this first thing in the morning, or the night before serving.

I like to serve it with baked or roasted sweet potatoes and steamed or parboiled leafy green or mixed vegetables.

1. Prepare Spicy Peanut Sauce at least 4 hours before serving to allow it to thicken. Add mustard if you like. Prep up to 48 hours ahead if desired.

2. Rinse chicken, pat dry with unbleached paper towel. If thick, pound to 1/2-inch thick with meat mallet or heavy skillet.

3. Arrange fillets in 3-quart glass bowl or oblong Pyrex container. Add peanut sauce and turn to coat. Cover with plate or lid; refrigerate 3 to 6 hours or overnight. Turn pieces once.

4. Preheat gas grill or broiler, or prepare medium-hot charcoal or wood fire. Position rack 2 to 4 inches from heat source. Remove chicken from sauce and reserve marinade.

5. Place chicken on grill rack or broiler pan coated with olive or coconut oil. Cook for about 3 to 4 minutes per side, until firm to the touch, juices run clear when pricked deeply with a fork, or same color throughout. Avoid overcooking. Transfer chicken to plates.

6. While chicken cooks, boil leftover marinade in a small saucepan for 2 minutes, simmer, and stir until thick, adding 2 tablespoons water or orange juice as needed. Serve chicken with sauce. (Sliced leftovers are great cold over green salad, with tomatoes, celery, cucumber, and scallions.)

Variations

* **Broiled (or Grilled) Pork Chops in Spicy Peanut Sauce:** Replace chicken with 2 pounds boneless pork loin chops 1- to 1 1/4-inches thick or 2 (1-pound) pork tenderloins. Grill or broil pork 5 to 6 inches from heat source, 5 to 7 minutes per side for chops, 8 to 10 minutes per side for tenderloins, or until firm, juices run clear, and, meat is still slightly rosy inside. Slice and serve with cooked peanut sauce.

Honey-Mustard Chicken with Ginger

Prep: 20 minutes ~ **Cooking:** 8 to 10 minutes ~ **Yield:** 6 servings

Ingredients & Directions

Chicken:
1 1/2 to 2 pounds skinless boneless chicken breast fillets, cut into 2-inch wedges

Honey-Mustard Marinade:
2 to 3 tablespoons extra-virgin olive oil

1/3 to 1/2 cup creamy white, yellow, or Dijon mustard (white mustard is my favorite)

2 tablespoons honey

1 tablespoon finely grated and minced fresh gingerroot **or** 1 teaspoon ground ginger

1/4 teaspoon ground red **or** black pepper

1 1/2 teaspoons unrefined coconut oil **or** olive oil to grease skillet or grill pan, optional

Nutrition

1 serving:
230 calories
30 g protein
7 g carbohydrate
9 g fat
15 mg calcium
128 mg sodium

Honey and mustard do wonders to moisten chicken breasts. Ginger adds a zingy taste.

This makes a delicious topping for mesclun greens or a main-course salad made with an assortment of raw, roasted, or grilled vegetables. A creamy carrot, squash, or tomato soup makes a great starter. For dessert, try Rosehip-Apple Compote, Apple-Apricot Compote, Chilled Cherry Gel, or Fruit Kabobs sprinkled with shredded, unsweetened coconut. (See Index for recipes.)

1. Add chicken to a glass or Pyrex pie plate or bowl. Mix marinade, pour over chicken, and stir to coat. Cover and refrigerate 6 to 8 hours, all day, or overnight.

2. Cook chicken pieces on grill, under broiler, or in lightly oiled, heavy-bottomed skillet, griddle, or grill pan over medium heat, about 3 minutes per side, or until firm, meat is beige throughout, and juices run clear when a test piece is cut in half.

3. Add a dash of water to any leftover marinade, bring to boil, and simmer 4 minutes. Baste chicken with mixture as it cooks.

4. Serve warm. Refrigerate leftovers and use within 3 days. (They're delicious cold.)

Variations

* In step 1, add 1 tablespoon minced fresh **or** 1 teaspoon dried rosemary, tarragon, dill, or basil.

* **Honey-Mustard Chicken with Chipotlé:** Replace ginger with 1/2 teaspoon ground chipotlé. Omit black pepper and garnish final dish with minced cilantro before serving.

* **Honey-Mustard Chicken Salad:** Serve chicken over heaping individual plates of raw spinach, arugula, or spring greens, minced scallions, parsley, red radishes, celery, fresh or sun-dried tomato slices, avocado, and a squeeze of lemon or lime juice. Add roasted onions, bell peppers, and/or carrots, if desired.

Sautéed Chicken Breast Fillets

Prep: 15 minutes ~ **Cooking:** 10 to 15 minutes ~ **Yield:** 4 servings

Ingredients & Directions

4 medium skinless, boneless chicken breast halves (about 1 1/4 pounds)

1/4 teaspoon finely ground unrefined, mineral-rich sea salt

1/4 to 1/2 teaspoon ground black pepper **or** 1 teaspoon lemon pepper

1/4 to 1/2 cup arrowroot starch

2 to 3 tablespoons unrefined coconut oil, clarified butter, ghee, **or** combination of oil and ghee

4 lemon wedges for garnish

Pan Sauce, optional:

1/4 cup homemade chicken stock, Bone-Building Broth (Page 278), **or** preservative-free chicken broth

1/4 cup white wine **or** balsamic vinegar

1/2 cup minced onion or shallots

1 clove garlic, minced, optional

1 teaspoon dried, crumbled tarragon, basil, oregano, **or** powdered Herbes de Provençe

Nutrition

4 ounces without sauce:

275 calories
35 g protein
9 g carbohydrate
11 g fat
18 mg calcium
100 mg sodium

A light flouring and brief sautéing seal in moisture and flavor. I use arrowroot in place of wheat or white flour. It's less allergenic and contains more calcium.

If you're serving this as a hot dish, you can make a quick pan sauce using the delicious browned bits in the bottom of the skillet. You can measure out all the ingredients for the sauce while the chicken cooks. For a cold dish, slice and fan leftovers over individual green salads.

1. Remove tenderloin from each breast half; pound with mallet or back of heavy skillet until even textured and flat. Sprinkle both sides of fillets and tenderloins with sea salt and pepper, and dredge one at a time in arrowroot. Shake gently over a plate to remove excess.

2. Turn on exhaust fan. Heat oil in heavy-bottomed, 12-inch skillet over medium-high heat. Tilt pan to spread oil. When sizzling, but not smoking, arrange fillets and tenderloins in skillet. Do not crowd pieces or heat will drop and chicken will not brown evenly or cook quickly. (If using a 10-inch skillet, add 1 1/2 tablespoons oil and cook in 2 batches.) Turn pieces only once, until golden brown, firm to touch, and clotted juices appear around tenderloin, 3 to 4 minutes per side for fillets, 2 to 3 minutes for tenderloins.

3. Transfer cooked chicken to plates. For sauce, reduce heat to medium, add onions or shallots, garlic if desired, and stir for 30 seconds. Immediately add broth or stock, wine or vinegar, and herbs. Reduce to about 1/4 cup (you can eyeball it), spoon over cutlets and serve.

4. Refrigerate leftovers and use within 3 days or freeze.

Variations

* **Omit pan sauce:** Served sautéed chicken cutlets with Cajun Ketchup, Better Barbecue Sauce, **or** Mango-Ginger Chutney (see Index for recipes), about 1/4 cup per person.

Tuscan Chicken or Turkey Casserole

Prep: 20 minutes ~ **Cooking:** 20 to 30 minutes ~ **Yield:** 4 to 6 servings

Ingredients & Directions

1 1/2 pounds skinless boneless chicken or turkey breast, cut into 2-inch chunks or wedges

1 packed cup fresh button, cremini, or shiitake mushrooms, quartered **or** 1/2 cup dried shiitake mushrooms soaked in warm water to cover, then quartered

1 1/2 tablespoons extra-virgin olive oil, clarified butter **or** ghee

1 medium onion, cut into thin crescents

1/2 teaspoon finely ground, unrefined sea salt **or** 1 tablespoon tamari soy sauce, optional

3 to 4 garlic cloves, minced

12 sun-dried tomato halves (about 1/3 cup), quartered

1 fresh red or gold bell pepper, halved, seeded, and cubed **or** 1/4 cup freeze-dried bell pepper bits (red, green, or combination; not hot pepper flakes!)

2 teaspoons dried oregano **or** basil, crumbled

1/2 to 3/4 cup Bone-Building Broth (Page 278), preservative-free chicken broth, homemade stock, white wine or filtered water

2 teaspoons arrowroot, dissolved in 1/4 cup cold or room temperature stock, broth, white wine, or filtered water

1/4 cup fresh, minced Italian, Chinese, or curly leaf parsley

1/4 teaspoon black pepper **or** 1/3 teaspoon lemon pepper, to taste

Nutrition

1 serving:
277 calories
37 g protein
12 g carbohydrate
(2 g fiber)
9 g fat
47 mg calcium
19 mg sodium

Unlike most western-style casseroles, this one doesn't require baking; it cooks quickly on top of the range, making it perfect for hot summer days and nights. For a stunning presentation, serve with a mesclun green salad or parboiled vegetable medley and a fresh fruit salad or cooked fruit dessert. If you don't like green peppers, substitute 2 large carrots.

1. Rinse poultry and pat dry with unbleached paper towel. Soak dried mushrooms in enough hot water to cover for 1 hour, or place in jar with cool water and refrigerate all day or overnight. Chop remaining vegetables and arrange in separate bowls. Cover and refrigerate if prepped ahead.

2. Heat oil in 10- to 12-inch wok, saucepan, or Dutch oven over medium heat. Add onions, stir and cook 3 to 4 minutes, until translucent around edges. Add sea salt or tamari if desired, then mushrooms, garlic, sun-dried tomatoes, bell peppers, and dried herbs, stirring for 1 minute after each addition. Scoot vegetables to sides of pan. Add chicken or turkey pieces to skillet. Stir and turn to brown on all sides. Add liquid, cover, reduce heat, and simmer 8 to 10 minutes, until poultry is tender, stirring periodically

3. Add dissolved arrowroot; simmer, and stir until thick. Remove from heat; stir in parsley and pepper, and serve. Refrigerate leftovers and use within 3 days.

Stewed Chicken with Carrots, Parsnips & Ginger

Prep: 20 to 30 minutes ~ **Cooking:** 40 to 60 minutes ~ **Yield:** 6 servings

Ingredients & Directions

1 medium onion, cut into thick crescents or 1-inch cubes

3 cups carrots, cut into diagonal wedges

3 cups small parsnips, peeled and cut into diagonal wedges

1 tablespoon peeled, minced fresh gingerroot

1 teaspoon minced garlic

3 (5-inch) strips kelp **or** kombu sea vegetable, cut into 1-inch pieces using shears

1/2 to 1 teaspoon unrefined sea salt **or** 1 to 2 tablespoons tamari soy sauce, optional

2 tablespoons extra-virgin olive oil, clarified butter, **or** ghee

4 pounds bone-in chicken parts, skinned **or** 2 pounds boneless, skinless thigh or breast fillets

1 cup filtered water, homemade stock, Bone-Building Broth (Page 278 or 306) **or** preservative-free chicken broth

1 bay leaf

1/2 teaspoon ground cinnamon

1/4 teaspoon ground red or black pepper

1/2 cup minced fresh parsley

Nutrition

1 serving dark meat:
351 calories
30 g protein
24 g carbohydrate
        (3 g fiber)
15 g fat
85 mg calcium
174 mg sodium

1 serving breast meat:
351 calories
39 g protein
24 g carbohydrate
        (3 g fiber)
11 g fat
89 mg calcium
179 mg sodium

All you need to complete this meal is a crisp green salad or sautéed leafy greens or Brussels sprouts. Select small parsnips, no larger than an average carrot—anything larger will usually be tough, woody, mealy, and bitter. Wait to buy the parsnips until after the first frost, so they'll be sweet.

1. Rinse chicken and pat dry. Heat oil in 3- to 4-quart stew pot or Dutch oven over medium-high heat. Lightly brown chicken in 2 batches and remove to a bowl.

2. Sauté onion in same pot, stirring until tender, about 5 to 7 minutes. Add carrots and parsnips. Stir, reduce heat to medium and cook 5 minutes. Add stock or broth, bay leaf, sea vegetable, salt if desired, then ginger, garlic, cinnamon, pepper, chicken, and any juices that have accumulated in the bowl. Gently turn to coat. Cover, bring to boil, and reduce heat so liquid just simmers.

3. Cook, turning chicken once or twice, until dark meat releases clear juices when pierced with sharp knife or breast meat is same color throughout, 35 to 45 minutes.

4. Remove from heat, add fresh parsley, and serve. Refrigerate leftovers and use within 3 days.

Variations

* **Stewed Chicken with Squash:** Replace carrots and parsnips with peeled kabocha, buttercup, Hokaido pumpkin, or butternut squash, cut into 2-inch cubes. Use ginger, garlic, cinnamon, and pepper, **or** substitute 1 tablespoon paprika, 1/2 teaspoon dried dill weed, and 1/4 teaspoon pepper.

Stewed Chicken with Zucchini, Mushrooms & Sun-Dried Tomatoes

Prep: 20 to 30 minutes ~ **Cooking:** 40 to 60 minutes ~ **Yield:** 6 servings

Ingredients & Directions

1 medium onion, cut into thick crescents

2 heaping cups button, cremini, or fresh shiitake mushrooms, rinsed and quartered, stems removed

4 cups zucchini, cut into 2x2-inch chunks

2 tablespoons extra-virgin olive oil

4 pounds bone-in chicken parts, skinned **or** 2 pounds boneless, skinless thigh or breast fillets

1 bay leaf

3 (5-inch) strips kelp **or** kombu sea vegetable, cut into 1-inch pieces with kitchen shears

3 medium garlic cloves (about 1 tablespoon), coarsely chopped

1/2 cup sun-dried tomato halves, quartered

1 cup filtered water, homemade stock, **or** Bone-Building Broth (Page 278), preservative-free chicken broth, **or** red wine

2 teaspoons dried Herbes de Provence **or** Italian herb blend

1/4 teaspoons ground red **or** black pepper **or** 1/2 teaspoon lemon pepper

1/2 to 1 teaspoon unrefined sea salt **or** 1 to 2 tablespoons tamari soy sauce, optional

1/2 cup minced fresh parsley for garnish

Lemon pepper

Nutrition

1 serving dark meat:

287 calories
30 g protein
8 g carbohydrate
(2 g fiber)
15 g fat
58 mg calcium
146 mg sodium

1 serving breast meat:

283 calories
38 g protein
8 g carbohydrate
(2 g fiber)
11 g fat
61 mg calcium
150 mg sodium

Make this when gardens and farmers' markets are brimming with zucchini and other summer squashes. Complete the meal with a crisp green salad, parboiled vegetable medley, or crudité-style parboiled vegetables with contrasting colors.

1. Chop vegetables. Rinse chicken, pat dry, and set aside.

2. Heat oil in heavy 3- to 4-quart Dutch oven or stew pot over medium-high heat. Lightly brown chicken in 2 batches and remove to bowl.

3. Sauté onion in same pan, stirring often until tender, about 5 to 7 minutes. Add mushrooms; reduce heat and cook until tender, about 5 minutes. Add bay leaf, sea vegetable, garlic, sun-dried tomato halves, liquid, herbs, pepper, optional sea salt, chicken, and any juices that have accumulated in the bowl. Turn to coat, cover, and bring to boil.

4. Reduce heat so liquid just simmers. Cook for 20 minutes, turning chicken once or twice. Add zucchini. Cover and cook 15 to 20 minutes more, until chicken is firm and juices run clear when pierced with sharp knife.

5. Garnish with parsley and pepper and serve. Refrigerate leftovers and use within 3 days.

Variations

* **Stewed Chicken with Zucchini, Mushrooms & Tomatoes:** Replace sun-dried tomatoes with 1 1/4 pounds halved, seeded, and sliced fresh tomatoes, **or** 1 (18-ounce) can chopped unsalted tomatoes.

Basic Herbed Turkey Burgers

Prep: 15 minutes ~ **Cooking:** 8 to 12 minutes ~ **Yield:** 4 servings

Ingredients & Directions

1 to 1 1/4 pounds lean ground turkey (breast or skinless dark meat), completely thawed

1 medium to large whole egg **or** 2 egg whites, optional

1 small red, yellow, or white onion, grated, **or** 4 trimmed and minced scallions, **or** 1 tablespoon dried onion flakes

1 1/2 teaspoons dried, crumbled Italian herbs:
    basil, oregano, thyme, sage, marjoram, rosemary, or combination, or Herbes de Provençe

1/4 teaspoon ground black pepper **or** 1/2 teaspoon lemon pepper

1 garlic clove, minced **or** 1/4 teaspoon garlic powder (not garlic salt)

Finely ground sea salt, optional

1 teaspoon unrefined coconut oil, clarified butter, **or** ghee

Nutrition

Dark meat patty:
202 calories
23 g protein
3 g carbohydrate
11 g fat
21 mg calcium
175 mg sodium

We enjoy burgers for breakfast, lunch, or dinner with Better Barbecue Sauce or Cajun Ketchup (Page 401), or a generous dollop of prepared mustard, with sautéed leafy greens and fresh fruit. For lunch or dinner, we sometimes replace cooked greens with a salad, and fruit with a root or tuber.

1. In a medium bowl, combine everything but the oil. Toss with clean bare hands to evenly distribute. Shape into 4 balls and flatten to 3/4-inch thick with a fork or your fingers. If desired form burgers on squares of parchment paper, cover with more parchment and refrigerate until cooking time.

2. Turn on exhaust fan. Heat oil in large, heavy stainless steel or cast iron skillet or grill pan over medium-high heat until hot but not smoking. Add burgers and brown for about 2 minutes per side. Cover, reduce heat to medium, and cook 6 more minutes or until no longer pink.

3. Serve warm with assorted vegetables. Refrigerate leftovers and use within 3 days.

Variations

* **Smoky Turkey Burgers:** Replace Italian herbs and garlic with 3/4 teaspoon dry mustard, 1/4 teaspoon ground chipotlé, 1/4 teaspoon turmeric, and 1 teaspoon Wright's Natural Liquid Hickory Smoke Seasoning.

* **Turkey Burgers with Cumin, Sage & Thyme:** Replace Italian herbs with 1/2 teaspoon each ground cumin, dried, rubbed sage, and dried, crumbled thyme. Omit garlic.

* **Turkey Chili Burgers:** Replace Italian herbs with 1 tablespoon chili powder blend. Serve with salsa or Better Barbecue Sauce (Page 401).

Notes: Transfer frozen meat to a pan in the refrigerator 24 to 36 hours ahead.

If pressed for time, cook unseasoned pre-formed turkey patties and top with Better Barbecue Sauce or Cajun Ketchup.

Basic Poultry Bone-Building Broth

Prep: 15 minutes ~ **Cooking:** 0 to 14 hours ~ **Yield:** 4 quarts

Ingredients & Directions

(For a large batch:)

3 to 4 pounds poultry raw or cooked bones, from whole carcasses, fryer parts, backs, necks, or wings of chicken, turkey, duck, guinea fowl, game hens, etc.

3 tablespoons lemon juice, organic red wine vinegar **or** raw apple cider vinegar

2 bay leaves **and/or** 2 to 3 (5-inch) pieces kelp, kombu **or** alaria sea vegetable

12 peppercorns, optional

1 teaspoon each dried rosemary and thyme, optional

1 large onion, quartered

1 large carrot, quartered, optional

5 to 6 quarts filtered water, or slightly more as needed to amply cover bones

Nutrition

1 cup:
Nutrition information not available

1. Combine ingredients in 8-quart stockpot. Add water to cover bones. Cover and bring to full rolling boil over medium heat. Reduce to medium-low to keep broth gently bubbling. Skim off foam that rises to surface during first 30 minutes.

2. Simmer 10 to 14 hours, or until broth appears milky. Add more water if needed to keep bones covered. To add more nutrients, mash with potato masher after 8 hours.

3. Uncover and simmer 1 hour longer, or until reduced to 4 quarts. Remove bones with large slotted spoon or pour through colander over extra-large bowl. Return broth to pot and place in sink filled with several inches of ice water. Cool for 30 minutes.

4. Strain and ladle into 1-quart Mason jars or freezer containers allowing 1 inch of head space in each container. Label, date, and refrigerate. Broth will thicken as it cools.

5. Skim off and discard fat layer before using or freezing broth. You can freeze some of the broth in ice cube trays and transfer to larger freezer containers. Use refrigerated broth within 10 days. Use frozen broth within 9 months.

Variations

* **Slow Cooker:** Combine all ingredients, except water, in 5- to 6-quart slow cooker. Add water to within 1 inch of top. Cover and cook on HIGH for 2 to 3 hours, if possible, then reduce heat to LOW and continue to cook for 8 to 10 hours.

I save all the bones from boning and cooking chicken, turkey, duck, and gamebirds—even if we've nibbled on them. I separate meat bones from poultry bones in recycled bags in the freezer. When I have enough, I make a thick, milky, gelatinous, mineral-rich broth. I read that a cup of bone stock/broth may contain as much calcium as a glass of milk. Because I make mine so thick, it probably contains more. I use it to make sautéed greens, Better Brussels Sprouts, Better Barbecue Sauce, Lean & Creamy Dressings, stir-fried vegetables, gravy, soup, and stews (see Index for recipes).

Note: Sea vegetables add trace minerals, including iodine and chelate heavy metals (including mercury) and radioactive isotopes from your body. I start cooking this in the morning or after lunch or supper, and let it to cook all day or night. If you're only cooking bones from breast parts, the broth won't turn milky, but it will still be delicious.

17 The Meat of the Matter

BEST BITES

Steak Tartare

Prep: 15 minutes ~ **Cooking:** 0 ~ **Yield:** 4 servings

Ingredients & Directions

1 to 1 1/4 pounds lean ground beef **or** bison (94 to 96 percent lean), frozen for at least 2 weeks and completely thawed

1/2 cup minced onions (Walla Walla Sweets or vidalias are very good)

1/4 cup minced shallots, optional

1/4 cup minced parsley leaves, no stems

2 tablespoons prepared mustard:
  Dijon, stone-ground, creamy white,
  jalapeno-, smoked green chili-, or garlic-flavored

1 to 2 egg yolks (they contain lipase which aids digestion)

1/2 teaspoon finely ground sea salt **or** 1 tablespoon tamari soy sauce, optional

1/4 to 1/3 teaspoon ground black pepper **or** chipotlé, or to taste

2 to 3 tablespoons fresh lemon juice, optional

Hot sauce, optional

Nutrition

1 serving beef:
175 calories
25 g protein
5 g carbohydrate
6 g fat
17 mg calcium
382 mg sodium

1. Combine everything except hot sauce in a 2-quart mixing bowl. Mix with fork. Form into a mound in a bowl or 4 smaller mounds on a platter.

2. Serve immediately, or cover and chill for 2 to 4 hours before serving.

3. Cover and refrigerate leftovers and use within 2 days.

Variations

* **Tex-Mex Steak Tartare:** Omit shallots, mustard, and lemon juice. Mince and add 2 garlic cloves, 2 seeded, finely minced small green chilies, 1 cup peeled, seeded, finely chopped tomato, and 1/4 cup lime juice. Refrigerate 2 to 4 hours. Serve over green salads with avocado or with guacamole and vegetable sticks.

When I was a young child, I loved Steak Tartare. I still do (so does Don). We've never gotten sick from it; probably because we use naturally raised (usually 100 percent grass-fed) beef frozen for at least 2 weeks. Rather than serve it as an appetizer, we enjoy it as a main dish, served on a bed of green salad with sliced avocado and lemon wedges, or with parboiled vegetables and one of our creamy tahini dressings (see Index for recipes), and with fresh fruit for dessert.

Note: Transfer frozen meat to a pan in the refrigerator 24 to 36 hours ahead. To grind your own meat, chop tenderloin, top round, or sirloin steak into 1/2-inch pieces. Place in a food processor fitted with a metal blade and pulse on and off until the pieces are about 1/8 inch in size, about 10 seconds. A Vita-Mix also works if you grind small batches.

Tex-Mex Raw Beef Salad

Prep: 10 minutes ~ **Cooking:** 0 ~ **Yield:** 6 servings

Ingredients & Directions

Meat:
1 1/2 to 2 pounds boneless lean beef **or** bison steak (sirloin, tenderloin, round tip, top round, etc.), frozen for at least 2 weeks

Marinade:
1/3 to 1/2 cup fresh lime juice **or** lemon juice

1 medium sweet red or white onion, sliced (about 3/4 cup)

2 small dried red chili peppers (chipotlé, ancho, Anaheim, or cayenne), seeded, and coarsely chopped

2 to 3 small to medium garlic cloves, chopped

1 teaspoon dried, crumbled oregano **or** 1 tablespoon minced fresh oregano leaves

1 tablespoon raw honey **or** agavé nectar (cactus honey)

1 to 2 tablespoons tamari soy sauce **or** 1/2 to 1 teaspoon finely ground unrefined sea salt

Nutrition

1 serving (sirloin tip or round):

152 calories
24 g protein
7 g carbohydrate
3 g fat
4 mg calcium
194 mg sodium

1. Slice steak into 1/4-inch wide strips, then crosswise into bite-size pieces when partially frozen. Arrange meat in shallow casserole or deep-dish glass pie plate.

2. Purée remaining ingredients in blender or food processor. Pour over meat, stir and turn to coat. Cover with lid or dinner plate. Refrigerate for 12 to 24 hours, stirring once or twice.

3. Serve chilled. Use within 3 days.

Variations

* **Tex-Mex Raw Salmon Salad:** Replace beef with thinly sliced or diced salmon fillets. Prepare as above.

This is a lot like Steak Tartare except the meat is thinly sliced rather than ground. I don't recommend anonymous meat from the supermarket. Look for 100 percent pasture-raised (grass-fed) beef or bison, or naturally raised meat from a natural foods market. According to some experts, freezing the meat for at least 2 weeks kills potential pathogens. Marinating in an acidic solution with spices also adds anti-bacterial and anti-microbial benefits and is traditional around the world.

I usually serve this 2 or 3 days in a row, spooned over heaping plates of salad greens and assorted raw vegetables. I top it off with avocado and tomato slices, or guacamole and jicama sticks. Or, I plate the meat with a parboiled vegetable medley and one of our creamy tahini dressings (see Index for recipes). For a light dessert, serve a fresh fruit salad or fruit kabobs dusted with coconut.

Speedy Moroccan-Spiced Pork Loin

Prep: 15 minutes ~ **Cooking:** under 15 minutes ~ **Yield:** 6 to 8 servings

Ingredients & Directions

2 pork tenderloins (about 2 pounds total)

1/2 teaspoon finely ground, unrefined sea salt

1/2 recipe (about 1/3 cup) Moroccan Barbecue Spice Mix (Page 399)

2 tablespoons extra-virgin olive oil, unrefined coconut butter, clarified butter, **or** ghee

1. Preheat oven to 450° F. Pat tenderloins dry with unbleached paper towel. If necessary remove thin silver skin by inserting sharp boning knife under membrane and cutting it away. Keep knife angled slightly toward silver skin. Lightly season with sea salt. Spread and press spice mix all over tenderloins.

2. Heat a heavy 12-inch (preferably cast iron) ovenproof skillet over medium-high heat until very hot. Add oil; carefully add tenderloins. Cook until well browned on the bottom, about 5 minutes. Turn tenderloins and immediately transfer skillet to hot oven.

3. Roast for 5 minutes, remove pan from oven, and test with instant-read thermometer. Meat should register 145° F. If not, return pan (but not thermometer) to oven and cook 1 or 2 more minutes; test again. Do not cook past 155° F or pork will be leathery.

4. Transfer tenderloins to meat cutting board, tent with foil and let rest for 5 minutes. Cut 1 tenderloin into 1/4-inch thick slices and serve. Cool, cover, and refrigerate second tenderloin. Store unused spice rub in airtight jar at room temperature. Use leftover pork within 3 days or freeze.

Variations

* Serve sliced pork loin topped with Moroccan Barbecue Sauce (Page 400).

* **Cajun-Spiced Pork Loin:** Replace Moroccan Spice Mix with preservative-free Cajun blend (fantastic with Cajun Barbecue Sauce (Page 401). Or try Jamaican Jerk Seasoning.

Nutrition

1 serving (6 per recipe):
282 calories
32 g protein
3 g carbohydrate
16 g fat
55 mg calcium
234 mg sodium

The inspiration for this easy entrée came from *Cooking for the Week* by Morgan, Taggart, and Taggart. Leftovers are wonderful for breakfast or used as a key component in main-course salads for lunch or dinner. The meat cooks quickly, so have your side dishes—a green salad or cooked leafy greens, and a colorful root, tuber, soup, or fruit—ready before you start the tenderloin.

Note: Calorie and fat counts will be lower for pasture-raised pork (the best) than for the grain-fed pork I used for the analysis. Prep time assumes you prepared the spice blend ahead.

Moroccan-Spiced Pork Chops

Prep: 10 minutes ~ **Cooking:** 15 minutes ~ **Yield:** 6 servings

Ingredients & Directions

1 3/4 to 2 pounds center-cut boneless pork loin, pork chops, **or** steaks (1- to 1 1/2- inches thick) — you can trim away visible fat, but I usually don't

1/4 to 1/2 teaspoon finely ground unrefined sea salt

1/2 teaspoon ground black pepper

1/3 cup Moroccan Barbecue Spice Mix (Page 399)

1 tablespoon extra-virgin olive oil, unrefined coconut butter, clarified butter, **or** ghee

1/2 cup homemade stock, preservative-free chicken broth, Bone-Building Broth (Page 278), white wine **or** 1 cup Moroccan Barbecue Sauce (Page 400)

1. Place chops on clean, dry plate. Sprinkle lightly with salt and pepper and roll in spice mix to coat both sides. Press so an even layer adheres.

2. Heat oil in heavy 12-inch skillet over medium-high heat until hot but not smoking. Arrange chops in skillet and cook until lightly golden, 2 to 3 minutes per side. Reduce heat to medium-low to keep chops sizzling. Cover and cook 10 to 12 more minutes, turning once or twice, until firm to the touch but not hard when pressed, juices run clear, or instant-read thermometer inserted into side of chop registers 145 to 155° F but no higher than 150 or 160° F.

3. Remove chops to platter. Cover loosely with foil for 5 minutes to allow juices to settle. Internal temperature will rise 5° F.

4. Add stock, broth, wine, or barbecue sauce to skillet. Raise heat, stir, scrape up browned bits, and simmer until syrupy. Spoon sauce over chops and serve. Refrigerate leftovers and use within 3 days or freeze.

Variations

* **To grill or broil:** Season chops; brush or rub with olive or coconut oil. Broil or grill 5 to 7 minutes per side or until meat tests done.

* **Cajun-Spiced Pork Chops:** Replace Moroccan Spice Mix with salt-free Cajun Spice Blend.

   Serve plain or with Cajun Ketchup (Page 401).

It only takes 10 minutes to make the spice mix and there are so many delicious ways to use it (see Index). Even if I'm cooking for two, I make a full recipe so we have leftovers.

Nutrition

4 ounces trimmed pork without sauce:

291 calories
33 g protein
7 g carbohydrate
15 g fat
56 mg calcium
157 mg sodium

With sauce:

328 calories
33 g protein
13 g carbohydrate
   (1 g fiber)
16 g fat
70 mg calcium
237 mg sodium

Note: The USDA recommends cooking pork to 160° F for medium, 170° F for well-done. Many of today's best food writers recommend 145 to 150° F for medium and 155 to 160° F for medium-well. At these temperatures, pork will still have a faint pink tinge, be perfectly safe to eat, and more tender than pork cooked to well-done. The parasite that causes trichinosis is killed at 137° F.

Seared Pork Chops with Cranberry, Onion & Chipotlé Sauce

Prep: 15 to 20 minutes ~ **Cooking:** 15 minutes ~ **Yield:** 6 servings

Ingredients & Directions

1 3/4 to 2 pounds center-cut boneless pork loin chops **or** steaks, **or** bone-in rib chops 1 to 1 1/2 inches thick — trim away visible fat if desired; I usually don't

1/2 teaspoon finely ground, unrefined sea salt

1/4 to 1/2 teaspoon ground black pepper

1 to 1 1/2 tablespoons extra-virgin olive oil, unrefined coconut oil, clarified butter, **or** ghee

Cranberry, Onion & Chipotlé Sauce:

1 large onion, cubed or cut into thin half-moon slices (about 2 cups)

1 tablespoon chipotlé spice rub, not straight chipotlé (see Sources in Appendix D)

1/2 cup fresh or hard apple cider **or** dry white wine

1/2 cup water, apple juice, salt-free chicken stock, preservative-free broth **or** Bone-Building Broth (Page 278 or 306)

1/2 cup dried, fruit-sweetened sulfite-free cranberries

2 to 3 teaspoons arrowroot dissolved in 3 tablespoons cold juice **or** water

Finely grated zest of 1 lime, optional

Nutrition

4 ounces trimmed meat plus sauce:

313 calories
32 g protein
16 g carbohydrate (2 g fiber)
14 g fat
30 mg calcium
231 mg sodium

1. Preheat oven to 400° F. Pat chops dry and season lightly with sea salt and pepper. Chop onions and measure ingredients for sauce.

2. Heat oil in heavy 12-inch ovenproof skillet over medium-high heat until hot but not smoking. Brown chops 3 minutes per side, then transfer skillet to hot oven and roast until instant-read thermometer inserted horizontally 2 inches into meat registers 155° F, about 7 to 10 minutes. Use thick oven mitts to remove pan.

3. Transfer chops to platter, leaving fat and juices in skillet. Loosely tent with foil to retain heat. Temperature will rise another 5 degrees.

4. Hold skillet with thick oven mitts, add onions, and stir over medium-high heat until lightly golden or soft. Add chipotlé blend and 1/2 cup juice or wine. Raise heat and cook away most of liquid. Stir in cranberries and 1/2 cup additional liquid and cook until reduced by one-half. Add dissolved arrowroot and juices that have pooled around chops; simmer and stir until thick. Add lime zest if desired.

5. While sauce cooks, thinly slice chops on the diagonal if desired. Spoon sauce over chops, and serve. Refrigerate leftovers and use within 3 days or freeze. Warm gently or serve cold.

This technique produces marvelously moist chops with almost no supervision. (I use it with other dried fruits, herbs, and spices, so don't stop at cranberries with chipotlé.)

When you return the pan to the range top resist the urge to grab the scorching hot handles with your bare hands! Have some Chinese Burn Cream on hand (see Chapter 9 for suppliers), just in case.

Complete the meal with a green salad or sautéed greens, and baked or roasted winter squash, sweet potatoes, or a puréed carrot or squash soup. Besides making a great lunch or dinner for the next day, leftovers are delicious for breakfast.

~Variations next page~

Variations

Seared Pork Chops with Cranberry, Onion & Chipotlé Sauce ~ continued

* **Broiled or Grilled Pork Chops with Chipotlé:** Season chops with sea salt and chipotlé spice rub, pressing so an even layer adheres. Let chops rest at room temperature for 1 hour, or cover loosely with parchment and refrigerate several hours or overnight. Rub chops with olive or melted coconut oil, and grill or broil for 5 to 7 minutes per side, or until done (145 to 150° F for medium, 155 to 160° F for medium-well). Serve without sauce or prepare sauce by sautéing onions in 1 tablespoon coconut or olive oil, ghee, **or** clarified butter.

* Replace chipotlé spice rub with 1/2 teaspoon ground chipotlé (smoked, dried Jalapeno pepper), 1/4 teaspoon ground chile molido, 1/4 teaspoon ground chile ancho, 1 1/2 teaspoons paprika, and 1/2 teaspoon onion powder.

* **Seared Pork Chops with Cranberry, Onion, Sage & Thyme Sauce**: Replace chipotlé spice blend with 1 teaspoon dried, rubbed sage, 3/4 teaspoon dried, crumbled thyme, plus 1 teaspoon Dijon or 1/2 teaspoon dry mustard powder. Replace lime juice with zest and juice of 1/2 orange.

* **Seared Pork Chops with Currant, Apricot & Onion Sauce:** In master recipe, replace black pepper with white pepper, and dried cranberries with 1/4 cup dried currants plus 1/4 cup chopped, pitted, sulfite-free dried Turkish apricots. Replace chipotlé seasoning with 1 teaspoon Quatre Epice (French 4-Spice). Replace lime zest with grated zest of 1/2 orange.

    Note: To make French 4-spice, combine 1 rounded teaspoon ground white pepper, 1/2 teaspoon ground nutmeg, a very scant 1/2 teaspoon ground ginger or cinnamon, and 2 generous pinches ground cloves.

* **Seared Pork Chops with 5-Spice Fruit Sauce:** Five-Spice is a magical mixture of the 5 major spices featured in Chinese cooking. This sweet and pungent blend includes star anise, szhechuan pepper, fennel or anise, and cinnamon or cloves. Two more spices may be chosen from licorice root, cardamom, and ginger. This recipe also works with chicken or duck breast.

* Replace dried cranberries with 1/4 cup dried, pitted plums (prunes) or raisins, and 1/4 cup sulfite-free dried, pitted apricots or combination prunes, apricots, and raisins. Replace chipotlé spice blend with 2 teaspoons Chinese 5-Spice and 1 teaspoon dry mustard. Use 1/2 cup chicken stock or broth plus 1/2 cup saké, white wine, **or** apple cider. Replace lime zest with 1 tablespoon brown rice vinegar or orange juice. Add grated zest of 1/2 orange if desired.

Stir-Fried Beef with Broccoli & Mushrooms

Prep: 20 to 30 minutes ~ **Cooking:** 10 minutes ~ **Yield:** 2 servings

Ingredients & Directions

8-ounce boneless steak, trimmed of visible fat:
eye of round, top round, round tip, flank, sirloin, NY strip, or tenderloin

1 1/2 to 2 tablespoons unrefined coconut oil, divided, **or** half coconut, half olive oil

1/4 teaspoon ground chipotlé **or** black pepper

1/2 cup onion, cut into thin crescents or small cubes

1/8 to 1/4 teaspoon finely ground, unrefined sea salt

1 cup button or cremini mushrooms, trimmed and thinly sliced

4 cups broccoli, florets cut in half and stems peeled and cut into thin rounds (from 1 medium bunch or about 1 pound untrimmed broccoli)

1 or 2 cloves minced garlic

2 teaspoons peeled, finely minced gingerroot

1 tablespoon lemon juice **or** brown rice vinegar, optional

1 tablespoon tamari soy sauce, optional

1/2 cup Bone-Building Broth (Page 278 or 306), **or** preservative-free chicken or beef broth, divided

Nutrition

1 serving:
338 calories
33 g protein
19 g carbohydrate
(8 g fiber)
15 g fat
8 g fiber
95 mg calcium
206 mg sodium

I vary the vegetables, meats, and spices. When cooking for more than 2 people, stir-fry in batches unless you have an enormous wok. Overcrowding produces soggy vegetables.

Serve with a cup of soup or cooked or fresh fruit.

1. Slice steak into quarter-inch wide strips, then crosswise into bite-size pieces when partially frozen. Wash and chop vegetables. Arrange in separate bowls according to kind.

2. Heat 1 1/2 to 2 teaspoons of oil in a 10- to 14-inch wok or heavy-bottomed frying pan over medium-high heat until hot. Add meat and cook 3 to 5 minutes, stirring every 20 seconds, until lightly browned and meat loses its raw color. Sprinkle with pepper and remove from pan.

3. Heat remaining oil in a wok or heavy skillet over medium-high heat. Add onions and stir for 3 to 4 minutes, until soft and lightly charred. Stir in mushrooms, broccoli stems, then florets, garlic, ginger, lemon juice or vinegar, tamari if desired, and 1/4 cup broth or stock.

4. Cover and steam 2 to 4 minutes, until vegetables are almost crisp-tender, adding additional stock or broth only as needed to moisten. Remove lid and stir 1 or 2 minutes. Add cooked meat, stir, and cook 1 minute more. Remove from heat and serve.

5. Refrigerate leftovers and use within 24 hours.

Variations

* Replace mushrooms with thinly sliced carrots **or** yellow bell peppers; or replace 2 cups of broccoli with 2 cups of cauliflower **or** thinly sliced red cabbage.

Stir-Fried Veggies with Last Night's Meat

Prep: 15 minutes ~ **Cooking:** 6 to 8 minutes ~ **Yield:** 1 servings

Ingredients & Directions

1/2 cup scallions, cut into 2-inch logs split lengthwise using all the white part and the first 2 inches of the green part, **or** 1/2 cup onion, cut into thin half-moons

Small pinch finely ground, unrefined sea salt (about 1/8 teaspoon)

1/2 cup red or yellow bell pepper, cut into 2-to 3-inch long, 1/2-inch wide strips

1 1/2 cups red or green cabbage, cut into thin strips or 2-inch cubes

1 1/2 cups broccoli, florets cut in half, stalks peeled and cut into thin rounds, tough part discarded

1 clove garlic, minced

1/2 teaspoon fresh gingerroot, peeled and minced

1 tablespoon extra-virgin olive oil **or** unrefined coconut oil

1/4 teaspoon ground black pepper **or** 1/2 teaspoon lemon pepper

1/2 teaspoon finely ground, unrefined sea salt **or** 1 tablespoon tamari soy sauce, optional

1/8 to 1/4 cup homemade or preservative-free beef or chicken broth, Bone-Building Broth (Page 278 or 306) **or** liquid from cooking meatballs

6 ounces of cooked meat, cut into 1/4x2-inch strips or 1-inch cubes:
> beef, bison, venison, pork, chicken breast, ostrich, or leftover meatballs

Nutrition

1 serving with lean beef:
366 calories
32 g protein
24 g carbohydrate
(11 g fiber)
17 g fat
171 mg calcium
340 mg sodium

What do you do with last night's chicken, turkey, beef, pork, or meatballs? Slip them into a stir-fry.

If cooking for 2, prepare vegetables in 2 batches to avoid overcrowding the wok. For desert, try a fruit compote, a chestnut dessert, macaroons, or sliced fresh fruit (see Index for recipes).

1. Wash and chop vegetables, garlic, and ginger. Arrange in separate bowls.

2. Heat oil in 10- to 12-inch wok over high or medium-high heat. Add ingredients in the following order, stirring for 1 to 2 minutes after each addition: scallions or onions, sea salt, bell pepper, cabbage, broccoli stems, florets, garlic, ginger, pepper, optional sea salt or tamari, and stock or broth.

3. Stir and cook until almost crisp-tender. Add cooked meat or poultry and cook 2 to 3 minutes more until food is warm. Serve immediately.

Variations

* Replace 1 cup cabbage with button, cremini, or shiitake mushrooms, **or** carrot slices.

* Use 1/2 cup each, thinly sliced onion, mushrooms, and carrots with 1 1/2 cups halved cauliflower florets and 1 cup of asparagus cut into 2-inch lengths with woody part removed.

* Use 1/2 cup red or white onion, 3/4 cup sliced mushrooms, 6 cups thoroughly washed, packed, and chopped spinach, and 1/2 cup red or yellow bell pepper strips.

Herbed Meatballs

Prep: 15 minutes ~ **Cooking:** 15 to 20 minutes ~ **Yield:** 24 meatballs; 4 servings

Ingredients & Directions

1/4 cup powdered, dried shan yao (Radix Dioscorea)
+ 1/4 cup preservative-free chicken or beef broth, stock,
Better Barbecue Sauce, Cajun Ketchup (Page 401), **or**
tomato sauce

1 medium to large egg **or** 2 egg whites, lightly beaten

1 1/2 teaspoons dried Italian or mixed herbs **or** 1 1/2 to
2 tablespoons minced fresh herbs:
    Italian blend, Herbes de Provençe, Fines Herbes or
    sage, thyme, marjoram, oregano, basil, thyme, or
    combination of several herbs

1/2 teaspoon ground cumin, optional

1/4 teaspoon ground chipotlé **or** black pepper

1 garlic clove, minced **or** 1/4 teaspoon garlic powder

1/4 cup fresh, minced parsley **or** 1 tablespoon dried parsley

1/2 cup minced onion **or** 1 tablespoon dried onion flakes

1/2 teaspoon finely ground, unrefined sea salt **or** 1 tablespoon
tamari soy sauce, optional

1 to 1 1/4 pounds 90 to 96 percent lean ground beef **or** bison

1/2 cup filtered water, Bone-Building Broth (Page 278 or 306)
or preservative-free chicken broth to simmer meatballs, or
enough to cover bottom of skillet by 1/4-inch, optional

Nutrition

1 serving (beef):
183 calories
26 g protein
6 g carbohydrate
                (1 g fiber)
6 g fat
32 mg calcium
68 mg sodium

You don't need to sauté or stir meatballs as they cook or serve them with pasta. They're great spooned over spaghetti squash with red sauce, or with a green salad or steamed, parboiled, or sautéed leafy greens, and a dab of flavored mustard. Transfer frozen meat to refrigerator 24 to 36 hours ahead.

1. In a medium bowl, combine powdered shan yao and 1/4 cup water, broth, stock, barbecue sauce, or ketchup. Add next 8 ingredients (egg through onion) and whisk well.

2. Crumble meat into a large bowl then top with step 1 ingredients. Mix with clean bare hands pulling mixture apart rather than squeezing and packing to evenly distribute seasoning. Do not overmix. Shape into 24 (1-inch) balls.

3. **To simmer:** Bring 1/4 inch water to boil in a 12-inch skillet. Add meatballs, cover, reduce heat and simmer 15 to 20 minutes, until meat is the same color throughout or only slightly pink in the center. Transfer to a plate. Simmer liquid to reduce to 1/4 cup and spoon over meat.

   To bake: Omit 1/2 cup filtered water or broth. Bake meatballs on parchment-lined baking sheet in preheated 350° F oven for 15 to 20 minutes, shaking pan occasionally, until done.

3. Serve warm. Refrigerate leftovers and use within 3 days or freeze.

Variations

* **Herbed Ostrich or Turkey Meatballs:** Replace beef with ground ostrich or skinless dark meat turkey. For ostrich or turkey breast, add 1/4 cup chopped pecans if desired.

Note: To bind meatballs without bread crumbs, I use dried shan yao (Radix Dioscorea), a starchy white tuber sold in Chinese markets and herb shops. I powder shan yao pieces in the blender. If you can't find it and you tolerate gluten, substitute 1/4 cup rolled oats then soak them in 1/4 cup water, stock, or broth for 2 to 6 hours before assembling the meatballs.

My Favorite Meatloaf

Prep: 20 to 30 minutes ~ **Cooking:** 60 minutes ~ **Yield:** 8 servings
---

Ingredients & Directions

1/2 cup powdered, dried shan yao (Radix Dioscorea)

3/4 cup Better Barbecue Sauce **or** Cajun Ketchup (Page 401), divided

2 garlic cloves, finely minced, optional

1/2 teaspoon finely ground, unrefined sea salt **or** 1 tablespoon tamari soy sauce

1/2 teaspoon ground red or black pepper

1 tablespoon dried celery bits **or** 3 stalks fresh celery, finely minced

1 slightly rounded tablespoon dried onion flakes **or** 1 cup minced scallions or onion

2 tablespoons dried parsley **or** 1 cup finely minced parsley leaves, stems removed

2 tablespoons dried carrot bits **or** 1 heaping cup grated fresh carrot

1 tablespoon dried bell pepper bits **or** 1/2 cup minced fresh red and/or yellow bell pepper

2 medium-large eggs **or** 4 egg whites

1 1/2 tablespoons dried, crumbled or ground Italian herb blend **or** 1/4 cup minced fresh herbs:
combination basil, oregano, thyme, sage, and/or marjoram

1 teaspoon ground cumin

2 pounds 93 to 96 percent lean ground beef, or bison (buffalo), **or** venison

Nutrition

1 slice plus 2 tablespoons sauce:

205 calories
27 g protein
8 g carbohydrate
(2 g fiber)
7 g fat
55 mg calcium
228 mg sodium

I make a full batch of this wheat-free and grain-free loaf even if I'm cooking for 2 people. We don't mind eating it 2 or 3 days in a row, and stashing some in the freezer.

Transfer frozen meat to a pan in the fridge 36 hours ahead to defrost.

1. Combine powdered shan yao and 1/2 cup barbecue sauce or ketchup in a medium-size bowl. Add optional garlic and next 10 ingredients (sea salt through cumin). Mix with fork to blend.

2. Lightly grease a 9x5-inch (8-cup) loaf pan or 9x9x2-inch pan and preheat oven to 350° F.

3. Crumble meat into a large bowl. Add ingredients from Step 1 and mix with clean bare hands, pulling mixture apart rather than squeezing and packing. Press into prepared pan. Top with remaining 1/4 cup barbecue sauce or ketchup.

4. Bake uncovered in center of oven for 1 hour or until firm to the touch, meat pulls away from sides, and an instant-read thermometer registers 160° F for beef, bison, venison, or pork, and 170° F for turkey. Cut into 8 slices and serve. Refrigerate leftovers and use within 3 days or freeze.

Variations

* **Buffaloaf or Turkey Meatloaf:** Replace beef with skinless ground turkey or bison.

* Replace Italian herbs with 2 teaspoons ground coriander, increase cumin to 2 teaspoons, and add 3/4 teaspoon ground allspice. Add garlic if desired, and proceed as indicated above.

Note: To bind my meatloaf, I use dried shan yao (Radix Dioscorea), a starchy white tuber sold in Chinese markets and herb shops. I powder shan yao pieces in the blender. If you can't find it and you tolerate gluten, substitute 1/2 cup rolled oats; omit barbecue sauce and ketchup from the loaf, then soak the oats in 1/2 cup water for 2 to 6 hours before assembling the loaf. If desired, spread 1/4 to 1/2 cup barbecue sauce or ketchup over loaf before baking or add it at the table.

Basic Herbed Burgers

Prep: 5 to 10 minutes ~ **Cooking:** 6 to 12 minutes ~ **Yield:** 4 servings

Ingredients & Directions

1 to 1 1/4 pounds 90 to 96 percent lean ground beef or bison, completely thawed

1 medium to large whole egg **or** 2 egg whites, optional

1 small red, yellow, or white onion, grated, 4 minced green onions (scallions) **or** 1 tablespoon dried onion flakes

1 1/2 teaspoons dried, crumbled herbs **or** 1 1/2 to 2 tablespoons fresh:
    basil, oregano, thyme, sage, marjoram, rosemary, or combination

1/4 teaspoon ground black pepper **or** 1/2 teaspoon lemon pepper

1 small to medium garlic clove, minced

1/2 teaspoon finely ground sea salt **or** 1 tablespoon tamari soy sauce, optional

1 teaspoon extra-virgin olive or coconut oil, clarified butter, **or** ghee

Nutrition	
1 serving beef:	
162 calories	
25 g protein	
5 g carbohydrate	(1 g fiber)
5 g fat	
22 mg calcium	
52 mg sodium	
1 serving bison:	
179 calories	
33 g protein	
5 g carbohydrate	(1 g fiber)
3 g fat	
33 mg calcium	
67 mg sodium	

1. In medium bowl, combine everything but oil. Toss with clean bare hands to evenly distribute herbs, spices, and egg. Shape into 4 balls. Flatten to 3/4- to 1-inch thick with fork or fingertips. If desired, separate burgers on squares of unbleached parchment and refrigerate for later.

2. Heat oil in heavy, stainless steel or cast iron skillet or grill pan over medium-high heat until hot but not smoking. Cook burgers for about 6 to 8 minutes for rare, 8 to 10 minutes for medium-rare, 10 to 12 minutes for well-done, turning once. You may cover skillet after browning each side for 2 minutes. Or, cook on preheated gas or charcoal grill.

3. Serve warm. Refrigerate leftovers and use within 2 days.

Variations

* **Basic Beef Burgers:** Omit herbs and spices. Include onion and pepper, or use preformed patties. Top with Better Barbecue Sauce or Cajun Ketchup (Page 401) or your favorite prepared mustard.

* **Garlic, Ginger & Scallion Burgers:** Replace dried herbs and pepper with 2 teaspoons peeled, finely grated fresh ginger. Increase garlic to 2 cloves, and replace sea salt with tamari.

Instead of buns and fries, we serve burgers with cooked greens or salad and a soup, roasted or baked vegetables, fruit, or some combination.

If you must have bread, look for 100 percent sprouted whole grain buns in natural foods stores or the health food freezer section of supermarkets or try our Steamed Buns recipe in Appendix D.

If you want mayonnaise, we have a recipe for that too (Page 424).

Note: Transfer frozen meat to refrigerator 24 to 36 hours ahead. If you plan to grill or broil, you can use fattier grass-fed meat (80 to 90 percent lean). Excess fat will drain off in cooking, producing a lean, moist, tender patty.

Basic Broiled Steak

Prep: 5 minutes ~ **Cooking:** 8 to 25 minutes ~ **Yield:** 5 servings

Ingredients & Directions

1 1/2 pounds boneless **or** 2 pounds bone-in steak (at least 1-inch thick):
> sirloin, tenderloin, fillet, NY strip, top loin, round tip, flank, London Broil, rib-eye, T-bone, porterhouse, club or sandwich steak, or other cut

1 tablespoon ground cumin **or** combination of cumin and dry mustard

1/2 teaspoon ground black pepper **or** lemon pepper, or to taste

Finely ground unrefined sea salt, optional

1 tablespoon extra-virgin olive oil, optional

1. Position broiler rack 2 to 3 inches from heat source for 3/4-inch thick steaks; 3 to 4 inches for 1- to 1 1/2-inch thick steaks, 4 to 6 inches for 1 1/2- to 2-inch thick steaks.

2. Pat steaks dry, lightly sprinkle and rub with sea salt if desired, and liberally coat with cumin or a combination of cumin and dry mustard and pepper. Let rest at room temperature for 30 minutes, or cover loosely with unbleached parchment and refrigerate overnight.

3. Preheat broiler 15 minutes before cooking (5 minutes for toaster oven). If using electric oven or toaster oven, add 1/4 cup water to bottom of broiler pan. (Liquid should not touch steaks.) Brush or rub steaks with oil, if desired. **Note:** During cooking, leave door of electric oven ajar; close door of gas oven.

4. Broil 1-inch thick steaks 4 to 6 minutes for rare, 8 to 11 minutes for medium, 12 to 16 minutes for well-done. Cook 1 1/2-inch or thicker steaks 13 to 20 minutes. Turn steaks once top side has browned. Test by pressing or cutting into center of bone-in steak or outside of boneless fillet.

5. Rest steaks on cutting board for 5 minutes, then slice and serve, or refrigerate. Deposit bones in a bag in the freezer for making broth or stock. Consume leftovers within 3 days.

Variations

* Replace beef with buffalo, bear, venison, caribou, elk, or other wild game meat.

* Sprinkle steak lightly with sea salt, rub liberally with a salt-free chili powder blend, Cajun blend, or Moroccan Barbecue Spice Mix (Page 399), and grill.

Nutrition

4 ounces rib eye, strip, top sirloin, or flank steak:

119 calories
23 g protein
3 g fat
50 mg sodium

4 ounces top round or sirloin tip:

131 calories
26 g protein
3 g fat
45 mg sodium

To save time and energy and reduce cleanup, I usually broil in a large toaster oven. I leave visible fat on steaks until after cooking; it adds moisture. With 100 percent grass-fed meat, you may not want to trim at all (just reduce added fats or oils in the rest of the meal). Warm steak is delicious with Better Barbecue Sauce or Herb-Roasted Mushrooms (see Index for recipes). Cold steak is great sliced over a green salad.

Press Test: To test meat, hang your hand by your side. Rare meat will feel flaccid, like the web between your thumb and forefinger. Make a loose fist and press again; that's medium-rare. Make a tight fist and press into the web; that's what well-done (really overdone) feels like.

Pan-Seared Steak

Prep: 10 minutes ~ **Cooking:** 8 to 12 minutes ~ **Yield:** 5 servings

Ingredients & Directions

1 1/2 pounds boneless **or** 2 pounds bone-in steak,
3/4- to 1 1/4-inch thick:
>   sirloin, tenderloin, fillet, or NY strip, top loin,
>   round tip, flank, London Broil, rib-eye, T-bone,
>   Porterhouse, or other

1/2 teaspoon coarsely ground black pepper
or 1 teaspoon lemon pepper, **or** 2 to 6 teaspoons ground
cumin

Finely ground, unrefined sea salt, optional

1 to 1/2 tablespoons extra-virgin olive or coconut oil,
clarified butter, **or** ghee, optional

1. Pat steaks dry. Sprinkle with pepper or cumin and
   salt if desired. Rub seasonings in with back of spoon.
   If desired rub steaks with oil to lightly coat. Let rest
   at room temperature for 30 minutes.

2. Open a window or turn on ventilator fan. Heat 12- to
   13-inch cast iron or heavy-bottomed stainless steel
   skillet or ridged grill pan over low heat for 5 to 10
   minutes or medium-high for 4 to 5 minutes. (High heat will damage
   lining on most non-stick surfaces.)

3. Raise heat to high 3 to 4 minutes before cooking. When almost
   smoking, add steak(s). Sear first side for 3 minutes. Turn meat with
   metal spatula or tongs. Sear second side until beads of moisture
   begin coming through crust, about 3 minutes for medium-rare.
   Cook 1 or 2 minutes more per side for medium. Test by cutting
   bone-in steak near bone, boneless steak near outside.

4. Transfer to platter or cutting board. Tent loosely with foil, let rest
   for 10 minutes, then cut into 4-ounce portions or thin strips or
   cubes for salad. Deposit bones into bags in freezer for making Bone-
   Building Broth (Page 306). Refrigerate leftovers and use within 3
   days.

Variations

* **Pan-Seared Filet Mignon:** Use 1 1/4-inch thick steaks. Cook
  3 1/2 to 4 minutes per side for rare, 4 1/2 to 5 minutes per side for
  medium.

* **1 1/2- to 2-inch thick steaks:** Increase cooking time for thicker
  steaks, turning twice.

Nutrition

4 ounces rib-eye, strip, top sirloin, or flank:

119 calories
23 g protein
3 g fat
50 mg sodium

4 ounces top round or sirloin tip:

131 calories
26 g protein
3 g fat
45 mg sodium

This technique is best for 1/2-inch to 1 1/4-inch thick steaks. Thicker steaks and bone-in fillets are best cooked on the grill or under the broiler. Great accompaniments include Better Barbecue Sauce (Page 401) or flavored mustard.

I like to slice and serve steak over individual green salads with assorted raw, parboiled, or roasted vegetables. Vary spices according to your tastes.

Note: I don't trim the visible fat before cooking; it adds moisture. If you trim, do so after cooking.

Balsamic Beef Roast with Onions & Mushrooms

Prep: 15 minutes ~ **Cooking:** 4 to 6 hours ~ **Yield:** 8 to 12 servings

Ingredients & Directions

3- to 3 1/2-pound boneless **or** 4- to 4 1/2-pound bone-in beef roast, patted dry with paper towel: tenderloin, sirloin, tri-tip, strip loin, chuck roast, or other

1 to 1 1/2 tablespoons unrefined coconut oil, extra-virgin olive oil, clarified butter, **or** ghee

1 teaspoon ground black pepper

2 teaspoons dry mustard **or** ground cumin

Finely ground, unrefined sea salt, optional

2 large onions, cut into thin rounds, half-moons, or crescents (about 3 cups sliced)

3 to 4 cups thinly sliced fresh button, cremini or shiitake mushrooms

1/2 cup balsamic vinegar **or** red wine

1 tablespoon arrowroot dissolved in 3 tablespoons cold water, balsamic vinegar, cider, **or** red wine, optional

Nutrition

4 ounces:
245 calories
38 g protein
7 g carbohydrate
(1 g fiber)
8 g fat
9 mg calcium
62 mg sodium

Long, slow cooking produces meat that melts in your mouth. It also provides more leeway in cooking so there is less chance of overcooking. You could start it, leave for work, and have your husband or kids remove it from the oven later, or use a slow cooker.

1. Sprinkle half the pepper, mustard or cumin, and optional sea salt over 1 side of roast. Rub in with fingers or back of spoon. Repeat on second side. Allow roast to rest at room temperature for 1 to 2 hours, or cover with unbleached parchment and refrigerate overnight.

2. Remove roast from refrigerator 1 hour before cooking. Preheat oven to 275° F.

3. Heat oil in heavy Dutch oven, cast iron skillet, or heavy-bottomed chef pan over medium-high heat for 2 to 3 minutes, swirling to coat pan. Brown for 3 to 5 minutes per side. Transfer to roasting pan. Add vinegar or red wine to sauté pan and stir to loosen stuck bits. Add onions and mushrooms. Stir and cook for 5 to 10 minutes and spoon over roast. Cover with tight-fitting lid or foil.

4. Bake for 2 to 3 hours. Uncover, turn roast over, spoon pan sauce over meat, replace cover, and bake 2 to 3 more hours, until fork tender. Time will vary with size of roast, pan, and oven.

5. Place roast on cutting board, tent with foil, and let rest for 15 minutes. Meanwhile, simmer pan juices, uncovered, on top of stove and stir until thick. If watery, add dissolved arrowroot, simmer, and stir to thicken.

6. Cut meat cross-wise (against the grain), into thin strips. Return meat to pan sauce. Warm briefly and serve. Refrigerate leftovers and use within 3 days or freeze.

Note: Meat will be more moist if you don't trim the fat until after cooking.

Variations

* Replace pepper and mustard with 1 tablespoon Greek, Italian, or French 4-Spice blend.

* **Slow Cooker:** Prepare as for steps 1 and 2. In step 3, transfer browned roast to 3 1/2- to 5-quart slow cooker. Top with deglazed pan juices and vegetables. Cover and cook on "LOW" for 6 to 8 hours. Reduce and thicken pan juices as in original recipe.

Basic Beef Roast

Prep: 15 minutes ~ **Cooking:** 40 to 60 minutes ~ **Yield:** 6 to 12 servings
---

Ingredients & Directions

3- to 6-pound boneless **or** bone-in beef roast, patted dry with paper towel:
> top or bottom round, eye of round, strip loin, or chuck arm, shoulder, blade roast, or other

2 tablespoons dry mustard, ground cumin, dried thyme and/or rosemary

1 teaspoon finely ground black pepper **or** 2 teaspoons lemon pepper

Finely ground, unrefined sea salt, optional

Nutrition

4 ounces:
240 calories
40 g protein
1 g carbohydrate
8 g fat
10 mg calcium
76 mg sodium

1. Sprinkle and rub half the seasonings over one side of bone-in roast. Turn and repeat on other side. For boneless roast, mix seasonings on large sheet of parchment, then roll roast in spice mixture to coat. Rest at room temperature for 1 to 2 hours or cover loosely with unbleached parchment and refrigerate overnight.

2. Remove from refrigerator 1 hour before cooking. Preheat oven to 250° F. (If your oven is more reliable at 225° F or even 200° F, use that temperature instead.) Place roast on rack in shallow roasting pan. If roast has little or no visible fat, place directly in bottom of pan.

3. Roast uncovered until meat thermometer registers 110° F. Raise oven temperature to 450° F and continue to cook, uncovered, until internal temperature reaches 125 to 130° F for medium-rare, 135 to 140° F for medium doneness, and outside is brown (about 10 to 15 minutes for a 4 to 6 pound roast). If you cook it any longer it will be overdone.

4. Cover roast and let rest at room temperature for 10 to 15 minutes to allow juices to settle.

5. Slice and serve warm with any pan juices, or cover and refrigerate. Leftover juices may be turned into a sauce or saved for soup or stew. Use within 3 days or freeze.

Prolonged low-temperature roasting helps prevent overcooking. You can leave the roast alone for 15 minutes at a time without worrying that you'll find it cooked to 180° F and completely ruined.

If you roast it at 450° F, the difference between rare and overdone might be a matter of a few minutes! However, finishing a slow roast at 450° F browns the outside and adds a rich flavor. (A digital instant-read thermometer is ideal.)

I often start a roast cooking first thing in the morning, so it's ready for lunch or dinner and the next couple of days.

Rule of thumb: about 20 minutes per pound.

Variations

* For a smaller roast, keep a closer eye on meat after raising heat to 450° F.

* **Beef Roast in Barbecue Sauce**: Serve roast with cold or gently warmed Better Barbecue Sauce (Page 401). Or, slice and slather leftover roast with barbecue sauce in a heat-proof dish and heat in a 300° F oven or toaster oven until warmed through.

Barbecued Beef Brisket

Prep: 30 minutes ~ **Cooking:** 2 1/2 to 3 1/2 hours ~ **Yield:** 8 to 10 servings

Ingredients & Directions

3 1/2- to 4 1/2-pound beef brisket (thin or first cut, flat or point, or whole brisket from a small steer)

1 tablespoon extra-virgin olive oil **or** unrefined coconut oil

1/2 to 1 teaspoon finely ground, unrefined sea salt, optional

1/2 teaspoon ground black pepper

1 tablespoon extra-virgin olive oil, unrefined coconut oil, clarified butter, **or** ghee

1 large or extra large onion thinly cut into rings or half-moons (about 2 packed cups)

1/2 cup water, stock **or** Bone-Building Broth (Page 278 or 306)

2 cups Better Barbecue Sauce (Page 401)

1 tablespoon apple juice concentrate **or** honey, optional

Nutrition

4 ounces meat plus sauce:
321 calories
39 g protein
14 g carbohydrate
　　　(3 g fiber)
12 g fat
30 mg calcium
192 mg sodium

Long slow cooking breaks down the otherwise tough fibers in brisket, making the meat melt in your mouth. Add 15 minutes to prep time if you don't have leftover barbecue sauce.

1. If you trim visible fat from brisket, leave at least 1/4-inch intact. Pat dry, rub with sea salt if desired, and allow to rest at room temperature for 1 hour. Preheat oven to 350° F (325° F for grass-fed beef, Piedmontese beef, buffalo, or venison) 15 minutes before cooking.

2. Heat 1 tablespoon oil in heavy Dutch oven or flame-proof casserole over medium-high heat for 2 to 3 minutes and swirl to coat. Add brisket, cook for 3 to 5 minutes per side, or until browned. Remove brisket to platter and sprinkle with pepper.

3. If meat released plenty of fat, you will not need additional oil. If dry, add 1 tablespoon oil to pan. Add onions, stir, and cook until soft and lightly browned, about 5 minutes. Add water, stock, or broth. Stir; add brisket and barbecue sauce, cover, and transfer to hot oven.

4. Bake until fork tender, 2 to 3 hours. Spoon sauce over roast several times. Transfer brisket to meat-designated cutting board. Cut crosswise, against the grain, into thin strips. Return sliced meat to sauce, warm briefly, and serve.

5. Refrigerate leftovers. Use within 3 days or freeze.

Note: A 5-pound brisket will serve 10 or more.

Variations

* **Barbecued Buffalo Brisket:** Replace beef with buffalo (bison) brisket.

* **Mini-brisket:** If cooking a 2-pound brisket from a small grass-fed steer, reduce everything by 1/2 except oil (100 percent grass-fed beef brisket is very lean). Serves 4 to 6.

* **Barbecued Chuck Roast:** Replace brisket with 4-pound boneless chuck roast. Serves 12.

Beef, Carrot & Sunchoke Stew

Prep: 30 minutes ~ **Cooking:** 1 3/4 hours ~ **Yield:** 6 servings
---

Ingredients & Directions

4 cups Bone-Building Broth (Page 278 or 306) **or** preservative-free chicken or beef broth

1/2 packed cup kelp **or** kombu, cut into 1/2-inch pieces with shears

2 medium or 1 jumbo onion, cubed (3 cups)

1/2 pound cremini or button mushrooms, wiped clean, stems trimmed, thickly sliced (2 1/2 cups)

3 to 4 medium to large carrots (4 cups)

4 to 6 sunchokes/Jerusalem artichokes, cut into 1-inch cubes (4 cups)

3 medium celery ribs, chopped (1 1/2 cups)

1 1/2 pounds beef or bison stew meat, cut into 1 1/4-inch cubes, patted dry

1/2 teaspoon ground black pepper

Finely ground, unrefined sea salt, optional

2 tablespoon unrefined coconut oil **or** extra-virgin olive oil, divided

3 large garlic cloves, coarsely chopped

2 large bay leaves

2 teaspoons Wright's Natural Liquid Hickory Smoke Seasoning

2 teaspoons dried, crumbled thyme **or** 2 tablespoons chopped fresh thyme leaves

1 1/2 teaspoons ground cumin

1/3 cup apple juice, fresh or hard apple cider, **or** red wine

10 sun-dried tomato halves, quartered, optional

2 tablespoons arrowroot starch, dissolved in 1/3 cup cold water, Bone-Building Broth (Page 278 or 306), preservative-free chicken or beef broth, **or** red wine

2 tablespoons tamari soy sauce, optional

1/2 cup minced fresh parsley **or** scallions for garnish

For a simple meal, all you need is to add a green salad or cooked leafy greens. The stew freezes well.

Nutrition

1 serving:
337 calories
31 g protein
36 g carbohydrate
(4 g fiber)
8 g fat
86 mg calcium
191 mg sodium

Note: If you can't find sunchokes, substitute turnips or fresh potatoes free of sprouts, and greenish colored skin. I prefer butterball, yellow Finn, or Yukon gold potatoes.

~Directions & Variations on next page~

Directions

1. Add stock or broth and seaweed to heavy 2- to 3-quart Dutch oven. Scrub sunchokes exceedingly well. Break off knobs, scrub and rinse around crevices to remove all traces of sand. Wash vegetables, chop, and arrange in separate bowls. Bring stock or broth to low boil over medium heat.

2. Dust meat with pepper and optional sea salt. Heat 1 tablespoon oil in 10- to 12-inch heavy stainless steel or cast iron skillet. Cook half the meat in skillet, turning to brown on all sides, about 8 minutes; transfer to boiling broth. Repeat with remaining beef. Deglaze skillet with 1/2 cup broth. Scrape up browned bits and add to boiling broth.

3. Add onions, mushrooms, carrots, sunchokes, and celery to boiling broth. Then add garlic, bay leaves, cumin, thyme, cider or wine, and optional dried tomatoes. Cover, reduce heat, and simmer for 1 1/2 hours, or until beef is tender, stirring occasionally. Uncover and simmer for 30 to 60 minutes. Discard bay leaf, taste, and adjust seasonings. Add dissolved arrowroot, simmer, and stir until thick. Ladle into bowls, garnish, and serve.

4. Use within 4 days or freeze.

Variations

* **Slow Cooker:** Brown meat, deglaze pan, and layer all ingredients (except arrowroot, 1/3 cup liquid, and garnish) in a 3 1/2-quart slow cooker. (Use a 5 1/2- to 7-quart slow cooker for double batch). Cover and cook on LOW for 8 to 10 hours.

* Replace beef with bison, venison, deer, elk, or other game meat, **or** lean lamb.

* **Lamb, Squash & Leek Stew:** Replace beef with lamb stew meat. Use shiitake mushrooms, or omit mushrooms altogether. Replace onions with 2 large leeks, split in half down the center and rinse thoroughly under running water to remove all traces of sand. Cut white part and most of green part into 1-inch pieces. Discard scruffy looking portion, usually the last 2 to 3 inches. Replace carrots and sunchokes with Hokaido, kabocha, buttercup, butternut, or honey delight squash, peeled and cut into 1-inch cubes. Omit liquid smoke. Replace red wine and apple juice with broth or stock. If desired replace cumin with dried, rubbed sage, or replace cumin and thyme with finely grated gingerroot.

* Experiment with other root vegetables and winter squashes. Try squash with shiitake mushrooms and onions; rutabaga with squash and onions; carrots with parsnips and onions; or a collection of roots, such as carrots, rutabaga, turnips, and parsnips with onions. If you replace dried tomatoes with fresh tomatoes, reduce liquid by 1 to 2 cups.

Beef, Carrot, & Sunchoke Stew ~ continued

Beef & Vegetable Stew

Prep: 45 minutes ~ **Cooking:** about 1 1/2 hours ~ **Yield:** 8 servings
---

Ingredients & Directions

3 to 4 cups Bone-Building Broth (Page 278 or 306), **or** preservative-free chicken or beef broth **or** 4 parts broth to 1 part red wine

3 (5-inch strips) kelp **or** kombu seaweed, cut into 1/2-inch squares (about 1/2 cup)

2 pounds boneless lean beef (round or chuck), cut into 1 1/2-inch cubes

2 small or 1 large yellow or white onion, cubed

1/2 pound shiitake, cremini, or button mushrooms, wiped with damp cloth, stems trimmed, caps quartered

3 carrots, cut into 1-inch chunks (about 2 cups)

2 small to medium turnips, cut into 1-inch chunks (about 2 cups)

2 small or 1 medium rutabaga, cut into 1-inch chunks (about 2 cups)

1 celery root bulb, peeled, trimmed, and cut into 1-inch chunks **or** 2 to 3 cups additional vegetables, such as carrots, turnips, and rutabaga

4 cloves minced garlic

3 to 4 tablespoon unrefined coconut oil, clarified butter, ghee **or** extra-virgin olive oil, divided

2 bay leaves

1 teaspoon ground black pepper **or** lemon pepper

1 teaspoon dried sage **or** dried, crumbled thyme

1/2 teaspoon ground cumin

10 unsalted sun-dried tomato halves, quartered, optional

2 tablespoons dried porcini or shiitake mushrooms powdered in spice-dedicated coffee grinder, optional

1/2 to 1 teaspoon unrefined sea salt **or** 1 to 2 tablespoons tamari soy sauce

1 1/2 to 2 tablespoons arrowroot dissolved in 1/3 cup cold Bone-Building Broth (Page 278 or 306), preservative-free chicken or beef broth, apple cider, **or** red wine

Fresh minced parsley, scallions and/or ground black pepper for garnish

Nutrition

1 serving:
242 calories
22 g protein
18 g carbohydrate
(2 g fiber)
9 g fat
47 mg calcium
247 mg sodium

The key to creating a great stew is to brown the meat and vegetables and deglaze the pan.

You can vary the vegetables or replace beef with bison or venison. You can use more liquid if you prefer a soupier consistency. Leftovers taste even better the second day and freeze well.

~Directions on next page~

Directions

Beef, & Vegetable Stew – continued

1. Add stock and seaweed to 2- to 3-quart Dutch oven. Pat meat dry and set aside. Chop vegetables and arrange in separate bowls. Bring stock to low boil.

2. Heat 1 tablespoon of oil in a large heavy cast iron skillet. Add half the meat to skillet. Stir to brown on all sides, about 5 minutes; transfer to boiling broth. Ladle 1/2 cup broth into skillet, scrape up browned bits, and add to stockpot.

3. Dry skillet over hot burner (dry with a towel if using a Creuset pot to avoid ruining the finish). Heat 1 tablespoon oil, brown remaining meat, and add to stockpot. Deglaze pan with 1/2 cup stock. Add browned bits and liquid from bottom of pan to stockpot.

4. Dry skillet over burner (unless using a Creuset). Heat 1 tablespoon of oil in skillet. Sauté onions and mushrooms until tender and browned, and add to stew. Deglaze pan with broth.

5. Dry skillet over burner. Heat 1 tablespoon of oil; sauté carrots, turnips, rutabaga, and celery root until lightly browned; add to stew. Deglaze pan with broth; return broth to stockpot with garlic, herbs, spices, optional sun-dried tomato, dried mushroom powder, and sea salt or tamari. Cover, reduce heat, and simmer 1 hour, or until meat and vegetables are tender.

6. Discard bay leaves. Adjust seasonings as desired. Add dissolved arrowroot and stir gently over medium heat until thick and clear. Remove from heat, ladle into bowls, garnish, and serve.

7. Refrigerate leftovers and use within 3 days or freeze.

Caveman Chili

Prep: 30 minutes ~ **Cooking:** 3 hours ~ **Yield:** 6 to 8 servings
---

Ingredients & Directions

3 (5-inch strips) kelp **or** kombu seaweed, cut into 1/2-inch squares (about 1/2 cup)

2 pounds trimmed boneless beef stew meat (round or chuck), cut into 2-inch cubes

1/2 teaspoon cracked or ground black pepper

1/2 teaspoon finely ground unrefined sea salt

2 tablespoons extra-virgin olive oil **or** unrefined coconut oil, divided

1 jumbo white or yellow onion, cut into 1-inch cubes (about 2 cups)

1 sweet red, orange, or yellow bell pepper, halved, seeded, and diced

2 tablespoons salt-free chili powder

1 1/2 teaspoons ground cumin

1 1/2 teaspoons dried oregano, crumbled

1/2 teaspoon ground chipotlé **or** 1 small dried jalapeno or red chili pepper, seeded and minced

3 to 4 garlic cloves, coarsely chopped

4 heaping cups cubed fresh red or low-acid gold tomatoes **or** salt-free canned tomatoes

1 cup diced celery, optional

1/2 cup minced fresh cilantro **or** parsley leaves for garnish

Ground black pepper for garnish, optional

Nutrition

1 serving:
260 calories
33 g protein
11 g carbohydrate
    (3 g fiber)
9 g fat
55 mg calcium
311 mg sodium

What's chili without cornbread? Delicious eaten with a spoon or spooned over individual bowls of baked, raked spaghetti squash, and garnished with sliced avocado or guacamole. A side salad completes the meal. You can substitute bison, pork loin, venison, bear, or moose for beef.

1. Pat meat dry with unbleached paper towel. Dust with pepper and sea salt if desired.

2. Heat half the oil in a heavy 3-quart Dutch oven or large, deep saucepan over medium-high heat until hot. Brown half the meat on all sides, about 5 minutes. Remove from pan. Repeat with remaining meat. Set meat aside.

3. Sauté onions in same pan, until lightly browned, about 5 minutes. Add bell pepper, chili powder, cumin, oregano, chipotlé or red pepper, and garlic. Stir for 2 minutes; add kelp or kombu, tomatoes, celery if desired, and meat with any accumulated juices. Cover, bring to boil, and reduce heat. Slip a heat deflector (flame tamer) under pot if using a gas stove. Simmer for 2 to 2 1/2 hours, until meat is fork tender.

4. Taste and adjust seasonings. Ladle into bowls, garnish, and serve. Refrigerate leftovers and use within 3 days or freeze.

~Variations on next page~

Variations

* Omit kelp or kombu. Season stew with 1 teaspoon unrefined sea salt **or** 2 tablespoons tamari.

* **Ground Beef, Chicken or Turkey Chili**: Omit stew meat. Sauté vegetables and spices. Add ground beef, chicken, or turkey. Stir and simmer 45 to 50 minutes. Taste and adjust seasonings.

* **Slow Cooker:** Brown meat, then combine all ingredients in slow cooker. Cover and cook on LOW for 6 to 8 hours. Consider making a double batch for the freezer.

Ben's Tomatillo Chili

Prep: 30 minutes ~ **Cooking:** 1 1/2 hours ~ **Yield:** 6 to 8 servings

Ingredients & Directions

2 fresh, raw Anaheim chilies

2 tablespoons extra-virgin olive oil

2 pounds beef (such as round or chuck blade), cut into 2-inch chunks

1 medium onion, diced

1 red bell pepper, halved, seeded, and diced

1 green or orange bell pepper, halved, seeded, and diced

2 or 3 (5-inch pieces) kelp **or** kombu seaweed, cut into 1/2-inch pieces with kitchen shears

2 garlic cloves, minced or pressed

1/4 teaspoon black pepper, or to taste

2 teaspoons salt-free chili powder, or to taste

1 teaspoon ground cumin

2 cups chopped tomatillos

1 1/2 to 2 pounds yellow tomatoes, peeled, seeded, and diced

1 cinnamon stick

1/3 cup fresh cilantro, chopped (garnish)

Finely ground, unrefined sea salt or tamari soy sauce, optional

Nutrition

1 serving:
285 calories
37 g protein
15 g carbohydrate
(4 g fiber)
9 g fat
38 mg calcium
1199 mg sodium

Paleo pen-pal Stacie Tolen and her husband, Ben, came up with this lovely avocado colored chili. Look for tomatillos (small green tomatoes with a wrinkled papery wrapper) at farmers' markets or in supermarkets. If you can't find fresh low-acid gold tomatoes, look for a salt-free canned version, or substitute red tomatoes.

For a simple supper, serve this stew with a tossed green salad and a fruit salad. It's also delicious over spaghetti squash with guacamole and a green salad or sautéed greens.

1. Rinse hot peppers, pat dry, and arrange on cookie sheet or in shallow baking pan. Roast in preheated 400° F oven or under broiler until skins are charred. With a spoon, transfer hot peppers to a glass bowl. Cover with a plate and allow to sweat for 10 minutes. Wearing gloves, peel off and discard skins. Chop flesh and seeds; set aside. Peppers may be roasted 24 hours ahead.

2. Heat oil in a wide 6- to 8-quart pot over medium heat. Stir and brown meat on all sides, about 5 minutes. Add onions and bell pepper; stir and cook until they start to soften. Add chopped hot peppers and remaining ingredients, except cilantro, the in order listed. Stir, cover, and bring to boil. Reduce heat, and simmer until cooked thoroughly, 30 to 45 minutes.

3. Remove cinnamon stick. Garnish with cilantro and serve. Refrigerate leftovers and use within 3 days or freeze.

Variations

* Use a pork and beef or pork and chicken combo. If using ground meat, sauté and brown onions first, then add meat, stir, and proceed as above.

* **Slow Cooker:** Brown 2 pounds of stew meat. Layer ingredients in 3 1/2- to 5-quart slow cooker. Cover and cook on LOW 6 to 8 hours.

Broiled Lamb Chops & Steaks

Prep: 10 minutes ~ **Cooking:** 9 to 12 minutes ~ **Yield:** 4 servings

Ingredients & Directions

4 double-rib **or** large shoulder, leg, **or** sirloin chops, 8 rib **or** T-bone (loin) chops, 4 boneless lamb leg sirloin steaks, **or** 12 trimmed riblets, 1- to 2-inches thick

2 garlic cloves, peeled and cut into thin slivers, optional

1/2 to 1 tablespoon extra-virgin olive oil, optional

1/2 teaspoon coarsely ground black pepper **or** lemon pepper

1/2 lemon or orange for garnish, cut into wedges, optional

Nutrition

4 1/2 ounces:
233 calories
35 g protein
11 g fat
17 mg calcium
84 mg sodium

1. Remove lamb from refrigerator 30 minutes before cooking. Position broiler rack 3 to 4 inches from heat source and preheat. Pat meat dry with unbleached paper towel and rest on broiler pan. To prevent splattering and avoid blowing a fuse, add 1/3 cup water to bottom of broiler pan if using an electric oven or toaster oven.

2. If using garlic, make small 1/2-inch deep slits on both sides of steaks with a paring knife; insert garlic slivers. Lightly brush or rub chops or steaks with oil if desired. Sprinkle and rub with pepper.

3. If broiling, leave oven door ajar for an electric range. Cook 3 1/2 to 5 minutes per side for medium-rare, 1 minute more for medium. Allow less time for small, single rib or loin chops, or chops less than 1-inch thick. Transfer to serving plates or cutting board.

4. Serve warm, garnished with lemon or orange wedges as desired.

5. Deposit bones in a bag in the freezer for making broth. Use leftovers within 3 days or freeze.

Variations

* Insert garlic and needles from 3 small fresh rosemary sprigs **or** 2 teaspoons dried, crumbled rosemary into slits in steaks or chops.

* **Grilled Lamb Chops:** Grill chops 4 inches from heat source using cooking times above.

* **Broiled Lamb Chops with Barbecue Sauce:** Season chops with garlic and pepper. Broil or grill and serve with Better Barbecue Sauce.

* **Broiled Lamb Chops with Chutney:** Season lamb chops or steaks with garlic and pepper. Broil as above. Serve with Mango, Peach, or Apricot Chutney (Page 404).

Leftover lamb is delicious warmed briefly and topped with Better Barbecue Sauce (Page 401) or sliced and served over crisp green salads topped with colorful raw or roasted vegetables and a splash of balsamic vinegar or citrus juice. Tiny bits of leftover lamb can stand in for bacon, served with soft-boiled or poached eggs, steamed broccoli, spinach, or asparagus, and fresh fruit for breakfast.

Note: Meat will be more moist if you don't trim the fat until after cooking.

Roasted Lamb Chops & Steaks

Prep: 10 minutes ~ **Cooking:** 10 to 12 minutes ~ **Yield:** 4 servings

Ingredients & Directions

4 double-rib **or** large shoulder, leg, **or** sirloin chops, 8 rib **or** T-bone (loin) chops, 4 boneless lamb leg sirloin steaks, **or** 12 trimmed riblets, 1-to 2-inches thick

3 garlic cloves, peeled and cut into thin slivers, optional

1/2 teaspoon coarsely ground black pepper **or** lemon pepper

1/2 to 1 lemon or orange cut in to wedges, optional

Nutrition

4 1/2 ounces trimmed of visible fat:

233 calories
35 g protein
11 g fat
17 mg calcium
84 mg sodium

1. Remove steaks or chops from refrigerator 30 minutes before cooking. Place oven rack in upper third of oven. Preheat to 500° F 15 minutes before cooking. Heat a large cast iron skillet, griddle, or shallow roasting pan in oven for 8 to 10 minutes.

2. Pat steaks or chops dry. If using garlic, make small 1/2-inch deep slits on both sides of steaks with paring knife. Insert garlic slivers. Lightly brush or rub with oil. Sprinkle and rub with pepper.

3. Wearing thick oven mitts, open oven door, pull out rack, and drop chops or steaks onto hot skillet. Close oven and roast for 10 to 12 minutes, or until instant-read thermometer inserted horizontally 2 inches into thickest part of chops registers 120° F for rare, 125 to 130° F for medium-rare, or 135° F for medium. Meat should be slightly pink inside.

4. Transfer meat to plates and serve garnished with lemon or orange wedges as desired. Deposit bones in a bag in the freezer for making Bone-Building Broth (Page 306). Refrigerate leftovers and use within 3 days or freeze.

Variations

*   Insert needles from 3 small fresh rosemary sprigs **or** 2 teaspoons dried, crumbled rosemary **or** Herbes de Provençe with the garlic.

*   **Roasted Lamb Chops with Barbecue Sauce:** Season chops or steaks with pepper **or** lemon pepper. Serve with Better Barbecue Sauce (Page 401).

*   **Roasted Lamb Chops with Chutney:** Season chops or steaks with garlic and pepper. Serve with Mango-Ginger Chutney or any of the variations on Page 404.

*   **Roasted Lamb Chops with Moroccan Spice Rub:** In step 1, season chops with black pepper and sea salt if desired. Coat both sides with Moroccan Spice Mix (Page 399), pressing to coat evenly. Serve with Moroccan-Spiced Barbecue Sauce (Page 400) if desired.

This cooking method is easy on the cook and so is cleanup. You can vary the herbs and spices; try a Turkish, Greek, or French blend. Leftovers are great warmed in a toaster oven or under the broiler and served with parboiled or steamed vegetables or sliced over individual green salads and drizzled with lemon or lime juice, or a splash of good balsamic vinegar.

Note: Meat will be more moist if you wait to trim the fat until after cooking.

Roast Leg of Lamb

Prep: 30 minutes ~ **Cooking:** 1 1/4 to 2 hours ~ **Yield:** 8 servings

Ingredients & Directions

5- to 6-pound bone-in leg of lamb **or** 4- to 6-pound boned and rolled leg or short leg

1 teaspoon ground black pepper **or** lemon pepper

1 teaspoon finely ground, unrefined sea salt, optional

1 1/2 tablespoons dried, crushed rosemary, thyme, sage **or** combination **or** 1/4 cup minced fresh rosemary leaves, thyme, sage, or combination

4 to 6 small to medium garlic cloves, cut into thin slivers lengthwise, optional

1 to 2 tablespoons extra-virgin olive oil (for very lean roasts)

1/3 cup apple juice concentrate, optional

Nutrition

4 1/2-ounces, trimmed:
237 calories
35 g protein
11 g fat
22 mg calcium
84 mg sodium

1. Position rack in center of oven and preheat to 500° F. Untie or cut away netting holding together a boneless leg of lamb; unroll meat, cut-side up, on a clean surface.

2. Sprinkle with half the pepper, salt, all the garlic, and half the dried herbs or fresh sprigs of thyme, rosemary, and sage. Re-roll meat around herbs and tie with twine at 1-inch intervals. Lightly rub roast with oil. If using bone-in leg, mix olive oil with pepper and herbs; poke 1/2-inch deep holes in top, bottom, and sides of roast with a thin-bladed knife. Stuff half of seasoning mixture into incisions.

3. Rest lamb fat side up in ovenproof skillet or roasting pan (I prefer cast-iron), that closely approximates size of roast. Cook in preheated oven for 20 to 30 minutes. Reduce heat to 375° F. After 45 minutes, rub reserved pepper and herbs over roast. Continue to cook and baste or brush with oil or apple juice concentrate for about 15 minutes, or until done. Lamb is rare when a thermometer inserted in the center reads 125° F; medium-rare at 130° F to 135° F. Well-done lamb will be dry and tough.

4. Remove roast from oven. Cover loosely with foil, let rest for 10 to 15 minutes then slice and serve. Save bones in a bag in the freezer for making Bone-Building Broth (Page 306).

5. Refrigerate leftovers and use within 3 days or freeze.

Variations

* Omit pepper, rosemary, thyme, sage, and garlic. Use 2 teaspoons Turkish Seasoning (cumin, garlic, paprika, black pepper, oregano, sumac, and cilantro) **or** Lamb Seasoning (Turkish oregano, rosemary, cumin, celery, sweet paprika, black pepper, onion, garlic, spearmint, and ginger) per pound of meat.

Roast leg of lamb makes a wonderful holiday centerpiece or special Sunday supper with leftovers for another couple of days or the freezer. To make slicing easier, have your butcher remove all bones (or at least the hip bones) from the leg. Cook 15 to 20 minutes per pound. If meat is boneless, figure 6 ounces of uncooked meat per person; if bone in, 8 to 10 ounces.

Jack Knorek, my former grass-fed beef connection in Michigan and Ohio, helped tweak this recipe.

Basic Meat Bone-Building Broth

Prep: 10 to 15 minutes ~ **Cooking:** 1 to 15 hours ~ **Yield:** 4 quarts

---

Ingredients & Directions

For a large batch

3 to 4 pounds meat bones, leg, marrow, or assorted bones (raw or from cooked meats):
> beef, bison, lamb, venison, pork bones, or other

5 to 6 quarts filtered water, or slightly more as needed

2 bay leaves **and/or** 2 or 3 (5-inch) pieces kelp, kombu **or** alaria sea vegetable

3 tablespoons lemon juice **or** 2 tablespoons raw apple cider vinegar

Nutrition

1 cup
Nutrition information not available

I save all bones from turkey, beef, bison, venison, and pork—even if they've been nibbled on—and use them to make this simple stock/broth.

1. Combine ingredients in an 8-quart stockpot. Add water to cover bones. Cover and bring to a full rolling boil over medium heat. Reduce to medium-low to keep broth gently bubbling. Skim off foam that rises to surface during first 30 minutes.

2. Simmer 10 to 14 hours or until broth appears milky. Add water if needed to keep bones covered.

3. Uncover and simmer 1 hour longer or until liquid is reduced to 4 quarts. Remove bones with large slotted spoon or pour through large colander over extra-large bowl. Return broth to pot and place in sink filled with several inches of ice water. Cool for 30 minutes.

4. Strain and ladle into 1-quart Mason jars or freezer containers allowing 1 inch of head space in each container. Label, date, and refrigerate. Broth will thicken as it cools.

5. Skim off and discard fat layer before using or freezing broth. You can freeze some of the broth in ice cube trays and transfer to larger freezer containers. Use refrigerated broth within 10 days. Use frozen broth within 9 months.

It adds phenomenal flavor to soups, stews, sauces, sautéed kale, collard, mustard or turnip greens, Brussels sprouts, stir-fried vegetables, gravy, Better Barbecue Sauce, Cajun Ketchup, Moroccan-Spiced Barbecue Sauce, and my Lean & Creamy Salad dressings (see Index for recipes).

Variations

* **Slow Cooker:** Combine all ingredients, except water, in 5- to 6-quart slow cooker. Add water to within 1 inch of top. Cover and cook on HIGH for 2 to 3 hours, if possible. Reduce heat to LOW and cook 8 to 10 more hours. In hot weather, you can cook broth on the porch.

Technically this is a stock, but I call it broth. You can use it to replace either one in a recipe, although you may need to thin it with water. I save raw and cooked meat bones, even if we've nibbled on them. Deposit them in bags in the freezer, storing lamb bones separately (they have a strong aroma). When I have enough bones, or need more stock or broth, I create a delicious, gelatinous broth packed with calcium, magnesium, phosphorus, boron, and glucosamine sulfate.

To save space in the freezer or fridge, I boil the broth down before storing it. Some sources say that a cup of bone broth can contain as much calcium as a glass of milk. My brew probably contains more because it's so concentrated. Don't be alarmed if it looks like milk when it's hot and thin Jell-O (from the gelatin released from the cartilage) after a night in the fridge.

Note: The sea vegetable is optional, but desirable. It adds flavor and minerals, helps tenderize the bones, and through a process called chelation, helps rid your body of heavy metals (like mercury from fish and other foods) and radioactive isotopes. If you buy meat by the half or quarter, ask the butcher to save all the bones so you can make gallons of broth. Leg bones contain the most marrow and gelatin.

18

Cooked Leafy Greens, Flowering Vegetables, & Shoots

Best Bites

Green Leafy Vegetables (Kale) & Citrus Fruit (Orange)

As the chart below shows, green leafy vegetables such as kale (as well as collard, mustard, and turnip greens) are more nutrient dense than fruits. We emphasize daily use of dark green leafy vegetables and recommend that you eat them at least twice a day. Other great greens to use include broccoli, bok choy, baby bok choy, tat soi (also called tat soy), choy sum, Brussels sprouts, and various cabbages. Dark green leaf lettuces also count toward your daily greens quota; these are featured in the salad chapter.

You can see from the comparison below how foolish it is to lump vegetables and fruits into a single food group as is done in many standard four-food-group diet plans. You can easily end up undernourished if you eat a large volume of fruits at the expense of vegetables.

(A 100-gram serving is roughly 3 1/2 ounces by weight.)

Nutrient	Kale*	Orange	Difference:
Calories	38	49	orange has 29 percent more
Protein	4.2 g	1.0 g	kale has 420 percent more
Calcium	179 mg	41 mg	kale has 437 percent more
Phosphorus	73 mg	20 mg	kale has 365 percent more
Iron	2.2 mg	0.4 mg	kale has 550 percent more
Potassium	378 mg	200 mg	kale has 189 percent more
Vitamin A	8900 IU	200 IU	kale has 4450 percent more
Vitamin C	125 mg	50 mg	kale has 250 percent more

These numbers are for raw kale. Values are nearly identical if kale is cooked for less than 8 minutes at boiling temperature, a common technique we use. (See Whole Boiled Greens, Page 310.) Even if boiled 15 minutes, less than half of the water soluble vitamins, such as C, will be destroyed. Since kale is twice as high in this nutrient as an orange, you can still get as much vitamin C from cooked kale as from an equal volume of raw orange.

Dark leafy green vegetables are very cool and cleansing, but some contain bitter compounds that can hinder digestion. It is important to know how to prepare them to maximize their benefits and minimize or avoid digestive distress. This is especially true of the very dark, hardy greens—kale, collards, mustard, and turnip greens—which are practically indigestible, and for many people unpalatable, served raw or when steamed for only a few minutes. Traditionally these really dark and fibrous greens have been cooked for at least 10 minutes. Proper temperature is essential to preserve their flavor, nutrients, a lively green color. Our recipes will guide you.

Dark Leafy Greens: The King of Calcium

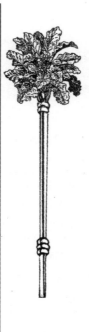

Type of Green	Calcium per cup	Calories per cup
Lambs quarters, cooked	464 mg	50
Bok choy	330 mg	32
Collards, cooked	304 mg	58
Turnip greens, cooked	252 mg	30
Mustard greens, cooked	196 mg	22
Chicory leaf, raw	180 mg	42
Spinach*	166 mg	42
Beet greens, boiled*	164 mg	40
Dandelion greens, cooked	146 mg	36
Dandelion greens, raw	102 mg	26
Chard, boiled*	102 mg	36
Kale, cooked	78 mg	38
Parsley, raw	78 mg	20
Dock, raw	58 mg	30
Endive, raw	26 mg	8
Watercress, cooked	40 mg	4

Notes on spinach, chard and beet greens: *The oxalic acid in these greens can bind with and reduce the absorption of the calcium and iron in these vegetables. Spinach, chard, and beet greens are less nutrient dense and less weather hardy than kale, collards, and other cabbage-family vegetables. We use spinach, chard, and beet greens infrequently. We rely mainly on greens that don't contain oxalates.*

Whole Boiled Greens

Prep: 15 minutes ~ **Cooking:** 10 to 15 minutes ~ **Yield:** 6 to 8 servings

Ingredients & Directions

3 quarts filtered water

1/2 teaspoon unrefined sea salt

1 1/2 to 2 pounds kale, collards, mustard **or** turnip greens (2 jumbo or 4 medium-size bunches)

Cool filtered water plus 1 tray of ice cubes to cool greens

Dressing, optional

Nutrition

1 heaping cup without dressing:

72 calories
4 g protein
14 g carbohydrate
   (2 g fiber)
180 mg calcium
90 mg sodium

1. Bring salted water to boil in 4-quart pot. Separate leaves and discard woody bottom portion of each stem and any rotten or yellowed pieces. Swish leaves in cold water. Rinse and run your fingers down each leaf and stem to remove sand. Strip stems from leaves.

2. Immerse stems and greens in boiling water. Boil *uncovered* over medium-high heat. After 3 or 4 minutes turn greens over and continue cooking until tender and vibrant green, about 4 more minutes for small, tender leaves, 5 to 8 minutes for larger leaves. You may need to cook greens in 2 batches, depending on size of pot.

3. Plunge greens and stems in ice water to stop the cooking and hold the color. Drain and wring to remove excess water. Cook and shock any remaining greens. Discard cooking water.

4. Arrange leaves on a cutting board. Roll up like newspaper and thinly slice into strips, then cut crosswise to make bite-size pieces. Or, cut each leaf in half, stack, and cut into 1-inch squares. Taste a bite of each stem. Discard if bitter or tough. Thinly slice remaining tender stems.

5. Toss with vinaigrette or drizzle with tahini or peanut dressing at the table.

6. Refrigerate leftovers in glass or stainless steel. Use within 3 days.

Variations

* For rollups, remove stems from cooked whole collards leaves. Place 2 tablespoons chicken, tuna, or egg salad, a meatball, or Steak Tartare on each leaf. Fold in sides, roll up package, secure with toothpick. Chill if desired and serve.

Cooking hardy greens removes bitter anti-nutrients and increases nutrient absorption of beta-carotene and vitamin C. Cooking the leaves whole retains more nutrients and saves time, since you don't have to chop vegetables before cooking or stir them while they cook. I cook several bunches at a time and we enjoy them for a 3 or 4 meals running.

For a cold salad, cool greens in ice water, drain, and dress in the kitchen or at the table. For a hot dish, follow instructions for Twice Cooked Greens (Page 312), or gently heat and serve greens as a bed for warm red sauce and meatballs.

FYI: One pound of raw greens will reduce to 3 or 4 cups.

Whole Boiled Greens with Onions & Spicy Peanut Sauce

Prep: 10 minutes ~ **Cooking:** 10 to 15 minutes ~ **Yield:** 6 servings
---

Ingredients & Directions

Vegetables:
3 quarts filtered water

1/2 teaspoon unrefined sea salt

1 1/2 to 2 pounds or 2 to 3 bunches kale **or** collards

Extra water to cool greens after cooking

1 tray ice cubes

1 medium red, yellow, or white onion, sliced into thin crescents or half-moons (1 1/2 cups)

Extra water to rinse and cool greens after cooking

Dressing, optional:
1 1/2 cups Spicy Peanut Sauce (Page 416)

1. Bring salted water to boil in 4-quart pot. Separate leaves and discard woody bottom portion of each stem and rotten or yellowed pieces. Swish leaves in cold water. Rinse and run your fingers down each leaf and stem to remove sand. Strip stems from leaves.

2. Boil onions uncovered for 1 minute. Remove with skimmer, plunge into ice water for 3 minutes, drain, and set aside. When water returns to boil, immerse greens. Cook *uncovered* over medium-high heat. After 3 or 4 minutes turn greens over and continue cooking, about 4 more minutes for small, tender leaves, 6 to 8 minutes for large leaves, or until tender and vibrant green. Cook large bunches in 2 batches.

3. Plunge greens in ice water to stop the cooking and the hold color. Drain and wring to remove excess water. Cook and shock any remaining greens. Discard cooking water.

4. Arrange leaves on cutting board. Roll up like newspaper and thinly slice into strips, then cut crosswise into bite-size pieces. Or, cut each leaf in half, stack, and cut into 1-inch squares and toss with parboiled onions.

5. Chill if desired and serve with dressing. Refrigerate leftovers in glass or stainless steel. Do not reheat. Use within 3 days

Nutrition

1 heaping cup vegetables:
93 calories
5 g protein
18 g carbohydrate
(3 g fiber)
2 g fat
190 mg calcium
90 mg sodium

1 heaping cup vegetables with 1/4 cup dressing:
189 calories
10 g protein
22 g carbohydrate
(4 g fiber)
9 g fat
199 g calcium
186–282 mg sodium

Dark leafy greens are an essential part of our daily diets. They add a brilliant color, cool flavor, vitamins, and minerals, including calcium to meals. We enjoy them for breakfast, lunch, or dinner, so I always cook enough for a few meals. To vary this chilled salad, I change the type of greens, colorful vegetables, dressing, or several of these.

Variations

* With or instead of onions, cut 2 carrots into thin rounds and/or 1/2 small head of cauliflower into florets. Parboil each for 1 to 3 minutes, chill, drain, and toss with greens or artfully arrange on platter.

* Replace Spicy Peanut Sauce with Macadamia-Dill Dressing, one of our tahini dressings, or 1/2 cup Very Easy Vinaigrette or Lemonette (see Index for recipes).

Twice-Cooked Greens

Prep: 20 minutes ~ **Cooking:** 5 to 10 minutes ~ **Yield:** 6 servings

Ingredients & Directions

2 tablespoons unrefined coconut oil, extra-virgin olive oil, clarified butter, **or** ghee

1 medium-large onion, cut into thin crescents or half-moons (about 1 1/2 cups)

2 small to medium garlic cloves, minced

1 1/2 teaspoons dried, rubbed sage, ground rosemary, cumin **or** dry mustard

1/4 teaspoon ground chipotlé **or** black pepper, or to taste

1/2 cup packed dulse **or** wild nori seaweed, sorted and cut into 1/4-inch pieces, optional

6 packed cups Whole Boiled Greens (Page 310) from 1 1/2 to 2 pounds untrimmed, uncooked kale, collards, mustard or turnip greens

1 tablespoon tamari soy sauce **or** 1/2 teaspoon finely ground, unrefined sea salt, optional

Nutrition

1 serving:
128 calories
5 g protein
17 g carbohydrate
(3 g fiber)
5 g fat
190 mg calcium
59 mg sodium

Parboiling whole leaves of kale, collards, turnip, or mustard greens reduces their strong bitter flavor. You can do this several hours ahead or the night before serving. Sautéing seals in the flavor and boosts absorption of vitamins, minerals, and antioxidants. I prepare enough for 2 or 3 meals and serve the leftovers at room temperature. They're fantastic for breakfast or in a pack lunch.

1. Heat oil in 10- to 13-inch heavy skillet, wok, or 4-quart casserole over medium-high heat. Add onion. Stir until tender and translucent, about 4 minutes. Add garlic, dried and crumbled herbs, and pepper; stir for 1 to 2 minutes.

2. Add dulse or wild nori, if desired, and chopped stems from greens. Stir and cook for 1 or 2 minutes. Add cut leaves and tamari or sea salt if desired. Stir for 2 to 4 minutes or until heated through. Transfer to serving bowl. Serve warm or cooled.

3. Refrigerate leftovers in glass or stainless steel container and use within 2 days.

Variations

* Add 1/2 pound quartered or thinly sliced fresh button, cremini, shiitake, or enoki mushrooms after onions have softened. Stir for 3 to 4 minutes, until tender, before adding herbs, spices, stems from greens, chopped leaves, and tamari.

* Add 1 to 1 1/2 cups thinly sliced daikon radish, carrot, celery, or bell pepper strips to onions. Cook until tender before adding herbs, spices, stems, and chopped leaves.

* Replace garlic and herbs with 1 rounded tablespoon peeled, finely minced or grated fresh gingerroot in step 2, or use combination of garlic and ginger. Add tamari if desired.

Sautéed Kale or Collards with Sunchokes & Sage

Prep: 15 minutes ~ **Cooking:** 15 minutes ~ **Yield:** 6 servings

Ingredients & Directions

1 large leek (about 2 cups trimmed and chopped)

2 cups cleaned, sunchokes, halved or quartered and cut in 1/2-inch slices

2 pounds or 3 bunches kale **or** collard greens (12 to 14 tightly packed cups after removing stems and discolored or yellowed leaves)

2 tablespoons extra-virgin olive oil **or** unrefined coconut oil, clarified butter **or** ghee

2 garlic cloves, minced or pressed

1 teaspoon dried, rubbed sage

1/2 teaspoon dry mustard **or** dried, crumbled thyme

1/2 teaspoon lemon pepper **or** 1/4 teaspoon ground chipotlé

1/2 packed cup dulse leaf **or** wild nori seaweed, sorted to remove small shells, stones, or mollusks, leaves cut into 1/2-inch pieces with kitchen shears, **or** 1/2 teaspoon unrefined sea salt **or** 1 tablespoon tamari soy sauce, optional

3/4 to 1 cup filtered water, Bone-Building Broth (Page 278 or 306), **or** preservative-free chicken broth

Nutrition

1 packed cup:
168 calories
6 g protein
26 g carbohydrate
(3 g fiber)
5 g fat
193 mg calcium
61 mg sodium

Sunchokes (also called Jerusalem artichokes) add an earthy flavor and nutty crunch to hardy greens. If you find the inulin in this starchy root difficult to digest, substitute thinly sliced celery and change the name of the recipe. You can also replace leeks with red onions, add sun-dried tomatoes, or use mustard or turnip greens.

1. Trim off root end of each leek and any hard or scruffy leaves. Make a long vertical slit down the length, 3/4 of the way through, starting 1 inch from root end. Hold leaves of leeks open and run water through each layer to remove sand. Slice into 1/2-inch rounds. Scrub sunchokes with a brush to remove sand. If knobby, break off knobs and rinse again. Trim sunchokes to remove pink, black, soft, or shriveled spots, then slice.

2. Wash and chop leeks. Separate leaves of kale or collard greens. Immerse in several changes of water or run water and your fingers down each leaf and stem to remove all traces of sand. Strip leaves from stems one at a time. Tear each leaf into bite-size pieces or stack and roll like a newspaper. Cut into 1-inch wide strips, then cut crosswise to make 1-inch squares. Discard stems.

3. Heat oil in a 12- to 13-inch saucepan or 4-quart Dutch oven over medium heat. Stir and cook leeks until tender, 3 to 4 minutes. Add sunchokes; stir for 2 minutes. Add garlic and sage, mustard or thyme, pepper or chipotlé, and optional ingredients desired: sea vegetable, sea salt, or tamari. Top with greens and 3/4 cup liquid.

4. Cover and bring to boil over medium-high heat. Reduce heat to medium-low and simmer, covered, until vibrant green and tender, 10 to 15 minutes. If pan becomes dry before greens are done, add 1/4 cup liquid. Serve warm or at room temperature.

5. Cover and refrigerate leftovers; use within 2 days or freeze.

Sautéed Kale or Collards with Onions & Garlic

Prep: 15 minutes ~ **Cooking:** 15 minutes ~ **Yield:** 6 servings

Ingredients & Directions

1 large onion, cubed or cut in crescents (about 2 cups)

2 pounds or 3 bunches kale **or** collard greens (12 to 14 tightly packed cups after removing stems and discolored or yellowed leaves)

2 tablespoons extra-virgin olive oil **or** unrefined coconut oil, clarified butter, **or** ghee

2 garlic cloves, minced or pressed

1/4 teaspoon ground black pepper **or** 1/2 teaspoon lemon pepper

1/2 packed cup dulse leaf **or** wild nori seaweed, sorted to remove small shells, stones, or mollusks, leaves cut into 1/2-inch pieces with kitchen shears, **or**
1/2 teaspoon unrefined sea salt **or** 1 tablespoon tamari soy sauce, optional

1 teaspoon ground cumin **or** dry mustard, optional

3/4 to 1 cup filtered water, Bone-Building Broth (Page 278 or 306), **or** preservative-free chicken broth

Hot sauce, optional

Nutrition

1 packed cup:

128 calories
5 g protein
17 g carbohydrate
    (3 g fiber)
5 g fat
185 mg calcium
59 mg sodium

1. Chop onions. Separate leaves of kale and collard greens and immerse in several changes of water. Run water and your fingers down each leaf and stem to remove all traces of sand.

2. Strip leaves from stems one at a time. Tear into bite-size pieces or stack and roll like newspaper. Cut into 1-inch wide strips, then cut crosswise to make 1-inch squares. Repeat. Discard stems.

3. Heat oil in a 13-inch skillet or 3- to 4-quart Dutch oven over medium heat. Add onions; stir and cook until tender, about 4 minutes; add garlic, pepper, and optional ingredients desired: cumin or mustard, and sea vegetable, sea salt, or tamari. Top with chopped or torn greens, then add 3/4 cup water or broth.

4. Cover and bring to boil. Reduce to medium or medium-low, and cook, covered, until vibrant green and tender, 10 to 15 minutes. If pan becomes dry before greens are done, add 1/4 cup liquid. Remove from heat and serve or chill for later. Use within 2 days or freeze.

~ Variations next page ~

Kale and collards are some of the most nutritious greens you can eat. They are packed with potassium, magnesium, calcium, iron, beta-carotene, vitamin K, vitamin C and fiber. Unlike spinach, they don't contain oxalic acid, so their calcium is more available. If I make this dish (or one like it) several times in a week, I vary the greens, herbs, spices, or added vegetables with each batch.

Note: Onions are essential. They sweeten and flavor the greens. Measuring ingredients helps ensure your food will be predictably delicious without having to taste as you cook or endlessly adjust the recipe.

FYI: The amount of greens called for may sound excessive, until you strip away the stems and see how the leaves shrink! I *always* make enough for 3 meals and rarely reheat them. They look and taste better cold or close to room temperature. Sometimes I make extra batches to freeze in pint-size containers. We just thaw them in the fridge or an ice chest when traveling.

Variations

Sautéed Kale or Collards with Onions & Garlic ~ continued

* Layer 1 1/2 cups thinly sliced celery over greens before covering.

* **Sautéed Kale or Collards with Onions & Broccoli:** In basic recipe, or any of the variations, replace a portion of kale or collards with peeled and thinly sliced broccoli stalks and bite-size florets. Cauliflower also works.

* **Sautéed Kale or Collards with Onions, Cumin & Chipotlé:** In step 3, add 1 teaspoon ground cumin, and 1 teaspoon dry mustard if desired. Replace black pepper or lemon pepper with 1/4 teaspoon ground chipotlé (smoked dried jalapeno pepper).

* **Sautéed Kale or Collards with Onions, Cumin & Thyme:** Omit mustard. Add 1/2 teaspoon ground cumin, 1 teaspoon dried, crumbled thyme, and 1/4 teaspoon black pepper **or** 1/2 teaspoon lemon pepper. (Combination of sage and thyme also works well.)

* **Sautéed Kale or Collards with Onions & Mustard:** Omit cumin and add 1 teaspoon dry mustard. Add 1/4 teaspoon black pepper **or** 1/4 ground chipotlé **or** 1/2 teaspoon lemon pepper.

* **Sautéed Kale or Collards with Onions & Sage:** Omit cumin and add 1 teaspoon dried, rubbed sage, 1/2 teaspoon dry mustard, and 1/4 teaspoon black pepper **or** 1/2 teaspoon lemon pepper.

* **Sautéed Kale or Collards with Ginger:** Omit cumin, black pepper, or lemon pepper. With garlic, add 2 teaspoons peeled, finely grated fresh ginger **or** 1 tablespoon bottled, or fresh ginger juice. Tamari soy sauce is also delicious with this combination.

* **Moroccan-Spiced Greens:** Include garlic in original recipe if desired, but omit cumin. Add 1 Tablespoon Moroccan Barbecue Spice Mix (Page 399), and 1/4 teaspoon ground black pepper **or** 1/2 teaspoon lemon pepper.

* **Sautéed Mustard/Turnip Greens with Onions:** Replace kale or collards with mustard or turnip greens in original recipe or any of the variations. These greens are fairly bitter. If you're new to eating hardy leafy greens, stick with the mild flavors of kale and collards or parboil mustard and turnip greens before sautéing. See Whole Boiled Greens (Page 310), and Twice-Cooked Greens (Page 312).

Sautéed Kale or Collards with Onions, Mushrooms & Garlic

Prep: 15 minutes ~ **Cooking:** 15 minutes ~ **Yield:** 6 servings
---

Ingredients & Directions

1 large onion, cubed or cut in crescents (about 1 1/2 cups)

2 cups cleaned, quartered button, cremini, or shiitake mushrooms, thinly sliced **or** 8 to 12 dried shiitake mushrooms, soaked, chopped, stems removed; water reserved for cooking)

2 pounds or 3 bunches kale **or** collards (12 to 14 tightly packed cups after removing stems and discolored or yellowed leaves)

2 tablespoons extra-virgin olive oil **or** unrefined coconut oil, clarified butter **or** ghee

2 garlic cloves, minced or pressed

1/2 packed cup dulse leaf **or** wild nori seaweed, sorted to remove small shells, stones, or mollusks, leaves cut into 1/2-inch pieces with kitchen shears, **or** 1/2 teaspoon unrefined sea salt **or** 1 tablespoon tamari soy sauce, optional

1/2 teaspoon lemon pepper **or** 1/4 teaspoon ground black pepper, optional

3/4 to 1 cup filtered water, Bone-Building Broth, (Page 278 or 306), **or** preservative-free chicken broth

Low sodium hot sauce, optional

Nutrition

1 packed cup:
136 calories
5 g protein
18 g carbohydrate
(3 g fiber)
5 g fat
187 mg calcium
60 mg sodium

Don and I have eaten cooked leafy greens once or twice a day for more than a decade. We love the flavor, color, and texture they add to meals. These greens are far more nutritious (and to us, more delicious) than spinach. We always make enough for 3 meals. Leftovers are great (unheated) for lunch, dinner, even breakfast, or frozen for future meals.

Since we eat greens so often, we like to vary the seasonings. If you make this recipe often enough, you will commit it to memory and eventually be able to follow it to a "T" without peeking. Measuring the ingredients helps ensure your food will be predictably delicious and allows you to avoid tasting as you cook or having to endlessly adjust the final result.

1. Chop onions. Separate leaves of kale or collard greens and immerse in several changes of water. Or run water and your fingers down each leaf and stem to remove all traces of sand.

2. Strip leaves from stems one at a time. Tear into bite-size pieces or stack and roll like newspaper. Cut into 1-inch wide strips, then cut crosswise to make 1-inch squares. Repeat. Discard stems.

3. Heat oil in a 13-inch skillet or 3- to 4-quart Dutch oven over medium heat. Add onions, stir, and cook until tender, about 4 minutes. Add mushrooms, garlic, and optional ginger, sea vegetable, sea salt, or tamari if desired. Top with chopped or torn greens, pepper, and 3/4 cup liquid.

4. Cover and bring to boil. Reduce to medium or medium-low, and simmer, covered, until vibrant green and tender, 10 to 15 minutes. If pan becomes dry before greens are done, add 1/4 cup liquid. Remove from heat and serve or chill for later. Use within 2 days or freeze.

~ Variations next page ~

Variations

Sautéed Kale or Collards with Onions, Mushrooms & Garlic ~ continued

* In step 3, layer 1 1/2 cups thinly sliced celery over greens before covering.

* **Sautéed Kale or Collards with Onions, Mushrooms & Zucchini:** In basic recipe or any of the seasoning variations that follow, replace part of the kale or collards with thinly sliced zucchini. Leftovers are delicious tossed with Better Barbecue Sauce (Page 401).

* **Sautéed Kale or Collards with Onions, Mushrooms, Cumin & Chipotlé:** Add 1 teaspoon ground cumin, 1 teaspoon dry mustard, if desired, and replace black pepper **or** lemon pepper with 1/4 teaspoon ground chipotlé (smoked dried jalapeno pepper).

* **Sautéed Kale or Collards with Onions, Mushrooms, Cumin & Thyme:** Add 1/2 teaspoon ground cumin, 1/2 teaspoon dried, crumbled thyme, and 1/4 teaspoon black pepper **or** 1/2 teaspoon lemon pepper. (Combination of sage and thyme also works well.)

* **Sautéed Kale or Collards with Onions, Mushrooms & Sage:** In step 3, add 1 teaspoon dried, rubbed sage, 1/2 teaspoon dry mustard, and 1/4 teaspoon black pepper, 1/2 teaspoon lemon pepper, **or** 1/4 teaspoon ground chipotlé.

* **Sautéed Kale or Collards with Onions, Mushrooms & Mustard:** Add 1 teaspoon dry mustard and 1/4 teaspoon black pepper or ground chipotlé **or** 1/2 teaspoon lemon pepper.

* **Sautéed Kale or Collards with Onions, Mushrooms, Basil & Garlic:** Add 1 teaspoon dried, crumbled basil, and 1/4 teaspoon black pepper **or** 1/2 teaspoon lemon pepper.

* **Sautéed Kale or Collards with Onions, Mushrooms & Herbs de Provençe:** With garlic, add 2 to 3 teaspoons dried, powdered Herbs de Provençe.

* **Sautéed Kale or Collards with Onions, Mushrooms & Ginger:** Omit black pepper or lemon pepper. With garlic, add 2 teaspoons peeled, finely grated fresh gingerroot **or** 1 tablespoon bottled, or fresh ginger juice. Tamari soy sauce is also delicious with this combination.

* **Moroccan-Spiced Greens with Mushrooms:** Include garlic in original recipe if desired. Add 1 Tablespoon Moroccan Barbecue Spice Mix (Page 399), and 1/4 teaspoon ground black pepper **or** 1/2 teaspoon lemon pepper.

* **Sautéed Mustard or Turnip Greens with Onions & Mushrooms:** Replace kale or collards with mustard or turnip greens in original recipe or any of the variations. These greens are fairly bitter. If you're new to eating hardy leafy greens, stick with the mild flavors of kale and collards or parboil mustard and turnip greens before sautéing. See Whole Boiled Greens (Page 310), and Twice-Cooked Greens (Page 312).

Sautéed Kale or Collards with Onions, Mushrooms & Sun-Dried Tomatoes

Prep: 15 minutes ~ **Cooking:** 15 minutes ~ **Yield:** 6 servings

Ingredients & Directions

12 sun-dried tomato halves, quartered with kitchen shears (about 1/2 cup)

1 large onion, cut in crescents (about 1 1/2 cups) **or** 2 medium leeks, trimmed, slit in half length-wise, washed exceedingly well to remove sand, and cut into 1-inch lengths (2 to 3 cups)

2 to 3 cups cleaned, quartered button, cremini, **or** shiitake mushrooms, thinly sliced

2 pounds or 3 bunches kale **or** collard greens (12 to 14 tightly packed cups after removing stems and discolored or yellowed leaves)

2 tablespoons extra-virgin olive oil **or** unrefined coconut oil, clarified butter **or** ghee

2 to 3 garlic cloves, minced or pressed

1/2 packed cup dulse leaf **or** wild nori seaweed, sorted to remove small shells, stones, or mollusks, leaves cut into 1/2-inch pieces with kitchen shears, **or** 1/2 teaspoon unrefined sea salt **or** 1 tablespoon tamari soy sauce, optional

2 teaspoons dried, powdered rosemary, sage, thyme, basil **or** Herbes de Provençe

1/2 teaspoon lemon pepper **or** 1/4 teaspoon black pepper

3/4 cup water used to soak tomatoes, filtered water, Bone-Building Broth (Page 278 or 306), preservative-free chicken broth **or** combination

Nutrition

1 packed cup:
150 calories
6 g protein
21 g carbohydrate
(4 g fiber)
5 g fat
192 mg calcium
65 mg sodium

Warm, chilled, or close to room temperature, these greens are delicious with eggs, fish, poultry, or meat, and a root, tuber, squash, or fruit dish. Sun-dried tomatoes add a brilliant color and rich flavor. Buy them packed in oil (most convenient) or dehydrated in packages or bulk bins. After you've used oil-packed tomatoes, don't throw out the oil; it's sublime for dressing green salads.

1. Chop sun-dried tomatoes with knife or shears. Add warm water to barely cover and soak. Wash and chop onion or leeks and set aside. Wash or wipe mushrooms clean. Remove last 1/4 inch of each stem and thinly slice mushrooms.

2. Separate leaves and immerse in several changes of water. Run water and your fingers down each leaf and stem to remove traces of sand.

3. Strip leaves of kale or collard greens from stems one at a time. Tear into bite-size pieces or stack and roll like newspaper. Cut into 1-inch wide strips, then cut crosswise to make 1-inch squares. Repeat. Discard stems.

~ Directions continued & Variations next page ~

Directions

4. Heat oil in a 13-inch skillet or 3- to 4-quart Dutch oven over medium heat. Add onions or leeks. Stir and cook until tender, about 4 minutes. Add mushrooms, garlic, rehydrated tomatoes, and optional sea vegetable, sea salt or tamari if desired. Top with greens, herbs, spices, and 3/4 cup liquid.

5. Cover and bring to boil. Reduce heat to medium or medium-low, and simmer, covered, until vibrant green and tender, about 10 to 15 minutes. If pan becomes dry before greens are done, add 1/4 cup liquid. Remove from heat and serve or chill for later. Use within 2 days or freeze.

Variations

* Replace kale or collards with mustard greens **or** use 1 pound kale, collard, or mustard greens with 1 pound of cauliflower florets or sliced zucchini.

Sautéed Kale or Collards w/ Mushrooms, Onions, & Sun-Dried Tomatoes ~ cont.

Southern-Style Greens

Prep: 20 minutes ~ **Cooking:** 15 minutes ~ **Yield:** 6 servings

Ingredients & Directions

1 cup tightly packed dulse sea vegetable leaf (not dulse granules or flakes!)

1 teaspoon dry mustard

1/3 to 1/2 teaspoon ground chipotlé

1 teaspoon Wright's Liquid Hickory Smoke Seasoning

3/4 cup filtered water, or slightly more as needed

1 medium to large onion, cut in thin half-moons (about 2 cups)

2 pounds or 3 bunches kale **or** collard greens (12 to 14 tightly packed cups after removing stems and discolored or yellowed leaves)

2 tablespoons extra-virgin olive oil **or** unrefined coconut oil, clarified butter **or** ghee

2 small garlic cloves, minced or pressed

1/2 to 3/4 cup filtered water, Bone-Building Broth (Page 278 or 306), **or** preservative-free chicken broth **or** homemade stock

Nutrition

1 packed cup:
173 calories
8 g protein
25 g carbohydrate
(5 g fiber)
5 g fat
284 mg calcium
149 mg sodium

Don devised this recipe during our vegan years to create a rich, smoky flavor without bacon. The secret is to use dulse (a purple-colored, slightly salty sea vegetable), chipotlé (smoked dried jalapeno pepper), natural liquid hickory smoke seasoning, and dry mustard. I serve this with omelets or soft-boiled eggs, leftover meat, and fruit for breakfast, or with chicken, turkey, or salmon, and sweet potatoes for lunch or dinner. Warm or close to room temperature, leftovers are always appreciated in our house.

1. Sort dulse to remove small stones and shells. Slice into 1/2-inch pieces with kitchen shears. Add to bowl with mustard, chipotlé, liquid smoke, and 3/4 cup water and set aside.

2. Wash and chop onions. Separate leaves of kale or collard greens. Immerse in several changes of water. Run water and your fingers down each leaf and stem to remove all traces of sand.

3. Strip leaves from stems one at a time. Tear each leaf into bite-size pieces or stack and roll like newspaper. Cut into 1-inch wide strips, then cut crosswise to make 1-inch squares. Discard stems.

4. Heat oil in 12- to 13-inch skillet or 3- to 4-quart Dutch oven over medium heat. Add onions. Stir and cook until tender, about 4 minutes. Add garlic and stir; add greens, dulse mixture, and 1/2 cup additional water, broth, or stock. Cover and bring to boil over medium-high heat. Reduce to medium or medium-low, and simmer, covered, until vibrant green and tender, 10 to 15 minutes. If pan becomes dry before greens are done, add 1/4 cup additional liquid.

5. Remove lid, stir, and serve. Refrigerate leftovers and use within 2 days, or freeze.

Oil-Free Sautéed Chinese Greens with Onions, Mushrooms & Celery

Prep: 15 minutes ~ **Cooking:** 10 to 12 minutes ~ **Yield:** 6 servings

Ingredients & Directions

2 pounds Chinese greens, about 12 packed cups, cut into 1-inch pieces (see notes below for chopping): bok choy, baby bok choy, tat soi, choy sum, or Chinese cabbage

1 medium red, white or yellow onion, cut into 1-inch cubes or thin crescents (1 to 1 1/2 cups)

1 1/2 cups fresh shiitake, button, or cremini mushrooms, washed, bottom 1/4 inch of stems removed, mushrooms cut into thin slices

1 heaping cup thinly sliced celery ribs

1 carrot, halved, and thinly sliced, optional

2 to 3 garlic cloves, minced

1 1/2 teaspoons peeled and grated gingerroot **or** 1 teaspoon ground cumin or dry mustard

1/4 teaspoon ground red **or** black pepper

1/2 teaspoon unrefined sea salt **or** 1 tablespoon tamari soy sauce, optional

1 cup filtered water, Bone-Building Broth (Page 278 or 306), **or** preservative-free broth; more as needed

1 tablespoon arrowroot dissolved in 3 tablespoons water **or** cool or cold stock or broth

4 to 6 teaspoons lemon-flavored cod liver oil **or** 1/4 cup Toasted Sesame Seeds (Page 405) for garnish, optional

Nutrition	**1 packed cup:**
	78 calories
	3 g protein
	16 g carbohydrate
	(4 g fiber)
	330 mg calcium
	51 mg sodium

1. Separate leaves of Chinese greens. Rinse thoroughly to remove all traces of sand. Discard yellowed or soggy leaves. For large greens, make a "V" slice to cut green leafy part away from thick white portion. Chop white portion into 1-inch wide strips, then crosswise to make 1-inch squares; transfer to a bowl. Cut green leafy portion into 1-inch squares; place in a separate bowl. If using other greens, cut leaves into 8-inch squares after discarding stems. Chop and measure remaining ingredients into separate bowls.

2. Heat 1/4 cup broth and onions in 12-inch skillet over medium-high heat. Add garlic, ginger, and pepper and stir to cook away liquid. Add mushrooms and 1/4 cup additional stock or broth. Stir and cook for 1 to 2 minutes. Add carrot if desired, then celery. If most of the liquid has cooked away, add 1/4 cup additional stock.

3. Add sea salt or tamari if desired, stir, add greens and 1/4 to 1/2 cup additional stock. Continue to stir and cook until almost tender. Add dissolved arrowroot, simmer and stir to thicken.

4. Remove from heat, portion onto plates. Garnish if desired and serve.

Variations

* If using broccoli, kale, collards, or mustard greens, cover, reduce heat, and cook until almost tender and vibrant green, about 6 to 9 minutes, then remove lid, stir, and cook away liquid, with or without arrowroot.

Sometimes I cook greens in broth or stock without oil, then we top them with poached or fried eggs, some other rich side dish, or lemon-flavored cod liver oil at the table. (It tastes better than it sounds!) Asian markets and farmers' markets are the best places to find fresh Chinese greens. Supermarkets also sell them, just make sure they look "alive," not wilted or yellowed.

Note: Don't buy already toasted sesame seeds; they'll be rancid. Buy raw sesame seeds. Store them in the fridge or freezer. Dry toast them and keep refrigerated.

Braised Baby Bok Choy with Ginger

Prep: 5 minutes ~ **Cooking:** 6 to 8 minutes ~ **Yield:** 4 servings

Ingredients & Directions

2 pounds baby bok choy or Shanghai bok choy (weigh, don't guess), 3 inches in length

1 1/2 tablespoons finely grated fresh ginger (use a microplane or smallest hole of box grater)

1 1/3 tablespoons unrefined coconut oil **or** extra-virgin olive oil

1 tablespoon tamari soy sauce

1-2 tablespoons filtered water, broth, **or** stock (optional)

Nutrition

1 serving (about 1 cup):
82 calories
4 g protein
7 g carbohydrate
(3 g fiber)
5 g fat
219 mg calcium
350 mg sodium

1. Cut 1/2 inch off bottom of each bunch of greens and separate leaves. Swish leaves in large bowl of water and transfer to colander. Run your finger and water down each leaf to remove all traces of sand. Drain but do not pat dry (moisture that clings to leaves is essential for steaming). Trim away shaggy or discolored leaves. Grate ginger; measure tamari and set aside.

2. Heat oil in 12- to 13-inch skillet or large wok over high heat until hot but not smoking. Add one-sixth of greens (about 1 heaping handful) at a time, stirring and turning in oil for about 30 seconds before adding another handful. When all greens are in skillet, sprinkle with ginger, stir, add tamari and 1 tablespoon water if desired. Cover, and steam for 3 to 4 minutes, until almost tender. Remove lid and cook away liquid.

3. Serve immediately. Cover and refrigerate leftovers. Use within 2 days. Do not reheat.

Variations

* **Braised Baby Bok Choy with Garlic:** Replace ginger with 2 to 3 cloves minced garlic.

* **Braised Bok Choy with Garlic or Ginger:** Replace baby bok choy with mature bok choy or choy sum. Cut stems into 1-inch pieces and leaves crosswise into 1-inch wide strips, about 12 cups total. Sauté stems for 3 minutes; add leaves, ginger or garlic, and tamari. Cover, and cook for 5 to 6 minutes, stirring periodically.

Baby bok choy is delicious and easy to prepare. It requires no chopping, cooks quickly, and goes well with everything. We enjoy it with eggs for breakfast, or with fish, fowl, or meat for lunch or dinner. Like mature bok choy, it's rich in calcium, iron, magnesium, beta-carotene, folic acid, potassium, and vitamin C. Leftovers are great served at room temperature.

Note: Look for bright green unwilted baby bok choy or Shanghai bok choy in Asian markets, large natural foods markets, and farmers' markets. These greens are often sold in 1 1/2 pound bags in Asian markets; break into another package as needed to have 2 pounds for the recipe. This dish does not freeze well.

Better Brussels Sprouts

Prep: 20 minutes ~ **Cooking:** 15 to 20 minutes ~ **Yield:** 6 cups

Ingredients & Directions

1 medium-large onion, cubed or cut into thin crescents (about 1 1/2 cups)

2 pounds Brussels sprouts (8 heaping cups halved or quartered)

2 tablespoons unrefined coconut oil, extra-virgin olive oil, clarified butter, **or** ghee

1/2 teaspoon ground chipotlé **or** black pepper

1/2 teaspoon dry mustard, ground cumin, **or** rubbed sage

2 garlic cloves, minced

1/2 packed cup dulse leaf **or** wild nori seaweed, sorted to remove small shells, stones, or mollusks, then cut into 1/2-inch pieces with kitchen shears **or** 1/2 teaspoon unrefined sea salt **or** 1 tablespoon tamari soy sauce, optional

1/2 to 1 cup filtered water, Bone-Building Broth (Page 278 or 306), **or** preservative-free chicken broth

Hot sauce **or** lemon pepper, added to taste, optional

Nutrition

1 packed cup:
118 calories
5 g protein
14 g carbohydrate
(5 g fiber)
5 g fat
55 mg calcium
30 mg sodium

I hated Brussels sprouts until I was 21. Then one of my early macrobiotic cooking teachers, Michelle Cowmeadow of Cornwall, England, showed me how to prepare them properly...and forever changed my tastes! Now, I buy Brussels sprouts 2 pounds at a time and enjoy them for lunch, dinner, and sometimes breakfast!

1. Rinse Brussels sprouts thoroughly and drain. One by one, trim 1/4 inch off the bottom of each stem; discard discolored leaves. Halve small sprouts; quarter large ones. Collect sprouts and loose leaves (they're delicious) in a large bowl or measuring container.

2. Heat oil in 13-inch skillet or heavy 3- to 4-quart pot over medium heat. Add onions; stir, and cook until tender, about 4 minutes. Add pepper or chipotlé, mustard, cumin or sage, garlic, and sea vegetable, sea salt or tamari, if desired. Add sprouts and 1/2 cup water or broth (increase to 3/4 cup if using sea vegetable). Stir, cover, and bring to boil over medium heat.

3. Reduce to medium-low and cook until tender, 12 to 15 minutes, stirring twice, top to bottom. If pan becomes dry before sprouts are tender, add additional 1/4 cup liquid. If much liquid remains, remove lid and simmer to reduce. Remove from heat and serve, adding hot sauce or lemon pepper as desired. Refrigerate leftovers and use within 2 days or freeze.

Variations

* Replace herbs and spices above with Herbes de Provençe **or** an Italian or Greek blend.

* After adding onions, add 2 cups sliced fresh button, cremini, or shiitake mushrooms and/or 1/2 cup thinly sliced sun-dried tomatoes. If you have not rehydrated the tomatoes, add 1/4 to 1/2 cup additional liquid to pan, as needed to moisten.

Secrets for Success:

1) Seek out smaller sprouts.

2) Reject those with yellowing, wilted, or loosely packed heads.

3) If possible, buy sprouts at a farmers' market, on the "tree" with the tender and tasty top leaves still attached. Don't toss those leaves; they're delicious and extraordinarily nutritious.

4) Halve or quarter the sprouts before cooking to reduce gas buildup and bitterness.

5) Cook Brussels sprouts until they're just fork tender.

Better Brussels Sprouts with Sunchokes & Sage

Prep: 20 minutes ~ **Cooking:** 15 to 20 minutes ~ **Yield:** 6 servings

Ingredients & Directions

2 pounds Brussels sprouts (about 8 heaping cups, halved or quartered)

1 medium-large onion, cubed or cut into thin crescents (about 1 1/2 cups)

1 1/2 cups thoroughly washed, halved or quartered sunchokes, cut into 1/2-inch thick slices

2 garlic cloves, minced

2 tablespoons unrefined coconut oil, extra-virgin olive oil, clarified butter, **or** ghee

1 teaspoon lemon pepper **or** 1/2 teaspoon pepper

1/2 teaspoon ground cumin

1/2 teaspoon dried, rubbed sage

1/2 packed cup dulse seaweed (dulse leaf), cut into 1/2-inch pieces with shears **or** 1 tablespoon tamari soy sauce **or** 1/2 teaspoon unrefined sea salt, optional

3/4 to 1 cup filtered water, Bone-Building Broth (Page 278 or 306), **or** preservative-free chicken broth **or** homemade stock

Nutrition

1 heaping cup:
144 calories
6 g protein
20 g carbohydrate
(5 g fiber)
5 g fat
61 mg calcium
32 mg sodium

Jerusalem artichokes (also called sunchokes), have nothing to do with Jerusalem and bear no resemblance to globe artichokes! These knobby tubers are members of the sunflower family. Served raw or lightly stir-fried, they're crunchy and reminiscent of water chestnuts. Cooked tender, they add an earthy potato-like flavor and texture to sautés, soups, and stews. Unlike other tubers, they should be refrigerated as soon as you bring them home.

1. Wash Brussels sprouts thoroughly, and drain. One by one, trim 1/4 inch from the bottom of each stem, and remove discolored leaves. Cut each sprout in half lengthwise; quarter large sprouts. Collect sprouts and any loose leaves in a large bowl or measuring container.

2. Chop onions, sunchokes, and garlic.

3. Heat oil in 13-inch skillet or heavy 3-quart pot over medium heat. Add onion; stir and cook until tender, 4 to 5 minutes. Add garlic, pepper or lemon pepper, mustard or cumin, and dulse, sea salt, or tamari if desired. Stir and add Brussels sprouts and 1/2 cup water, stock, or broth (increase to 3/4 cup if using sea vegetable).

4. Cover and bring to boil over medium heat; reduce to medium-low, and cook until fork tender, about 15 minutes, stirring twice, top to bottom. If pan becomes dry before sprouts are tender, add an additional 1/4 cup liquid. If much liquid remains, remove lid and simmer to reduce.

5. Remove from heat and serve. Refrigerate leftovers. Use within 2 days or freeze.

Variations

* **Sautéed Broccoli with Sunchokes:** Replace Brussels sprouts with broccoli florets and peeled, thinly sliced stalks. Reduce cooking time to 10 minutes.

Note: Wash and scrub sunchokes impeccably to remove all traces of sand from the outer surface and crevices. If knobby, break off the knobs and rinse again. Do not peel, and wait to slice until just before cooking because they discolor quickly. Cut away any pink, black, or discolored stubbles.

Creamy Broccoli-Avocado Soup

Prep: 20 minutes ~ **Cooking:** 30 minutes ~ **Yield:** 6 servings

Ingredients & Directions

4 cups homemade chicken stock, Bone Building Broth (Page 278) **or** preservative-free chicken or vegetable broth, divided

1 medium onion (about 1 cup), thinly sliced or diced

2 to 3 small cloves finely chopped garlic

1/2 teaspoon unrefined sea salt, or to taste

1/4 to 1/2 teaspoon ground chipotlé (smoked dried Jalapeno pepper), start with less.

1/2 teaspoon ground cumin, optional

3 packed cups broccoli, stalks peeled and thinly sliced, tops cut into florets, tough part discarded

2 large ripe avocados, seeded, peeled, and chopped

1/4 cup minced scallions, parsley or cilantro leaves, **or** red or yellow bell pepper for garnish

Hot sauce **or** ground black pepper **or** lemon pepper, optional

Nutrition

1 cup:
149 calories
4 g protein
11 g carbohydrate
(6 g fiber)
10 g fat
37 mg calcium
174 mg sodium

1. Combine 2 cups broth or stock with onion, garlic, sea salt, and chipotlé, in a 2-quart pot. Add cumin if desired. Cover and bring to boil over medium heat; reduce heat to low and simmer 15 minutes.

2. Add remaining broth and broccoli. Bring to boil, cover, reduce heat, and simmer 15 minutes until vegetables are tender. Do not boil or overcook broccoli.

3. In blender, Vita-Mix, or food processor, purée vegetables, liquid, and avocado in batches, holding top down with a towel and starting on low to avoid splattering.

4. Return soup to pot and warm gently. Ladle into bowls, garnish, and serve. Add hot sauce or black pepper to individual portions if desired. May also be served chilled.

5. Refrigerate and use within 3 days.

Variations

* Substitute zucchini, summer squash, or asparagus for broccoli and change the name of the recipe. Serve with a green salad, cooked greens or cauliflower.

* For milder flavor, omit chipotlé. Add 1/2 teaspoon ground black pepper **or** lemon pepper and 1/4 teaspoon ground nutmeg **or** 1 teaspoon dried or 1 tablespoon fresh dill weed. Add hot sauce to servings if desired.

Avocado adds a rich taste and creamy texture to green vegetable soups without milk or cream. I got the idea from a "California Avocado Zucchini Soup" recipe created by the California Avocado Commission. I replaced zucchini with broccoli, increased the volume of vegetables and servings, and changed the seasonings. Fish, poultry, or meat and a bright yellow, orange, or red vegetable or fruit dish complete the meal. A green salad is optional.

Steamed Broccoli

Prep: 15 minutes ~ **Cooking:** 4 to 8 minutes ~ **Yield:** 4 to 6 servings

Ingredients & Directions

2 to 4 cups filtered water

1 large or 2 medium bunches broccoli, cut into florets, stems peeled and thinly sliced, woody bottoms of stems discarded (about 2-pounds or 6 to 7 packed cups, trimmed)

1/2 bunch small red radishes, cut into thin rounds or 1 cup daikon radish, cut into thin half-moons

6 scallions, trimmed, white part and part of green stems cut into 1-inch lengths

Nutrition

1 serving:
58 calories
5 g protein
10 g carbohydrate
(5 g fiber)
86 mg calcium
44 mg sodium

1. Pour 1 inch of water into 2 1/2- to 3-quart saucepan. Add metal folding accordion steamer. Water should rise to just below bottom of steamer. Alternatively, pour 2 inches of water into a stockpot. Add pasta insert, place bamboo steamer tray inside wok, or rest bamboo tray on rim of pot. Bamboo tray's diameter must match diameter of the pot it rests on.

2. Cover and bring to boil over medium-high heat. Add sliced broccoli stems. Cover, cook 2 to 3 minutes. Add florets, radish slices, and scallions. Cover, cook 2 to 5 more minutes, until broccoli is bright green and crisp-tender.

3. Remove lid with mitts and promptly transfer vegetables to serving bowl to avoid overcooking. Serve plain or with dressing. Refrigerate leftovers and serve without reheating. Use within 2 days.

Variations

* **Steamed Broccoli & Cauliflower:** Use a 50:50 ratio. Top with shredded purple cabbage or thinly sliced red onion, red radishes, or carrots for more color.

* **Steamed Broccoli & Yellow Wax Beans:** Trim and cut 3/4 pound of yellow wax beans into 1-inch slices. Sprinkle over 3/4 pound of broccoli florets. Add a handful of red onion slices (about 1/2 cup) if you like. Delicious with butter or any tahini dressing.

* **Steamed Cauliflower & Green Beans:** Trim and chop 1/2 pound of green beans into 1-inch slices. Sprinkle over 1 pound of chopped cauliflower florets in place of broccoli. Add a handful (about 1/2 cup) of red onion slices if you like. Cook until crisp-tender. Basil & Garlic Mayonnaise (Page 424) makes a great coating. Tahini dressings (see Index for recipes) also work well.

* **Steamed Cauliflower & Asparagus:** Use 1 pound each of cauliflower and asparagus, cut into 1-inch lengths. Discard woody bottom part of asparagus spears. Add red onion slices if desired. Cook until crisp-tender. Delicious with butter, Lemonette, Vinaigrette, or Shallot & Chive Mayonnaise (see Index for recipes).

Bite-size young broccoli buds (broccolini) are sweet, tender, and require almost no trimming. Look for them or regular broccoli at farmers' markets. Avoid broccoli wrapped in cellophane because plastic traps moisture and makes a bitter-tasting gas build up in the vegetables. I always use the green leaves attached to the stalks; they're rich in calcium and delicious.

I enjoy broccoli served plain or topped with a creamy tahini dressing, Spicy Peanut Sauce, a drizzle of lemon-flavored cod liver oil, Practically Paleo Pesto, homemade Aioli, or some other flavored mayonnaise (see Index for recipes). The same dressings work equally well if you substitute other vegetables for broccoli.

~ Variations continued next page ~

Variations

Steamed Broccoli ~ continued

* **Steamed Cauliflower & Snow Peas:** Use cauliflower and snow peas (about 1 1/2 pounds combined) in place of broccoli. Add thinly sliced red radishes, purple cabbage, celery, carrot rounds, or several of these (about 1 cupful) if your side dishes aren't very colorful. Cook until crisp-tender. This is delicious with Spicy Peanut Sauce (Page 416) **or** Very Easy Vinaigrette (Page 422).

* **Steamed Green Beans & Red Onions:** Trim 1 pound of green beans and cut into 1-inch lengths. Cut 1 medium red onion into thin crescents or half-moons. Layer in steamer basket and cook until crisp tender, about 3 to 5 minutes. Great condiments for this include Practically Paleo Pesto, Sesame-Garlic Sauce, Basil & Garlic Mayonnaise, or Aioli (see Index for recipes). If I'm not including a green salad in a meal with this, I usually serve it on a bed of shredded lettuce or radicchio.

* **Steamed Baby Turnips with Tops:** Use 1 bunch of baby turnips with tops, roots cut into thin rounds, greens washed thoroughly, and thinly sliced, and stems discarded. Steam root pieces for 2 to 4 minutes. Add sliced tops and cook 6 to 8 more minutes until tender. This is delicious dabbed with butter **or** coconut oil (when served hot) or served cold with a tahini dressing or flavored mayonnaise at the table (see Index for recipes).

* **Steamed Baby Bok Choy:** Start with 1 to 1 1/2 pounds of baby bok choy. Separate leaves from core. Rinse well to remove all traces of sand. Cook leaves whole or cut into 1-inch long pieces. Trim rough portions away from stem, then slice. Add other vegetables if desired (onions, celery, mushrooms, carrots, radish slices) and steam 4 to 6 minutes until fork tender.

Simmered Broccoli with Herbs

Prep: 15 minutes ~ **Cooking:** 6 to 8 minutes ~ **Yield:** 4 servings

Ingredients & Directions

1/4 inch filtered water, salt-free poultry stock, **or** diluted Bone-Building Broth (Page 278 or 306)

1/4 teaspoon ground black pepper **or** chipotlé (smoked, dried jalapeno)

1/2 teaspoon dry mustard **or** ground sumac

1/2 teaspoon dried, crumbled oregano, basil or ground cumin

1/4 to 1/2 teaspoon finely ground, unrefined sea salt **or** 1 to 2 teaspoons tamari, optional

1/2 cup onion, cubed or cut into thin crescents

6 heaping cups broccoli, cut into florets, stalks peeled, and thinly sliced stems, woody part discarded (1 pound)

> **Nutrition**
> **1 cup:**
> 57 calories
> 5 g protein
> 9 g carbohydrate
> (5 g fiber)
> 70 mg calcium
> 37 mg sodium

1. Add ingredients to 10-inch skillet in the order listed. Use a 12- to 13-inch skillet for a double batch. Cover and bring to boil over medium-high heat. Reduce heat to medium and steam for 5 to 6 minutes, until barely tender but still vibrant green and firm. Liquid should be absorbed.

2. Promptly remove lid and transfer vegetables to a bowl or individual plates. If much liquid remains, simmer to reduce, and spoon over vegetables.

3. Cover and refrigerate leftovers. Serve cold or close to room temperature; use within 2 days.

Variations

* Replace mustard/sumac and herbs with 1 1/2 teaspoons peeled, minced fresh ginger.

* **Simmered Broccoli & Mushrooms:** Add 1 cup thinly sliced shiitake, button or cremini mushrooms with onions.

* **Simmered Broccoli & Bell Peppers:** Add 1 cup sliced or diced red, orange, or gold bell pepper to broccoli. Onions are optional.

* **Simmered Broccoli & Cauliflower:** Replace half the broccoli with cauliflower cut into florets and core thinly sliced. Optional: Add 1 cup diced red, yellow, or orange bell pepper.

* **Simmered Cauliflower & Green Beans:** Use cauliflower and green beans. Add 1 handful of thinly sliced carrot as desired.

In contrast to steaming—where the vegetables are placed above liquid—these vegetables are arranged in the bottom of a saucepan with seasonings and a minimum of liquid. At the end, the liquid should be completely absorbed.
I serve the vegetables as is, or drizzle with flax oil, lemon-flavored cod liver oil, or a sprinkle of lightly toasted, coarsely chopped nuts.

FYI: This method works for Chinese broccoli, asparagus, cauliflower, cabbage, even carrots.

Mustard-Glazed Broccoli

Prep: 15 minutes ~ **Cooking:** 8 minutes ~ **Yield:** 4 servings

Ingredients & Directions

1/4 cup filtered water, salt-free chicken stock or broth **or** white wine as needed to just cover bottom of pot or wok 1/4 inch

1 1/2 to 2 teaspoons tamari soy sauce **or** 1/4 to 1/3 teaspoon unrefined sea salt

2 cloves minced garlic, optional

4 scallions, cut into 1-inch logs **or** 2/3 cup onion, thinly sliced in half-moons or rings

5 cups chopped broccoli florets and peeled, thinly sliced stalks or core

1/2 to 2/3 cup cold water, homemade stock, preservative-free chicken broth **or** Bone-Building Broth (Page 278 or 306)

1/2 teaspoon arrowroot powder

1 tablespoon Dijon or white mustard **or** 2/3 teaspoon dry mustard

Nutrition

1 serving:
56 calories
4 g protein
10 g carbohydrate
(5 g fiber)
71 mg calcium
190 mg sodium

For a rich taste without oil, try this technique. Thickening the pan juices with arrowroot creates a flavorful sauce. You can use this procedure as the foundation for a pseudo stir-fry. If you aren't crazy about broccoli, substitute cauliflower.

1. Add stock, water, or wine to skillet or wok to barely cover bottom. Add tamari or sea salt, and garlic if desired. Warm over medium-high heat; stir; bring to low boil. Add broccoli stems, then florets. Stir, cover, and simmer over medium heat for about 3 to 4 minutes, until almost tender.

2. In separate saucepan, combine water or stock, arrowroot, and mustard. Stir to dissolve. Simmer over medium heat until thick and clear. Pour sauce over crisp-tender vegetables. Stir to thicken and coat broccoli. Remove from heat, transfer to medium-size bowl or plates, and serve.

3. Refrigerate leftovers and use within 24 hours.

Variations

* Add 1 cup thinly sliced button, cremini, or shiitake mushrooms after or instead of onions.

* Replace onion or 1 cup of broccoli with 1 thinly sliced carrot or celery stalk, or 5 thinly sliced small red radishes.

* **Glazed Broccoli Almondine:** Sprinkle broccoli with 3 tablespoons of lightly toasted, chopped almonds when pouring sauce on vegetables.

Parboiled Broccoli

Prep: 15 minutes ~ **Cooking:** 6 to 8 minutes ~ **Yield:** 8 servings
---

Ingredients & Directions

1 1/2 quarts filtered water (6 cups)

1/2 teaspoon unrefined sea salt

2 large bunches broccoli (about 4 pounds or 12 to 14 cups trimmed and chopped)

Additional filtered water and ice for chilling

1. Bring salted water to boil in covered 2-quart pot over medium-high heat. Add pasta insert submerged in at least 3 inches of water, or have a large skimmer handy.

2. Immerse broccoli in a bowl of water. Swish to remove all traces of sand. Rinse well. Trim off but save and cook green leaves. They're rich in calcium! Discard bottom inch from each broccoli stalk (it's usually tough). Chop off stalks 1 to 2 inches below florets and remove skin with a vegetable peeler. Thinly slice stems. Cut tops into bite-size florets.

3. Plunge half the broccoli in boiling water. Cook uncovered—1 to 2 minutes for crisp, 2 to 3 minutes for crisp-tender. Quickly remove with skimmer or pasta insert, plunge in ice water, and chill 3 minutes to stop the cooking and hold the color. Drain and squeeze to remove water. Repeat with remaining broccoli.

4. Serve plain or dressed, or refrigerate in a covered bowl or wide-mouth jar. Use within 2 days.

Nutrition

1 packed cup:
48 calories
4 g protein
8 g carbohydrate
(4 g fiber)
72 mg calcium
50 mg sodium

Variations

* Parboil half the broccoli, plunge in ice water; drain, and refrigerate for later or tomorrow. Eight minutes before serving, parboil remaining broccoli, drain, and serve warm.

* **Parboiled Broccoli & Cauliflower:** Replace half the broccoli with cauliflower.

* Cut 1 red or white onion, 2 medium carrots, **or** 8 small red radishes into thin rounds. Parboil for 30 to 60 seconds. Quickly immerse in ice water, drain, and toss with broccoli.

People who don't usually like raw broccoli or find it difficult to digest often change their minds after they try this dish. Dipped briefly in lightly salted boiling water, broccoli loses its bitterness and gains a more brilliant color and subtle sweetness. Sometimes I serve it plain; sometimes I toss a bowl of the broccoli with Very Easy Vinaigrette, Lemonette, Practically Paleo Pesto or Pistou, or add Spicy Peanut Sauce or a tahini dressing (see Index for recipes) at the table. Undressed leftovers look and taste fresh the second day, so I always cook enough for 2 or 3 meals.

Note: 10 to 12 cups of raw broccoli yields about 8 to 9 cups cooked.

About Parboiled Salads

I was first introduced to the Japanese technique Ohitashi almost 18 years ago. To many people "boiled salad," conjures up visions of soggy boiled lettuce, cucumber, and tomatoes, so I prefer to use the term, "parboiled salad." As with blanching, you cut the vegetables into thin or bite-size pieces, cook briefly in boiling water, chill in ice water, and drain.

We salt the water to create osmotic pressure to minimize loss of minerals from the vegetables into the water. (Remember high school biology?) Whether you're making a salad or creating a crudité plate, parboiling pays. Hard vegetables become more tender and digestible, without overcooking. Colors become more brilliant. Bitter flavors are toned down, sweet flavors are enhanced. I find many people who dislike raw broccoli, cauliflower, cabbage, onions, and red radishes, enjoy these same vegetables parboiled and frequently ask for seconds.

To maintain the unique flavor of each vegetable, cook each kind separately, but in the same water. That way the carrots won't taste like broccoli, and the cauliflower won't taste like onions. This is not a soup! Order of cooking is important. Start with mildest or sweetest-tasting vegetables (carrots or onions). Finish with strong, bitter, or pungent vegetables (broccoli, asparagus, celery, cabbage, daikon, mustard greens) or those colors that might bleed (red radish or purple cabbage).

Shocking cooked vegetables (plunging them into cold water) stops the cooking and holds their vibrant colors. Draining is just as crucial. Do it twice to remove all traces of water, otherwise dressing will pool in the bottom of the bowl. You can toss vegetables together in a serving bowl, artfully arrange them on a platter for a composed salad, or refrigerate them in separate jars for a salad bar effect. Dress an entire bowlful (I usually don't) or just enough for a meal, or let each person dress his or her portions to taste at the table. If you're serving rich side dishes, you might want to forego the dressing.

Essentials:

(1) sturdy vegetable knife, such as a Mac or Caddie knife or chef knife

(2) 3-quart pot with lid

(3) large stainless steel colander nestled inside a larger stainless steel bowl

(4) skimmer, deep fry basket, or pasta insert

(5) ice and water

(6) large platter, bowls, or wide-mouth jars for serving and storing

Vegetables to Parboil

* onions, scallions, or leeks, cut into thin crescents, rings, half-moons, or 1-inch lengths
* carrots, cut into thin rounds, half-moons, quarter moons, or match sticks
* pea pods, snap peas, or snow peas with fibrous string removed, vegetable cut into 1-inch lengths
* cauliflower and broccoli, cut into 1-inch florets, stems and cores peeled and thinly sliced
* green beans or yellow wax beans, ends trimmed, beans left whole or halved
* fennel, base trimmed, upper stalks removed, bulb cut into 1/2-inch thick strips
* asparagus, bottom part snapped off, remaining portion cut into 1 1/2-inch lengths
* celery ribs, cut into thin diagonal slices
* red or white radishes, cut into thin rounds, half-moons, quarter-moons, or matchstick slices
* rutabaga, cut into matchsticks, or quartered and thinly sliced
* green or red cabbage, thinly sliced or cut into 1-inch squares
* kale, collards, or mustard greens, cut into thin strips or bite-size squares
* bok choy, tat soy, choy sum, cut into paper thin strips or squares
* arugula, watercress, or other young salad greens, stems removed, leaves cut into bite-size pieces
* Jerusalem artichoke, scrubbed and cut into 1/4-inch thin rounds or half-moons
* zucchini or summer squash, cut into 1/8- to 1/4-inch thick rounds, half or quarter-moons

Basic Parboiled Salad/Vegetable Medley

Prep: 20 minutes ~ **Cooking:** 10 to 15 minutes ~ **Yield:** 6 to 8 servings

Ingredients & Directions

2 quarts filtered water

1/2 to 3/4 teaspoon unrefined sea salt
(about 1/4 teaspoon per quart)

Additional filtered water and ice for chilling

1 medium onion, halved and cut into thin crescents or
half-moon slices (1 to 1 1/2 cups)

2 medium-large carrots, cut into thin rounds or half-
moons (about 1 1/2 to 2 cups)

1/2 small to medium cauliflower, cut into 1-inch florets,
core trimmed and thinly sliced (3 cups)

1 bunch broccoli, stems peeled and thinly sliced, bottom
inch discarded if woody, cut into 1-inch florets (5 to 6
cups total)

1 bunch red radishes, trimmed and cut into thin slices
(about 2 cups)

Nutrition

Entire recipe:
451 calories
28 g protein
84 g carbohydrate
(38 g fiber)
444 mg calcium
797 mg sodium

1 1/2 to 2 cups:
75 calories
5 g protein
14 g carbohydrate
(6 g fiber)
74 mg calcium
133 mg sodium

A parboiled salad is a great make-ahead dish for sit-down meals, buffets, potlucks, pack lunches, or dip trays. People who don't usually like raw broccoli, cauliflower, or radishes often ask for seconds. For a delicious topping, try Sesame Pesto, Sesame, Garlic & Chive, Sesame-Dill, Tahini-Tarragon, or Macadamia-Dill dressings, or Spicy Peanut Sauce (see Index for recipes).

1. Salt water, cover, and bring to boil in 3-quart pot over medium-high heat. Add pasta insert submerged in at least 3 inches of water or have large skimmer handy. Wash vegetables, chop, and arrange in separate bowls. Fill large bowl with ice and water.

2. Cook vegetables, uncovered, one variety at a time, in this order: onions 30 to 60 seconds; carrots 1 to 2 minutes; cauliflower 1 to 3 minutes; broccoli 1 to 3 minutes; red radishes 30 to 60 seconds.

3. After cooking each vegetable, remove with skimmer and plunge in ice water. Remove from cold water, drain and squeeze to remove excess moisture. Add more ice to bowl as needed. Let water to return to boil before adding a new vegetable; start timing once water returns to boil.

4. Discard cooking water. Toss vegetables in a serving bowl, artfully arrange on platters, or transfer to separate bowls or jars for a salad bar effect in the fridge.

5. Toss entire salad with vinaigrette before serving, or allow each person to dress portions to taste at the table. Refrigerate leftovers and use within 2 days or freeze. Do not reheat.

Note: These salads freeze fairly well. We've taken them on plane and car trips, or moving by U-Haul. Simply defrost in the fridge or an ice chest, dress if desired, and serve.

~ Variations next page ~

Variations

Follow basic parboiling procedure described but change the vegetables. Cook thin or fragile or watery vegetables (scallions, radishes, pea pods, celery, zucchini, arugula, watercress) for 30 to 60 seconds. Cook hard vegetables (onions, carrots, rutabagas, sunchokes, cabbage, broccoli, cauliflower, asparagus, fennel, green beans, and wax beans) for 1 to 3 minutes, until crisp tender. See Page 331 for order in which to cook vegetables.

* Combine cauliflower, savoy cabbage, red radishes, yellow wax beans, and yellow bell peppers.

* Combine cauliflower, green beans, and red bell peppers or red radish slices.

* Mix cauliflower and watercress with red radish slices.

* Try asparagus with cauliflower and carrots.

* Combine asparagus with red radishes and yellow bell peppers. Add cauliflower if you like.

* Use asparagus and cauliflower with yellow summer squash, and red radish slices.

* Try bok choy with carrots, scallions, and celery slices.

* Use savoy cabbage, carrots, celery, and scallions. Add broccoli if desired.

* Use Chinese cabbage with a smaller volume of scallions and carrots.

* Use broccoli with red radishes and onion rings. Add yellow wax beans if desired.

* Use broccoli with leeks, carrots, and daikon radish.

* Try broccoli and cauliflower with carrots. Add red radish rounds if desired.

* Try broccoli and cauliflower with sunchokes, celery, onions, and carrots.

* Try broccoli, purple cabbage, onion rings, and yellow summer squash.

* Combine broccoli, yellow summer squash, carrots, and red radish slices.

Broccoli & Cauliflower with Sun-Dried Tomatoes & Basil Vinaigrette

Prep: 20 minutes ~ **Cooking:** 10 minutes ~ **Yield:** 6 to 8 servings

Ingredients & Directions

Vegetables:
4 cups broccoli, cut into bite-size florets

4 cups cauliflower, cut into bite-size florets

2 cups thinly sliced red onion rounds or half-moons, celery, or daikon (white radish) cut into paper thin half-moons or halved, seeded and sliced yellow bell peppers

Sun-Dried Tomatoes & Basil Vinaigrette:
12 oil-packed, sun-dried tomatoes, drained and thinly sliced (such as Mediterranean Organic brand) **or** dry-packed tomatoes, soaked briefly in warm water to barely cover, drained and thinly sliced; save liquid

2 tablespoons organic balsamic vinegar, red wine vinegar **or** brown rice vinegar

1 1/2 to 2 tablespoons extra-virgin olive, unrefined sesame **or** flax oil

1 to 2 tablespoons tamari soy sauce

1 or 2 garlic cloves, finely minced or pressed

1 1/2 teaspoons dried basil, crumbled **or** 1 1/2 to 2 tablespoons minced fresh basil leaves

1/4 teaspoon ground black pepper, white pepper, or lemon pepper, or to taste

Nutrition

1 serving (about 1 1/2 cups):
106 calories
5 g protein
13 g carbohydrate
(6 g fiber)
4 g fat
52 mg calcium
264 mg sodium

This simple salad is perfect for a potluck, buffet, or picnic. For convenience, chop the vegetables and mix the dressing ahead, then cook close to serving time. Or, prepare the entire dish 2 to 6 hours before serving. Cover and refrigerate in warm weather. Leftovers look and taste great the next day, so I always make enough another meal or two.

1. Layer vegetables on steamer rack in 3- to 4-quart pot over 2 inches of boiling water. Cover and cook until crisp-tender, about 6 to 8 minutes. Or, parboil vegetables separately, but in the same water until crisp-tender. (See parboiled salads.) If you don't plan to serve right away, plunge vegetables in ice water and drain well, twice.

2. Mix sun-dried tomatoes and vinaigrette ingredients in non-metallic bowl. Toss with drained vegetables, and serve, or cover and refrigerate for several hours. Do not reheat.

3. Serve chilled or close to room temperature. Refrigerate leftovers and use within 2 days.

Variations

* Replace basil with powdered rosemary, or dill weed and change the name of the dressing.

* Replace cauliflower with yellow wax beans, or broccoli with green beans.

Crudité Platter of Seasonal Vegetables

Prep: 20 minutes ~ **Cooking:** 10 to 15 minutes ~ **Yield:** 12 servings

Ingredients & Directions

3 quarts filtered water

1/2 to 3/4 teaspoon unrefined sea salt (1/4 teaspoon per quart)

Additional filtered water and ice for chilling

3 medium carrots (about 3 cups), cut into sticks suitable for dipping

1 medium cauliflower, 5 to 6 inches in diameter (about 5 to 6 cups), cut into florets with enough of stem attached to make a handle for holding

1 pound asparagus (about 4 cups), woody bottom portion discarded where it breaks easily and remaining stems cut into 1 1/2- to 2-inch lengths

1 medium-size sweet red bell pepper, halved, cored, seeded, stemmed, cut into 1-inch wide strips

1 sweet yellow bell pepper, halved, cored, seeded, stemmed, cut into 1-inch wide strips

Nutrition

Entire recipe:
565 calories
35 g protein
104 g carbs
(32 g fiber)
1 g fat
784 mg calcium
797 mg sodium

1 heaping cup:
47 calories
3 g protein
9 g carbohydrate
(3 g fiber)
65 mg calcium
65 mg sodium

Unlike raw crudités, most people find these vegetables more tender, tasty, and digestible.

You can prepare the vegetables up to 8 hours before company arrives. Second-day leftovers are great for pack lunches or quick meals at home. I vary vegetables with the season. For company, consider serving vegetables with a selection of 2 or 3 dips or dressings.

1. Arrange each kind of vegetable in a separate bowl.

2. Bring salted water to boil in large pot over medium-high heat. Immerse pasta insert in at least 3 inches of water or have a large skimmer ready to promptly retrieve vegetables.

3. Cook each variety of vegetables separately, but in the same water in this order: carrots 30 to 60 seconds, cauliflower 1 to 3 minutes, asparagus 60 seconds, peppers 30 seconds.

4. After cooking each vegetable, remove with skimmer and plunge in ice water. Remove from cold water, drain and squeeze to remove excess moisture. Add more ice to bowl as needed. Let water return to boil before adding a new vegetable; start timing once water returns to boil. When done, discard cooking water.

5. Arrange vegetables on one or more platter(s). Serve 2 or 3 dips or dressings in small custard cups in the center or on the side. Refrigerate leftovers and use within 3 days or freeze. Do not reheat.

FYI: As an appetizer, figure 1/2 to 1 cup cooked vegetables per person. As a side salad figure 1 1/2 to 2 cups per person if you will not be serving a tossed salad or other cooked greens.

Jazzed-Up Spinach

Prep: 10 minutes ~ **Cooking:** 10 to 12 minutes ~ **Yield:** 3 servings

Ingredients & Directions

1/3 cup filtered water **or** preservative-free chicken broth, homemade stock **or** Bone-Building Broth (Page 278 or 306)

1 small onion, thinly sliced (about 1/2 cup)

1 cup fresh button, cremini, oyster, or shiitake mushrooms, thinly sliced

1 garlic clove, minced

1/4 teaspoon ground black pepper **or** 1/2 teaspoon lemon pepper

1/4 teaspoon dry mustard **or** ground turmeric

1/4 teaspoon finely ground, unrefined sea salt **or** 1 1/2 teaspoons tamari soy sauce, optional

1 (12-ounce) package loose-leaf frozen spinach

2 teaspoons arrowroot starch dissolved in 1 to 2 tablespoons cold water, broth or stock

1 tablespoon flax oil, lemon-flavored cod liver oil, **or** butter, optional

Nutrition

1 cup:
76 calories
5 g protein
13 g carbohydrate
(4 g fiber)
192 mg calcium
111 mg sodium

Spinach is rich in chlorophyll, carotenoids, and vitamin C—potent inhibitors of cancer and macular degeneration. Cooking neutralizes the oxalic acid naturally present in spinach, freeing up more of the calcium for absorption. Experiment with different seasonings. Make a double recipe if you want leftovers for the next day.

1. Add water or broth, mushrooms, garlic, pepper, mustard, optional sea salt or tamari, and spinach, in that order, to a heavy 2-quart saucepan or skillet.

2. Cover and bring to boil over medium heat without stirring. Reduce heat and simmer, undisturbed for 3 to 4 minutes, until spinach begins to soften. Stir, cover, and simmer 4 more minutes, until tender. Add dissolved arrowroot, simmer, and stir to thicken.

3. Remove from heat and serve. Drizzle with oil or dab with butter if desired.

4. Refrigerate any leftovers and use leftovers within 24 hours.

Variations

* Replace dry mustard with 1/4 teaspoon each of dried, crumbled basil and oregano.

* Replace black pepper with ground chipotlé (smoked dried jalapeno pepper).

* Replace frozen spinach with frozen (unsalted) kale, collards, or mustard or turnip greens.

Note: Look for frozen spinach sold in bags; it thaws and cooks more quickly and evenly than solid blocks of frozen spinach.

Steamed Spinach

Prep: 10 minutes ~ **Cooking:** 3 to 4 minutes ~ **Yield:** 4 servings

Ingredients & Directions

2 pounds loose spinach (16 loosely packed cups, stems removed) **or** 3 (10-ounce) bunches

2 cups filtered water for steaming

4 teaspoons extra-virgin olive, coconut, or flax oil **or** butter

Hot sauce **or** lemon pepper, to taste

1. **To clean curly or large spinach leaves:** Hold 1 spinach leaf between thumb and forefinger of 1 hand. With other hand, pinch leaf close to stem and peel forward so stem comes off back of leaf. Drop leaf in bowl; discard stem. Repeat with remaining leaves.

2. Fill sink or large bowl with cold water. Swish leaves gently in water, lift out, drain in colander. Rinse bowl or drain sink. Repeat twice. Feel bottom of bowl or sink. If you find more than a grain or two of grit, wash and drain spinach again.

3. Add 1 or 2 inches of water to 2- to 3-quart saucepan fitted with vegetable steamer or pasta insert. Cover and bring to boil. Add spinach, cover and cook until leaves are bright green and tender, about 3 to 4 minutes. Or steam spinach in the bottom of the large saucepan with about 1/4 cup water until tender.

4. Drain spinach in colander, press out excess water, transfer to bowl, and toss with oil or butter. Add hot sauce or lemon pepper and serve. Refrigerate leftovers and use within 24 hours.

Nutrition

1 serving:
96 calories
8 g protein
8 g carbohydrate
(4 g fiber)
5 g fat
204 mg calcium
156 mg sodium

If possible, buy fresh locally grown spinach; it's sweeter, more tender and will last longer in the refrigerator than spinach from another region. Avoid bunches or bags with dried, yellowed or wilted leaves, and dark, slimy spots. Wash it impeccably to remove all traces of sand; the tiniest bit of grit will ruin the meal.

Variations

* **Cold Spinach Rolls:** Plunge cooked spinach in ice water. Drain and squeeze to remove excess moisture. Shape plain spinach into a 1-inch thick log with a bamboo sushi mat. Cut into 1-inch long slices. To serve, dip 1 end of each log into a custard cup of Practically Paleo, Pesto, Pistou, Spicy Peanut Sauce, or one of our tahini dressings (see Index for recipes).

* Replace half the spinach with arugula, endive, watercress, beet greens, Swiss chard, or young tender mustard greens. Remove stems, wash, and cook as above.

Note: 16 cups of raw spinach can cook down to 3 cupsful, so buy and cook more than you think you need. You don't have to destem young, flat leaf, baby spinach, but you should rinse even prewashed greens.

Sautéed Cabbage

Prep: 10 minutes ~ **Cooking:** 15 minutes ~ **Yield:** 6 servings

Ingredients & Directions

2 tablespoons unrefined coconut oil **or** extra-virgin olive oil

1 medium or 1/2 large onion, cut into thin crescents, half-moon, or 1/2-inch diced pieces

2/3 cup tightly packed dulse sea vegetable, sorted to remove small stones and shells, and cut into small pieces with kitchen shears **or** substitute 1/2 teaspoon unrefined sea salt **or** 1 tablespoon tamari soy sauce

1 medium-size head savoy **or** green cabbage (2 1/2 to 3 pounds), cut into thin strips or 1/2-inch cubes (about 12 to 14 packed cups)

1 tablespoon sweet Hungarian paprika

1 teaspoon ground cumin

1/2 teaspoon ground black pepper **or** 1/2 teaspoon lemon pepper, or to taste

1/2 to 1 cup filtered water, preservative-free chicken broth **or** Bone-Building Broth (Page 278 or 306)

Nutrition

1 serving:
107 calories
3 g protein
13 g carbohydrate
(5 g fiber)
5 g fat
99 mg calcium
74 mg sodium

Cabbage becomes sweeter and less bitter with sufficient cooking. Most people also find it more digestible. I think it tastes even better the second day, so I always prepare enough for 2 or 3 meals. Try it with poached or fried eggs, hamburgers, or turkey breast, and fresh or stewed fruit for breakfast, lunch or dinner. It's also delicious with cooked fish or poultry and a beet, squash, sweet potato or carrot soup or side dish.

1. Heat oil in heavy sauté pan, cast iron skillet, or wok over medium-high heat. Add onions and cook, stirring continuously until soft, about 4 to 5 minutes. Add dulse, sea salt, or tamari, and cabbage. Stir over medium heat for about 3 minutes.

2. Add paprika, cumin, and pepper. Stir and raise heat to high. Add 1/2 cup water, stock, or broth to barely cover the bottom of pot. Add additional 1/4 cup liquid if using dulse. Cover, bring to boil, reduce heat, and simmer until tender, 8 to 10 minutes.

3. Remove lid and add 1/4 cup additional liquid if needed to moisten pan. Cover and simmer 5 to 7 more minutes, or until tender. Remove lid, stir, and serve. Refrigerate leftovers and use within 2 days.

Variations

* **Moroccan-Spiced Cabbage:** Replace paprika and cumin with 1 tablespoon Moroccan Barbecue Spice Mix (Page 399).

* **Sautéed Cabbage with Curry:** Omit paprika and cumin. Add 2 to 3 teaspoons curry powder.

FYI: You can freeze portions for up to 2 months. Defrost and warm briefly or serve close to room temperature.

Steamed Asparagus

Prep: 10 to 15 minutes ~ **Cooking:** 4 to 15 minutes ~ **Yield:** 7 to 8 cups

Ingredients & Directions

2 pounds asparagus, the thicker the better

2 to 4 cups filtered water

Lemon pepper **or** ground black pepper, optional

2 tablespoons lemon juice **or** balsamic vinegar, optional

1. Rinse asparagus. One at a time, bend each spear about 2 inches from bottom. It will break (more or less) where the tender part ends and the woody part begins. Discard woody part. Peel extremely thick stalks by laying stalks flat on cutting board, and one at a time, applying a vegetable peeler from the base to the flower.

2. Rest metal steamer or pasta insert in wide 3-quart or larger pot filled with 1 1/2 to 2 inches of water. Or, omit steamer and use a tall and narrow pot that allows spears to stand upright with or without the aid of a 16-ounce can with the top and bottom removed. Cover pot and bring to boil over high heat.

3. Stand asparagus upright in a tall pot, or arrange on a steamer basket in a shallow pan. Cover and steam over high heat until thickest part of stalk is easily pierced with thin-bladed knife, 2 minutes if tiny; 4 minutes if small, 5 to 6 minutes if medium thickness, 7 to 10 minutes if large.

4. Drain and arrange asparagus on plates. Serve immediately or rinse under cold water, pat dry, and cut into 1-inch lengths. Chill as is, or toss with Very Easy Vinaigrette or Lemonette (see Index for recipes).

5. If cold, remove from refrigerator 20 minutes before serving. Use within 2 days.

Nutrition

1 cup (12 spears):
48 calories
4 g protein
8 g carbohydrate
(2 g fiber)
36 mg calcium
20 mg sodium

Asparagus is a shoot, not a leafy green, but I sometimes serve it instead of greens in a meal. Look for locally grown asparagus in the spring and summer. Spears should be firm, crisp, and well rounded with compact (unwilted) tips free of slime and decay. Avoid flat, limp, cracked, or dehydrated stalks. Before cooking, be sure to snap off the woody portion.

The spears are delicious plain, dipped in 6- to 10-year old balsamic vinegar, or lightly dressed with Vinaigrette, Lemonette, Practically Paleo Pesto, a Tahini Dip, or Homemade Mayonnaise with herbs. (See Index for recipes). Halve recipe if desired.

Variations

* **Asparagus Lemonette:** Toss cooled, drained, chopped asparagus with 1/4 cup thinly sliced scallions and 1/4 to 1/2 cup Lemonette (Page 421). Cover and chill for 3 hours.

* **Asparagus with Tarragon:** Toss cooled, drained, chopped asparagus with a mixture of 1/4 cup lemon juice or balsamic vinegar, 2 tablespoons chopped fresh tarragon, 2 tablespoons extra-virgin olive or flax oil, and 1/3 teaspoon ground black pepper.

* Combine 1 pound of trimmed asparagus and 3/4 pound of cauliflower, cut into bite-size pieces. Steam until tender. Serve warm or chilled, dressed or undressed.

Sautéed Summer Squash with Better Barbecue Sauce

Prep: 20 minutes ~ **Cooking:** 15 minutes ~ **Yield:** 6 servings

Ingredients & Directions

2 tablespoons extra-virgin olive oil **or** unrefined coconut oil

1 medium-large onion, cut into thin half-moons or crescents (1 1/2 to 2 cups)

8 ounces shiitake, cremini or button mushrooms, wiped clean with a damp cloth, ends trimmed and mushrooms thinly sliced (about 1 1/2 cups)

3 medium or 4 small garlic cloves, minced

2 to 2 1/2 pounds summer squash or zucchini (smaller is better), cut into 1/2-inch thin rounds, halved if large, ends discarded (about 8 packed cups)

1 teaspoon dried oregano, crumbled

3/4 to 1 cup Better Barbecue Sauce (Page 401)

1/4 teaspoon black pepper **or** ground chipotlé (smoked dried jalapeno pepper)

1/4 cup minced fresh parsley or basil leaves, optional

Nutrition

1 serving:
141 calories
5 g protein
18 g carbohydrate
(5 g fiber)
6 g fat
51 mg calcium
65 mg sodium

This is not a leafy greens dish, but I sometimes serve it as a substitute in some meals. I like to make this first thing in the morning to serve with fried or poached eggs, burgers, pork chops, or turkey and fresh fruit. (Sometimes I steam or parboil broccoli or cauliflower to go with it.) I gently warm leftovers in the toaster oven the next day.

1. Chop vegetables and set aside in separate bowls. Heat oil in a 3-quart heavy-bottomed Dutch oven or 13-inch skillet over medium heat. Add onions, stir and cook until tender, about 5 minutes. Add mushrooms and oregano, stir and cook for 2 minutes. Add garlic, and zucchini or summer squash. Stir, cover, and reduce heat to medium-low. Simmer until zucchini is almost tender and translucent, 10 to 12 minutes.

2. Uncover, add pepper and 3/4 cup barbecue sauce, stir and cook, uncovered, until tender and aromatic, about 4 minutes. Garnish with parsley or basil. Stir, remove from heat, and serve.

3. Refrigerate leftovers in heat-proof container for ease of reheating. Use within 3 days.

Variations

* **Sautéed Zucchini & Cauliflower with Better Barbecue Sauce:** Use 1 to 1 1/2 pounds of zucchini with 1 pound of cauliflower, cut into bite-size florets.

* **Sautéed Summer Squash with Broccoli & Better Barbecue Sauce:** Use 1 to 1 1/2 pounds of yellow summer squash plus 1 to 1 1/4 pounds of broccoli florets and peeled, sliced stalks above.

Note: Start with fresh, firm, zucchini or summer squash free of dents gashes, and soft spots; the smaller the better (from 2 to about 8 inches long or so). Overgrown summer squash is usually fibrous and watery.

19 Side Salads & Main Dish Salads

BEST BITES

TIPS FOR WASHING & CHOPPING SALAD GREENS

Clean Those Greens!

Nothing spoils a salad faster than grit. If you inadvertently neglect thorough cleaning, you'll put a bad taste in everyone's mouth. A quick run under the faucet is not enough. Discard any wilted or shaggy outer leaves. Separate leaves and place in a large bowl or sink filled with cold water. Swish for 30 to 60 seconds. Remove leaves one at a time so dirt and grit remain in the water. Repeat with fresh water until water is clear or no traces of sand remain in the bottom of bowl or sink. Spinach, arugula, and parsley may require 3 or 4 washes. Carefully inspect every leaf for grit. If dirt remains, rinse each leaf individually under cold running water.

Dry 'em, You'll Like 'em

If you don't dry salad greens thoroughly, they will spoil prematurely and the salad dressing will slide off and puddle in the bottom of the bowl, leaving the flavor behind.

A salad spinner is the best tool for this job. Don't overfill it or it won't work properly and you'll bruise the leaves. Fill the spinner 1/2 to 2/3 full with lettuce. (If you overfill it it won't spin.) If desired, spritz lettuce with diluted grapefruit seed extract or food-grade hydrogen peroxide to disinfect, then rinse again before you spin dry. If your spinner retains water, remove the salad basket and dump out the water.

A salad spinner doubles as storage unit and allows air to circulate. It prolongs shelf life of salad greens and eliminates the need for plastic bags. If you need to wash more greens than will fit in your spinner, gently stuff clean, dry greens in a cotton or linen drawstring bag or arrange on a clean white or unbleached cotton-linen towel, roll up, and store in an open bowl in the fridge.

Tear with Care

Salad greens are easily bruised. Leave young, tender, baby greens whole. Tear or gently cut mature leaf lettuces into bite-size pieces. Romaine and other firm lettuces should be sliced or torn as close to serving time as possible to avoid bruising and discoloration. Firmer vegetables (radishes, carrots, bell peppers, cucumbers, scallions, and parsley) may be cut to last longer. Chopped celery should be used within 24 to 48 hours; it gets funky fast. Ditto for jicama.

Seeding cucumbers and tomatoes

Have you ever wondered why some recipes call for peeling and seeding (actually deseeding) cucumbers and removing the seeds from tomatoes? They make cucumbers and tomatoes more delicious and reduce or eliminate their propensity to cause intestinal gas. Seeding also makes tomatoes easier to eat without spraying seeds and juices.

To peel and seed a cucumber: I peel cucumbers whether they are waxed or not. Since the ends of cucumbers are often bitter, run the vegetable peeler from the middle to the ends, to avoid spreading any bitterness to the center section. Cut cucumber in half lengthwise, run a teaspoon down the exposed center to scrape out the seeds and discard. Turn cucumber halves cut side down and thinly slice. Cut slices in half again if you want smaller pieces. Whatever you don't use right away you can stuff into a pint jar, cover, and refrigerate. Add them to salads over the next 4 to 5 days.

To seed a tomato: Core tomato and cut it in half bisecting the midline. (If it was the Earth, you'd cut along the equator.) With the end of a chopstick or point of a paring knife, scrape seeds into a bowl and discard. Cut fruit into wedges, thin slices, or dice. Store extra sliced tomato in a pint-size glass jar, cover, refrigerate, and use within 3 days. I often cut cherry or grape tomatoes in half, so I don't spray myself or someone else with tomato juice when I bite into them

To peel a tomato: Cut a small "X" in the bottom of the tomato with a paring knife to make it easier to peel. Try to cut the skin and as little flesh as possible. Dip tomato in boiling water for 1 or 2 minutes. Remove, plunge in cold water, drain, and peel. Seed if desired and slice.

Dressing for Success

I usually serve dressing—other than a rich vinaigrette—on the side so each person can dress his/her salad to taste. This also ensures that the leftover salad will look good the next day. If I'm serving a rich vinaigrette, I generally prefer to toss the entire salad with dressing to make a little bit of oil go a long way. I do this just before serving, adding dressing a little at a time to coat each leaf without drowning it.

Parboiled salads may be dressed at the table with a creamy tahini or peanut butter dressing, or tossed lightly with vinaigrette in the kitchen. Tossed salads need to be dressed moments before serving so they don't wilt and lose their appeal; parboiled salads are sturdy enough to be tossed with vinaigrette, then chilled until serving time if you want the dressing to permeate and marinate the vegetables.

> Note
> Pickling cucumbers are small, and less seedy; it's usually unnecessary to peel or seed them.

Your Basic Green Salad

Prep: 15 minutes ~ **Yield:** 4 to 6 servings

Ingredients & Directions

Salad greens:
6 to 8 cups packed salad greens, washed well, dried, and cut or torn into bite-size pieces (Page 342):

> romaine, red leaf, green leaf, oak leaf, Boston, buttercrunch, bib, lollo rosso lettuce, or some combination of 2 or more mild lettuces

Select 2 to 3 colorful mix-ins, about 2 to 3 cups:
Burpless/English cucumber, regular cucumber, **or** kirby (pickling) cucumber, peeled, halved, quartered, seeded, and thinly sliced for easier digestion

Sweet red, orange, or gold bell peppers, seeded, sliced, diced, or finely minced

Daikon (white) radish, grated or thinly sliced into matchsticks

Red radish, thinly sliced into rounds or half-moons

Carrots **or** beets trimmed and finely grated

Red, gold, or orange tomatoes, halved, seeded and sliced or diced

Minced parsley leaves **or** fennel fronds, stems removed

Scallions (green onions; white plus most of the green part), trimmed and minced

Red or sweet white onions, cut into thin rings, half-moons, or minced

Sunflower, alfalfa, clover **or** onion sprouts

Water chestnuts (not canned), peeled and thinly sliced

Jicama, peeled and thinly sliced, diced, or cubed

Dressing (Pick 1):
1 cup Lean & Creamy Mustard, Italian, French **or** Basil-Balsamic Dressing (Page 417 to 418)

1 cup Mustard-Tahini Dressing (Page 411)

1 cup Macadamia-Dill Dressing (Page 413)

Nutrition

1 serving without dressing:
28 calories
2 g protein
3 g carbohydrate
    (2 g fiber)
27 mg calcium
6 mg sodium

1 serving with 1/4 cup Lean & Creamy Mustard Dressing:
149 calories
5 g carbohydrate
    (2 g fiber)
15 g fat
34 calcium
137 mg sodium

1 serving with 1/4 cup Mustard-Tahini Dressing:
138 calories
5 g protein
9 g carbohydrate
    (3 g fiber)
8 g fat
45 mg calcium
153 mg sodium

You can assemble scrumptious salads in mere minutes if you keep a salad spinner filled with clean greens next to wide-mouth jars stuffed with a colorful assortment of thinly sliced vegetables on the top shelf of the refrigerator. Vary combinations and dressings meal to meal and day to day. Add sliced or diced fish, poultry, beef, bison, pork, or lean lamb for one-dish dining.

1. Layer vegetables in a 4-quart bowl, or 4 smaller bowls with fitted lids for lunches. You may prepare salad to this point, cover with plates or snap-on lid(s) and refrigerate until serving time.

2. When ready to eat, lightly drizzle dressing over salad and toss to coat, or serve dressing on the side.

3. Cover and refrigerate leftovers. Use within 24 hours if dressed, within 2 days if undressed.

~ Variations next page ~

Variations

Your Basic Green Salad ~ continued

* **Arugula, Onion & Tomato Salad:** Use arugula for all or half of the greens. Add sweet white or red onions, red, orange, or yellow tomatoes, and sunflower sprouts with tomatoes.

* **Lettuce, Cucumber, Jicama & Red Onion Salad:** Combine red, green leaf, or romaine lettuces. Add peeled, sliced cucumber, jicama, and red onion rings. Add minced parsley, if desired.

* **Lettuce, White Radish & Tomato Salad:** Use 1 or 2 types of lettuce, fresh parsley, white radish cut into thin rounds or matchsticks, and sliced or diced tomato or cherry, plum or pear tomatoes. **Optional:** minced scallions or thin rings of sweet white onions or grated carrot. Alternatively, use red radishes and yellow or orange tomatoes in the salad.

* **Lettuce, Cucumber, Celery & Red Radish Salad:** Combine romaine or red leaf lettuce, green leaf, or mixed salad greens with peeled, seeded, thinly sliced cucumber and quartered, thinly sliced red radishes.

* **Zesty Lettuce, Tomato & Daikon Salad with Sunflower Sprouts**: Use 1 or 2 types of lettuce. Add arugula or radicchio, daikon radish (white radish cut into thin matchsticks or quarter-moon slices), diced red or low-acid gold tomatoes, and sunflower sprouts.

* **Lettuce, Sweet Pepper & Red Radish Salad:** Use 1 or 2 lettuces, fresh parsley, thinly sliced red radishes, and yellow bell pepper. Add minced scallions or thin rings of red or sweet white onions as desired. Minced jicama makes a crunchy addition.

* **Lettuce, Parsley & Pepper Salad:** Use 1 or 2 lettuces, fresh parsley, and 1 or 2 varieties of sweet bell peppers. If desired add peeled and thinly sliced cucumbers or fresh water chestnuts.

* **Lettuce, Carrot, Water Chestnut & Celery Salad with Scallions:** Use 1 or more lettuces. Add grated carrots, peeled and thinly sliced fresh water chestnuts, celery, and scallions. If you can't find fresh water chestnuts, substitute peeled, sliced jicama.

* **Chopped Salad:** Cover a large platter or individual dinner plates with shredded or torn lettuce. Arrange 3 to 5 kinds of vegetables over the lettuce in mounds, rows, or like spokes on a wheel. Along with raw vegetables, I sometimes include roasted onions, mushrooms, and/or bell peppers. For one-dish dining, add mounds or rows of sliced, cubed, diced or flaked chicken, turkey breast, lean pork, beef, fish, or hard-boiled egg. Set out 2 or 3 salad dressings for use at the table (see list in main recipe).

Spinach Salad with Tahini Dressing

Prep: 20 minutes ~ **Yield:** 6 servings

Ingredients & Directions

Salad ingredients:

9 to 10 cups spinach leaves, washed, dried, stems removed, leaves torn into bite-size pieces

1 to 2 cups curly or flat leaf parsley, watercress, mustard cress, **or** arugula leaves, washed, dried, and minced, stems removed

1 large or 4 small red, orange, or gold tomatoes, halved, seeded, and sliced thin or diced

1 bunch scallions (green onions; green and white part), trimmed and minced, **or** sweet white onion

1/2 cup fresh, roughly chopped whole basil leaves, stems removed, optional

1 ripe avocado, halved, pitted, and cut into bite-size pieces, optional

1 to 1 1/2 cups Sesame, Garlic & Chive, Mustard-Tahini, **or** Sesame-Dill Dressing (Page 411 to 412)

1. Layer vegetables in a 4-quart bowl, or 4 smaller bowls with lids for lunches. Prepare up to this point and if desired cover bowl(s) with plates or lid(s), and refrigerate until serving time.

2. When ready to serve, lightly drizzle with dressing and toss to coat, or serve dressing on the side.

3. Cover and refrigerate leftovers. Use within 24 hours if dressed, 2 days if undressed.

Variations

* Replace scallions with 2 cups Roasted Onions (Page 373).

* Replace Tahini Dressing with Lean & Creamy Mustard, French, or Basil-Balsamic Dressing, or Poppy Seed-Orange Drizzle (see Index for recipes).

* Top each portion of salad with 3 to 4 ounces flaked fish, sliced chicken, turkey breast, or pork loin for one-dish dining. Dress pack lunches just before serving.

Nutrition

1 serving without dressing:

101 calories
5 g protein
9 g carbohydrate
(4 g fiber)
5 g fat
107 mg calcium
67 mg sodium

1 serving with 1/4 cup Tahini Dressing:

211 calories
8 g protein
15 g carbohydrate
(5 g fiber)
13 g fat
125 mg calcium
214 mg sodium

Fresh locally grown spinach will keep for an entire week in the fridge if you store it in a cotton-canvas bag instead of plastic. Cloth allows the vegetables to breathe. Carefully wash spinach in several changes of water. One sandy bite can spoil the meal. To skip trimming, tearing, and sorting, buy prewashed baby spinach, but give it a quick rinse and whirl in your salad spinner for safety.

Note: If the avocados at the market are rock hard, buy them a week ahead to give them time to ripen at room temperature. You might want to buy 1 or 2 extras, just in case you get a bad one.

Spinach Salad with Parboiled Broccoli, Cauliflower & Carrots

Prep: 30 minutes ~ **Yield:** 6 servings

Ingredients & Directions

1 to 1 1/2 quarts filtered water plus 1/4 teaspoon unrefined sea salt

6 cups spinach, washed, spun dry, stems removed, large leaves torn into bite-size pieces

1/2 large red onion, cut into thin half-moon slices (1 cup)

2 small to medium carrots, cut into thin coin-like rounds (2 cups)

2 1/2 to 3 cups broccoli, cut into bite-size florets, stems peeled and thinly sliced, tough part discarded

2 1/2 to 3 cups cauliflower, cut into bite-size florets, cores trimmed and thinly sliced

1/2 recipe (1/4 cup plus 2 tablespoons) Very Easy Vinaigrette **or** Lemonette (Page 422 or 421)

Nutrition

1 serving without dressing:

70 calories
5 g protein
13 g carbohydrate
 (6 g fiber)
95 mg calcium
77 mg sodium

1 serving with vinaigrette:

157 calories
5 g protein
13 g carbohydrate
 (6 g fiber)
9 g fat
95 mg calcium
79 mg sodium

1. Boil water in a 2-quart saucepan over high heat. Wash spinach, sort to remove stems, and spin dry. Wash and chop remaining vegetables and arrange in separate bowls. Add spinach to a 3- to 4-quart serving bowl. Fill another bowl with ice water.

2. Parboil vegetables separately, but in the same water in this order: onions 1 minute, carrots 1 to 2 minutes, broccoli 2 to 3 minutes, cauliflower 2 to 3 minutes, until crisp-tender. After cooking each vegetable remove with a skimmer and plunge in ice water. Remove from cold water, drain, and squeeze to remove excess moisture. Add more ice to the bowl as needed.

3. Arrange cooked, cooled, and drained vegetables over raw spinach. At this point, you can cover and refrigerate salad until serving time if desired.

4. Toss with dressing and serve immediately. Cover and refrigerate leftovers and use within 24 hours.

Variations

* Replace Lemonette or Vinaigrette with 1 to 1 1/4 cups Lean & Creamy Mustard, Italian, or Basil-Balsamic Dressing, or a tahini dressing (see Index for recipes).

Parboiling makes the carrots and cruciferous vegetables more colorful and digestible and the salad more substantial. Parboil the vegetables ahead if you like. (I always make enough for 2 days.) Double the recipe for more people, but dress only the portion you plan to serve within 24 hours.

To save time, look for prewashed baby spinach at your local farmers' market or natural foods store. You still need to wash it, then dry in a salad spinner or with cotton dish towels. You can store washed, dried, unused greens in your salad spinner on the top shelf of the fridge.

Mesclun/Baby Greens Salad

Prep: 15 minutes ~ **Yield:** 4 to 6 servings

Ingredients & Directions

8 cups spring greens, baby greens, mesclun, **or** field greens, washed and spun dry

1 cup edible flowers **or** thinly sliced celery, celery tops, minced scallions or parsley leaves

Freshly ground black pepper, optional

Dressing, select 1:
3/4 cup Lean & Creamy Mustard, Basil-Balsamic, Italian, or French Dressing (Page 417 to 419)

3/4 cup Poppy Seed-Orange/Pineapple Drizzle (Page 420)

3/4 cup Tahini Dressing, any flavor (Page 411 to 412)

1. Top salad greens with sliced or minced vegetables in a 3-quart bowl.

2. Drizzle salad with dressing and toss to coat. Taste and add a little more dressing as needed. Serve immediately. Or serve undressed allowing each person to dress his or her salad to taste.

3. Cover and refrigerate leftovers; if dressed use within 24 hours.

Variations

* **Mesclun Greens with Berries:** Omit scallions and parsley. Layer 3 cups of washed, drained blueberries, raspberries, or hulled, sliced strawberries or 1/3 to 1/2 cup dried, fruit-sweetened berries or cherries over greens. Sprinkle with edible flowers if available and toss with Lean & Creamy Basil-Balsamic Dressing, Poppy Seed-Pineapple, or Poppy Seed-Cherry Drizzle and garnish with 1/4 cup toasted walnuts or pecans if desired.

* **Mesclun Green & Pear Salad with Toasted Pecans:** Top salad greens with 1 cup of edible flowers, 2 peeled, cored, and thinly sliced ripe, but firm, bosc, spartlett, or anjou pears, freshly ground black pepper, 1/4 cup lightly toasted pecans (Page 406), and enough Basil-Balsamic Dressing or Poppy Seed-Pineapple, or Poppy Seed-Cherry Drizzle to lightly coat.

Nutrition

1 serving without dressing:
20 calories
2 g protein
3 g carbohydrate
(2 g fiber)
64 mg calcium
75 mg sodium

1 serving with 3 tablespoons Lean & Creamy Mustard Dressing:
111 calories
2 g protein
5 carbohydrate
(2 g fiber)
9 g fat
69 calcium
173 mg sodium

Mesclun and *misticanza*, French and Italian terms for mixture, refer to a centuries-old tradition of collecting young, tender field greens for the salad bowl. These flavorful and nutritious greens are often labeled *Young Spring Greens, Field Greens,* or *Mixed Baby Greens* in farmers' markets, natural foods stores, and supermarkets. Rinse and spin them dry even if the package says "prewashed." One-pound bags are more economical and yield 8 to 10 generous servings.

Mesclun Greens with Herb-Roasted Mushrooms, Onions & Walnuts

Prep: 15 minutes ~ **Yield:** 4 to 6 servings

Ingredients & Directions

8 cups washed and dried mesclun greens, early greens, baby greens **or** spring mix:
> mixture of lettuces with endives, chicories, spinaches, mustard greens, cress, arugula, and often fresh herbs and/or edible flowers

2 cups Herb-Roasted Mushrooms (Page 375)

2 cups Roasted Onions or Leeks (Page 373)

1 cup thinly sliced celery or celery tops

1/4 to 1/2 cup lightly toasted walnuts (Page 406)

1 cup Toasted Dulse (Page 397), crumbled, optional

1/2 teaspoon freshly ground black pepper, or to taste

3 to 4 tablespoons of 5- to 10-year old balsamic vinegar

Nutrition

1 serving:
203 calories
6 g protein
21 g carbohydrate
(5 g fiber)
11 fat
54 mg calcium
56 mg sodium

Roasted mushrooms and toasted walnuts add a rich meaty flavor and texture to baby greens and sweet roasted onions. Roast mushrooms and onions, toast nuts, and wash and dry greens in advance; layer and toss ingredients just before serving.

1. Layer greens, mushrooms, onions or leeks, celery, and nuts in a 4-quart bowl or 4 smaller bowls with lids for pack lunches. Prepare to this point, cover, and refrigerate until serving time.
2. When ready to serve, sprinkle dulse over salad if desired, then pepper. Drizzle with vinegar, toss to coat, and serve.
3. Cover and refrigerate leftovers. If dressed, use within 24 hours, if undressed, within 2 days.

Variations

* Add 1 or 2 cups of halved, seeded, and diced fresh tomatoes in season.

* Omit vinegar and toss salad with 1/2 to 2/3 cup Lean & Creamy Mustard Dressing (Page 411), or Basil-Balsamic Dressing (Page 418), just before serving.

* Replace walnuts with 2 sliced or diced ripe avocados.

Note: Even though bags of baby greens are sold ready to eat, you will be wise to give them a good rinse and drain; then spin dry in a salad spinner. You can store the greens in the spinner in the fridge if you like.

FYI: One pound of baby greens will yield 8 to 10 generous servings, enough for 2 to enjoy every day for almost a week. I complete the meal with fish, chicken, turkey, or pork, and baked or roasted sweet potatoes, carrots, a colorful soup, or fruit.

Spring Green & Marinated Beet Root Salad with Fluffy Tahini

Prep: 15 minutes ~ **Yield:** 4 to 6 servings

Ingredients & Directions

8 to 10 cups washed mesclun greens, baby greens, spring salad mix **or** baby spinach, **or** shredded romaine or red and green leaf lettuce, spun dry

1 cup peeled, halved, seeded, and thinly sliced English cucumbers **or** pickling cucumbers

3 cups Marinated Beet Root Salad (Page 366), including some of the juices

1 medium-large or 2 small oranges, peeled, seeded, and sectioned to remove the inner skin

1/2 to 1 cup Fluffy Tahini (Page 409)

Nutrition

1 serving:
216 calories
7 g protein
29 g carbohydrate
(7 g fiber)
8 g fat
130 mg calcium
236 mg sodium

1. Layer greens in a 4-quart bowl or divide among 4 to 6 large plates with sides or bowls with fitted lids. Arrange cucumbers, marinated beets, some of marinade from beets, and orange slices, over greens. Top with tahini and serve. (Dress only portions of salad you plan to serve immediately.)

2. Cover and refrigerate leftovers and use within 24 hours.

Variations

* Replace Fluffy Tahini with 1/2 cup of lightly toasted walnuts (Page 406).

* Replace Marinated Beet Root Salad with peeled, sliced Roasted Beets (Page 366). Toss salad with 1/2 to 3/4 cup Poppy Seed-Orange or Pineapple Drizzle (Page 420) just before serving.

I like the brilliant blush and sweet taste of marinated beets added to simple side salad. To make assembly even easier, make beet salad and Fluffy Tahini a day ahead. If you buy prewashed greens, it's still a good idea to wash and spin them dry before serving. I store the greens in a salad spinner on the top shelf of the fridge so they're ready to go.

Nutty Apple & Green Salad
with Fruity Balsamic-Mustard Vinaigrette

Prep: 30 minutes ~ **Yield:** 6 servings

Ingredients & Directions

2 small or 1 large head dark green leaf lettuce, washed, dried, and torn into bite-size pieces:
> Boston, bib, oak leaf or green leaf, or combination of mild greens with chicory, escarole, radicchio, or arugula (8 to 10 cups)

1 medium cucumber, peeled, halved, quartered, and thinly sliced (about 2 cups)

1/2 to 1 Walla Walla Sweet **or** Vidalia onion, cut into thin rings or crescents (about 2 cups)

3 ribs celery, washed and thinly sliced

1/3 to 1/2 cup toasted walnuts **or** pecans (Page 406), coarsely chopped

1/2 cup unsulphured raisins **or** 4 cups seedless grapes, halved

1/4 cup minced fresh peppermint leaves, optional

1 large or 2 medium tart-sweet apples washed, cored, peeled if waxed, halved, and diced:
> pink lady, gala, Fuji, braeburn, or jonathan

Fruity Balsamic-Mustard Vinaigrette (3/4 cup):

2 tablespoons organic balsamic vinegar

1/4 cup flax oil, unrefined sesame oil, **or** combination

1/4 cup apple juice, apple cider **or** apple-berry juice blend

1 1/2 teaspoons prepared mustard (stone-ground, yellow, Dijon, or white)

1 or 2 pinches finely ground, unrefined sea salt, optional

Freshly ground black pepper, to taste

1   Layer salad ingredients in a 4-quart bowl or divide among 6 smaller containers for pack lunches. If desired prepare to this point, cover with plates or snap-on lid(s), and refrigerate. Add apples at serving time.

2.   Mix vinaigrette ingredients in a small jar. Cover and refrigerate if prepared in advance.

3.   When ready to serve, drizzle dressing over salad, toss, to coat, divide among 6 large plates, and serve. Refrigerate leftovers and use within 24 hours.

Variations

*   Replace Fruity Balsamic-Mustard Vinaigrette with 1 to 1 1/4 cups Poppy Seed-Pineapple Drizzle, Lean & Creamy Mustard or Basil-Balsamic Dressing (see Index for recipes).

*   For one-dish dining, divide salad into 4 to 6 portions. Top each with 3 to 5 ounces of sliced skinless chicken, turkey breast, salmon, or pork loin or chops.

Nutrition

1 serving without dressing:

143 calories
3 g protein
22 g carbohydrate
(4 g fiber)
5 g fat
55 mg calcium
27 mg sodium

1 serving with 2 tablespoons dressing:

237 calories
3 g protein
24 g carbohydrate
(4 g fiber)
14 g fat
56 mg calcium
45 mg sodium

Here's a takeoff on the classic Waldorf salad. Adding fruit to green salads often encourages kids and adults to take second helpings. Try different salad greens, apples, and nuts.

Nutty Spring Green & Orange Salad
with Sweet Citrus Vinaigrette

Prep: 30 minutes ~ **Yield:** 6 servings

Ingredients & Directions

Salad:

8 cups washed, dried, and torn, mixed salad greens: Boston, bib, butter, oak leaf, red or green leaf combined with a smaller volume of arugula, chicory, sorrel, or watercress, stems removed

2 cups Belgian endive **or** radicchio, washed and spun dry

1/2 to 1 medium Walla Walla Sweet **or** Vidalia onion, cut into thin rings or half-moons

3 to 4 medium-size, seedless oranges, peeled, sectioned, and cut into bite-size pieces, pith removed

1/2 cup lightly toasted walnuts **or** pecan halves (Page 406), chopped in half

1/4 cup fresh, roughly chopped mint leaves **or** edible flower, optional

1 cup Toasted Dulse (Page 397) crumbled, optional

Sweet Citrus Vinaigrette (3/4 cup):

2 tablespoons lemon juice **or** organic balsamic vinegar

1/4 cup flax oil, unrefined sesame oil, **or** combination

1/4 to 1/3 cup freshly squeezed orange juice (from about 1 medium orange)

1 1/2 teaspoons creamy white, yellow, or Dijon mustard

1/4 teaspoon finely ground black pepper

1 shallot **or** 1 clove garlic, minced, optional

1 pinch finely ground sea salt, optional

Nutrition

1 serving without dressing:

117 calories
4 g protein
11 g carbohydrate
(4 g fiber)
7 g fat
70 mg calcium
9 mg sodium

1 serving with 2 tablespoons dressing:

211 calories
4 g protein
13 g carbohydrate
(4 g fiber)
16 g fat
17 mg calcium
27 mg sodium

Citrus fruits and nuts encourage kids and adults to take first—and second—helpings of this delicious salad. Vary the ingredients as you like. If you don't enjoy raw onions, try parboiled onions or minced scallions, or omit the onions altogether. For one-dish dining, top each salad with roasted, grilled, or poached salmon, chicken breast, or pork loin.

1. Layer salad ingredients in a 4-quart bowl or divide among 6 smaller containers for pack lunches. Prepare salad to this point, cover, and refrigerate until serving time.

2. Mix vinaigrette ingredients in small jar or blender. Refrigerate in a tightly covered jar if prepared in advance.

3. When ready to serve, drizzle dressing over salad and toss to coat; divide among 6 large plates and serve. Refrigerate leftovers and use within 24 hours.

Variations

* Replace Citrus Vinaigrette with 1 to 1 1/4 cups Poppy Seed-Pineapple or Orange Drizzle, Lean & Creamy Mustard **or** Basil-Balsamic Dressing (see Index for recipes).

* **Spring Green, Orange & Avocado Salad:** Use sweet red onions. Replace nuts with 1 halved, pitted, and cubed ripe avocado.

Roasted Onion, Sweet Pepper & Spring Green Salad

Prep: 30 minutes ~ **Yield:** 4 to 6 servings

Ingredients & Directions

8 to 10 cups packed dark leaf lettuces, washed, dried, sliced thinly or torn into 1 1/2-inch pieces:
romaine, red, green or oak leaf lettuce with arugula, radicchio, curly endive, frisée, or escarole; or prewashed spring salad mix, baby salad greens, or mesclun

2 Roasted (red or gold) Bell Peppers (Page 376), thinly sliced or diced (2 cups)

2 cups Roasted Onions (Page 373)

2 cups thinly sliced celery with tops **or** minced parsley leaves

1/2 cup toasted walnuts **or** pecans (Page 406)

1/2 cup loosely packed, Toasted Dulse (Page 397) crumbled, optional

Juice of 1 lime **or** 2 to 3 tablespoons balsamic vinegar

Nutrition

1 serving:
229 calories
8 g protein
23 g carbohydrate
(3 g fiber)
12 g fat
113 mg calcium
69 mg sodium

1. Layer lettuce, peppers, onions, and celery in a 4-quart bowl or 4 (1-quart) bowls with fitted lids for lunches. Prepare salad to this point, cover, and refrigerate until serving.

2. Sprinkle with nuts, sea vegetable if desired, and lime juice or vinegar. Toss and serve immediately. Cover and refrigerate leftovers and use within 24 hours.

Variations

* To reduce fat content, prepare onions as for Balsamic Roasted Onions (Page 373).

* Replace nuts with 1 large or 2 small halved, seeded, and diced avocados.

* Replace all or half the nuts or avocado with 1/2 to 1 cup Lean & Creamy Basil-Balsamic Dressing **or** Lean & Creamy Mustard Dressing (see Index for recipes).

This is a great make-ahead dish for potlucks, dinner parties, or picnics. You can roast the vegetables up to 24 hours ahead, toast nuts several days in advance, and wash and spin greens early in the day or the night before serving. (Nuts actually keep a long time, but they smell more fragrant immediately after toasting.)

Roasted vegetables and nuts are so flavorful, you don't need a dressing. But, if you want one, I've listed some suggestions in the third variation.

For a main course, top salad portions with sliced chicken or turkey breast, fish, or lean pork loin.

Roasted Onion, Tomato & Spring Green Salad

Prep: 15 to 30 minutes ~ **Yield:** 4 to 6 servings

Ingredients & Directions

8 to 10 packed cups dark leaf lettuces, washed, dried, sliced thinly or torn into 1 1/2-inch pieces:
romaine, red, green or oak leaf lettuce with or without arugula, radicchio, curly endive, frisée, or escarole, watercress, or mustard cress

2 to 3 cups Roasted Onions (Page 373)

1 large or 2 medium tomatoes, sliced, seeded, and diced (2 cups)

1/2 to 1 cup minced celery and/or celery leaves

1 cup English, pickling, or regular cucumber, peeled, halved, seeded, and thinly sliced

1 cup loosely packed, Toasted Dulse (Page 397) crumbled, optional

1 cup Lean & Creamy Mustard, Italian, or Basil-Balsamic Dressing (Page 417 to 419) **or** 1 to 1 1/3 cups Sesame-Dill Dressing (Page 412), **or** Sesame-Pesto Dressing (Page 414)

1. Layer vegetables in 4-quart bowl or 4 (1-quart) bowls with snap-on lids for pack lunches. You may prepare the salad up to this point, cover with a plate or fitted lid(s), and refrigerate until serving time.

2. Dress salad and toss to coat or allow each person to dress his or her salad at the table.

3. Cover and refrigerate leftovers. If dressed use within 24 hours, if undressed, within 2 days.

Variations

* Add 2 to 3 cups Herb-Roasted Potatoes (Page 390).

Nutrition

1 serving (no dressing):

124 calories
6 g protein
17 g carbohydrate
(7 g fiber)
4 g fat
75 mg calcium
18 mg sodium

1 serving with 1/4 cup Lean & Creamy Mustard Dressing:

245 calories
6 g protein
20 g carbohydrate
(7 g fiber)
16 g fat
82 calcium
149 mg sodium

1 serving with 1/4 cup Sesame-Dill Dressing:

233 calories
9 g protein
23 g carbohydrate
(8 g fiber)
12 g fat
100 mg calcium,
138 mg sodium

Roasted vegetables make salad more interesting and inviting. If you roast a couple of pans of vegetables at a time, make it a habit to cook meat with 2 or 3 meals in mind, and prepare salad dressing to last for 1 or 2 weeks at a time, you can assemble this flavor-packed salad in mere minutes. If you're out of dressing, drizzle the salad with lime juice or a good balsamic vinegar and sprinkle with toasted, walnuts, pine nuts, pumpkin seeds, or diced avocado.

Note: For one-dish dining, all you need to do is fan sliced chicken, turkey breast, or lean beef roast, steak, or lamb over each serving plate before serving.

Steak, Sun-Dried Tomato & Green Salad with Onions & Avocado

Prep: 30 minutes ~ **Yield:** 4 servings

Ingredients & Directions

8 cups romaine, red or green leaf lettuce, or spinach (stems removed), washed, dried, thinly sliced

2 cups arugula, watercress, escarole, **or** Belgian endive, washed, dried, and thinly sliced, optional

1 cup minced celery stalk or leaves

1 cup thoroughly washed, dried, and minced parsley leaves, stems removed

1/2 cup minced scallions **or** 1/2 cup sweet white onion (raw or roasted)

12 sun-dried tomato halves

8 to 12 cloves of Roasted Garlic (Page 402)

1 pound lean beef **or** bison (steak or roast cut), broiled, roasted, or grilled, and thinly sliced

2 to 3 ripe, medium-large avocados, halved, seeded, and diced

1 lime, juiced (about 2 tablespoons)

1 cup Toasted Dulse (Page 397) **or** 1/4 cup dulse or nori sea vegetable flakes, optional

Coarsely ground black pepper **or** lemon pepper **or** low-salt hot sauce, to taste

Nutrition

1 serving:
354 calories
32 g protein
16 g carbohydrate
(9 g fiber)
19 g fat
66 mg calcium
80 mg sodium

1. If sun-dried tomatoes have not been soaking in oil, barely cover with warm water; soak for 30 minutes, until tender; drain, and reserve the liquid to toss over the salad before serving. If using oil-packed tomatoes, save the oil for dressing salads. Thinly slice tomatoes with shears.

2. Divide the first 7 ingredients (lettuce through garlic) among 4 large dinner plates or containers with lids. Prepare to this point if desired, then cover and refrigerate.

3. Layer warm or chilled meat over salad portions. Toss avocados with lime juice and spoon over salad. Add dulse if desired. Sprinkle with pepper or dot with hot sauce and serve.

4. Refrigerate leftovers and use within 24 hours.

Cooking lunch from scratch is impractical, if not impossible, for most people. Sometimes even dinner is a challenge. The solution: Wash and chop salad vegetables and bake, broil, or roast beef on Sunday or the night before you need them. Assemble the ingredients for pack lunches or dinner on the fly, preferably with 2 days' meals in mind. Experiment with different salad greens, different vegetables, and different kinds of meat or poultry.

Variations

* Add 2 cups of Roasted Onions or Balsamic Roasted Onions (Page 373).

* **Steak, Sun-Dried Tomato, Potato & Green Salad with Onions & Avocado:** Add 2 to 3 cups Herb-Roasted Potatoes (Page 390). Use raw or roasted onions.

* Replace dried tomatoes with 2 cups halved, seeded, and sliced red, yellow or orange tomatoes.

* Replace avocado and lime with a Lean & Creamy Dressing **or** Tahini Dressing (see Index for recipes).

Salmon Salad with Black Pepper, Pineapple & Basil-Balsamic Dressing

Prep: 30 minutes ~ **Yield:** 4 servings

Ingredients & Directions

1 1/4 pounds wild caught uncooked salmon fillet, cut into 4 pieces

Extra-virgin olive oil

Finely ground black pepper **or** lemon pepper

Finely ground sea salt, optional

8 to 10 cups spring salad, baby salad greens, Italian or mesclun mix

2 cups fresh pineapple, cut into small bite-size cubes

1 cup thinly sliced or minced celery with tops **or** edible flowers

1/2 medium-size, sweet orange bell pepper, cored, seeded, and minced

1/2 cup minced sweet white or red onion **or** scallions

1/4 cup unsweetened or fruit-sweetened, sulfite-free dried cherries

1/4 cup minced mint leaves, stems removed; omit if you can't find

1 cup peeled, sliced fresh water or canned water chestnuts, optional but desirable

1/2 to 1 cup Toasted Dulse (Page 397) crumbled, optional

1 cup Lean & Creamy Basil-Balsamic Dressing (Page 416)

Nutrition

1 serving without dressing:

295 calories
30 g protein
24 g carbohydrate
(4 g fiber)
9 g fat
122 mg calcium
169 mg sodium

1 serving with 1/4 cup Basil-Balsamic Dressing:

418 calories
30 g protein
27 g carbohydrate
(4 g fiber)
21 g fat
130 mg calcium
288 mg sodium

For smooth assembly, prepare salmon and dressing in advance. Keep clean salad greens in a spinner on the top shelf of the fridge, and chopped vegetables in jars in the side door. You can slice the pineapple up to 24 hours in advance. Look for fresh water chestnuts in the produce section of Asian or natural foods supermarkets. Once you try them, canned water chestnuts will never be as satisfying. If you don't like bell peppers, leave them out.

1. Preheat broiler, toaster oven, or grill. Mist or brush salmon with oil and sprinkle with pepper, and sea salt if desired. Bake, broil, or grill until firm to the touch, a thin-bladed knife inserts easily, and flesh is almost the same color throughout, 8 to 10 minutes per inch of thickness.

2. Wash and chop vegetables and fruit. Arrange greens, vegetables, fruits, and herbs of 4 large dinner plates or in 4 containers with fitted lids. Arrange salmon over salad portions.

3. Dress only portions you plan to serve immediately. Drizzle dressing over salad, toss to coat, and serve. If you're dressing and tossing the entire salad for a group, flake salmon first.

4. Refrigerate leftovers and consume within 24 hours

Variations

* Replace Basil-Balsamic Dressing with Poppy Seed-Pineapple Drizzle (Page 420).

* **Salmon, Cranberry & Green Salad:** Omit pineapple and replace cherries with 1/2 cup dried fruit sweetened cranberries. Round out the meal with Baked Sweet Potato (Page 386), Creamy Carrot Soup (Page 370), **or** Tomato, Squash & Ginger Bisque (Page 381).

Practically Paleo Cobb Salad

Prep: 45 to 60 minutes ~ **Yield:** 4 to 6 servings

Ingredients & Directions

1 medium to large head romaine lettuce **or** 1 1/2 romaine hearts, washed, dried, and thinly sliced or torn into 1 1/2-inch bite-size pieces (7 to 8 cups)

1 bunch (about 1 cup) arugula, radicchio, **or** curly leaf endive, washed, dried, and chopped

2 medium red or gold tomato, halved, seeded, and chopped (1 to 1 1/2 cups)

1/4 cup washed, dried, and minced curly or flat leaf parsley leaves, stems removed

3 scallions (including some of the green part), washed, trimmed, and minced

3 small skinless chicken breast halves, baked, broiled, grilled, and thinly sliced (about 1-pound)

1 ripe avocado, halved, peeled and diced

1/4 cup lemon juice from about 1 medium lemon

1 medium-size Hard-Boiled Egg (Page 220) peeled and diced, optional

3/4 to 1 cup Toasted Dulse (Page 397) **or** hickory-smoked dulse leaf crumbled, optional

Dressing, pick one:

1 to 1/2 cups Mustard-Tahini, Cumin-Curry, Coriander-Tahini Dressing, Sesame, Garlic & Chive Dressing, **or** Sesame-Pesto Dressing (Page 411 to 414)

1 to 1 1/2 cup Lean & Creamy Mustard Dressing (Page 417)

Nutrition

1 serving with 1/4 cup Tahini Dressing:

433 calories
45 g protein
17 g carbohydrate
(8 g fiber)
21 g fat
103 mg calcium
265 mg sodium

1 serving with 1/4 cup Lean & Creamy Dressing:

445 calories
42 g protein
14 g carbohydrate
(7 g fiber)
25 g fat
85 mg calcium
248 mg sodium

I've taken great liberties with the classic Cobb. For a rich smoky flavor without bacon, replace the chicken with Roasted Smoky Turkey Breast (Page 258); it's worth making just for the leftovers. And don't forget the dulse leaf, a salty, smoky tasting sea vegetable. You can buy hickory-smoked dulse for an even smokier taste.

You can prep the ingredients several hours in advance, refrigerate them in separate containers, and assemble the salad 15 minutes before serving. Increase or decrease items as you like. Leftovers are perfect for pack lunches. For a light dessert, serve a fresh fruit plate, fresh watermelon, grapes, or Fruit Kabobs (Page 434).

1. Up to 1 hour before serving, layer everything but the avocado, lemon, and dressing in a 5- to 6-quart bowl. Toss avocado with lemon; sprinkle over salad, and bring to the table.

2. If you plan to serve the entire salad, lightly dress and toss to coat, and serve. For less than 4 people, dress individual portions to taste at the table.

3. Cover, and refrigerate leftovers, and use within 2 days.

Variations

* Replace chicken with Roasted Smoky Turkey Breast (Page 258).

Chicken, Sweet Potato & Green Salad

Prep: 20 minutes ~ **Yield:** 2 servings

Ingredients & Directions

4 to 6 cups dark leaf lettuce, washed, dried, and sliced thinly or torn into 1 1/2-inch pieces:
>   romaine, red leaf, green leaf or oak leaf lettuce, or lettuce with arugula, or spinach

1/2 large red or gold bell pepper, halved, seeded and thinly sliced (about 3/4 cup)

1/2 cup halved, thinly sliced red radishes, optional

1/3 cup minced parsley leaf, scallions, chives, **or** celery tops

2 baked small to medium sweet potatoes (Page 386), skinned, and cubed:
>   Jersey sweets (white sweet potatoes), Beauregard, Japanese sweet potatoes, or red garnet or jewel yams

2 small chicken breast halves, cooked and sliced (6 to 8 ounces)

2 to 4 tablespoons toasted pecans (Page 406), optional

1/2 cup Toasted Dulse (Page 397) crumbled, optional

1/2 cup Lean & Creamy Mustard **or** Basil-Balsamic Dressing (Page 417 or 418)

Nutrition

1 serving without dressing or nuts:

317 calories
31 g protein
37 g carbohydrate
(8 g fiber)
5 g fat
108 mg calcium
105 mg sodium

1 serving with 1/4 cup Basil-Balsamic Dressing:

437 calories
31 g protein
40 g carbohydrate
(8 g fiber)
17 g fat
116 mg calcium
224 mg sodium

1. Divide and layer all ingredients except the dressing on 2 large dinner plates, 2 large Pyrex pie plates, or in 2 containers with lids. If desired, prepare salad up to this point, cover with dinner plates or snap-on lids, and refrigerate until serving time.

2. Just before serving, drizzle with dressing and toss to coat. For pack lunches transport dressing in small, tightly closed bottles and dress just before serving.

3. Cover and refrigerate extra portions and use within 24 hours.

Variations

* For a hot meal cook or warm leftover chicken and whole sweet potatoes just before serving.

* Replace salad dressings and nuts with Poppy Seed-Pineapple Drizzle (Page 420), **or** Spicy Peanut Sauce (Page 416).

* **Turkey, Sweet Potato & Green Salad:** Replace chicken with Roasted Smoky Turkey Breast (Page 258), **or** Quick Smoky Turkey (Page 261).

You can assemble this colorful main-course salad quickly if you wash greens, toast nuts, bake sweet potatoes and chicken, and make dressing the day or night before you need them (or use this recipe to transform dinner into tomorrow's lunch). To serve 2 people, 2 days in a row, double everything, and dress your portions just before serving. If you need more calories, increase the nuts or use slightly larger sweet potatoes or more chicken.

Individual Crudité Plates

Prep: 15 to 20 minutes ~ **Yield:** 2 servings

Ingredients & Directions

4 ounces of cooked chicken breast, cut into thin strips

3 1/2 ounces peeled, deveined, boiled or broiled shrimp or prawns

2 Hard-Boiled Eggs (Page 220), cut into half lengthwise, **or** Angeled Eggs (Page 221)

1 large carrot, cut into sticks, raw or parboiled (Page 355)

2 cups broccoli, cut into florets and parboiled (Page 330)

2 cups cauliflower, cut into florets and parboiled (Page 330)

2 celery ribs, cut into half, then into sticks

1/2 to 2/3 cup Mustard-Tahini Dressing (Page 411), Sesame-Pesto Dressing (Page 414), **or** Tahini Tartar Sauce (Page 410)

1/2 cup Better Barbecue Sauce **or** Cajun Ketchup (Page 401)

Nutrition

1 serving:
435 calories
42 g protein
28 g carbohydrate
(10 g fiber)
18 g fat
167 mg calcium
512 mg sodium

1. Slice cooked chicken breast. Steam or broil shrimp until tails curl and flesh turns pink.

2. Divide vegetables, chicken, shrimp, and eggs between 2 serving plates or platters, arranging ingredients like spokes on a wheel, spiraling out from center, leaving empty space in the center. Vegetables that don't fit may be arranged on a separate platter.

3. Divide Mustard-Tahini Dressing, Sesame-Pesto or Tahini Tartar Sauce between 2 custard cups; place 1 custard cup in the center of each plate. Divide barbecue sauce or ketchup between 2 custard cups and serve alongside.

4. Cover and refrigerate unused portions and use within 24 hours.

Variations

* Other good vegetables for plate: trimmed, raw red radishes, endive, romaine hearts, peeled, seeded, sliced cucumber spears, or parboiled red, yellow, or orange bell pepper strips, sugar snap peas, pea pods, yellow wax beans, broccoflower, or asparagus.

* Replace chicken with turkey breast or lean meatballs. Adjust portions up or down as you like.

In France, the term *"crudité"* refers to an assortment of individual vegetables dressed and arranged in sections on the same plate. To Americans, the term refers to a tray of sliced raw carrots, celery, broccoli, and cauliflower served with a dip. I do it differently. I parboil most of the vegetables to remove bitter flavors and make them more tender and digestible, and I often add meat, fish, poultry or hard-boiled eggs to make a light meal. For desserts consider a fruit salad, Fresh Fruit Gel, Fruit Kabobs, Date-Coconut Rolls Stuffed with Nuts, or Chocolate-Dipped Dates (see Index for recipes).

Surf & Turf Salad

Prep: 20 minutes ~ **Yield:** 2 servings

Ingredients & Directions

4 to 6 cups packed dark leaf lettuces, washed, dried, and sliced thinly or torn into 1 1/2-inch pieces:
> romaine, red leaf, green leaf, or oak leaf lettuce with arugula, Radicchio, curly endive, frisée, escarole, or prewashed spring salad mix, baby greens, **or** mesclun

1 cup halved red or gold cherry or pear tomatoes **or** 2 Roma tomatoes, sliced, seeded, and diced

1 cup Roasted Onions (Page 373) **or** Roasted Mushrooms (Page 375)

3/4 cup peeled, seeded, quartered, and thinly sliced cucumber

1/4 cup minced fresh curly or flat leaf parsley **or** basil leaves, stems removed

2 tablespoons toasted pine nuts (Page 406)

1/4 to 1/2 head Roasted Garlic (Page 402), optional

1/2 cup loosely packed, toasted, crumbled wild nori **or** dulse sea vegetable (Page 397), optional

4 ounces water-packed tuna **or** cooked white meat fish

4 ounces cooked chicken or turkey breast, lean beef, **or** bison, trimmed of fat

1 Hard-Boiled Egg (Page 220), peeled and diced, optional

1/2 cup Lean & Creamy Basil-Balsamic, Mustard, French, **or** Italian Dressing (Page 417 to 419)

Nutrition

1 serving without dressing:
224 calories
38 g protein
20 g carbohydrate
(5 g fiber)
10 g fat
71 mg calcium
112 mg sodium

1 serving with 1/4 cup Basil-Balsamic Dressing:
347 calories
38 g protein
23 g carbohydrate
(5 g fiber)
22 g fat
79 mg calcium
231 mg sodium

Making a salad the focal point of a meal allows you to use up leftover vegetables and small portions of meat. If you've roasted vegetables, made dressing, and washed salad greens in advance, prep time will be minimal.

Use this recipe as a model for making colorful main-course salads with whatever you have on hand. For a satisfying last course, serve sliced fresh fruit, a fruit gel, or compote. Mix the fish and meat into both salads, or decide who gets the surf and who gets the turf.

1. Divide salad greens between 2 large Pyrex pie plates, dinner plates with sides, or quart bowls with snap-on lids for lunches. Layer remaining ingredients except meat and dressing over greens. You may prepare to this point, then cover and refrigerate.

2. If desired, briefly warm meat before arranging over salad(s). To serve, add dressing to individual plates, a little at a time. Toss to coat, adding more as needed.

Variations

* Omit dressing and increase nuts to 1/2 cup. Drizzle each salad with meat pan juices and a good balsamic vinegar. Or, replace the nuts and dressing with 1 diced avocado and 2 lime wedges.

Tuna, Beet & Green Salad

Prep: 20 to 30 minutes ~ **Yield:** 2 servings

Ingredients & Directions

3 cups raw broccoli, parboiled (Page 330)

1 1/2 cups raw cauliflower, parboiled (Page 330)

1 cup yellow or orange bell pepper strips, parboiled (Page 335)

1 1/2 to 2 cups Marinated Beet Root Salad (Page 366)

6 to 8 ounces cooked fresh tuna **or** drained, water packed, no-salt tuna

1/4 cup minced curly or flat leaf parsley, scallions, chives, **or** combination of 2 of these

1 Hard-Boiled Egg (Page 220), peeled and diced, optional

4 tablespoons dulse flakes, optional

1/2 to 2/3 cup Mustard-Tahini, Sesame-Dill, or Sesame-Pesto Dressing (Page 411, 412, 414) **or** 1/3 cup Homemade Mayonnaise (Page 424)

1. Parboil vegetables 1 at a time in boiling water, cooking bell peppers for 1 minute, broccoli for 2 minutes, and cauliflower 2 to 3 minutes, then plunge in ice water and drain well.

2. Divide parboiled vegetables between 2 large dinner plates with sides or 1-quart bowls with fitted lids. Top with beet salad and some of the salad juices.

3. Combine tuna, parsley, scallions, or chives, and dressing or mayonnaise in a small bowl. Stir and spoon over vegetables. Garnish with hard-boiled egg and dulse if desired.

4. Cover and refrigerate unused portions and use within 24 hours.

Variations

Turkey, Beet & Green Salad: Replace tuna with 6 to 8 ounces of sliced turkey breast, or peeled and deveined shrimp, boiled or steamed for 2 to 3 minutes until tails curl and flesh turns pink.

*   Replace broccoli with asparagus.

Nutrition

1 serving with tahini dressing:

357 calories
31 g protein
40 g carbohydrate
(13 g fiber)
8 g fat
154 mg calcium
414 mg sodium

1 serving with mayonnaise:

443 calories
29 g protein
30 g carbohydrate
(11 g fiber)
11 g fat
132 mg calcium
240 mg sodium

Raw broccoli and cauliflower contain goitrogens that can inhibit thyroid function. Parboiling inactivates the goitrogens. It also removes bitterness, makes the vegetables more digestible, more colorful, and sweeter.

I make this main-course salad after I've made Marinated Beet Root Salad. (Don't even think about using canned beets; their flavor and nutritional value are negligible.) I parboil the vegetables fresh, or use vegetables I cooked the previous day. Freshly cooked tuna tastes best; if you use canned, make sure it's packed in water without salt, MSG, or broth (which may contain MSG even if the label doesn't say so).

Basic Coleslaw

Prep: 30 minutes ~ **Marinating:** 1-6 hours ~ **Yield:** 8 cups; 8 to 12 servings

---

Ingredients & Directions

(16 to 18 packed cups):

12 cups shredded hard green cabbage or combination red and green cabbage

2 cups coarsely grated carrot

1 to 2 cups finely minced white, yellow, or red onion

1 to 2 cups minced celery with tops

2 teaspoons unrefined sea salt (such as Celtic)

2 cloves minced garlic, optional

Dressing, select one, optional:

1 1/4 to 1 1/2 cups Tahini Dressing:
  Sesame-Dill, Mustard-Tahini, Sesame, Garlic &
  Chive, Sesame-Pesto, or other (Page 411 to 414)

1 1/4 to 1 1/2 cups Spicy Peanut Sauce (Page 416)

3/4 to 1 cup Homemade Mayonnaise, plain or flavored (Page 424)

1 cup Fluffy Tahini (Page 409) plus 1/4 cup raw apple cider vinegar **or** red wine vinegar **or** lemon juice

Nutrition

1 serving w/out dressing:

59 calories
2 g protein
13 g carbohydrate
    (4 g fiber)
80 mg calcium
sodium unknown

1 serving w/tahini dressing:

126 calories
4 g protein
16 g carbohydrate
    (5 g fiber)
5 g fat
96 mg calcium
sodium unknown

Salting and crushing the vegetables may sound like extra work, but it's worth it. People in Asia and Europe have been doing it for centuries. Here's why: It breaks down the tough fibers, releases water, and concentrates the nutrients, producing a more tender, flavorful, and digestible salad that will keep for 10 days in the refrigerator (5 days in a cooler if you change the ice daily). With practice you'll learn this versatile recipe by heart. A mandolin makes slicing fast and effortless.

1. Combine all ingredients except dressing in large mixing bowl. Knead salt into vegetables with your hands until cabbage starts to shrink and release water, 5 to 6 minutes.

2. Pack salad into the bottom of bowl. Cover with smaller plate that fits inside the rim; place a jug of water on plate to press on vegetables. Alternatively, pack into a 3 1/2- to 4-quart Asian style pickle press and tighten the top. Leave at room temperature for 1 to 6 hours to release more water; refrigerate in very hot weather.

3. Drain in a colander or strainer over a large bowl, squeezing cabbage, 1 handful at a time to remove salty liquid. Reserve liquid if you plan to store half or more of the salad undressed for more than 4 days; otherwise discard juices.

4. Taste salad. If too salty, rinse with cold, filtered water, drain thoroughly, and dress.

5. Refrigerate dressed coleslaw in a covered jar or bowl and use within 4 days. Pack undressed slaw into 1 or 2 wide-mouth quart jars and top with salty juices from step 2. Use undressed salad within 10 days.

Note: If you're cooking for 2, dress half of the salad, then refrigerate the rest, covered with the salty juices. Drain and dress later in the week.

~ Variations next page ~

Variations

Basic Coleslaw ~ continued

* Replace half the carrots with peeled and grated rutabaga (choose small rather than larger roots for best results) or use seeded, diced, or cubed sweet red, orange, or yellow bell pepper.

* Replace 1 1/2 cups of cabbage or carrot with thinly sliced small red radishes. If desired, add 1 halved, seeded, and cubed or diced red or yellow bell pepper.

* Use savoy or nappa cabbage, cut into 1-inch squares; replace onion with 1 bunch of trimmed scallions, cut into 1-inch lengths; replace celery (or 2 cups cabbage) with quartered, thinly sliced pickling cucumbers or peeled, seeded, and sliced regular cucumbers.

* For an Asian-flavored dressing, combine mayonnaise with 1 teaspoon dry mustard, 2 cloves minced or pressed garlic, 2 teaspoons ginger juice **or** peeled and finely grated fresh ginger, and 1/4 teaspoon ground red pepper. Garnish with toasted sesame seeds if desired.

* **Coleslaw with mayonnaise:** Dress the entire salad with about 1/3 cup of plain mayonnaise. Add 2 tablespoons lemon juice or cider vinegar **or** wine vinegar if desired. Add 1 tablespoon dried dill weed or 3 tablespoons minced fresh dill weed, 1 teaspoon dry **or** 2 teaspoons prepared mustard, and 1/2 teaspoon ground black pepper **or** 1/4 teaspoon ground chipotlé. Alternatively, use herbed mayonnaise.

* Replace creamy dressings with 1/4 cup extra-virgin olive or flax oil mixed with 3 to 4 tablespoons raw apple cider vinegar or red wine vinegar, 2 cloves of pressed garlic, 1/2 teaspoon celery seed and 1/2 teaspoon ground black pepper or to taste.

* To extend the salad or add more color to any of the variations, surround the bowl of coleslaw with parboiled broccoli florets when serving.

* **Hot slaw:** Undressed coleslaw may be steamed until tender. This is delicious on a cold day, served with or without butter, flax oil, or lemon-flavored cod liver oil.

20 Roots, Tubers, Squash & Other Vegetables

BEST BITES

Marinated Beet Root Salad

Prep: 30 minutes ~ **Cooking:** 40 to 60 minutes ~ **Yield:** 8 to 9 cups

Ingredients & Directions

Vegetables:

3 pounds small to medium-size beets with tails and stubs but not leaves, washed

2 bay leaves

Filtered water to completely cover beets

3 cups water to cook onions, optional

2 medium onions (sweet onions are good raw), cut into thin half-moons

Beet Vinaigrette:

1/2 cup balsamic vinegar

1/4 teaspoon ground black pepper

1 1/2 teaspoons dry mustard

1 1/2 teaspoons ground cumin

4-inch piece fresh horseradish root, peeled and finely grated, optional

1/2 cup thoroughly washed, dried, chopped, fresh parsley leaves, optional

1 cup Fluffy Tahini (Page 409) **or** 1 cup toasted walnuts (Page 406), chopped, optional

1. Cover beets and bay leaves with water in large pot. Cover, bring to boil, reduce heat, and simmer until tender and skewer inserts easily, 30 to 60 minutes, depending on size.

2. Slice onions. If you prefer, cook for 60 seconds in 3 cups boiling water and drain. Save water to drink or add to soup. Set onions aside.

3. Mix vinaigrette ingredients in 3- to 4-quart Pyrex bowl. Toss with onions and set aside.

4. Plunge beets in ice water. Drain, remove tops and tails; slip off skins with knife. Cut small beets into thin rounds; cut large beets into half- or quarter-moons. Toss with onions. Add horseradish and/or parsley if desired. Marinate at room temperature for 2 hours or refrigerate for at least 3 hours before serving.

5. Serve with Fluffy Tahini or toasted walnuts if desired. Use within 1 week or freeze.

Variations

* Replace balsamic vinegar with raw apple cider vinegar and add 2 tablespoons tamari. See box for nutrition information.

* **Roasted Beets:** Wrap raw beets in aluminum foil and bake in a 400° F oven for 40 to 60 minutes, or until skewer inserts easily. Continue with steps 2 through 5.

Nutrition

1/2 cup:

48 calories
1 g protein
11 g carbohydrate
            (2 g fiber)
19 mg calcium
99 mg sodium

**Variation
1/2 cup serving:**

48 calories
2 g protein
10 g carbohydrate
            (2 g fiber)
18 mg calcium
174 mg sodium

People who don't ordinarily like beets have changed their minds after trying this salad. The secret is to cook fresh beets; don't even think of using canned. Forget the hype about beets being high on the glycemic index; they have a low-glycemic load and they're very nutritious. Served with a complete protein, cooked greens or salad, and nuts, seeds, or oil, the meal will have a moderate glycemic index

---

FYI: Halve recipe when cooking for 2 or 3 people.

Creamy ABC Bisque

Prep: 15 minutes ~ **Cooking:** 30 minutes ~ **Yield:** 6 servings

---

Ingredients & Directions

1/2 to 3/4 cup unsalted, unroasted whole or halved cashews

1 cup boiling water

3 medium-large blond or golden beets (3 1/2 to 4 cups, cut into 1/2-inch diced pieces)

1 large or 2 small tart-sweet apples, cored, peeled if desired, and quartered (about 2 heaping cups):
    Fuji, gala, braeburn, golden delicious, criterion, early gold or ginger gold

1 1/4 teaspoons apple pie spice **or** pumpkin pie spice **or** 2 tablespoons grated fresh gingerroot

1 tablespoon minced or grated lemon zest **or** orange zest, colored part only

2 1/2 cups filtered water **or** preservative-free chicken broth, **or** diluted Bone-Building Broth (Page 278) **or** combination, additional 1/2 cup if needed to blend

1/2 to 1 cup apple juice/cider

2 tablespoons lemon juice **or** orange juice

1/8 teaspoon stevia extract powder, optional

3 to 4 tablespoons minced fresh fennel fronds **or** mint leaves for garnish

Nutrition

1 serving:
137 calories
3 g protein
21 g carbohydrate
        (5 g fiber)
5 g fat
28 mg calcium
72 mg sodium

Apples and puréed cashews add a rich taste and creamy texture to this surprising starter or final course. Look for golden beets at your local farmers' market. They will be pale gold or slightly pink on the outside, golden inside. The taste is surprisingly mild. Peeled and puréed, they produce a lemon-yellow soup that frequently fools people who say they don't like beets.

1. Chop cashews, cover with 1 cup hot water, and soak at room temperature for 3 hours or refrigerate in a jar for up to 12 hours.

2. Layer cashews, beets, apples, pie spice, and lemon rind in 2-quart saucepan and cover with water or water plus broth used for boiling cashews. Cover, bring to boil, reduce heat, and simmer until beets are tender, about 35 minutes.

3. Purée soup in 2 batches in food processor or blender, adding apple juice, lemon juice or orange juice, and extra water as needed to create 6 cups of smooth soup. Warm gently over low heat, stirring frequently. Ladle soup into cups or bowls, garnish with fennel or mint, and serve. Use within 4 days.

Variations

* **Creamy Carrot, Apple & Cashew Bisque**: Replace beets with carrots.

Oven-Fried Parsnips with Pie Spice

Prep: 20 minutes ~ **Cooking:** 35 to 40 minutes ~ **Yield:** 8 servings

Ingredients & Directions

2 pounds small parsnips, scrubbed, rinsed, peeled, and trimmed

2 tablespoons clarified butter, ghee, **or** extra-virgin olive oil or coconut oil

2 teaspoons apple pie spice **or** pumpkin pie spice

1/2 teaspoon finely ground, unrefined sea salt **or**
1 tablespoon tamari soy sauce

1. Preheat oven to 400° F. Line a 14x19x2-inch or 18x9x2-inch baking pan with unbleached parchment paper for easy cleanup.

2. Cut parsnips into 3-inch by 1/2-inch sticks. Toss with oil, spice, and salt in a large mixing bowl. Arrange in prepared pan being careful not to crowd.

3. Roast, uncovered, turning parsnips after 15 minutes. Cook for 35 to 40 minutes or until tender and lightly golden.

4. Serve warm. Cover and refrigerate leftovers, and use within 3 days.

Variations

* Replace pie spice with cinnamon **or** 2 tablespoons juice from peeled, finely grated, and squeezed fresh gingerroot. (Use a microplane or the smallest hole of a cheese grater.)

* **Oven-Fried Carrots & Parsnips with Pie Spice:** Use half carrots and half parsnips.

* For a sweeter taste, douse parsnips or carrots and parsnips with 1/2 cup apple juice before roasting. When juice cooks away vegetables will caramelize.

* **Oven-Fried Sweet Potatoes:** Replace parsnips with red garnet or jewel yams, or white (Jersey) sweet potatoes. Use cinnamon, pie spice, **or** ground rosemary with dried thyme. Peel if desired.

* **Roasted Parsnips:** Omit pie spice, salt, and tamari. Roast as instructed above.

Nutrition

3/4 cup:
118 calories
3 g protein
19 g carbohydrate
5 g fat
41 mg calcium
126 mg sodium

Parsnips make a great alternative to French fries. Although they're high on the glycemic index, they actually have a low-glycemic load because of their bulk. We serve them with eggs, fish, chicken, turkey, or lamb, and cooked leafy greens or a tossed salad.

Good parsnips are essential. Search for parsnips after a frost, when their natural sugars develop. Select the smallest roots you can find. Large, overgrown roots are usually tough, dry, and bitter.

Roasted Carrots

Prep: 15 minutes ~ **Cooking:** 40 to 50 minutes ~ **Yield:** 6 servings

Ingredients & Directions

2 pounds carrots, scrubbed, rinsed, trimmed, and peeled
if desired

1 medium onion, cut into 1 1/2-inch chunks, optional

2 tablespoons extra-virgin olive oil **or** coconut oil

2 teaspoons Garam Masala spice blend

1. Preheat oven to 400° F. Add oil to 14x9x2-inch or
   18x9x2-inch roasting pan or 2 (9-inch) cake pans.

2. Cut carrots into 2- to 3-inch lengths, then cut in
   half lengthwise and in half lengthwise again to make
   sticks. Add to roasting pan and toss with spices and
   oil.

3. Roast uncovered until tender and evenly browned, 40
   to 50 minutes, stirring every 15 minutes.

4. Serve warm or chilled. Cover and refrigerate leftovers and use
   within 3 days.

Nutrition

1 serving (about 3/4 cup):

119 calories
2 g protein
14 g carbohydrate
(6 g fiber)
5 g fat
53 mg calcium
61 mg sodium

These tender, tasty, caramelized carrot sticks look like French fries, only they're orange. They pair well with burgers, fish steaks, or pork chops and salad. I always make enough for 3 meals, to serve 3 days in row. They're delicious warm, or chilled, as a side dish, or added to a tossed green side salad or main-course salad with meat. Don't be shy; give the variations a try.

Variations

* **Roasted Carrots with Ginger:** Omit Garam Masala. After carrots
  have roasted for 30 minutes, toss with 2 tablespoons ginger juice
  made from peeled, finely grated, and squeezed fresh ginger. (Use a
  microplane or ginger grater and discard pulp.)

* **Roasted Carrots with Rosemary:** Substitute 2 teaspoons dried,
  powdered rosemary plus 1/4 teaspoon ground black pepper for
  Garam Masala.

* **Roasted Carrots with Mustard Seeds:** Omit Garam Masala. After
  carrots have roasted for 20 minutes, add 2 tablespoons of whole
  yellow mustard seeds and continue roasting until done, stirring
  occasionally.

* **Roasted Carrots and Turnips:** Peel and quarter 1 pound of small
  unwaxed turnips and toss with 1 cup of carrots cut into small
  wedges. Replace Garam Masala with 2 teaspoons dried, powdered
  rosemary, thyme, **or** mixed Italian herbs.

* **Roasted Winter Squash:** Peel, halve, and seed a 3-pound butternut
  squash. Cut into 2-inch square- or triangle-shaped pieces. Toss with
  oil and Garam Masala, cinnamon, apple or pumpkin pie spice, **or** 2
  tablespoons ginger juice. Roast.

Note: Garam Masala is a blend of cardamom, cinnamon, cloves, cumin, black pepper, and coriander sold in natural foods stores. If you don't like strong spices, try one of the variations, especially the one with ginger, or prepare the carrots without spices.

Creamy Carrot Soup with Ginger

Prep: 20 minutes ~ **Cooking:** 20 to 30 minutes ~ **Yield:** 6 servings

Ingredients & Directions

1 tablespoon unrefined coconut oil, clarified butter **or** ghee

1 medium onion, finely chopped

1/2 to 1 teaspoon finely ground, unrefined sea salt

1 tablespoon peeled, finely minced fresh gingerroot

1 1/2 pounds carrots, sliced into 1/2-inch thick rounds (about 4 packed cups)

2 cups poultry stock, Basic Poultry Bone-Building Broth (Page 278), preservative-free chicken broth, **or** filtered water

1/3 to 1/2 cup apple juice or cider **or** water plus 1/8 teaspoon stevia extract powder

1/2 teaspoon dried ground ginger, optional

1/2 cup coconut milk (Thai Kitchen, premium *not lite*), thoroughly blended

1/2 cup water, stock, **or** broth as needed to blend

Freshly grated nutmeg, minced scallions, chives, parsley **or** fennel fronds for garnish

Nutrition

1 cup serving:
106 calories
1 g protein
12 g carbohydrate
(3 g fiber)
6 g fat
28 mg calcium
344 mg sodium

Coconut milk adds a creamy taste and texture without dairy products and with less than half the fat and calories of cream. Look for Thai Kitchen or Edward and Sons coconut milk in natural food stores or the ethnic aisle of supermarkets. These are the purest brands—free of added sugar, sulfites, or other preservatives.

1. Warm oil in 2- to 3-quart saucepan over medium heat. Add onions. Stir and cook until tender, about 4 minutes, adding salt to draw out moisture. Add fresh ginger, stir for 1 minute. Add carrots, stock or broth, apple juice or water plus stevia, and dried ginger. Bring to low boil, reduce heat, and simmer until carrots are tender, about 30 minutes.

2. In blender or food processor, purée soup and coconut milk a few cups at a time. (Hold down top with a dishtowel and start on low to prevent splattering.) Add additional 1/4 cup juice, stock, broth, or water as needed to thin.

3. Return soup to saucepan and warm briefly, without boiling. Ladle into bowls, garnish, and serve. Refrigerate leftovers and use within 4 days.

Variations

* Replace ginger with 1 small clove of garlic and 1/8 teaspoon each of ground white pepper and nutmeg.

* **Creamy Carrot Soup with Cumin & Dill:** Omit ginger. Add 1/2 teaspoon ground cumin in step 1. Blend in 1 teaspoon dried or 1 tablespoon fresh dill weed in step 2.

* **Creamy Carrot Soup with Curry:** Reduce fresh ginger to 1 1/2 teaspoons and replace dried ginger with 1/2 teaspoon curry powder.

* Replace half the coconut milk with 1 1/2 tablespoons roasted, unsalted almond butter.

Simmered Carrots with Sunchokes

Prep: 20 minutes ~ **Cooking:** 35 to 45 minutes ~ **Yield:** 6 cups; 8 servings

Ingredients & Directions

1/2 to 3/4 cup water **or** salt-free stock **or** Bone-Building Broth, to barely cover bottom of pot

1 (8-inch) piece kelp **or** kombu, cut into 1/2-inch pieces with shears, **or** 1 whole bay leaf

1 teaspoon ground cumin **or** 1/2 teaspoon cumin and 1/2 teaspoon dried ginger

1/2 teaspoon lemon pepper **or** 1/4 teaspoon ground chipotlé

1 medium onion, cut into 1-inch cubes or wedges, optional

1/2 teaspoon finely ground, unrefined sea salt **or** 1 tablespoon tamari soy sauce, optional

4 cups carrots, cut into 2x1-inch wedges, or halved lengthwise and cut into 2-inch pieces

4 cups sunchokes (Jerusalem artichokes), cut into 2x1-inch wedges

1/4 cup minced parsley, scallions, **or** chives for garnish, optional

1/2 cup Fluffy Tahini (Page 409) **or** toasted walnuts (Page 406), coarsely chopped, for garnish, optional

Nutrition

1 serving:
121 calories
4 g protein
27 g carbohydrate
(4 g fiber)
50 mg calcium
54 mg sodium

This colorful stove-top dish requires just enough water to create steam. At the end all of the liquid should be cooked into the vegetables. To round out the meal, I serve sautéed leafy greens or a crisp green salad and salmon, chicken, turkey, pork chops, or burgers.

Sunchokes contain a blood sugar-balancing starch called inulin, and a pesky carbohydrate called *FOS* (fructo-oligo-saccharide). It's the FOS that can increase the production of intestinal gas for some people. If you're one of them, take digestive enzymes with the meal, or substitute turnips or potatoes for sunchokes.

1. Add 1/4-inch water, stock, or broth to 3- to 4-quart heavy-bottomed pot. Add kelp, kombu or bay leaf, cumin, pepper, and optional onion, sea salt or tamari if desired.

2. Rinse and scrub vegetables. Peel if waxed or marred. Scrub sunchokes exceedingly well to remove all traces of sand. If knobby, break off knobs, rinse and scrub again. Cut carrots and sunchokes into similar sized chunks and place in separate bowls.

3. Layer carrots and sunchokes in pot. Cover and bring to boil without stirring. Reduce heat to medium-low, and simmer until fork tender, 35 to 45 minutes.

4. Stir gently with large, wide wooden spoon without mashing. If liquid remains, remove lid and simmer away liquid. Garnish and serve warm. Refrigerate leftovers and use within 3 days.

Variations

* **Simmered Carrots with Ginger:** Replace sunchokes with carrots. Replace cumin and pepper with 1/2 teaspoon dried ginger or 2 teaspoons peeled, minced, fresh ginger.

* **Simmered Carrots & Parsnips:** Use carrots and peeled small parsnips. Substitute ground cinnamon for cumin and ground ginger for pepper.

* **Simmered Potatoes:** Substitute peeled, cubed potatoes for onions, carrots, and sunchokes. Use cumin or substitute 1 teaspoon Italian herbs. Add 1/4 teaspoon pepper and sea salt. Serve with butter, coconut oil or flax oil, or as part of a main-course salad.

Sautéed Sunchokes with Dulse

Prep: 20 minutes ~ **Cooking:** 30 minutes ~ **Yield:** 6 to 8 servings

Ingredients & Directions

1 packed cup raw dulse sea vegetable, sorted to remove small shells and stones

Filtered water to soak sea vegetable

1 large onion, thinly sliced into crescents or half-moons

2 tablespoons extra-virgin olive oil **or** unrefined coconut oil

3 small to medium-size garlic cloves, coarsely chopped

6 to 8 cups washed, cubed sunchokes/Jerusalem artichokes

1 teaspoon ground cumin **or** dried, rubbed sage

1 teaspoon lemon pepper **or** 1/4 teaspoon ground black pepper

1 bay leaf, optional

1/2 teaspoon unrefined sea salt **or** 1 tablespoon tamari, optional

1/2 cup filtered water, Bone-Building Broth (Page 278) or 306), **or** preservative-free chicken broth

1/4 cup minced scallions, chives, or parsley for garnish

> **Nutrition**
>
> **1 serving:**
> 135 calories
> 4 g protein
> 22 g carbohydrate
> (3 g fiber)
> 4 g fat
> 28 mg calcium
> 52 mg sodium

Jerusalem artichokes (also called sunchokes) bear no resemblance to globe artichokes and have absolutely nothing to do with Jerusalem. Sunchokes are light-cream colored, round or oblong, and usually the size of fingerling potatoes, sometimes with protruding knobs. For sunchoke selection and storage tips, see Chapter 10.

1. Do not rinse dulse. After sorting, snip into 1/2-inch pieces with kitchen shears. Soak in enough water to barely cover. Meanwhile, chop onions. Scrub and rinse sunchokes, break off any knobs and scrub the crevices with a brush under running water. Slice sunchokes into 1 1/2- to 2-inch chunks or wedges. Chop garlic and set aside.

2. Heat oil in large cast iron skillet or Dutch oven over medium heat. Add onions, stir, and cook until almost translucent around the edges. Add sea salt or tamari if desired, then garlic, cumin or sage, pepper, and bay leaf. Add sunchokes.

3. Remove dulse from water. Add dulse and water to skillet, holding back any gritty material in bottom of bowl. Stir and add 1/2 cup water, broth, or stock.

4. Cover and bring to low boil, reduce heat to medium-low and simmer without stirring, until sunchokes are tender and juicy, 20 to 30 minutes. Remove lid, stir, and simmer away liquid. Remove from heat, garnish, and serve. Refrigerate leftovers and use within 3 days.

Variations

* **Sautéed Potatoes with Dulse:** Replace sunchokes with peeled, unblemished, firm white or yellow potatoes free of sprouts and green skin.

FYI: Sunchokes contain a blood sugar-balancing starch called inulin and a pesky carbohydrate called FOS (fructo-oligo-saccharides), which gives some people gas. You'll know if you're one of them. This dish goes well with cooked kale or collard greens and salmon.

Roasted Onions

Prep: 5 minutes ~ **Cooking:** 40 to 50 minutes ~ **Yield:** 3 to 4 cups; 6 to 8 servings

Ingredients & Directions

2 to 2 1/2 pounds white, yellow or red onions (3 jumbo or 4 to 6 large), 8 to 10 cups:
Spanish, yellow, white, or vidalia, Walla Walla, **or** Maui onion

2 tablespoons extra-virgin olive oil **or** unrefined coconut oil

1/4 teaspoon ground black pepper **or** lemon pepper

1 1/2 teaspoons dried, crumbled thyme, sage, rosemary, oregano, or combination

4 shallots, peeled and quartered **or** 1/2 head garlic, optional

Nutrition

1 serving:
103 calories
2 g protein
13 g carbohydrate
(3 g fiber)
5 g fat
37 mg calcium
5 mg sodium

1. Preheat oven to 400° F. Break garlic head into individual cloves, peel, and set aside.

2. Trim, halve, peel, and cut each onion into sixths or eighths to make wedges, into 1-inch cubes, or thin crescents or half-moons. Combine onions, oil, pepper, and herbs in a 9x9x2-inch baking pan and toss to coat. Use a 13x9x2-inch pan for a double batch.

3. Roast uncovered for 15 minutes. Stir top to bottom. Add garlic or shallots if desired. Roast for 15 minutes and stir again. Roast 10 to 15 minutes longer or until lightly golden and tender.

4. Serve or cool, and refrigerate in covered glass container or jar. Use within 4 days.

Variations

* Substitute Fine Herbes or Herbes de Provençe for oregano, thyme, and rosemary.

* **Roasted Balsamic Onions (half the fat of main recipe):** Use 1 tablespoon oil and add 2 tablespoons balsamic vinegar. Cover pan with a lid or foil. Roast for 20 minutes uncover, stir, and roast 20 minutes longer.

* **Roasted Pearl Onions:** Plunge 4 pints of pearl onions into boiling water for 1 minute. Drain and rinse under cold water. Cut off ends and slide off skins, leaving onions whole. Arrange in 1 large or 2 small roasting pans that will hold onions in 1 layer. Roast as instructed in the master recipe.

Roasted onions are sweet and delicious. They add a rich taste and texture to tossed green salads and main-dish salads made with fish, poultry, or lean red meat. Unlike most roasted vegetable preparations, you can arrange onions several layers deep in the pan because they shrink so much.

I often make this first thing in the morning (and in the toaster oven during hot weather) with several days in mind. Leftovers are great chilled or warmed in the toaster oven. Try different kinds of onions, different herbs and spices.

Grilled Onion Rings

Prep: 10 minutes ~ **Cooking:** 12 minutes ~ **Yield:** 4 servings

Ingredients & Directions

4 small to medium-size red onions (about 1 1/4-pounds)

1 tablespoon unrefined coconut oil **or** extra-virgin olive oil

2 teaspoons coarsely ground rosemary, sage, thyme **or** favorite blend

1/2 teaspoon lemon pepper **or** ground black pepper, or to taste

Finely ground, unrefined sea salt, optional

Nutrition

1 serving:
94 calories
2 g protein
14 g carbohydrate
(1 g fiber)
4 g fat
38 mg calcium
6 mg sodium

1. Cut off ends of onions; peel back and remove skins. Slice onions into rounds, about 1/3-inch thick using a mandoline, chef knife, or sturdy vegetable knife. (Don't cut them too thin or they will stick, burn, or fall through the grill grates.)

2. Brush both sides of each onion ring with oil. Dust with herbs, pepper, and sea salt if desired.

   On the grill: Place onion rings on grill grates. Cook 5 to 6 minutes per side, or until onions darken around the edges and rings begin to separate.

   In grill pan: Turn on a ventilator fan. Lightly brush large a grill pan with oil and warm on moderate heat until piping hot. Add onion rings to cover bottom of pan. (You might need to cook in 2 batches). Cook onions for 4 to 5 minutes per side, or until slightly charred, soft, and rings begin to separate.

3. Serve warm or refrigerate and serve cold. Refrigerate leftovers and use within 4 days.

Grilled onions taste slightly smoky and sweet. They make a fantastic topping for burgers, pork chops, omelets, and green salad. Leftovers are good on fried or poached eggs served with steamed broccoli or asparagus, and fresh fruit for breakfast. If you don't have a covered grill or porch for winter grilling, use a grill pan on top of the range.

Herb-Roasted Mushrooms

Prep: 10 minutes ~ **Cooking:** 40 to 50 minutes ~ **Yield:** 6 servings

---

Ingredients & Directions

2 pounds fresh button **or** cremini mushrooms

1 medium-size red, white, or yellow onion, cut into
1/4-inch thick rings or crescents, optional

2 tablespoons extra-virgin olive oil

2 teaspoons dried, crumbled thyme, oregano, rosemary,
or Herbes de Provençe

1/4 teaspoon ground black pepper **or** 1/2 teaspoon
lemon pepper

1. Preheat oven to 400° F. Rinse or wipe mushrooms
   clean with damp cloth to remove all traces of dirt.
   Trim away and discard about 1/4 inch from each
   stem end. Halve or quarter mushrooms larger than
   1 1/2- to 2-inches in diameter. Add to a shallow 12x9x2-inch or
   14x9x2-inch roasting pan, jellyroll pan, or 2 (9-inch) cake pans.
   Add onion if desired. Toss with oil, dried herbs, and pepper.

2. Roast, uncovered, until lightly golden, tender, and aromatic, 30 to
   40 minutes, stirring twice. Exact time will depend on size and type
   of pan, mushrooms, and accuracy of your oven.

3. Serve warm or chilled. Cover and refrigerate leftovers and use
   within 4 days.

Variations

* **Herb-Roasted Shiitake Mushrooms:** Replace button or cremini
  mushrooms with fresh (not dried) shiitake mushrooms. They're a bit
  pricey, but worth every penny. Check Asian markets and farmers'
  markets for the best deals. Shiitakes are packed with antioxidants
  and immune-enhancing compounds.

* **To reduce the fat by one half:** Use only 1 tablespoon of oil and pour
  1/4 cup white wine over mushrooms. Roast until tender, stirring
  every 15 minutes.

Nutrition

1 serving:
80 calories
3 g protein
6 g carbohydrate
5 g fat
13 mg calcium
2 mg sodium

Roasted mushrooms
have a rich, robust
flavor. I like to cook this
for dinner and 2 more
meals. Or, I
might assemble
and cook it the
morning, so it's
ready for later
and the next
2 days. These
mushrooms are
delicious cold,
close to room
temperature, or
warmed briefly
in a toaster oven.

I toss them with lettuce
or baby greens for a
side salad. Sometimes I
add sliced fresh or sun-
dried tomatoes, Roasted
Onions, Roasted
Carrots, Roasted Bell
Pepper strips, or several
of these (see Index for
recipes). I add warm
or chilled fish, poultry,
or lean meat and salad
dressing for a main-dish
salad.

Roasted Bell Peppers

Prep: 15 minutes ~ **Cooking:** 10 to 30 minutes ~ **Yield:** 8 to 12 servings

Ingredients & Directions

4 medium-large bell peppers, about 6 to 9 ounces each: red, orange, yellow, green, or combination of 2 to 3 colors

1 to 2 teaspoons extra-virgin olive oil **or** unrefined coconut oil

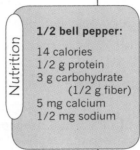

Nutrition

1/2 bell pepper:

14 calories
1/2 g protein
3 g carbohydrate
   (1/2 g fiber)
5 mg calcium
1/2 mg sodium

1. Preheat oven to 400° F or broil. Rinse and cut 1/4 inch from top and bottom of each pepper. Gently remove and discard stem from top lobe. Core peppers and remove seeds. Cut each pepper in half, lay flat, skin side down, and trim away ribs and remaining seeds. Arrange strips, tops, and bottom lobes, skin side up, on oiled or foil-lined 17x11-inch baking sheet or jellyroll pan. Flatten strips with the palm of your hand.

2. **To roast:** Place baking sheet(s) in oven. Cook uncovered for 30 minutes, until tender, golden, and edges of peppers start to shrivel and top has browned or blackened slightly.

   To broil: Move oven rack to top position. If rack is more than 3 1/2 inches from heating element, set an upside down roasting pan or jelly roll pan under the baking sheet to lift it. Broil peppers until spotty, about 5 minutes; turn pan 180° and roast until skins are charred and puffy but flesh is still firm, about 5 minutes longer.

3. Transfer peppers to clean paper bag or heat-proof mixing bowl. Close bag or cover bowl with a dinner plate. Let peppers steam for 30 minutes.

4. Peel and discard skins. Cut peppers into thin, long strips, cubes, or dice, and transfer to wide-mouth jar or glass container with lid. Cover, refrigerate, and use within 4 days.

Variations

* See Index for Roasted Onion, Sweet Pepper & Spring Green Salad.

I like to prepare peppers first thing in the morning or in the evening when I have the oven fired up for other things. I typically toss cooled pepper strips with romaine, spinach, or baby greens, and other colorful raw, roasted, or parboiled vegetables. For one-dish dining (great for pack lunches), top salad servings with sliced, chicken, turkey breast, or pork loin, and drizzle with balsamic vinegar, Very Easy Vinaigrette, or a Lean & Creamy Dressing (see Index for recipes).

Baked Spaghetti Squash

Prep: 15 minutes ~ **Cooking:** 90 minutes ~ **Yield:** 4 to 6 servings

Ingredients & Directions

1 spaghetti squash, about 3 pounds

4 teaspoons unrefined coconut oil **or** extra-virgin olive **or** butter

1/2 teaspoon ground black pepper **or** lemon pepper, or to taste

Dulse flakes **or** green nori flakes, optional

1. Preheat oven to 350° F. Rinse squash, poke with fork, thin-bladed knife, or metal skewer in half a dozen places, and place in shallow baking pan with sides.

2. Bake for 90 minutes or until fork tender. When baking smaller squash (less than 3 pounds), reduce cooking time to about 1 hour or until tender but not mushy.

3. Allow squash to cool 10 minutes, then transfer to cutting board. Cut in half lengthwise. Remove seeds and pulp with an ice cream scoop; discard. Using a fork, rake flesh onto a large platter or bowl to create spaghetti-like strands.

4. Toss all the squash or individual servings with oil or butter, pepper, and dulse or nori flakes. Serve warm. Refrigerate leftovers and use within 3 days.

Variations

* Omit oil and pepper. Stir-fry onions, mushrooms, celery, carrots, garlic, and ginger in coconut oil. Add crisp-tender cooked spaghetti squash strands and a dash of tamari soy sauce. Serve with grilled, broiled, or baked salmon, shrimp, pork, or chicken.

* To steam squash, halve lengthwise, remove seeds and quarter squash lengthwise. Cover and steam flesh side down on rack over 1 inch of boiling water until tender but not mushy, about 15 minutes. Rake flesh and serve.

Nutrition

1/2 cup:
44 calories
1 g protein
22 g carbohydrate
(4 g fiber)
1 g fat
15 mg calcium
1 mg sodium

Spaghetti squash—a thin yellow-skinned oblong, almost football-shaped fruit—is often called vegetable spaghetti because it separates easily into spaghetti-like strands after cooking. A great pasta impostor, you can toss it with garlic-infused olive oil, coconut oil or butter, and black pepper, Practically Paleo Pesto, or top it with chili or Better Barbecue Sauce and meatballs (see Index for recipes).

Spaghetti squash has a high water and fiber content and very little carbohydrate. The flavor may be starchy or fairly sweet, depending on the age, ripeness at picking, storage temperature, and length of cooking. Look for specimens with clean, hard skins free of soft spots, decay, or cracks.

Steamed Squash Crescents

Prep: 15 minutes ~ **Cooking:** 20 to 30 minutes ~ **Yield:** 6 to 8 servings

Ingredients & Directions

1 medium-large winter squash:
    kabocha, Hokaido, buttercup, honey delight, or sweet
    mama **or** 3 small delicata or sweet dumpling

4 to 8 teaspoons coconut oil, real creamery butter **or**
flax oil **or** 1/4 to 1/2 cup Fluffy Almond Butter
(Page 408), for garnish, optional

1. Rinse squash and remove skin with a sturdy
   vegetable peeler. Place on a folded kitchen towel on
   a cutting board. Slice off stems. Cut squash in half
   top to bottom with a sturdy vegetable knife, rocking
   it back and forth to press through squash. Discard
   seeds. Cut squash into crescents, triangles, or 2-inch
   cubes. Arrange on bamboo or metal steamer trays.

2. Rest a metal steamer basket in 2- to 4-quart pot over 1 1/2 inches
   of water. Or, stack 2 bamboo trays inside a wok filled with 2 inches
   of water or place trays on rim of pot with matching diameter.

3. Cover trays or pot with a lid. Bring water to boil over medium-high
   heat; reduce heat to medium with steam rising. Cook 20 to 30
   minutes, or until fork tender and fragrant. Check water level during
   cooking, adding more *boiling* water to bottom of pot as needed to
   keep steam rising and pot from boiling dry. Transfer to serving bowl.

4. Garnish as desired and serve. Refrigerate leftovers and use within 3
   days or freeze.

Variations

* For a quick and nourishing breakfast, figure 1 to 1 1/2 cups cooked,
  cubed squash per person plus 1/2 cup Protein-Coconut Cream
  (Page 470). Dust with cinnamon or pie spice.

* Turn leftover squash into Squash Pudding Pie **or** Tomato, Squash &
  Ginger Bisque (see Index for recipes).

Nutrition

1/2 cup cubed squash:

55 calories
1 g protein
11 g carbohydrate
          (4 g fiber)
1 g fat
15 mg calcium
1 mg sodium

Kabocha squash, and Hokaido "pumpkin," Japanese winter squash, are round, and slightly flat on top with a dark green exterior and deep orange, slightly dry flesh. Look for them in Asian markets, farmers' markets and natural foods stores. (Honey delight, buttercup, and sweet mama are similar and good substitutes.) Delicata and sweet dumpling are smaller, bright yellow all over with stripes. For best results, see squash selection tips in Chapter 10.

Simmered Squash

Prep: 10 minutes ~ **Cooking:** 40 to 45 minutes ~ **Yield:** 6 to 8 servings

Ingredients & Directions

1 (5-inch) strip kelp **or** kombu sea vegetable, optional

1/2 to 2/3 cup filtered water to barely cover bottom of pot

1 teaspoon ground cinnamon **or** apple pie spice
or 1/2 teaspoons dried ginger powder

1 medium-large onion (1 1/2 to 2 cups), cut into 1-inch cubes, optional

10 cups hard sweet squash, peeled and cut into
1 1/2- to 2-inch cubes or wedges:
    kabocha, buttercup, butternut, honey delight,
    sweet dumpling or Hokaido pumpkin

2 to 3 tablespoons unrefined coconut oil, flax oil, real creamery butter, **or** 1/2 cup Fluffy Almond Butter (Page 408), **or** 1/2 cup toasted walnuts (Page 406), coarsely chopped, optional

> **Nutrition**
>
> **1 serving
> (without topping):**
>
> 91 calories
> 4 g protein
> 19 g carbohydrate
>   (4 g fiber)
> 70 mg calcium
> 2 mg sodium

1. If desired, snip kelp into 1/2-inch pieces with shears and add to a heavy-bottomed 4-quart pot. Add 1/4-inch of water to pot. Add spices, onions if desired, and cubed squash.

2. Cover and bring to boil over medium heat without stirring. Reduce heat and simmer until tender and syrupy, about 45 minutes. Lift lid to check after 25 minutes. If liquid has cooked away, add 3 to 4 tablespoons of water. Liquid should be absorbed at the end of cooking.

3. Stir gently with large, wide wooden spoon being careful not to mash. Serve warm. Garnish individual portions as desired.

4. Refrigerate leftovers and consume within 3 days.

Variations

* For a quick breakfast, serve 1 to 1 1/2 cups of cooked, cubed squash per person (warm or close to room temperature). Top each serving with 1/2 cup Protein-Coconut Cream (Page 470).

* Turn leftover squash into Squash Pudding Pie (Page 384), **or** Tomato, Squash & Ginger Bisque (Page 381).

This is a takeoff on a Japanese technique that uses only enough water to barely cover the bottom of the cooking pot and create steam. At the end of cooking, all the juices should be absorbed into the vegetables. Ripe winter squash requires no sugar or honey. If you happen to get an under-ripe dud—or one grown in nutrient poor soil—add a dash of stevia, date sugar, honey, or agavé nectar.

Basic Baked Squash Halves

Prep: 5 minutes ~ **Cooking:** 30 to 45 minutes ~ **Yield:** 4 to 8 servings

Ingredients & Directions

2 sweet dumpling, or delicata squash (1 1/2 to 1 3/4 pounds each) **or** 1 (3- to 3 1/2-pound) kabocha, Hokaido, buttercup, or butternut squash

Extra-virgin olive oil, clarified butter **or** unrefined coconut oil to grease pan, optional

Ground cinnamon **or** apple pie spice, optional

2 tablespoons unrefined coconut oil, flax oil, butter **or** 1/2 cup Fluffy Almond Butter (at the table), optional

1. Preheat oven to 350° F. Wash and scrub squash, leaving skin intact. Snap or cut stem off with a sturdy knife. Place squash on a folded kitchen towel on a cutting board. Rock a sturdy vegetable or chef knife back and forth, pressing through squash. Discard seeds. Brush or mist cut sides with coconut or olive oil and dust with cinnamon or pie spice if desired.

2. Arrange squash cut side *down* in 1 or 2 cake pans or baking sheets with sides. Bake uncovered in center of oven until tender, easily pierced with fork, and slightly golden on the bottom, 30 to 40 minutes.

3. Quarter large squash halves. Garnish as desired and serve or cover and refrigerate. Eat leftovers within 3 days.

Variations

* For a quick breakfast, serve 1 to 1 1/2 cups of cooked, cubed squash per person (warm or close to room temperature). Top each serving with 1/2 cup Protein-Coconut Cream (Page 470).

* Turn leftover squash into Squash Pudding Pie (Page 384), **or** Tomato, Squash & Ginger Bisque (Page 381).

Nutrition

1/2 cup
55 calories
1 g protein
11 g carbohydrate
(4 g fiber)
1 g fat
15 mg calcium
1 mg sodium

Baked squash is incredibly sweet if you pick the right variety and prepare it properly. It should be heavy for its size. The stem should be dry, and any markings on the skin should be deep, dark orange.

Halved and baked cut side *down*, so they don't dry out, and without foil, water, or cover, the natural sugars caramelize. If you get a dud, you can sweeten it with honey, agavé nectar, date sugar, or stevia and vanilla. Leftovers are convenient and delicious gently warmed in a toaster oven.

One sweet dumpling or delicata will yield about 1 cup of mashed squash and can stand in for potatoes or pumpkin in a meal or recipe.

Tomato, Squash & Ginger Bisque

Prep: 10 minutes ~ **Cooking:** 20 minutes ~ **Yield:** 4 small servings

Ingredients & Directions

1 cup chopped white or yellow onion

1 tablespoon finely minced or grated fresh gingerroot

1 clove minced garlic

1/2 cup canned, unsalted, diced tomato

1/4 to 1/2 cup Bone-Building Broth (Page 278) **or** preservative-free chicken broth

1 (10- to 12-ounce) package frozen, preferably organic, winter squash, defrosted **or** 1 1/2 cups cooked and puréed winter squash the texture of applesauce

3/4 cup lite coconut milk **or** 1/4 cup premium coconut milk plus 1/2 cup water or broth

1/4 teaspoon ground black pepper

1/4 teaspoon stevia extract powder **or** 1 to 2 tablespoons honey or agavé nectar **or** 1/2 teaspoon finely ground unrefined sea salt, or to taste

Minced parsley, scallions, **or** chives for garnish

Nutrition

1 cup:
89 calories
2 g protein
14 g carbohydrate
(2 g fiber)
3 g fat
12 mg calcium
4 mg sodium

Here's an easy way to way to transform leftover cooked or frozen squash into a soothing starter. This is a takeoff on a recipe I developed for Barry and Lynn Sears' *Zone Meals in Seconds* (HarperCollins 2004). Don't even think about using canned squash; it's not nearly as nutritious or delicious as fresh or frozen. If your squash turns out to be a dud or you make this without salt, add a dash of honey, agavé nectar, or a pinch of stevia to deepen the flavor.

1. Layer onions, ginger, garlic, tomato, 1/2 cup stock, and squash in a medium saucepan. Cover and bring to a low boil. Reduce heat and simmer for 20 minutes, until squash is tender and soup has thickened.

2. Add coconut milk to soup. Season with pepper and stevia, honey, or sea salt. Taste and adjust as needed. For a smoother texture, purée in a blender or food processor starting on low and holding the top down with a towel. Return soup to saucepan and warm gently without boiling. If too thick, add 1/4 cup broth or water.

3. Ladle into 4 soup bowls, garnish, and serve. Use leftovers within 3 days or freeze.

Variations

* **Curried Tomato-Squash Bisque:** Replace garlic with 1/2 teaspoon curry powder and reduce ginger to 2 teaspoons.

* **Quick Creamy Squash-Ginger Bisque:** Replace tomato with 1/2 cup broth or water and use twice as much squash in step 1.

* For a richer taste, sauté onions in 1 tablespoon coconut oil, clarified butter or ghee before combining ingredients, or use 1/2 cup premium coconut milk plus 1/4 cup water in step 2.

Note: For larger portions, double everything. For a thicker texture, increase squash by 50 percent and stock by only 1/4 to 1/2 cup.

Soothing Ginger, Squash & Apple Soup

Prep: 20 minutes ~ **Cooking:** 45 minutes ~ **Yield:** 6 to 8 servings
---

Ingredients & Directions

2 to 3 teaspoons unrefined coconut oil, clarified butter **or** ghee

1 small onion, thinly sliced (about 2/3 cup)

1 teaspoon unrefined, mineral-rich sea salt (such as Celtic)

1 tablespoon peeled, minced fresh gingerroot **or** bottled ginger juice

1/2 teaspoon dried ginger

4 cups peeled, and cubed winter squash:
    kabocha, Hokaido, buttercup, butternut, sweet dumpling, **or** delicata squash

2 cups tart or tart-sweet apples (about 1 pound), cored, peeled, and chopped:
    pink lady, gala, Fuji, or braeburn

1 cup apple cider **or** apple juice

2 to 3 cups Bone-Building Broth (Page 278), preservative-free chicken broth, **or** water

1/4 teaspoon ground black pepper, optional

1/2 cup full-fat thoroughly blended preservative-free coconut milk

1/4 cup finely minced fresh fennel fronds, parsley leaves **or** chives

Nutrition

1 cup:
111 calories
2 g protein
15 g carbohydrate
    (2 g fiber)
5 g fat
25 mg calcium
237 mg sodium

This soup is a wonderful way to celebrate the fall harvest. It goes well with fish, poultry, or pork, and cooked leafy greens or coleslaw. For best results, you want a really ripe squash. See squash selection tips in Chapter 10.

1. Heat oil in a large, heavy saucepan over medium heat. Add onion and salt; stir until tender and almost translucent, about 4 minutes. Add ginger. Stir and cook for 1 minute. Add squash, apples, cider or juice, and broth or water. Cover, bring to low boil, reduce heat, and simmer 45 minutes, until tender. Wash, spin dry, and chop garnish and set aside.

2. Purée soup with coconut milk using an immersion blender or in 3 batches in a blender or food processor until smooth. Add additional liquid as needed, a little at a time. Taste, adjust seasonings as desired.

3. Return soup to saucepan and warm gently without boiling. Ladle into bowls, garnish, and serve. Use leftovers within 4 days or freeze.

Variations

* **Soothing Ginger, Squash & Orange Soup:** Replace apple and apple juice with peeled, seeded, and sectioned orange with membranes removed, and orange juice.

* **Soothing Ginger, Squash & Pear Soup:** Replace apple and juice with pear and pear nectar.

* **Soothing Squash Soup with Pie Spice:** Replace ginger with 1 teaspoon apple or pumpkin pie spice.

Hungarian Squash Soup

Prep: 30 minutes ~ **Cooking:** 30 minutes ~ **Yield:** 6 servings

Ingredients & Directions

Vegetables:

1 small onion, finely chopped (about 1 cup)

1 garlic clove, minced or pressed (about 1/2 teaspoon)

3 cups hard, sweet squash, peeled, halved, seeded, and cut into 1-inch cubes:
Hokaido, kabocha, buttercup, honey-delight, delicata or sweet dumpling

1/2 to 1 teaspoon unrefined, mineral-rich sea salt

1 cup Bone-Building Broth (Page 278) **or** preservative-free chicken broth

Thickener and seasonings:

2 cups preservative-free lite coconut milk **or** almond milk

1 tablespoon raw apple cider vinegar **or** 1 1/2 tablespoons lemon juice

2 tablespoons arrowroot

1 1/2 teaspoons mild paprika

1 teaspoon dried dill weed

2 tablespoons finely chopped, fresh parsley

1 cup Bone-Building Broth (Page 278), preservative-free chicken broth **or** filtered water

1/8 to 1/4 teaspoon stevia extract powder **or** 1 to 2 tablespoons honey **or** agavé, optional

Minced scallions **or** fresh or dried chives for garnish

Nutrition

1 serving:
108 calories
3 g protein
13 g carbohydrate
(3 g fiber)
5 g fat
26 mg calcium
177 mg sodium

The inspiration for this sweet, creamy dairy-free soup comes from a Hungarian squash and yogurt dish from *Laurel's Kitchen*. I like to serve this with broiled or baked salmon, chicken, or turkey breast, and sautéed greens or Brussels sprouts. For a festive finale, try Stewed Pears with Anise or Apple-Apricot Compote with caraway and chopped, toasted walnuts (see Index for recipes).

1. Layer onion, garlic, squash, sea salt, and 1 cup broth in 2-quart pot. Cover, bring to low boil, reduce heat, and simmer 15 to 20 minutes, until squash is almost tender.

2. Meanwhile, blend or whisk coconut or almond milk, vinegar, arrowroot, paprika, dill, parsley, and broth or water. Add to soup and bring to low boil, stirring constantly. Reduce heat and simmer to thicken, 12 to 15 minutes.

3. Taste. If additional sweetness is desired, add 1/8 teaspoon stevia or 1 tablespoon honey. Stir, taste, and adjust as needed. Ladle into cups, garnish, and serve. Refrigerate leftovers and use within 4 days.

Variations

* Replace lite coconut milk with 1 cup premium coconut milk plus 1 cup water (this adds 2 fat grams per serving).

Squash Pudding Pie

Prep: 30 minutes ~ **Cooking:** 1 hour ~ **Yield:** 1 10-inch pie; 8 slices

Ingredients & Directions

3 cups baked or simmered and mashed hard, sweet squash, scooped from skin:
> butternut, buttercup, sweet dumpling, delicata, kabocha, sweet mama or Hokaido

3/4 cup thoroughly blended, preservative-free unsweetened, coconut milk

1/4 cup honey, agavé nectar **or** maple syrup

3 whole eggs **or** 6 egg whites **or** 1/4 cup dried, powdered egg whites blended with 3/4 cup water

1 1/2 tablespoons arrowroot starch/powder

2 teaspoons apple pie spice **or** pumpkin pie spice

1 1/2 teaspoons pure vanilla extract **or** maple extract, preferably non-alcoholic

1/3 teaspoon finely ground, unrefined sea salt, optional

1 tablespoon additional honey, agavé nectar **or** maple syrup **or** 1/4 teaspoon white stevia extract powder, optional

Nutrition

1 serving (whole eggs):
154 calories
3 g protein
21 g carbohydrate (3 g fiber)
6 g fat
23 mg calcium
30 mg sodium

1 serving (whites only)
139 calories
4 g protein
20 g carbohydrate (3 g fiber)
5 g fat
15 mg calcium
48 mg sodium

1. Preheat oven to 350° F. In food processor, Vita-Mix, or hand food mill, combine all ingredients except stevia and mix until smooth. Mixture should be thick. If too stiff to blend, add 1/4 cup water. Taste. Add 1 more tablespoon honey and/or 1/4 teaspoon stevia if a sweeter taste is desired. Pie will become sweeter and more concentrated as it bakes.

2. Pour into oiled 10-inch deep-dish pie plate. Smooth with spatula. Bake in center of oven until firm, slightly golden, and dry around edges, about 60 minutes. Allow to cool, cover with foil, and refrigerate. (Pie will firm up in refrigerator.)

3. Cut into 8 slices and serve. Use within 4 days or freeze.

Variations

* In step 1, replace arrowroot with 4 teaspoons unflavored gelatin.

* Omit pie spice. Combine and add 1 teaspoon cinnamon, 3/4 teaspoon dried ginger, 1/4 teaspoon nutmeg, and 1/8 teaspoon ground cloves or allspice. Or, replace pie spice with 1 1/2 tablespoons finely grated fresh gingerroot plus 1/2 teaspoon dried ginger powder.

Not just for Thanksgiving, this antioxidant-packed pudding is delicious throughout the fall and winter. It's low in sugar and fat, and dairy-, gluten-, and grain-free. Select a sweet variety of squash and cook it thoroughly. Canned pumpkin is usually watered down and tastes like the can. If you don't have fresh squash, substitute frozen. If pumpkin is more popular in your house, call it "Pumpkin Pudding Pie."

Silver Dollar Sweet Potatoes

Prep: 30 minutes ~ **Cooking:** 25 to 35 minutes ~ **Yield:** 6 servings

Ingredients & Directions

2 tablespoons melted, unrefined coconut oil **or** extra-virgin olive oil

2 teaspoons apple pie spice **or** ground ginger or cinnamon, or as needed

4 large **or** 6 medium sweet potatoes or yams (about 2 to 2 1/2 pounds):
> Jersey sweets, white sweet potatoes, Beauregard, or Japanese sweet potatoes, or red garnet or jewel yams

1. Preheat oven to 400° F. Put oil in custard cup and set out spices.

2. Rinse and scrub sweet potatoes with bristle brush. Pat dry. Remove rough sections and any soft or black spots. Peel if desired. Cut into 1/3-inch thick rounds with sturdy vegetable or chef knife or use a mandoline for potato chip-like texture. Cut into 1/2-inch thick rounds for softer, French fry-like texture.

3. Working quickly to keep sweet potatoes from oxidizing, lightly brush cut surfaces with oil, dust with spices, rub spiced halves together, and arrange on 2 large cookie sheets or shallow baking pans. (For easy cleanup, line with unbleached parchment paper.)

4. Bake 15 minutes. Flip slices with metal spatula if desired, and bake 10 to 15 minutes longer, until just tender and serve. Refrigerate leftovers and use within 3 days.

Nutrition

1 serving:
205 calories
3 g protein
38 g carbohydrate
(4 g fiber)
5 g fat
52 mg calcium
15 mg sodium

Don't wait for the holidays to serve sweet potatoes. They're delicious all year round and handy for pack lunches or quick meals at home. These mouthwatering medallions are rich in potassium and beta-carotene and lower in fat and sodium than French fries. The aroma during baking or reheating under the broiler reminds me of oatmeal cookies or cinnamon toast. People who don't usually like sweet potatoes or yams often devour these with delight.

Variations

* Gently warm leftovers in toaster oven or under broiler for 1 to 3 minutes. Check frequently to avoid burning.

* **Sweet Potato Fries:** Omit spices. Use only enough oil to lightly grease baking pans or line with unbleached parchment. In step 2, gently beat 3 to 4 large egg whites in a 3-quart bowl until frothy. Slice sweet potatoes, promptly add to egg whites, and turn to coat thoroughly. Arrange on prepared sheets and bake.

* **Baked Spiced Sweet Potato Halves:** To save time, cut raw sweet potatoes in half lengthwise. Rub or brush cut sides with oil or ghee and dust with pie spice or cinnamon. Rub 2 spiced halves together to spread seasonings. Place cut side down on baking sheet lined with unbleached parchment for ease of clean up. Bake until bottom side is golden brown and tubers are tender when poked with a fork or skewer, 20 to 40 minutes, depending on size.

Basic Baked Sweet Potatoes

Prep: 5 minutes ~ **Cooking:** about 1 hour ~ **Yield:** 8 servings

Ingredients & Directions

4 large **or** 6 to 8 small to medium sweet potatoes (about 2 pounds)
Jersey sweets (white sweet potatoes), Beauregard or Japanese sweet potatoes, or red garnet or jewel yams

Unrefined coconut oil, butter, macadamia nut butter, chopped Toasted Nuts (Page 406), Fluffy Almond Butter (Page 408) **or** Fluffy Tahini (Page 409), optional

1. Preheat oven to 400° F. Scrub and rinse sweet potatoes. Pat dry but do not peel. Remove rough, soft, or black spots. If desired, poke holes in each tuber in several spots with skewer or thin-bladed knife. Arrange in shallow baking pan with sides; line with unbleached parchment for easy cleanup if desired. Do not cover or add water.

2. Bake 50 to 60 minutes or until sweet potatoes are soft when squeezed. If possible, turn them after 30 minutes so they cook evenly. Jumbo sweet potatoes may take 90 minutes to soften.

3. Serve warm, garnishing as desired. Cover and refrigerate leftovers and use within 3 days.

Variations

* For a quick breakfast, serve 1 cup of cooked sweet potato per person (warm or close to room temperature). Top each serving with 1/2 cup Protein-Coconut Cream (Page 470).

* Turn leftover sweet potato into a custard-like pie. See Squash Pudding Pie (Page 384).

Nutrition

4 ounce serving without nuts or oil:

120 calories
2 g protein
28 g carbohydrate
(3 g fiber)
32 mg calcium
11 mg sodium

In our house, we serve sweet potatoes all year. I usually cook 6 at a time, to serve 3 days in a row. Leftovers are great warm or close to room temperature on a hot day or in a pack lunch. They pair well with pork, fish, or poultry, and cooked leafy greens or a tossed green salad.

FYI: What you see labeled as yams are usually *sweet potatoes*. True yams are a tropical vegetable that is starchy, not sweet, and rarely sold in the United States. Numerous varieties of sweet potatoes exist. Don's and my favorites are white sweet potatoes (Jersey sweets) and Japanese sweet potatoes, which are firmer and more dense than red garnet or jewel yams, and less mushy when cooked.

Sweet potatoes, members of the morning glory family, are totally unrelated to common potatoes, and unlike potatoes, sweet potatoes don't contain solanine, a poisonous alkaloid. Sweet potatoes are rich in beta-carotene, potassium, fiber, trace amounts of folic acid, and vitamin C. They'll be sweet and delicious without sugar if they are properly cured before you get them, free of bruises and moldy spots, and thoroughly cooked. Baking is best. Boiling and steaming make them watery; microwaving produces micro-flavors.

Mashed Sweet Potatoes with Lime

Prep: 15 to 20 minutes ~ **Cooking:** 1 1/2 hours ~ **Yield:** 8 servings

Ingredients & Directions

6 medium to large sweet potatoes (about 1/2 pound each, 3 pounds total):
> red garnet or jewel yams, or Beauregard or Japanese sweet potatoes

Juice of 1/2 lime

1/4 teaspoon ground black pepper

3 tablespoons flax oil, unrefined coconut oil, butter, macadamia nut butter **or** 2/3 cup chopped, toasted pecans (Page 406), optional

1. Preheat oven to 400° F. Scrub and rinse sweet potatoes. Pat dry but do not peel. Remove rough, soft, or black spots. If desired, poke holes in each tuber in several spots with skewer or thin-bladed knife. Arrange in shallow baking pan with sides; line with unbleached parchment for easy cleanup. Do not cover or add water.

2. Bake for 50 to 60 minutes, or until soft when squeezed with oven mitts. If possible, turn sweet potatoes after 20 to 30 minutes so they bake evenly.

3. When cool enough to handle, slip off and discard skins. Mash or purée with lime juice and pepper. Spoon into oiled heat-proof casserole.

4. Warm in preheated 300° F oven or toaster oven for 30 minutes. Top individual portions with oil, nut butter, or nuts if desired. Refrigerate leftovers and use within 3 days or freeze.

Variations

* **Mashed Sweet Potatoes with Orange & Ginger:** Replace lime juice with 1/4 cup orange or tangerine juice. Omit pepper. Add 1 teaspoon finely grated orange or tangerine zest, 1/2 teaspoon ground ginger and 2 teaspoons ginger juice or very finely grated ginger.

Nutrition

1 serving without oil or nuts:

183 calories
3 g protein
42 g carbohydrate
(5 g fiber)
48 mg calcium
17 mg sodium

Thoroughly baked sweet potatoes are delicious without sugar, syrup, or marshmallows—unless you get a real dud.

My sister-in-law, Nancy, shared this scrumptious recipe with me more than 7 years ago and it's been a favorite ever since. It's easy on the cook, popular with children, and it reheats and freezes well. (We've eaten this dish unheated when we've been on the road.)

We enjoy this throughout the fall, winter, and early spring served with fish or poultry, and a crisp green salad or sautéed greens. For a fabulous and easy finale for company, try My Favorite Macaroons, Chocolate-Almond Meringues, or Stewed Pears with Anise & Apricots (see Index for recipes).

Yam Power Popovers

Prep: 15 minutes ~ **Cooking:** 20 to 25 minutes ~ **Yield:** 6 popovers

Ingredients & Directions

Dry ingredients:

Unrefined coconut oil, ghee, **or** clarified butter to liberally grease muffin tins

3/4 cup sweet potato flour **or** 3/4 cup powdered YAMMIT (from about 1 cup YAMMIT granules)

1/3 cup arrowroot starch (aka arrowroot flour)

1 1/2 teaspoons non-aluminum baking powder, such as Rumford

1 1/4 teaspoons apple pie spice **or** pumpkin pie spice free of sugar, MSG, hydrogenated fats, and preservatives (We use Frontier.)

Wet ingredients:

4 medium to large chicken eggs **or** 3 duck eggs (add a dash of water if needed to yield 1 cupful)

1 teaspoon pure vanilla **or** maple extract

1. Preheat oven to 350° F. Generously grease 6 muffin cups or line with unbleached muffin papers. Mix dry ingredients in medium bowl and set aside.

2. In blender, food processor, or bowl, whip eggs and vanilla until frothy, 2 minutes. Add dry ingredients and blend, whip, or beat until smooth and all lumps are dissolved.

3. Evenly divide batter between prepared muffin cups. Bake until puffy, firm to the touch, and toothpick inserted in center of popover comes out clean, 20 to 25 minutes.

4. Run knife around edges and invert muffins over a plate. When cool, cover and refrigerate. Use within 10 days or freeze. Serve plain or with butter or coconut oil.

Variations

* Reduce sweet potato flour to 1/2 cup and increase arrowroot to 2/3 cup.

* Replace pie spice with 1/2 teaspoon ground cinnamon, 1/2 teaspoon ground ginger, and 1/4 teaspoon ground nutmeg or cardamom.

* Replace whole eggs with 1 cup liquid egg whites, **or** beat 1/3 cup dried, powdered egg whites with 1 cup filtered water until frothy, scraping sides with spatula. Add 1 tablespoon melted coconut oil or butter to liquids. See box for nutrition info.

Nutrition

1 popover:
186 calories
5 g protein
32 g carbohydrate
(1 g fiber)
4 g fat
41 mg calcium
183 mg sodium

**Varation
(with whites)**
1 popover:
175 calories
6 g protein
32 g carbohydrate
(1 g fiber)
3 g fat
24 mg calcium
207 mg sodium.

Don devised these sweet, moist muffins. They look and taste remarkably like pumpkin bread, but contain no gluten, grain, dairy products (unless you use butter), or sugar. The secret is sweet potato flour or Jay Robb's YAMMIT, made from dried, powdered sweet potatoes. If you can't find this crucial ingredient at your local health food store, you can order it by mail (see Sources in Appendix D).

FYI: This recipe doubles and freezes well.

Basic Baked Potatoes

Prep: 5 minutes ~ **Cooking:** 30 to 60 minutes ~ **Yield:** 8 servings

Ingredients & Directions

2 pounds small, medium, or large potatoes with smooth, unwrinkled skins:
> yellow Finn, Yukon gold, butterball, fingerling, new, russet, Idaho, or heirloom variety

Unrefined coconut oil, Practically Paleo Pesto or Pistou (Page 415), Aioli or Pesto Flavored Mayonnaise (Page 425), optional

Minced scallions, chives, parsley **or** pepper, optional

1. Preheat oven to 425° F. Lightly scrub and rinse potatoes. Trim away any rough, brown or black spots, and any sprouts. Discard potatoes with green on surface or under skin. Pat dry; do not peel. If desired, poke potatoes in 3 places with a paring knife or skewer to keep them from exploding in the oven. Arrange in a shallow baking pan. Do not cover or add water.

2. Bake 3- or 4-ounce potatoes for 30 minutes, 5- to 7-ounce spuds 45 to 50 minutes, and 8- to 10-ounce tubers, 45 to 60 minutes or until easily pierced with a knife or skewer. If possible, turn potatoes over halfway through cooking.

3. Serve warm. Halve lengthwise and add your favorite topping. Cover and refrigerate leftovers and use within 3 days.

Variations

* **Baked Spiced Potato Halves:** Cut raw potatoes in half lengthwise. Lightly brush cut sides with oil and dust with paprika and lemon pepper; **or** ground cumin, oregano, and thyme; **or** chili powder; **or** Italian herb blend. Rub spiced halves together. Place cut side down on baking sheet lined with unbleached parchment for easy cleanup. Bake until bottom side is golden brown and tubers are tender when poked with skewer, 20 to 40 minutes, depending on size.

* Cube leftover baked potatoes and serve warm or close to room temperature as part of a side salad or a main-course salad with fish, poultry, pork, or lean meat.

Nutrition

5 ounce serving without fat:

116 calories
3 g protein
26 g carbohydrate
    (1 g fiber)
11 mg calcium
5 mg sodium

To save energy, in hot weather, or if I have nothing else to bake, I use a toaster oven. Two-inch potatoes further reduce cooking time and energy use.

Note: Always store potatoes in a cool, dry, and dark place with air circulation—not in a sunny spot or the fridge. Exposure to sunlight makes them sprout and produces solanine, a toxic alkaloid. Refrigerated potatoes may mold or become soggy from excess moisture. Discard potatoes with greenish skin and avoid buying potatoes with sprouts.

Herb-Roasted Potatoes

Prep: 10 minutes ~ **Cooking:** 30 to 45 minutes ~ **Yield:** 8 servings

Ingredients & Directions

2 pounds firm, unwrinkled potatoes, free of soft or dark spots, sprouts, and greenish skins:
> Yukon gold, yellow Finn, butterball, or other

2 tablespoons extra-virgin olive or coconut oil **or** clarified butter or ghee

2 teaspoons dried, crumbled herbs or herb blend:
> basil, oregano, thyme, sage, rosemary, or some combination, or Herbes de Provençe

1/4 teaspoon black pepper **or** 1/2 teaspoon lemon pepper

Nutrition

1 serving:
119 calories
2 g protein
20 g carbohydrate
(1 g fiber)
4 g fat
12 mg calcium
4 mg sodium

1. Preheat oven to 400° F. Scrub and rinse potatoes. Trim away rough spots, eyes, or sprouts. (Discard any potatoes with greenish skins; the solanine they contain can make you sick.)

2. Cut potatoes in half lengthwise and place cut side down on a cutting board. Cut each half into 2 to 4 pieces lengthwise, then crosswise to make 1-inch wedges. Toss with oil, herbs, and spices to coat and arrange in an 18x9x2-inch pan lined with parchment for easy cleanup.

3. Roast in center of oven 20 minutes. Turn wedges with a metal spatula, scraping to remove stuck bits, and roast until tender and slightly golden, 15 to 20 more minutes.

4. Serve warm or chilled. Cover and refrigerate leftovers and use within 4 days.

Variations

* **Save time:** Buy baby potatoes (fingerlings or 1 to 2 inches long). Wash, trim if needed, halve, and toss with oil, herbs, and spices; add to prepared pan. Bake, shaking or stirring every 15 minutes, until tender.

* **Herb-Roasted Potatoes & Onions:** Slice 1 medium red, yellow, or white onion into thin crescents; toss with potatoes before roasting. Onions will shrink as they cook and resemble bacon bits by the time potatoes are done.

* **Herb-Roasted Potatoes & Carrots:** Use a combination of potatoes and carrots for a colorful effect and sweet taste.

Potatoes rank 80 on the glycemic index, but don't rule them out. They're packed with potassium, filling, and relatively low in calories—as long as you don't drown them in gobs of butter or sour cream. For a blood-sugar balancing meal, serve with a modest portion of protein and a generous helping of cooked kale, collards, broccoli, asparagus, or a tossed green salad. Leftovers make a great breakfast or dinner side dish and are fantastic added to a main-course salad with meat.

Steamed Corn on the Cob

Prep: 5 minutes ~ **Cooking:** 7 to 10 minutes ~ **Yield:** 6 servings

Ingredients & Directions

Enough filtered water to cover bottom of pot

6 medium to large ears of freshly picked sweet corn

Real butter **or** Practically Paleo Pesto or Pistou (Page 415), optional

1. Add 1/2 inch of water to a medium or large saucepan. For more than 6 ears, use a stockpot and up to 1 inch of water. Remove cornhusks. Reserve corn silk for making tea if desired.

2. If pot is large and shallow, rest ears of corn flat in pot. If pot is narrower, cut each ear into 3 pieces or break each in half with your hands.

3. Cover pot, bring to boil over medium high heat, and cook for 7 to 10 minutes, until tender.

4. Transfer corn to a platter or serving plates with tongs. Serve plain or with a spread. Save cooking liquid.

5. Refrigerate leftovers and use within 2 days or remove from cobs and freeze.

Variations

* Cut leftover sweet corn off the cob. Add to a tomato or winter squash soup, stew, chili, salsa, omelet, green salad, parboiled vegetable medley, or sautéed greens.

Nutrition

1 medium ear (7 inches):

89 calories
3 g protein
17 g carbohydrate
(2 g fiber)
2 mg calcium
14 mg sodium

1 large ear (7¾ to 9 inches):

146 calories
5 g protein
27 g carbohydrate
(4 g fiber)
3 mg calcium
21 mg sodium

We don't eat a lot of corn, but when we want it, we find freshly picked, locally grown corn free of GMOs (genetically modified organisms). The key to great corn is to cook it the day it's picked or the day after, before the sugars turn to starch. I usually cook enough for the next day. Leftovers are delicious on or off the cob.

I round out the meal with salmon, sea bass, chicken, beef, or pork chops and sautéed leafy greens, a crisp green salad, or a parboiled vegetable medley with dressing. Fresh fruit completes the meal if we're still hungry.

I cook corn in a minimal amount of water to preserve more nutrients and flavor. We drink the delicious broth or use it to make soup. Even the corn silk can be used. If you cut off the brown part, simmer it in water for 15 minutes, strain, and chill, you have a cooling and refreshing drink.

21 Salad Dressings, Sauces, Sprinkles, Spice Rubs & Relishes

BEST BITES

Ghee and Clarified Butter

Prep: 10 minutes ~ **Cooking:** 1 to 2 hours ~ **Yield:** 1 1/2 cups ghee plus 1/2 cup solids

Ingredients & Directions

1 pound raw, unsalted butter, cut into 1-inch pieces

1. Melt butter in a 2-quart saucepan over medium heat. Do not use a high flame. Do not stir. When completely melted, butter will begin to sizzle as moisture and air are driven off.

2. When white foam (milk solids) begins to accumulate and thicken on top, reduce heat (3 or 4 on electric range) and start skimming solids off with a teaspoon without removing the clear oil. Do not disturb bottom of pan. Some solids will sink; they may be left there until after ghee is poured off.

3. When oily portion becomes clear and sediment on the bottom becomes golden, ghee is almost done. Do not allow solids to burn. When all the water has evaporated, sound of cooking oil will change from boiling to sizzling or frying, and bubbling will stop. Oil should be clear.

4. Remove from heat. Allow to cool for 5 to 10 minutes and pour into an impeccably clean glass jar. Scrape bits from bottom of pan into bowl with skimmed milk solids. Discard solids or cover, refrigerate, and serve over steamed or baked vegetables.

5. When cool, cover, and store ghee at room temperature or in the refrigerator. Use to replace oil, margarine, and butter when sautéing or roasting vegetables, fish, or meat, cooking eggs, or oiling baking pans. Consume ghee within 6 months. Use milk solids within 4 days.

Nutrition

1 teaspoon:
5 g fat
45 calories

To make clarified butter, chop butter, heat on low for 15 minutes, strain through cheesecloth, and chill. Ghee is cooked longer, has a nuttier flavor, and is stable enough to keep at room temperature for 6 months. Ghee and clarified butter can be used interchangeably.

Butter is a perfectly nutritious food made by Mother Nature. It's more stable in storage and in cooking than vegetable oils, and always preferable to man-made margarine or shortening. Although butter is often blamed for rising rates of cancer, heart disease and obesity, it can't be the cause. Per capita consumption has declined by more than 50 percent since the early 1900s. The real villain is refined and polyunsaturated vegetable oils; per capita consumption of these has increased by more than 600 percent since 1910.

Unlike vegetable oil, butter contains water (which reduces its shelf life) and milk solids (which easily burn during sautéing). For centuries people in France and India have countered these drawbacks by creating clarified butter in France, and ghee in India.

Note: If possible, buy organic or biodynamic butter or butter from grass-fed cows.

Vegetables from the Seven Seas

Most Americans are unfamiliar with sea vegetables—plants that have nourished life longer than humans have been on Earth. However, the Vikings, Celts, Russians, Australians, Chinese, Japanese, Koreans, Native Americans, Irish, Danish, Icelandic, Welsh, Scottish, coastal African, and Mediterranean people all revered sea plants for their healthful properties, particularly for pregnant, lactating and nursing mothers and children.

Although their calorie count is negligible, sea vegetables provide the 56 minerals and trace elements our bodies require in a well-balanced form. By weight they pack 10 to 20 times the minerals found in land vegetables, including a healthy punch of potassium, iodine, chlorophyll, B vitamins, fiber, and modest amounts of calcium, magnesium, beta-carotene, chromium, niacin, riboflavin, iron, zinc, and naturally occurring sodium. Although product labels and some authors claim that sea vegetables contain vitamin B12, it is an analog. B12 found in sea plants is not biologically active. True B12 is found only in products of animal origin.

Good Food & Medicine

For thousands of years, sea vegetables have been used as food and medicine in Asia. In Chinese medicine, sea vegetables are classified as cooling and softening. They have been used for dispersing congestion, dissolving hard tumors, removing fat, suppressing coughs, and reducing internal heat, high blood pressure, edema and goiter (enlargement of the thyroid from insufficient dietary iodine). Mannitol, a constituent of seaweed, is believed to help reduce acute glaucoma and edema of the brain.

Science suggests that the softening and downward motion of sea plants may keep you regular. Sea vegetables hold several times their weight in water as they pass through the digestive tract, where the alginic acid they contain forms a lubricating gel that increases the bulk of your stool and accelerates transit time. Studies in Japan and at the Harvard School of Public Health show that moderate consumption of sea vegetables in the kelp family (consumed as 5 percent of the diet) inhibits cancer growth and can bring about total remission of active cancerous tumors. *(Japanese Journal of Experimental Medicine 44:543-46. Cancer Research 44: 2758-61.)* Sea vegetables have been shown to dissolve non-cancerous fatty and cholesterol deposits.

Sort Sea Veggies
Sort sea vegetables to remove small shells or stones before toasting. We urge you to follow recipes when working with these and other unfamiliar foods.

Detoxify Heavy Metals Naturally

Research indicates that the alginic acid forms a gel in the intestines. After safely binding with heavy metals, such as mercury, cadmium, and strontium, it pulls these potentially toxic elements out of the body, through a process called chelation, allowing for safe elimination through the bowels (*Canadian Medical Association Journal,* 1968, vol. 99, no 4). Early findings were confirmed at McGill University in Montreal in the early 1970s.

Strange New Food or Old Friend?

Does the idea of eating sea vegetables leave you queasy? You may already be eating them in minute amounts in ice cream, soups, sauces, salad dressings, puddings, and various packaged mixes. When cooked, Irish Moss (one sea vegetable) forms a gel, called caragheen or caragheenan, which manufacturers strain and use as a thickener in many commercial foods.

Sea vegetables come in a wide array of colors ranging from reddish to brownish to greenish. Some resemble ribbons, spaghetti, threads, flat, wide lasagna noodles, or crinkly sheets of paper. Flavors may remind you of tuna, caviar, bacon, beef jerky, or herbs. If you're not fond of one, try another. Different seasonings, preparations and proportions yield different eating experiences. Persevere and you may come to crave the slightly salty, primitive taste of sea plants. Eventually they may become a permanent fixture in your pantry.

Aren't They High in Sodium?

Although sea vegetables contain sodium and many taste salty, they contain far less sodium per teaspoon, tablespoon, or cupful than salt. Most sea vegetables contain 3 to 4 times as much potassium as sodium, ideal, even for individuals who suffer from hypertension.

Laver (wild nori) contains even less sodium than dulse (71 milligrams sodium and 187 milligrams potassium per 7-gram or 1/3-cup portion). Sea vegetable flakes and granules made from nori, kelp, or dulse—sold plain or flavored with spices—can be used to replace salt at the table. Sheets of sushi nori can be used to replace tortillas, to make wraps for vegetables and meat, or torn or sliced over food as a garnish.

Wild nori and dulse are delicious lightly toasted and crumbled over salads, steamed vegetables, and fried or poached eggs. You can also chop or snip sea vegetables with kitchen shears, and sauté with onions, roots, tubers, or leafy green vegetables. Many varieties require presoaking. Consult the library, package backs, and people who harvest sea vegetables for additional recipes. Jill Gussman's *Vegetables from the Sea* is full of gorgeous pictures and great ideas.

---

1 Pound = 10

You don't need to eat sea vegetables in great quantity to reap their benefits. One dried pound is the equivalent of 10 pounds of sopping wet sea vegetables. When soaked, sea vegetables expand again, some more than others. Start with a small amount.

Nutrition Facts:

Applewood smoked dulse, a salty & smoky sea vegetable

Serving size: 1/3 cup (7 grams), **Calories:** 18

		% of DV*
Carbohydrate (gm)	3	1
Dietary fiber (gm)	2	9
Fat (gm)	0	0
Sugars (gm)	0	0
Protein (gm)	2	3
Iodine (mcg)	365	243
Sodium (mg)	122	5
Potassium (mg)	547	16
Magnesium (mg)	19	6
Phosphorus (mg)	29	3
Calcium (mg)	15	2
Chromium (mcg)	11	9
Zinc (mcg)	26	2
Iron (mg)	2	19
Riboflavin (mg)	0.14	10
Niacin (mg)	0.16	1
Vitamin B6 (mg)	0.63	42

* Percent Daily Values (DV) are based on a 2,000-calorie diet.
Source: Maine Coast Sea Vegetables Inc., Franklin, Maine 04634, www.seaveg.com

Toasted Dulse

Prep: 4 minutes ~ **Cooking:** 10 to 20 minutes ~ **Yield:** 2 cups; 8 servings

Ingredients & Directions

2 to 3 packed cups dry dulse leaf, sorted to remove small shells, stones, or mollusks

1. **Quick toasting:** Pull dulse leaves apart to expose more surface area and spread on a 9- to 10-inch cast iron skillet, baking pan, or cookie sheet. Toast in a preheated 200° F oven for 15 minutes or at 250° F for 5 to 10 minutes until lightly crisped. Watch closely to avoid burning. Reduce roasting time if using a toaster oven.

   Slow toasting: You must have a gas oven with a pilot light. Pull dulse leaves apart to expose more surface area and spread on a 9- to 10-inch cast iron skillet, baking pan, or cookie sheet. Leave pan in oven all day or overnight with just the pilot light on. It will be crisp within 8 to 12 hours.

2. When cool, pack into a pint jar, cover tightly, and store indefinitely at room temperature.

3. Crumble over foods at the table or powder in a spice-dedicated coffee grinder or blender.

Variations

* **Toasted Wild Nori:** Replace dulse with wild nori, which is not the same as sushi nori sheets. See box for nutrition information.

* For a richer flavor, coat baking pan with 2 teaspoons extra-virgin olive or coconut oil before adding sea vegetable and toasting.

Nutrition

1/4 cup dulse:

18 calories
1 g protein
1 g carbohydrate
1 g fat
13 mg calcium
109 mg sodium

**Variation
1/4 cup wild nori (laver):**

21 calories,
2 g protein
3 g carbohydrate
12 mg calcium
101 mg sodium

Dulse is a purple sea plant native to the Atlantic Coast. Although you can soak it, chop it, and add it to salads or sautéed vegetables, it's particularly good lightly toasted in a slow oven, then crumbled or sprinkled over green salads, steamed vegetables, fried or poached eggs, or egg salad. The flavor reminds me of potato chips and bacon.

You can toast it, stuff it into a quart jar, and store it at room temperature for months. It's handy to add to anything at the table when you want a salty taste or added crunch. As an added bonus, it's rich in potassium, trace minerals, and extraordinarily low in calories.

Note: For a smoky bacon-like flavor, use natural hickory-smoked dulse from Maine Coast Sea Vegetables (see Appendix D).

Dulse, Dried Onion & Sea Cress Sprinkles

Prep: 10 minutes ~ **Yield:** 1 1/2 cups

Ingredients & Directions

1/2 cup dulse flakes

1/2 cup green sea cress flakes (nori or ao-nori flakes)

1/2 cup dried onion granules (**not** onion salt, flakes, or powder)

1. Combine ingredients in mixing bowl. Stir to evenly distribute.

2. Transfer to small jars or spice bottles with lids. Store at room temperature away from sunny windows. Use within 1 year. If mixture cakes up, stir with fork or chopstick.

Variations

* **Dulse, Nori & Garlic Sprinkles:** Replace 2 tablespoons of onion granules with garlic granules.

* **Dulse, Nori, Cumin & Garlic Sprinkles:** Replace 1/4 cup onion granules with 2 tablespoons ground cumin plus 2 tablespoons garlic granules.

* **Dulse-Onion Sprinkles:** If you can't find green nori flakes, combine 1/2 cup dulse flakes with 1/4 cup onion granules.

* **Dulse-Pumpkinseed Sprinkle with Garlic:** Combine 1/2 cup dulse flakes with 1 cup lightly toasted, coarsely ground, green, hulled pumpkinseeds. Add 1 tablespoon garlic granules. Add 1 tablespoon onion granules if desired.

* **Grind your own sea flakes:** Start with raw, unroasted sea vegetables, sorted to remove small stones and shells. Pulverize in a blender, Corona mill, or high-powered grinder.

Nutrition

1 teaspoon or tablespoon:
0 calories

This mineral-rich condiment makes a low-sodium alternative to salt at the table. Try it over scrambled, poached, fried, or soft-boiled eggs, cooked greens, chicken, or a green salad. Look for dulse and sea cress flakes in the bulk herb-spice or Asian-macrobiotic section of natural foods stores or by mail (see Appendix D).

Note: Do not use kelp *granules* here, unless they are very fine or they'll be gritty against your teeth. Onion granules are preferable to onion powder, which clumps.

Moroccan Barbecue Spice Mix

Prep: 15 minutes ~ **Cooking:** 3 to 4 minutes ~ **Yield:** about 2/3 cup

Ingredients & Directions

1/4 cup whole coriander seeds

1/4 cup whole fennel seeds

2 tablespoons whole cumin seeds

1 teaspoon whole shelled cardamom seeds

2 teaspoons whole cloves

1. Toast all ingredients in a dry medium skillet over moderate heat, stirring until fragrant, about 3 minutes. Cool on a plate.

2. Finely grind in spice-dedicated coffee grinder or mortar and pestle. Pour into airtight jar.

3. **To use:** Season steaks, chops, fish, or beef or pork roast with coarsely ground black pepper and sea salt. Roll meat in a portion of spice mix; press firmly to coat evenly.

4. Allow seasoned meat to rest at room temperature for 15 to 30 minutes, or cover loosely with unbleached parchment and refrigerate for up to 4 hours before roasting or sautéing. (See Index for Moroccan-Spiced Salmon, Moroccan-Spiced Pork Chops, or Moroccan-Spiced Pork Loin.)

5. Store spice mix at room temperature. Best if used within 1 month, but it will keep longer.

Nutrition

Entire recipe without meat:

186 calories
33 g carbohydrate
6 g fat
600 mg calcium
70 mg sodium

1 tablespoon:

19 calories
3 g carbohydrate
1/2 g fat
60 mg calcium
7 mg sodium

Paleo Chef Bruce Sherrod modified a Moroccan spice rub found in the Searchable Online Archive of Recipes (SOAR). He eliminated the salt and sugar, halved the number of ingredients, and toasted the spices to create a more intense flavor. I liberally rub this mouthwatering mix over salmon, pork, or beef, or add it to sautéed kale, collards, or cabbage in cooking.

Note: If you're starting with whole cardamom pods, put 1 tablespoon of pods on a cutting board, rock over them with a heavy-bottomed skillet, pull away and discard the shells, then measure the black seeds. Crack more pods as needed. Or buy shelled cardamom seeds in the bulk spice section of natural foods stores.

Moroccan Barbecue Sauce

Prep: 15 minutes ~ **Cooking:** 20 to 30 minutes ~ **Yield:** about 2 1/3 cups; 9 servings

Ingredients & Directions

1 tablespoon extra-virgin olive oil **or** unrefined coconut oil

1 cup minced fresh onion

1/2 teaspoon unrefined sea salt **or** 1 tablespoon tamari soy sauce

4 cloves minced garlic

1 large or 2 small shallots, minced (about 1/4 cup)

1 1/2 to 2 tablespoons Moroccan Barbecue Spice Mix (Page 399)

1 tablespoon Harissa, or to taste, **or** a low-sodium hot sauce **or** 1/4 teaspoon ground red pepper.

1 (6-ounce) can (salt-free, sugar-free) tomato paste

1 1/4 cups water **or** diluted or full-strength Bone-Building Broth (Page 278 or 306) **or** preservative-free chicken broth

2 tablespoons raw apple cider vinegar **or** 3 tablespoons lime juice

1/4 teaspoon stevia extract powder

1 tablespoon agavé nectar **or** honey (optional, but good)

Nutrition

1/4 cup
51 calories
2 g protein
7 g carbohydrate
(1 g fiber)
2 g fat
13 mg calcium
116 mg sodium

1. Heat oil in a 1-quart saucepan over medium heat. Add onions and stir until tender, about 5 minutes. Add sea salt or tamari, garlic and shallots, and stir for 1 to 2 minutes. Add remaining ingredients and whisk until smooth.

2. Bring to low boil, cover, reduce heat, and simmer with lid ajar, stirring periodically until mixture thickens, 20 to 30 minutes.

3. Pour sauce into a wide-mouth glass jar. Cover and refrigerate. Use within 2 weeks or freeze.

Variations

* **Shortcut:** Skip sautéing. Replace fresh onion with 1 tablespoon dried onion flakes. Combine and whisk all ingredients in a saucepan. Bring to boil, reduce heat, and simmer.

This is a modification of a recipe by Bruce Sherrod—the wizard behind the Moroccan Barbecue Spice Mix. It's wonderful over Moroccan-Spiced Salmon, Moroccan-Spiced Pork Loin, Moroccan-Spiced Pork or Lamb Chops, broiled or grilled Chilean sea bass, roast beef, chicken, burgers, or meatballs. (See Index for recipes.)

I usually make this with tomato paste so I can add my homemade Bone-Building Broth. If you don't have this or good low-sodium stock, replace water or stock and tomato paste with 2 1/4 cups crushed unsalted canned tomatoes. Recipe may be doubled.

FYI: Look for Tunisian hot sauce in Indian groceries or try one of the substitutions listed in the above recipe.

Better Barbecue Sauce

Prep: 20 minutes ~ **Cooking:** 20 to 30 minutes ~ **Yield:** about 2 1/3 cups; 9 servings

Ingredients & Directions

1 tablespoon extra-virgin olive oil **or** unrefined coconut oil

1 cup minced fresh onion **or** 1 tablespoon dried onion flakes

1/2 teaspoon unrefined sea salt **or** 1 tablespoon tamari soy sauce

3 cloves minced garlic **or** 1 teaspoon garlic powder

1 teaspoon ground cumin (preferably ground fresh)

1 teaspoon dry mustard

1/3 teaspoon ground chipotlé (smoked dried jalapeno pepper)

1 teaspoon dried, crumbled basil

1 teaspoon dried, crumbled oregano, optional

1 (6-ounce) can salt-free, sugar-free tomato paste

1 1/4 cups water, preservative-free chicken broth **or** diluted or full-strength Bone-Building Broth (Page 278 or 306)

2 tablespoons raw apple cider vinegar **or** 3 tablespoons lime juice

1/4 teaspoon stevia extract powder

1 tablespoon agavé nectar **or** honey **or** vegetable glycerine, optional

Nutrition

1/4 cup:
45 calories
1 g protein
6 g carbohydrate
(1 g fiber)
2 g fat
12 mg calcium
119 mg sodium

What makes this mild, slightly smoky sauce better than anything sold in a bottle? It's lower in calories, carbohydrate, sugar, and sodium, and free of preservatives, artificial flavorings, and trans fats. I use it liberally at the table the way you'd use ketchup or tomato sauce, over meatballs, meatloaf, burgers, steaks, roasts, chicken, turkey, pork chops, even salmon. Recipe may be doubled.

1. Heat oil in a 1-quart saucepan over medium heat. Add onions and stir until tender, about 5 minutes. Add remaining ingredients and whisk until smooth. Bring to low boil, cover, reduce heat, and simmer with lid ajar to reduce splattering, stirring periodically until mixture thickens, 20 to 30 minutes.

2. Pour into wide-mouth glass jar; allow to cool. Cover and refrigerate. Use within 2 weeks or freeze.

Variations

* **Shortcut:** Skip sautéing. Combine and whisk ingredients in a saucepan; bring to boil, reduce heat, and simmer.

* **Cajun Ketchup:** Replace garlic, cumin, mustard, chipotlé, basil, and oregano with 1 tablespoon mild salt-free Cajun spice blend. If desired, replace honey with real maple syrup.

Note: Calcium content will be higher and the flavor richer if you use Bone-Building Broth.

Roasted Garlic

Prep: 5 minutes ~ **Cooking:** 45 to 60 minutes ~ **Yield:** 8 servings

Ingredients & Directions

2 whole, preferably large, heads of garlic with cloves intact

2 to 3 teaspoons extra-virgin olive oil

1 sprig fresh thyme **or** rosemary (optional)

1. Preheat oven to 325° F. To expose garlic cloves and make it easy to remove them from the skins after roasting, cut top 1/4 inch off each garlic head with a sharp knife. Without breaking cloves apart, peel off as much papery coating as possible, leaving a thin covering in place.

2. Place garlic on a 10-inch square sheet of aluminum foil or foil lined with a similar-size piece of unbleached parchment. Sprinkle oil and optional thyme or rosemary over garlic. Pull foil up to enclose garlic and then fold down to seal tightly.

3. Bake until tender and easily pierced with knife, about 50 to 60 minutes at 325° F. Cooking time will be 15 to 20 minutes less in toaster or convection oven.

4. Serve hot, chilled, or at room temperature. Squeeze garlic from skins in kitchen or at the table. Refrigerate leftovers in tightly covered jar. Use within 5 days or squeeze garlic from skins, purée in a food processor, and freeze. Slice off and thaw pieces as needed.

Nutrition

Entire recipe:
212 calories
8 g protein
24 g carbohydrate
9 g fat

1/4 head garlic:
27 calories
1 g protein
3 g carbohydrate
1 g fat

Roasted garlic has a more mild, mellow, rich, and slightly smoky flavor. You can use it more liberally than raw garlic. We like it squeezed over green salads, added to dips like guacamole, seasoning pastes such as pesto or pistou, homemade mayonnaise, tahini dressings, soups, and salsas.

Variations

* **Roasted Garlic in a Casserole Dish:** Place 4 heads of garlic in an 8x8x2-inch baking dish. Add 1/4 cup water or preservative-free chicken stock or broth. Drizzle with oil and top with 2 sprigs of fresh thyme or rosemary if desired. Cover with foil, a heat-proof saucer, or fitted lid. Bake for 30 minutes, baste with oil and broth mixture from pan, cover and keep baking until tender, 15 to 20 minutes more. Reduce time by 1/3 in convection oven.

Note: If garlic is the only thing you're cooking, use a toaster oven to save energy and avoid overheating your kitchen. Recipe may be doubled, tripled, or quadrupled. Assemble extra batches in separate foil packages for even cooking.

Guacamole

Prep: 10 minutes ~ **Yield:** 2 cups; 6 servings

Ingredients & Directions

1/4 cup minced onion **or** shallot, rinsed under cold water to reduce heat

2 to 3 raw cloves of garlic, finely minced or pressed **or** 1 head of Roasted Garlic (Page 402)

1/3 to 1/2 teaspoon ground chipotlé, ancho, **or** cayenne pepper, **or** hot sauce to taste

1/2 cup Toasted Dulse (Page 397), crumbled **or** 1/4 teaspoon finely ground, unrefined sea salt

1 medium tomato (about 1 cup), seeded and diced, optional

2 large **or** 3 medium avocados, ripe and slightly soft but not mushy

3 tablespoons fresh lemon juice **or** lime juice, or to taste

2 to 3 tablespoons minced fresh cilantro leaves for garnish, optional

1. Combine onion or shallot, garlic, chipotlé, and dulse or sea salt in small bowl. Add tomato if desired.

2. Cut avocados in half lengthwise with a paring knife. Twist sides apart as if to unscrew. Pop out pits and reserve. Scoop flesh into a non-metallic bowl and coarsely mash with a fork or potato masher, leaving mixture slightly lumpy. Stir in onion mixture and citrus juice.

3. Taste and adjust seasonings. Garnish and serve immediately or tuck pits into guacamole to reduce discoloration. Cover tightly and refrigerate up to 4 hours.

4. Remove pits before garnishing and serving. Use within 24 hours.

Variations

* **Bruce's Avocado Sour Cream:** Omit onion, or shallot, garlic, red pepper, dulse, tomato, and cilantro. Whip mashed avocado and lime juice with an electric mixer or in a food processor until smooth. Serve over broiled chicken breast, roasted turkey breast, grilled fish, or salad.

Nutrition

1 serving (about 1/3 cup):
128 calories
2 g protein
7 g carbohydrate
(4 g fiber)
10 g fat
10 mg calcium
9 mg sodium

Guacamole is great without chips. The cool creamy texture is perfect for dipping crunchy raw carrot, celery, daikon radish, or Jicama sticks or crisp-tender parboiled broccoli and cauliflower florets. Guacamole also makes a great topping for turkey or chicken breast, beef or bison burgers, or over a green salad in place of dressing. Make a double batch for company or more than 4 people.

FYI: Dulse, a purple colored sea vegetable sold in natural foods stores, adds a slightly salty taste with far less sodium and more minerals than salt. If you use salt, look for an unrefined, mineral-rich brand, such as Celtic Sea Salt. You won't want to go back to regular table salt or refined sea salt once you try it.

Mango-Ginger Chutney

Prep: 15 to 20 minutes ~ **Cooking:** 20 minutes ~ **Yield:** 2 cups; 6 servings

Ingredients & Directions

1/4 cup lemon juice

1 tablespoon lime juice (from about 1/2 lime)

1/4 cup dried currants **or** raisins

1/4 cup dried, pitted, chopped dates **or** 1/3 teaspoon stevia extract powder

3 tablespoons peeled, minced fresh ginger root

1/4 to 1/3 teaspoon cayenne pepper **or** 1 small dried red chile pepper

1 cinnamon stick

2 cups ripe mango, cut into 1/2- to 1-inch pieces (from 2 small to medium fruits, peeled with vegetable peeler, sliced, and pitted), **or** substitute unsweetened, cubed, frozen mango

1/2 cup minced onion, optional

1/2 to 3/4 cup 100 percent pure apple juice **or** pineapple juice

Nutrition

1 serving:
96 calories
23 g carbohydrate
(2 g fiber)
15 mg calcium
3 mg sodium

Choose chutney when you want a sweet and spicy topping for grilled, roasted, or broiled beef, pork, salmon, or chicken breast. The inspiration for this came from a recipe by Lisa Turner in "Ginger A Spice for All Reasons," (January 2001, *Great Life* magazine). Additional seasoning ideas came from Mark Bittman's *How to Cook Everything*.

1. Layer ingredients in a 1 1/2-quart saucepan. Bring to boil, reduce heat, and simmer uncovered until soft and slightly thick, about 20 to 25 minutes, stirring occasionally. If liquid cooks away before fruit is tender, add a little more juice or water and cook until soft.

2. Discard cinnamon stick. Stir fruit mixture and serve immediately or transfer to jar. Cover and refrigerate. Serve hot, warm, or at room temperature. Use within 1 week or freeze.

Variations

* **Curried Mango-Mustard Chutney:** Omit ginger and cinnamon. Add 1 tablespoon curry powder and 1 tablespoon yellow mustard seeds. Use ground cayenne or whole chile pepper.

* **Ginger-Peach Chutney:** Replace mango with 3 to 4 fresh peaches. Dip peaches in boiling water until skins loosen, about 30 seconds. Plunge in ice water and slide skins off. Remove from water. Pit and chop fruit, and cut into bite-size pieces.

* **Mixed Fruit Chutney with Ginger:** For mangoes, substitute 2 or more kinds of stone fruit (peaches, apricots, plums, and nectarines). Peel and prep about 6 to 8 small stone fruits **or** 2 packed cups fruit as for Ginger-Peach Chutney. Use seasonings in master recipe, or 1 tablespoon curry powder, 1 tablespoon yellow mustard seeds, and 1/4 to 1/3 teaspoon cayenne pepper **or** 1 small dried red chili pepper.

Note: Double or triple this recipe if you like but use a large and wide pot to allow the juices to cook away quickly. To save time, substitute frozen unsweetened mango cubes from the supermarket or a natural foods store.

Toasted Seeds

Prep: 10 minutes ~ **Cooking:** 8 to 10 minutes ~ **Yield:** about 2 1/4 cups; 36 servings

Ingredients & Directions

2 cups unsalted raw, shelled seeds, sorted to remove smell stones or hulls:
> pumpkin (green, hulled variety), sunflower, or sesame

1. Rinse seeds in a fine mesh strainer. Drain thoroughly. Heat only 1 type of seed in a large dry wok or cast iron skillet over medium heat, stirring continuously until dry. (If toasting more than 1 variety of seeds, do them separately to accommodate different cooking times.) Sesame seeds and pumpkinseeds will pop as they dry. If seeds start popping out of the pan, reduce heat on gas burner or lift skillet off electric burner until heat is reduced. Continue stirring.

2. Stir and toast until lightly browned and aromatic, 8 to 12 minutes. Sesame seeds are done when easily crushed between your thumb and forefinger. Pumpkinseeds will be puffy, slightly golden, and easily powdered with your fingers. Transfer seeds to a shallow bowl.

3. Cool and refrigerate in a covered glass jar or freeze

Variations

* **Sesame-Nori Sprinkle:** In a ridged mortar with a pestle, grind 1 cup toasted sesame seeds with 1/4 cup toasted, powdered wild nori seaweed (Page 397). Or, pulse in blender or food processor until coarsely ground. Use as a substitute for salt at the table to garnish salads or cooked vegetables. Replace sesame with sunflower seeds or pumpkinseeds. Refrigerate.

* **Pumpkinseed Sprinkle with Dulse:** Replace nori with toasted dulse, or grind 1 cup lightly toasted pumpkinseeds to a coarse powder. Combine with 1 cup dulse flakes, purchased from natural foods store or by mail. Refrigerate.

Nutrition

Entire recipe (pumpkinseeds):

1606 calories
68 g protein
50 g carbohydrate
(10 g fiber)
126 g fat
118 mg calcium
50 mg sodium

1 tablespoon (pumpkinseeds):

45 calories
2 g protein
1 g carbohydrate
4 g fat
3 mg calcium
1 mg sodium

Toasting brings out a rich taste. It also deactivates substances in raw seeds that can inhibit digestion. To avoid burning, I toast seeds on top of the stove, so I can watch and stir them constantly. I sprinkle the finished seeds over raw or parboiled vegetable salads, fruit salads, or steamed, sautéed, or marinated leafy greens for a nutty texture. Go easy though, half a cup of seeds will set you back 360 calories.

Note: Look for refrigerated *raw* seeds in natural foods markets and co-ops. Once home, keep them in the fridge or freezer. Green hulled pumpkinseeds, sold in natural foods stores, are easier to toast, grind, and crush, since they don't have a hard shell found on seeds from common pumpkins.

Toasted Nuts

Prep: 5 minutes ~ **Cooking:** 10 to 15 minutes ~ **Yield:** 2 cups; 32 servings

Ingredients & Directions

2 cups unsalted *raw*, shelled nuts (select 1 variety for each baking sheet):

walnut, pecan, or cashew halves, whole cashews, almonds, hazelnuts, pistachios, macadamia nuts, or pine nuts

1. Preheat oven to 350° F (or 300° F if your oven runs hot). Scatter nuts one layer deep in a dry baking pan with sides. Use 2 pans for 2 different types of nuts.

2. Toast pine nuts for 4 to 6 minutes. Toast larger nuts for 10 to 15 minutes, checking and stirring frequently. Set a timer and watch nuts closely; they burn easily. Nuts are done when lightly golden and aromatic. Do not allow nuts to darken or they will be bitter and unpleasant. Discard burned nuts.

3. Cool in shallow bowl. Store in covered jar in refrigerator.

Variations

* **Stove-Top Toasted Pine Nuts:** Toast in a hot, dry cast iron skillet or wok on the range top, over medium or medium-low heat. Stir or shake pan continuously to prevent burning, 5 to 6 minutes. This method does not work for almonds, walnuts, pecans, hazelnuts, or cashews

* **Toasted Nuts with Dulse:** Combine 1 cup toasted, coarsely chopped nuts with 1/4 to 1/2 cup crumbled Toasted Dulse (Page 397). Adjust proportions to your taste. Use as a garnish for salads or cooked vegetables at the table.

Nutrition

Entire recipe (walnuts):

1402 calories
30 g protein
28 g carbohydrate
(14 g fiber)
130 g fat
208 mg calcium
4 mg sodium

1 tablespoon (walnuts):

44 calories
1 g protein
1 g carbohydrate
4 g fat
7 mg calcium

Ready-to-eat toasted nuts are usually rancid when you buy them and notoriously high in sodium. Many companies also roast them in oil or oil and sugar, which add excess calories. You're better off buying whole raw nuts (shelled or unshelled) or nut halves (sold refrigerated, if possible).

Avoid slivered, crushed nuts, or nut pieces, which are usually rancid.

Nuts should always be stored in the refrigerator or freezer.

Toasting nuts is no trouble. It only requires a few minutes of hands-on prep. The payoff: a tantalizing, rich taste that provides more flavor from fewer nuts. Toasting also deactivates substances in nuts that can inhibit digestion.

You don't need oil to roast or toast nuts—they are already 70 to 80 percent fat. One handful packs 400 calories. Rather than eat them out of hand, we suggest using them to garnish chicken, turkey, or fruit salad, green salads, baked squash, sweet potatoes, or cooked fruit compotes. For a delicious dessert, we stuff nuts into Date-Coconut Rolls or whole dried apricots.

Homemade Almond Butter

Prep: 10 minutes ~ **Yield:** 3 cups

Ingredients & Directions

4 cups toasted, unsalted, almonds (Page 406)

1/3 cup unrefined coconut oil **or** unrefined palm oil, additional 2 tablespoons only if needed

4 drops vitamin E oil

1. **In Vita-Mix:** Add nuts to container with 1/4 cup oil and vitamin E oil. Secure 2-part lid, select HIGH, and turn on. Insert tamper through lid and push nuts into blades. Add additional oil through top of lid only if needed to blend. In 1 to 2 minutes you will hear a high-pitched chugging sound. Once nut butter begins to flow freely through the blades the motor sound will change from a high pitch to a low laboring sound. Turn off immediately.

   In food processor: Add nuts, 1 or 2 tablespoons coconut or palm oil (you shouldn't need more), and vitamin E oil to a food processor fitted with a metal blade. Secure lid and process until smooth. Add 2 more tablespoons of oil if needed.

2. Scrape nut butter into wide-mouth glass jars. Cover and refrigerate. It will keep for months.

Nutrition

1 tablespoon:
87 calories
3 g protein
2 g carbohydrate
(1 g fiber)
8 g fat
31 mg calcium

If you like almonds, you'll love almond butter. It's slightly sweet and just as versatile as peanut butter. It's less allergenic and contains more calcium. Spread it on sliced apples or celery sticks. Use it as a healthy fat source in fruit smoothies. Dilute to make a dip for fruit such as Chocolate or Vanilla Protein-Nut Spread (Page 464). Or transform into Fluffy Almond Butter (Page 408) and serve over fruit compote or sliced fresh or frozen bananas.

Variations

* **Homemade Cashew Butter:** Substitute lightly toasted, unsalted, cashews. This is outstanding in Protein-Nut Spread or used to make Fluffy Cashew Butter (Page 408).

* **Homemade Macadamia Nut Butter:** Substitute macadamia nuts. Reduce added oil to 2 to 3 tablespoons. Drizzle over fruit compote, Date-Coconut Rolls, or Baked Sweet Potatoes (see Index for recipes).

* **Homemade Walnut or Hazelnut Butter:** Substitute lightly toasted walnuts **or** hazelnuts. Wrap nuts in a clean kitchen towel and rub to remove skins before grinding. Serve over Date-Coconut Rolls, Baked Sweet Potatoes, sliced bananas, **or** in Protein-Nut Spread (see Index for recipes).

* **Homemade Peanut Butter:** Substitute lightly toasted peanuts in the master recipe. Wrap toasted nuts in a clean kitchen towel and rub to remove skins before grinding.

FYI: Buy raw, shelled nuts and lightly toast before grinding. Nuts sold already roasted have less flavor and are usually salted, coated with oil, or rancid.

Fluffy Almond Butter

Prep: 5 minutes ~ **Yield:** 1 cup; 8 servings

Ingredients & Directions

1/2 cup lightly toasted, unsalted, unsweetened almond butter

1/2 cup warm filtered water

1/4 to 1/2 teaspoon finely ground, unrefined sea salt, optional

1. Don't discard oil on top of a new jar of nut butter. Process contents of jar in a food processor, Vita-Mix, or large suribachi (Japanese ridged mortar) with a pestle until smooth. Return almond butter to original jar and refrigerate unused portion.

2. Dissolve optional salt in warm water. Add almond butter and mix or blend until smooth.

3. Scrape into a wide-mouth jar. Cover and refrigerate for at least 4 hours or until thick before serving. Use within 4 days if unsalted, 1 week if salted.

Nutrition

2 tablespoons:
109 calories
4 g protein
3 g carbohydrate
(3 g fiber)
9 g fat
89 mg calcium

To make almond butter more spreadable and less caloric, I often emulsify it with warm water. After it chills, it thickens, and fluffs up. It's delicious spooned over baked sweet potatoes, winter squash, fruit compote or sliced fresh or frozen bananas for a delicious snack or dessert. Although it may be tempting to dilute an entire jar of nut butter—don't. It'll sour after about 4 days if unsalted, and a week to 10 days if salted.

Variations

* **Fluffy Cashew Butter:** Replace almond butter with lightly roasted cashew butter. Try this over Stewed Pears with Anise, winter squash, sweet potato, or Marinated Beet Root Salad (see Index for recipes).

* **Fluffy Peanut Butter:** Buy unsalted, unsweetened, peanut butter without added oil. Organic is best since peanuts are usually grown in rotation with chemically treated cotton. (See note about freshly ground nut butter from stores).

* **Peanut-Honey Drizzle or Almond-Honey Drizzle:** A delightful drizzle for a tart batch of Rosehip-Apple Compote, Cranberry-Apple Compote, or Apple-Apricot Compote (see Index for recipes).
    To yield 1 1/4 cups sauce, combine 1 cup Fluffy Peanut or Almond Butter, 1/4 cup honey or agavé nectar, and 1 teaspoon vanilla or almond extract. Chill 3 or more hours until thick, or freeze for a faster set. Spoon over fruit and serve.

Note: Nut butter made fresh in stores with do-it-yourself grinders is not dense enough for this recipe. Select a bottled brand free of added salt, sugar, hydrogenated oil, and soybeans, or use homemade almond butter (Page 407).

Fluffy Tahini

Prep: 5 minutes ~ **Yield:** 1 cup; 8 servings

Ingredients & Directions

1/2 cup raw or lightly toasted unsalted sesame tahini

1/3 to 1/2 teaspoon finely ground unrefined sea salt

1/2 cup warm filtered water

1. Don't discard oil on top of a new jar of tahini. Process contents of jar in food processor, Vita-Mix, or large suribachi (Japanese ridged mortar) with a pestle until smooth. Return tahini to original jar and refrigerate unused portion.

2. Dissolve salt in warm water and mix with tahini until smooth.

3. Spoon into a wide-mouth jar, cover, and refrigerate for at least 4 hours or until thick before serving. Use within 4 days if unsalted, 10 days if salted.

Variations

* **Sesame-Garlic Sauce:** In step 2, add 1/4 cup lemon juice and 1 entire head of Roasted Garlic, about 3 to 4 tablespoons (Page 402), and a dash of black pepper. Serve as a topping for steamed or poached fish, a dip for raw vegetable sticks or parboiled crudités, or as a substitute for mayonnaise. If mixture becomes too thick, add 1 to 2 tablespoons additional water.
  Yield: 1 1/2 cups. See box for nutrition information.

Nutrition

2 tablespoons:
110 calories
2 g protein
5 g carbohydrate
(1 g fiber)
5 g fat
11 mg calcium
61 mg sodium

Variation
2 tablespoons:
76 calories
3 g protein
5 g carbohydrate
(1 g fiber)
6 g fat
11 mg calcium
40 mg sodium

Tahini taken right from the jar is often stiff and hard to spread. If you emulsify it with warm water, it becomes more spreadable and less calorie dense. After the mixture cools and thickens, it fluffs up. We use it in place of sour cream, yogurt, or butter over baked sweet potatoes, Marinated Beet Root Salad, or fruit compote.

Tahini Tartar Sauce

Prep: 15 minutes ~ **Yield:** 1 1/2 cups; 12 servings

Ingredients & Directions

1/2 cup well-blended, unsalted sesame tahini

1/2 cup warm filtered water

1/4 to 1/2 teaspoon finely ground, unrefined sea salt

1/3 cup peeled, seeded, and finely minced English (burpless) cucumbers **or** pickling cucumbers

2 tablespoons minced scallions, red onion, shallots, **or** chives

2 tablespoons minced, fresh parsley **or** tarragon

2 tablespoons fresh lemon juice

1/2 teaspoon lemon pepper **or** 1/4 teaspoon ground black pepper, or to taste

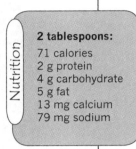

Nutrition

2 tablespoons:
71 calories
2 g protein
4 g carbohydrate
5 g fat
13 mg calcium
79 mg sodium

This creamy concoction reminds me of tartar sauce. I start with sesame tahini, a paste made from hulled, puréed sesame seeds. I use minced cucumbers to replace salty pickles. (Substitute rinsed capers or minced organic dill pickles if you like.) I serve this sauce over grilled, baked, or poached fish, chicken breast, parboiled broccoli, cauliflower, green beans, or asparagus. It also makes an excellent dip for raw or parboiled crudités.

1. Blend warm water and salt in a small non-metallic bowl, suribachi, Vita-Mix, or food processor until smooth. Add tahini and blend until smooth. Add remaining ingredients and blend again. Taste and add more lemon juice and pepper if desired. Transfer to a pint jar.

2. Cover and refrigerate for at least 3 hours or until thick before serving.

3. Use within 2 weeks.

Variations

* To reduce sodium and increase minerals, replace salt with 1/2 packed cup raw dulse leaf, sorted to remove small shells and stones, finely minced with kitchen shears, and soaked briefly in water to cover, **or** use toasted, crumbled, and sorted dulse leaf and omit soaking.

* **Middle Eastern Tahini Tartar Sauce:** Use scallions **or** onions, parsley, and 2 teaspoons each of minced fresh basil and oregano **or** 2/3 teaspoon each of dried, crumbled basil and oregano. Add pepper to taste.

* **Tartar Sauce Made with Mayonnaise:** Replace tahini and water with 1 cup of Homemade Mayonnaise (Page 424). If mayonnaise contains salt, omit salt in original recipe.

Mustard-Tahini Dressing

Prep: 15 minutes ~ **Yield:** 2 cups; 8 servings

Ingredients & Directions

1/2 cup raw or lightly toasted, unsalted sesame tahini

1/2 cup warm filtered water

1/2 to 3/4 teaspoon finely ground, unrefined sea salt

1/4 cup cold filtered water for dressing

1/4 cup lemon juice **or** 3 tablespoons raw apple cider vinegar

1 to 2 tablespoons prepared Dijon, yellow, or stone-ground mustard

2 teaspoons onion powder optional

1 raw clove minced or pressed garlic **or** 4 cloves of Roasted Garlic (Page 402), optional

Nutrition

1/4 cup:
110 calories
3 g protein
6 g carbohydrate
(1 g fiber)
8 g fat
18 mg calcium
147 mg sodium

1. Don't discard the oil on top of a new jar of tahini. Process contents of jar in a food processor, Vita-Mix, or large suribachi (Japanese ridged mortar) until smooth. Return tahini to original jar and refrigerate unused portion.

2. Dissolve sea salt in warm water then mix with tahini until smooth. Add remaining ingredients and blend until smooth.

3. Pour into wide-mouth jar. Cover and refrigerate for at least 3 hours or until thick before serving. Add 2 to 4 tablespoons water if too stiff. Use within 2 weeks.

Variations

* In place of Dijon mustard, use a specialty mustard such as smoked green chili, red chili, roasted garlic, sun-dried tomato, or horseradish-flavored mustard.

* **Tahini-Tarragon Dressing:** Add 1 tablespoon dried **or** 3 tablespoons minced fresh tarragon leaves.

* **Sesame, Garlic & Chive Dressing:** Omit mustard, onion powder, and garlic. Mince or press and add 2 cloves of raw garlic **or** 8 cloves of Roasted Garlic (Page 402). Stir 1/2 cup minced fresh chives **or** 2 tablespoons freeze-dried chives in by hand.

This recipe transforms a single tablespoon of tahini into 3 or 4 tablespoons of creamy, dairy-free dressing with a fraction of the fat found in most dressings. I serve this over tossed green salads, parboiled broccoli, cauliflower, asparagus, or mixed vegetables. I also use it as a dip for raw vegetables or as a substitute for mayonnaise in chicken, turkey, tuna, or egg salad.

Note: To prepare as dip, omit 1/4 cup cold filtered water.

Sesame-Dill Dressing

Prep: 15 minutes ~ **Yield:** 2 cups; 8 servings

Ingredients & Directions

1/2 cup raw or lightly toasted, unsalted sesame tahini

1/2 cup warm filtered water

1/2 to 3/4 teaspoon finely ground, unrefined sea salt

1/4 cup cold filtered water for dressing

1/4 cup lemon juice **or** 3 tablespoons raw apple cider vinegar

1/4 cup minced fresh scallions (green onions) **or** 1 tablespoon dried onion flakes

2 teaspoons dry dill weed **or** 2 tablespoons fresh dill weed, minced

2 teaspoons dried chives **or** 2 tablespoons minced fresh chives

1 teaspoon wet or dry mustard, optional

2 cloves of garlic, minced or pressed, optional

1/2 teaspoon lemon pepper, optional

Nutrition

1/4 cup:
109 calories
3 g protein
6 g carbohydrate
(1 g fiber)
8 g fat
25 mg calcium
120 mg sodium

Here is another wonderful way to use sesame tahini. You can make this thick (as a dip) or thinner for a salad dressing for raw, steamed, or parboiled vegetables, coleslaw, tossed green salads, or poached fish. It also makes a marvelous reduced-fat substitute for mayonnaise.

1. Don't discard oil on top of a new jar of tahini. Process contents of jar in food processor, Vita-Mix, or large suribachi (Japanese ridged mortar) with a pestle until smooth. Return tahini to original jar and refrigerate unused portion.

2. Dissolve sea salt in warm water then mix with tahini until smooth. Add remaining ingredients and blend until smooth.

3. Pour into a wide-mouth jar. Cover and refrigerate for at least 3 hours or until thick before serving. Add 2 to 4 tablespoons water if too stiff. Use within 2 weeks.

Variations

* Substitute 1 1/2 tablespoons salt-free dill blend for onion, dill, chives, and garlic. I prefer Frontier brand or Spice Hunter brand *Deliciously Dill* (dried onion, dill, lemon peel, ginger, garlic, and chives).

* **Cumin, Curry, Coriander & Tahini Dressing:** Substitute 1 teaspoon curry powder, 1/2 teaspoon ground cumin, and 1/2 teaspoon ground coriander with 1/8 to 1/4 teaspoon ground black pepper for dill, chives, garlic, and lemon pepper.

* **Curried Tahini Dressing:** Substitute 4 teaspoons curry powder and 1 1/2 teaspoons finely grated ginger for dill, chives, garlic, and lemon pepper.

Note: Omit 1/4 cold filtered water when making dip.

Macadamia-Dill Dressing

Prep: 15 minutes ~ **Yield:** 1 3/4 cups; 8 servings

Ingredients & Directions

1/2 cup raw or lightly toasted, unsalted, unsweetened macadamia nut butter

1/2 cup warm filtered water

1/2 to 3/4 teaspoon finely ground, unrefined sea salt

1/4 cup cold filtered water for dressing (omit for dip)

1/4 cup lemon juice **or** 3 tablespoons raw apple cider vinegar

1/4 cup minced fresh scallions (green onions)
or 1 tablespoon dried onion flakes

2 teaspoons dry dill weed **or** 2 tablespoons minced fresh dill weed

2 teaspoons dried chives **or** 2 tablespoons minced fresh chives

1 teaspoon wet or dry mustard, optional

2 garlic cloves, minced or pressed, optional

1/2 teaspoon lemon pepper, optional

Nutrition

1/4 cup:
135 calories
2 g protein
5 g carbohydrate
(1 g fiber)
12 g fat
17 mg calcium
145 mg sodium

1. Don't discard oil on top of a new jar of nut butter. Process contents in food processor, Vita-Mix, blender, or large suribachi (Japanese ridged mortar) with a pestle until smooth. Return nut butter to original jar, and refrigerate unused portion.

2. Dissolve salt in warm water and mix with nut butter until smooth. Add remaining ingredients and blend until smooth.

3. Pour into a wide-mouth jar. Cover and refrigerate for at least 4 hours or until thick before serving. Use within 2 weeks.

Variations

* Replace onion, dill, chives, and garlic with 1 1/2 tablespoons salt-free dill blend, such as Spice Hunter *Deliciously Dill* salt-free blend (dried onion, dill, lemon peel, ginger, garlic, and chives) or similar blend by Frontier.

I like the creamy texture and rich taste of macadamia nut butter. It's a great source of heart-healthy monounsaturated fats. It's thinner than most nut butters, but still makes a great dressing for parboiled vegetables, coleslaw, or tossed green salads, especially with tomatoes, scallions, or carrots. Look for unsalted, unsweetened macadamia nut butter in natural foods stores. Once you open a jar, store it in the refrigerator. Like all nuts and nut butters, it spoils rapidly at room temperature and it's too pricey to toss.

Sesame-Pesto Dressing

Prep: 20 minutes ~ **Yield:** 2 1/2 cups; 10 servings

Ingredients & Directions

1/2 cup unsalted, raw or roasted sesame tahini

1/2 cup warm filtered water

1/2 to 3/4 teaspoon finely ground, unrefined sea salt

1/4 cup cold water

1/4 cup lemon juice **or** balsamic vinegar

1/4 minced fresh parsley

1 1/2 packed cups fresh basil leaves with stems and blackened leaves removed

2 to 3 small to medium cloves garlic, minced **or** 1 head of Roasted Garlic (Page 402)

1/2 teaspoon lemon pepper, optional

Nutrition

1/4 cup:
87 calories
3 g protein
5 g carbohydrate
(1 g fiber)
6 g fat
27 mg calcium
141 mg sodium

This luscious low-calorie creamy, green dip and dressing is dairy-free but packed with flavor. It's perfect for potlucks, pack lunches, parties, and family meals. It usually encourages people to take second helpings of vegetables. It's also great for dressing parboiled vegetable medleys, steamed vegetables, seeded and chopped tomatoes on a bed of greens, or as a dip for raw or blanched vegetables.

1. If opening a new jar of tahini, don't discard oil on top. Process contents of jar in food processor, Vita-Mix, or large suribachi (Japanese ridged mortar) with a pestle until smooth. Return tahini to original jar and refrigerate unused portion.

2. Dissolve salt in warm water then mix with tahini until smooth. Add remaining ingredients, process until smooth, and pour into wide-mouth jar.

3. Cover and refrigerate for at least 3 hours or until thick before serving. Add 2 to 3 tablespoons water if too stiff to pour. Use within 2 weeks.

Variations

* **Sesame Green Goddess Dressing:** Omit basil. Add 1/4 cup minced parsley leaves, 1/4 cup minced chives, 2 tablespoons minced fresh tarragon leaves, and 1/8 teaspoon ground red or black pepper. Add 1/4 cup minced dill and 1 teaspoon Dijon mustard if desired.

Note: Basil makes the mixture discolor quickly. Don't make a double batch unless you're expecting company or sharing it with a friend or neighbor.

Practically Paleo Pesto

Prep: 20 minutes ~ **Cooking:** 5 to 15 minutes (for nuts) ~ **Yield:** 2 cups; 16 servings
---

Ingredients & Directions

2 packed cups fresh basil leaves, washed, dried, stems removed

1/4 cup toasted walnuts **or** pine nuts (Page 406)

1/4 cup fresh parsley leaves, washed and dried, stems removed

1 teaspoon finely ground, unrefined sea salt, or to taste

2 to 3 medium to large garlic cloves, chopped or crushed

2 tablespoons fresh lemon juice

1/2 cup extra-virgin olive oil **or** flax oil

Additional oil **or** preservative-free chicken broth, optional

3 drops vitamin E oil

Nutrition

2 tablespoons:
75 calories
1 g carbohydrate
8 g fat
11 mg calcium
115 mg sodium

1. Process all ingredients in blender, Vita-Mix, or food processor and blend until smooth, stopping to scrape sides with spatula. For thinner consistency, add a dash of oil, broth, or stock with motor running. Transfer to a clean wide-mouth jar that allows very little air space.

2. Cover and refrigerate. After each use, top with thin layer of olive oil to prevent oxidation.

3. Use within 1 week, or freeze in ice cube trays and transfer frozen cubes to sealed containers in freezer and use within 2 months.

Variations

* **Practically Paleo Pumpkinseed Pesto:** Replace nuts with lightly toasted pumpkinseeds. Use hulled green pumpkinseeds sold in natural foods stores.

* **Practically Paleo Mint Pesto:** Replace basil with fresh mint leaves. Reduce garlic to 1 clove. Add 1 tablespoon lemon juice and 1/4 teaspoon ground black pepper. Serve with lamb, duck breast, or green salad.

* **Practically Paleo Pistou:** Omit nuts. Add 1/4 teaspoon freshly ground black pepper, or to taste. This will eliminate 17 grams of fat and 189 calories from master recipe.

Unlike conventional pesto, this one is made without Parmesan cheese. If you need to avoid nuts, try the take-off on *Pistou*—the French Provençal version of pesto without nuts. Either can be used to baste salmon, white meat fish, or chicken before baking, roasting, or grilling. It can also be stuffed under the skin of chicken breasts before baking. Toss sauce with parboiled vegetables, sliced fresh tomatoes, or diced chicken breast for a salad, or spoon over grilled fresh tuna or pork at the table.

Note: Do not use flax oil if you plan to heat or cook with this sauce.

Spicy Peanut Sauce

Prep: 15 to 20 minutes ~ **Yield:** 1 1/2 cups; 9 servings

Ingredients & Directions

1/2 cup crunchy or smooth roasted unhydrogenated, unsalted, unsweetened peanut butter

1/2 cup warm filtered water, additional tablespoon as needed

1 to 2 tablespoons tamari soy sauce **or** 1/2 to 1 teaspoon finely ground unrefined sea salt

1/4 cup raw apple cider vinegar **or** lime juice

1/2 to 3/4 teaspoon ground chipotlé (start with less)

3 medium garlic cloves, minced or pressed

1/4 cup minced, fresh scallions or cilantro

2 to 4 tablespoons cold water for dressing (omit for a thick dip)

1. Don't discard oil on top of new jar of peanut butter. Blend contents of jar in bowl, suribachi, or food processor until smooth. Return peanut butter to original jar, and refrigerate unused portion.

2. Combine salt or tamari, warm water, and peanut butter in blender, food processor, or suribachi. Blend until smooth. Add vinegar, chipotlé, garlic, and blend again. Add 2 to 4 tablespoons cold water. Stir scallions or cilantro in by hand.

3. Pour into jar, cover, and refrigerate for at least 4 hours or until thick before serving. Use within 10 days.

Variations

* **Sweet Peanut Sauce:** Omit chipotlé, garlic, and scallions. Add 3/4 teaspoon cinnamon **or** 1 tablespoon finely minced or grated fresh ginger or ginger juice or purée, 1/8 teaspoon stevia extract powder, and 1 to 2 tablespoons honey or agavé nectar. Serve over plain chicken breasts, baked sweet potatoes, squash, steamed or parboiled carrots, broccoli, or mixed vegetables.

* **Spicy Peanut-Orange & Chipotlé Sauce:** Replace warm water with orange juice. This makes a fantastic marinade and sauce for pork, shrimp, or chicken breasts (Page 271).

Nutrition

1/4 cup:
96 calories
5 g protein
4 g carbohydrate
      (1 g fiber)
7 g fat
9 g calcium
96 to 192 mg
      sodium

Peanut butter and the rich smoky taste of chipotlé create a dazzling dip for parboiled or raw crudités, a delicious dressing for steamed or parboiled vegetables, green salads, and main-course salads made with pork, shrimp, or chicken breast. I modeled this on a recipe I found years ago in *Flat Breads and Flavors* by Naomi Duguid and Jeffrey Alford.

Note: Peanut butter made in markets with do-it-yourself grinders is not dense enough for this recipe. Find a bottled brand of natural peanut butter free of added salt, sugar, hydrogenated oil, and soybeans or use homemade peanut butter (Page 407).

Lean & Creamy Mustard Dressing

Prep: 15 minutes ~ **Cooking:** 5 minutes ~ **Yield:** 2 1/4 cups; 9 servings

Ingredients & Directions

1 cup salt-free chicken stock, Bone-Building Broth (Page 278), **or** preservative-free chicken broth

1/2 to 1 teaspoon unrefined sea salt (reduce or omit if using salted broth)

1 clove garlic, minced or pressed, optional

1 1/2 to 2 tablespoons arrowroot powder (less with thick Bone-Building Broth; more with water or thin stock or broth)

1/2 cup additional stock, broth **or** water

1/2 cup extra-virgin olive oil **or** flax oil **or** unrefined sesame oil

1/3 cup lemon juice **or** 1/4 cup raw apple cider vinegar

1/4 teaspoon ground chipotlé **or** black pepper

1 1/2 tablespoons Dijon mustard **or** 1 teaspoon dry mustard

2 teaspoons apple fiber powder, optional

1/4 teaspoon stevia extract powder **or** 6 to 8 drops stevia extract liquid

Nutrition

1/4 cup:
121 calories
3 g carbohydrate
12 g fat
7 calcium
131 mg sodium

1. Bring 1 cup of stock or broth and salt to boil in small saucepan. Add garlic now if desired or in step 3 below. Simmer and stir to dissolve salt. Dissolve arrowroot in remaining 1/2 cup liquid. Add to saucepan, and stir or whisk over medium-low heat until thick and clear.

2. Cool at room temperature or chill for at least 1 to 2 hours.

3. Whisk remaining ingredients into thickened broth, or process in blender. Pour into jars, label, cover, and refrigerate. Use within 3 weeks.

Variations

*   To reduce fat to 8 grams per serving, reduce oil to 1/3 cup.

*   **Lean & Creamy Honey-Mustard Dressing:** Omit stevia. Add 2 tablespoons honey or agavé nectar (cactus honey) in Step 1.

*   Add 1 teaspoon dried crumbled oregano, basil, or tarragon, in step 2.

This dressing reminds me of mayonnaise, only it's not as thick or as rich. It's delicious on tossed side salads and main-course salads. If possible, use our gelatin-rich Bone-Building Broth (Page 278) for added calcium, flavor and a thicker texture or use homemade chicken stock or broth.

Note: Apple fiber thickens the dressing and adds calcium and fiber. Look for it in natural foods stores or order it by mail (see Sources in Appendix D).

Lean & Creamy Basil-Balsamic Dressing

Prep: 20 minutes ~ **Cooking:** 5 minutes ~ **Yield:** 2 1/4 cups; 9 servings

Ingredients & Directions

1 cup salt-free chicken stock, Bone-Building Broth (Page 278), **or** preservative-free chicken broth

1/2 to 1 teaspoon unrefined sea salt (reduce or omit if using salted broth)

1 1/2 to 2 tablespoons arrowroot powder (less with thick Bone-Building Broth; more with water or thin stock or broth)

1/2 cup additional stock, broth **or** water

1/2 cup extra-virgin olive oil **or** flax oil

1/4 to 1/3 cup balsamic vinegar

1/3 cup fresh basil leaves **or** 1 1/2 tablespoons dried basil

3 small to medium garlic cloves, minced

1/4 teaspoon ground chipotlé **or** black pepper

2 teaspoons Dijon or yellow mustard **or** 1/2 teaspoon dry mustard

2 teaspoons apple fiber powder, optional

1/4 teaspoon stevia extract powder **or** 6 to 8 drops stevia extract liquid

Nutrition

1/4 cup:
123 calories
3 g carbohydrate
12 g fat
8 mg calcium
119 mg sodium

1. Bring 1 cup of stock or broth and salt to boil in small saucepan. Simmer and stir to dissolve salt. Dissolve arrowroot in remaining 1/2 cup liquid. Add to saucepan, and stir or whisk over medium-low heat until thick and clear.

2. Cool at room temperature or chill for at least 1 to 2 hours.

3. Whisk remaining ingredients into thickened broth, or process in blender. Pour into jars, label, cover, and refrigerate. Use within 3 weeks.

Variations

* To reduce fat to 8 grams per serving, reduce oil to 1/3 cup.

* **To omit stevia:** Substitute 1 tablespoon honey or agavé nectar in Step 1.

This creamy, reduced fat dressing goes well with almost any green salad. It's also delicious over main-course salads and greens mixed with fruit. If possible, use thick gelatin-rich Bone-Building Broth (Page 278) rather than thin stock or broth for extra calcium, boron, glucosamine sulfate, a rich flavor, and thicker texture.

Note: I often make a double batch. It doesn't take any more time than a single batch. It keeps well and it's great to share a bottle with friends, neighbors, or dinner guests.

Lean & Creamy French Dressing

Prep: 15 minutes ~ **Cooking:** 5 minutes ~ **Yield:** 2 1/4 cups; 9 servings

Ingredients & Directions

1 cup salt-free chicken stock, Bone-Building Broth (Page 278), **or** preservative-free chicken broth

1/2 to 1 teaspoon unrefined sea salt (reduce or omit if using salted broth)

1 1/2 to 2 tablespoons arrowroot powder (less with thick Bone-Building Broth; more with water or thin stock or broth)

1/2 cup stock, broth, **or** water

1/2 cup extra-virgin olive oil **or** flax oil

1/4 cup organic red wine vinegar **or** raw apple cider vinegar **or** 1/3 cup lemon juice

1 tablespoon dried crumbled, basil, oregano, thyme, chives, parsley, or some combination

1/2 teaspoon ground black pepper

1 teaspoon dry mustard **or** 1 tablespoon Dijon or yellow mustard

1/4 teaspoon stevia extract powder **or** 6 to 8 drops stevia extract liquid **or** 1 tablespoon honey

2 teaspoons apple fiber powder, optional

2 cloves minced garlic, optional

Nutrition

1/4 cup:
121 calories
3 g carbohydrate
12 g fat
7 calcium
105 mg sodium

Unlike most commercial salad dressings this one doesn't contain refined, polyunsaturated, or partially hydrogenated oils, sugar, preservatives, or MSG. I serve this over tossed green salads and main-course salads. Use gelatin-rich Bone-Building Broth for added calcium, flavor, and thickness.

1. Bring 1 cup of stock or broth and salt to boil in small saucepan. Simmer and stir to dissolve salt. Dissolve arrowroot in remaining 1/2 cup liquid. Add to saucepan and stir or whisk over medium-low heat until thick and clear.

2. Cool at room temperature or chill for at least 1 to 2 hours.

3. Whisk remaining ingredients into thickened stock or broth or process in blender. Pour into jars, cover, and refrigerate. Use within 3 weeks.

Variations

* Use combination of basil, chives, and parsley. Include 2 garlic cloves. Add 1/4 teaspoon celery seed and 2 teaspoons ground paprika.

* **Lean & Creamy Tomato French Dressing:** Replace 1 cup of water with preservative-free tomato juice. Add 1 tablespoon onion powder and 2 teaspoons dried, crumbled basil, oregano, chives, parsley, or a combination. If tomato juice contains sodium, omit salt from recipe.

* **Lean & Creamy Italian Dressing:** Omit mustard. Increase dried herbs to 2 tablespoons; use a combination of basil, oregano and thyme plus 1 tablespoon dried onion powder.

Poppy Seed-Pineapple Drizzle

Prep: 10 minutes ~ **Cooking:** 30 to 45 minutes ~ **Yield:** 2 3/4 cups; 11 servings

Ingredients & Directions

4 cups pineapple juice

1/2 teaspoon unrefined sea salt, optional

3 to 4 tablespoons poppy seeds

2 teaspoons minced fresh sage leaves **or** 3/4 teaspoon dried, rubbed sage, optional

1/4 teaspoon finely ground black pepper, optional

1 1/2 tablespoons arrowroot powder dissolved in 3 tablespoons cool or cold filtered water

1/2 cup extra-virgin flax oil **or** combination flax and unrefined sesame oil

3 drops vitamin E oil

1 teaspoon apple fiber powder, optional

1 tablespoon Dijon, yellow, or plain white mustard, optional, but delicious

1. Bring juice and optional salt to boil in shallow 2-quart saucepan. Add poppy seeds, sage, and pepper. Reduce heat and simmer, uncovered until thick and reduced by one-half, 30 to 45 minutes.

2. Add dissolved arrowroot and stir over medium-low heat until thick and clear, about 4 minutes.

3. Cool at room temperature, or refrigerate for at least 1 to 2 hours. Whisk in flax oil—or a combination of flax and unrefined sesame oil—vitamin E oil, and optional apple fiber and mustard. Pour into bottles, label, and refrigerate.

4. Use within 3 weeks or freeze in 1 or 2 canning jars with 1 inch of headspace.

Nutrition

1/4 cup:
160 calories
1 g protein
15 g carbohydrate
(1/2 g fiber)
11 g fat
50 mg calcium
2 mg sodium
(85 mg with salt)

Variation with orange juice, 1/4 cup:
145 calories
1 g protein
11 g carbohydrate
11 g fat
43 mg calcium
86 mg sodium

This is my rendition of a sweet sauce created by Chef Jeff McKahon of Rohr Fish & Seafood in Toledo, Ohio. It contains less than half the fat found in most salad dressings and has fabulous flavor. It's almost guaranteed to encourage friends and family members to take second helpings of salad. Try it over a tossed green salad, dark leaf lettuce paired with fresh or dried fruit, shrimp, chicken, or pork. Consider making a double batch for company or to last for a couple of weeks.

Variations

* **Poppy Seed-Orange Drizzle:** Replace pineapple juice with orange juice without pulp. See box for nutrition information.

* **Poppy Seed-Cherry Drizzle:** Replace pineapple juice with cherry or cherry-apple-grape juice. Add juice of 1 lemon (about 1/4 cup) in step 3 with mustard. **Yield:** 3 cups.

* Omit oil. Use poppy seed drizzle to coat fresh fruit salad just before serving.

Lemonette Dressing

Prep: 10 minutes ~ **Yield:** 3/4 cups; 6 servings

Ingredients & Directions

1/4 cup fresh lemon juice

1/4 teaspoon ground black pepper, or to taste

2 teaspoons Dijon, creamy white, or stone-ground mustard

1 to 2 garlic cloves (1/2 to 1 teaspoon) minced or pressed, optional

1/8 to 1/4 teaspoon finely ground, unrefined sea salt, optional

1/2 cup extra-virgin olive oil or flax oil **or** combination

1/4 teaspoon finely ground, unrefined sea salt, optional

1 tablespoon warm water

1 teaspoon minced or grated lemon zest, yellow part only, optional

Nutrition

2 tablespoons:
166 calories
0 g carbohydrate
18 g fat
22 mg sodium

Replace vinegar with lemon juice and vinaigrette becomes *lemonette*. Use more oil relative to citrus juice if you don't like a strong sour flavor. Always use the highest quality, extra-virgin oils sold in dark bottles.

1. Combine ingredients except water and citrus zest in blender or small food processor. Cover and blend. With machine running, add 1 tablespoon warm water and blend until smooth.

2. Taste, adjust as needed, and pour into small jar. Add grated citrus zest if desired. Cover, shake, and serve or refrigerate. Use within 2 weeks for best flavor.

Variations

* **Limonette:** Replace lemon juice and zest with lime juice and zest. Omit mustard but add garlic.

* **Orange Lemonette:** Replace lemon juice with 1/4 cup orange juice plus 1 tablespoon lemon juice. Blend, taste, and add 2 teaspoons minced fresh or dried dill weed if desired. To reduce fat, use 1/4 cup each of lemon and orange juice. Stir in 2 teaspoons orange zest if desired.

* **Shallot Lemonette:** Use garlic if you like. Increase pepper to 1/2 teaspoon. Add 2 minced shallots, and 1 1/2 teaspoons dried, crumbled **or** 2 tablespoons chopped fresh basil leaves.

* **Shallot & Mustard Lemonette:** Add 2 teaspoons Dijon or creamy white mustard to Shallot Lemonette.

* **Italian Lemonette:** Omit mustard. Add 1 tablespoon fresh **or** 1 teaspoon each of dried, crumbled basil, oregano, and thyme or rosemary leaves.

* **French Lemonette:** Add 2 teaspoons dried **or** 2 rounded tablespoons minced, fresh herbs (basil, thyme, chives, dill, oregano, parsley, or some combination).

* **Mediterranean Lemonette:** Omit mustard. Add 2 garlic cloves, 2 1/2 tablespoons minced fresh parsley, and 2 teaspoons minced fresh or 1/2 teaspoon dried thyme leaves.

FYI: Olive oil dressings naturally thicken in the refrigerator. Store them in the side of the fridge, or remove a bottle 20 minutes before serving to warm and liquefy.

Very Easy Vinaigrette

Prep: 5 minutes ~ **Yield:** 3/4 cups; 6 servings

Ingredients & Directions

1/4 cup quality vinegar: balsamic, red wine, **or** raw apple cider vinegar

1/4 teaspoon ground black pepper, or to taste

1 large or 2 small garlic cloves, minced or pressed, about 1/2 to 1 teaspoon

1/2 cup extra-virgin olive oil, flax oil **or** combination

1/4 teaspoon finely ground, unrefined sea salt, optional

1 tablespoon warm water

Nutrition

2 tablespoons:
173 calories
1/2 g carbs
18 g fat
3 mg sodium

1. Combine ingredients except warm water in blender or small food processor. Cover and blend. With machine running, add 1 tablespoon warm water and blend until smooth.

2. Taste, adjust as needed, pour into small jar, cover, and refrigerate or serve.

3. Use within 2 weeks for best flavor.

Variations

* Add 2/3 to 1 tablespoon Dijon, creamy white, or yellow mustard.

* **Shallot Vinaigrette:** Use garlic if you like. Increase pepper to 1/2 teaspoon, add 2 minced shallots, and 1 1/2 teaspoons dried, crumbled **or** 2 tablespoons chopped, fresh basil leaves.

* **Shallot & Mustard Vinaigrette.** Add 2 teaspoons Dijon or creamy white mustard to Shallot Vinaigrette.

* **Shallot & Raspberry Vinaigrette:** Use raspberry vinegar. Replace garlic with 2 chopped shallots and increase pepper to 1/2 teaspoon. If desired add 2 tablespoons chopped fresh basil or tarragon leaves **or** 1 1/2 teaspoons dried, crumbled herbs.

* **Italian Vinaigrette:** Use balsamic or red wine vinegar. Add 1 tablespoon fresh **or** 1 teaspoon each of dried, crumbled basil, oregano, and thyme or rosemary leaves.

* **French Vinaigrette:** Add 2 teaspoons Dijon mustard and 2 teaspoons dried **or** 2 rounded tablespoons minced fresh herbs (basil, thyme, chives, dill, oregano, parsley, or some combination).

* **Mediterranean Vinaigrette:** Add 2 1/2 tablespoons minced fresh parsley and 2 teaspoons minced fresh **or** 1/2 teaspoon dried, crumbled thyme.

A blender and a splash of hot water produce a lighter, creamier vinaigrette. A good rule of thumb is 1 part (tablespoon) vinegar to 2 or 3 parts (tablespoons) oil. Use more oil relative to vinegar if you don't like strong sour flavors.

Not just for tossed salads, this is delicious tossed with parboiled vegetables for a cold asparagus, green bean, cauliflower, broccoli, or mixed-vegetable salad.

FYI: Always use unrefined, virgin pressed oils sold in dark bottles. Olive oil dressing thickens in the refrigerator. Store it in the side door or remove the bottle 15 to 20 minutes before serving to allow it to warm and liquefy.

Tangerine & Shallot Vinaigrette

Prep: 5 minutes ~ **Yield:** 1 cups; 8 servings

Ingredients & Directions

2 teaspoons finely grated tangerine zest, colored part only

1 shallot, finely chopped

2 tablespoons balsamic vinegar, regular or berry flavored

1/4 cup freshly squeezed tangerine juice, preferably with pulp

1/2 cup flax oil **or** combination olive or unrefined sesame and flax oil

4 drops vitamin E oil

1/4 teaspoon finely ground, unrefined sea salt, optional

1/4 teaspoon ground red pepper, or to taste

1 tablespoon warm water

1. Combine all ingredients except warm water in blender or small food processor. Cover and turn on machine. While it's running, add 1 tablespoon warm water and blend until smooth.

2. Taste, adjust as needed, and pour into a small jar. Cover and refrigerate or serve.

3. Use within 1 week for best flavor.

Variations

* Add 1 tablespoon Dijon, creamy white, or yellow mustard.

* **Tangerine, Shallot & Tarragon Vinaigrette:** Replace red pepper with 1 teaspoon dried **or** 1 tablespoon minced fresh tarragon. Add 2 teaspoons Dijon mustard as desired.

* **Orange & Shallot Vinaigrette:** Replace tangerine zest and juice with orange zest and juice

For the best flavor and nutrition, use only unrefined, virgin pressed oils sold in dark bottles.

Nutrition

Entire recipe:
1031 calories
14 g carbohydrate
108 g fat
15 mg calcium
13 mg sodium

2 tablespoons:
129 calories
2 g carbohydrate
14 g fat
2 mg calcium
1 mg sodium

Note: Olive oil dressings naturally thicken in the refrigerator. Store in the side door of the fridge or remove the bottle 20 minutes before serving to soften. Flax oil produces a milder flavor and is easy to pour right from the refrigerator.

Homemade Mayonnaise

Prep: 15 minutes ~ **Yield:** 1 1/3 to 1 1/2 cups

Ingredients & Directions

1 medium-large (free-range) egg **or** 2 egg yolks

1 teaspoon dry mustard **or** 2 teaspoons Dijon mustard

1/8 to 1/4 teaspoon ground chipotlé **or** black pepper

2 tablespoons lemon juice **or** 1 tablespoon raw apple cider vinegar, or to taste

1/3 cup virgin pressed flax oil, unrefined sesame oil, **or** combination

2/3 cup extra-virgin olive, at room temperature

4 drops vitamin E oil

1/2 teaspoon finely ground, unrefined sea salt

2 to 4 tablespoons lukewarm filtered water, optional

1. Combine everything except oil and water in blender or food processor. Cover and process for 30 seconds. With motor running, slowly drizzle oil through top feeder until thick. Turn off, taste, and adjust seasonings if desired.

2. Add 2 to 4 tablespoons lukewarm water with machine running. Scrape mayonnaise into impeccably clean 16-ounce glass jar. Cover, refrigerate, and use within 1 week.

Nutrition

Entire recipe:
2026 calories
7 g protein
4 g carbohydrate
221 g fat
47 mg calcium
975 mg sodium

1 tablespoon:
96 calories
negligible protein
negligible carbs
11 g fat
2 mg calcium
46 mg sodium

Supermarket mayonnaise is made from refined and often hydrogenated oils, which have been linked to cancer, heart disease, and other degenerative diseases. Health foods brands are better, but still contain refined polyunsaturated oils and sugar. Homemade mayonnaise is the healthiest choice and incredibly easy to make in a food processor or blender. It has a more pronounced color from carotenes present in virgin pressed oils and a stronger flavor.

Variations

* For a milder flavor, use 1/4 cup flax oil, 1/4 cup unrefined sesame oil, and up to 1/2 cup olive oil.

* **Basil & Garlic Mayonnaise:** In step 2, add 1 cup fresh basil leaves and 2 to 3 cloves of minced raw garlic **or** 1/2 head Roasted Garlic (Page 402) and 2 tablespoons lemon juice. Blend, taste, and adjust as needed. This is fantastic tossed with lightly steamed or parboiled green beans cut in 1-inch lengths, green beans with cauliflower or yellow wax beans with broccoli served on a bed of shredded romaine or radicchio. It is also great in chicken, turkey, egg, or potato salad with minced sun-dried tomatoes, scallions, and celery. It can also be used like tartar sauce over poached, baked, steamed or grilled fish, pork loin, or chicken breast.

* **Herbed Mayonnaise:** In step 2, stir in 2 tablespoons lemon juice and 1 1/2 tablespoons crumbled, dried herbs **or** 1/4 cup plus 2 tablespoons chopped fresh dill, tarragon, chervil, chives, basil, oregano, or any of these with parsley. If desired, add 2 cloves finely minced garlic 6 cloves Roasted Garlic (Page 402). This is a wonderful topping for white meat fish, parboiled broccoli, cauliflower, green beans, and in chicken, turkey, egg or potato salad.

Note: If eating raw eggs make you uneasy, soft boil them for 2 minutes.

Be sure to buy unrefined, virgin pressed oils sold in dark bottles, which protect the oil from oxidation.

~ Variations continued next page ~

Variations

Homemade Mayonnaise ~ continued

* **Shallot & Chive Mayonnaise:** In step 2, stir in 3 tablespoons finely minced shallots and 1/2 cup minced fresh chives **or** 2 tablespoons freeze-dried chives. Use as a dip for parboiled vegetables, steamed asparagus or broccoli, or a topping for baked potatoes or fish.

* **Garlic Mayonnaise (Aioli):** Finely mince and blend in 4 small cloves raw garlic **or** an entire head of Roasted Garlic (Page 402), about 3 to 4 tablespoons, squeezed from the skin, 3 teaspoons lemon juice, 1/8 teaspoon black pepper, and 3 tablespoons warm filtered water. Toss with parboiled or cold steamed broccoli, yellow wax beans, or cauliflower with green beans. Use as a dip for crudités, parboiled vegetables, or to make turkey, tuna, or egg salad, or Angeled Eggs (Page 221).

* **Horseradish Mayonnaise:** At the end of step 2, add 1 1/2 tablespoons peeled, finely grated fresh horseradish, more as desired, and 1 tablespoon lemon juice. Spoon over rare roast beef, bison, or pork loin or serve over cooked white meat fish, roasted or baked beets, sliced tomatoes, or grilled vegetables.

22

Just Fruit

Best Bites

Baked Apples with Date-Nut Filling

Prep: 30 minutes ~ **Cooking:** 1 hour ~ **Yield:** 6 servings

Ingredients & Directions

Filling:

1/3 cup packed, dried, sulfite-free raisins

1/3 cup packed, dried, pitted dates

1/3 cup unsalted, unsweetened almond butter **or** cashew butter

1/4 cup orange juice concentrate

1 teaspoon pure vanilla **or** maple extract (preferably non-alcoholic)

1 1/4 teaspoons apple pie spice

Apples:

6 medium-large tart-sweet apples (8 ounces each):
early gold, ginger gold, golden delicious, braeburn,
gala, Fuji, pink lady, or Cortland

1/3 cup filtered water

1. Preheat oven to 350° F. Combine filling ingredients in food processor or Vita-Mix. Process until smooth. Alternatively, mince dried fruits and mix filling in a bowl.

2. Wash apples and core twice to create a wide cavity. Remove apple bits from around seeds and core; mince and add to filling. Peel upper 1/3 of each apple to keep skins from splitting during cooking, or remove entire peel.

3. Fill apples, mounding extra filling on top. Arrange in a 9-inch round, square, or oblong baking pan. Add water to pan. Cover pan with parchment then aluminum foil, or a tight-fitting lid. Bake in preheated oven for 60 minutes or until fork tender.

4. Simmer pan juices in saucepan to reduce to 1/4 cup then spoon over apples. Serve warm or close to room temperature. Use leftovers within 4 days.

Variations

* Substitute 1 1/2 teaspoons peeled, finely grated fresh gingerroot **or** 1/3 teaspoon dried ginger plus 3/4 teaspoon ground cinnamon, 1/8 teaspoon ground nutmeg, and 1/8 teaspoon ground cloves for apple pie spice.

* **Slow Cooker:** Place stuffed apples in a 3 1/2- to 6-quart slow cooker with 1/3 cup water. Cover and cook on LOW 3 to 4 hours or until fork tender. Transfer apples to serving bowls. Cook juices on HIGH to reduce to 1/4 cup. Spoon over apples and serve.

You don't need butter or brown sugar to make irresistible baked apples. These are wonderful warm or close to room temperature.

Nutrition

1 serving:
292 calories
4 protein
53 g carbohydrate
(10 g fiber)
9 fat
93 mg calcium
3 mg sodium

Note: I use eating apples rather than cooking apples because they hold their shape better. Cooking apples usually collapse into an applesauce mess. I use Frontier apple pie spice.

Apple-Apricot Compote

Prep: 20 minutes ~ **Cooking:** 30 minutes ~ **Yield:** 6 cups; 8 servings

Ingredients & Directions

1/2 cup filtered water

1/3 cup unsulphured raisins

1/3 cup dried, unsulphured, unsweetened Turkish dried apricots

1 teaspoon ground cinnamon **or** apple pie spice

8 medium or 6 large tart or tart-sweet apples (1 to 3 varieties), about 3 to 3 1/2 pounds:
cameo, empire, gala, granny smith, Cortland, Fuji, pink lady, cameo, ginger gold, Melrose, jonagold or braeburn

1 tablespoon arrowroot starch dissolved in 3 tablespoons cold water, optional

1/16 to 1/8 teaspoon stevia extract powder **or** 1/4 teaspoon powdered licorice root, optional

1/2 cup chopped, Toasted Nuts (Page 406) **or** 1/2 cup Fluffy Almond Butter (Page 408) for garnish, optional

Nutrition

1 serving (about 3/4 cup):
139 calories
32 g carbohydrate (5 g fiber)
1 g fat
20 mg calcium
1 mg sodium

1. Add water to barely cover bottom of 3- to 4-quart pot. Add raisins, apricots, and spices. Wash and core apples, and peel if waxed or desired. Halve, cut into thin half-moon slices or 1/2-inches wedges, and add to pot.

2. Cover and bring to boil. Reduce heat, and simmer until tender and sauce-like, 20 to 30 minutes.

3. Uncover and stir gently. If watery, remove lid and cook away moisture or add dissolved arrowroot. Simmer and stir to thicken. If fruit is not sweet enough, sprinkle and stir in stevia in small amounts (it's 100 to 300 times sweeter than sugar), or add powdered licorice.

4. Serve warm or close to room temperature. Garnish with nuts or Fluffy Almond Butter if desired. Refrigerate in sealed jars and use within 5 days.

Variations

* **Apple-Prune Compote with Chinese 5-Spice:** Substitute 1 1/2 teaspoons Chinese 5-spice powder for cinnamon or pie spice. Replace raisins or apricots with pitted prunes if desired.

* Substitute 1 tablespoon peeled, minced fresh ginger or ground caraway, anise, or fennel seeds for cinnamon or pie spice.

I love apples and ate them almost daily during the fall and winter when we lived in Ohio, Michigan, and Washington State. I vary the dried fruits, apples, and spices. Leftovers are delicious with any meal, from breakfast to dinner.

Eating apples hold their shape and retain texture better than cooking apples.

Dress this up with a sprinkle of chopped nuts or drizzle with macadamia nut butter before serving.

Note: For holiday gift giving, fill pint or quart canning jars with compote. Add a ribbon and a recipe card (giving credit to our book and us), and give the gift of health.

Rosehip-Apple Compote

Prep: 20 minutes ~ **Cooking:** 20 to 30 minutes ~ **Yield:** 8 servings

Ingredients & Directions

1/2 cup filtered water, to just cover bottom of pot

1/2 cup dried, cut and de-seeded rosehips, golden pit pieces removed **or** 3 tablespoons fine rosehip powder

1/2 cup unsulphured raisins **or** chopped, pitted prunes

1/3 cup halved, dried unsulphured, unsweetened apricots, halved, optional

1 teaspoon ground cinnamon, pumpkin pie spice **or** apple pie spice, optional

6 large tart or tart-sweet apples (1 or 2 varieties), about 3 to 3 1/2 pounds:
    granny smith, macintosh, braeburn, jonagold, gala, cameo, Fuji, or pink lady

1 tablespoon arrowroot starch dissolved in 3 tablespoons cold water, optional

1/8 teaspoon stevia extract powder **or** 1/4 teaspoon powdered licorice root, optional

1/2 cup chopped Toasted Nuts (Page 406) **or** Fluffy Almond Butter **or** Fluffy Peanut Butter **or** Peanut- or Almond-Honey Drizzle (Page 408), Fluffy Tahini (Page 409) **or** 1/4 cup plain macadamia nut butter for garnish, optional

Nutrition

1 serving:
199 calories
1 g protein
47 g carbohydrate
(6 g fiber)
1 g fat
31 mg calcium
228 mg sodium

More than a decade ago Don devised this delightfully sweet, tart, and tangy dessert.

We've served it in the early autumn, for Thanksgiving, Christmas, and on through Easter. Buy dried, cut, de-seeded rosehips, which resemble small flakes, or purchase fine rosehip powder sold in natural foods stores or by mail from Frontier Herbs (see Sources in Appendix).

1. Add water to barely cover bottom of 3- to 4-quart pot. Add sorted rosehips or rosehip powder, raisins or prunes, and optional apricots and spice. Wash, core, and peel apples. Grate 1 apple into the pot. Cut remaining apples into 1 1/2-inch wedges or thin half-moon slices and add to pot. Cover and bring to boil without stirring.

2. Reduce heat and simmer until tender and sauce-like, 20 to 30 minutes. Remove lid and stir. If watery, simmer uncovered until thick, or add dissolved arrowroot, simmer and stir to thicken. If too tart, stir in 1/8 teaspoon stevia extract powder or 1/4 teaspoon powdered licorice.

3. Remove from heat. Serve warm or chilled with optional garnish of choice. Refrigerate in glass. Use within 5 days.

Variations

*   Substitute 1 1/2 teaspoons peeled, finely grated fresh gingerroot **or** 1/3 teaspoon dried ginger plus 3/4 teaspoon ground cinnamon, 1/8 teaspoon ground nutmeg, and 1/8 teaspoon ground cloves for apple pie spice.

FYI: The sodium content sounds high, but don't rule this out. It's from the rosehips, which have a lot of naturally occurring sodium in addition to vitamin C and bioflavonoids.

Note: For holiday gift giving, fill pint or quart canning jars with compote. Add a ribbon and a recipe card (giving credit to our book and us), and give the gift of health.

Stewed Pears with Anise & Apricots

Prep: 15 minutes ~ **Cooking:** 25 to 35 minutes ~ **Yield:** 6 to 8 servings
---

Ingredients & Directions

1/2 cup filtered water

1/3 to 1/2 cups unsulphured raisins (depending upon desired sweetness)

1/3 to 1/2 cup dried, pitted, unsulphured Turkish apricots, coarsely chopped

1 tablespoon whole anise seeds **or** 2 teaspoons ground anise powder

Coarsely grated zest of 1/2 orange or tangerine, colored part only, optional

6 medium-size ripe, fragrant, but still firm, unblemished pears (about 2 1/2 pounds):
   bosc, comice, bartlett, spartlet, anjou, or others

1 tablespoon arrowroot starch dissolved in 3 tablespoons cool or cold water, optional

1/4 to 1/2 cup lightly toasted, coarsely chopped pecans, walnuts, or almonds (Page 406) **or** 1/4 cup macadamia nut butter for garnish, optional

Nutrition

1 serving:
141 calories
1 g protein
32 g carbohydrate
                (4 g fiber)
1 g fat
29 mg calcium
1 mg sodium

Raisins, dried apricots, anise seeds, and water create succulent licorice-like syrup for pears without added sugar. More than 5000 varieties of pears exist worldwide and more than 100 are grown in the United States. Check your local farmers' market for exotic and heirloom varieties.

1. Add water to 3-quart pot. Add raisins, apricots, anise, and optional orange or tangerine zest. Wash, halve, core, and cut pears into bite-size chunks and add to pot. Pears will release more liquid as they cook.

2. Cover and bring to boil over medium heat without stirring. Reduce heat and simmer, undisturbed until tender, 20 to 25 minutes. Stir gently with a wide spoon, being careful not to mash. For a thicker consistency, add arrowroot mixture, simmer and stir. Remove from heat.

3. Ladle into dessert cups or parfait glasses. Garnish with nuts or nut butter if desired, and serve warm or at room temperature. Refrigerate leftovers and use within 5 days.

Variations

* **Stewed Pears with Apricots, Prunes & 5-Spice:** Replace anise with 2 teaspoons Chinese 5-spice powder and raisins with thinly sliced, pitted prunes.

* **Stewed Pears with Apricots & Ginger:** Include apricots. Replace anise with 1 1/2 tablespoons peeled and finely minced or grated fresh gingerroot.

* **Chocolate Sauce:** Combine 4 ounces of unsweetened bakers chocolate, 1/2 cup regular or lite coconut milk, 1/2 cup honey or agavé nectar, 1/8 to 1/4 teaspoon stevia extract liquid or powder, and 1 teaspoon pure vanilla extract in a small saucepan. Melt over low heat. Stir and spoon over pear compote. Garnish with coarsely chopped toasted pecans or walnuts if desired.

Chocolate-Avocado Mousse

Prep: 20 to 30 minutes ~ **Yield:** 3 heaping cups; 6 servings

Ingredients & Directions

1 cup cold filtered water

4 teaspoons unflavored gelatin (bulk beef gelatin or Knox)

1/2 cup chopped, soft, pitted dates (such as medjool)

2 medium large ripe avocados (1 pound or 2 to 2 1/2 cups halved, seeded, peeled, and diced)

1/4 cup to 1/2 cup unsweetened cocoa powder, adjusted to taste

2 teaspoons nonalcoholic vanilla extract **or** 1 teaspoon pure vanilla extract in alcohol

1/2 teaspoon stevia extract powder

1/2 teaspoon ground cinnamon

2 tablespoons dark rum **or** 1 teaspoon natural rum extract, optional

3/4 cup cold water **or** ice

Finely grated zest of 1 small to medium orange, colored part only

Nutrition

1 serving:
199 calories
4 g protein
19 g carbohydrate
(5 g fiber)
12 g fat
18 mg calcium
8 mg sodium

An unlikely but delicious combination of cocoa, avocado, and dates makes a delightful dessert without dairy and with a fraction of the fat contained in conventional confections. It's easy to make and packed with potassium, antioxidants, and flavor.

1. Slowly sprinkle gelatin over 1 cup cool or cold water in small saucepan. Warm over low heat, without stirring until completely dissolved, 1 to 2 minutes. Cover and remove from heat.

2. Add gelatin mixture to blender or food processor with dates and process until frothy, about 60 seconds; turn off machine. Add remaining ingredients except orange zest. Cover and blend until smooth, stopping to scrape sides with spatula.

3. Taste and add more cocoa if desired. Fold in orange zest by hand; scrape into 6 small bowls or wine goblets.

4. If you did not use ice, chill for 3 hours until set, before serving. Refrigerate and use within 5 days or freeze.

Variations

* Substitute 1/3 cup plus 1 tablespoon agavé nectar or light-colored honey for dates, and reduce cold water or ice by 1/4 cup.

FYI: The avocados should be ripe and yield to pressure, but not mushy. Buy 1 or 2 extras just in case. You can always add them to a salad, salsa, or guacamole.

Cranberry-Apple Compote

Prep: 20 minutes ~ **Cooking:** 25 minutes ~ **Yield:** 8 cups; 12 servings

Ingredients & Directions

1 cup unsulphured raisins **or** chopped, pitted dates

2 cups cranberries, fresh or frozen, rinsed and drained

1/2 cup filtered water **or** apple juice

1 tablespoon finely grated orange zest, colored part only, **or** 1 teaspoon dried orange peel

2 tablespoons peeled, minced fresh gingerroot, optional

5 large tart-sweet apples (2 1/2 pounds), cored and peeled if desired, divided:
    granny smith, pink lady, jonagold, jonathan, macintosh, braeburn, gala, cameo, or Rome

1/4 to 1/3 teaspoon stevia extract powder **or** powdered licorice root, optional

1 tablespoon arrowroot dissolved in 3 tablespoons cold water, optional

3/4 cup chopped Toasted Nuts (Page 406), Fluffy Almond Butter, Peanut- or Almond-Honey Drizzle (Page 408), **or** Fluffy Tahini (Page 409), optional

Nutrition

3/4 cup:
122 calories
1 g protein
29 g carbohydrate
    (6 g fiber)
2 mg calcium
2 mg sodium

1. Layer raisins, cranberries, water or juice, and orange zest in a 4-quart pot. Add ginger if desired. Grate 1 apple into pot. Cut remaining apples into 1 1/2- to 2-inch pieces or thin half-moon slices and add to the pot.

2. Cover and bring to boil over medium-high heat, without stirring. Reduce heat and simmer until tender, 20 to 30 minutes.

3. Stir gently with a large wide spoon without mashing. Taste. Sprinkle and stir in stevia or licorice in tiny increments if a sweeter taste is desired. For a thicker consistency, add dissolved arrowroot; simmer, and stir. Serve warm or chilled, garnishing as desired.

4. Refrigerate leftovers in a covered glass container and use within 5 days.

Variations

* **Cranberry Applesauce:** At end of step 3, purée fruit in blender or food processor.

* For a scrumptious snack, top each serving of compote with 1/4 cup Vanilla or Chocolate Protein-Nut Spread **or** Protein-Coconut Cream, **or** 2 tablespoons Fluffy Almond Butter **or** Peanut-Honey Drizzle (see Index for Recipes).

This sweet- and tart-tasting compote has been a holiday tradition in our home for more than a decade. It's easy to assemble. You can serve it instead of cranberry sauce, as a side dish, turkey topping, or dessert. The high pectin content of granny smith and pink lady apples makes a natural thickener. Other varieties may require thickening with arrowroot.

Note: For holiday gift giving, fill pint or quart canning jars with compote. Add a ribbon and a recipe card (giving credit to our book and us), and give the gift of health.

Fruit Kabobs

Prep: 20 minutes ~ **Yield:** 12 skewers, 4 servings

Ingredients & Directions

4 cups fresh, fully ripened fruit, 3 to 5 varieties:
pineapple, cantaloupe or honeydew melon, peaches,
pears, apples, nectarines, peeled kiwi, mango,
or papaya, cut in 1-to 1 1/2-inch chunks, sliced
bananas, or whole strawberries.

1/2 tablespoon fresh lemon, lime or orange juice

Topping, select 1:

1 cup plain, Chilled Coconut Milk (Page 449)

1 cup Vanilla or Chocolate Protein-Coconut Cream
(Page 470)

1 cup Fluffy Almond Butter (Page 408)

Nutrition

**1 serving
(fruit only):**
76 calories
1 g protein
17 g carbohydrate
(3 g fiber)
13 mg calcium
7 mg sodium

Here's an elegant way to serve fruit. Select 3 or 4 fruits for the most striking presentation.

Figure 1 or 2 kabobs per person for dessert; 3 or 4 per person with 1/4 cup of sauce for a snack. If you plan to serve the kabobs with eggs, fish, or meat, and a salad or cooked greens, replace the topping with a light dusting of shredded, sulfite-free unsweetened, coconut.

1. Slice and pit fruit close to serving time. Drizzle apple, pear, peach, or banana slices with lemon juice to prevent oxidation.

2. Thread fruit onto 12 skewers, alternating colors and varieties. Leave space between each piece and at least 1 inch on the end of each stick for holding. Serve at room temperature or chilled.

3. Use leftover fruit within 24 hours as a side dish, in a smoothie or Total Juice, or freeze for future smoothies or Frosty Fruit Whips (see Index for recipes).

Variations

* Papaya, Pineapple & Peach Kabobs

* Pineapple, Peach & Plum Kabobs

* Cantaloupe, Strawberry, Nectarine & Banana Kabobs

* Cantaloupe, Strawberry & Peach Kabobs

* Strawberry, Kiwi & Peach Kabobs

* Strawberry, Cantaloupe & Kiwi Kabobs

Basic Fruit Salad

Prep: 20 minutes ~ **Yield:** 8 (1 cup) servings

Ingredients & Directions

Fruit:

8 cups fresh, fully ripened, washed, sliced or diced fruit
(2 to 5 varieties):

> strawberries, blueberries, raspberries,
> blackberries, Marionberries, lingonberries,
> sweet or sour (pitted) cherries, seedless grapes,
> honeydew, cantaloupe or crenshaw melon,
> peaches, nectarines, plums, apricots, kiwi, papaya,
> mango, pineapple, banana, or star fruit, pears,
> apples or kiwi

Seasonings:

Juice of 1 lime, 1 medium orange **or** 3 tablespoons balsamic vinegar

1/2 teaspoon cinnamon or apple pie spice
or 3 tablespoons ginger juice, optional

1 to 2 tablespoons honey **or** agavé nectar for tart fruits, optional

Garnish:

1/2 cup unsweetened, sulfite-free, shredded coconut **or** chopped, Toasted Nuts (Page 406), optional

Nutrition

1 cup fruit (average of fruits without nuts):

77 calories
1 g protein
17 g carbohydrate
(3 g fiber)
2 g fat
14 mg calcium
7 mg sodium

You almost don't need a recipe but people often get in ruts and forget to try new combinations. I usually limit the salad to 3 or 4 fruits so we have more variety throughout the week. Use as much fruit from your region or bioregion as possible. It will be fresher, more flavorful, and often less costly, particularly if you buy it directly from the farmer.

1. Combine fruit in a 2 1/2- to 3-quart nonmetallic bowl. Combine seasonings of your choice and toss with fruit. Garnish with coconut or nuts if desired, and serve.

2. Refrigerate leftovers in covered glass bowl or wide-mouth jar. Use within 24 hours, or freeze on cookie sheets, then transfer to bags or freezer containers and use to make Frosty Fruit Whips, Better Balanced Smoothies, or Protein Popsicles (see Index for recipes).

Variations

* **Fruit Salad with Poppy Seed Glaze:** Omit seasonings. Just before serving, toss fruit with 1 cup of Poppy Seed-Pineapple or Poppy Seed-Orange Glaze (Page 420).

* **Fruit Salad with Vanilla Protein-Coconut Cream:** For a blood sugar-balancing breakfast or snack, figure 2 to 2 1/2 cups fruit per person plus 1/2 cup Protein Coconut Cream (Page 470).

Frozen Bananas

Prep: 10 to 15 minutes ~ **Yield:** 6 to 12 servings

Ingredients & Directions

6 to 12 ripe or slightly over-ripe bananas (more as desired), rinsed, peeled, and thinly sliced

1. Spread banana slices on 1 or more cookie sheets. Freeze until firm.

2. Transfer banana slices to cup, half pint, or pint-size freezer containers; fill to top. If containers are not full, top each container with a piece of unbleached parchment paper cut to size, then cover with a tight-fitting lid to prevent or reduce discoloration and freezer burn.

3. Label, date, and freeze. **Note:** Bananas will keep better (and last longer) in a chest freezer.

4. Use within 3 weeks for best results.

Nutrition

1 cupful:
157 calories
2 g protein
35 g carbohydrate
    (4 g fiber)
1 g fat
9 mg calcium
2 mg sodium

Frozen bananas are great for smoothies, Frosty Fruit Whips (Page 475), and Frozen Banana Delight (Page 437). Let the bananas fully ripen—but not turn mushy or alcoholic—before freezing. To save money, buy organic bananas after they've been marked down. For ease of serving, store the slices in freezer containers with snap-on lids. Snack-size containers are ideal. Avoid large containers. Bananas that are thawed and frozen in large containers turn black.

Frozen Banana Delight

Prep: 5 minutes ~ **Yield:** 4 servings

Ingredients & Directions

4 large ripe sweet bananas **or** 3 to 4 cups sliced, bananas, frozen (Page 436)

1/2 to 3/4 cup Fluffy Almond Butter, Fluffy Cashew Butter, **or** Fluffy Peanut Butter (Page 408)

1 teaspoon nonalcoholic vanilla extract

1. Empty frozen bananas into 4 shallow bowls. Allow to soften for 10 to 15 minutes.

2. Mix Fluffy Almond Butter, Fluffy Cashew Butter, or Fluffy Peanut Butter with vanilla. Spoon sauce over bananas and serve. If you haven't added cocoa powder to the sauce, you can sprinkle it over your serving(s) and stir as you eat, if desired.

Nutrition

1 serving without cocoa:

279 calories
6 g protein
38 g carbohydrate
(7 g fiber)
10 g fat
89 mg calcium
4 mg sodium

Variations

* **Unfrozen Banana Delight:** Replace frozen bananas with peeled, sliced fresh bananas.

* **Cocoa-Nut Butter Sauce:** Add 4 tablespoons unsweetened cocoa and 3 to 4 tablespoons water to Fluffy Almond Butter, Fluffy Cashew Butter, or Fluffy Peanut Butter. It adds only 18 calories, 1 gram of carbohydrate, and 1 gram of fat per serving.

* **Frozen Cocoa-Banana Swirl:** Alternate layers of mashed banana and Cocoa-Nut Butter sauce in 2 pint-size freezer containers. Cover and freeze for at least 4 hours until firm. Serve with an ice cream scoop and use within 7 days.

* Replace Fluffy Nut Butter with 1 cup Vanilla or Chocolate Protein-Nut Spread (Page 464), 1/4 cup per person and per banana.

This is one of my favorite snacks. It reminds me of ice cream, but it's a lot more nutritious. You can assemble it in a few minutes—if you keep sliced frozen bananas in the freezer and a jar of Fluffy Nut Butter in the fridge. Bananas have gotten a bad rap for being high on the glycemic Index, but don't rule them out. They're a product of nature: sweet, delicious, and packed with potassium. To reduce their glycemic Index, just serve them with nuts or nut butter.

Chilled Cherry Gel

Prep: 20 minutes ~ **Cooking:** 10 minutes ~ **Yield:** 6 to 8 servings

Ingredients & Directions

2 cups apple juice **or** cherry juice, divided

1 1/2 tablespoons unflavored gelatin

1 quart fresh sweet cherries, washed, and drained
(3 packed cups pitted or frozen, not thawed):
    bing, Rainier, royal ann, or fresh (not bottled)
    maraschino cherries

1 tablespoon arrowroot starch dissolved in reserved
1/4 cup of juice

1/3 cup lightly toasted, coarsely chopped Toasted
Almonds (Page 406), **or** Fluffy Almond Butter
(Page 408), optional

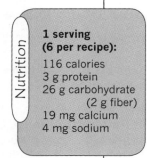

Nutrition

**1 serving
(6 per recipe):**

116 calories
3 g protein
26 g carbohydrate
(2 g fiber)
19 mg calcium
4 mg sodium

1. Pour 1/4 cup juice into a shallow bowl. Slowly
   sprinkle with gelatin and let stand for 5 minutes until no dry spots
   remain. Pit cherries and set aside. Reserve 1/4 cup juice.

2. Combine remaining 1 1/2 cups juice and cherries in a medium-size
   saucepan. Bring to a low boil. Add dissolved arrowroot, simmer and
   stir until thick and clear, about 3 minutes. Remove from heat.

3. Pour 1/2 cup of hot juice over gelatin and stir to dissolve then
   combine with remaining hot mixture. Ladle into 6 wine glasses or
   dessert cups. Allow to cool. Refrigerate for at least 3 hours, until
   set, before serving.

4. Serve plain or garnished with chopped, toasted nuts or Fluffy
   Almond Butter.

Variations

* At the end of step 3, add 1 teaspoon nonalcoholic vanilla extract **or**
  1/2 teaspoon nonalcoholic almond extract and 1 teaspoon of grated
  lemon, orange, **or** tangerine zest (finely grated rind, colored part
  only).

* Experiment with mango, peeled and sliced apricots, peaches,
  nectarines, berries, grapes, or pears. **Note:** Enzymes in raw
  pineapple, papaya, or kiwi may prevent gel from setting.

If you can't find fresh, locally grown cherries, use frozen pitted sweet unsweetened cherries. During our vegan-macrobiotic days, Don and I made this with agar agar, the vegetarian equivalent of gelatin. Both versions taste identical, but you have to use 2 or 3 times as much agar agar, it takes longer to cook, and costs $10 an ounce ($160 a pound). I use bulk or bottled gelatin from a natural foods store. Knox unflavored gelatin works equally well.

Basic Fresh Fruit Gel

Prep: 15 minutes ~ **Cooking:** 5 minutes ~ **Yield:** 8 to 10 servings

Ingredients & Directions

2 tablespoons unflavored gelatin

1 cup cool or cold filtered water **or** fruit juice for a sweeter taste

3 cups apple juice **or** apple-apricot, apple-berry, or cherry juice, divided

1 slightly rounded tablespoon arrowroot dissolved in 1/2 cup reserved juice

2 cups of fresh fruit (1 fruit or combination of 2 to 3 varieties):
> blueberries, raspberries, mulberries, pitted sweet cherries, sliced strawberries, melon balls, seedless red or green grapes, pitted, peeled, and sliced apricots, peaches, or nectarines

1 teaspoon nonalcoholic vanilla extract, optional

1 teaspoon finely grated lemon, lime, or orange, zest (colored part only), optional

1/2 cup coarsely chopped Toasted Nuts (Page 406), optional

Nutrition

1 serving (blueberry-apricot):
110 calories
3 g protein
25 g carbohydrate
(2 g fiber)
1 g fat
15 mg calcium
5 mg sodium

1. Sprinkle gelatin over 1 cup cool or cold filtered water or juice and set aside.

2. Heat 2 1/2 cups juice in saucepan over medium heat. Dissolve arrowroot in 1/2 cup reserved juice, add to pan, bring to a low boil, stir until arrowroot thickens and turns clear, about 3 minutes, and remove from heat.

3. Add hot juice to gelatin mixture and stir to dissolve. Add vanilla and citrus zest if desired.

4. Arrange raw fruit in an oblong pan or large bowl or divide between 8 small bowls or goblets. Pour hot juice over fruit and cool for 30 minutes, then refrigerate until set, about 4 hours.

   Alternatively, pour hot juice into an oblong pan or bowl and chill until the consistency of unbeaten egg whites. Stir in fresh fruit and turn into a 4-cup mold and chill until firm.

5. Garnish with nuts if desired and serve. Refrigerate leftovers and use within 5 days.

If you love, or once loved, the jiggly texture of Jell-O, you'll like this refreshing remake of a 1970s classic. Unlike packaged products and the stuff sold in cafeterias, this is made from 100 percent real fruit and fruit juice. It's easy to make, fun to eat, and you can vary it almost endlessly.

Use bulk beef gelatin from a natural foods store or Knox unflavored gelatin.

Note: The enzymes in pineapple, papaya, and kiwi may prevent the gelatin from setting unless you cook these fruits first and add them with the juice in step 1.

FYI: The basic rule of thumb is 1 tablespoon unflavored gelatin for every 2 cups liquid. If you add fruit you need to use slightly more gelatin, or add arrowroot to make the mixture set up. If you inadvertently make your gel too firm, cube and purée it in a food processor or blender, pour into bowls, and chill for a fluffy mousse-like texture.

Dried Apple Rings/Apple Chips

Prep: 30 minutes ~ **Drying:** 8 to 14 hours ~ **Yield:** 3 quarts; 1 1/4 pounds; 24 (1/2 cup) servings

Ingredients & Directions

1 quart unsweetened apple cider **or** apple, pineapple, or orange juice (there will be some leftover)

6 pounds firm-crisp, sweet or tart-sweet eating apples (about 15 medium-size apples):
    Cortland, Melrose, gravenstein, pink lady, gala, Fuji, braeburn, ginger gold, mutsu, yataka, cameo, jonathan, jonagold, adina, or other

Ground cinnamon, ginger, apple pie spice **or** pumpkin pie spice

1. Divide juice between 2 (3-quart) non-metallic bowls. Set out 10 dehydrator trays. Line bottom tray with a fruit roll sheet to catch drips. Line remaining trays with fruit roll sheets or screens if you have enough.

2. Wash and core 6 apples. Peel if desired or apples are non-organic. Cut into 1/4-inch thick rounds with sharp knife or mandoline and immerse in juice. Fill both bowls with fruit. With tongs, remove apple slices from first bowl and arrange on trays without overlapping. Lightly dust with spice. Repeat with apples from second bowl.

3. Core and slice more apples and immerse to fill 1 bowl, then the other. Repeat steps above to fill trays. Refrigerate leftover juice and use within 4 days.

4. Dry apples at 130 to 135° F for 8 to 10 hours or until slices bend but contain no pockets of moisture when tested. For a crunchier texture, dry for 10 to 14 hours until easily snapped in half. Exact time will depend on type of dehydrator and number of trays.

5. Cool apple slices at room temperature. Transfer to airtight jars, Pyrex containers with fitted lids, or plant-based cellulose bags. Store at room temperature. For longer shelf life, refrigerate or freeze. Thoroughly dried fruits should keep for 18 to 24 months at room temperature or 5 to 8 years in a freezer at 0° F.

Variations

  * **Pear & Apple Chips:** Replace apples with Asian pear-apples.

Nutrition

Entire recipe:
1876 calories
428 g carbs
    (72 g fiber)
12 g fat
206 mg calcium
11 mg sodium

1/2 cup serving:
78 calories
18 g carbohydrate
    (3 g fiber)
1/2 g fat
9 mg calcium
negligible sodium

Here's a great alternative to candies, cookies, chips, and granola bars for pack lunches, snacks, hiking, backpacking, and traveling. During the holidays, paleo pen pal Stacie Tolen hangs these on the Christmas tree. I include dried apple rings in holiday gift baskets. I like to make large batches several weeks in a row to stock up for the winter. Taken right from the freezer apple chips are delightfully crunchy, like crackers.

FYI: Double estimated prep time if you don't have an apple corer and mandoline or someone to help you.

Basic Applesauce

Prep: 30 to 60 minutes ~ **Yield:** about 6 cups; 8 servings

Ingredients & Directions

4 pounds of one variety sweet or tart-sweet apples (8 large to 12 medium), washed, cored, peeled, diced:
> gravenstein, yellow newton, pink lady, ginger gold, early gold, braeburn, gala, Fuji, Cortland, macoun, jonathan, or jonagold

1 cup unsweetened apple cider **or** apple juice

3/4 teaspoon ground cinnamon, ginger **or** apple pie spice

Pinch of unrefined sea salt, optional

1/4 to 1/3 teaspoon stevia extract powder **or** 2 to 3 tablespoons honey or agavé nectar, optional

1. Combine all ingredients except stevia or honey in a wide 3- to 4-quart saucepan or non-reactive Dutch oven. Cover and bring to boil over medium heat. Reduce heat to low, and simmer until tender and the consistency of jam, about 45 to 60 minutes. If too thin, remove lid and simmer to thicken.

2. Mash apples against the side of the pot with a wide wooden spoon or press a potato masher against the bottom of the pot. Taste and adjust with a tiny bit of stevia (it's 100 to 300 times sweeter than sugar) or honey if a sweeter taste is desired.

3. Serve hot, warm, or close to room temperature. Refrigerate in tightly sealed wide-mouth jars. Use within 1 to 2 weeks, or freeze, leaving 1/2 inch of headspace in each container.

Nutrition

Entire recipe:
1220 calories
287 g carbs
(49 g fiber)
8 g fat
165 mg calcium
8 mg sodium

3/4 cup:
152 calories
36 g carbohydrate
(6 g fiber)
1 g fat
21 mg calcium
1 mg sodium

Homemade applesauce tastes so much better than anything from a can or bottle. The best time to make it is during the fall and winter when you can get locally grown apples from an orchard, farmers' market, or a natural foods store that supports farmers in your region.

Variations

* Wash apples, but don't peel or core. Remove stems and cut fruit into 1 1/2-inch pieces. Combine ingredients and cook. Transfer cooked apples and pan juices to a food mill fitted with a medium disk. Purée, leaving skin, seeds, and core behind.

* Omit ground spices. Add 4 (3-inch) pieces of cinnamon sticks, 2 to 3 pieces of star anise, 4 (1/2-inch thick) slices of fresh ginger, **or** 4 whole cloves. Cook as above. Remove and discard cinnamon, star anise, ginger or cloves before puréeing.

* **Apple & Apricot, Apple & Peach, or Apple & Cherry Sauce:** Replace 1 pound of apples with pitted apricots, peaches, or sweet cherries.

* Turn your applesauce into Apple Leather (Page 442).

FYI: Use the timesaving variation on the left if you own a non-electric hand food mill (Moulinex, Foley, Cuispro, Norpro, or other).

Uncooked Apple Leather

Prep: 30 minutes ~ **Drying:** 8 to 12 hours ~ **Yield:** 2 sheets; 6 servings

Ingredients & Directions

2 1/2 pounds sweet or tart-sweet apples (about 5 large apples), washed, cored, peeled, and diced: gravenstein, newton, pink lady, ginger gold, early gold, braeburn, gala, Fuji, Cortland, yataka, or other variety

1/3 to 3/4 cup unsweetened apple cider **or** apple or orange juice, as needed to blend

3/4 to 1 teaspoon ground cinnamon, ginger **or** apple pie spice

2 teaspoons finely grated orange or tangerine rind, optional

1 teaspoon nonalcoholic vanilla extract, optional

1/4 to 1/3 teaspoon stevia extract powder **or** 2 to 3 tablespoons honey or agavé nectar, optional

Unrefined coconut oil to grease fruit-roll sheets

Nutrition

Entire recipe:
753 calories
177 g carbs
(31 g fiber)
5 g fat
98 mg calcium
5 mg sodium

**1 serving
(6 per recipe):**
126 calories
30 g carbohydrate
(5 g fiber)
16 mg calcium,

Homemade fruit leather is a great people pleaser. Pack it with lunches, in picnic baskets, or gift baskets. For the best flavor, pick locally grown fruit in volume or purchase it directly from a grower in the summer and fall. In early autumn, I usually make multiple batches of this at least 4 weeks in a row to stock the refrigerator and freezer for winter, spring, and holiday gift giving. Try single fruits or a combination of 2.

1. Oil 2 round (13-inch) fruit roll sheets or 1 (10x20-inch) square solid sheet. Rest on trays.

2. Add 1/3 of apples to Vita-Mix, blender or food processor with 1/3 cup juice and remaining ingredients except stevia, honey, and oil. Process until smooth, adding more apples, a handful at a time. Add more juice as needed to yield an applesauce texture and 5 cups purée. Add stevia or honey in tiny amounts if a sweeter taste is desired.

3. Pour and spread purée over sheets until uniformly distributed and 1/4-inch thick.

4. Dry at 120 to 130° F until leathery, pliable, easily peeled off sheets, and no thick, wet, or sticky spots remain on top or underside. If top is dry and bottom is not, flip leather over.

5. Remove leather from trays. Cover with a similar sized piece of unbleached parchment paper and roll tightly while warm. Cut each roll into 3 rolls. Pack in wide-mouth jars, stainless steel canisters, or plant-based cellulose bags closed with twist ties. To prolong shelf life beyond several weeks or months (or in hot weather), refrigerate or freeze in cellulose bags slipped inside zip-locking freezer bags. Label and date. They will keep almost indefinitely in the freezer.

Variations

* **Apple Leather from Cooked Applesauce:** Spread 4 to 5 cups cooked applesauce (Page 441) over 2 or 3 dehydrator trays. Dry.

* **Apple & Cherry, Apple & Peach, or Apple & Berry Leather:** Replace half the apples with rinsed, drained, and pitted sweet cherries, peaches, or berries. Add softer fruit to blender first. Add as little juice as possible. If too thin, blend in more fruit.

Raw Peach Leather

Prep: 15 to 20 minutes ~ **Drying:** 8 to 12 hours ~ **Yield:** 3 sheets; 6 to 9 servings

Ingredients & Directions

8 medium or 10 small, ripe peaches (2 to 2 1/4 pounds unpitted), washed, quartered, skins on (about 6 cups without pits)

1/4 cup apple juice **or** peach juice

1/8 teaspoon ascorbic acid (vitamin C) powder **or** 1 tablespoon lemon juice

1/2 teaspoon ground cinnamon **or** apple pie spice **or** 2 teaspoons peeled, minced fresh gingerroot

1 tablespoon honey, agavé nectar **or** fruit juice concentrate

1 teaspoon nonalcoholic vanilla extract, optional

1/8 to 1/4 teaspoon stevia extract powder **or** 1 to 3 teaspoons honey **or** agavé nectar, optional

Unrefined coconut oil to oil dehydrator sheets

1. Add peaches to Vita-Mix, blender, or food processor with apple juice, lemon juice or ascorbic acid, cinnamon or other spice, 1 tablespoon honey, agavé, or fruit juice concentrate, and optional vanilla. Cover and blend until smooth, to yield 4 1/2 to 5 cups purée. Taste, then add optional stevia or additional honey, agavé nectar, or fruit juice concentrate in tiny increments if desired.

2. Oil 3 round (13-inch) fruit-roll sheets or 1 to 2 (10x20-inch) square solid sheet(s). Slowly pour and spread purée over sheets until uniformly distributed and 1/4-inch thick.

3. Dry at 120 to 135° F until leathery, pliable, easily peeled off sheets and no thick, wet, or sticky spots remain on top or bottom. If top is dry and bottom is not, flip leather over.

4. Remove leather from trays. Cover with a similar sized piece of unbleached parchment paper. Roll tightly while warm. Cut each roll into 2 to 3 shorter rolls. Pack into wide-mouth jars, or stuff rolls into plant-based cellulose bags and close with twist ties. To freeze, put each bag into a zip-locking freezer bag. Label and date. To prolong shelf life, refrigerate or freeze.

Nutrition

Entire recipe:
485 calories
8 g protein
113 g carbs
    (17 g fiber)
58 mg calcium
1 mg sodium

**1 serving
(6 per recipe):**
81 calories
1 g protein
19 carbohydrate
    (3 g fiber)
10 mg calcium
negligible sodium

Superb fruit rolls start with fresh, locally grown, vine-ripened fruits. I prefer to buy them from a farmers' market so I can choose from varieties I can't find in supermarkets. If the fruits are hard, store at room temperature and give them 3 or 4 days to ripen and smell fragrant before making leather. Just don't let them turn soggy and rot.

Variations

* **Apricot Leather:** Replace peaches with fresh, ripe apricots.

* **Nectarine Leather:** Replace peaches with fresh, ripe nectarines.

* **Berry &, Peach, Cherry & Peach, or Apple & Peach Leather:**
Replace 1/3 to 1/2 of peaches with fresh blueberries, strawberries, pitted sweet cherries, or peeled and cored sweet apples. Increase sweetener as needed.

23 Nut-Based Sweets & Treats

The Basics of Beating Egg Whites

Stiffly beaten egg whites are a must for such things as meringues and macaroons, which are some of the easiest flourless baked goods to make. Because egg whites are far more finicky than yolks or whole eggs, special care must be taken to select bowls and utensils and to separate the whites from the yolks. Secrets for success:

1. Separate whites from yolks when the eggs are cold, then allow the whites to come to room temperature for 1 to 2 hours before beating.

2. Cover and refrigerate unused yolks and use in scrambles, omelets, meatloaf, burgers, or to make mayonnaise. Or smear raw egg yolk over your face, allow it dry, then rinse off, for a healing, pore cleansing vitamin A-rich facial.

3. Start with impeccably clean non-plastic bowls. Slightly dirty or plastic bowls will retain oils from foods previously stored in them. This can prevent whites from whipping. Copper bowls are ideal, but stainless steel or Pyrex will do. Beaters must be spotless.

4. Separate eggs in to 3 bowls to avoid letting traces of yolks spoil whites. Transfer the yolk back and forth between the halved eggshell, letting the white drop into a small bowl. Gently drop the unbroken yolk into a separate bowl or small jar; if yolk breaks, set the entire egg aside. Even a tiny trace of yolk can prevent the whites from forming stiff peaks. Transfer the pure egg white to a 1- to 1 1/2-quart non-plastic bowl.

5. Repeat continuing to add pure whites to the larger bowl until you have 4 pure whites. (Use a larger bowl for a double batch).

6. Beat whites until frothy. Add the amount of cream of tartar specified in the recipe and beat until stiff peaks form and the tips of the whites stand straight when the beaters are turned off and lifted away.

Copper Bowl is Best
If you can afford it or already have a copper bowl, use it to beat the whites. It will produce the stiffest and most voluminous egg white foam you can imagine and the whites will rarely deflate after you add the coconut or other ingredients.

My Favorite Macaroons

Prep: 30 minutes ~ **Cooking:** 20 minutes ~ **Yield:** 20 to 24 macaroons

Ingredients & Directions

4 egg whites from large or extra-large eggs (1/2 to 2/3 cup)

1/4 teaspoon cream of tartar, unless using a copper bowl

1/3 cup honey **or** agavé nectar (cactus honey)

1/4 teaspoon white stevia extract powder

1 1/2 teaspoons nonalcoholic vanilla extract **or** 1 teaspoon pure vanilla extract in alcohol

1 1/3 cups unsweetened, sulfite-free, finely shredded coconut, additional 1/2 cup only as needed for extra-large eggs

Unrefined coconut oil to grease baking sheets

1. Separate whites from yolks; transfer pure whites to an impeccably clean 1- to 1 1/2-quart measuring container, or copper, glass or stainless steel bowl (see Page 446).

2. Preheat oven to 300° F or lower if your oven runs hot. Line a large cookie sheet with unbleached parchment paper and lightly mist or rub with oil. (Oil bleached parchment, if used).

3. Using an electric beater on high, beat *room temperature* whites until frothy. Add cream of tartar. Beat until stiff peaks form when beaters are lifted away. Or remove beater and hold bowl upside down; if whites are beaten sufficiently, they will not fall out.

4. Reduce speed to low. Gradually add honey or agavé nectar, stevia, and vanilla. Turn off and fold in coconut with a wide wooden spoon. Don't panic if whites deflate. Add additional coconut, a little at a time, if batter is very wet from using extra-large eggs.

5. Drop batter by level tablespoons onto prepared baking sheet(s), creating an oval shape. If desired, use 2 spoons to make a round shape.

6. Bake in center of oven until set and slightly brown around edges, 18 to 20 minutes. Cool on baking sheet, and transfer to airtight container. Store at room temperature for up to 2 weeks, refrigerate for up to 4 weeks, or freeze for longer storage.

Variations

* **My Favorite Coconut-Orange Macaroons:** Replace vanilla with 1 teaspoon orange extract.

* **My Favorite Cocoa Macaroons:** Add 2 tablespoons sifted unsweetened cocoa.

Nutrition

1 macaroon (20) per batch):
55 calories
1 g protein
8 g carbohydrate
        (1/2 g fiber)
2 g fat
14 mg sodium

1 macaroon (24) per batch):
46 calories
1 g protein
6 g carbohydrate
        (1/2 g fiber)
2 g fat
12 mg sodium

These wheat-free, dairy-free treats are easy to assemble. After analyzing the nutrition label for "Jennie's Macaroons," the healthiest commercial macaroons on the market—made from sulfite-free unsweetened coconut, honey, and egg whites—I devised a lower sugar version by replacing a portion of the honey with stevia.

Note: Test your oven for accuracy with an oven thermometer that stays in the oven if you have not done so recently. Older ovens may run much hotter or cooler than the temperature dial indicates; adjust oven temperature accordingly. If the oven is too hot, macaroons and other items will burn on the outside before the inside is done. If the oven is too cool, food will be undercooked in allotted time.

FYI: Fine coconut flakes are a must. If you buy medium- or large-flaked coconut, grind in a blender or food processor, fluff with a fork, then measure. Recipe may be doubled.

Chocolate-Pecan Meringues

Prep: 20 to 30 minutes ~ **Cooking:** 1 hour ~ **Yield:** 16 to 24 cookies

Ingredients & Directions

3 large or 4 small egg whites (1/2 cup)

1/4 teaspoon cream of tartar, unless using a copper bowl

1/3 cup date sugar **or** granulated honey, additional tablespoon for a strong sweet-tooth

3 tablespoons unsweetened cocoa, sifted to remove lumps

1/4 teaspoon white stevia extract powder

1/3 cup finely ground raw pecans

1. Carefully separate egg yolks from whites and transfer pure whites to an impeccably clean 1 to 1 1/2 quart metal or Pyrex bowl or measuring container (Page 446).

2. Preheat oven to 200° F. Line a large cookie sheet with unbleached parchment paper. Grease lightly with coconut oil or butter as desired.

3. Using an electric mixer, beat *room temperature* whites on high until frothy. Add cream of tartar. Beat until stiff tips of peaks stand straight when beaters are lifted. Volume will increase to 3 to 4 cups. Reduce speed to low and gradually add granulated sweetener, cocoa, and stevia. Turn off mixer and fold in pecans with a wide spoon. Don't panic if whites deflate.

5. Drop mixture onto prepared baking sheet to create oval cookies: by rounded teaspoons to yield 24 cookies, or level tablespoons to yield 16 larger cookies. If desired, use 2 spoons to give the cookies a round upward shape or use a pastry bag to create a star shape.

6. Bake in center of oven 45 minutes for smaller cookies, 1 hour for larger cookies. Do not open oven door. Turn off oven. Allow meringues to cool in oven. Transfer to a jar, cookie tin, or other covered container. Meringues will soften in the container.

7. Store at room temperature or in the refrigerator. Use within 4 weeks or freeze.

Variations

* **Chocolate-Macadamia Meringues:** Replace finely ground pecans with raw finely ground macadamia nuts.

* **Chocolate-Almond Meringues:** Replace finely ground pecans with raw finely ground almonds.

* For more light and airy meringues, increase granulated sweetener to 1/2 cup and reduce stevia to 1/8 teaspoon.

Nutrition

1 macaroon (16) per batch):

41 calories
2 g protein
6 g carbohydrate
(1 g fiber)
1 g fat
7 mg calcium
14 sodium

1 macaroon (24) per batch):

27 calories
1 g protein
4 g carbohydrate
(1 g fiber)
1 g fat
5 mg calcium
9 mg sodium

Meringues are light, airy, and amazingly low in fat. This recipe calls for less sugar than other meringues so the cookies aren't as airy but they are still delicious. Since they don't contain grains or dairy products, they're perfect for people on gluten-, grain-, and dairy-free diets. Stevia and date sugar add sweetness with less sugar and fewer calories. Recipe may be doubled.

FYI: Look for a brand of date sugar free of oats, which reduce the sugar's concentration requiring you to use twice as much. Oats also cause problems for people with celiac sprue or other gluten sensitivity. The label should say: date powder or dried, powdered dates.

Notes: Test oven for accuracy. Use blender or food processor to grind nuts.

Chilled Coconut Milk & Coconut Cream

Prep: 10 minutes ~ **Yield:** 1 3/4 cup

Ingredients & Directions

1 (14-ounce) can unsweetened, preservative-free coconut milk (Thai Kitchen, regular, not lite)

1. Shake unopened can. Rinse top of can and completely remove lid. Contents may have separated. Pour into an impeccably clean wide-mouth 16-ounce jar. Whisk, or cover and shake until smooth. If thick or uneven, process in a blender or food processor. Cover and refrigerate.

2. Coconut milk will thicken within several hours or overnight and will rarely separate again.

3. Use within 5 days or freeze in ice cube trays for longer storage. Frozen cubes will last almost indefinitely. If mixture turns sour or moldy in the fridge, discard and start over.

Nutrition

Thai Kitchen Premium Coconut Milk, 14-ounce can:

770 calories
28 g carbohydrate
7 g protein
70 g fat
217 mg sodium

1/4 cup serving:

110 calories
4 g carbohydrate
1 g protein
10 g fat
31 mg sodium

In warm weather, canned coconut milk will be liquid at room temperature. When cool or cold, contents of the can may appear thick or chunky on top and watery on the bottom. This is normal. Don't toss it out unless it smells like spoiled milk, which is rare! If it's too thick to blend by hand, purée in a blender or food processor before using.

We buy unsweetened coconut milk in cans, often by the case through a wholesale buying club or natural foods store. Many supermarkets stock it on the ethnic aisle; read labels carefully. Most brands contain added sugar, preservatives, sulfites, or other additives. Don and I have found 2 exceptional brands free of additives: *Thai Kitchen* and *Native Forest*.

Coconut milk is delicious in puddings and fruit smoothies, spooned over fresh fruit, or added to a soup, sauce, or casserole. But, don't drink it straight—it's much more calorie dense than milk. You can use it cup for cup to replace cream or half and half. It contains half the fat and calories of cream. It can also be diluted with 1 to 4 parts water to replace milk, buttermilk, or yogurt in cooking or baking.

Coconut milk won't whip like cream. For volume or thickness you need to add egg yolks, beaten whites, arrowroot or potato starch, or unflavored gelatin, and then cook the mixture.

Note: Our recipes include nutrition breakdowns using Thai Kitchen coconut milk. All of our recipes use premium coconut milk rather than light unless otherwise specified.

FYI: The liquid inside a fresh coconut is *not* coconut milk. It's *coconut water!* Coconut milk comes from blending coconut meat with water to produce a creamy liquid. You can make it from scratch, using fresh, whole coconuts, an ice pick, hammer, and food processor, or Vita-Mix, but it's time consuming unless you find young coconuts with soft meat you can scoop out with a spoon.

Dairy-Free Cocoa-Coconut Pots de Crème

Prep: 30 minutes ~ **Cooking:** 1 hour ~ **Yield:** 4 to 6 servings

Ingredients & Directions

Unrefined coconut oil to grease custard cups

1/2 cup hot filtered water

2 large or 3 medium Date-Coconut Rolls **or** soft, pitted dates, (40 grams weight), broken into pieces **or** 3 to 4 tablespoons date sugar

1 cup unsweetened premium coconut milk

2 teaspoons unflavored gelatin

2 large egg yolks **or** 1 large or jumbo egg

1/4 cup unsweetened cocoa powder

1 tablespoon lightly roasted, unsalted, unsweetened almond butter

2 to 3 teaspoons non-alcoholic vanilla extract **or** 1 teaspoon pure vanilla in alcohol plus 1 to 2 teaspoons vegetable glycerine

1/2 teaspoon stevia extract powder

1/4 teaspoon ground cinnamon

Nutrition

1 serving (4 per batch):
236 calories
5 g protein
18 g carbohydrate (3 g fiber)
16 g fat
38 mg calcium,
36 mg sodium

1 serving (6 per batch):
158 calories
3 g protein
12 g carbohydrate (2 g fiber)
10 g fat
25 mg calcium
24 mg sodium

This dairy-free, low-sugar spin on a French classic has been a hit with cooking students, chocolate fiends, friends, kids, and several professional chefs I know.

Look for Chattfield's or Health Best date sugar, made from dried, powdered dates, without oat flour. The flour reduces the sugar's concentration, requiring you to use twice as much and oats are off limits for people with severe gluten intolerance, such as celiac sprue.

1. Preheat oven to 325° F. Grease 4 to 6 (6-ounce) ramekins or ovenproof custard cups. Take out a shallow oblong baking pan; if glass line with a cloth dish towel to prevent breakage. Boil about 5 cups of water.

2. Purée 1/2 cup hot water with dates, Date-Coconut Rolls, or date sugar in blender or food processor. Add remaining ingredients and process until smooth, stopping to scrape sides with a spatula. Pour 1/4 cup of purée into each cup, and evenly divide the remaining purée.

3. Arrange cups in baking pan and place on a rack in center of preheated oven. Add very hot water to the pan, surrounding cups to within 1-inch of the top.

4. Bake for 60 minutes or until custards are almost set in the center with a light crust on top. Remove cups from water and cool for 30 minutes. Cover and refrigerate for at least 3 hours, or overnight, before serving. Custard will set up as it cools.

Note: If you can't find pure date sugar or Date-Coconut Rolls, substitute maple granules or granulated honey.

Variations

* **Dairy-Free Mocha Pots de Crème:** Replace 1/2 cup hot water with Roasted Chicory & Dandelion Root "Coffee" (Page 495) **or** 1/2 cup of brewed Raja's Cup, an antioxidant-rich coffee-like beverage sold in natural foods stores.

Date-Coconut Rolls Stuffed with Nuts

Prep: 5 minutes ~ **Yield:** 4 servings

Ingredients & Directions

4 large or 6 to 8 small Date-Coconut Rolls (about 80 grams in weight)

1/4 to 1/2 cup toasted almonds, walnuts, pecan halves, **or** macadamia nuts (Page 406)

1. Stuff each date roll with 1 tablespoon of whole nuts or nut halves.

2. Serve immediately, cover and chill, or pack in a lunch.

Variations

* **Date-Coconut Rolls Frosted with Nut Butter:** Replace nuts with 1/4 to 1/3 cup lightly toasted, unsalted, unsweetened almond, macadamia, hazelnut or cashew butter. (This will add about 5 grams of fat and 45 calories per serving, but it's worth it!) Place each date roll in a small dessert cup and frost with 1 tablespoon of nut butter. Serve with spoons for dessert.

Nutrition

1 serving (with almonds):
125 calories
1 g protein
17 g carbohydrate
          (2 g fiber)
6 g fat
13 mg calcium
3 mg sodium

1 serving (with pecans):
119 calories
1 g protein
18 g carbohydrate
          (2 g fiber)
5 g fat
6 mg calcium
3 mg sodium

If you're looking for a sweet cookie or candy-like treat for dessert, this is it! We prefer Date-Coconut Rolls because they're softer and easier to stuff with nuts than plain pitted dates.

Date-Coconut Rolls are pitted dates put through a grinder twice, shaped into logs, and rolled in unsweetened, sulfite-free coconut. Although you can make them in a food processor, you can buy them from the produce section of natural foods stores or by mail or through the Internet (see Sources in the Appendix).

The combination of date rolls and lightly toasted pecans reminds us of pecan pie filling!

Note: Different brands of date rolls may vary in density, size, and sweetness. Some are firmer and more calorie dense, others are softer or less sweet. Experiment to find your favorite source.

Date-Nut Balls

Prep: 5 to 10 minutes ~ **Yield:** 16 servings

Ingredients & Directions

1 cup (8 ounces by weight) lightly toasted walnut or pecan halves **or** almonds (Page 406)

1 cup dried pitted dates **or** Date-Coconut Rolls (about 6 ounces by weight)

2 tablespoons warm or hot water, additional 2 tablespoons only as needed

1/2 teaspoon cinnamon **or** apple pie spice

2 teaspoons finely grated orange zest, colored part only

1/2 to 1 tablespoon apple fiber powder, optional

1/4 cup shredded, unsweetened, sulfite-free coconut **or** unsweetened cocoa or carob powder, optional

1. Grind nuts to a powder in blender or food processor, pour into 2-quart bowl, and set aside.

2. Pulse pitted dates in a blender or food processor with 2 tablespoons water, spices, and orange zest. Add additional water only as needed to blend. Add date purée to nuts. **Note:** If using Date-Coconut Rolls omit water, tear into pieces, and combine with pulverized nuts, spices, and optional orange zest.

3. Mix and knead with clean bare hands to form a smooth ball. If too wet, add apple fiber powder or carob or cocoa powder. With wet hand, form dough into 16 tablespoon-size balls. If you like roll them in coconut or unsweetened carob or cocoa powder.

4. Cover and freeze briefly or chill for at least 3 hours until firm. Refrigerate and use within 1 month or freeze.

Nutrition

Entire recipe with pecans:
1421 calories
16 g protein
149 g carbs
(25 g fiber)
85 g fat
151 mg calcium
5 mg sodium

1 serving:
89 calories
9 g carbohydrate
(2 g fiber)
5 g fat
9 mg calcium
negligible sodium

The nuts in this recipe keep the dates in this dessert from being too cloyingly sweet. These tasty treats, a takeoff on several recipes, are ideal for picnics, potlucks, pack lunches, Halloween, or Christmas parties. The combination of dates with toasted pecans reminds us of pecan pie filling!

Variations

* **Pumpkinseed Date-Nut Balls:** Replace nuts with toasted, hulled green pumpkinseeds (Page 405), **or** 1/2 cup walnuts plus 1/2 cup pumpkinseeds, measured then pulverized.

* **Fig Date-Nut Balls:** Use half dates, half dried black mission figs **or** Turkish figs (remove stems) with toasted almonds, walnuts, **or** cashews. You may need to add a little more water. Sometimes I also add 1/4 cup of carob powder.

* **Apricot, Date & Walnut Balls:** Use half dates, half dried, Turkish apricots and toasted almonds, walnuts, **or** pecans.

Dark Chocolate-Dipped Dates

Prep: 15 minutes ~ **Yield:** 8 servings

Ingredients & Directions

Coconut oil **or** butter to oil double boiler or bowl

4 ounces unsweetened baker's chocolate bar (e.g., Ghirardelli, Valrhona, or Hershey's), broken or chopped into pieces

8 large or 16 small Date-Coconut Rolls (8 ounces by weight)

1 tablespoon unsweetened, sulfite-free shredded coconut, optional

Finely grated zest of 1 medium orange, optional

1. Lightly oil a double boiler or small saucepan. Set out an 8x10-inch sheet of wax paper or unbleached parchment paper.

2. Melt chocolate in a double boiler over hot—but not boiling—water orin a small saucepan over very low heat. Stir periodically until melted, then remove from heat.

3. Flatten date rolls to 1/2-inch thick. One at a time, with tongs or cooking chopsticks, dip date rolls in chocolate, turning to coat all sides. Transfer to paper. Scrape remaining chocolate from bowl and evenly spoon over date rolls. Dust lightly with coconut or orange zest if desired.

4. Allow dates to cool at room temperature or refrigerate or freeze for a faster set.

5. Cover and refrigerate. Consume within 3 weeks for best results.

Nutrition

Entire recipe:
1292 calories
21 g protein
163 g carbs
    (29 g fiber)
62 g fat
64 mg calcium
23 mg sodium

1 serving:
162 calories
3 g protein
20 g carbohydrate
    (5 g fiber)
8 g fat
15 mg calcium
3 mg sodium

This is one very quick, very easy, and very delicious dessert. Bar the guilt—chocolate is rich in antioxidants and the sweetness in this recipe comes from dates, a great potassium source, not refined sugar.

Date-Coconut Rolls are pitted dates put through a grinder twice, rolled in sulfite-free, unsweetened coconut, and shaped into logs. You can buy them in natural foods markets or by mail or through the Internet. If you can't find them, substitute 8 ounces (by weight) of large, soft, pitted dates.

Variations

* For a less-intense chocolate taste, and more sweetness, use only 3 ounces unsweetened chocolate.

* **Dark Chocolate-Dipped Date & Pecan Rolls:** Replace Date-Coconut Rolls with Date-Pecan Rolls (date rolls rolled in chopped, toasted pecan pieces), sold in natural foods stores and by mail. Or stuff 3 toasted pecan halves into each date roll before dipping in chocolate.

* For smaller servings, after flattening each date roll in step 3, cut each in half to make 2 smaller logs. Dip in chocolate and garnish as desired. **Yield:** 16 to 32 small pieces.

Dried Figs with Fennel Seeds & Nuts

Prep: 5 minutes ~ **Yield:** 4 servings

Ingredients & Directions

1 cup sulfite-free dried figs (about 160 grams by weight), halved

2 to 4 tablespoons whole or ground fennel seeds

1/4 to 1/2 cup lightly toasted almonds, cashews, **or** walnut or pecan halves (Page 406)

1. Slice each fig in half lengthwise. Scatter whole or ground fennel seeds on a small plate.

2. Dip each fig half in seeds and arrange on a clean plate. Press 2 toasted nuts or nut halves into each fig half.

3. Cover and refrigerate leftovers in hot weather.

Variations

* **Dried Figs with Anise Seeds:** For a licorice-like taste, replace fennel with 3 to 4 tablespoons anise seeds, or anise seeds ground to a powder in a spice-dedicated coffee grinder.

* Replace almonds with raw or lightly toasted cashew or macadamia nuts.

Nutrition

1 serving (1/4 cup figs plus 1 tablespoon nuts):

169 calories
3 g protein
29 g carbohydrate
(6 g fiber)
5 g fat
92 mg calcium
0 sodium

Figs contain more antioxidant polyphenols than cherries, grapes, or strawberries and more fiber and minerals than most other fruits and vegetables. A 1/4-cup serving (5 or 6 small dried figs) packs 244 mg of potassium, 50 mg of calcium, 1 mg of iron, 5 grams of fiber, and only 108 calories. We stock up on sulfite-free dried figs from a natural food store and enjoy them for dessert.

FYI: More than a dozen varieties of figs exist. We're partial to black mission figs, named for the mission fathers who planted the fruit trees along the California coast. (Other varieties may be used, provided they are fresh, firm, sweet and have not been allowed to ferment and sour.) Dipping the figs in fennel or anise seeds sweetens the breath and is thought to aid digestion. Nuts add texture and richness and counterbalance the intense sweetness of the figs.

Trail Mix

Prep: 15 to 20 minutes ~ **Yield:** 2 cups; 8 servings

Ingredients & Directions

1 cup sulfite-free, whole nuts, seeds, or nut halves, toasted (Page 405 to 406), choose 2 to 4 varieties:
> almonds, walnuts, pecans, hazelnuts, pistachios, cashews, macadamia nuts, sunflower seeds, green, hulled pumpkinseeds, or large raw flakes of unsweetened coconut

1 cup unsweetened **or** fruit-sweetened, sulfite-free, pitted dried fruits, choose 2 to 4 varieties, and chop if large:
> raisins, date pieces, dried pears, peaches, nectarines, Turkish apricots, figs, prunes, cranberries, blueberries, cherries, mulberries, Marionberries, bilberries, lycii berries (wolf berries), papaya, mango, or pineapple

1. Combine ingredients in a large bowl. Stir and transfer to pint or quart jars or small containers for snacks. Cover and refrigerate.

2. Use within 1 year. It will keep longer in the freezer.

Nutrition

Entire recipe:
1320 calories
36 g protein
133 g carbs
   (21 g fiber)
72 grams fat
286 mg calcium
13 mg sodium

1/4 cup:
165 calories
5 g protein
17 g carbohydrate
   (3 g fiber)
9 g fat
36 mg calcium
2 mg sodium

Commercial trail mix often contains fruits treated with sugar, sulfites, and oil, and nuts that have been over roasted, cooked in oil, and salted. For the healthiest mix, start with unsweetened or fruit sweetened dried fruits free of sulfites. Buy raw nuts, and dry toast them lightly at home. Vary the ratio of nuts to dried fruit as you like.

Variations

* **Cranberry-Nut Trail Mix:** Mix 1/4 cup each toasted green pumpkinseeds, sunflower seeds, cashews, and walnut halves with 1/2 cup raisins, 1/4 cup date pieces, and 1/4 cup fruit sweetened dried cranberries.

* **Fig-Nut Mix:** Mix toasted cashews, macadamia nuts, and large raw flakes of coconut with chopped dried pineapple, papaya or mango, and date pieces.

* **Hunza Mix:** Mix toasted almonds and walnuts, and sunflower seeds if desired. Add a combination of dried apricots, raisins, and mulberries if you can locate them.

* **Eye Bright Mix:** This is a takeoff on a mixture we discovered in a local herb shop. Combine chopped dried apricots, lycii berries, dried blueberries, and bilberries with 1 or 2 of the following: toasted almonds, pecans, and walnuts.

* Make a small batch of trail mix for 1: 1/4 cup of dried fruits plus 1/4 cup of nuts.

FYI: Any way you make it, trail mix is calorie dense: one handful (about 1/2 cup) packs 300 to 400 calories. This is good for backpackers, active kids, athletes, and others with very high calorie needs...but not so good for anyone who is inactive, has a slow metabolism, or is trying lose weight. If you fall into the latter group, measure out 1/4 cup for a snack or dessert and stop.

Roasted Chestnuts

Prep: 30 to 50 minutes ~ **Cooking:** 30 minutes ~ **Yield:** 5 cups; 10 servings

Ingredients & Directions

2-pounds fresh chestnuts, in the shell

Water to cover

1. Cover chestnuts with fresh water and soak for 1 to 3 hours to facilitate removal from the shells.

2. Preheat oven to 350° F. Remove chestnuts from water. Cut an "X" in the end or flat side of each shell with a sharp paring knife, or snip the ends with kitchen shears so shells will peel back as the nuts roasts and keep the nuts from exploding in the oven.

3. Scatter chestnuts 1 layer deep in 1 or 2 unoiled shallow baking pans with sides. Roast uncovered for 20 to 30 minutes, rolling nuts over halfway through. Or, place chestnuts directly on a preheated grill with tightly packed grates. Close lid, and roast for 30 minutes.

4. Pour roasted chestnuts into a paper bag. Fold the top down and allow to steam for 15 minutes.

5. When cool enough to handle, peel back shells and inner skins to reveal chestnut meats. Discard nuts with greenish, grayish or black spots or mold.

6. If chestnuts are hard or you plan to purée them, cover with water or apple juice, bring to boil, reduce heat, and simmer until very soft. Remove lid and cook away liquid.

7. Serve warm or at room temperature, or cover and refrigerate in wide-mouth jars. Use within 5 days or freeze.

Variations

* **Chestnut, Squash & Ginger Bisque:** Add 1/2 cup roasted, peeled chestnuts to Quick Creamy Squash-Ginger Bisque (Page 381) or Soothing Ginger, Squash & Apple Soup before cooking soup. Taste before adding honey or stevia.

* See Index for additional chestnut recipes.

* Add roasted, peeled chestnuts to a vegetable stir fry, a stew with onions, carrots, and parsnips or winter squash, with or without chicken, beef, or pork, or toss into a winter fruit salad.

Nutrition

1/2 cup serving:

176 calories
3 g protein
38 g carbohydrate
2 g fat
21 mg calcium
2 mg sodium

Chestnuts are more like a fruit than a nut. Whereas most nuts derive 70 to 80 percent of calories from fat and provide 800 calories per cup, chestnuts are only 9 percent fat and 5 to 10 percent protein, and contain about 350 calories a cup. Eighty percent of their calories come from sweet-tasting complex carbohydrates. If you serve them for dessert, let everyone peel them at the table.

I don't recommend boiling chestnuts in the shell; you'll lose too much flavor in the water.

Note: Before picking chestnuts from unknown trees, consult a book or on-line guide to edible plants with illustrations and/or photographs.

Chestnut Tips

Tips for storing and sorting fresh chestnuts

1. Buy more than you think you need. Some may be moldy and you won't know it until you remove the peels.

2. Pack in loosely covered containers or plastic bags poked with holes. Unshelled raw chestnuts keep for months in the refrigerator or a cold attic or garage, longer in the freezer.

   Note: Chestnuts are not to be mistaken for Chinese water chestnuts—a different species entirely—nor with poisonous, look-alike horse chestnuts. Look for fresh chestnuts in supermarkets, farmers' markets, and specialty stores in the fall and winter. Steam-peeled dried chestnuts (ready to soak and boil) are sold in Asian and Italian markets.

Tips for using frozen, peeled chestnuts

Cooked and peeled, fresh chestnuts are sold in the freezer section of gourmet and Asian markets. Although they are ready-to-eat, they will be more tender, delicious, and digestible if cooked briefly before serving, giving them a chance to absorb the flavors of the foods with which they will be served.

1. Defrost and add them to a soup, stew, stir fry, or sauté, during the final 10 to 20 minutes of cooking, longer if you've failed to defrost them or prefer a softer texture.

2. If you plan to purée frozen chestnuts, simmer in water, juice, or stock until fork tender, 20 to 45 minutes, uncover and cook away most of the liquid, then include remaining liquid in the final dish. Alternatively, add the chestnuts to a soup and cook for 30 to 40 minutes, then purée.

Boiled, Steam-Peeled Chestnuts

Prep: 15 minutes ~ **Cooking:** 30 minutes to 3 hours ~ **Yield:** 4 cups

Ingredients & Directions

2 cups dried, steam-peeled chestnuts (11 ounces dry weight)

4 cups filtered water

3 cups additional water if boiling chesnuts

Dried, steam-peeled chestnuts cost more than fresh, but save time. You don't have to soak them, cut "Xs" in each nut, or roast and peel them one by one. Look for them in Italian and Oriental markets, or specialty catalogs (see Appendix D).

Nutrition

1/2 cup:
149 calories
3 g protein
32 g carbohydrate
(4 g fiber)
1 g fat
11 mg calcium
3 mg sodium

1. Combine chestnuts and water in a medium-size bowl or saucepan. Soak at room temperature for 6 to 8 hours or overnight uncovered or covered loosely with a bamboo mat or clean kitchen towel. Refrigerate in extremely hot weather. Do not pour off soak water. Cook chestnuts in their soak liquid, which contains much of the flavor and sweetness.

2. **To pressure cook:** Pour chestnuts and soak water into a small- or medium-size pressure cooker. Seal cooker and bring to pressure over medium heat. When hissing loudly, reduce heat to medium-low and cook for 25 minutes. Allow pressure to come down naturally, or immerse cooker in a sink or large bowl filled with several inches of cold water to reduce pressure faster.

    To boil: Pour chestnuts and soak water into a 2- to 3-quart pot. Add 3 more cups of water. Cover and bring to boil over medium-high heat, reduce heat to medium-low, and simmer until tender, about 2 to 3 hours. Check often, adding more water as needed to cover and prevent burning.

3. When tender, remove lid and simmer away liquid. Any remaining liquid should be used in the dish to which the chestnuts are added. Refrigerate cooked chestnuts in a covered, preferably glass, container. Use within 5 days.

Variations

* Blend cooked chestnuts with cooked carrots, parsnips, winter squash, or sweet potatoes, unsweetened coconut milk or water, and orange or tangerine juice, to make a sweet purée for a festive fall or winter meal. Add finely grated orange or tangerine zest and a dash of vanilla or maple extract. Garnish with chopped toasted pecans, walnuts, or butter before serving.

    See Index for additional chestnut recipes.

FYI: Dried chestnuts are not ready to eat! They are hard as rocks and must be rehydrated and cooked in their soak water until tender before you can eat them or add them to a soup, stew, casserole, compote, vegetable purée, pudding, or salad.

Raisin-Glazed Chestnuts

Prep: 20 minutes ~ **Cooking:** 1 to 3 hours ~ **Yield:** 8 servings

---

Ingredients & Directions

Chestnuts:

2 cups dried, steam-peeled chestnuts (11 ounces dry weight)

1 cup apple cider or apple juice

3 cups water (additional 2 cups as needed to boil)

Raisin sauce:

1 cup apple cider or apple juice

1 cup water

1/2 cup raisins

Reserved chestnut cooking liquid (about 1/4 to 1/2 cup)

1/4 teaspoon finely ground, unrefined sea salt

1/2 teaspoon cinnamon

Glaze:

2 tablespoons arrowroot **dissolved in** 1/2 cup cold water

Nutrition

1 serving:
219 calories
3 g protein
47 g carbohydrate
(5 g fiber)
2 g fat
22 mg calcium
63 mg sodium

Plump and juicy raisins surround sweet, succulent chunks of chestnuts. Slightly softer than Jell-O and firmer than pudding, this luscious, low-fat dessert makes a great final course after a rich meal. A little goes a long way. I figure 1/2 to 2/3 cup per person.

1. **Chestnuts:** Combine chestnuts, juice, and 3 cups water in a medium-size bowl or saucepan. Soak at room temperature for 8 hours or overnight uncovered or covered loosely with a bamboo mat or kitchen towel. Refrigerate in hot weather. Do not pour off soak liquid.

2. **To pressure cook:** Pour chestnuts and soak liquid into a small- or medium-size pressure cooker. Seal cooker, bring to pressure over medium heat, reduce heat to medium-low and cook for 25 minutes. Allow pressure to come down naturally or immerse cooker in sink filled with several inches of cold water for a faster release. Simmer to reduce liquid to about 1/2 cup.

   To boil: Pour chestnuts and soak liquid into a 2- to 3-quart pot. Add 2 more cups water. Cover and bring to boil over medium-high heat. Reduce to medium-low and simmer until tender, about 3 hours. Check often, adding water as needed to cover and prevent burning Drain and reserve cooking liquid. Simmer to reduce liquid to about 1/2 cup.

3. **Raisin sauce:** Combine raisins, apple cider or juice, water, chestnut cooking liquid, salt, and cinnamon. Bring to boil, reduce heat to low, and simmer for 10 minutes.

4. **Glaze:** Add dissolved arrowroot to raisin sauce. Stir and simmer over medium-low heat until thick and clear. Add chestnuts, stir, and spoon into serving cups. Allow to cool before serving.

FYI: Look for steam-peeled, whole dried chestnuts in Italian and Oriental markets or see Appendix D.

Chestnut-Apple Compote

Prep: 20 minutes ~ **Drying:** 30 to 40 minutes ~ **Yield:** 12 to 16 servings

---

Ingredients & Directions

2 cups roasted fresh chestnuts (Page 456), boiled or pressure cooked, dried, peeled chestnuts, cooked to the crisp-tender stage, (Page 458), **or** frozen, cooked chestnuts, defrosted

1 tablespoon apple pie spice

1/2 cup raisins

1/2 cup sulfite-free Turkish dried apricots, halved

1/2 cup dried pitted prunes, halved

3/4 cup filtered water (include any chestnut cooking water)

12 small or 8 large tart-sweet apples (1 to 3 varieties), 3 1/2 to 4 pounds:
> Cortland, jonathan, jonagold, granny smith, cameo, braeburn, Melrose, or pink lady

1 tablespoon arrowroot starch dissolved in 3 tablespoons cold water, optional

1/2 cup toasted walnut or pecan halves, coarsely chopped (Page 406) **or** 3/4 cup Fluffy Almond Butter (Page 408), for garnish, optional

Nutrition

1 serving (about 3/4 cup):

188 calories
2 g protein
44 g carbohydrate
(6 g fiber)
27 mg calcium
2 mg sodium

1. Layer cooked chestnuts, pie spice, raisins, and dried apricots in a 3- to 4-quart pot. Add water. Wash, core, and peel apples. Cut in to 1 1/2-inch pieces and layer over dried fruit.

2. Cover and bring to boil over medium heat, without stirring. Reduce heat and simmer until tender, about 30 minutes. Uncover and stir gently. If much liquid remains, remove lid and cook away liquid, or add dissolved arrowroot, simmer, and stir to thicken, 3 to 4 minutes.

3. Remove from heat. Serve warm or close to room temperature.

4. Refrigerate leftovers and use within 5 days.

Variations

* Replace pie spice with 1 teaspoon ground cinnamon and 1 teaspoon dried orange peel **or** 1 heaping tablespoon finely grated fresh orange zest, plus 3/4 teaspoon ground ginger (powder), 1/4 teaspoon each of ground fenugreek and nutmeg, and 1/8 teaspoon ground cloves.

Chestnuts are more like a fruit than a nut, incredibly low in fat, rich in complex carbohydrates, sweet, and delicious. Purchase dried, peeled chestnuts in Asian or Italian markets or specialty mail order catalogs. Buy cooked, peeled, and frozen chestnuts in gourmet or Oriental markets, or find fresh chestnuts in the shell at farmers' markets or the produce section of supermarkets throughout the fall and winter.

Note: If you're not expecting company, make half the recipe or pack extra portions into 16-ounce jars, tie with colorful ribbons, and share with family and friends.

Chestnut-Chocolate Pudding

Prep: 30 minutes ~ **Cooking:** 0 to 1 hour ~ **Yield:** 3 heaping cups; 6 servings

Ingredients & Directions

2 slightly rounded cups boiled or pressure cooked chestnuts (Page 458), roasted chestnuts (Page 456) **or** thawed, frozen chestnuts, simmered until fork tender

3/4 cup water (include any chestnut cooking water), additional water as needed to blend

1/2 to 3/4 cup unsweetened, sulfite-free coconut milk (regular or premium, not lite)

1/2 cup unsweetened cocoa powder

1/4 cup honey **or** agavé nectar

1/4 teaspoon stevia extract powder

2 teaspoons nonalcoholic vanilla extract **or** 1 teaspoon pure vanilla extract in alcohol

1/2 teaspoon natural rum flavoring **or** 2 tablespoons rum, optional

Finely grated zest (colored part only) of 1 orange or tangerine, optional

1/4 cup pitted sweet cherries, raspberries, or sliced fresh strawberries for garnish, optional

Nutrition

1 serving:
234 calories
3 g protein
42 g carbohydrate
(2 g fiber)
6 g fat
22 mg calcium
13 mg sodium

If you're a fan of chocolate pudding, try this unusual dessert made from chestnuts. It's one of our favorite treats. It looks like chocolate frosting, but it's a lot better for you.

1. In a blender, food processor, or Vita-Mix, combine 1 cup cooked chestnuts, 3/4 cup water, 1/2 cup coconut milk with cocoa powder, honey or agavé nectar, stevia, vanilla, and optional rum flavoring and orange zest. Cover and process until smooth, stopping to scrape the sides with a spatula. Add remaining chestnuts and blend until smooth, adding additional water and/or coconut milk a little at a time as needed to produce a smooth, frosting-like texture. Pudding will thicken even more as it cools. Adjust sweetness if needed.

2. Transfer pudding to a non-metallic bowl, glass jar, or individual parfait or dessert cups. Cover and refrigerate. Garnish with cherries or berries before serving if desired. Use within 5 days or freeze.

Variations

*   Replace coconut milk with 1/4 cup toasted almond or hazelnut butter plus 1/4 cup water.

FYI: If using roasted, peeled chestnuts, or peeled frozen chestnuts from a gourmet or Asian market (they are only partially cooked), cover with water, bring to boil, and simmer until fork tender, 1/2 to 1 hour, then cook away most of the liquid. Use chestnut cooking water in the pudding.

Chestnut-Chocolate Mousse

Prep: 30 minutes ~ **Cooking:** 5 minutes to 1 hour ~ **Yield:** 3 1/2 to 4 cups; 6 servings

---

Ingredients & Directions

1 1/3 to 1 1/2 cups boiled or pressure cooked chestnuts (Page 458), roasted chestnuts (Page 456) **or** 1 (8-ounce) package thawed, frozen chestnuts, simmered until fork tender

1 1/2 cups filtered water (include any chestnut cooking water)

1 tablespoon plus 1 teaspoon unflavored gelatin (Knox or bulk beef gelatin)

1/2 cup unsweetened, sulfite-free coconut milk (regular or premium, not lite), thoroughly blended

3 ounces unsweetened bakers chocolate bars (e.g., Ghirardelli, Valrhona, Hershey's), broken or chopped into pieces

1/4 to 1/3 cup honey **or** agavé nectar

1/2 teaspoon stevia extract powder

2 teaspoons apple fiber powder,

2 teaspoons nonalcoholic vanilla extract **or** 1 teaspoon pure vanilla extract in alcohol

1/2 teaspoon natural rum flavoring **or** 2 tablespoons rum, optional

Finely grated zest of 1 orange, colored part only, optional

4 to 6 thin slices of orange for garnish, optional

Nutrition

1 serving:
268 calories
5 g protein
36 g carbohydrate
(4 g fiber)
11 g fat
21 mg calcium
12 g sodium

I have fond memories of watching my mother melt unsweetened chocolate with sugar, add vanilla, and fold the bitter-sweet sauce into part-skim ricotta cheese. Her mousse was dense and delicious. This recipe uses different ingredients but produces a velvet texture much like the original; gelatin is the key. Honey and stevia replace the sugar as the sweeteners.

1. Slowly sprinkle gelatin over 1 1/2 cups of cool or cold water in a 1- to 1 1/2-quart saucepan. Heat slowly without stirring until gelatin melts completely, 3 to 4 minutes. Remove from heat.

2. Combine coconut milk, chocolate, and honey or agavé nectar in a small saucepan over medium-low heat. Remove from heat when melted.

3. Combine gelatin mixture, cooked chestnuts, and melted chocolate mixture in a blender, food processor, or Vita-Mix. Add stevia, apple fiber powder, vanilla, optional rum flavoring, and orange zest. Cover and blend until smooth, stopping to scrape sides with a spatula. Add a dash more stevia or honey if a sweeter taste is desired.

4. Divide mixture among 6 containers and chill for at least 4 hours until firm before serving; chill in a medium bowl and serve with a wet ice cream scoop; or pour into a pie plate, chill until set, then slice and serve.

5. Garnish with orange slices if desired. Use within 1 week.

FYI: If using roasted, peeled chestnuts, or peeled frozen chestnuts from a gourmet or Asian market (they are only partially cooked), cover with water, bring to boil, and simmer until fork tender, 1/2 to 1 hour, then cook away most of the liquid. Use chestnut cooking water in the mousse.

B<small>EST</small> B<small>ITES</small>

Protein-Nut Spread

Prep: 20 minutes ~ **Yield:** 2 1/2 cups

Ingredients & Directions

3/4 cup boiling, filtered water

3/4 cup unsweetened, salt-free, roasted almond **or** cashew butter, thoroughly mixed

5 (1-ounce) scoops unsweetened vanilla egg white protein
or 1 1/2 cups dried, powdered egg whites

2 teaspoons pure vanilla extract in a nonalcoholic base
or 1 teaspoon vanilla in alcohol

1/2 cup cool or cold filtered water, additional 1/4 cup as needed

1/2 teaspoon stevia extract powder **or** 10 to 12 drops stevia extract liquid

1 to 2 tablespoons honey **or** agavé nectar, if using unsweetened protein powder

> **Nutrition**
>
> **2 tablespoons (with almond butter):**
>
> 93 calories
> 8 g protein
> 3 g carbohydrate
> (2 g fiber)
> 5 g fat
> 48 mg calcium
> 65 mg sodium

1. Mix hot water and nut butter in a 2-quart bowl, large suribachi, or food processor until smooth and creamy. Add remaining ingredients and blend until smooth, scraping bottom and sides of the container.

2. Add 1/2 cup cool water. If too stiff to blend, add 2 to 4 additional tablespoons water. Taste and adjust sweetness if desired, adding 1/16 to 1/8 teaspoon stevia extract powder, 3 to 6 drops stevia extract liquid, or 1 to 2 teaspoons honey or agavé nectar at a time.

3. Scrape into a wide-mouth jar or smaller containers. Cover and refrigerate for at least 3 hours or until thick before serving. Use within 2 weeks.

Don came up with the prototype for this irresistible frosting-like spread for apples, strawberries, and bananas, during our early experiments with the *Zone* Diet. Besides being a source of heart-smart fats, it also happens to be packed with protein and is extraordinarily low in sugar. Kyle McCullough, a friend and former cooking student, helped develop chocolate and vanilla variations. For a sweet tooth snack or blood-sugar-balancing mini-meal, figure 1/4 to 1/2 cup of spread and 1 medium to large apple or 1 or 2 bananas per person. You won't be sorry.

Variations

* For a chocolate taste without cocoa or caffeine, replace water with strong Roasted Chicory & Dandelion Root "Coffee" (Page 495), and add 3 tablespoons carob powder.

* **Chocolate Protein-Nut Spread:** Add 3 tablespoons unsweetened cocoa or substitute chocolate egg white protein powder.

* **Butterscotch Protein-Nut Spread:** Replace vanilla with 1 teaspoon natural butterscotch extract, such as Pickford's.

* **Chocolate-Covered Strawberries:** Friend and fellow cooking coach Judy Stone of Ann Arbor, Michigan, came up with this. Rinse and hull fresh strawberries and pat dry. One at a time dip strawberries into freshly made Chocolate Protein-Nut Spread with an hors d'oeuvre fork, coat well, and arrange on parchment or wax-paper-lined trays. Chill before serving.

Chocolate-Protein Pudding

Prep: 20 minutes ~ **Yield:** 3 1/2 to 4 cups; 3 to 6 servings

Ingredients & Directions

1 cup cold filtered water

4 teaspoons unflavored gelatin (i.e., bulk beef gelatin or Knox)

1/2 cup blended, unsweetened coconut milk

4 Date-Coconut Rolls (80 grams by weight) **or** 12 small pitted dates

2 tablespoons unsalted, unsweetened roasted almond butter

2 to 3 teaspoons apple fiber powder

2 tablespoons unsweetened cocoa

2 tablespoon carob powder for sweetness and depth of flavor

1/2 cup dried, powdered egg whites **or** unsweetened vanilla egg white protein

2 teaspoons nonalcoholic vanilla extract **or** 1 teaspoon vanilla in alcohol

4 ice cubes, as needed to yield 3 1/2 to 4 cups total volume

1. Slowly sprinkle gelatin over 1 cup cool or cold water in small saucepan. Gently warm over low heat without stirring until completely dissolved. Remove from heat. Add pitted dates or date rolls, cover, and soak for 15 to 30 minutes until soft.

2. Pour gelatin-water-date mixture into blender or food processor, and add remaining ingredients, except ice. Cover and process until smooth, stopping to scrape sides with a spatula. Add ice, cover, and blend until smooth.

3. Pour into 3 (12-ounce) serving dishes for substantial snacks or 6 small dishes for dessert. Chill for at least 3 hours or freeze briefly until set. Use within 5 days or freeze.

Variations

* If using sweetened egg white protein, reduce non-alcoholic vanilla by one-half if used, and use only 2 to 3 date rolls or 6 to 8 pitted dates. Stir, taste, and adjust as needed.

* **Chocolate-Protein Pudding Pops:** These remind me of Fudgesicles I ate as a child. Lunch, dinner, potluck, and party guests love them. Pour blended mixture into 6 Popsicle molds or paper cups. Freeze until firm. Run warm water over molds to release pops or transfer cups to the counter 15 minutes before serving, to soften. Serve with spoons.

Nutrition

1/3 recipe:
347 calories
20 g protein
34 g carbohydrate
    (5 g fiber)
17 g fat
112 mg calcium
231 mg sodium

1/6 recipe:
174 calories
10 g protein
17 g carbohydrate
    (3 g fiber)
7 g fat
56 mg calcium
115 mg sodium

Don devised this delicious protein-rich blender pudding. The texture reminds me of my mother's unconventional and very dense ricotta chocolate mousse. We enjoy it for snacks or mini-meals, but you could serve smaller portions for dessert. Date-Coconut Rolls—soft pulverized dates shaped into logs and rolled in coconut—are easier to purée than plain pitted dates. Apple fiber powder, made from dried, powdered apple peels, adds density and texture; if you don't have it, you can omit it without hurting the pudding.

Note: Shake unopened can of coconut milk. Rinse top and completely remove lid. Contents may have separated. Pour into an impeccably clean wide-mouth 16-ounce jar. Whisk, or cover and shake until smooth. If thick or uneven, process in blender or food processor. We use Thai Kitchen coconut milk and NOW Foods apple fiber powder.

Chocolate Protein-Prune Pudding

Prep: 20 minutes ~ **Yield:** 3 cups; 3 to 6 servings

Ingredients & Directions

1 cup cold or room temperature filtered water

4 teaspoons unflavored gelatin (i.e., bulk beef gelatin)

1/4 cup packed pitted prunes (about 6 prunes)

3 Date-Coconut Rolls (60 grams by weight) **or** 9 small pitted dates (weigh them)

2 tablespoon unsweetened cocoa

2 tablespoon carob powder for sweetness and depth of flavor

1 1/2 tablespoons unsalted, unsweetened, almond butter

1 tablespoon apple fiber powder

2 teaspoons nonalcoholic vanilla extract **or** 1 teaspoon pure vanilla in alcohol

1/2 cup dried, powdered egg whites **or** unsweetened vanilla egg white protein

1 tablespoon flax oil plus 3 drops vitamin E oil

2 to 3 large ice cubes (about 1/2 to 2/3 cup)

Nutrition

1/3 recipe:
305 calories
21 g protein
34 g carbohydrate
(5 g fiber)
11 g fat
103 mg calcium
210 mg sodium

1/6 recipe:
152 calories
10 g protein
17 g carbohydrate
(3 g fiber)
5 g fat
51 mg calcium
105 mg sodium

Prunes become infinitely more enticing combined with dates, coconut milk, cocoa, carob, and almond butter. Don gets credit for dreaming up this dish and making it a winner from the very first bite. Besides being delicious, it's low in sugar, dairy-free, and rich in antioxidants, protein, and friendly fats. It's easy to make and fun to eat for a blood sugar-balancing snack.

1. Slowly sprinkle gelatin over 1 cup cool or cold water in small saucepan. Gently warm over low heat without stirring until completely dissolved. Remove from heat. Add pitted prunes, and date rolls or pitted dates. Cover and soak for 15 to 30 minutes until soft.

2. Pour water-gelatin-date mixture into blender or food processor. Add remaining ingredients, except ice. Cover and process until smooth, stopping to scrape sides with a spatula. Add ice, cover, and blend until smooth.

3. Pour into 3 (12-ounce) serving dishes for substantial snacks or 6 small dishes for dessert. Chill for at least 3 hours or freeze briefly until set. Use within 5 days or freeze.

Variations

* If using sweetened egg white protein, reduce non-alcoholic vanilla by one-half and use only 2 to 3 Date-Coconut Rolls or 6 to 8 pitted dates.

* **Chocolate Protein-Prune Pudding Pops:** Pour blended mixture into 6 to 8 Popsicle molds or paper cups. Freeze until firm. Run molds under warm water to release or transfer cups to the counter 15 minutes before serving with spoons.

Notes: Gelatin is essential, but apple fiber powder is optional.

Shake unopened can of coconut milk. Rinse top and completely remove lid. Contents may have separated. Pour into an impeccably clean wide-mouth 16-ounce jar. Whisk, or cover and shake until smooth. If thick or uneven, process in blender or food processor.

We use Thai Kitchen coconut milk and NOW Foods apple fiber powder.

Don's Smoothie Base

Prep: 20 minutes ~ **Yield:** 3 heaping cups; 6 servings

Ingredients & Directions

1 cup cool or cold filtered water

2 tablespoon unflavored gelatin

1 (14-ounce) can unsweetened coconut milk
(1 3/4 cups), premium not lite

6 (1-ounce) scoops vanilla or chocolate egg white protein
or 2 cups dried, powdered egg white

1/4 to 1/2 teaspoon stevia extract powder or liquid **or**
1 to 2 tablespoons raw honey if egg white protein is
unsweetened

2 teaspoons nonalcoholic vanilla extract **or** 1 teaspoon
pure vanilla in alcohol (omit if using vanilla egg white protein)

1 teaspoon dried ginger **or** 1 tablespoon peeled, sliced or grated
fresh gingerroot

1/2 cup ice water

Nutrition

**1 serving,
without fruit:**
238 calories
28 g protein
6 g carbohydrate
12 g fat
296 mg sodium

1. Slowly sprinkle gelatin over 1 cup cool or cold water in a saucepan.
Warm over low heat without stirring until gelatin melts and
dissolves completely. Cover and let stand 2 minutes, then purée in
blender or Vita Mix for 30 seconds until frothy.

2. Add egg white, optional stevia or honey and vanilla, then ginger,
and water. Blend until smooth, stopping to scrape sides with a
spatula.

3. Divide mixture between 6 wide-mouth (16-ounce) containers with
tight lids. Cover, label, and refrigerate for up to 6 days or freeze for
longer storage.

4. To serve, add 1 Smoothie Base portion to blender. If frozen, transfer
to refrigerator several hours before serving or overnight. Add 1 to
1 1/2 cups fresh or frozen unsweetened fruit. Blend until smooth,
stopping to scrape sides with a spatula.

5. Pour smoothie into container that held smoothie base or a
16-ounce glass and serve. For a snack that will keep for several
hours unrefrigerated, pour into freezer-safe thermos and freeze for
several hours.

Variations

* **To add 5 to 7 grams of fat and 45 to 70 calories per serving:** Add 2
to 3 tablespoons macadamia nut butter or flax oil to the base.

* **Don's favorite fruits to add:** Cherries, blueberries, peaches, or
cherries with blueberries, or strawberries with banana. (Calories
from fruit not included above.)

* **Cocoa-Banana Shake:** Add 1 tablespoon carob powder and
1 tablespoon unsweetened cocoa powder, 1 peeled, sliced, large
banana, and 2 teaspoons apple fiber powder to 1 serving of
Smoothie Base. Blend and serve for a quick meal or substantial
snack.

If you want a smoothie for a snack, light supper, or quick breakfast during the week, make a batch of this on Sunday. Mark containers with labels or colored rubber bands if other family members want smoothie bases and have different calorie needs.

Purée with fresh or frozen fruit for a quick breakfast. Or, if you have access to a blender at work, before leaving home, spoon frozen fruit over a portion of Smoothie Base, stash the container in an insulated tote with your lunch, and refrigerate at work. For a snack or light meal, buzz in a blender and drink or eat with a spoon.

Note: We use Thai Kitchen coconut milk and NOW Foods apple fiber powder.

Rachel's Smoothie Base

Prep: 15 to 20 minutes ~ **Yield:** 3 heaping cups; 7 servings

---

Ingredients & Directions

1 cup cool or cold filtered water

2 tablespoons unflavored gelatin

1 (14-ounce) can unsweetened coconut milk (1 3/4 cups total), premium not lite

5 (1-ounce) scoops vanilla or chocolate egg white protein **or** 1 2/3 cups dried, powdered egg white

1/4 to 1/2 teaspoon stevia extract powder or liquid **or** 1 to 2 tablespoons raw honey if egg white protein is unsweetened

2 teaspoons nonalcoholic vanilla extract **or** 1 teaspoon pure vanilla in alcohol (omit if using vanilla egg white protein)

1 teaspoon dried ginger **or** 1 tablespoon peeled, sliced or grated fresh gingerroot

1/2 cup ice water

Nutrition

1 serving, without fruit:
189 calories
20 g protein
5 g carbohydrate
10 g fat
217 mg sodium

1. Slowly sprinkle gelatin over 1 cup cool or cold water in a saucepan. Warm over low heat, without boiling or stirring until gelatin melts and dissolves completely. Cover and let stand 2 minutes, then purée in a blender or Vita-Mix for 30 seconds, until frothy.

2. Add remaining ingredients and blend until smooth, stopping to scrape sides with a spatula.

3. Divide mixture between 7 (16-ounce) wide-mouth containers with tight lids. Cover, label, and refrigerate for up to 6 days or freeze for longer storage.

4. To serve, add 1 Smoothie Base portion to a blender. If frozen, transfer to refrigerator several hours before serving or overnight. Add 1 to 1 1/2 cups fresh or frozen unsweetened fruit and blend until smooth, stopping to scrape the sides with a spatula.

5. Pour smoothie into container that held smoothie base or a 16-ounce glass and serve. For a snack that will keep for several hours unrefrigerated, pour into freezer-safe thermos and freeze for several hours.

Variations

* **For 5 more fat grams and 45 to 50 calories per serving:** Add 2 tablespoons macadamia nut butter or flax oil to the base.

* **To add 4 to 7 more protein grams and 16 to 28 calories per serving:** Add 1 to 2 extra scoops egg white protein.

* **Rachel's favorite fruits to add:** Peaches, nectarines, apricots, blueberries, strawberries, pitted, unsweetened cherries, seedless watermelon, mango, pineapple, or a mixture of 2 or 3 fruits. Refer to Better Balanced Smoothies and Frosty Fruit Whips (see Index for recipes) for delicious fruit combinations.

If you make this on the weekend and refrigerate or freeze portions in pint jars or thick or hard plastic HDPE containers, you can whip up a smoothie for a protein-rich snack or light meal in minutes. Coconut milk adds a creamy texture and immune-enhancing fatty acids. Gelatin thickens and keeps the ingredients from separating. Stevia adds a sweet taste without calories, carbohydrates, or artificial sweeteners.

Note: We use Thai Kitchen coconut milk and NOW Foods apple fiber powder. Mark containers with labels or colored rubber bands if other family members want smoothie bases and have different calorie needs.

Macadamia Nut Smoothie Base

Prep: 15 to 20 minutes ~ **Yield:** 6 servings

Ingredients & Directions

1 cup cool or cold filtered water

2 tablespoons unflavored gelatin

1/2 cup unsalted, unsweetened macadamia nut butter

6 (1-ounce) scoops vanilla **or** chocolate egg white protein

1/4 to 1/2 teaspoon stevia extract powder or liquid **or** 1 to 2 tablespoons raw honey if egg white protein is unsweetened

2 teaspoons nonalcoholic vanilla extract **or** 1 teaspoon pure vanilla in alcohol (omit if using vanilla egg white protein)

1 cup ice cold water

1. Slowly sprinkle gelatin over cold water in a saucepan. Warm over low heat without boiling or stirring until gelatin melts and dissolves completely. Cover and let stand for 2 minutes.

2. Put gelatin mixture and remaining ingredients in a blender or food processor. Blend until smooth, stopping to scrape sides with a spatula.

3. Divide between 6 wide-mouth (16-ounce) containers with tight lids. Cover and label, then refrigerate for up to 5 days or freeze for longer storage.

4. To serve, add 1 Smoothie Base portion to blender. If frozen, transfer to refrigerator several hours before serving or overnight. Add 1 to 1 1/2 cups fresh or frozen unsweetened fruit and blend until smooth, stopping to scrape sides with a spatula.

5. Pour smoothie into container that held smoothie base or 16-ounce glass and serve. For a snack that will keep for several hours unrefrigerated, pour into freezer-safe thermos and freeze for several hours.

Variations

* **To reduce protein and fat calories:** Use only 1/3 cup macadamia nut butter and 4 to 5 scoops of egg white protein **or** 1 to 1 1/4 cups dried, powdered egg white.

Nutrition

Entire recipe (using stevia):

1680 calories
174 grams protein
30 g carbohydrate
96 g fat
64 mg calcium
1560 mg sodium

1 serving (smoothie base only):

280 calories
29 g protein
5 g carbohydrate
16 g fat
11 mg calcium
260 mg sodium

Make this smoothie base on the weekend and you can quickly assemble Better-Balanced Smoothies or Frosty Fruit Whips for snacks or mini-meals all week. Unflavored gelatin is essential; it thickens the base and keeps the mixture from separating. Macadamia nut butter adds monounsaturated fats and stevia provides the sweetness.

If you have a blender at work, before leaving home top a smoothie base with 1 to 1 1/2 cups of frozen fruit, chill in an insulated tote, and refrigerate at work. For a snack or fourth meal, blend (add a banana if you need more calories).

Note: The high sodium content comes from the egg whites, which are naturally rich in sodium.

Vanilla Protein-Coconut Cream

Prep: 20 minutes ~ **Yield:** 5 servings

Ingredients & Directions

2/3 cup cold filtered water

2 teaspoons unflavored gelatin

1 (14-ounce) can unsweetened coconut milk

4 (1-ounce) scoops vanilla egg white protein, about
1 1/4 cups **or** plain dried, powdered egg white (reduce
or omit stevia if protein powder contains stevia or any
other sweetener)

2 teaspoons nonalcoholic pure vanilla extract
or 1 teaspoon pure vanilla in alcohol (if using unflavored
egg white powder, add 1 to 2 teaspoons honey)

1/8 to 1/4 teaspoon stevia extract powder
or 1 to 2 tablespoons honey **or** agavé nectar

1/4 teaspoon ground nutmeg **or** 2 teaspoons peeled,
finely minced fresh gingerroot, optional

Nutrition

1 serving:
241 calories
22 g protein
7 g carbohydrate
14 g fat
251 mg sodium

For a quick, protein-rich breakfast or substantial snack, enjoy this dairy-free, sugarless sauce over individual servings of fresh berries, mixed fruit, or baked winter squash. If you make it on the weekend or mid-week, you'll have the fixings for several delicious breakfasts.

1. Slowly sprinkle gelatin over water in small saucepan. Heat slowly without stirring until gelatin melts completely. Stir, then process in blender or bowl of food processor.

2. Shake unopened can of coconut milk. Rinse top of can and completely remove lid. Combine coconut milk with remaining ingredients. Cover and blend until smooth, stopping to scrape down sides with spatula. Taste and add dash more stevia, or honey if a sweeter taste is desired. Divide mixture between 5 containers and cover with tight-fitting lids.

3. Chill for at least 5 hours before serving. If a fluffy texture is desired, whip in blender or with beaters before serving. Use within 5 days or freeze to prevent spoiling.

Variations

* For a higher protein sauce, use 6 scoops of egg white protein.

* **Almond Protein-Coconut Cream:** Replace vanilla with 1/2 teaspoon pure almond extract, adding an additional 2 teaspoons honey or agavé nectar if needed.

* **Chocolate Protein-Coconut Cream:** Replace vanilla egg white protein with chocolate egg white protein or add 2 tablespoons unsweetened cocoa powder.

Note: Coconut fat has anti-viral, antifungal, and anti-microbial properties—so you can enjoy it without guilt! The bad press about coconut was processed food propaganda.

Better Balanced Banana-Almond Smoothie

Prep: 10 minutes ~ **Yield:** 1 serving; 1 1/2 to 2 cups

Ingredients & Directions

1/3 to 1/2 cup cool or cold filtered water

1 (1-ounce) scoop vanilla egg white protein **or** 1/3 cup dried, powdered egg whites

1 teaspoon nonalcoholic vanilla extract **or** 1/2 teaspoon pure vanilla in alcohol

1/8 teaspoon apple pie spice, cinnamon, or cardamom

1 1/2 tablespoons roasted, unsalted, unsweetened almond butter

1 (8- to 9-inch) ripe or over-ripe banana, sliced **or** about 3/4 to 1 cup sliced, frozen banana

3 to 6 ice cubes, optional

1/16th to 1/8 teaspoon stevia extract powder, optional, if a sweeter taste is desired

Nutrition

1 serving:
406 calories
31 g protein
38 g carbohydrate
　　　(9 g fiber)
15 g fat
130 mg calcium
261 mg sodium

When I was growing up my mother used to make a creamy banana Julius by blending bananas, milk, non-fat milk powder, sugar, vanilla, and ice. This recipe reminds of that drink, only it's thicker, richer in fat and protein, and substantial enough to be a quick meal on the go or generous snack.

1. Combine all ingredients except ice and stevia in the order listed in a blender. Cover and process until smooth, stopping to scrape sides with a spatula. Taste and add 1/16 teaspoon optional stevia if a sweeter taste is desired. Blend and taste again. Your probably won't need more stevia, but if you do, add an additional 1/16 teaspoon.

2. For a frostier texture or more volume, add ice and blend again. Pour into a 12- to 16-ounce glass and serve immediately or freeze in a thermos and use a short time later. Bananas discolor quickly.

Variations

* **For 45 additional calories:** add 1 teaspoon flax oil or additional 1/2 tablespoon almond butter.

* **Better Balanced Banana-Macadamia Nut Smoothie:** Replace almond butter with macadamia nut butter.

* **Better Balanced Cocoa-Banana Smoothie:** Add 2 to 3 teaspoons unsweetened cocoa powder or use chocolate egg white protein.

* **Better Balanced Banana-Coconut Smoothie:** Replace almond butter with 1/4 cup plus 2 tablespoons unsweetened, sulfite-free premium coconut milk, such as Thai Kitchen.

Better Balanced Cherry Smoothie

Prep: 15 minutes ~ **Yield:** 1 1/2 to 2 cups; 1 serving

Ingredients & Directions

1/4 cup thoroughly blended, unsweetened coconut milk (premium, not lite)

1/4 cup filtered water

1 (1-ounce) scoop vanilla egg white protein **or** 1/3 cup dried, powdered egg whites

1/2 teaspoons nonalcoholic vanilla extract **or** 1/4 teaspoon pure vanilla in alcohol if protein powder is unflavored

1/3 teaspoon dried ginger **or** 1 teaspoon minced gingerroot

1 cup fresh or frozen, pitted unsweetened sweet cherries

1 teaspoon apple fiber powder, optional

1/16 to 1/8 teaspoon stevia extract powder **or** stevia extract liquid if egg white protein is unsweetened, optional
3 to 4 ice cubes, optional

Nutrition

1 serving:
388 calories
28 g protein
39 g carbohydrate
(6 g fiber)
13 g fat
31 mg calcium
291 mg sodium

1. Combine all ingredients except stevia and ice in the order listed in a blender. Cover and process until smooth, stopping to scrape sides with a spatula. Taste and adjust with stevia in tiny increments if a sweeter taste is desired.

2. For a frostier texture, add ice and blend again. Pour into a tall glass and serve immediately, or chill or freeze briefly in a 16-ounce wide-mouth thermos.

Variations

* **Better Balanced Chocolate-Cherry Smoothie:** Add 2 to 3 teaspoons unsweetened cocoa powder or use chocolate-flavored egg white protein.

* **Better Balanced Melon-Cherry Smoothie:** For a lower-carbohydrate count, use 1/2 cup cherries and 3/4 to 1 cup fresh or frozen honeydew, cantaloupe, canary, or crenshaw melon.

* **Better Balanced Mango-Cherry Smoothie**:** Replace half the cherries with cubed fresh or frozen mango. Taste before adding stevia; you may not need it.

    ** **Note:** Texture is more important than color when shopping for mangoes. If mangoes are hard, allow them to ripen on the counter or store in a closed paper bag punched with holes along with a ripe banana or apple. Check daily to catch them before they spoil.

This refreshing recipe makes a great breakfast for people who don't have time for a sit-down meal. We sometimes serve it as a substantial snack or a light supper on days we eat an early afternoon supper and have to work in the evening. To make this a regular part of your repertoire, stock up on frozen, pitted, sweet but unsweetened cherries, sold in supermarkets everywhere.

FYI: Because cherries are so sweet you probably won't need to add any sweetener to the main recipe or to the mango variation.

Note: Shake unopened can of coconut milk. Rinse top and completely remove lid. Contents may have separated. Pour into an impeccably clean wide-mouth 16-ounce jar. Whisk, or cover and shake until smooth. If thick or uneven, purée in blender or food processor. We use Thai Kitchen coconut milk and NOW Foods apple fiber powder.

~ Variations continued next page ~

Variations

Better Balanced Cherry Smoothie ~ continued

* **Better Balanced Morning Mango Smoothie:** Replace cherries with cubed fresh or frozen mango. Add 2 teaspoons lime juice if desired. Taste before adding stevia; you may not need it.

* **Better Balanced Mango-Macadamia Smoothie:** Replace cherries with cubed fresh or frozen mango and replace coconut milk with 1/4 cup water plus 2 to 3 teaspoons unsalted macadamia nut butter. Taste before adding stevia; you may not need it.

* **Better Balanced Mango-Pineapple-Strawberry Smoothie**: Replace cherries with 1 to 1 1/2 cups fresh or frozen mango, pineapple, and strawberry pieces (you can buy them as a mix in the freezer section of supermarkets).

* **If you don't have coconut milk:** Substitute 1/4 cup water plus 2 to 3 teaspoons macadamia nut butter **or** flax oil, **or** 1 tablespoon almond butter.

* **To add 5 to 10 more fat grams and 45 to 90 additional calories:** Replace 1/8 to 1/4 cup of water with coconut milk, or add 1 to 2 teaspoons flax oil **or** 1/2 to 1 tablespoon almond butter to the master recipe or any of the variations.

Better Balanced Blueberry Smoothie

Prep: 15 minutes ~ **Yield:** 1 1/2 to 2 cups; 1 serving

Ingredients & Directions

1/4 cup thoroughly blended, unsweetened coconut milk
(premium, not lite)

1/4 cup filtered water

1 (1-ounce) scoop vanilla egg white protein **or** 1/3 cup
dried, powdered egg whites

1/16 to 1/8 teaspoon stevia extract powder **or** stevia
extract liquid if egg white protein is unsweetened

1/2 teaspoons nonalcoholic vanilla extract
or 1/4 teaspoon pure vanilla in alcohol if protein powder
is unflavored

1 to 1 1/2 cups fresh or frozen unsweetened blueberries

1/4 teaspoon dried ginger, cinnamon **or** 1 teaspoon
peeled, minced, or grated gingerroot

1 teaspoon apple fiber powder, optional

3 to 4 ice cubes, optional

Nutrition

1 serving:
318 calories
26 g protein
30 g carbohydrate
(5 g fiber)
10 g fat
1 mg calcium
304 mg sodium

Berries are loaded with vitamins, minerals, fiber, flavor, and antioxidants. Try this delicious, protein-rich drink for a light snack or evening meal. Use frozen fruit for a soft-serve ice cream-like texture, or use fresh or thawed fruit for a drinkable delight. Other berries may be used, but raspberries and boysenberries result in a seedy texture.

1. Combine all ingredients except stevia and ice in the order listed in a blender. Cover and process until smooth, stopping to scrape sides with a spatula. Taste and adjust with stevia in tiny increments if a sweeter taste is desired.

2. For a frostier texture, add ice and blend again. Pour into a tall glass and serve immediately, or chill or freeze briefly in a 16-ounce wide-mouth thermos.

Variations

* **Better Balanced Cocoa-Blueberry Smoothie**: Add 2 to 3 teaspoons unsweetened cocoa or use chocolate-flavored egg white protein. Sounds strange, tastes great, and adds antioxidants.

* **Better Balanced Blueberry-Banana Smoothie:** Use 1/2 to 1 cup blueberries with 1/2 to 1 banana. If desired add 2 teaspoons cocoa or use chocolate-flavored egg white protein.

* **Better Balanced Blueberry-Mango Smoothie:** Replace 1/2 cup blueberries with fresh or frozen mango cubes.

* **If you don't have coconut milk:** Substitute 1/4 cup water plus 2 teaspoons macadamia nut butter or flax oil, **or** 1 tablespoon almond butter.

* **To add 5 to 10 more fat grams and 45 to 90 additional calories:** Replace 1/8 to 1/4 cup of water with coconut milk, **or** add 1 to 2 teaspoons flax oil **or** 1/2 to 1 tablespoon almond butter to the master recipe or any of the variations.

Note: Shake unopened can of coconut milk. Rinse top and completely remove lid. Contents may have separated. Pour into an impeccably clean wide-mouth 16-ounce jar. Whisk, or cover and shake until smooth. If thick or uneven, purée in blender or food processor. We use Thai Kitchen coconut milk and NOW Foods apple fiber powder.

Speedy Smoothie or Fast Frosty Fruit Whip

Prep: 10 minutes ~ **Yield:** 1 servings

Ingredients & Directions

1 portion Rachel's Smoothie Base (Page 468), thoroughly chilled and set

1/8 teaspoon dried ginger **or** 1 teaspoon peeled, minced or grated gingerroot

1 1/2 cups frozen, unsweetened fruit (1 or combination of 2 to 3 fruits):
  peaches, apricots, nectarines, strawberries, blueberries, pitted sweet but unsweetened cherries, pineapple, mango, papaya, bananas, seedless watermelon, cantaloupe, canary, crenshaw or honeydew melon

3 to 4 ice cubes, optional

Nutrition

1 serving (peach):
309 calories
22 g protein
34 g carbohydrate
          (5 g fiber)
12 g fat
14 mg calcium
217 mg sodium

1. Add ingredients to a blender or Vita-Mix in the order listed.

2. **Blender:** Cover and start on low, then turn to high or ice crushing mode until smooth.

   Vita-Mix: Select VARIABLE speed number 1. Turn on and quickly increase speed to number 10, then HIGH. Remove lid plug. Insert tamper through lid opening and push contents into blades until smooth. A loud pulling sound indicates the mix has formed 4 mounds in the container, about 60 seconds.

3. Turn off machine and scrape sides with a spatula to make sure fruit and ice are completely crushed. Blend again if chunks remain, then spoon into container that held smoothie base, a 16-ounce parfait glass, or wide-mouth thermos.

4. Serve within 15 minutes or, freeze for several hours in a thermos for a portable snack or mini-meal. Consume frozen mixture within 4 hours of leaving home if you are not storing it in a thermos or cooler.

Variations

* **For 45 more calories:** add 1 teaspoon flax oil **or** macadamia nut butter.

* **Rachel's favorites:** cherries combined with peaches, cantaloupe, canary or honeydew melon, or blueberries with peaches, seedless watermelon, or other melon.

* **Don's favorites:** cherries, blueberries, or cherries with strawberries, blueberries, or banana.

For faster frosties and smoothies, make a batch of smoothie base on the weekend, and refrigerate or freeze it in individual portions. For a scrumptious snack or light meal, take out a premeasured portion, add fresh or frozen fruit, blend, and serve. Use fresh or thawed fruit for a drinkable delight. Use frozen fruit if you want a soft serve ice cream-like treat.

Peach Frosty Fruit Whip

Prep: 15 minutes ~ **Yield:** 1 1/2 to 2 cups; 1 serving

Ingredients & Directions

1/3 cup cool or cold filtered water

2 teaspoons unflavored gelatin (beef gelatin)

2 teaspoons apple fiber powder, optional

1 (1-ounce) scoop vanilla egg white protein **or** 1/3 cup dried, powdered egg whites

1/16 to 1/8 teaspoon stevia extract powder **or** stevia extract liquid if egg white protein is unsweetened

1/2 teaspoon nonalcoholic vanilla extract **or** 1/4 teaspoon pure vanilla in alcohol, if protein powder is unflavored

1/8 teaspoon ground nutmeg **or** 1 teaspoon peeled, minced or grated gingerroot

1/4 cup blended, chilled, unsweetened coconut milk (premium, not lite)

1 1/2 to 1 3/4 cups frozen, unsweetened sliced peaches

3 to 4 cup ice cubes, optional

1. Slowly sprinkle gelatin over cool or cold water in a small saucepan. Warm over low heat, without stirring until gelatin dissolves and turns clear, about 2 minutes. Remove from heat and process in a blender for 30 seconds until frothy.

2. Add remaining ingredients, except fruit and ice. Cover and blend until smooth. Turn off and scrape sides with a spatula to remove lumps. Add frozen fruit, cover and process until smooth, stopping to scrape sides. Taste and add stevia if a sweeter taste is desired. If mix sets up too fast add 2 tablespoons cold water. If it's too thin add ice 2 cubes. Blend until smooth.

3. Serve immediately, chill for 10 minutes, or freeze briefly in a 16-ounce wide-mouth thermos for a snack to go.

Variations

* **Blueberry-Peach Frosty Fruit Whip:** Replace 1/3 to 1/2 of peaches with frozen blueberries.

* **Blueberry Frosty Fruit Whip:** Blueberries are loaded with antioxidants and flavor. Replace peaches with 1 1/2 cups frozen blueberries, **or** 1 cup frozen blueberries plus 1/2 cup ice.

* **Cherry-Peach Frosty Fruit Whip:** Use 1 cup frozen peaches plus 1/2 cup frozen, pitted sweet unsweetened cherries, **or** 1/2 cup frozen peaches plus 1/2 cup frozen, pitted sweet cherries and 1/2 cup ice.

~ Variations continued next page ~

Nutrition

1 serving:
348 calories
32 g protein
32 g carbohydrate
(4 g fiber)
10 g fat
1 mg calcium
291 mg sodium

Variation 1 (pg 477):
1 serving:
347 calories
32 g protein
30 g carbohydrate
(5 g fiber)
11 g fat
30 mg calcium
294 mg sodium

Variation 2 (pg 477)
1 serving:
407 calories
33 g protein
39 g carbohydrate
(6 g fiber)
13 g fat
31 mg calcium
291 mg sodium

Several years ago, I discovered that hot water, gelatin, frozen fruit, protein powder, and coconut milk congeal almost instantly in the blender, creating a thick, soft-serve like treat. Since then, I've come up with numerous fun flavors. Because this recipe is rich in protein, we don't serve it as dessert. We consider it a special snack or mini meal. If you make it often enough, you can commit the recipe to memory. Always measure, so you produce consistently great results and avoid overdoing it with the coconut milk or stevia.

Note: Shake unopened can of coconut milk. Rinse top and completely remove lid. Contents may have separated. Pour into an impeccably clean wide-mouth 16-ounce jar. Whisk, or cover and shake until smooth. If thick or uneven, purée in blender or food processor. We use Thai Kitchen coconut milk and NOW Foods apple fiber powder.

Variations

Peach Frosty Fruit Whip ~ continued

* **Strawberry-Mango Frosty Fruit Whip:** Replace peaches with 1 cup frozen strawberries plus 1/2 cup frozen, unsweetened mango chunks. See box for nutrition information (Variation 1).

* **Cherry Frosty Fruit Whip:** Like blueberries, cherries are loaded with antioxidants and flavor. Since frozen, pitted sweet but unsweetened cherries are available in supermarkets everywhere, there's no reason not to stock up. Replace peaches with 1 cup frozen, pitted, unsweetened cherries plus 1/2 cup ice. Taste before adding stevia. You may not need it. See nutrition box for information (Variation 2).

* **If you don't have coconut milk:** Substitute 1/4 cup water plus 2 teaspoons macadamia nut butter or flax oil.

* **To add 5 to 10 more fat grams and 45 to 90 additional calories:** Replace 1/8 to 1/4 cup of water with coconut milk, **or** add 1 to 2 teaspoons flax oil **or** 1/2 to 1 tablespoon almond butter to master recipe or any of the variations.

FYI: Have all the ingredients on the counter before you start and work quickly. If you don't get the perfect texture the first time, keep practicing. Apple fiber powder isn't essential, but it creates a thicker texture and reduces the glycemic effect of this snack (see Appendix for mail order suppliers). Grated apples will not produce the same effect.

Mocha Frosty

Prep: 15 minutes ~ **Yield:** 1 servings

Ingredients & Directions

1 to 1 1/2 cups strong Chicory and Dandelion Root "Coffee" (Page 495)

1/3 cup boiling filtered water

2 teaspoons unflavored gelatin (beef gelatin, such as Knox)

2 teaspoons apple fiber power

1 1/2 tablespoons roasted almond **or** hazelnut butter

1 (1-ounce) scoop vanilla or chocolate egg white protein **or** 1/3 cup dried, powdered egg white

1/8 **to** 1/4 teaspoon stevia extract powder **or** stevia extract liquid if protein powder is unsweetened

1 teaspoon nonalcoholic vanilla extract **or** 1/2 teaspoon vanilla in alcohol

1/8 **to** 1/4 teaspoon additional stevia extract powder **or** stevia extract liquid **or** 1 to 3 teaspoons honey or agavé nectar, as needed to sweeten

1/4 teaspoon ground cinnamon **or** apple pie spice

2 ice cubes

This high-protein, low-carbohydrate, caffeine-free concoction makes a great blood sugar-balancing snack that reminds me of the A & W Frosties I was wild about when I was growing up. Some of my students say this rivals Starbuck's coffee creations, which I've never tried. I brew the Chicory & Dandelion Root "Coffee" and freeze it in ice cube trays a day or more in advance.

Nutrition

1 serving:
315 calories
35 g protein
11 g carbohydrate
(7 g fiber)
14 g fat
185 mg calcium
260 mg sodium

1. Pour Chicory & Dandelion Root "Coffee" in ice cube tray(s). Freeze until hard.

2. Add boiling water to blender. Cover and turn on low. Slowly sprinkle gelatin through top feeder and blend for 30 seconds, holding top down with a towel to prevent splattering. Turn off and scrape sides with spatula.

3. Add apple fiber, nut butter, protein powder, vanilla, and spice. Cover and blend until smooth, stopping to scrape sides with spatula. Turn to ice crushing mode. Add 4 "coffee" ice cubes and blend. Add 3 to 4 more "coffee" cubes through top feeder, stopping to push ice down with a spatula and scrape sides. If desired, add 1 or 2 plain ice cubes for a frostier texture. Add stevia or honey if a sweeter taste is desired.

4. Pour into a tall glass and serve. For a thicker consistency, chill or freeze for 15 minutes.

Variations

* **Coconut-Mocha Frosty:** Replace 1/3 cup hot water with hot unsweetened coconut milk and omit nut butter. Nutrition profile will be almost identical.

* **For a richer taste and 50 more calories:** Increase almond butter to 2 tablespoons.

Note: Look for apple fiber powder in small bags or jars in natural foods stores or buy it by mail from NOW Foods. It adds fiber and texture. Fresh apples are not a substitute.

Caffeine-Free, High-Protein Roastaroma Mocha

Prep: 5 minutes ~ **Steeping:** 10 minutes ~ **Yield:** 1 large serving

Ingredients & Directions

2 cups boiling hot filtered water

2 Celestial Seasonings Roastaroma tea bags

1 (1-ounce) scoop vanilla or chocolate egg white protein **or** 1/3 cup dried, powdered egg whites

1/8 to 1/4 teaspoon stevia extract powder or liquid **or** 2 to 3 teaspoons of honey or agavé nectar, or some combination if protein powder is unsweetened

1/4 cup well mixed, unsweetened, preservative-free coconut milk (premium, not lite)

Nutrition

1 cup serving:
210 calories
25 g protein
5 g carbohydrate
10 g fat
291 mg sodium

1. Pour boiling water over tea bags, cover, and steep for 10 to 12 minutes.

2. Remove tea bags, add vanilla or chocolate protein powder and coconut milk; stir or whisk to dissolve. Taste; adjust with stevia, honey, agavé or some combination if desired.

3. Divide between 2 mugs and serve, or pour into a thermos, seal, and take with you to work or the gym.

Variations

* Replace coconut milk with 1/4 cup homemade cashew or almond milk. Calorie counts will vary with different nut milk recipes. To reduce fat, replace regular coconut milk with lite coconut milk.

Roastaroma—a caffeine-free, herbal tea made from roasted barley, roasted barley malt, roasted chicory root, roasted carob, cinnamon, allspice, and star anise—is sold in supermarkets, drug stores, and natural foods markets. If you're strictly avoiding gluten, replace Roastaroma with Raja's Cup, a robust antioxidant-rich herbal brew that looks like coffee but contains no caffeine, gluten, or refined ingredients. Look for it in natural foods stores.

If you're weaning yourself from coffee, mochas, and lattés, this protein-packed snack might brighten your morning—or afternoon. The protein helps balance your blood sugar level. Coconut milk adds a rich creamy taste, without cream. Stevia and honey replace sugar.

Note: Shake unopened can of coconut milk. Rinse top and completely remove lid. Contents may have separated. Pour into an impeccably clean wide-mouth 16-ounce jar. Whisk, or cover and shake until smooth. If thick or uneven, purée in a blender or food processor. I use Thai Kitchen unsweetened coconut milk and NOW Foods apple fiber powder.

Blueberry-Protein Popsicles

Prep: 20 minutes ~ **Yield:** 8 servings

Ingredients & Directions

1 cup thoroughly blended, unsweetened coconut milk (premium, not lite), divided

2 to 3 teaspoons unflavored gelatin (beef gelatin or Knox)

2 (1-ounce) scoops vanilla or chocolate egg white protein **or** 2/3 cup dried, powdered egg whites (if unsweetened, add 1/8 to 1/4 teaspoon stevia extract powder or liquid **or** 2 teaspoons honey or agavé nectar)

1 teaspoon nonalcoholic vanilla or almond extract

1/2 teaspoon ground cinnamon **or** 2 teaspoons peeled, minced or grated gingerroot

2 cups fresh **or** 2 1/2 cups frozen, unsweetened, blueberries

2 teaspoons lemon juice or orange juice

1 tablespoon honey **or** agavé nectar, optional

Nutrition

1 serving:
114 calories
7 g protein
7 g carbohydrate
(1 g fiber)
6 g fat
2 mg calcium
73 mg sodium

These sweet and creamy Popsicles are packed with vitamins, minerals, antioxidants, and protein. Coconut milk makes them creamy without dairy products and it adds immune enhancing fatty acids. These make a great dessert or blood sugar-balancing snack on a hot day. Experiment with different fruits singly or in combination.

1. Slowly sprinkle gelatin over 1/2 cup coconut milk in a small saucepan. (If coconut milk is thick from chilling, first warm it over low heat to liquefy.) Let stand for a few minutes until no dry spots are visible. Warm over low heat until dissolved. Stir, cover, and remove from heat.

2. Pour mixture into a blender or food processor and purée for 30 seconds until frothy. Cool for 10 minutes. Add remaining ingredients and blend until smooth, stopping to scrape sides with a spatula. Taste, adjust sweetness if desired, and blend again.

3. Pour into 8 (4-ounce) Popsicle molds or paper cups, leaving 1/4-inch headspace. Top molds with lids or freeze cups until slushy (about 1 hour) then slip a stick into the center of each cup if desired. Freeze until firm, at least 3 hours.

4. Run molds under warm water or rest in a pan of water for several minutes to release pops or peel off paper as you eat. To serve without sticks, remove cups from freezer 15 minutes before serving with spoons. Use within 3 weeks to avoid freezer burn.

Variations

* **Mango-Protein Popsicles:** Replace blueberries with mango chunks and use ginger above.

* **Cherry-Protein Popsicles:** Replace blueberries with cherries.

* **Apricot-Protein Popsicles:** Replace blueberries with apricots or apricots and bananas.

Note: Shake unopened can of coconut milk. Rinse top and completely remove lid. Contents may have separated. Pour into an impeccably clean wide-mouth 16-ounce jar. Whisk, or cover and shake until smooth. If thick or uneven, process in blender or food processor. I use Thai Kitchen unsweetened coconut milk and NOW Foods apple fiber powder.

25 Jerky & Pemmican

BEST BITES

Drying Meat

Drying is the oldest means of preserving food. Prior to refrigerators and modern freezers, drying made meat available during lean times and for travel. Today dried meat still makes a convenient meal or snack at home, work, or on the road. Unfortunately, commercial jerky is usually made from factory-farmed beef or turkey. It's cured with one or more forms of sugar, an excessive amount of salt, plus sodium nitrate and laced with MSG, hydrogenated or partially hydrogenated fats, artificial colorings and flavorings, and preservatives. Avoid this stuff!

To enjoy the taste and convenience of dried meat while protecting your health you'll have to make it yourself. It's easy to do. I sometimes make several batches per week, several weeks in a row, and store the bulk in the freezer. Refrigerated jerky will last for months. Frozen jerky will last for years if tightly packed to prevent freezer burn.

Properly dried jerky will keep at room temperature for 1 to 2 months. In the absence of preservatives, or if improperly dried, jerky can start to spoil or turn moldy, particularly in hot or damp weather. When traveling in warm or muggy weather, keep jerky in a cooler or near an ice bag.

Ten Good Reasons to Make Your Own Beef & Turkey Jerky

1) You can eliminate unwholesome ingredients: refined salt, sodium nitrate and nitrite, sugar, artificial colorings and flavorings, hydrogenated fats and oils, and other preservatives and additives.
2) You can control the sodium content. You can omit the salt altogether or lightly season the meat with unrefined sea salt or naturally brewed tamari soy sauce.
3) You can use hormone- and antibiotic-free lean meats, poultry, or fish you've caught or bought.
4) You can use beef, bison, venison, deer, elk, bear, ostrich, or emu.
5) You can vary the herbs and spices according to what you like and what you have on hand.
6) You can adjust the degree of dryness and texture to your liking.
7) You will save money. (Jerky sold in natural foods stores is pricey.)
8) You will enjoy a fresher, better-tasting product.
9) You can use it as a convenient snack or as a sausage or bacon substitute for breakfast.
10) Jerky makes a gift for travelers, hikers, cyclists, and students. It makes a great birthday, anniversary, Christmas, Chanukah, graduation, or housewarming present. It may be one of the most remembered gifts of the season.

Homemade is Best: While jerky makes for a great snack at home or on the go, it's best to make your own. Commercial jerky is usually made from factory-farmed beef/turkey and contains sugar, excessive salt, and even MSG.

Good Reasons to Add Raisins to Jerky

What's a good substitute for the preservative, sodium nitrate, used widely in beef jerky and other processed meats and foods? It's raisin purée, according to researchers in the food science department at Oregon State University in Corvallis.

OSU food scientist Mark Daeschel, a specialist in natural antimicrobials, and his team found ground-up raisins as effective as sodium nitrate at inhibiting growth of bacteria and other harmful microbes, including E. coli, staphylococcus aureus and Listeria monocytogenes. The biggest benefit is that—unlike sodium nitrates—raisins don't break down into cancer-causing chemicals during digestion. Dried grapes add significant amounts antioxidants and fiber improve the flavor and texture of jerky, and reduce the amount of total fat and sodium per serving.

For a preservative effect the raisins must make up 10 to 15 percent of the jerky by weight. That means 10 to 15 grams of raisins for every 85 to 90 grams of meat. If kitchen math isn't your forté, don't fret, we've done the math for you. In the recipes in this chapter, we'll walk you through the process of making natural beef, bison, and turkey jerky using the amazing antioxidant powers of dried fruits.

Do other dried fruits work? You bet. Dried blueberries, bilberries, lycii berries (also known as wolfberries), pitted prunes (also sold as dried plums), dried apricots, cherries, and cranberries also contain beneficial protective properties. Raisins and prunes are the mildest, cranberries are the most tart. Experiment to find your favorite combinations.

Look for unsweetened, or fruit-sweetened, sulfite-free dried fruits free of added oils. Some companies add polyunsaturated vegetable oils to dried fruits.

Ground Turkey Jerky with Raisins

Prep: 30 minutes ~ **Drying:** 12 to 18 hours ~ **Yield:** About 1 pound (5 cups); 16 servings

Ingredients & Directions

Meat:
2 pounds lean ground skinless dark meat turkey **or** a combination of light and dark meat

Raisin purée:
1 loosely packed cup sulfite-free raisins

Scant 1/4 cup hot water, additional 2 tablespoons as needed to blend

Seasonings:
1 1/2 teaspoons dried, crumbled herbs (combine 2 to 3 herbs or your favorites and blend)
    basil, oregano, thyme, sage, marjoram, or combination

1/2 to 1 teaspoon ground cumin **or** dry mustard

1/2 teaspoon ground black pepper **or** ancho or Anaheim pepper, chile molido, **or** ground chipotlé (smoked dried jalapeno pepper powder)

2 garlic cloves, minced or pressed **or** 1 teaspoon garlic powder

2 tablespoons freeze-dried onion flakes **or** 1 tablespoon onion powder, optional

1 teaspoon finely ground unrefined sea salt **or** 2 tablespoons tamari soy sauce, optional

Unlike jerky made from steak, ground turkey jerky made with raisin purée is moist and easy to chew. It has a subtle sweetness without refined sugars. It's packed with antioxidants and keeps well without preservatives. It's also much lower in sodium than conventional store-bought jerky.

Nutrition

1 ounce made with dark meat and without salt or tamari:

119 calories
11 g protein
7 g carbohydrate
   (1/2 gram fiber)
5 g fat
9 mg calcium
81 mg sodium
   (196 with salt)

1 ounce made with light meat and without salt or tamari:

112 calories
16 g protein
7 g carbohydrate
   (1/2 gram fiber)
2 g fat
9 mg calcium
81 mg sodium
   (196 with salt)

1. Add raisins and hot water to a food processor or Vita-Mix. Soak for at least 30 minutes. Process until pulverized, adding additional water 1 tablespoon at a time only as needed to blend. Mixture may be coarse. Don't make it too wet.

2. Break meat apart in a shallow 1-quart bowl. Add raisin purée and seasonings and mix well with clean, bare hands to evenly distribute seasoning. Form into tablespoon-size balls, then flatten to 1/4- to 3/8-inch thick, or use a jerky press or jerky gun to yield uniform strips, tubes, or discs.

3. **Oven drying:** Preheat oven to 140° F. Line 2 to 4 cookie sheets or roasting pans with aluminum foil folded up at the corners to catch drips and top with a roasting rack. Arrange meat without overlapping. Hold oven door ajar with a wooden spoon. Dry for 12 to 18 hours or until a test piece is slightly brittle when bent. Turn meat over after the first 6 to 8 hours. For crispier jerky, dry until a test piece splinters when bent.

   Food dehydrator: Arrange meat without overlapping on as many trays as needed. Dry at 145° F for 12 to 18 hours.

FYI: When grinding the raisins, add as little water as possible. Allow a longer drying time than for jerky made without raisin purée because the ground meat will be very moist. I usually start the meat drying after dinner or before going to bed.

~ Directions continued & Variations next page ~

Directions

4. Pat off beads of oil with unbleached paper towel. Cool and store in sealed jars, cellulose or wax paper bags, or heavy zip-locking freezer bags. Label and date. This will keep for at least 1 to 2 months at room temperature, 3 or more months in the refrigerator, and indefinitely in the freezer.

Variations

* Replace herbs, cumin, mustard, pepper, and dried onion with 1 tablespoon Italian blend, Herbes de Provençe, Fines Herbes, Turkish seasoning, Quatre Epices, Cajun blend, **or** our Moroccan Barbecue Spice Mix (Page 399).

* **Ground Turkey Jerky with Sausage Seasonings:** Omit dried herbs, pepper, garlic, and onion flakes. Add 1 teaspoon dry mustard, 1/2 teaspoon ground turmeric, 1/2 teaspoon ground cumin, 1/2 teaspoon ground chipotlé, and 4 teaspoons natural liquid hickory smoke seasoning (such as Wright's).

* **Ground Turkey Jerky with Cumin, Garlic, and Pepper:** Substitute 1 teaspoon ground cumin and 1 teaspoon dried, rubbed sage or thyme; add 2 cloves of minced garlic **or** 1 teaspoon garlic powder, and 1/2 teaspoon ground black pepper for herbs and spices.

* Substitute dried, pitted prunes (check to remove all pits before puréeing even if the package says pitted), sulfite-free, unsweetened or fruit-sweetened dried apricots, cranberries, blueberries, sweet cherries, or dry-pack sun-dried tomato halves paired with Italian herbs, Herbs de Provençe, or your favorite savory blend for raisins. You may need to add more hot water to rehydrate and purée dried tomatoes.

* **Ground Turkey Jerky with 5-Spice:** Use dried apricots with pitted prunes and ground turkey. Replace the herbs, cumin, mustard, garlic, and pepper with 2 to 3 teaspoons Chinese 5-spice powder.

* **Ground Beef/Bison Jerky:** Replace ground turkey with lean or extra lean (90 to 96 percent lean) ground beef **or** bison.

* **Ground Chicken Jerky:** Replace ground turkey with ground chicken.

Ground Turkey Jerky with Raisins ~ continued

Ground Beef, Bison, or Venison Jerky with Italian Herbs

Prep: 30 minutes ~ **Drying:** 10 to 14 hours ~ **Yield:** About 10 ounces; 2 pints
---

Ingredients & Directions

2 pounds extra-lean (96 percent lean) or lean (92 percent) ground meat:
> beef (ground round, sirloin, or grass fed beef),
> bison, bear, or venison

1 teaspoon each of dried, crumbled basil and oregano

1 teaspoon lemon pepper **or** 1/2 teaspoon ground black pepper

3 garlic cloves, minced or pressed **or** 1 teaspoon garlic powder

2 tablespoons dried onion flakes, optional

1 teaspoon finely ground unrefined sea salt
or 2 tablespoons tamari soy sauce, optional

Nutrition

1 ounce made without salt or tamari:

115 calories
19 g protein
1/2 g carbs
3 g fat
8 mg calcium
40 mg sodium
(224 with salt)

1. Break meat apart in a shallow 1-quart bowl. Add remaining ingredients. Mix well with clean, bare hands to evenly distribute spices. Form into tablespoon-size balls, and flatten to 1/4-to 3/8-inch thick, or use a jerky press or jerky gun to yield uniform strips, tubes, or discs.

2. **Oven drying:** Preheat oven to 140° F. Line 2 to 4 cookie sheets or roasting pans with aluminum foil folded up at the corners to catch drips and top with a roasting rack. Arrange meat without overlapping. Hold oven door ajar with a wooden spoon. Dry for 10 to 14 hours or until a test piece is slightly brittle when bent. Turn the meat after the first 6 to 8 hours. For crispier jerky, dry until a test piece splinters when bent.

   Food dehydrator: Arrange meat without overlapping on as many trays as needed. Dry at 145° F for 10 to 14 hours.

3. Pat off beads of oil with unbleached paper towel. Cool and store in sealed jars, cellulose or wax paper bags, or heavy zip-locking freezer bags. Label and date. This will keep for at least 1 to 2 months at room temperature, 3 or more months in the refrigerator, and indefinitely in the freezer.

Variations

* **Ground Beef Jerky with Cumin, Garlic, and Pepper:** Substitute 1 1/2 teaspoons ground cumin and 1 teaspoon dried, rubbed sage or thyme for basil and oregano. Include 2 or 3 cloves of minced garlic **or** 1 teaspoon garlic powder, and 1/2 teaspoon ground black pepper.

* **Ground Beef Jerky with Sausage Seasonings:** Omit oregano and pepper. Add 1 teaspoon dry mustard, 1/2 teaspoon ground turmeric, 1/2 to 3/4 teaspoon ground chipotlé, and 4 teaspoons natural liquid hickory smoke seasoning (such as Wright's).

* **For a crisp, cracker-like texture:** Whip 4 teaspoons dried powdered egg whites in 1/4 cup water until smooth and frothy. Mix into ground meat with spices.

Ground beef jerky is economical and easy to make. The meat shrinks a lot, so I usually make a double or triple batch to stock the refrigerator and freezer. For the best texture and keeping quality, add 1 cup of puréed raisins, prunes, or puréed dried tomatoes to the meat, as noted in the ground turkey recipe (Page 484).

FYI: Fatty meat is a no-no; it's messy and the fat oxidizes during drying, leading to rapid spoilage. Freeze wild game meats at 0° F for at least 30 days before drying to kill potential parasites.

Basic Beef, Bison & Venison Jerky Strips

Prep: 30 minutes ~ **Drying:** 10 to 14 hours ~ **Yield:** 8 ounces; 1 quart

Ingredients & Directions

2 pounds boneless beef, bison **or** venison steak or roast, trimmed of visible fat:
> eye of round, strip steak, round tip, tenderloin, sirloin, flank, or sandwich steak

2 teaspoons lemon pepper **or** 1/2 teaspoon ground chipotlé

1/2 to 1 tablespoon garlic powder

1 tablespoon dried thyme, sage, **or** finely ground rosemary, optional

1 teaspoon finely ground unrefined sea salt
or 2 tablespoons tamari soy sauce, optional

Nutrition

1 ounce made without salt or tamari:
123 calories
23 g protein
1 g carbohydrate
3 g fat
3 mg calcium
51 mg sodium
(280 with salt)

The flavor and nutritional value of homemade jerky surpasses anything sold in stores. Invest in a food dehydrator if you plan to make jerky regularly. It's more efficient than the oven and allows you to dry more meat at once.

1. Meat is easiest to slice when partially frozen. Using a sharp knife cut meat across the grain into 1/4- to 3/8-inch thick slices. (Cut a boneless roast into 1/2- to 1-inch wide pieces.) Thinner slices yield crunchier jerky; thicker slices produce chewier jerky.

2. Arrange meat in a single layer on pie plates, platters, or an oblong glass pan. Mix seasonings, sprinkle over meat, and toss and press to coat. If time permits cover meat with parchment paper or another pie plate and refrigerate for 4 to 8 hours to allow flavors to penetrate.

3. **Oven drying**: Preheat oven to 140° F. Line 2 to 4 cookie sheets or roasting pans with aluminum foil folded up at the corners to catch drips and top with a roasting rack. Arrange meat without overlapping. Hold oven door ajar with a wooden spoon. Dry for 10 to 14 hours or until a test piece is slightly brittle when bent. Turn meat after the first 6 to 8 hours. For crispier jerky, dry until a test piece splinters when bent.

   Food dehydrator: Arrange meat without overlapping on as many trays as needed. Dry at 145° F for 10 to 14 hours.

4. Pat off beads of oil with unbleached paper towel. Cool and store in sealed jars, cellulose or wax paper bags, or heavy zip-locking freezer bags. Label and date. This will keep for at least 1 to 2 months at room temperature, 3 or more months in the refrigerator, and indefinitely in the freezer.

Variations

* **Jerky with Juniper Berries:** Substitute 1 tablespoon juniper berries powdered in a spice-dedicated coffee grinder. Add 1 to 2 teaspoons garlic powder, and 1/2 teaspoon ground black pepper **or** 1 teaspoon lemon pepper. Add sea salt or tamari for best results.

Notes: To save time, ask your butcher to cut steaks or boneless round or loin roasts into paper-thin slices.

Freeze venison or other wild game meats at 0° F for at least 30 days before drying to kill any parasites that may be present.

Make a double or triple batch if space and time permit.

Moroccan-Spiced Jerky

Prep: 30 minutes ~ **Drying:** 10 to 14 hours ~ **Yield:** 8 ounces; 1 quart

Ingredients & Directions

2 pounds boneless beef, bison **or** venison steak or boneless roast, trimmed of visible fat:
  eye of round, strip steak, round tip, tenderloin, sirloin, flank, or sandwich steak

1/4 cup Moroccan Barbecue Spice Mix (Page 399)

1 teaspoon finely ground unrefined sea salt **or** 2 tablespoons tamari soy sauce, optional

2 tablespoons honey as a natural preservative, optional

1. Meat is easiest to slice when partially frozen. Using a sharp knife cut meat across the grain into 1/4- to 3/8-inch thick slices. (Cut a boneless roast into 1/2- to 1-inch wide pieces.) Thinner slices yield crunchier jerky; thicker slices produce chewier jerky.

2. Arrange meat in a single layer on pie plates, platters, or an oblong glass pan. Mix seasonings, sprinkle over meat, and toss and press to coat. If time permits cover meat with parchment paper or another pie plate and refrigerate for 4 to 8 hours to allow flavors to penetrate.

3. **Oven drying:** Preheat oven to 140° F. Line 2 to 4 cookie sheets or roasting pans with aluminum foil folded up at the corners to catch drips and top with a roasting rack. Arrange meat without overlapping. Hold oven door ajar with a wooden spoon. Dry for 10 to 14 hours or until a test piece is slightly brittle when bent. Turn meat after the first 6 to 8 hours. For crispier jerky, dry until a test piece splinters when bent.

   Food dehydrator: Arrange meat without overlapping on as many trays as needed. Dry at 145° F for 10 to 14 hours.

4. Pat off beads of oil with unbleached paper towel. Cool and store in sealed jars, cellulose or wax paper bags, or heavy zip-locking freezer bags. Label and date. This will keep for at least 1 to 2 months at room temperature, 3 or more months in the refrigerator, and indefinitely in the freezer.

Variations

* **Chili-Flavored Jerky:** Replace Moroccan Spice Blend with 1 1/2 to 2 tablespoons chili powder, 2 teaspoons garlic powder or granules, and 1 teaspoon ground cumin.

* For additional varieties, replace Moroccan Spice Mix with 2 to 3 tablespoons Fines Herbes, Herbes de Provence, Italian, Mediterranean, salt-free Cajun blend, or Jamaican Jerk seasoning.

Nutrition

1 ounce made without salt, tamari, or honey:

137 calories
23 g protein
3 g carbohydrate
3 g fat
34 mg calcium
53 mg sodium
  (280 with salt)

You can't buy Moroccan Barbecue Spice Mix in stores, but you can buy the ingredients for it: whole coriander, fennel, cumin, cardamom seeds, and cloves. It only takes 10 or 15 minutes to assemble. This is one of many ways I use it to add interest to meat, fish, poultry, and vegetables.

Notes: To save time, ask your butcher to cut steaks or boneless round or loin roasts into paper-thin slices for jerky. Freeze venison or other wild game meats at 0° F for at least 30 days before drying to kill any parasites that may be present.

Pemmican

According to *Neanderthin* author Ray Audette, pemmican was manufactured for 200 years by the Hudson Bay Company from buffalo hunted on the Northern Plains. Natives of North America relied heavily on this a high-energy food made from dried, powdered meat and rendered buffalo fat, often with the addition of dried berries, herbs or spice. The appeal was portability and a long shelf life without refrigeration, ideal attributes for travel food. Although some natural foods stores sell a granola bar under the "pemmican" name, don't be misled, the real McCoy is a purely carnivorous creation.

Although the combination of ingredients may sound strange or unappealing at first, many people—Don and myself included—enjoyed it from the first bite. Many of our friends and their kids took to it immediately. Pemmican was one of the first solid foods eaten and enjoyed by Ray Audette's son, and favored by Grayson Haak's classmates when he and his dad brought enough of this mud colored "cupcake" to school for his peers to try.

Pemmican makes a great snack or meal for the urban hunter-gatherer with high-calorie needs. Wrapped in multiple lettuce leaves and paired with a fresh apple or grapes, it makes a great meal on a plane or train, or when your time is limited but your hunger is not.

If you want to try it, you can't go out and buy it. You'll have to take a chance and make it at home. It takes some time (Page 490), but once made it will last for a long time, particularly in the refrigerator or freezer.

Lard, Beef Suet, and Tallow

An important ingredient for making pemmican is tallow, which is made from rendered suet (pronounced "soo-it"), the storage fat from the area around the kidneys of large animals, such as cattle, deer, elk, caribou, or buffalo. Suet is whitish in color, tasteless, solid in the refrigerator and at room temperature. The composition of tallow and suet are considerably different from the external fat found in or around muscle meat. Whereas pan drippings from muscle meat are rich in polyunsaturated fatty acids and spoil easily when exposed to light, heat or oxygen, suet and tallow contain fewer polyunsatures and more saturated fats, and have a longer shelf life.

For cooking or making pemmican, suet must be rendered (clarified) to make tallow. Rendering removes the solids, leaving a clear liquid that hardens as it cools and has excellent keeping qualities. Be aware, suet from lamb and mutton has a much stronger fragrance and flavor that many people find overwhelming. Beef and bison tallow are more mild and versatile.

Ask your butcher for beef suet or special order it from the person who supplies you with pasture-raised beef or from a natural foods market in your area. Suet should come from animals raised without hormones and antibiotics. Suet from pasture-raised or grass-fed animals will be even more nutritious.

Rendering Fats

Rendering fat (Page 490) consists of melting it over a low heat to cook off the moisture and remove all connective tissue and impurities to improve the keeping quality of the fat. It's not as unpleasant as it sounds at first. Since the process requires very little attention, you can start it when you're in the kitchen, then go on to other tasks, periodically checking to see how it's doing. If you render more suet than you need for making a batch of pemmican, save the extra tallow for your next batch or use it for frying or scrambling eggs, cooking omelets, or other foods. Pan drippings left from cooking rich cuts of beef, pork, bacon, lamb, or other meat are not interchangeable with or as stable as suet or tallow.

Fat left from cooking grass-fed meat or wild game may be saved and used for sautéing, browning, or braising vegetables or lean meats if you clarify it to remove impurities and improve the keeping quality. Collect the fat in the refrigerator for a week. Place it in a pan and warm over low heat until liquid. When hot, pour through cheesecloth and strain out and discard any solids or impurities. Pour into a jar. Cool, cover, and refrigerate.

Coconut and olive oil are poor substitutes for tallow. They melt too easily at room temperature, turning pemmican cakes to mush.

Basic Procedure for Making Pemmican

Prep: 30 to 60 minutes ~ **Yield:** 12 muffin-sized cakes; 12 servings

Ingredients & Directions

1 pound suet (storage fat), yields about 1 1/2 cups liquid tallow

1 pound dried meat from about 6 pounds raw lean meat or about 4 1/2 cups powdered (Page 487)

1. **Rendering suet to make tallow:** Cut tallow into small pieces. Place in a 10-inch cast iron or stainless steel skillet and melt over very low heat until moisture evaporates. It should bubble slowly but not sizzle like frying fat. Do not allow mixture to smoke. Allow pan to cool and repeat. Alternatively, place tallow pieces in a cast iron or ovenproof skillet in a preheated 250° F oven for approximately 2 hours.

2. **Straining tallow:** Place a fine metal strainer over a heat-proof bowl. Pour liquid fat through the strainer, pressing the solids with the back of a large spoon. Discard solids (rinds). What's left is tallow.

3. **Grinding the meat:** Powder dried meat in a blender, food processor, or Vita-Mix in several small batches, about 1 large handful or cup at a time. Pour into a medium-size bowl or jar for longer storage.

4. **Assembling pemmican:** Gently warm and melt tallow if solid. Allow to cool until lukewarm. Pour warm (but not hot) tallow over pulverized meat a little at a time, stirring with a wooden spoon. Add only enough to moisten and create a thick, paste-like consistency.

5. If desired stir in finely ground sea salt, dried herbs, spices, dried berries, or some combination. While mixture is warm, scoop and pack into 12 muffin tins. Cool at room temperature or in the refrigerator. Cakes will harden as they cool.

6. Store pemmican in cellulose or wax paper bags, liners saved from boxes of herb tea, stainless steel food tins, or stack in quart mason jar. Store in the coldest part of the house, or in the refrigerator. Freeze what you don't think you will consume within a month. Use pemmican and tallow within 1 year for best results.

~ Variations next page ~

Nutrition

1 pemmican cake:
481 calories
46 g protein
0 carbohydrate
33 g fat
100 mg sodium.

Pemmican is the paleolithic equivalent of a protein bar. It makes a convenient and portable calorie-dense snack or meal, as is or wrapped in lettuce leaves, and eaten with a piece of fresh fruit or a cup of juice. It keeps for extended periods without refrigeration. You can make extra batches to freeze.

Note: Do not add piping hot tallow to ground meat in step 4 or your pemmican will be gritty and almost inedible. The tallow should be cool enough to touch without burning your fingers.

For convenience, render a double or triple batch of tallow, pour it into muffin tins, and refrigerate or freeze in airtight containers for extended storage. You can dry and grind extra meat in advance, and assemble pemmican at a later date. Suet comes from fat located around the kidneys of a steer or other animal; it's higher in stearic acid—and therefore less susceptible to becoming rancid—than the fat found in and around muscle meat. Contrary to popular belief, neither suet nor tallow is 100 percent saturated. Half the fat in these products is oleic acid, the same fatty acid found in olive oil.

Variations

Basic Procedure for Making Pemmican ~ continued

* **Salt-Seasoned Pemmican:** Add 1 teaspoon finely ground unrefined sea salt to powdered meat before adding the liquid fat (tallow).

* **Pemmican with Berries:** Add 3/4 to 1 cup of unsweetened or fruit-sweetened dried blueberries, wild cherries, currants, choke cherries, raisins, or other dried fruit free of added sugars, hydrogenated oils, sulfites, and other preservatives to the warm mixture before packing into muffin tins.

* **Herbed Pemmican:** In step 4, add 2 to 3 teaspoons of dried, crumbled herbs (basil, oregano, thyme, marjoram, or combination, or powdered Herbs de Provençe or Italian herb blend) and 1/2 teaspoon ground black pepper and 1 to 2 teaspoons dried, powdered garlic (**not** garlic salt!) if desired. Prepare with or without 1 teaspoon unrefined sea salt.

* **Pemmican with Pepper & Garlic:** In step 4, add 2 teaspoons ground black pepper and 2 teaspoons garlic powder to the meat mixture. Prepare with or without 1 teaspoon unrefined sea salt.

* **Pemmican with Vegetables:** In step 4, add 2 tablespoons onion powder and 1/2 cup minced, sun-dried tomato bits. If desired also add 1 tablespoon dried, crumbled herbs or a blend, such as Italian herbs or Herbs de Provençe. Add 1 teaspoon finely ground unrefined sea salt **or** 2 tablespoons tamari soy sauce if desired.

* **Pizza-Flavored Pemmican:** In step 4, add 2 teaspoons each dried, crumbled basil, oregano, thyme, garlic powder, and onion powder, 1/2 teaspoon ground black pepper **or** ground chipotlé, and 1 teaspoon finely ground unrefined sea salt **or** 2 tablespoons tamari soy sauce. If desired, add 1 tablespoon dried parsley and/or 1/2 cup minced sun-dried tomato halves. Add slightly more tallow to moisten as needed.

* **Smoky Pemmican:** In step 4, add 1 tablespoon dry mustard powder, 1/2 teaspoon ground chipotlé, 1 tablespoon liquid hickory smoke seasoning (Wright's brand is the purest), and 1 teaspoon finely ground unrefined sea salt **or** 2 tablespoon tamari.

* **Judy's Pemmican:** Combine 3 cups of dried powdered beef or venison with 1 cup of dried, powdered liver and/or heart. (Slice organ meats into thin pieces and dry as per jerky instructions, Page 487, or buy desiccated liver powder from a natural foods store.) Add 3/4 cup dried, unsweetened or fruit-sweetened cherries, blueberries, Marionberries, or raisins. Season with 1 teaspoon each dried onion powder, ground black pepper, and finely ground unrefined sea salt, 1 tablespoon kelp powder (**not** kelp granules) **or** 1/4 cup toasted, crumbled dulse. Add 1 1/2 cups liquid tallow, or as needed to moisten.

26 Better Beverages

BEST BITES

A Healthful Alternative to Coffee

If you're cutting back on coffee or simply searching for a robust alternative to black, green, or herbal teas, roasted chicory and dandelion roots may make the brew for you.

Roasted chicory roots make a wonderful caffeine-free coffee extender or substitute. In the Deep South, roasted chicory root has been blended with coffee for decades to make French Market Coffee. Chicory root contains lactucin and lactucopicrin, which have a mildly sedating effect.

Roasted dandelion root also makes an excellent coffee substitute.

Use of chicory and dandelion roots dates back to the time of the Egyptian pharaohs. They have been employed to detoxify the liver and to remedy acne, age spots, anemia, arthritis, asthma, diabetes, jaundice, spleen problems, gout, gallstones, hepatitis, hypoglycemia, high blood pressure, loss of appetite (in the underweight person), liver disorders, rheumatism, eczema, elevated cholesterol, and constipation.

Bitter flavors stimulate peristalsis and elimination. These roots contain substances that increase the flow of bile, necessary for proper liver function and metabolism of fat and cholesterol. Herbalists have used chicory and dandelion root to reduce symptoms of PMS. By improving liver function these herbs help the body maintain hormonal balance.

To reduce your intake of coffee, make a 50:50 mix of ground coffee (use shade-grown organic coffee if possible) with roasted chicory and/or dandelion root. Gradually decrease the amount of coffee and increase the amount of chicory and/or dandelion root as desired. Or just jump in and enjoy the roasted root brew itself.

Roasted Chicory & Dandelion Root "Coffee"

Prep: 5 minutes ~ **Cooking:** 15 minutes ~ **Yield:** 6 cups

Ingredients & Directions

6 cups filtered water

4 tablespoons roasted chicory root pieces or grinds **or** roasted dandelion root pieces or grinds, **or** combination of the 2

1 teaspoon licorice root powder **or** licorice root grinds, optional

Nutrition

1 cup:
negligible calories, protein, carbohydrate, fat

1. **In a saucepan:** Boil water in a 3-quart glass, ceramic, or stainless steel pot. Add roasted chicory and/or dandelion root pieces or grinds and optional licorice root. If using larger pieces of roasted chicory or dandelion root, simmer 5 more minutes. Cover, reduce heat, and simmer for 15 minutes. If too strong, add more water. Strain before serving or refrigerating.

   In a percolator: Add roasted chicory and/or dandelion root to metal basket of stainless steel stovetop percolator (lined with an unbleached paper liner) with optional licorice root, reduce heat and percolate for 15 minutes. If using an electric percolator, follow manufacturer's suggestions.

   In a drip coffee maker: Line the basket with a dioxin-free coffee filter. Add finely ground roasted chicory and/or dandelion root, water, and optional licorice root, and follow manufacturer's instructions.

2. Serve hot, black, or with nut milk or coconut milk. Sweeten as desired. Reheat or pour into 1 or more thermos bottles and seal to keep warm for several hours. Refrigerate leftover "coffee" in a glass jar. Reheat gently in a saucepan and use within 5 days.

Roasted and brewed, chicory and dandelion roots have a robust coffee-like flavor and fragrance. Unlike coffee, they're caffeine-free. And you can make a pot, refrigerate the leftovers, and reheat as needed. Dilute a strong brew with water or coconut milk, or use it to make a Mocha Frosty, or Dairy-Free Mocha Pots de Creme. For an alternative to milk or cream, try unsweetened coconut milk or homemade almond, cashew, or macadamia nut milk.

For a sweet taste, add dried, minced licorice root or licorice root powder to the pot, or sweeten individual cups of this beverage with a tiny pinch of stevia extract powder, a few drops of stevia extract liquid, a dash of kiwi concentrate, or a teaspoon of honey or agavé nectar before serving.

Note: If you can't find roasted chicory and dandelion root pieces or grinds in health foods stores in your area, refer to Sources in Appendix.

Cardamom-Spiced Chicory & Dandelion Root "Coffee"

Prep: 5 minutes ~ **Cooking:** 10 minutes ~ **Yield:** 8 servings

Ingredients & Directions

1 cup unsweetened coconut milk, blended well

7 cups filtered water

12 small cardamom pods, coarsely ground in mortar or spice mill

3 tablespoons roasted chicory root grind plus
3 tablespoons roasted dandelion root grinds
or 3 dandelion and 3 chicory root tea bags

1 teaspoon nonalcoholic vanilla or almond extract, optional

15 to 20 drops stevia extract liquid
or 1/4 to 1/3 teaspoon stevia extract powder **or** 1/4 cup honey or agavé nectar

Nutrition

1 cup:
63 calories
2 g carbohydrate
6 g fat
1 mg calcium
7 mg sodium

A delicious, caffeine-free twist on a classic Arabic drink, this brew is easy to assemble and reheats well. In place of milk, I use Thai Kitchen coconut milk or nut milk. Instead of sugar, I use stevia, raw honey or agavé nectar. This brew won't make you jittery or cause any of the problems associated with coffee. Look for roasted chicory and dandelion root pieces or grinds in the bulk herb-spice section of your local natural foods store or order them by mail.

1. Combine water, crushed cardamom, and roasted root coffee/grinds or tea bags in a 3- to 4-quart saucepan. Cover, bring to boil, reduce heat, and simmer 5 to 10 minutes. Do not boil

2. Remove from heat. Steep for 10 to 15 minutes. Add optional vanilla or almond extract.

3. Ladle "coffee" through a fine-mesh strainer into a teapot or second saucepan. Discard solids. Add coconut or nut milk. Heat gently, remove from heat, whisk in stevia or honey, a little at a time, taste, and adjust as needed. Serve immediately or transfer to a thermos.

4. Refrigerate leftovers in a glass jar. Reheat gently on top of the stove and use with 3 days.

Variations

*   Use only roasted dandelion root grinds, or only roasted chicory root grinds.

*   **Roasted Chicory & Dandelion Chai:** Add 3 cinnamon sticks, 1/8 teaspoon ground allspice and 1/8 teaspoon ground nutmeg to saucepan before heating. If desired add a few cracked peppercorns, and 1 teaspoon minced fresh gingerroot for a spicier taste.

Note: If opening a new can of coconut milk, shake thoroughly. If mixture is uneven or thick on top and watery on bottom, transfer contents to a blender, process until smooth, and pour into an impeccably clean jar. Cover and refrigerate what you don't plan to use immediately.

Nut Milk

Prep: 3 minutes ~ **Cooking:** 0 ~ **Yield:** 4 cups

Ingredients & Directions

1 cup raw shelled almonds **or** cashews

4 cups boiling hot filtered water, divided

1/4 teaspoon stevia extract powder or liquid
or 2 tablespoons honey or agavé nectar, optional

1. **In a Vita-Mix:** Add nuts and 2 cups of hot water to a Vita-Mix container. Secure 2-part lid. Select VARIABLE speed number 1. Cover the top with a towel, and turn machine on. Quickly increase speed to number 10. Turn to HIGH for 2 minutes. Add additional 2 cups hot water, turn to LOW and repeat.

   In a blender: Combine nuts and 2 cups hot water in blender. Cover top with a towel, turn on machine, and pulse or grind for 2 minutes, add remaining water, and blend until smooth and frothy.

2. Line a fine-mesh sieve with cheesecloth and place it over a large bowl. Pour nut milk into sieve and press mixture with a spoon. Lift up sides of cloth, twist ends, and squeeze to extract more liquid.

3. Add sweetener if desired and refrigerate in glass jar(s). Use within 5 days or freeze. Leftover pulp may be used as a body scrub in the bath.

Variations

* **For creamier almond milk:** Blanch almonds. Drop almonds into a pot of boiling water. Cover, remove from heat, and allow to cool. Drain and discard water. Slip skins off almonds with your thumb and index finger before blending.

* **For creamier cashew milk:** Soak cashews in filtered water for 6 to 8 hours before blending (soak in the refrigerator in hot weather). If too thick, add additional water.

* **Macadamia Nut Milk:** Replace cashews with macadamia nuts. Strain if desired.

Nutrition

1 cup unstrained almond milk:

209 calories
8 g protein
3 g carbohydrate
18 g fat
92 mg calcium

1 cup unstrained cashew milk:

161 calories
5 g protein
5 g carbohydrate
13 g fat
16 mg calcium

Commercial nut milks are diluted to reduce the fat content and sweetened with sugar.

If you want the real McCoy, you'll have to make it yourself. It's easy to do in a blender, food processor, or Vita-Mix. We don't serve nut milk as a beverage (it's far more calorie dense than cow's milk), instead, we use it in cooking to replace milk or cream in soups, sauces, and special occasion desserts. If you want to serve it as drink, you'll need to dilute it.

Don's Coconut Drink

Prep: 5 to 10 minutes ~ **Cooking:** 0 ~ **Yield:** 1 quart

Ingredients & Directions

1/2 cup unsweetened, sulfite-free coconut milk, premium, not lite

3 1/2 to 3 3/4 cups filtered water

1 1/4 (1-ounce) scoops vanilla egg white protein

2 tablespoons honey **or** agavé nectar, less if using sweetened egg white protein

4 cups hot filtered water, divided

1. If you're opening a new can of coconut milk, shake well, remove the lid completely, and whisk or stir thoroughly. If the mixture is stiff, uneven, or coarse, purée the entire contents of the can in a blender or food processor, then pour into a clean jar. Refrigerate whatever you do not use immediately, or freeze in ice cube trays.

2. Purée the measured amount of coconut milk, water, egg white protein, and honey into a blender or food processor until smooth. Pour into 1 or more jars, cover, and refrigerate. Use within 6 days or freeze in 8-ounce containers with headspace.

Variations

* Replace vanilla egg white protein with dried, powdered egg white. Add 1 teaspoon nonalcoholic vanilla or almond extract.

* Replace half the honey with 1/16 to 1/8 teaspoon stevia extract powder **or** 4 to 6 drops stevia extract liquid. Taste and adjust with a dash more stevia as needed.

Nutrition

1 cup:
127 calories
8 g protein
3 g carbohydrate
6 g fat
88 mg sodium

Coconut milk makes a great substitute for half-and-half and cream, but at 40 grams of fat per cup, premium (full-fat) coconut milk is too rich to drink straight. Lite coconut milk is still rich at 16 grams of fat a cup. However, if you dilute full-fat coconut milk with water, add vanilla egg white protein, and honey or agavé nectar, you end up with a composition similar to cow's milk, ideal as a beverage for athletes and other active people who need more calories between meals.

FYI: To use coconut milk to replace milk in cooking or baking, you can dilute coconut milk with water, stock, or fruit juice, depending upon the recipe, or add a smaller amount of undiluted coconut milk to a recipe.

Note: Look for a brand of coconut milk that's free of preservatives, additives, sugar, sulfites, and sodium benzoate. The best tasting and purest brand I've found is Thai Kitchen.

Basic Herb Tea

Prep: under 5 minutes ~ **Steep:** 10 to 20 minutes ~ **Yield:** 4 to 6 servings

Ingredients & Directions

4 cups filtered water

1/8 to 1/2 cup loose dried herbs, leaves, roots, flowers, spices, and/or fruits; single item or blend of several ingredients (1 to 3 teaspoons per cup water):
chamomile, rosehip, alfalfa, red clover, peppermint, spearmint, lemon verbena, other herb, or herbal tea blend (including dried orange or lemon peel, roots, barks, spices, etc.)

1. Bring water to boil. Place tea in a strainer insert, tea ball, or directly in a non-metallic teapot. Pour boiling water over tea. Cover and allow to steep for 10 to 20 minutes.

2. Remove insert or strain out herbs/leaves; compost if possible. Serve tea at once, pour into a thermos or thermal carafe that has not been used for coffee, or chill for later.

3. Refrigerate leftover tea to serve cold and use within 4 to 5 days.

Nutrition

1 cup serving: negligible calories, protein, carbohydrate, calcium

Variations

* **Use tea bags:** Boil water, add 1 tea bag per 1 1/2 to 2 cups hot water. Steep 5 to 10 minutes, then squeeze tea bag against the cup with a spoon and remove.

* **Peppermint Tea:** Use this drink to sooth an upset stomach, bloodshot eyes, a fever, a dry, sore throat, or a cold with several of these symptoms.

* **Peppermint-Ginger Tea:** Prepare peppermint tea adding 1/2 teaspoon finely grated gingerroot. Great for indigestion or a cold.

* **Spearmint-Ginger Tea:** Prepare as for Peppermint & Ginger Tea.

* **For a sweet taste:** Add 1 licorice root tea bag to other herb tea, or sweeten each cup of tea with 2 to 5 drops stevia extract liquid or a toothpick-size pinch of stevia extract powder or licorice root powder.

* **Sun Tea:** Add herbs to a jar with cold water. Cover and place in the sun for 4 to 6 hours, until tea is dark. Strain, sweeten if desired, and chill before serving.

A wide assortment of herb teas can be found in conventional and natural foods markets and teashops. Try a single herb—such as rosehips, peppermint, spearmint, chamomile, lemon verbena–or a blend of several ingredients. Brewed loose herbs provide the best flavor; tea bags offer convenience. Read labels carefully to avoid products that contain caffeine, artificial flavorings or colorings, and sweeteners other than licorice or stevia.

Note: Brewing time will vary with the type and form of tea and your personal preference. For 1 cup of tea, figure about 1 teaspoon of processed finely ground herbs and up to 1 tablespoon of coarse herbs.

Ethiopian Tea

Prep: 3 minutes ~ **Steep:** 10 to 15 minutes ~ **Yield:** 4 to 6 servings

Ingredients & Directions

4 cups filtered (but not distilled) water

3 to 4 teaspoons loose Ethiopian Tea blend

1. Bring water to boil. Place tea in a strainer insert, tea ball, or directly in a non-metallic teapot. Pour boiling water over tea, cover, and allow to steep for 10 to 15 minutes.

2. Remove insert or strain out herbs/leaves and compost if possible. Serve tea at once or pour into a thermos or thermal carafe that has not been used for coffee, or chill the tea for later. No sweetener is required for this blend.

3. Refrigerate leftover tea and use within 4 to 5 days.

Nutrition

1 cup serving: negligible calories, protein, carbohydrate, calcium

This delightfully sweet and spicy tea, made for the Emperor of Ethiopia, contains no sugar, caffeine, or artificial flavorings. The exquisite flavor comes from orange and lemon peels, cloves, chamomile, rosehips, wood betony, and cinnamon.

FYI: A 2-ounce jar of Ethiopian tea makes up to 25 cups of tea. If you're in Ann Arbor or Ferndale, Michigan, you can buy it at the Blue Nile Restaurant. Otherwise, you can order it by phone, mail, or Internet from Rafal Spice Company (refer to Source section in Appendix D).

Cinnamon-Spiced Tea

Prep: 3 minutes ~ **Cooking:** 15 minutes ~ **Yield:** 6 servings

Ingredients & Directions

1 1/2 teaspoons dried licorice root (bits) **or** 2 licorice root tea bags

2 to 3 cinnamon sticks (they look like the bark of a tree rolled into scrolls)

2 to 3 teaspoons grated fresh gingerroot

3 to 4 cardamom pods, crushed with a knife or in a mortar, optional

1/8 teaspoon ground black pepper, optional

6 cups filtered water

Nutrition

1 cup: negligible calories, protein, carbohydrate, calcium

1. For best results do not use a metal pot, which can interact with the herbs. Combine all ingredients in a Chinese clay pot, sold in Asian markets, or a glass or ceramic teapot or saucepan.

2. Cover and bring to boil. Reduce heat and simmer for 15 minutes.

3. Remove from heat. Strain and serve warm. Refrigerate leftovers. Reheat, and use within 4 days.

Variations

* **Cinnamon Tea:** Here is another variation from India. Combine 5 (2-inch long) cinnamon sticks with 6 cups water. Cover, bring to boil, reduce heat, and simmer 15 to 20 minutes until tea is a lovely shade of rust and cinnamon twigs unravel. Strain and serve warm or chilled, with or without an itsy-bitsy pinch of stevia extract powder or liquid or licorice root powder per cup of tea.

Licorice root powder, tea bags, and dried and coarsely chopped pieces can be found in the bulk herb and spice section of natural foods stores, in Asian markets, and specialty herb shops. The powder can be added to a cup of tea as a sweetener in place of stevia. The tea bags may be steeped in hot water then used to sweeten tea. The coarse bits must be simmered for at least 15 minutes to release their flavor.

Cinnamon is slightly spicy, warming, and used widely in China and India to aid digestion after meals or to take the chill off a cold day. Licorice root sweetens the pot, soothes and tonifies the digestive organs, and helps regulate blood sugar levels.

Note: Do not use more licorice than called for. Too much licorice can cause heartburn, burping, gas, or bloating.

Licorice-Ginger Tea

Prep: under 5 minutes ~ **Cooking:** 15 minutes ~ **Yield:** 8 servings

---

Ingredients & Directions

1 1/2 to 2 teaspoons dried licorice root (bits) **or** 2 licorice root tea bags **or** 1/3 teaspoon powder

8 cups filtered water

3 tablespoons finely grated fresh gingerroot, peeled if desired

1. Bring licorice and water to boil in a glass, clay, or ceramic pot. If possible, avoid using a metal or stainless steel pot, which can chemically interact with the herbs and make them less effective. Add ginger, reduce heat and simmer 5 minutes for tea bags, 10 to 15 minutes for licorice bits, until aromatic.

2. Remove from heat and steep for 10 minutes, or pour through a bamboo or fine-mesh tea strainer and serve immediately. If too spicy, dilute with additional warm water.

3. Refrigerate leftovers in a glass jar. Warm gently without boiling and use within 5 days.

Nutrition

1 cup: negligible calories, protein, carbohydrate, calcium

Licorice root sweetens this tea and soothes your throat and stomach, but beware how much you use. Too much licorice can cause heartburn, burping, gas, or bloating.

Ginger is warming, stimulates digestion and circulation, revs the metabolism, and may be helpful when you're fighting an infection or at the first sign of a cold.

Variations

* **Peppermint-Licorice Tea:** Omit ginger. Simmer licorice root for 10 to 15 minutes, then add 2 tablespoons dried peppermint leaves. Cover and remove from heat; allow to steep for 5 to 10 minutes. If using licorice root powder, simply combine it with boiling hot water and peppermint leaves, then cover and steep for 10 minutes. Do not boil.

* **Hot Ginger Tea:** Add 2 tablespoons peeled and finely grated fresh gingerroot (a microplane grater is ideal) to 4 cups hot water. Cover and steep for 10 minutes. Strain, sweeten with stevia or honey if desired, and serve.

Iced Ginger Elixir

Prep: 10 minutes ~ **Cooking**: 0 ~ **Yield:** 8 to 10 cups

Ingredients & Directions

1/4 cup peeled and thinly sliced fresh gingerroot

4 cups boiling water

4 cups cool or cold filtered water, additional 2 cups water as needed

1/4 to 1/2 teaspoon stevia extract powder **or** liquid, or to taste

Nutrition

1 cup:
4 calories
1 g carbohydrate

1. Combine ginger and 1/2 cup hot water in a blender, Vita-Mix, or food processor. Hold top down with a towel. Process on LOW and slowly increase to HIGH. Add remaining 3 1/2 cups hot water, and blend, holding top down and starting on low. Pour into a glass container and let steep uncovered for 1 to 2 hours.

2. Place a fine sieve and mesh strainer over a bowl. If possible line strainer with 2 layers of rinsed and squeezed cheesecloth. Pour tea into strainer and press with a spoon. Gather edges of cheesecloth or pick up pulp one handful at a time and squeeze to extract liquid. Discard solids.

3. Add 4 cups cool or cold water to the tea. Whisk in stevia (or honey) and taste. If too spicy, add additional water, 1 cup at a time. Adjust sweetness in tiny increments if desired.

4. Refrigerate. Serve cool or cold, with or without ice and use within 1 week.

Variations

* **Iced Ginger & Lemon Elixir:** Add 1/4 cup lemon juice per quart of tea. If you don't have lemons, substitute lime juice for a **Ginger & Lime Elixir**.

* **Iced Ginger Elixir with Honey:** Replace stevia with 1/3 cup raw honey or agavé nectar.

Good for what ails you, this soothing drink can quench your thirst on a hot day, aid digestion and help heal a host of maladies.

Look for fresh gingerroots with smooth, unblemished skin free of mold, wrinkled or soft spots. If the roots are packed in plastic don't buy them; they're usually moldy. The best and least expensive source for fresh ginger is an Asian market or a farmers' market if you live where ginger grows. Natural foods stores are a close second; supermarkets are another option.

FYI: Store fresh gingerroot at room temperature in an open bowl. It will keep for weeks. Storing ginger in the refrigerator can cause it to mold. Storing it in the freezer leads to loss of flavor and fragrance.

Low-Carb Lemonade

Prep: 10 minutes ~ **Yield:** 1 quart

Ingredients & Directions

4 cups filtered water

Juice and pulp of 2 lemons (organic if possible)

1/8 to 1/4 teaspoon stevia extract powder
or 1/4 to 1/2 teaspoon stevia extract liquid

1. Rinse lemons, press and roll on a cutting board to soften the pulp. Remove zest (colored part only) with a microplane grater or the smallest holes of a cheese grater and set aside.

2. Halve and juice lemons. If desired scrape a spoon across the flesh to remove pulp. Discard seeds.

3. Combine water, lemon juice, pulp, zest, and stevia in a tall pitcher or quart jar and whisk well. Taste and add 1/16 to 1/8 teaspoon additional stevia if a sweeter taste is desired.

4. Serve over ice, or cover and chill for later. If too lemony, dilute with additional water. Refrigerate in a non-plastic container and use within 1 week.

Variations

* **Low-Carb Limeade:** Replace lemon with 3 to 4 limes.

* **Quick Lemon & Gingerade:** Add 2 tablespoons juice from finely grated, squeezed, fresh gingerroot or bottled ginger juice. Or, replace 2 cups of water with 2 cups of Hot Ginger Tea (Page 502).

* **Low-Carb Orangeade:** Follow the basic recipe for lemonade, replacing 1 cup cold water with 1 cup fresh-squeezed orange juice and reduce stevia by one-half. Taste and adjust as needed.

* **Kiwi-Sweetened Lemonade:** Replace stevia with 1 to 2 tablespoons kiwi concentrate (trutina dulcem), such as TriMedica brand.

* **Honey Lemonade:** Omit stevia and sweeten with 2 to 4 tablespoons honey **or** agavé nectar.

Nutrition

Entire recipe (with pulp)

104 calories
2 g protein
24 g carbohydrate
(10 g fiber)
132 mg calcium
6 mg sodium

1 cup serving:

26 calories
6 g carbohydrate
(3 g fiber)
33 mg calcium
2 mg sodium

If you love—or once loved—lemonade but don't want the sugar or artificial sweeteners found in most recipes, try this. The sweetness comes from Stevia Rebaudiana, the leaf of a South American plant. The trick is to use stevia sparingly. Since it's *100 to 300 times* sweeter than sugar, depending upon the form, you don't need much. Brands may differ in flavor and concentration, so always start with less than you think you need, taste, and adjust in minuscule amounts as needed.

FYI: I prefer brands of stevia that don't contain FOS, maltodextrin, or other starches that dilute the herb and, in the case of FOS, cause gas and bloating for many people.

Red Zinger Punch

Prep: 5 minutes ~ **Yield:** 1 quart

Ingredients & Directions

2 cups boiling filtered water

2 to 4 Celestial Seasonings Red Zinger tea bags, depending on desired strength

2 cups cold filtered water

1/4 teaspoon stevia extract powder **or** 8 to 12 drops stevia extract liquid, or to taste

1. Add tea bags to a 1-quart heat-proof measuring container with a spout or a heat-proof quart Mason jar. Add boiling water. Cover loosely with a lid, plate, or saucer. Steep for 10 minutes.

2. Remove tea bags, squeeze, and discard (compost if possible). Add cold water and a small amount of stevia. Whisk, taste, and adjust with a tiny bit of additional stevia if needed. Pour tea into jars or empty juice bottles, cover and chill.

3. Serve as is or over ice. Use within 2 weeks.

Nutrition

1 cup serving: negligible calories, protein, carbohydrate, calcium

This delightful drink—great for parties, picnics, and hot summer days—looks like punch but contains no sugar or artificial sweeteners. Use a light hand with stevia, an herbal sweetener that's *100 to 300 times* sweeter than sugar, depending upon the brand and concentration.

Variations

* For a zesty taste, add the juice of 1/2 to 1 lime.

* **Raspberry Zinger Punch:** Use Raspberry Zinger tea bags.

* **Lemon Zinger Punch:** Use Lemon Zinger tea bags.

* **Blackberry Zinger Punch:** Use Blackberry Zinger tea bags.

* **Iced Ruby Burst (Red Bush) Punch:** Look for African Red Bush Tea, also called Rooibos tea. It's rich in antioxidants, like green tea, but caffeine free. *Seelect South African Ruby Burst Tea* comes in 3 delicious fruity flavors.

* Freeze fresh apple, pineapple, **or** orange juice in ice cube trays. Toss a few fruit flavored cubes into each glass of stevia-sweetened tea for a treat.

* Omit stevia. Use 2 cups of cold water and 2 cups of apple or pineapple juice in the master recipe.

Note: Look for a brand of stevia that doesn't contain FOS, maltodextrin, or other vegetable starches.

Vita-Mix Beet-Apple Blend

Prep: 10 minutes ~ **Yield:** 2 servings

Ingredients & Directions

1 large or 2 small apples (about 10 ounces), washed, cored, peeled, and quartered:
> Fuji, gala, pink lady, jonathan, jonagold, Cortland, braeburn, Melrose, golden delicious, ginger gold, red delicious, or other crisp sweet or tart-sweet apples

1 small to medium beet (about 4 ounces), trimmed, peeled, and quartered (1/2 to 3/4 cup)

4 to 5 ice cubes (1 to 1 1/4 cups)

1/8 teaspoon stevia extract powder **or** 4 to 6 drops stevia extract liquid **or** 2 teaspoons honey or agavé nectar

1/4-inch thick sliced fresh, peeled, gingerroot **or** 1/4 teaspoon ground cinnamon **or** pie spice

1 teaspoon non-alcoholic vanilla **or** almond extract, optional

Nutrition

1 serving:
84 calories
20 g carbohydrate
(4 g fiber)
13 mg calcium
27 mg sodium

This recipe produces a thick and creamy smoothie-like drink we enjoy with eggs, fish, or meat, and cooked leafy greens for breakfast, lunch, or a light dinner. Tart apples produce a drink that tastes remarkably like cranberry-apple juice.

1. Add ingredients to Vita-Mix in the order listed. Add lid and insert tamper. Start on VARIABLE SPEED number 1 and walk up to number 10, then turn to HIGH and run until smooth, about 1 minute.

2. Pour into 2 (8-ounce) glasses or coffee mugs. Drink or eat with a spoon!

Variations

* **For a more calorie dense drink:** Use 3 small or 1 1/2 to 2 large apples.

* **Beet-Orange Blend:** Replace apples with 2 peeled oranges **or** 1 cup of fresh orange juice (**or** 1/4 cup orange juice concentrate plus 3/4 cup additional ice). Taste before adding sweetener.

* **Beet, Orange & Apple Blend:** In the variation above, use 1 small to medium apple, 1/2 small beet (about 1/2 cup), and 1 peeled orange with seeds and white pith removed.

FYI: Unlike conventional juices, this contains all the goodness of whole fruits and vegetables and 2 to 8 times more vitamin C, magnesium, potassium, calcium, beta-carotene and fiber. It's lower on the glycemic index, and there's no waste.

Vita-Mix Carrot-Peach Blend

Prep: 10 minutes ~ **Yield:** 2 servings

Ingredients & Directions

2 large or 4 small peaches (about 1 pound), washed, quartered, seeds removed

1 large or 2 small carrots, washed and cut into 1-inch pieces (about 1 cup)

4 to 5 large ice cubes (1 to 1 1/4 cups)

1/8 teaspoon stevia extract powder, 4 to 6 drops stevia extract liquid **or** 2 teaspoons honey or agavé nectar

1/4-inch thick sliced fresh, peeled, gingerroot **or** 1/4 teaspoon ground cinnamon or pie spice

Nutrition

1 serving:
113 calories
3 protein
25 g carbohydrate
(5 g fiber)
20 mg calcium
12 mg sodium

1. Add ingredients to the Vita-Mix in the order listed. Add the lid and insert the tamper. Start on VARIABLE SPEED number 1 and walk up to number 10, then turn to HIGH and run until smooth, about 1 minute. Pour into 2 glasses or coffee mugs.

2. Drink or eat with a spoon!

Variations

* **Carrot-Pineapple Blend:** Replace apple with 1 cup diced pineapple.

* **Carrot-Orange Blend:** Replace apples with 2 medium oranges, peeled and seeded (valencias are ideal), **or** 1/4 cup orange juice concentrate plus 3/4 cup additional ice or water. Taste before adding any sweetener.

* **Carrot-Nectarine Blend:** Replace peaches with fresh or frozen nectarines. Apricots also work.

This is one of our favorite summer fruit blends. We serve it for breakfast or lunch with meat or eggs and a colorful salad or cooked leafy greens. It contains all the vitamins, minerals, antioxidants, and fiber that are missing from conventional juices. Besides making the drink thick, the fiber reduces the glycemic index. Best of all, a Vita-Mix is much easier to clean than a juicer.

Vita-Mix Carrot-Apple Blend

Prep: 10 minutes ~ **Yield:** 2 servings

Ingredients & Directions

1 large or 2 small apples (about 10 ounces), washed, cored, peeled, and quartered:
> Fuji, gala, pink lady, jonathan, jonagold, Cortland, braeburn, Melrose, golden delicious, ginger gold, red delicious, or other crisp sweet or tart-sweet apples

1 medium carrot, trimmed and cut into 1-inch pieces (about 1 cup)

4 to 5 large ice cubes (1 to 1 1/4 cups)

1/8 teaspoon stevia extract powder, 4 to 6 drops stevia extract liquid **or** 2 teaspoon honey or agavé nectar

1/4-inch thick slice fresh, peeled, gingerroot **or** 1/4 teaspoon ground cinnamon or pie spice

1 teaspoon nonalcoholic vanilla **or** almond extract, optional

1/4 cup filtered water, optional

Nutrition

1 serving:
68 calories
17 g carbohydrate
(4 g fiber)
10 mg calcium
4 mg sodium

This makes a delicious snack or a side dish for breakfast or lunch. Unlike conventional carrot juice, this is made from the whole carrot, so it's more nutritious and contains 45 percent more vitamins, minerals, antioxidants, phytonutrients and all the fiber present in whole fruits and vegetables. It's lower on the glycemic index than extracted juice. There's no pulp to toss and no mess to clean up.

1. Add ingredients to Vita-Mix in the order listed. Add lid and insert tamper. Start on VARIABLE SPEED number 1 and walk up to number 10, then turn to HIGH and run until smooth, about 1 minute.

2. Pour into 2 glasses or coffee mugs. Drink or eat with a spoon!

Variations

* **For a more calorie dense dish:** Use a large carrot **or** 3 small or 1 1/2 to 2 large apples.

* **Carrot, Pineapple & Apple Blend:** Use 1 small to medium carrot, 1 small to medium apple, and 1 cup diced pineapple.

Vita-Mix Apple, Banana & Orange Blend

Prep: 10 minutes or less ~ **Yield:** 2 servings

Ingredients & Directions

1 large or 2 small apples (about 10 ounces), washed, cored, peeled, and quartered:
> Fuji, gala, pink lady, jonathan, jonagold, Cortland, braeburn, Melrose, golden delicious, ginger gold, red delicious, or other crisp sweet or tart-sweet apples

1 ripe medium banana, peeled and halved

1 medium seedless orange, peeled

1/4-inch thick slice fresh, peeled, gingerroot **or** 1/4 teaspoon ground cinnamon or pie spice

1/8 teaspoon stevia extract powder **or** 4 to 6 drops stevia extract liquid

1 teaspoon nonalcoholic vanilla **or** almond extract, optional

4 to 5 large ice cubes (1 to 1 1/4 cups)

1/4 cup filtered water, optional

Nutrition

1 serving:
169 calories
1 protein
39 g carbohydrate
1 g fat
       (7 g fiber)
44 mg calcium

This drink makes a delicious breakfast side dish, dessert, or afternoon snack. If you prefer a thinner drink, use less fruit or more ice. For a rich, creamy and satisfying snack, add 1/4 cup unsweetened coconut milk.

1. Add ingredients to Vita-Mix in the order listed. Add lid and insert tamper. Start on VARIABLE SPEED number 1 and walk up to number 10, then turn to HIGH and run until smooth, about 1 minute.

2. Pour into 2 glasses or mugs. Drink or eat with a spoon. Serve immediately.

Variations

* **Apple, Banana, Orange & Pineapple Blend:** This comes from the Vita-Mix Cookbook. Combine 1/2 large or 1 small apple, 1/2 to 1 ripe banana, 1/2 of a peeled, seedless or seeded orange, and 1/2 cup pineapple.

* **Apple, Banana & Mango Blend:** Replace 1/2 orange with 1/2 cup diced mango.

* **Apple, Banana & Strawberry Blend:** Replace orange with 1 cup fresh or frozen, unsweetened strawberries.

* **Apple, Strawberry & Pineapple Blend:** Use 1 medium to large apple, 1/2 to 1 cup hulled strawberries, and 1/2 to 1 cup diced fresh pineapple with ginger, stevia, and optional vanilla.

Vita-Mix Pineapple, Peach & Pear Blend

Prep: 10 minutes or less ~ **Yield:** 2 servings

Ingredients & Directions

1 cup sliced fresh or frozen unsweetened pineapple

1 large peach **or** 1 cup sliced frozen peaches

1 large ripe (but firm) pear, halved and pitted, stem removed

4 to 5 large ice cubes (1 to 1 1/4 cups)

1/8 teaspoon stevia extract powder **or** 4 to 6 drops stevia extract liquid

1/4-inch thick sliced fresh, peeled, gingerroot **or** 1/4 teaspoon apple pie spice

1 teaspoon nonalcoholic vanilla **or** almond extract, optional

1/4 cup filtered water optional

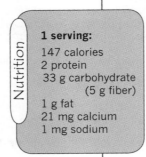

1 serving:
147 calories
2 protein
33 g carbohydrate
    (5 g fiber)
1 g fat
21 mg calcium
1 mg sodium

Nutrition

Try this vitamin-, fiber-, and antioxidant-packed fruit drink with eggs, fish, or meat and a green salad or cooked leafy greens for breakfast, lunch, or a light dinner. For a rich, creamy and satisfying snack, add 1/4 cup unsweetened coconut milk.

1. Add ingredients to Vita-Mix in the order listed. Add lid and insert tamper. Start on VARIABLE SPEED number 1 and walk up to number 10, then turn to HIGH and run until smooth, about 1 minute.

2. Pour into 2 glasses or mugs. Drink or eat with a spoon!

Variations

* **Pineapple, Peach & Banana Blend:** Replace pear with 1 medium banana.

* **Pineapple, Peach & Mango Blend:** Replace pear with 1/2 to 1 cup sliced mango.

* **Pineapple, Peach & Berry Blend:** Replace pear with 1 cup blueberries **or** strawberries.

* **Banana-Peach Blend:** Use 1 banana and 2 peaches.

Appendix A:

Alternative Sweeteners

Wondering what to use to sweeten your tea or special occasion treats? Besides honey, date sugar, and dried puréed dates, we use stevia and agavé nectar. Both are widely available in natural foods stores, by mail, and over the Internet.

Stevia, the Sweet Leaf

Stevia is a non-caloric herbal sweetener extracted from the leaf of a South American plant, *Stevia Rebaudiana*, a shrub with incredibly small leaves that are 50 times sweeter than table sugar.

Stevia has been in use since the 16th century, when natives of Paraguay began using the leaves to sweeten maté, a traditional herbal beverage. The sweet green leaves have also been used therapeutically by indigenous people, as an antiseptic and aid to wound healing.

In recent times, stevia has been used as a sweetener in Paraguay, Brazil, Korea, Thailand, China, and several other countries, with no reported adverse affects. In Japan, stevia is the low-calorie sugar substitute of choice, capturing up to 47 percent of the sweetener market. Toxicity tests and more than 30 years of continuous use in Asia attest to the safety of this sweetener.

Top Secret Sweetener

Although stevia was first introduced to the United States in 1918, very few Americans have heard of it. The reason? Stevia—a product of nature that cannot be patented—threatens the multi-billion dollar artificial sweetener industry, which has lobbied heavily to keep the sweet leaf off the market.

In the 1980s stevia was used in several commercial herbal teas in the United States. In 1991 the Food and Drug Administration (FDA) labeled the leaf an "unsafe food additive," blocked importation into the United States, and demanded that manufacturers remove it from their products even though there was no indication that stevia might be harmful to humans.

Retailers and consumers lobbied to have stevia added to the Generally Recognized As Safe (GRAS) list of foods, herbs, and nutrients because of its historical use, but permission was denied. Products with shorter and less honorable track records, such as saccharin, remained on the market.

Book banning and burning?

In 1996, FDA officials ordered the Stevita Co., of Arlington, Texas, to destroy all copies of *Stevia Rebaudiana: Nature's Sweet Secret* by

David Richard, *The Stevia Story* by Donna Gates and Linda and Bill Bonvie, and *Cooking with Stevia* by James Kirkland. The books were viewed as "product labeling" for the herb the Stevita Co. sold, an act deemed illegal. Products containing stevia were suddenly considered "adulterated food products." (If this sounds like a violation of our constitutional rights to freedom of speech and press, it is!)

As a result of the passage of the Dietary Supplement, Health Education Act (DSHEA), consumers once again have access to stevia, but the herb may not be called, labeled, or sold as a *sweetener*—only as a "dietary supplement." Commercially, stevia cannot be added to teas or other food products, with the exception of protein powders, which are classified as "dietary supplements."

These regulations curtail the spread of stevia and protect huge market interests, not you, the consumer. If the FDA deems stevia safe for use as a dietary supplement, why wouldn't it be safe as an ingredient in foods and teas?

A Cut Above

Unlike caloric sweeteners, stevia is non-cariogenic and has no effect on blood glucose levels. It's safe for dieters, diabetics, those with hypoglycemia, and individuals who want to avoid the adverse affects of sugar and other concentrated, caloric, or artificial sweeteners. Individuals following ketogenic, low-carb, anti-fungal, and candida diets can use stevia without problems.

Unlike artificial sweeteners, stevia is non-toxic and has a record of safe and continuous use for hundreds of years. At this time, no adverse affects have been attributed to the herb or its extracts. The only downside is a bitter taste if you use too much. This can be avoided by precisely measuring stevia extract and adding it to recipes in tiny pinches or several drops at a time.

Shopping for stevia

Green stevia leaves and the powder made from them represent the least concentrated form of the herb. They posses the most therapeutic value (great for facial masks and other applications) but also have what many describe as a strong licorice-like flavor. Nevertheless, they may be added to foods and beverages, including fruit smoothies.

White stevia extract powder is sold straight as well as diluted with maltodextrin (a bland carbohydrate), erythritol (a granulated filler from fruits, vegetables, and grains), or FOS (fructo-oligo-saccharides) to create a more dilute product sold in single-serving packets, like sugar or artificial sweeteners. We avoid these products in favor of pure stevia extract powder and liquid. Products that contain FOS—a pesky indigestible carbohydrate—can cause excruciating gas and intestinal bloating for many individuals.

Pure, undiluted white stevia extract powder and liquid range from 100 to 300 times sweeter than sugar. A concentration of steviosides and rebaudiosides (a group of molecules, called glycosides) from the leaves give the extract its extraordinary taste. The more steviosides and rebaudiosides, the higher the quality and the less chance of an after taste. Many consumers prefer these products even though they lack the therapeutic properties of the whole green leaf.

Stevia extract powder may also be blended with dried, powdered agavé (cactus honey), a low-glycemic sweetener made from the leaf of the agavé plant; agavé masks the slight bitterness of stevia that some people object to. A blend of stevia and agavé is made and marketed by KAL and sold in individual serving packets. You can create a similar effect by combining stevia extract powder or liquid with a small amount of honey, agavé nectar, maple granules, dates, date purée, date sugar, or other sweet fruits in recipes as we do.

Stevia extract liquids are sold in two ways: bottled in alcohol or a non-alcoholic glycerin base. They are interchangeable, but many prefer the flavor of products in an alcohol-free base. These colorless liquids are easy to use and ideal for sweetening hot or iced tea because they dissolve immediately.

Using Stevia

Stevia is heat stable, so you can add it to hot foods and beverages and use it in cooking and baking. In contrast to some artificial sweeteners, stevia is stable when combined with acid fruits.

The biggest problem for people is knowing how much to use. *There is no hard and fast formula that says "add this much stevia to replace this much sugar, honey, or maple syrup."* There are more than 150 methods for extracting the sweetest portion of the stevia plant. The percentage and concentration of steviosides and flavor may vary from one brand to another. You may need to try more than one brand to find your favorite.

Stevia is so concentrated that only minuscule amounts are needed to produce a sweet taste. More is not better; too much will produce an unpleasant bitter aftertaste. If a range is given in a recipe, always start with the smaller volume, stir or blend well, taste, and work your way up SLOWLY if you desire a sweeter taste. Although 1/16 of a teaspoon might not sound like much, it's often adequate to sweeten a 12- to 16-ounce fruit smoothie or mug of tea. A 1/8 teaspoon measuring spoon is helpful. (Half of one of these spoons will yield 1/16 of a teaspoon.) You may only need 1/8 to 1/4 teaspoon of stevia extract to sweeten a bowl of oatmeal or cup of plain yogurt, and less if you're using a sweetened protein powder. A quarter teaspoon of stevia extract powder is usually sufficient to sweeten a quart of lemonade.

The price may seem high—until you realize that a $10 (2-ounce bottle) of alcohol-free stevia extract liquid provides 350 to 400 servings. Also note that stevia is non-perishable, so you don't need toss it out even if it's been in your kitchen for a year or more. Like arrowroot and most other dried foods, stevia is shelf stable.

Cooking and Baking with Stevia

Sugar provides both sweetness and volume in recipes. When you replace sugar and caloric syrups with stevia, particularly in baked goods, you must adjust liquid and dry ingredients up or down to compensate for the sweetener you're omitting. If you reduce granulated sugar by 1/2 cup, you must reduce the liquids or increase the dry ingredients by the same amount. If you reduce a liquid sweetener by 1/2 cup, you must add 1/3 to 1/2 cup of extra liquid—juice or water—or omit 1/3 to 1/2 cup of dry ingredients. Sounds complicated, but it's not.

For the best flavor combine a small amount of honey, agavé, maple syrup, date syrup, fruit juice concentrate, date or raisin purée, granulated honey, maple crystals, or date sugar, with a minute amount of stevia in a recipe.

When modifying a dessert recipe that yields 4 to 6 servings, start with half the amount of sweetener called for in your original recipe, then add 1/4 teaspoon of white stevia extract powder or liquid. Stir, taste, and add additional stevia 1/8 teaspoon at a time, stirring well after each addition. You probably won't need more than 1/2 teaspoon of stevia in such a recipe. White or brown sugar may be replaced with date sugar, powdered honey, maple granules, or xylitol (birch bark sweetener). Corn syrup, rice syrup, and barley malt may be replaced with honey, agavé nectar, or maple syrup.

Baked goods made with little or no sugar don't brown much so you need to test them with a toothpick. Before experimenting with stevia, we suggest you follow the recipes in this book—My Favorite Macaroons, Chocolate-Almond Meringues, Cocoa Coconut Pots de Crème, Chocolate Avocado-Mousse, Chestnut-Chocolate Pudding, and Protein-Nut Spread (see Index for recipes)—then use these as guides for modifying other recipes. If you don't get exactly the taste or texture you're after, make adjustments until you get the desired result.

All about Agavé Nectar - A Spirited Sweetener

Agavé, a cactus-like plant native to Mexico, has been a source of food and fiber for more than 9000 years. If you've ever ingested tequila, you've imbibed a product of this pineapple-shaped plant. Agavé syrup is yet another.

General Guidelines for Using Stevia

* Place a tiny pinch of green stevia leaves in a cup of tea.

* Start with 3 to 4 drops of stevia extract liquid or an amount of stevia extract powder that fits on the end of a toothpick for 1 cup or mug of tea; stir, taste, and add more as needed.

* Add 1/4 teaspoon stevia extract powder or 8 to 12 drops of the liquid to 1 quart of lemonade.

* Add 1/16 to 1/8 teaspoon stevia extract powder or 4 to 8 drops of stevia extract liquid along with 1/2 teaspoon of nonalcoholic vanilla or maple extract for a smooth flavor to sweeten 1 cup of plain yogurt or oatmeal. Stir, taste, and adjust as needed. Oatmeal benefits from the addition of cinnamon, ginger, apple, or pumpkin pie spice. When sweetening yogurt, in addition to the stevia and vanilla, adding fresh fruit, chopped or puréed with the yogurt, produces the best flavor. Also, use full-fat or low-fat, rather than non-fat yogurt, which can have a chalky taste.

* When using stevia packets, which are diluted with fruit or vegetable starches, add 1/4 of the packet to a food or beverage, stir, taste, then add more only if needed.

From Sap to Sweetener

Although agavé syrup has only been on the market since the 1990s, it's been harvested on a small scale for local consumption for thousands of years.

The agavé plant produces hundreds of offspring during its 8-year lifecycle. Indians native to central Mexico, and familiar with the plant's cycles, harvest the plant when it has reached its prime and before it dies. To collect agavé sap they slice off the top off of living agavé plant, hollow out the center, cap the plants with stones, then wait for the plants to release their nectar into the hollow cavity. Several days later, the harvesters return to remove the milky white "juice" with ladles.

The process of turning the sap into syrup is similar to what bees do to make honey. Bees add enzymes to the complex sugars contained in the nectar collected in their hive. The enzymes break the carbohydrates into simple sugars producing a sweet and highly concentrated energy source we call honey. Similarly, humans use enzymes to transform the complex sugar from agavé juice into a simple sugar or sweetener known as agavé nectar.

Originally this natural liquid sweetener was made from the Blue Agavé plant, which is also used to produce tequila. During the 1990s demand for Blue Agavé increased and drove the price so high that manufacturers had to find more plentiful wild sources of agavé for making syrup.

Sweet as Honey

Agavé nectar has the same caloric value as sucrose. However, like honey agavé is 25 to 50 percent sweeter than sugar, so you don't need as much to achieve the same level of sweetness. Three-quarters of a cup of agavé nectar can replace 1 cup of sugar in a recipe. When baking, if you replace 1 cup of sugar with 3/4 cup of agavé, reduce the liquids by 1/3 and lower the oven temperature by 25 degrees. In salad dressings, fruit sauces, smoothies, or popsicles, where only a small amount of sweetener is called for, agavé syrup may be used interchangeably with table sugar or liquid sweeteners without adjusting the liquid or dry ingredients.

Advantages of Agavé

Agavé nectar has a high fructose (90 percent) and low glucose (10 percent) content. This composition slows the absorption of the sugars, and gives the syrup a low glycemic rating compared to sugar, honey, maple syrup, molasses, corn syrup, rice syrup, and barley malt.

The exact glycemic rating depends on whether the chart you consult uses white bread or pure glucose as the standard. With white bread as the standard (GI = 100), most varieties of wild agavé syrup have a GI of 32 to 46, depending upon the variety of agavé. Blue Webber Agave has a glycemic Index of 11 to 16. By comparison, honey has a GI of 104. Sucrose (white sugar) has a GI of 92, and crystalline or liquid fructose (purified fruit sugar) comes in at 32 on the Glycemic Index.

Whereas the color and flavor of honey can vary widely from one variety to the next, agavé syrup has a milder and more consistent flavor. Light agavé syrup is the most subtle. Dark amber agavé syrup has a slight maple- or molasses-like flavor. Agavé syrup dissolves readily in both hot and cold liquids. It has a long shelf life stored at room temperature. Unlike honey it doesn't crystallize over time so it's always easy to pour and measure. All this and it costs less than honey, maple syrup, rice syrup, or barley malt.

Look for agavé syrup in natural foods stores and over the Internet. Some companies provide both organic and kosher certification. See Appendix D for brand recommendations.

Menus for Special Occasions & Holidays

July 4th Party/Summer Buffet
Carrot, jicama, and celery sticks with
  Guacamole
Herbed (Turkey, Beef, or Bison) Burgers with
  Better Barbecue Sauce
Baked or Grilled Chicken Thighs with Cumin
  & Lime
Marinated Beet Root Salad with Fluffy Tahini
Spinach Salad with Creamy Tahini Dressing
Fruit Salad **or** fresh watermelon
Low-Carb Lemonade
Iced Ginger Elixir

Barbecue or Picnic by the Pool
Broiled or Grilled Chicken Parts with Herbs
Cajun-Spiced Pork Chops with Cajun Ketchup
Steamed Corn on the Cob with Practically
  Paleo-Pesto
Parboiled Crudité Platter of Seasonal
  Vegetables with Sesame, Garlic & Chive Dip
  and Spicy Peanut Sauce.
Mesclun Green & Pear Salad with Toasted
  Pecans
Chilled Cherry Gel

Late Summer Luncheon
Creamy Carrot Soup with Cumin & Dill
Quick Smoky Simmered Salmon with Chipotlé
Roasted Onion, Tomato & Spring Green Salad
  with Lean & Creamy Basil-Balsamic Dressing
Blueberry-Protein Popsicles
Chocolate-Protein Pudding Pops
Iced Spearmint Tea
Raspberry Zinger Punch

Casual Summer Luncheon with Friends
Creamy Carrot Soup with Ginger
Salmon Salad with Black Pepper, Pineapple &
  Basil-Balsamic Dressing
Dark Chocolate-Dipped Dates **or**
  Chocolate-Almond Meringues
Iced Peppermint Tea

Light Summer Lunch with Friends
Practically Paleo Cobb Salad
Steamed Corn on the Cob with Fruit Salad
  dusted with shredded, unsweetened coconut
Iced Ginger Elixir

Casual Summer Dinner Party with Friends
Strawberry, Shrimp & Pineapple Kabobs with
  Poppy Seed-Pineapple Drizzle
Sesame-Buttered Seafood
Spinach Salad with Parboiled Broccoli,
  Cauliflower & Carrots with Very Easy
  Vinaigrette
Iced Peppermint Tea
Dark Chocolate-Dipped Dates

Summer/Fall Buffet 1
Raw carrot, celery & jicama sticks with
  Sesame-Pesto Dip
Broiled or Grilled Lamb Chops with Herbs
Arctic Char in Parchment Packets
Spinach Salad with Parboiled Broccoli,
  Cauliflower & Carrots with Lemonette
Fruit Kabobs garnished with shredded,
  unsweetened coconut
Dark Chocolate-Dipped Dates **or** Date-Nut
  Balls
Red Zinger Punch
Iced Ginger Elixir

Summer/Fall Buffet 2
Parboiled Broccoli, Cauliflower & Carrot Sticks
  with Guacamole & Sesame-Dill Dip
Baked Chicken Thighs with Cumin & Lime
Broiled or Grilled Burgers with Cajun Ketchup
Mesclun Green Salad with Lean & Creamy
  Basil-Balsamic Dressing
Chilled Cherry Gel
Date-Nut Balls **or** My Favorite Macaroons
Low-Carb Lemonade

Summer Brunch Buffet 1
Spinach & Egg Pie
Herbed-Salmon Burgers (muffin-size)
Herb-Roasted Potatoes
Fruit Kabobs with Almond-Honey Drizzle
Assorted herbal teas

Summer Brunch Buffet 2
Egg & Vegetable Pie Italiano
Herbed-Salmon Burgers (muffin size)
Yam Power Popovers (mini-muffin size) **or**
  Herb-Roasted Potatoes
Braised Baby Bok Choy with Ginger
Fruit Salad garnished with shredded,
  unsweetened coconut
Assorted herbal teas

Perfect Patio Dining
Parboiled Carrot Sticks with Guacamole
Baked Chicken Thighs with Cumin & Lime
Sautéed Sunchokes with Dulse
Basic Coleslaw with Sesame, Garlic & Chive
    Dressing and Parboiled Broccoli
Chocolate-Avocado Mousse **or** Chestnut-
    Chocolate Pudding
Roasted Chicory & Dandelion Root "Coffee"

Summer/Fall Light Lunch with Friends
Steak, Sun-Dried Tomato & Green Salad with
    Onions & Avocado
Herb-Roasted Potatoes
Fruit Salad with Poppy Seed Glaze
Peppermint Tea

Autumn Harvest Brunch
Salmon & Egg Scramble
Egg & Vegetable Pie Italiano
Herb-Roasted Potatoes & Carrots
Sautéed Kale with Onions & Mushrooms
Fresh Fruit Salad
Assorted herbal teas
Roasted Chicory & Dandelion Root "Coffee"

Autumn Harvest Dinner with Friends
Roasted Red Snapper with Rosemary, Garlic,
    Lemon, Pepper & Crab Meat Filling
Silver Dollar Sweet Potatoes with Pie Spice
Mesclun Greens with Roasted Mushrooms,
    Onions & Walnuts
Dark Chocolate-Dipped Dates
Roasted Chicory & Dandelion Root "Coffee"
Ginger-Licorice Tea

Autumn Harvest Celebration
Tomato, Squash & Ginger Bisque
Arctic Char or Escolar in Parchment Packets
Nutty Apple & Green Salad with Fruity
    Balsamic-Mustard Vinaigrette
Raisin-Glazed Chestnuts
My Favorite Macaroons
Roasted Dandelion & Chicory Root "Coffee"

Hungarian Inspired Harvest Meal
Hungarian Squash Soup
Baked Salmon or Sea Bass with Mustard
    Sauce & Herbs
Sautéed Cabbage garnished with Toasted
    Dulse
Apple-Apricot Compote with Caraway
    garnished with toasted walnuts
Roasted Dandelion & Chicory Root "Coffee"

Laid Back Thanksgiving Dinner
Roasted Smoky Turkey Breast
Mashed Sweet Potatoes with Lime
Better Brussels Sprouts
Mesclun Greens with Roasted Mushrooms,
    Onions & Walnuts
Cranberry-Apple Compote with Almond-Honey
    Drizzle
Roasted Chicory & Dandelion Root "Coffee"
Cinnamon-Spiced Tea

No-Frills Thanksgiving Dinner
ABC Bisque
Roasted Chicken with Lemon & Thyme
Sautéed Collards with Sunchokes & Sage
Squash Pudding Pie
Roasted Chicory & Dandelion Root "Coffee"
Cinnamon-Spiced Tea

Thanksgiving Dinner with Hors d'oeuvres
Crudité platter of raw carrot, daikon radish
    and celery sticks and Parboiled Broccoli
    florets with Macadamia-Dill Dip, Spicy-
    Peanut Dip, and Angeled Eggs

Herbed-Orange Roasted Turkey Breast **or**
    Smoky Roasted Turkey Breast
Yam Power Popovers
Nutty Apple & Green Salad with Fruity
    Balsamic-Mustard Vinaigrette
Herb-Roasted Mushrooms
My Favorite Macaroons (vanilla and/or
    chocolate)
Ethiopian Tea or Cardamom Spiced Chicory &
    Dandelion Root "Coffee"

Down-Home Winter Dinner
My Favorite Meat & Vegetable Loaf with Better
    Barbecue Sauce
Herb-Roasted Potatoes or Oven-Fried Parsnips
    with Ginger
Coleslaw with Mayonnaise **or** Sesame-Dill
    Dressing
Apple-Apricot Compote with toasted walnuts
Chicory & Dandelion Root "Coffee"

Equinox Celebration
Barbecued Beef or Buffalo Brisket
Herb-Roasted Potatoes **or** Roasted Parsnips
Sautéed Kale or Collards with Mushrooms &
    Sage
Chestnut-Apple Compote with toasted Pecans
Cinnamon Tea
Chicory & Dandelion Root "Coffee"

Party Hors d'oeuvres For Any Occasion
Crudité platter of parboiled carrot and daikon
  radish sticks, broccoli and cauliflower florets
Sesame-Dill Dip and Spicy-Peanut Dip
Angeled Eggs
Broiled Scampi with Herb Paste

Christmas Eve or New Year's Eve Buffet
Broiled Scampi with Herb Paste
Herbed Meatballs with Cajun Ketchup
Angeled Eggs on a bed of shredded lettuce
Mesclun Greens with Lean & Creamy Basil-
  Balsamic Dressing
Crudité Platter of Seasonal Vegetables
Sesame, Garlic & Chive Dip and Macadamia-
  Dill Dip
My Favorite Macaroons (orange and chocolate)
Date-Nut Balls **or** Dark Chocolate-Dipped
  Dates
Cinnamon-Spiced Tea **or** Ethiopian Tea
Roasted Chicory & Dandelion Root "Coffee"

Christmas or New Year's Eve Dinner 1
Tomato, Squash & Ginger Bisque or Creamy
  Carrot Soup with Ginger
Baked Sea Bass with Mustard & Herbs
Sautéed Kale or Collards with Cumin &
  Chipotlé
Cranberry-Apple Compote **or** Rosehip-Apple
  Compote with Almond-Honey Drizzle
Ginger Tea
Roasted Chicory & Dandelion Root "Coffee"

Christmas/New Years Day Dinner 2
Roast Leg of Lamb **or** Barbecued Beef Brisket
  with Better Barbecue Sauce
Oven-Fried Parsnips with Pie Spice
Better Brussels Sprouts with Sunchokes &
  Sage
Chestnut-Apple Compote with toasted pecans
Cardamom-Spiced Chicory & Dandelion Root
  "Coffee"
Ginger Tea

Dessert and Tea Tray for a Special Event
My Favorite Macaroons (vanilla, chocolate, and
  orange flavors)
Dark Chocolate-Dipped Dates
Date-Nut Balls
Roasted Chicory & Dandelion Root "Coffee"
Ginger Tea
Cinnamon Tea

Meat & Potatoes Makeover
Garlic, Ginger & Scallion Burgers
Roasted Carrots
The Basic Coleslaw with Herbed Mayonnaise
Chocolate-Avocado Mousse **or** Frozen Banana
  Delight
Roasted Chicory & Dandelion Root "Coffee"

Valentine's Day Dinner 1
Moroccan-Spiced Salmon **or** Pork Chops with
  Moroccan Barbecue Sauce
Mesclun Greens with Macadamia-Dill Dressing
  or Lean & Creamy Mustard Dressing
Roasted Parsnips with Pie Spice
Dairy-Free Cocoa Coconut Pots de Crème
Roasted Chicory & Dandelion Root "Coffee" **or**
  Ginger Tea

Valentine's Dinner 2
Roasted Red Snapper with Rosemary, Garlic,
  Lemon, & Pepper
Mesclun Greens with Lean & Creamy Basil-
  Balsamic Dressing
Marinated Beet Root Salad with Fluffy Tahini
  or ABC Bisque
My Favorite Macaroons (chocolate and orange)
Roasted Chicory & Dandelion Root "Coffee" or
  Ginger Tea

Mother's Day Brunch
Scrambled Eggs with Tomato & Tarragon **or**
  Smoky Salmon & Egg Scramble
Twice-Cooked Greens
Yam Power Popovers
Roasted Chicory & Dandelion Root "Coffee" **or**
  Ginger Tea

Mother's Day Dinner
Creamy Carrot Soup with Ginger
Seared Pork Chops with Currant, Apricot &
  Onion Sauce
Sautéed Kale or Collards with Onions,
  Mushrooms & Garlic
Rosehip-Apple Compote topped with toasted
  walnuts **or** Chestnut-Chocolate Pudding

Cinco de Mayo/Spring Celebration
Seared Pork Chops with Cranberry, Onion &
  Chipotlé Sauce
Sautéed Kale or Collards with Sunchokes &
  Sage
Chocolate-Avocado Mousse
Cinnamon Tea
Roasted Chicory & Dandelion Root "Coffee"

Southwest and French Fusion Meal
Guacamole with raw carrot, celery, and jicama
  sticks
Ben's Tomatillo Chili over Baked Spaghetti
  Squash
Mesclun Greens with Lean & Creamy French
  Dressing
Dairy-Free Cocoa Coconut Pots de Creme
Chicory & Dandelion Root "Coffee"

Indian Inspiration
Broiled or Grilled Chicken Breasts with
  Mango-Ginger Chutney
Whole Boiled Greens with Cauliflower, Carrots
  & Onions with Cumin, Curry, Coriander &
  Tahini Dressing
Dried Fig Halves with Anise & Toasted
  Almonds
Cinnamon-Spiced Tea or Ginger Tea

Late Winter/Spring Buffet of Light Bites
Parboiled Crudité Plate with Macadamia-Dill
  Dip and Sesame-Pesto Dip
Angeled Eggs
Baked Chicken Thighs with Cumin & Lime
Herbed Meatballs with Cajun Ketchup
Nutty Spring Green & Orange Salad with
  Sweet Citrus Vinaigrette
Chocolate & Vanilla Protein-Nut Spread with
  strawberries & sliced apples
Date-Nut Balls
Assorted herbal teas

Fall/Winter/Early Spring Dinner
Soothing Ginger, Squash & Apple Soup
Speedy Moroccan-Spiced Pork Loin
Coleslaw with Shallot & Chive Mayonnaise
  surrounded by Parboiled Broccoli florets
Raisin-Glazed Chestnuts garnished with
  toasted pecans
Ginger Tea

Easter Dinner
Roast Leg of Lamb
Roasted Onion, Sweet Pepper & Spring Green
  Salad with Lean & Creamy Mustard Dressing
Roasted Parsnips with Pie Spice **or** Slow-
  Simmered Carrots with Sunchokes
Raisin-Glazed Chestnuts **or** Rosehip-Apple
  Compote with Peanut-Honey Drizzle
Roasted Chicory & Dandelion Root "Coffee"
Peppermint Tea

Winter Citrus Celebration
Macadamia-Orange Roughy in Orange & White
  Wine Reduction Sauce
Crudité Platter of blanched, beautifully
  arranged vegetables
  with a duo of dressings:
    Sesame-Dill Dressing
    Lemonette
Coconut-Orange Macaroons
Roasted Chicory & Dandelion Root "Coffee"

An Evening with Friends
Creamy Carrot Soup with Ginger
Baked Sea Bass **or** Escolar with Mustard &
  Herbs
Parboiled Vegetable Medley with Sesame-Dill
  Dressing
Stewed Pears with Anise & Apricots and
  toasted pecan garnish
Cardamom-Spiced Chicory & Dandelion Root
  "Coffee"
Cinnamon-Spiced Tea

Spring/Summer Celebration
Savory Shrimp & Coconut Bisque
Herbed Salmon Cakes with Citrus
Simmered Squash with Cinnamon
Mustard-Glazed Broccoli
Raisin-Glazed Chestnuts
Ethiopian Tea
Ginger Tea

Tables of Equivalents & Substitutions

Abbreviations

teaspoon	=	tsp.
tablespoon	=	tbsp.
ounce	=	oz.

U.S. Measurements & Equivalents

A few grains	less than 1/8 teaspoon
1 small (two-finger) pinch	1/8 teaspoon
1 big (three-finger) pinch	1/4 teaspoon
1 teaspoon	1/3 tablespoon
3 teaspoons	1 tablespoon
4 tablespoons	1/4 cup
5 1/3 tablespoons	1/3 cup
8 tablespoons	1/2 cup or 4 ounces (volume)
16 tablespoons	1 (8-ounce) cup or 8 ounces (volume)
1/4 cup	4 tablespoons
1/3 cup	5 1/3 tablespoons (5 tablespoons + 1 teaspoon)
3/8 cup	1/4 cup + 2 tablespoons
5/8 cup	1/2 cup + 2 tablespoons
7/8 cup	3/4 cup + 2 tablespoons
1 cup	1/2 pint or 8 fluid ounces
2 cups	1 pint or 16 fluid ounces
2 pints	1 quart (liquid)
4 pints	1 gallon
1 gill (liquid)	1/2 cup or 4 ounces
1 pint (liquid)	4 gills or 16 fluid ounces
1 quart (liquid)	2 pints
1 gallon (liquid)	4 quarts or 16 cups

Dry Measure Volume Equivalents

(For large volumes of raw fruits and vegetables)

This	**equals this**
1 quart	2 pints
8 quarts	1 peck
4 pecks	1 bushel
1 pound	16 ounces (weight)
1 kilo	2.2 pounds

Table of Equivalents

Food	Measure	Equivalent
Almonds	1 pound in shell	1 1/4 cups shelled
Almonds	1 cup shelled	6 ounces by weight
Almonds	1 ounce by weight	1/4 cup
Apples	1 pound (3 medium)	2 1/2 cups peeled and sliced
Apples	1 (5 ounce)	3/4 to 1 cup sliced
Apricots	1 pound dried	3 cups
Apricots	1 pound fresh	8 to 10 medium
Asparagus	1/2 pound	6 to 8 stalks
Asparagus	1 pound fresh	3 1/2 cups cut into pieces
Avocado	2 medium fruits	1 pound
		2 to 2 1/2 cups cubed
Bananas	1 pound (3 to 4)	1/2 cup mashed
		2 cups sliced
Beets	1 pound trimmed	2 cups cooked and sliced
Blueberries	1 pint	2 cups
Bok choy	1 pound raw	6 to 8 cups chopped
Broccoli	1 pound raw	4 cups trimmed and chopped
Brussels sprouts	1 pound fresh	4 cups chopped
Butter	1 stick	1/2 cup (8 tablespoons)
	1 pound (4 sticks)	2 cups
Cabbage, regular	1 pound fresh	4 to 4 1/2 cups shredded
	2 pounds raw	9 cups shredded or sliced
Cabbage, Chinese	1 1/2 pounds	6 to 8 cups sliced
Carrots	1 pound raw (6 to 7 carrots)	3 cups sliced or shredded
		1 1/3 cups cooked and puréed
		2 1/2 cups diced
Cauliflower	1 pound fresh	1 1/2 cups sliced
Cashew nuts	1 pound shelled	3 1/4 cups
Celery	1 large rib (1/4 pound)	1/2 cup sliced or chopped
Celery root (celeriac)	1 pound	3 cups sliced or grated
Cherries	1 pound fresh	2 1/2 to 3 cups pitted
Chestnuts	3 cups chestnut flour	1 pound
	1 1/2 pounds in the shell	1 pound or 2 1/2 cups peeled
	1 pound shelled	35 to 40 large chestnuts
	1 cup dried, steam peeled	6 ounces (weight)
Chicken	3- to 4-pound bird	3 to 4 cups cooked meat
	1 pound with bones/skin	1 cup diced
	1 large boned breast	2 cups cooked meat
Chocolate, unsweetened	1 ounce (1 square)	2 tablespoons grated
Cocoa	8-ounce can	2 cups
Coconut	1 medium, fresh	4 cups shredded
		2 1/2 cups coconut milk
	3 1/2 ounces flaked	1 1/3 cups
Coconut milk	14-ounce can	1 3/4 cups

Table of Equivalents ~ Continued

Food	Measure	Equivalent
Collard greens	1 1/2 to 2 pounds raw	12 to 14 packed cups, stemmed, chopped
	1 pound raw	3 to 4 cups, stemmed and cooked
Corn	2 medium ears	1 cup kernels
Cranberries	12-ounce bag	3 cups
Cucumber	2 medium	3 cups peeled and sliced
Currants	10 ounces dry	2 cups
Dates, pitted	8-ounce package	1 1/4 to 1 1/2 cups chopped
Eggs (large)	5 whole	1 cup
	1 medium-size white	2 tablespoons
	8 medium-size whites	1 cup
	1 medium-size yolk	1 tablespoon
	12 to 14 yolks	1 cup
Figs, dried	1 pound	3 cups chopped
Garlic	1 medium clove	1/2 teaspoon minced
	2 medium cloves	1 teaspoon minced
Ginger, fresh	2-inch piece	2 tablespoons minced or grated
	1/4 cup finely grated	1 to 2 tablespoons juice
Grapefruit	1 medium	2/3 cup juice
Hazelnuts	1 pound in shell	3 cups shelled
Herbs	1 tablespoon fresh	1 teaspoon dried
Horseradish, fresh	1 tablespoon grated	2 tablespoons bottled
Jerusalem artichokes	1 pound	2 1/2 cups trimmed and sliced
Leeks	2 pounds trimmed	4 cups sliced or chopped
		2 cups cooked
Kale, raw	1 1/2 to 2 pounds	12 to 14 cups, stemmed and chopped
Lemons	1 medium	3 tablespoons juice
		2 teaspoons grated zest
Limes	1 medium	1 1/2 to 2 tablespoons juice
		1 teaspoon grated zest
Lobsters	2 pounds	1/2 cup cooked meat
Macadamia nuts	7-ounce jar	1 1/2 cups
Mushrooms	1/4 pound fresh	1 cup sliced
		1 1/2 cups chopped
	3 ounces dried	1 pound fresh
Mustard	1 teaspoon dry	1 tablespoon fresh
Nectarines	1 pound (3 to 4)	2 cups sliced
Nut meats	4 ounces by weight	1 cup
Oil	2 cups	16 fluid ounces
Onions raw	1 pound	2 medium or 1 extra large
Onion	1 medium (4 ounce)	3/4 to 1 cup
	1 large (8 ounce)	1 1/2 to 2 cups
Oranges	1 medium	1/3 cup juice
		2 to 3 tablespoons grated zest

Food	Measure	Equivalent
Pecans	2 1/2 pounds in shell	1 pound shelled
	1 pound in shell	2 cups shelled
	1 pound shelled	4 cups halved or chopped
Peppers, bell	1 large	1 1/2 cups chopped
Pineapple	1 medium	3 cups cubed flesh
Pistachios	1 pound shelled	3 1/2 cups shelled
Plums	1 pound (6 medium)	2 1/2 cups halved, pitted
Pumpkin fresh	3 to 4 pounds	3 1/2 cups cooked and puréed
Raisins, seedless	4 ounces	3/4 cup
Raspberries	1 pint	1 3/4 to 2 cups
Scallions	1 bunch (6 to 7)	1/3 cup chopped (white only)
Scallops	1 pound	2 cups
Seeds, raw, shelled	4 cups	1 pound
Seeds, raw	1 cup	4 ounces dry weight
	1/4 cup	1 ounce
Shallots	1 large (1/2 ounce)	1 tablespoon minced
Shrimp	2 pounds in the shell	1 1/2 pounds shelled
	1 pound	10 to 15 jumbo
		16 to 20 large
		25 to 30 medium
		30 to 35 small
Spinach, fresh	1 pound raw	16 chopped, packed cups
	2 pounds loose **or** 2 (10-ounce) bags	1 1/2 cups cooked and chopped
Squash, winter	3 pounds	3 cups cooked and puréed
Tomatillos	1 pound (10-12)	2 (13-ounce cans), drained
Tomatoes	1 pound (3 medium)	1 1/2 cups peeled and seeded
	28-ounce can	2 cups drained pulp
Tomato paste	6-ounce can	3/4 cup
Tomato sauce	8 ounces	1 cup
Turnips	1 pound (4 medium)	2 1/2 cups cooked
Walnuts	1 pound in shell	2 cups shelled
	1 pound shelled	3 1/2 cups chopped

Uncooked to Cooked Yields

Food	Dry Unprepared Volume	Cooked Volume
Seeds and nuts		
Nuts to nut butters	2 cups walnuts or almonds	1 cup nut butter
Vegetables		
Broccoli	1 pound (4 stalks)	5 to 6 cups chopped
		4 cups cooked
Bok choy	7 to 9 cups raw, chopped	4 to 5 cups cooked
Brussels sprouts	3 cups sliced, raw	2 to 2 1/2 cups cooked
Brussels sprouts	2 pounds	8 cups trimmed, chopped
		6 cups cooked
Carrots	1 1/2 pounds	4 cups chopped
		4 cups steamed or thick purée
Carrots, raw	2 pounds	5 cups roasted
Cabbage, red	5 cups chopped, raw	4 cups cooked
Cabbage, green	6 to 7 cups chopped, raw	4 cups cooked
Cabbage, regular	1 pound	4 to 4 1/2 cups shredded
		2 cups cooked
Cauliflower	1 1/2-pound head	5 cups raw
		4 1/2 cups cooked
Collard greens	8-ounce bunch, raw	1 1/2 to 2 cups cooked
	1 pound raw	3 to 4 cups cooked
	12 to 14 cups, chopped, no stems	4 to 5 cups cooked
Green peas, fresh	8 ounces by weight	1 1/2 cups raw or cooked
Kale	8-ounce bunch, raw	2 cups cooked
Mustard greens	8 to 14 packed cups raw, chopped	2 to 4 cups cooked
Potatoes	1 pound raw, peeled	2 cups baked and mashed
Red radishes	1 (7-ounce) bunch	1 1/2 cups sliced, raw
		1 1/4 cups cooked
Sweet potatoes/yams	1 pound raw	2 cups cooked, less if mashed
	2 medium sized	1 1/2 cups cooked, mashed
Watercress	6 cups raw	2 cups cooked
Fruit		
Apples or pears	2 cups chopped	1 cup cooked
Apples	6 pounds raw	9 cups cooked
Applesauce	9 cups	5 cups apple butter

Table of Substitutions

Replace this	With this
1 tablespoon cornstarch	2 1/2 teaspoons arrowroot
1 tablespoon kuzu root starch	1 1/3 tablespoons arrowroot starch
2 teaspoons kuzu root starch	1 tablespoon arrowroot starch
2 tablespoons agar agar flakes	1 tablespoon unflavored gelatin
1/2 teaspoon vinegar	1 teaspoon lemon **or** lime juice
1 tablespoon lemon juice	1/2 tablespoon apple cider **or** red wine vinegar
1 teaspoon vegetable oil	1 teaspoon coconut, flax, **or** olive oil
1 teaspoon butter or margarine	1 teaspoon olive oil **or** coconut oil
1 teaspoon lemon juice	1/2 teaspoon apple cider vinegar
1 tablespoon nuts	1 1/2 teaspoons nut butter
1 tablespoon peanut butter	1 tablespoon almond butter **or** cashew butter
1 teaspoon minced fresh ginger	1 teaspoon bottled fresh ginger **or** bottled ginger juice
1 small to medium garlic clove	1/2 teaspoon minced
	1/8 teaspoon garlic powder
1 large garlic clove	1 teaspoon minced **or** 1/4 teaspoon garlic powder
1 teaspoon dried herbs	1 tablespoon minced fresh herbs
1 cup minced fresh vegetables	1/4 cup dried vegetables flakes
1 large stalk fresh celery	1 tablespoon dried celery flakes
1 large fresh bell pepper	1 to 2 tablespoons dried bell pepper bits
1 medium to large fresh onion	1 tablespoon dried onion flakes
1 to 2 tablespoons minced, fresh vegetables	1 teaspoon dried vegetable bits
4 1/4 pounds fresh tomatoes	1/4 pound sun-dried tomatoes
17 pounds fresh tomatoes	1 pound sun-dried tomatoes
2 pounds fresh apples	1 quart dried apple rings
6 pounds fresh apples	1 1/4 pounds dried apple rings
1 cup milk	1/3 cup coconut milk + 2/3 cup water, stock, **or** juice
1 cup cream (in cooking or baking)	1 cup premium, unsweetened coconut milk
1 cup low-fat milk (in cooking or baking)	1/3 cup lite coconut milk + 2/3 cup water
1 cup sweetened condensed milk	1/2 cup coconut milk + 1/2 cup water + 3 tablespoons honey **or** agavé nectar **or** 1/4 teaspoon stevia extract
1 cup sugar	1 cup xylitol (granulated birch bark sweetener)
	1 cup date sugar (made without oats or oat flour)
	1 cup chopped pitted dates **or** raisins
	1 cup date purée **or** raisin purée
	1 cup maple granules **or** maple syrup
	3/4 cup honey **or** agavé nectar
1 whole egg	2 egg yolks + 1 tablespoon water
	2 egg whites
2 egg yolks	1 whole egg
2 egg whites **or** 1 whole egg	4 teaspoons dried, powdered whites + 1/4 cup water
4 egg whites **or** 2 whole eggs	8 teaspoons dried, powdered whites + 1/2 cup water

Mail Order & Internet Sources for Unusual & Hard to Find Foods & Herbs

Most of the foods listed below can be found in large natural foods markets, health food co-ops and through co-op buying clubs. If you cannot find a particular ingredient in your area, contact one of the companies listed below or ask your local retailer if s/he will order the product for you.

Note: *For kitchen equipment and sources, refer to Chapter 9.*

AGAVE NECTAR (cactus honey)

Madhava Honey
4689 Ute Highway
Longmont, CO 80503
Phone: (303) 823-5166
Fax: (303) 823-5755
www.madhavahoney.com/agave.htm
Email: info@madhavahoney.com

Sweet Cactus Farms
10627 Regent Street
Los Angeles, CA 90034
Phone: (310) 733-4343
Fax: (310) 733-4353
www.sweetcactusfarms.com
Email: agave@sweetcactusfarms.com

The Grain and Salt Society
273 Fairway Drive
Asheville, NC 28805
Order online or call (800) TOP-SALT
or (800) 867-7258
Fax: (828) 299-1640
www.celtic-seasalt.com

APPLE CIDER VINEGAR, raw, unpasteurized

Eden Foods
701 Tecumseh Road
Clinton, MI 49236
Phone: (888) 441-EDEN **or** (888) 441-3336
or (888) 424-3336
www.edenfoods.com

ARROWROOT STARCH

American Natural Snacks
405 Golfway West Drive
St. Augustine, FL 32095-8837
Phone: (800) 238-3947
Fax: (904) 940-2234
www.ans-natural.com
Email: anscustsrv@ansbrands.com

Frontier Natural Products Co-op
P.O. Box 299
3021 78th Street
Norway, IA 52318
Phone: (800) 669-3275
www.frontiercoop.com

Natural Lifestyle Supplies Mail Order Market
16 Lookout Drive
Asheville, NC 28804-3330
Phone: (800) 752-2775
www.natural-lifestyle.com

APPLE FIBER POWDER

NOW Foods, corporate office
For store listing contact:
395 Glen Ellyn Road,
Bloomingdale, IL 60108
Phone: (800) 999-8069
www.nowfoods.com

To mail order NOW Foods products contact:
Fruitful Yield
154 South Bloomingdale Road
Bloomingdale, IL 60108
Phone: (800) 469-5552
www.fruitfulyield.com

CHESTNUT FLOUR

Empire Chestnut Company
3276 Empire Road SW
Carrollton, OH 44615-9515
Phone: (330) 627-3181
www.empirechestnut.com

CHESTNUTS, Fresh

Diamond Organics
The Organic Food Catalog
P.O. Box 2159, Freedom, CA 95019
Phone: (888) ORGANIC **or** (888) 674-2642
www.diamondorganics.com

Empire Chestnut Company
3276 Empire Road SW
Carrollton, OH 44615-9515
Phone: (330) 627-3181
www.empirechestnut.com

Ladd Hill Orchards
15500 Southwest Roberts Road
Sherwood, OR 97140
Phone: (503) 625-1248
Fax: (503) 625-1937
www.laddhillchestnuts.com
Email: Laddhill1@aol.com

CHESTNUTS, dried, peeled

Diamond Organics
The Organic Food Catalog
P.O. Box 2159, Freedom, CA 95019
Phone: (888) ORGANIC **or** (888) 674-2642
www.diamondorganics.com

Empire Chestnut Company
3276 Empire Road SW
Carrollton, OH 44615-9515
Phone: (330) 627-3181
www.empirechestnut.com

Gold Mine Natural Foods
7805 Arjons Drive
San Diego, CA 92126
Phone: (800) 475-FOOD **or** (800) 475-3663
www.goldminenaturalfood.com

Ladd Hill Orchards
15500 Southwest Roberts Road
Sherwood, OR 97140
Phone: (503) 625-1248
Fax: (503) 625-1937
www.laddhillchestnuts.com
Email: Laddhill1@aol.com

Natural Lifestyle Supplies Mail Order Market
16 Lookout Drive
Asheville, NC 28804-3330
Phone: (800) 752-2775
www.natural-lifestyle.com

CHICORY ROOT, roasted pieces and grinds
Frontier Natural Products Co-op
P.O. Box 299
3021 78th Street
Norway, IA 52318
Phone: (800) 669-3275
www.frontiercoop.com

CHIPOTLÉ, GROUND

Conscious Light Botanicals
4160 N. Craftsman Court #103
Scottsdale, AZ 85251
Phone: (480) 970-6157
www.consciouslight.com

Spice House
1941 Central St.
Evanston, IL 60201
Phone: (847) 328-3711
www.thespicehouse.com

Spice Hunter
184 Suburban Road
San Luis Obispo, CA 93401
Phone: (800) 444-3061
www.spicehunter.com

CHIPOTLÉ SPICE BLEND

Conscious Light Botanicals
4160 N. Craftsman Court #103
Scottsdale, AZ 85251
Phone: (480) 970-6157
www.consciouslight.com

COCONUT OIL, unrefined, virgin-pressed

Coconutoil-online.com
Mid-American Marketing Corporation
P.O. Box 295
1531 East Main Street
Eaton, OH 45320
Phone: (800) 922-1744
www.coconutoil-online.com

Garden of Life Inc.
770 Northpoint Parkway
Suite 100
West Palm Beach, FL 33407
Phone: (800) 622-8986
Fax: (561) 575-5488
www.gardenoflifeusa.com
Email: info@gardenoflifeusa.com

Omega Nutrition, Mail Order Distribution
6515 Aldrich Road
Bellingham, WA 98226
Phone: (360) 384-1238
Order Line only:
(800) 661-FLAX (3529)
www.omeganutrition.com

Omega Nutrition Canada
1695 Franklin Street,
Vancouver, BC V5L 1P5
Phone: (604) 253-4677
Fax: (604) 253-4228

COCONUT, unsweetened, shredded, sulfite-free

Bob's Red Mill (large flaked coconut)
Natural Foods Inc.
5209 S.E. International Way
Milwaukee, OR 97222
Phone: (800) 349-2173
www.bobsredmill.com

Bulkfoods.com
3040 Hill Avenue
Toledo, OH 43607
Phone: (419) 324-0032
www.bulkfoods.com

Coconutoil-online.com
Mid-American Marketing Corporation
P.O. Box 295
1531 East Main Street
Eaton, OH 45320
Phone: (800) 922-1744
www.coconutoil-online.com

Edward & Sons Trading Co. (finely flaked coconut)
P.O. Box 1326
Carpinteria, CA 93014
Phone: (805) 684-8500
Fax: (805) 684-8220
www.edwardandsons.com

Gold Mine Natural Foods (finely flaked coconut)
7805 Arjon's Drive
San Diego, CA 92126
Phone: (800) 475-FOOD **or** (800) 475-3663
www.goldminenaturalfood.com

COCONUT MILK, unsweetened, shredded, sulfite- & preservative-free

Edward & Sons Trading Co.
P.O. Box 1326
Carpinteria, CA 93014
Phone: (805) 684-8500
Fax: (805) 684-8220
www.edwardandsons.com

Thai Kitchen
Epicurean International
Suite 100
1919 Market Street
Oakland, CA 97607
Phone: (510) 268-0209
www.thaikitchen.com

COD LIVER OIL, lemon-flavored

Carlson's
15 College Drive
Arlington Heights, IL 60004-1985
Phone: (800) 323-4141
www.carlsonlabs.com

DANDELION ROOT, roasted, pieces

Alvita Herbal Teas
A Division of TWINLAB Division
American Fork, UT 84003

Available on line from the following companies:
www.vitaminlife.com
www.frontierherbs.com
www.loaves-n-fishes.com
www.enknatural.com
www.herbsmd.com
www.betterhealthstore.com
www.cdnf.com

Frontier Natural Products Co-op
P.O. Box 299
3021 78th Street
Norway, IA 52318
Phone: (800) 669-3275
www.frontiercoop.com

DATES & DATE-COCONUT ROLLS

Bulkfoods.com
3040 Hill Avenue
Toledo, OH 43607
Phone: (419) 324-0032
www.bulkfoods.com

Diamond Organics
The Organic Food Catalog
P.O. Box 2159
Freedom, CA 95019
Phone: (888) ORGANIC **or** (888) 674-2642
www.diamondorganics.com

Jewel Date Co.
84675 Avenue 60
Thermal, CA 92274
Phone: (760) 399-4474
www.jeweldate.com
Email: jeweldate@aol.com

Sun Organic Farm
P.O. Box 409
San Marcos, CA 92079
Phone: (888) 269-9888
www.sunorganic.com

DATE SUGAR

Chattfield's Date Sugar
American Natural Snacks
405 Golfway West Drive
St. Augustine, FL 32095-8837
Phone: (800) 238-3947
Fax: (904) 940-2234
www.ans-natural.com
Email: anscustsrv@ansbrands.com

Diamond Organics
The Organic Food Catalog
P.O. Box 2159
Freedom, CA 95019
Phone: (888) ORGANIC **or** (888) 674-2642
www.diamondorganics.com

Healthbest (Nature's Best)
(Wholesale only; will provide list of retailers in your area.)
105 South Puente Street
Brea, CA 92821
Phone: (800) 800-7799
www.naturesbest.net

Jewel Date Co.
84675 Avenue 60
Thermal, CA 92274
Phone: (760) 399-4474
www.jeweldate.com
Email: jeweldate@aol.com

DULSE FLAKES & OTHER SEA VEGETABLE FLAKES

Frontier Natural Products Co-op
P.O. Box 299
3021 78th Street
Norway, IA 52318
Phone: (800) 669-3275
www.frontiercoop.com

Gold Mine Natural Foods
7805 Arjon's Drive
San Diego, CA 92126
Phone: (800) 475-FOOD **or** (800) 475-3663
www.goldminenaturalfood.com

Maine Coast Sea Vegetables
3 Georges Pond Road
Franklin, ME 04634
Phone: (207) 565-2907
www.seaveg.com

Mendocino Sea Vegetable Company
P.O. Box 455
Philo, CA 95466
Phone: (707) 895-2996
Fax: (707) 895-3270
www.seaweed.net

Natural Lifestyle Supplies Mail Order Market
16 Lookout Drive
Asheville, NC 28804-3330
Phone: (800) 752-2775
www.natural-lifestyle.com

EGG WHITE PROTEIN, vanilla & chocolate

Jay Robb Enterprises Inc. (sells Yammit)
5670 El Camino Real, Suite D
Carlsbad, CA 92008
Phone: (877) JAY ROBB
or (760) 448-2860
www.jayrobb.com

EGG WHITES, dried, powdered

Jay Robb Enterprises Inc. (sells Yammit)
5670 El Camino Real, Suite D
Carlsbad, CA 92008
Phone: (877) JAY ROBB
or (760) 448-2860
www.jayrobb.com

Hickman's Egg Ranch
7403 North 91st Avenue
Glendale, AZ 85305
Phone: (623) 872-1120
Fax: (623) 872-9220
www.hickmanseggs.com

Just Whites
Deb El Foods Corporation
4510 Edison Avenue
Colorado Springs, CO 80940
Elizabeth, NJ 07206
Phone: (800) 356-3876
www.thehomemarketplace.com

NOW Foods, corporate office
For store listing contact:
395 Glen Ellyn Road,
Bloomingdale, IL 60108
Phone: (800) 999-8069
www.nowfoods.com

To mail order from NOW Foods contact:
Fruitful Yield
154 South Bloomingdale Road
Bloomingdale, IL 60108
Phone: (800) 469-5552
www.fruitfulyield.com

ETHIOPIAN TEA

Rafal Spice Company
2521 Russell Street
Detroit, MI 48207
Phone: (800) 228-4276
www.rafalspicecompany.com

FLAX OIL, virgin-pressed

Barlean's
4936 Lake Terrel Road
Ferndale, WA 98248
Phone: (800) 445-3529
www.barleans.com

Flora Oils
P.O. Box 73, 805 E. Badger Road
Lynden, WA 98264
Phone: (360) 354-2110 **or** (800) 498-3610

Omega Nutrition, Mail Order Distribution
6515 Aldrich Road
Bellingham, WA 98226
Phone: (360) 384-1238
Order Line only:
(800) 661-FLAX (3529)
www.omeganutrition.com

Omega Nutrition Canada
1695 Franklin Street
Vancouver, BC V5L 1P5
Phone: (604) 253-4677
Fax: (604-253-4228

GELATIN, unflavored

Great Lakes
PO Box 917
Grayslake, IL 60030
Phone: (800) 232-0328
www.greatlakesgelatin.com

Bulkfoods.com
3040 Hill Avenue
Toledo, OH 43607
Phone: (419) 324-0032
www.bulkfoods.com

NOW Foods, corporate office
For store listing contact:
395 Glen Ellyn Road
Bloomingdale, IL 60108
Phone: (800) 999-8069
www.nowfoods.com

To mail order from NOW Foods contact:
Fruitful Yield
154 South Bloomingdale Road
Bloomingdale, IL 60108
Phone: (800) 469-5552
www.fruitfulyield.com

GINGER TEA BAGS

Triple Leaf Inc.
P.O. Box 421572
San Francisco, CA 94142
Phone: (800) 552-7448 **or** (650) 588-8406
www.tripleleaf-tea.com
Email: triple@tripleleaf-tea.com

HERBS & SPICES, non-irradiated and organic

Conscious Light Botanicals
4160 N. Craftsman Court #103
Scottsdale, AZ 85251
Phone: (480) 970-6157
www.consciouslight.com

Frontier Natural Products Co-op
P.O. Box 299
3021 78th Street
Norway, IA 52318
Phone: (800) 669-3275
www.frontiercoop.com

Gold Mine Natural Foods
7805 Arjon's Drive
San Diego, CA 92126
Phone: (800) 475-FOOD **or** (800) 475-3663
www.goldminenaturalfood.com

Natural Lifestyle Supplies Mail Order Market
16 Lookout Drive
Asheville, NC 28804-3330
Phone: (800) 752-2775
www.natural-lifestyle.com

Spice Hunter
184 Suburban Road
San Luis Obispo, CA 93401
Phone: (800) 444-3061
www.spicehunter.com

KIWI CONCENTRATE

(Trimedica Slim Sweet low glycemic, natural sweetener)
Life's Vigor Health & Beauty Care
13916 Searspoint Avenue
Bakersfield, CA 93314
Phone: (661) 589-1818
www.lifesvigor.com/Trimedica

MEATS, 100 PERCENT GRASSFED

(State by state listing of sources across the United States & Canada)

www.eatwild.com

Greatbeef
www.greatbeef.com

MUSTARD, CREAMY, WHITE, ORGANIC

True Natural Taste
30029 Torrepines Place
Agoura Hills, CA 91301
Phone: (818) 597-9983
Fax: (818) 597-9984
www.truenaturaltaste.com
Email: info@truenaturaltaste.com

ONION FLAKES, freeze-dried

Frontier Natural Products Co-op
P.O. Box 299
3021 78th Street
Norway, IA 52318
Phone: (800) 669-3275
www.frontiercoop.com

Natural Lifestyle Supplies Mail Order Market
16 Lookout Drive
Asheville, NC 28804-3330
Phone: (800) 752-2775
www.natural-lifestyle.com

ROSEHIPS, dried, de-Seeded

Frontier Natural Products Co-op
P.O. Box 299
3021 78th Street
Norway, IA 52318
Phone: (800) 669-3275
www.frontiercoop.com

SALAD DRESSING
(Ingredients: 100 PERCENT extra-virgin olive oil, balsamic and red wine vinegar, lemon juice, fresh garlic, Realsalt, and black pepper)

Syd & Diane's Incredible Dressing
5829 Monroe Street
Sylvania, OH 43560
Phone: (800) 807-8012

SEA SALT, unrefined, mineral-rich (including Celtic brand sea salt)

Diamond Organics
The Organic Food Catalog
P.O. Box 2159
Freedom, CA 95019
Phone: (888) ORGANIC **or** (888) 674-2642
www.diamondorganics.com

Gold Mine Natural Foods
7805 Arjon's Drive
San Diego, CA 92126
Phone: (800) 475-FOOD **or** (800) 475-3663
www.goldminenaturalfood.com

Natural Lifestyle Supplies Mail Order Market
16 Lookout Drive
Asheville, NC 28804-3330
Phone: (800) 752-2775
www.natural-lifestyle.com

The Grain and Salt Society
273 Fairway Drive
Asheville, NC 28805
Order online or call -800-TOP-SALT
or (800) 867-7258
Fax: (828) 299-1640
www.celtic-seasalt.com

SEA VEGETABLES, American and Canadian

Gold Mine Natural Foods
7805 Arjon's Drive
San Diego, CA 92126
Phone: (800) 475-FOOD **or** (800) 475-3663
www.goldminenaturalfood.com

Maine Coast Sea Vegetables
3 Georges Pond Road
Franklin, ME 04634
Phone: (207) 565-2907
www.seaveg.com

Maine Seaweed
Larch Hanson
P.O. Box 57
Steuben, ME 04680
Phone: (207) 546-2875

Mendocino Sea Vegetable Company
P.O. Box 455
Philo, CA 95466
Phone: (707) 895-2996
Fax: (707) 895-3270
www.seaweed.net

Natural Lifestyle Supplies Mail Order Market
16 Lookout Drive
Asheville, NC 28804-3330
Phone: (800) 752-2775
www.natural-lifestyle.com

STEVIA EXTRACT POWDER & LIQUID

Diamond Organics
The Organic Food Catalog
P.O. Box 2159
Freedom, CA 95019
Phone: (888) ORGANIC **or** (888) 674-2642
www.diamondorganics.com

Gold Mine Natural Foods
7805 Arjon's Drive
San Diego, CA 92126
Phone: (800) 475-FOOD **or** (800) 475-3663
www.goldminenaturalfood.com

Jay Robb Enterprises Inc. (sells Yammit)
5670 El Camino Real, Suite D
Carlsbad, CA 92008
Phone: (877) JAY ROBB
or (760) 448-2860
www.jayrobb.com

(Kal brand stevia extract powder and liquid)
Nutraceutical Corporation
1400 Kearns Boulevard, 2nd Floor
Park City, UT 84060
(800) 365-5966
www.nutraceutical.com

NOW Foods, corporate office
For store listing contact:
395 Glen Ellyn Road,
Bloomingdale, IL 60108
Phone: (800) 999-8069
www.nowfoods.com

To mail order NOW Foods products contact:
Fruitful Yield
154 South Bloomingdale Road
Bloomingdale, IL 60108
Phone: (800) 469-55552
www.fruitfulyield.com

Nu Naturals Inc.
2220 West 2nd Avenue #1
Eugene, OR 97402
Phone: (541) 344-9785
or (800) 753-4372 (HERB)
www.nunaturals.com

Wisdom Natural Herbs
Wisdom of the Ancient Herbal Teas
2546 West Birchwood Avenue, Suite #104
Mesa, AZ 85202
Phone: (800) 899-9908
Fax: (480) 966-3805
www.wisdomnaturalbrands.com
Email: info@wisdomnaturalbrands.com

SUMAC BERRIES, ground

Epicentre
659 Red Pine Lane
Bridge North, Ontario, Canada KOL 1HO
Phone: (705) 292-5247
Fax: (705) 292-7378
www.theepicentre.com
Note: This company grinds sumac without salt.

Great American Spice Company
P.O. Box 80068
Fort Wayne, IN 46898
Phone: (260) 420-8118
or (888) 502) 8058
www.americanspice.com

Seasoned Pioneers LTD
101 Summers Road
Brunswick Business Park
Liverpool, L3 4BJ UK
Phone (UK only): 0800-0682348
Phone/Fax: +44 (0)151-709 9330
www.seasonedpioneers.co.uk
Email: info@seasonedpioneers.co.uk

VITAMIN-E OIL

NOW Foods, corporate office
For store listing contact:
395 Glen Ellyn Road
Bloomingdale, IL 60108
Phone: (800) 999-8069
www.nowfoods.com

To mail order NOW Foods products contact:
Fruitful Yield
154 South Bloomingdale Road
Bloomingdale, IL 60108
Phone: (800) 469-5552
www.fruitfulyield.com

100 PERCENT SPROUTED WHOLE GRAIN FLOUR

Casados Farms
Juanita Casados
Box 852
San Jan Pueblo, NM 87566
Phone: (505) 852-2433

Essential Eating Sprouted Flour Company
P.O. Box 337
Torreon, NM 87061
Phone: (877) 384-0337
Fax: (866) 870-0776
www.creatingheaven.net
Email: foodproducts@creatingheaven.net

100 PERCENT SPROUTED WHOLE GRAIN BREAD

Food for Life
P.O. Box 1434
Corona, CA 92878
Phone: (909) 279-5090
www.foodforlife.com

Oasis Breads
440 Venture Street
Escondido, CA 92029
Phone: (760) 747-7390
Fax: (760) 747-4854
www.oasisbreads.com
Email: bread@oasisbreads.com

Trader Joe's (Main office)
538 Mission St.
South Pasadena, CA 91031
For a state-by-state listing of locations visit:
www.traderjoes.com

YAMMIT, YAM AND SWEET POTATO FLOUR

Jay Robb Enterprises Inc. (Yammit)
5670 El Camino Real, Suite D
Carlsbad, CA 92008
Phone: (877) JAY ROBB
or (760) 448-2860
www.jayrobb.com

Special Foods (sweet potato flour)
9207 Shotgun Court
Springfield, VA 22153
Phone: (703) 644-0991
Fax: (703) 644-1006
www.specialfoods.com

Appendix E:

Buying Clubs across the United States

You can save money on refrigerated, frozen, dried and bottled natural foods, and natural foods products by joining or starting a co-op buying club. To learn more about the benefits of co-op buying clubs, please refer to "Money-Saving Moves" in Chapter 10.

To join an existing club or start your own, contact one or more of the following companies by letter, by phone, or by visiting their Web sites. They need not be located in your city or state; most companies deliver across several states.

Blooming Prairie
A subsidiary of United Natural Foods Inc.
(UNFI)
(Serves supermarkets, natural foods stores, buying clubs, and restaurants and covers 12 states.)
2840 Heinz Road
Iowa City, IA 52240
Phone: (800) 323-2131 **or**
(319) 337-6448
www.blooming-prairie.com

Mountain People's NW
A subsidiary of United Natural Foods Inc.
(UNFI)
(Serves supermarkets, natural foods stores, buying clubs, and restaurants. Covers more than 6 states.)
PO Box 1856
Auburn, WA 98071
Phone: (800) 679-6733 **or**
(253) 333-6769 **or**
Local calls (530) 889-9531
www.unfiw.com

Natural Farms, Inc.
(Covers 7 states.)
2077 S. Stoughton Road
Madison, WI 53716
Phone: (866) 333-9907 **or**
(608) 663-1060
Fax: (608) 663-1061
www.naturalfarms.org
Email: naturalfarmswebsite@hotmail.com

United Natural Foods Incorporated
(Covers all states.)
71 Stow Drive
Chestferfield, NH 03443
Phone: (603) 256-3000
www.unfi.com

Ozark Cooperative
1601 Pump Station Road
Fayetteville, AR 72701
Phone: (800) 967-2667 **or**
(479) 521-4920
Fax: (479) 521-9100
Message line (800) 967-2667
www.ozarkcoop.com

Tucson Cooperative
350 S. Toole Ave
Tucson, AZ 85701
Phone: (800) 350-2667
www.tcwfoodcoop.com

Appendix F:

Recommended Reading

Prime Picks:

Coming Home to Eat: The Pleasures and Politics of Local Foods by Gary Paul Nabhan (W.W. Norton & Co., 2002)

Why Grassfed is Best by Jo Robinson (Vashon Island Press, 2000)

A Cry Unheard: New Insights into the Medical Consequences of Loneliness by James J. Lynch, Ph.D. (Bancroft Press, 2000)

The Cholesterol Myths: Exposing The Fallacy That Saturated Fats & Cholesterol Cause Heart Disease by Uffe Ravsnkov, M.D., Ph.D. (New Trends Publishing, 2000)

Nutrition and Physical Degeneration by Weston A. Price, D.D.S. (Keats Publishing, 1998)

Appleton, Nancy, Ph.D., *Lick the Sugar Habit* (Warner Books, 1988)

Audette, Ray with Troy Gilchrist, *Neanderthin* (St. Martin's Press, 1999)

Bond, Geof, *Natural Eating* (Griffin Publishing Group, 2000)

Boynton, Herb, Mark F. McCarty, and Richard D. Moore, M.D., *The Salt Solution* (Avery, 2001)

Braly, John, M.D., and Ron Hoggan, M.A., *Dangerous Grains* (Avery, 2002)

Brockman, Henry, *Organic Matters* (Terra Books, 2001)

Burkitt, Dennis P., and Hubert C. Trowell, editors, *Western Diseases: Their Emergence and Prevention* (Harvard University Press, 1981)

Cohen, Mark, Ph.D., *Health and the Rise of Civilization* (Yale University Press, 1993)

Cordain, Loren, Ph.D., *The Paleo Diet* (John Wiley & Sons, 2002)

Crawford, Michael and Sheilagh, *What We Eat Today: The Food Manipulators vs. the People* (Stein & Day, 1972)

Crawford, Michael, Ph.D., and David Marsh, *Nutrition and Evolution* (Keats Publishing, 1995)

De Cava, Judith, B.S., C.N.C., C.W.C., *Cholesterol Facts & Fantasies* (Brentwood Academic Press, 1994)

Diamond, Jared, Ph.D., "The Worst Mistake In the History of the Human Race," *Discover,* May 1987, pp. 64-66

Eaton, Randall L., Ph.D., *The Sacred Hunt: Hunting As A Sacred Path* (Sacred Press, 1998)

Eaton, S. Boyd, M.D., Marjorie Shostak, and Melvin Konner, M.D., Ph.D., *The Paleolithic Prescription* (Harper & Row, 1988)

Enig, Mary, Ph.D., *Know Your Fats: The Complete Primer for Understanding the Nutrition of Fats, Oils, and Cholesterol* (Bethesda Press, 2000)

Fife, Bruce, N.D., *The Healing Miracles of Coconut Oil* (Healthwise Publications, 2001)

Gittleman, Ann Louise, Ph.D., *Get the Salt Out* (Crown Trade, 1996)

Gittleman, Ann Louise, Ph.D., *The Fat Flush Plan* (McGraw-Hill, 2002)

Harris, Marvin, Ph.D., *Cannibals and Kings: The Origins of Cultures* (Random House, 1977)

Harris, Marvin, Ph.D., and Eric B. Ross, Ph.D., editors, *Food and Evolution: Toward a Theory of Human Food Habits* (Temple University Press, 1987)

Lynch, James J., Ph.D., *A Cry Unheard: New Insights into the Medical Consequences of Loneliness* (Bancroft Press, 2000)

Mindell, Earl, Ph.D., *Unsafe at Any Meal* (Warner Books, 1987)

Murray, Michael, N.D., and Joseph Pizzorno, N.D., *Encyclopedia of Natural Medicine, 2nd edition* (Prima Publishing, 1998)

Nabhan, Gary Paul, *Coming Home to Eat: The Pleasures and Politics of Local Foods* (W.W Norton & Co., 2002)

Price, Weston A., D.D.S., *Nutrition and Physical Degeneration* (Keats Publishing, 1998)

Ravsnkov, Uffe, M.D., Ph.D., *The Cholesterol Myths: Exposing The Fallacy That Saturated Fats & Cholesterol Cause Heart Disease* (New Trends Publishing, 2000)

Robinson, Jo, *Why Grassfed is Best: The Surprising Benefits of Grassfed Meat, Eggs, and Dairy Products* (Vashon Island Press, 2000)

Schmid, Ron, N.D. *Traditional Foods Are Your Best Medicine* (Inner Traditions, 1997)

Sears, Barry, Ph.D., and Lynn Sears, *Zone Meals In Seconds* (HarperCollins, 2004)

Simopoulos, Artemis, M.D., and Jo Robinson, *The Omega Plan* (HarperCollins, 1998)

Smith, Melissa Diane, *Going Against the Grain: How Reducing and Avoiding Grains Can Revitalize Your Health* (McGraw Hill, 2002)

Sporek, Karel, *Salt and the Seven Deadly Ills* (1st Books, 2001)

Stefansson, Vilhjalmur, *Cancer: Disease of Civilization* (Hill and Wang, 1960)

Yudkin, John, M.D., *Pure, White and Deadly* (Penguin Books, 1988)

Keys to Making the Most Nutritious & Digestible Bread

Many people find it hard to go against the grain. Even if you decide to follow a grain-free diet or to consume cereals only occasionally, other family members may insist on having bread. If you occasionally want bread without the hazards associated with conventional or commercially baked products, you have a couple of options: buy 100 percent sprouted whole grain bread (see Appendix D for suggested brands) or make it yourself.

Why use sprouted flour?

One hundred percent sprouted whole grain flour is a vast improvement over even the freshest whole grain flour. This flour is made from whole grains that have been soaked, sprouted, dehydrated, and then ground. Soaking and sprouting increase the available nutrients and inactivate phytates in whole grains that bind with minerals and interfere with digestion and absorption. We recommend using this flour as a one-for-one substitute for conventional flour in bread and other recipes.

Sprouted flour may be ordered by mail (see Appendix D for sources). Many people prefer the texture and lightness of breads made from hard *white* whole wheat flour or spelt flour to hard red wheat bread flour. Hard white whole wheat flour is a whole grain flour made from a special type of bread wheat with a lighter color and texture. Spelt flour comes from an ancient grain believed to be the precursor of our modern wheat.

Currently, the only sprouted flour on the market is made from spelt. If you're ambitious, have plenty of time, and the right equipment, you can sprout whole grains—spelt, hard red wheat, hard *white* whole wheat, kamut, or a combination of several grains—dehydrate, then grind them to make your own flour. If not, you can buy sprouted spelt flour. Eventually additional varieties of sprouted flours may become available.

Bread Making Tips and Techniques

(1) **Follow instructions to the letter and measure meticulously.** For consistently good results, follow the recipe. If you don't you're apt to add too much flour or water and get inconsistent results.

Bread Myths

There are many myths about bread making. What follows are our answers to those myths, as well as tips, techniques, and recipes we developed during the many years we practiced and taught a grain-based diet, paired with what we later learned about the benefits of using sprouted grains.

Myth number 1: You need sugar to feed the yeast

Most bread recipes call for sugar, but you don't need it. The yeast feeds on the starches in the flour and the bread rises well without sweeteners. The longer you let dough rise, the more time yeast has to work.

Note: To allow longer rising time without letting bread over-rise and become yeasty, use room temperature water, less yeast, or a combination of the two.

Myth number 2: You need to add oil for moist bread

Fat—oil, butter, or margarine—is included in many recipes to moisten the dough, but it adds unnecessary calories. There are better ways to make moist and tender bread without adding fat or oil. One of the best ways is to steam rather than bake the dough.

Myth number 3: 100 percent whole grain bread is inherently heavy

Because 100 percent whole grain flour contains more fiber than refined white flour, it requires a higher ratio of water to flour and more cautious mixing and kneading. The coarse fibers in whole grains soak up more water than refined flour, but they take longer to do so. White bread dough is smooth immediately after kneading. Whole grain dough becomes smoother after rising, when the yeast has broken down the starches enveloped in the fiber.

The stickiness of whole grain dough can fool you into adding too much flour, creating dry, heavy dough that rises only slightly. The key is to add as little flour as possible during kneading.

Turning dough, particularly whole grain dough, onto a floured surface is almost guaranteed to make you add too much flour. Prevent this by kneading dough in a lightweight, stainless steel mixing bowl 12- to 18-inches across. Using a bowl allows you add minute amounts of flour, knead thoroughly, avoid dusting the entire kitchen and prevent sticking.

Myth number 4: Bread must be baked

Western bread is usually shaped into large loaves, baked, and sliced. Asian breads are more often made in the form of small buns, called steamed buns, or flat loaves, and cooked over steam on top of the range. A single, double, or triple batch of buns can be cooked with 1 pot and 1 burner if you have enough stacking trays. Steamed buns take less time and fuel to cook, and won't overheat your kitchen.

Steamed buns aren't just for Chinese meals. They can stand in for sandwich loaves, baguettes, dinner rolls, and burger buns. They also freeze well.

Myth number 5: Unleavened bread is best

Unleavened bread may sound like a good idea, but it's actually more difficult to digest than leavened bread. Leavening with yeast, a sourdough starter, or desem (a collection of airborne yeasts) breaks down phytates (antinutrients) contained in the fiber complex of whole grains. The result is more nutritious and digestible bread.

Myth number 6: Dry bread should be tossed

Bread can be dry without being ready for the refuse pile. Bread made without oil, butter, margarine, shortening, sugar, syrup, or dough conditioners dries out faster, but it is still good. To revive dry bread, wrap it in an unbleached cotton or linen (not paper) napkin or a dish towel (one without a fuzzy texture) and gently steam on a rack or tray for 1 to 3 minutes. Don't steam too long or the bread will become soggy.

Note: A microwave oven will not produce the same results as steam. Steam adds energy and moistens dry bread; a microwave oven scrambles the molecules, creating heat through friction. Although microwaved bread may initially appear moist, it turns hard and dry within minutes. Bread heated by steam stays moist longer and tastes better.

(2) Use the right tools. The right tools can be the difference between success and failure. For a list of essentials, consult the box on the right.

(3) Use a slow-rising method if possible. Try our Slow-Rise recipe or the Standard-Rise Bread Dough with half the amount of yeast called for and room-temperature water to give the yeast more time to work. If you allow the dough to rise at room temperature, your bread will have more flavor.

(4) Whenever possible, steam, rather than bake bread. Although dough recipes we provide may be shaped and cooked as pita breads, dinner rolls, loaves, focaccia, pizza, baguettes, boules, braids, or crowns, breads cooked over steam are the most nutritious and often the most digestible.

Kneading Notes

Kneading stretches the dough and the protein matrix developing gluten, the structure that helps bread rise and hold its shape. Five to 10 minutes or approximately 100 strokes should be sufficient.

Kneading Steps:

1. Oil an 8- to 12-quart stainless steel bowl with olive oil, coconut oil, clarified butter, or ghee and set aside. After kneading, you will put the dough in this bowl, cover it and let the bread rise.

2. In a second 8- to 12-quart stainless steel bowl, stir yeast into the minimal amount of flour called for in the recipe.

3. Add warm water and stir with a large sturdy spoon. Add 1/2 cup flour a few tablespoons at a time. Go slowly. It's better for the dough to be too wet than too dry.

4. When the dough becomes difficult to mix with a spoon, switch to your hands. Knead with one hand, keeping fingers closed, and add flour with the other.

5. Slightly cup your hand to scoop the dough toward you, fold toward center of bowl, and then push it away using the heel of your hand. Repeat once; give the bowl a quarter clockwise turn, and continue. At first, the dough will look like cookie dough; within 5 minutes it will be stiffer. The dough should come away from the sides of the bowl as you knead.

Bread Making Tools

* **Dry measuring cups for flour** (stainless steel is more accurate and durable than plastic)

* **Liquid measuring cups for water** (glass is best)

* **Measuring spoons** (stainless steel is more accurate and durable than plastic)

* **Oversized 12- to 16-quart stainless steel mixing bowls for mixing, kneading, and rising**

* **Large mixing spoon** (the sturdier the better)

* **Candy thermometer or other instant-read thermometer to test the water**

* **12-inch bamboo or metal steamer trays to cook buns** (2 to 6 trays and 1 lid)

* **9-inch heat-proof dinner plates to cook bun dough** (one for each steamer tray; 2 plates for a single batch, 4 for a double batch)

* **Food scale or ruler and sharp knife** (to weigh and/or divide the dough into equal portions)

* **Cotton or linen napkins or kitchen towels** (to wrap and steam dry bread)

6. If the dough sticks to the sides of the bowl, it's too wet and needs more flour. Add 1/4 cup at a time, and only enough to create a smooth dough that pulls away from the sides to form a smooth ball. It takes time for the fibers in whole grains to soak up water. Be patient. Too much flour will result in a dry, stiff dough and brick-like bread. When in doubt, knead more before adding flour beyond the initial 3 cups called for in the recipe for a single batch of dough.

7. When the dough feels fairly firm and slightly elastic, rub your palms together so stuck bits of dough come off your hands into the bowl, and incorporate them into the ball of dough. For the final kneading, it works best to move the bread bowl to a folded towel or mat on the floor and knead with the bowl in front of you, putting your weight into it. If this sounds too awkward, move the bowl to a table slightly lower than your hips so you'll have more leverage as you knead.

How do you know when you're done kneading?
The dough:
1). is moist,
2). pulls away from the sides of the bowl to form a smooth ball,
3). springs back to the touch when dented with your fingertips, (it can stick a little, as long as it's not coming off in big chunks on your hands or the sides of the bowl),
4). it has a texture like pizza dough and you could roll it out, and
5). it has the same consistency as your earlobe or is soft and smooth like a baby's bottom.

Note: If the dough doesn't spring back to the touch, it's too dry. You can mix in a little water by repeatedly moistening your hands, but this is tricky.

Be aware that whole grain dough may have some cracks in it even after the initial kneading because the fiber doesn't form gluten.

Best Rising Places

1) room temperature, away from hot appliances or cold drafts
2) a sunny windowsill or counter top in warm weather
3) near, but not on, a radiator
4) in a gas oven with only the pilot light on
5) in an electric coven with just the light on
6) in an oven preheated to 140° F for 15 minutes, then turned off

Basic Bread Dough

Prep: 20 to 30 minutes ~ **Rising:** 2 to 4 hours as needed ~ **Yield:** 8 large buns or rolls

Ingredients & Directions

Dry ingredients:

3 to 3 1/2 cups 100 percent sprouted spelt flour, slightly more only if needed (see Appendix for sources)

2 teaspoons active dry yeast (more for a faster rise, less for a slower rise)

Wet ingredients:

1 1/3 cups warm filtered water

1 teaspoon unrefined sea salt (if coarse, dissolve in warm water)

Virgin-pressed olive or coconut oil, butter, **or** ghee to grease the bowl used for rising

1. Reserve 1/2 cup flour. Measure 2 1/2 cups flour into a 12- to 18-inch stainless steel mixing bowl. Sprinkle with yeast, stir, and make a well in the center.

2. Warm salted water over moderate (not high) heat until hot to the touch, no hotter than 100 to 110° F. Stir water to dissolve salt. Test with instant-read thermometer. If too hot, allow to cool.

3. Use a large spoon to mix warm water into flour to form a soft dough. Add remaining 1/2 cup flour, a little at a time. When too stiff to stir with a spoon, begin kneading with one hand, using the other hand to add flour and turn the bowl.

4. Knead dough in the bowl, adding as little flour as possible—only enough to keep the dough from being too sticky or wet. (See Kneading Notes Page 539 to 540). Knead until dough is elastic, supple, and pulls away from the sides to form a smooth ball. Add more flour a tablespoon at a time, only if necessary.

5. Rest the ball of dough in an oiled 3-quart Pyrex bowl for a single batch or an 8- to 12-quart mixing bowl for a double batch. Cover a 3-quart bowl with a 9- to 10-inch dinner plate (oil the bottom to keep the dough from sticking as it rises). Cover a larger bowl with a larger upside down bowl. Or rest an oiled cooling rack over the bowl and cover with a clean, damp kitchen towel.

6. Allow the dough to rise in a warm place for approximately 1 to 2 hours, or at room temperature for 2 to 4 hours, or until it has nearly doubled in bulk.

~Directions continued and Variations on next page~

Nutrition

Entire recipe (using 3 1/2 cups flour):
1495 calories
52 g protein
293 g carbs
 (39 g fiber)
13 g fat
104 mg calcium
1840 mg sodium

1 large bun (8 per batch):
187 calories
7 g protein
37 g carbohydrate
 (5 g fiber)
2 g fat
13 mg calcium
230 mg sodium

1 small bun (10 per batch):
150 calories
5 g protein
29 g carbohydrate
 (4 g fiber)
1 g fat
10 mg calcium
184 mg sodium

This basic dough is amenable to a wide range of breads (buns, boules, dinner rolls, sandwich loaves, pita pockets, focaccia, etc.). We favor steaming because it is energy efficient, cooks on top of the stove and at a lower temperature than baking, and produces a marvelously moist texture. Use one of the slow-rise variations on Page 542 for maximum nutrition, digestibility, and flavor. If you plan to let the dough rise overnight, start it after dinner or just before going to bed.

Note: Although our recipe calls for sprouted spelt flour, you can substitute sprouted whole wheat bread flour, or sprouted kamut flour, if available. If you use a combination of several sprouted flours, the majority must be made up of grains that contain gluten. Recipes may be doubled or tripled. Use a large enough bowl to mix and let dough rise.

Directions

7. Gently punch dough down and knead a couple of turns in the bowl, folding the dough in on itself. If you're not ready to cook it, cover again, and allow the dough to rise and double again. (You can do this several times if you like.) Alternatively, after punching down, cover and refrigerate dough for up to 24 hours, then bring to room temperature and allow to rise one more time before proceeding.

8. Shape dough according to the Steamed Bun recipe. Allow it to rise one more time until it has doubled in bulk, about 1/2 to 2 hours, depending on ambient temperature. Don't let it over-rise. Cook according to directions for Steamed Buns (Page 543) or your favorite type of bread.

Variations

* **Rapid-Rise Dough:** Replace active dry yeast with 2 teaspoons rapid-rise yeast. Heat water to 125° F. After kneading dough, shape it into buns, let rise once, then cook according to directions for Steamed Buns (Page 543). Or, shape and bake as for your favorite type of bread.

* **Slow-Rise Dough 1:** Reduce active dry yeast to 1 teaspoon. Use room-temperature water. If salt is coarse or chunky, dissolve in warm water, then cool to 70 to 80° F. Let rise at *room temperature* until doubled in bulk, 4 to 6 hours in warm weather, 8 to 10 hours or overnight in cold weather. Punch down dough. If you're not ready to cook it yet, allow it to rise a second time, punch down, then shape and cook as directed for Steamed Buns (Page 543) or your favorite type of bread.

* **Slow-Rise Dough 2:** Reduce active dry yeast to 1/3 teaspoon. Use room-temperature water. If salt is coarse or chunky, dissolve in warm water, then cool to 70 to 80° F. Let dough rise at *room temperature* until doubled in bulk, 6 to 8 hours or overnight, then punch down, shape and cook as for Steamed Buns (Page 543) or your favorite type of bread.

* **Mixed-Grain Bread Doughs:** For a single batch, replace 1/2 to 1 cup of spelt or wheat flour with one of the following whole grain flours— buckwheat, barley, kamut **or** millet flour, **or** non-GMO (non genetically modified) yellow or blue cornmeal. When using more than one kind of flour, add the flour used in the smallest amount first, reserving 1 cup of wheat or spelt flour to add in small increments as needed.

Basic Bread Dough ~ continued

Steamed Buns

Prep: 15 minutes ~ **Rising:** 1/2 to 2 hours ~ **Cooking:** 20 minutes ~ **Yield:** 8 large buns

Ingredients & Directions

1 recipe Basic Bread Dough, from 3 to 3 1/2 cups of flour (Page 541)

Unrefined coconut oil **or** extra-virgin olive oil **or** butter to oil dinner plates

1. Oil two 9-inch heat-proof plates for a single batch.

2. **For *Rapid-Rise Dough*:** Shape dough immediately after mixing and kneading.

   For *Standard or Slow-Rise Dough*: Let dough rise once in a covered bowl. Shape into a uniform 8-inch log. With a ruler and a sharp knife, cut into 8 equal pieces.

3. **To shape:** Put 1 piece of dough in the palm of your left hand. Fold the top edge toward the center (as if closing the petals of a flower). Give the dough a quarter turn and pull an overlapping piece of dough toward the center. Repeat until smooth, round and all sides have been tucked in.

4. Place the ball seam side down in your left hand. Cup your right hand over the top and gently roll to make a smooth ball. Seams should disappear quickly as you fold the dough in on itself.

5. Arrange 4 large balls of dough seam side down on each oiled plate, leaving 1-inch of space between each ball. Put each plate on a 10 1/2- to 12-inch bamboo steamer tray. Stack trays and cover.

6. Allow dough to rise in a warm place 15 to 30 minutes for Rapid-Rise Dough, longer at room temperature, or until doubled in bulk (1 to 3 hours for Basic or Slow-Rise Dough).

7. Heat 2 inches of water to boiling in a wok or a wide, deep 4- to 6-quart pot that allows 2 to 4 inches between the water and the bottom of the steamer. Diameter of pot should match the diameter of the trays. If a wok is used, bamboo trays should rest inside the rim but the water should not touch the bottom of the tray.

8. When boiling water is steaming, reduce heat to medium or medium-high, and start timing. Water must maintain a steaming boil for the entire cooking time: 15 minutes for a single batch, 20 minutes for a double or triple batch. Immediately turn off the heat, but don't peek! Let buns rest, covered, over the warm pot for 10 minutes to complete the cooking process. If using an electric range, move the pot off the hot burner to cool.

Nutrition

**1 bun
(8 per batch):**
187 calories
7 g protein
37 g carbohydrate
         (5 g fiber)
2 g fat
13 mg calcium
230 mg sodium

**1 small bun
(10 per batch):**
150 calories
5 g protein
29 g carbohydrate
         (4 g fiber)
1 g fat
10 mg calcium
184 mg sodium

Unfilled buns can replace loaf bread, burger buns, English muffins, or dinner rolls. You can cook a single, double, or triple batch in 20 minutes using 1 pot and burner if you have enough steamers. Buns may be frozen.

You will need 2 stacking 12-inch bamboo steamer trays for a single batch, 4 for a double batch, and 6 for triple batch. Each tray should be large enough to hold a 9-inch heat-proof dinner plate with 1/8 to 1/4-inch of space around each plate. (You can try lining the trays with unbleached parchment but we've never done it that way.)

If you don't have bamboo trays, improvise. Use large, stacking stainless steel steamers, 1 or more stockpots fitted with accordion style vegetable steamers elevated on aluminum cans with the tops and bottoms removed, or 1 or 2 roasting pans fitted with large meat racks elevated at least 3 inches above the water. The top tray, stock pot, or roasting pans must have tight fitting lids.

~Directions continued on next page~

Directions

9. Uncover. Remove buns with a spatula. Cool on a rack or place in a towel-lined bread basket. Store in sealed bags in the refrigerator. Use within 2 weeks or freeze.

10. To reheat, moisten and freshen leftover or dry buns, slice buns in half and wrap in an uncolored cotton-linen towel and steam over rapidly boiling water for 1 to 3 minutes, then serve.

How to Fill Steamed Bun Dough

Figure no more than 1 to 3 tablespoons of filling per bun (2/3 to 1 3/4 cups of filling for an entire batch). For rich fillings, such as pesto or a buttery garlic filling, figure 2 teaspoons per bun.

1. In step 3, flatten each ball of dough into a 4- to 5-inch round in the palm of your hand. Don't roll out all of the balls of dough at once or they will dry out. Flatten and fill one at a time. Don't roll dough too thin or filling will leak out.
2. Spoon filling into the center of each piece of dough.
3. Pull 1 edge of the circle of dough up over filling to form a semi-circle or half-moon and pinch shut.
4. Tuck edges toward the center to form a ball; turn the ball over so the seam is on the bottom.
5. Roll dough gently between cupped hands, keeping seam-side down. Don't press hard or filling will ooze out.
6. Place bun seam-side down on well-oiled plate. Repeat with each ball. Cover and allow to rise.
7. Cook on plates as directed in recipe for Steamed Buns

Great filling ideas
* Pesto or Pistou
* Barbecued chicken or pork
* Curried chicken
* Mashed roasted garlic with olive oil or butter
* Peanut or almond butter with fruit-sweetened jelly
* Roasted garlic tapenade (sold in bottles)
* Sun-dried tomato tapenade (sold in bottles)

Steamed Buns ~ continued

Appendix H:

Proper Preparation of Whole Grains

Whole grains are relatively difficult to digest unless properly prepared. For thousands of years before the invention of industrial grain processing, traditional agrarian cooks used long soaking and cooking to make whole grains more digestible.

Most whole grains must be soaked at least 24 hours—on the verge of sprouting—to inactivate antinutrients such as enzyme inhibitors and phytates, and to initiate the hydration and breakdown of complex starches. Long cooking completes the predigestion process by thoroughly hydrating the starch molecules, required to render them vulnerable to our starch digestion enzymes.

Even rolled, cracked, or ground whole grains need soaking and longer cooking than commonly applied. To make rolled grains, the whole grains are briefly steamed, then rolled flat with large heavy rollers (nothing is removed from the whole grain). Rolled, cracked, and ground grains still contain antinutrients that need to be eliminated and starches that are difficult to digest unless soaked at least 12 hours and cooked for at least 30 minutes.

Only 100 years ago this was common knowledge, in part because packages of rolled oats recommended overnight soaking and cooking for 30 minutes or more. However, the packages changed with the fast pace of life, introduction of processed foods, and loss of traditional culinary lore.

Whole grains can be cooked in the water in which they are soaked. If your digestion is especially weak, after the soaking period you can pour off and measure the soaking water and replace it with an equal amount of fresh water, stock, or broth before cooking the grain.

The following table lists commonly used whole grains that are prepared by boiling, along with amount of water to use in soaking/ cooking, time required for soaking, and time for simmering after bringing to a boil.

Whole Grain (1 cup)	Water (cups)	Soaking time (hours)	Cooking time (minutes)
Amaranth	2	24 to 48	30 to 45
Barley*	2–3	24 to 48	60 to 90 (overnight for hot cereal)
Buckwheat	2	24 to 48	30
Millet	2–3	24 to 48	30 to 45
Oat groats	4	24 to 48	60 to 720 (1 to 12 hours)
Quinoa	2	12 to 24	15 to 45
Rice, brown	2	24 to 48	60 to 90
Rye*	2	24 to 48*	60 to 90
Teff	2	12 to 24	30 to 45
Wheat*	2	24 to 48*	60 to 90
Rolled grain, such as			
Rolled oats	2	12 to 24	30 to 45
Cracked grain**	2	12 to 24	30 to 45

Amount of water listed is for boiling and simmering. When pressure cooking whole grains, you may wish to reduce water by 1/2 cup for each cup of dry grain.

* Barley, rye and wheat are best digested if fully sprouted for 3 to 4 days in their whole state, or rolled or cracked and soaked prior to cooking.

** Includes polenta, corn grits, and steel cut oats. For steel oats, figure 1 cup dry grain to 3 1/2 to 4 cups water. Steel cut oats may be cooked overnight on LOW in a slow cooker.

Note: When shopping for rolled grains, such as oatmeal, always choose thick or old-fashioned over quick-cooking or instant oatmeal. For hot cereal, whole, steel cut, or rolled oats may be soaked during the day, then cooked overnight on low in a slow cooker.

Endnotes

Chapter 1: Finding *The Garden of Eating*

Introductory excerpt: Ni M, trans. *The Yellow Emperor's Classic of Medicine.* Boston: Shambhala, 1995:50.

1. Price W. *Nutrition and Physical Degeneration.* New Canaan, CT: Keats Publishing, 1998.

2. Cordain L, Eaton SB, Brand Miller J, Lindeberg S, Jensen C. An evolutionary analysis of the aetiology and pathogenesis of juvenile-onset myopia. *Acta Opthalmol Scand* 2002;80:125-135.

3. Cordain L, Lindeberg S, Hurtado M, Hill K, Eaton SB, Brand-Miller J. Acne vulgaris: A disease of western civilization. *Arch Dermatol* 2002;138:1584-90.

4. Murray M, Pizzorno J. *Encyclopedia of Natural Medicine, 2nd edition.* Rocklin, CA: Prima Publishing, 1998:194.

5. Burkitt DP, Trowell HC, eds. *Western Diseases: their emergence and prevention.* Cambridge MA: Harvard University Press, 1981:xv.

6. Eaton SB, Konner M, Shostak M. *The Paleolithic Prescription.* New York: Harper & Row, 1988.

7. Stefansson V. *Cancer: Disease of Civilization.* New York: Hill and Wang, 1960.

8. Diamond J. The Worst Mistake in the History of the Human Race. *Discover* 1987 (May):64-66.

9. Hopfenberg R, Pimentel D. Human population numbers as a function of food supply. *Environment, Development, and Sustainability* 2001;3:1-15.

10. Cohen MN. The Significance of Long Term Changes in Human Diet and Food Economy. In: Harris M, Ross EB, eds. *Food and Evolution.* Philadelphia, PA: Temple University Press, 1987.

11. Eaton SB, Konner M, Shostak M. *The Paleolithic Prescription.* New York: Harper & Row, 1988: 77. See also: Cordain L, Miller J, Mann N. Scant evidence of periodic starvation among hunter-gatherers. *Diabetologia* 1999;42:383-384.

12. Frisch RE. Fatness and fertility. *Scientific American* 1988 (March):88-95.

13. Eades MR, Eades MD. *Protein Power Lifeplan.* New York: Warner Books, 2000:15.

14. Bond G. *Natural Eating.* Torrance, CA: Griffin Publishing Group, 2000:131.

15. Liedloff J. *Understanding the Continuum Concept.* Accessed on the World Wide Web 9/19/2003, at <www.continuum-concept.org/cc_defined>.

16. Liedloff J. *The Continuum Concept.* New York: Random House, 1977.

17. Marieb EN. *Human Anatomy and Physiology,* Fifth Edition. New York: Benjamin Cummings, 2001: 673.

18. Crawford M, Marsh D. *Nutrition and Evolution.* New Canaan, CT: Keats, 1995:232.

Chapter 2: Native Nutrition

1. Price W. *Nutrition and Physical Degeneration.* New Canaan, CT: Keats, 1998:256-266.

2. Nowak RM. Walker's Mammals of the World Online. Johns Hopkins University Press, 1997. <www.press.jhu.edu/books/walkers_mammals_of_the_world/sirenia/sirenia.html>, accessed on the World Wide Web 8/13/2003.

3. Cordain L, Miller JB, Eaton SB, Mann N, Holt SHA, Speth JD. Plant-animal subsistence ratios and macronutrient energy estimations in worldwide hunter-gatherer diets. *Am J Clin Nutr* 2000;71: 682-92.

4. Price, op cit:265.

5. Crawford M, Marsh D. *Nutrition and Evolution.* New Canaan, CT: Keats, 1995:171-72.

6. Price, op cit:107.

7. Crawford, Marsh, op cit:170.

8. Abrams HL. The Preference for Animal Protein and Fat: A Cross-Cultural Survey. In Harris M, Ross EB, eds. *Food and Evolution.* Philadelphia, PA: Temple University Press, 1987):207.

9. Cordain L, Watkins BA, Florant GL, Kehler M, Rogers L, Li Y. Fatty acid analysis of wild ruminant tissues: Evolutionary implications for reducing diet-related chronic disease. *Eur J Clin Nutr* 2002;56:181-191.

10. Robinson, J. *Why Grassfed is Best.* Vashon, WA: Vashon Island Press, 2000.

11. Enig M. *Know Your Fats.* Silver Spring, MD: Bethesda Press, 2000:284.

12. Schmid RF. *Traditional Foods Are Your Best Medicine.* Rochester, VT: Healing Arts Press, 1997.

13. Eaton SB, Konner M, Shostak M. *The Paleolithic Prescription.* New York: Harper & Row, 1988.

14. Lee R, DeVore I, eds. *Kalahari Hunter-gatherers: Studies of the !Kung San and Their Neighbors.* Cambridge, MA: Harvard University Press, 1976.

15. Harris DR. Aboriginal Subsistence in a Tropical Rain Forest Environment. In Harris M, Ross EB, eds. *Food and Evolution.* Philadelphia, PA: Temple University Press, 1987:357-86.

16. Cordain L, et al. Plant-animal subsistence ratios and macronutrient energy estimations in worldwide hunter-gatherer diets. *Am J Clin Nutr* 2000;71:682-692, see 684-685.

17. Darby M. Meat and Wapatos: The post-glacial distribution of Sagittaria latifolia in North America and the implications of this with regards to the diet of late Pleistocene, early Holocene hunter-gatherers. Paper presented at the 63rd Annual National Meeting of the Society of American Archaeologists Conference, Seattle, 1996. Also Darby MC. Meat Bias dietary ratios. The Paleolithic Diet Symposium List, PALEODIET@MAELSTROM.STJOHNS.EDU, 9/16/2003 11:29 PM.

18. Enig, op cit:91.

19. Sebastian A, Frassetto LA, Sellmeyer DE, Merriam RL, Morris RC. Estimation of the net acid load of the diet of ancestral preagricultural Homo sapiens and their hominid ancestors. *Am J Clin Nutr* 2002;76:1308-16.

20. Remer T, Manz F. Potential renal acid load of foods and its influence on urine pH. *J Am Dietetic Assn* 1995;95(7):791-97. Our averages differ from Remer and Franz because we included all fresh and dried fruits and all fresh vegetables, but excluded all processed meats, in our calculations; Remer and Franz excluded dried fruits and spinach but included processed meats in their calculations. Remer and Franz did not calculate values for kale, collards, or other alkali-rich dark greens. These greens and dried fruits are part of our plan.

Chapter 3: Friendly Foods

1. Yerkes RM. *The Great Apes.* New Haven, CT: Yale University Press, 1929. Cited by Groves B. The design of our digestive organs and digestive enzymes today. Accessed on the World Wide Web, 8/7/2003, at <www.second-opinions.co.uk/carn_herb_comparison>.

2. Whitney EN, Rolfes SR. *Understanding Nutrition.* Minneapolis/St. Paul, MN: West Pub. Co., 1993: 200-03.

3. Murray M, Pizzorno J. *Encyclopedia of Natural Medicine, 2nd edition.* Rocklin, CA: Prima Publishing, 1998:233-34.

4. Scrimshaw NS. Iron Deficiency. *Scientific American* 1991 (Oct.):46-52.

5. Whitney, Rolfes, op cit:406-24.

6. Hokin BD, Butler T. Cyanocobalamin (vitamin B12) status in Seventh-day Adventist ministers in Australia. *Am J Clin Nutr* 1999 Sept;70(3 Suppl):576S-578S.

7. Lin Y, Dueker SR, Burri BJ, Neidlinger TR, Clifford AJ. Variability of the conversion of beta-carotene to vitamin A in women measured by using a double-tracer study design. *Am J Clin Nutr* 2000 June;71(6):1545-54.

8. Hickenbottom SJ, Follett JR, Lin Y, Dueker SR, Burri BJ, Neidlinger TR, Clifford AJ. Variability in conversion of beta-carotene to vitamin A in men as measured by using a double-tracer study design. *Am J Clin Nutr* 2002 May;75(5):900-7.

9. Nierenberg DW, Dain BJ, Mott LA, Baron JA, Greenberg ER. Effects of 4 years of oral supplementation with beta-carotene on serum concentrations of retinol, tocopherol, and five carotenoids. *Am J Clin Nutr* 1997 Aug;66(2):315-9.

10. Healthy News You Can Use—Vegetarians have elevated homocysteine levels. *Townsend Letter for Doctors and Patients* 2001 (April). Reports a study published in *Annals of Nutrition and Metabolism* 2000;44:135-38, which found low methionine and B12 levels and elevated homocysteine levels among vegans and vegetarians compared to omnivores, with the vegans suffering most.

11. Mazess R. Bone mineral content of North Alaskan Eskimos. *Am J Clin Nutr* 1974;27:916.

12. Munger RG, Cerhan JR, C-H Chiu B. Prospective study of dietary protein intake and risk of hip fracture in postmenopausal women. *Am J Clin Nutr* 1999;69:147-152.

13. Roughead ZKF, Johnson LK, Lykken GI, Hunt JR. Controlled High Meat Diets Do Not Affect Calcium Retention or Indices of Bone Status in Healthy Postmenopausal Women. *J Nutr* 2003 April 1;133(4):1020-1026.

14. Kerstetter JE, O'Brien KO, Insogna KL. Low Protein Intake: The Impact on Calcium and Bone Homeostasis in Humans. *J Nutr* 2003 March 1;133(3):855S- 861.

15. Chiu JF, Lan SJ, Yang CY, Wang PW, Yao WJ, Su LH, Hsieh CC, School of Public Health, Kaohsiung Medical College, Taiwan. Long-term vegetarian diet and bone mineral density in postmenopausal Taiwanese women. *Calcif Tissue Int* 1997 Mar;60(3):245-9.

16. Liao EY, Wu XP, Deng XG, et al. Age-related bone mineral density, accumulated bone loss rate and prevalence of osteoporosis at multiple skeletal sites in Chinese women. *Osteoporos Int* (England) 2002 Aug;13(8):669-76.

17. Heaney RP. Age related osteoporosis in Chinese women. *Am J Clin Nutr* 1999;69(6):1291-92.

18. Cordain L. Cereal Grains: Humanity's Double Edged Sword. *World Rev Nutr Diet* 1999;84:19-73.

19. McDonald L. *The Ketogenic Diet: A complete guide for dieters and practitioners*. Kearney, NE: Morris Publishing, 1998:35.

20. Schaefer O. Eskimos (Inuit). In: Burkitt DP, Trowell HC, eds. *Western Diseases: Their Emergence and Prevention*. Cambridge, MA: Harvard University Press, 1981:114.

21. Murray, Pizzorno, op cit: 381. Also: Wurtman RJ, Wurtman JJ. Carbohydrates and Depression. *Scientific American* 1989 (January):68-75.

22. Bushinsky DA. Acid-base imbalance and the skeleton. *Eur J Nutr* 2001;40(5):238-244.

23. Sebastian A, Harris ST, Ottaway JH, Todd KM, Morris RC. Improved mineral balance and skeletal metabolism in postmenopausal women treated with potassium bicarbonate. *NEJM* 1994 June 23;330(25):1776-1781.

24. Sebastian A, et al. Diet Evolution, and Aging: The pathophysiological effects of the post-industrial inversion of the potassium-to-sodium and base-to-chloride ratios in the human diet. *Euro J Nut* 2001;40(5):200-213.

25. Tucker KL, Hannan MT, Chen H, Cupples LA, Wilson PW, Kiel DP. Potassium, magnesium, and fruit and vegetable intakes are associated with greater bone mineral density in elderly men and women. *Am J Clin Nutr* 1999 April 1;69(4):727 - 736.

26. New SA, Robins SP, Campbell MK, Martin JC, Garton MJ, Bolton-Smith C, Grubb DA, Lee SJ, Reid DM. Dietary influences on bone mass and bone metabolism: further evidence of a positive link between fruit and vegetable consumption and bone health? *Am J Clin Nutr* 2000 Jan. 1;71(1): 142 - 151.

27. Stefansson V. Adventures In Diet, Part III. *Harper's Monthly* 1936 (Feb):189.

28. World Cancer Research Fund & American Institute for Cancer Research, 1997.

29. Munoz de Chavez M, Chavez A. Diet that prevents cancer: recommendations from the American Institute for Cancer Research. *Int J Cancer Suppl* (United States)1998;11:85-9.

30. Lindeberg S. On the Benefits of Ancient Diets. <www.panix.com/~paleodiet/lindeberg/>

31. Lu HC. *Chinese Foods For Longevity* NY: Sterling,1990:17.

32. Willcox BJ, Willcox DC, Suzuki M. *The Okinawa Program.* New York: Clarkson Potter, 2001:17.

Chapter 4: Problems With Farmed Foods

1. Cohen MN. The Significance of Long Term Changes in Human Diet and Food Economy. In Harris M, Ross EB, eds. *Food and Evolution.* Philadelphia, PA: Temple University Press, 1987.

2. Cordain L. Cereal Grains: Humanity's Double Edged Sword. *World Rev Nutr Diet* 1999;84:19-73.

3. Freed DLJ. Editorial: Do dietary lectins cause disease? *BMJ* 1999 April 17;318:1023-1024.

4. Allan CB, Lutz W. *Life Without Bread.* Chicago: Keats, 2000:136-139.

5. Jarvis WT. Why I Am Not a Vegetarian. <www.acsh.org/publications/priorities/0902/vegetarian.html>.

6. Braly J, Hoggan R. *Dangerous Grains.* New York: Avery, 2002.

7. Cordain L. *The Paleo Diet.* New York: John Wiley and Sons, 2002:53-55.

8. Bahna S. *Allergies to Milk.* New York: Grune and Stratton, 1980.

9. Grant WB, Moore A. The Role of Sugars in Ischemic Heart Disease. *Townsend Letter for Doctors and Patients* 1999 (February/March):80-86.

10. Scott FW, Kolb H. Cows' Milk and Insulin-Dependent Diabetes Mellitus. *Lancet* 1996 Aug 31;348:613.

11. Cramer DW, et al. Galactose Consumption and Metabolism in Relation to the Risk of Ovarian Cancer. *Lancet* 1989;2:66-71.

12. Schauss A. *Diet, Crime, and Delinquency.* Berkeley CA: Parker House, 1981:13-14.

13. Agranoff B. Diet and Geographical Distribution of Multiple Sclerosis. *Lancet* 1974;2:1061.

14. Alter M. Multiple Sclerosis and Nutrition. *Arch Neurol* 1974;31:267.

15. Dohan FC, et al. Relapsed schizophrenics: More rapid improvement on a milk and cereal free diet. *Br J Psych* 1969;115:595-96.

16. Dohan FC, Grasberger JC. Relapsed schizophrenics: Early discharge from the hospital after cereal-free, milk free diet. *Am J Psychiatry* 1973;130:685-88.

17. Crawford M, Marsh D. *Nutrition and Evolution.* New Canaan, CT: Keats, 1995:241.

18. Williams RJ. *Nutrition Against Disease.* New York: Pitman, 1971:269-270.

19. Ravnskov U. *The Cholesterol Myths: Exposing the Fallacy that Saturated Fat and Cholesterol Cause Heart Disease.* Washington, D.C.: New Trends Publishing, 2000:32-38, 99.

20. Williams RJ, op cit:300.

21. Robinson J. *Why Grassfed is Best.* Vashon, WA: Vashon Island Press, 2000:18-23.

22. Schmid RF. *Traditional Foods Are Your Best Medicine.* Rochester, VT: Healing Arts Press, 1997):160-168.

23. Feskanich D, et al. Milk, dietary calcium, and bone fractures in women: A 12 year prospective study. *Am J Public Health* 1997;87:992-997.

24. Feskanich D, Willett WC, Colditz GA. Calcium, vitamin D, milk consumption, and hip fractures: a prospective study among postmenopausal women. *Am J Clin Nutr* 2003 Feb. 1; 77(2):504-11.

25. Weinsier RL, Krumdieck CL. Dairy foods and bone health: examination of the evidence. *Am J Clin Nutr* 2000 Sept. 1;72(3): 681-89.

26. Heaney RP, Weaver CM. Calcium absorption from kale. *Am J Clin Nutr* 1990 Apr.; 51(4):656-657.

27. National Academy of Sciences. *Recommended Dietary Allowances, ninth edition.* Washington, D.C.: National Academy Press, 1980:128.

28. Sclafani A. Dietary Obesity Models. In: Bjorntorp P, Brodoff BN, eds. *Obesity.* New York: JB Lippincott, 1992:241-248.

29. Murray M, Pizzorno J. *Encyclopedia of Natural Medicine, 2nd edition.* Rocklin, CA: Prima Publishing, 1998. Check index for "sugar".

30. Yudkin J. *Pure, White and Deadly.* New York: Penguin, 1986.

31. De Stefani E, Deneo-Pellegrini H, Mendilaharsu M, et al. Dietary Sugar and Lung Cancer: A Case-Control Study in Uruguay. *Nutrition and Cancer* 1998;31(2):132-7.

32. Brody J. New Data on Sugar and Child Behavior. *New York Times* 1990 May 10.

33. Jones TW, et al. Enhanced Adrenomedulary Response and Increased Susceptibility to Neuroglycopenia: Mechanisms Underlying the Adverse Effects of Sugar Ingestion in Healthy Children. *Journal of Pediatrics* 1995;126(2):171-77.

34. Grimes DS. Refined Carbohydrate, Smooth-Muscle Spasm and Disease of the Colon. *Lancet* 1976;1:395-97.

35. Cornee J, et al. A Case-Control Study of Gastric Cancer and Nutritional Factors in Marseille, France. *European Journal of Epidemiology* 1995;11(1):55-65.

36. Slattery ML, Benson J, Berry TD, et al. Dietary sugar and colon cancer. *Cancer Epidemiol Biomarkers Prev* (United States)1997 Sept.; 6(9):677-85.

37. Calza S, Ferraroni M, La Vecchia C, et al. Low-risk diet for colorectal cancer in Italy. *Eur J Cancer Prev* (England) 2001 Dec;10(6):515-21.

38. Franceschi S, La Vecchia C, Russo A, et al. Low-risk diet for breast cancer in Italy. *Cancer Epidemiol Biomarkers Prev* (United States)1997 Nov; 6(11):875-9.

39. Franceschi S, Favero A, La Vecchia C, et al. Food groups and risk of colorectal cancer in Italy. *Int J Cancer* (United States)1997 Jul 3;72(1):56-61.

40. Rossignol AM, Bonnlander H. Prevalence and severity of the premenstrual syndrome. Effects of foods and beverages that are sweet or high in sugar content. *J Reprod Med* (United States), 1991 Feb.;36(2):131-6.

41. Dahl LK. Salt Intake and Salt Need. *NEJM* 1958 June 5:1152-57.

42. Boynton H, McCarty MF, Moore R. *The Salt Solution.* New York: Penguin Putnam Inc., 2001.

43. National Academy of Sciences. *Recommended Dietary Allowances, ninth edition.* Washington, D.C.: National Academy Press,1980:170.

44. Sebastian A, et al. Diet Evolution, and Aging: The pathophysiological effects of the post-industrial inversion of the potassium-to-sodium and base-to-chloride ratios in the human diet. *Euro J Nut* 2001;40(5):200-213.

45. Svardsudd K. Moderate alcohol consumption and cardiovascular disease: is there evidence for a preventive effect? *Alcohol Clin Exp Res* (United States) 1998 Oct. 22(7 Suppl):307S-314S.

46. Sasaki S. Alcohol and its relation to all-cause and cardiovascular mortality. *Acta Cardiol* (Belgium) 2000 Jun.;55(3):151-6

47. Coppere H, Audigier JC. Trends of mortality from cirrhosis in France between 1925 and 1982. *Gastroenterol Clin Biol* (France) 1986 Jun-Jul;10(6-7):468-74.

48. Folts JD. Potential health benefits from the flavonoids in grape products on vascular disease. *Adv Exp Med Biol* (United States) 2002;505:95-111.

49. Vinson JA. Teufel K, Wu N. Red wine, dealcoholized red wine, and especially grape juice, inhibit atherosclerosis in a hamster model. *Atherosclerosis* 2001 May;156(1):67-72.

50. Freedman JE, Parker C, Li L, et al. Select flavonoids and whole juice from purple grapes inhibit platelet function and enhance nitric oxide release. *Circulation* (United States) 2001 , Jun 12; 103(23):2792-8.

Chapter 5: A Short Fat Primer

1. Abrams HL. The Preference for Animal Protein and Fat: A Cross-Cultural Survey. In: Harris M and Ross EB, eds. *Food and Evolution.* Philadelphia, PA: Temple University Press, 1987: 207.

2. Brisson GJ. *Lipids In Human Nutrition.* Englewood: Jack K. Burgess, Inc., 1981:107.

3. Bettelheim FA, Brown WH, March J. *Introduction to General, Organic, & Biochemistry,* sixth edition. Brooks/Cole, 2001:482.

4. Enig M. *Know Your Fats.* Silver Spring, MD: Bethesda Press, 2000:270.

5. Ibid., p. 60.

6. Sporek K. *Salt and the Seven Deadly Ills.* 1st Books, 2001:188-190.

7. Marieb EN. *Human Anatomy and Physiology,* fifth edition. New York: Benjamin Cummings, 2001: 983.

8. Enig, op cit:31.

9. Gurr MI. *Role of Fats in Food and Nutrition.* London: Elsevier Applied Science, 1992.

10. Brisson, op cit, Chapters 4 and 5.

11. Ravnskov U. *The Cholesterol Myths: Exposing the Fallacy that Saturated Fat and Cholesterol Cause Heart Disease.* Washington D.C.: New Trends Publishing, 2000.

12. Crawford M, Marsh D. *Nutrition and Evolution.* New Canaan, CT: Keats, 1995:127-128.

13. Whitney EN, Rolfes SR. *Understanding Nutrition.* Minneapolis/St. Paul, MN: West Pub. Co., 1993: 141.

14. Li D, Sinclair A, Wilson A, Nakkote S, Kelly F, Abedin L, Mann N, Turner A. Effect of dietary alpha-linolenic acid on thrombotic risk factors in vegetarian men. *Am J Clin Nutr* 1999;69:872-82.

15. Schmidt MA. *Smart Fats.* Berkeley, CA: Frog Ltd., 1997:48-49. Dr. Schmidt cites:

    a) Agren JJ, et al. Fatty acid composition of erythrocyte, platelet, and serum lipids in strict vegetarians. *Lipids* 1995;30(4):365-69.

    b) Reddy S, Sanders TAB, Obeid O. The influence of maternal vegetarian diet on essential fatty acid status of the newborn. *Eur J Clin Nutr* 1994;48:358-68.

    c) Sanders TAB, Reddy S. The influence of a vegetarian diet on the fatty acid composition of milk and the essential fatty acid status of the infant. *J Pediatr* 1992;120:S71-77.

16. Pauletto P, et al. Blood Pressure and Atherogenic Lipoprotein Profiles of Fish-Diet and Vegetarian Villagers in Tanzania: The Lugalawa Study. *The Lancet* 1996 Sept. 21;348:784-88.

17. Rizek RL, Welsh SO, Marston RM, Jackson EM. Levels and Sources of Fat in the U.S. Food Supply and in Diets of Individuals. In: *Dietary Fats and Health.* Champaign, IL: American Oil Chemists' Society, 1983:13-43.

18. Bettleheim, et al, op cit:273.

19. Enig, op cit:187.

20. Brisson, op cit:62.

21. Ransnkov, op cit: 224.

22. Brisson, op cit:54-55.

23. Institute of Medicine, National Academies. <www.iom.edu/includes/dbfile.asp?id=13083>, accessed on the World Wide Web 8/28/2003.

24. Enig, op cit:85-86.

25. Simopoulos AP. Essential fatty acids in health and chronic disease. *Am J Clin Nutr* 1999 Sept.;70(3 Suppl):560S-569S.

26. Simopoulos A, Leaf A, Salem N. Essentiality of and recommended dietary intakes for omega-6 and omega-3 fatty acids. *Ann Nutr Metab* 1999;43:127-30.

27. Enig M. *Know Your Fats.* Silver Spring, MD: Bethesda Press, 2000.

28. Ravnskov U. Myth 7: Polyunsaturated Oils are Good For You. In: *The Cholesterol Myths: Exposing the Fallacy that Saturated Fat and Cholesterol Cause Heart Disease.* Washington D.C.: New Trends Publishing Inc., 2000:217-234.

29. Braden LM, Carroll KK. Dietary polyunsaturated fat in relation to mammary carcinogenesis in rats. *Lipids* 1986;21:285-88.

30. Toborek M, Lee YW, Garrido R, Kaiser S, Hennig B. Unsaturated fatty acids selectively induce an inflammatory environment in human endothelial cells. *Am J Clin Nutr* 2002;75:119-125.

31. Liu G, Bibus DM, Bode AM, Ma WY, Holman RT, Dong Z. Omega 3 but not omega 6 fatty acids inhibit AP-1 activity and cell transformation in JB6 cells. *PNAS* 2001 June 19;98(13):7510-7515.

32. Robinson J. Nutritional Benefits of Grassfarming. On the World Wide Web on 9/2/2003 at <www.eatwild.com/nutrition.html#10>. Cites: Dolecek TA, Grandits G. Dietary Polyunsaturated Fatty Acids and Mortality in the Multiple Risk Factor Intervention Trial (MRFIT). *World Rev Nutr Diet* 1991;66:205-16,

33. Simopoulos AP, Robinson J, *The Omega Plan.* New York: HarperCollins, 1998:86-98.

34. Schmidt MA. *Smart Fats.* Berkeley, CA: Frog, Ltd., 1997.

35. Watkins BA, Li Y, Lippman HE, Seifert MF. Omega-3 polyunsaturated fatty acids and skeletal health. *Exp Biol Med* (Maywood) 2001 Jun;226(6):485-97.

36. Sardi B. Vitamin D Is For Cancer Defense. *Nutrition Science News* 2000 March;5(3):100-102.

37. Gannage-Yared MH, et al. Hypovitaminosis D in a sunny country: relation to lifestyle and bone markers. *J Bone Mineral Research* 2000 Sept.;15(9):1856.

38. Downing D. Vitamin D—Time for Reassessment. *Journal of Nutritional & Environmental Medicine* 2001 Dec;11(4):237-9.

39. National Institutes of Health Clinical Center. Facts About Dietary Supplements, Vitamin D. Accessed 10/1/2003 on the World Wide Web at <www.cc.nih.gov/ccc/supplements/vitd>.

40. Vieth R. Vitamin D supplementation, 25-hydroxyVitamin D concentrations, and safety. *Am J Clin Nutr* 1999 May;69(5):842-56.

41. Vieth R. Vitamin D Nutrition and its Potential Health Benefits for Bone, Cancer and Other Conditions. *Journal of Nutritional & Environmental Medicine* 2001 Dec;11(4):275-91.

42. Thomas MK, Lloyd-Jones DM, Thadhani RI, Shaw AC, Deraska DJ, et. al. Hypovitaminosis D in Medical Inpatients. *New Engl J Med* 1998;338(12):777-83.

43. Utiger RD. The Need For More Vitamin D. *New Engl J Med* 1998;338(12):828-29.

44. On 10/2/2003, I (Don) searched Medline using the question "Do omega-3 fatty acids suppress immunity?" and turned up 200 matches. Some relevant articles are:

    a) Harbige LS. Dietary n-6 and n-3 fatty acids in immunity and autoimmune disease. *Proc Nutr Soc* (England) 1998 Nov.;57(4):555-62.

    b) Wu D, Meydani SN. Omega-3 polyunsaturated fatty acids and immune function. *Proc Nutr Soc* (England)1998 Nov.; 57(4):503-9.

    c) Hughes DA, Pinder AC. Omega-3 polyunsaturated fatty acids inhibit the antigen-presenting function of human monocytes. *Am J Clin Nutr* (United States) 2000 Jan.;71(1 Suppl):357S-60S.

45. Cordain L, Watkins BA, Florant GL, Kehler M, Rogers L, Li Y. Fatty acid analysis of wild ruminant tissues: Evolutionary implications for reducing diet-related chronic disease. *Eur J Clin Nutr* 2002;56:181-91.

46. Robinson J. *Why Grassfed is Best.* Vashon, WA: Vashon Island Press, 2000.

47.   Robinson J. Nutritional Benefits of Grassfarming. Cites: Ip C, Scimeca JA, et al. Conjugated linoleic acid. A powerful anti-carcinogen from animal fat sources. *Cancer* 1994;74(3 suppl):1050-4. Accessed on the World Wide Web at <www.eatwild.com/nutrition.html#10> on 9/2/2003.

48.   Robinson J. What is CLA? Cites: Aro A., Mannisto S, Salminen I, Ovaskainen ML, Kataja V, and Uusitupa M. Inverse Association between Dietary and Serum Conjugated Linoleic Acid and Risk of Breast Cancer in Postmenopausal Women. *Nutr Cancer* 2000;38(2):151-7. Accessed on the World Wide Web at <www.eatwild.com/cla.html> on 9/2/2003.

49.   Robinson J. Grassfarming and Human Health: Two new studies suggest that grassfed meat and dairy products may reduce the risk of breast cancer. Cites: Bougnoux, P, Lavillonniere F, Riboli E. Inverse relation between CLA in adipose breast tissue and risk of breast cancer. A case-control study in France. *Inform* 1999;10(5):S43. Accessed on the World Wide Web on 9/2/2003, at <www.eatwild.com/health.html#how researchers>.

50.   Robinson J. More evidence that milk from grassfed cows may reduce breast cancer risk. Cites: Stanton C, et al. CLA—A Health-Promoting Component of Animal and Milk Fat. *The Dairy Products Research Center No. 26*. ISBN: 1 84170 118 1. Accessed on the World Wide Web on 9/2/2003 at <www.eatwild.com/news.html#evidence>.

51.   Kris-Etherton PM, Zhao G, Binkoski AE, Coval SM, Etherton TD. The effects of nuts on coronary heart disease risk. *Nutr Rev* 2001 Apr;59(4):103-11.

52.   Hu FB, Stampfer MJ, Manson JE, Rimm EB, Colditz GA, Rosner BA, Speizer FE, Hennekens CH, Willett WC. Frequent nut consumption and risk of coronary heart disease in women: prospective cohort study. *BMJ* 1998 Nov 14;317(7169):1341-5.

53.   Dreher ML, Maher CV, Kearney P. The traditional and emerging role of nuts in healthful diets. *Nutr Rev* 1996 Aug;54(8):241-5.

54.   Hu FB, Stampfer MJ. Nut consumption and risk of coronary heart disease: a review of epidemiologic evidence. *Curr Atheroscler Rep* 1999 Nov;1(3):204-9.

55.   Fraser GE. Nut consumption, lipids, and risk of a coronary event. *Clin Cardiol* 1999 Jul; 22 (7 Suppl):III:11-5.

56.   Enig M. *Know Your Fats*. Silver Spring, MD: Bethesda Press, 2000:106.

57.   Fife B. *The Healing Miracles of Coconut Oil*. Colorado Springs, CO: Piccadilly Books Ltd., 2001.

58.   Price W. *Nutrition and Physical Degeneration*. New Canaan, CT: Keats, 1998.

Chapter 6: Organic Matters

1.   Rifkin J. *Entropy: Into the Greenhouse World*. New York: Bantam, 1989:194.

2.   How safe is our produce? *Consumer Reports* 1999 (March).

3.   Rifkin, op cit:156.

4.   Ren H, et al. The superiority of organically cultivated vegetables to general ones regarding antimutagenic activities. *Mutat Res* 2001;20:496(1-2):83-88.

5.   Worthington V. Effect of Agricultural Methods on Nutritional Quality: A Comparison of Organic with Conventional Crops. *Alternative Therapies in Health and Medicine* 1998; 4(1):58.

6.   Brockman H. *Organic Matters*. Congerville, IL: TerraBooks, 2001.

7.   Jenkins JC. *The Humanure Handbook*. Grove City, PA: Jenkins Publishing, 1994.

8.   Hopfenberg R. Pimentel D. Human population numbers as a function of food supply. *Environment, Development, and Sustainability* 2001;3:1-15.

9.   Quinn D. Reaching for the Future with All Three Hands. Accessed on the World Wide Web on 8/7/2003 at: <www.ishmael.org/Education/Writings/kentstate.shtml>. See also Quinn's books *Ishmael, My Ishmael, The Story of B*, and *Beyond Civilization*.

10.   Frisch RE. Fatness and fertility. *Scientific American* 1988 (March):88-95.

11.   Schell O. *Modern Meat: Antibiotics, Hormones, and the Pharmaceutical Farm*. New York: Random House, 1984.

12. Department of Animal Science, Oklahoma State University, <www.ansi.okstate.edu/breeds>.

13. Rifkin, op cit:149.

14. Robinson J. Hog factories move in, Hog farmers move out. Cites: The Multiple Benefits of Agriculture — An Economic, Environmental and Social Analysis. White Bear Lake, MN: The Land Stewardship Project, November 2001. Accessed on the World Wide Web on 9/2/2003 at <www.eatwild.com/news.html>.

Note: Page references in *italic* refer to figures; those in **boldface** refer to tables.

About the Authors

Chef Rachel Albert-Matesz earned a bachelor's degree in sociology and communications from the University of Washington (Seattle). She has been a cooking instructor, consultant, healthy cooking coach, and food and health writer for 18 years. From 1988 to 1989, Rachel was head chef for Rachel's Natural Foods Cafe in Seattle. She has led more than 650 cooking classes in Ohio, Michigan, California, Washington, and Arizona.

Previous works include *Gourmet Wholefoods, Cooking with Rachel*, and *The Nourishment for Life Cookbook*. All but *Cooking with Rachel* are out of print. More than 200 of Rachel's articles have appeared in national magazines, including *Natural Home, Living Without, The Herb Companion, Herbs for Health, Yoga Journal, Let's Live, Oxygen Women's Fitness Magazine, Muscle & Fitness, Muscle & Fitness Hers, Conscious Choice, Well Being Journal, Veggie Life, Vegetarian Times, Vegetarian Journal*, and *Macrobiotics Today*. Rachel's articles also appeared in *Fit, New Body*, and *Vegetarian Gourmet*, which are no longer in print.

Chef Rachel developed 130 recipes for two books by best-selling author Barry Sears, including 90 recipes for *Zone Meals in Seconds* (HarperCollins 2004). In December of 2002, she moved to and began teaching cooking classes in gourmet kitchen shops and private homes in Phoenix, Scottsdale, Tempe, and Chandler, Arizona, and became a faculty member in the nutrition department at the Southwest Institute of Healing Arts in Tempe.

Don Matesz holds bachelor's and master's degrees in philosophy from the University of Toledo, Ohio, a diploma in Comprehensive Nutrition from the American Academy of Nutrition, Corona Del Mar, California, and Chinese Herbology Practitioner Certification from the Institute of Chinese Herbology, Oakland, California. He is a member of Mensa.

More than 40 of Don's articles have appeared in health and fitness magazines, including *Alternative Medicine, Well Being Journal, Conscious Choice, Herbs for Health, Herb Quarterly, Oxygen Women's Fitness Magazine, Vegetarian Times, Vegetarian Journal, Veggie Life*, and *Macrobiotics Today*. His articles also appeared in *Vegetarian Gourmet, In Context, Fitt Journal*, and *Exercise Protocol*, which are no longer in print. He currently is a nutrition columnist for *Acupuncture Today*.

In 2003 Don began working on a master's degree in Oriental Medicine at the Phoenix Institute of Herbal Medicine and Acupuncture (PIHMA) in Phoenix, Arizona.

The Garden of Eating was a 7-year joint effort. Don wrote chapters 1 through 7 and Appendix G and H. Rachel contributed chapters 8 through 26 and the remainder of the Appendix.

Rachel and Don are available for public presentations. You may reach them by email at chefrachel@TheGardenOfEatingDiet.com **or** dmatesz@TheGardenOfEatingDiet.com **or** by phone: (602) 840-4556. Write to them care of:
Planetary Press, P.O. Box 97040, Phoenix, AZ 85060-7040

Quick Order Form

Telephone Orders: Call Planetary Press (602) 840-4556
Have your Visa, Mastercard, Discover, or American Express card ready.
Postal Orders: Make checks payable to and mail to

Planetary Press
P.O. Box 97040
Phoenix, AZ 85060-7040

For info about orders: PlanetaryPress@earthlink.net
On-line orders: www.TheGardenOfEatingDiet.com

Please do not remove this form from the book. Xerox and use it or give to a friend.

Please send the following books or booklets. I understand that I may return any of them for a full refund, if I am not completely satisfied for any reason.

Qty.	Title	U.S. Price	CN Price	Total
	The Garden of Eating	$29.95	$38.95	
	Shopping list for sample month of menus	$5.00	$6.50	
Shipping & Handling	**Shipping within the U.S.:** Add $6 *per book* for Media Mail/$12 for U.S. Priority Add $1.50 per *shopping list* for First Class/ $4 for U.S. Priority **Shipping to Canada:** Add $11 *per book* for Surface Rate/$22 for Priority Add $2.50 *per shopping list* for Surface/$6 for Priority International shipping rates vary by country. For all other international orders, visit our Web site: www.TheGardenOfEatingDiet.com.			
	Sales tax <u>(AZ residents only)</u>, add 6.3%)			
	Total enclosed			

Please send FREE information on
* Cooking class   * One-on-one coaching   * Speaking/seminars   * Consulting

PLEASE PRINT

Name: _____

Address:_____ City_____ State_____

Zip_____ Telephone: (___)_____ Fax_____

Email address: _____

Method of Payment

☐ Check ☐Money Order ☐ Credit Card: Visa, MasterCard, American Express, Discover

Card number_____   Name on card_____

Signature_____   Expiration Date_____

☐check if you would you like your book autographed. To whom would you like it dedicated?

_____

How or where did you hear about *The Garden of Eating?*_____

Quantity discounts are available. Call (602) 840-4556 for more information. Thank you for your order.